Indian Administration

Structure, Performance and Reform

Indian Administration

Structure, Performance and Reform

By:
Rumki Basu

ADROIT

Adroit Publishers

NEW DELHI • KATHMANDU

ISBN : 978-81-87393-73-3

2019

Published by
ADROIT PUBLISHERS 4675/21, Ganpati Bhawan, Ansari Road,
Daryaganj, New Delhi-110 002, INDIA, Phone : 011-23266030
adroitpublishers@gmail.com

Typeset in Garamond Premium Pro by Arun Sharma,
Akriti Graphic Solution, Delhi-110081 E-mail: arun263923@gmail.com,
Ph: 9999414390

Dedicated to:

The public administrators,
at all levels,
central, state and local,
who work hard to serve
the citizens and the public interest in difficult conditions
and problematic terrain
with an abiding sense of duty
and have held the
country together........

Contents

Preface

It is necessary that we, the citizens of India, understand the public administrative system under which we are governed, a system that has grown out of a long evolutionary process and should aim to build itself into a world-class public governance system to meet the needs of 21st-century India. We are the world's largest democracy and the citizens have constitutional rights, liberties and responsibilities. Our constitution is the world's longest written constitution, which has clearly defined the functions and powers of all our public institutions. India has one of the largest administrative networks in the world with a mandate to administer 3.3 million sq. km. of territory with a population of 1.3 billion. Despite governance deficits the Indian state has survived largely due to the innate strength of our democratic system sustained largely by politico-administrative regimes, which held our nation together through the trials and tribulations of its post-independence history.

Today, India is one of the leading players on the world stage. There is a need to create a public administrative system, commensurate with our global status as the fastest growing economy and the world's largest democracy. Good governance should be citizen-centric with efficiency and effectiveness in public service delivery. Older democracies of the West have graduated to bi-party systems where there are no sharp policy breaks unless required and good governance is always the result of a right understanding between the permanent and the political executive. Today, good governance needs to be guaranteed as the fundamental right of every Indian citizen.

The book has 19 chapters. Every effort has been made to cover most university courses on Indian Administration besides the UPSC civil services main exam syllabi on public administration. Information on Government of India laws, acts, and public policies have been updated. Every chapter is informative and analytical, and is presented in a student friendly format. Suggested Readings are given in every chapter.

In writing this book, I have greatly benefited from the works of eminent scholars on Indian constitution, politics, government and administration. I owe a deep sense of gratitude to all of them. A list of Suggested Readings has been given at the end of every chapter to acknowledge my debts and facilitate further reading. For facts and data, as far as possible, official documents have been relied upon. Finally, I must confess to having freely borrowed from my earlier publications. They are quite a few to be listed meticulously everywhere. I look forward to the response of my students, friends and critics on the book and apologize in advance for all errors, inadvertently made.

Rumki Basu

Introduction: Change and Continuity in Indian Administration

The Indian governmental machinery constitutes politico-administrative regimes at three levels (Central, State and Local) with a mandate to administer 3.3 million sq. km. of territory with a population of 1.3 billion. With its size and heterogeneity India is no easy state to govern. Despite India's multi-religious, multi-racial and multi-lingual society being united by a common history, civilizational identity and territory, the vast majority of Indian citizens have multiple identities in terms of their religion, caste, language, or region. The same person may belong to different groups depending upon the criteria of religion, language or community. Since society gets divided both horizontally and vertically it would be difficult to find any majoritarian hegemonic monoliths in Indian society. Every religion has its sects, languages and dialects, castes and sub-castes. Members of almost every religious group would be divided by language and region, just as members of every linguistic group by religion or caste.

India is fifth in global GDP and third in purchasing power parity but its ranking in human development is 130 out of 189 nations in the HD index published annually by the UNDP. It has the fastest growing economy and the second largest population in the world with a 400 million strong middle class and the largest number of youth population in the workforce. Despite governance deficits the Indian state has survived largely due to the innate strength of our democratic system sustained largely by politico-administrative regimes, which could hold the young nation together through the trials and tribulations of its post-independence history.

An outstanding feature of Indian administration is its remarkable resilience to radical change, though it is not averse to adaptation whenever required. The basic structure of revenue administration of the Mughal period was carried over to the British period and continues to function with minor modification even today. Except for introducing information technology, its core premises and structures remain unchanged. The police and large parts of criminal justice administration are still governed by the Acts and Codes introduced during the British rule in the 19th century. The constitutional moorings of Indian administration have evolved with successive Acts in the British colonial period, beginning with the Regulating Act of 1773.

Though Indian administration can be studied from the Mauryan dynasty onwards, its transition to modernity started with the British period of Indian history. Beginning with the Secretariat system at the Centre and the states, ministries and departments, the district administrative system, the collectorates, urban municipal bodies, the civil service personnel structure, the budgetary system, and general office procedure have all remained resilient to major structural changes though modern functional adaptations have been made. These are piecemeal changes, certainly not transformational in nature. The structure and framework of the civil services shows a connection from the British era till date. It is in the functioning and diversity of tasks that the civil service is substantively different in nature and scope today.

Politico-administrative Relations

The Parliamentary system of India gives its elected governments considerable power and control over the bureaucracies, though the ground reality does not match the Weberian model of bureaucracy on which, the Indian model is essentially based. The central bureaucracy in India has had great power for long to influence legislation, develop major new policies and programmes and determine the manner and extent to which policies get executed. The political executive have often lacked the time or the expertise to exert proper control or leadership over the bureaucracies. Bureaucracies became powerful in India over a period of time. While the Indian bureaucracy today has lost many of its discretionary powers in the age of liberalization, they are still able to influence and shape legislation, and their views and inputs may strongly shape policy discourse in the years to come.

After 1947, India adopted a socialist pattern of economic policy, especially in the early years after independence, when capital was scarce and the base of local entrepreneurship was weak. Bureaucracies had great powers in programme development, regulation and implementation. The Indian public officials were not very responsive towards the citizens, therefore the gulf between them remains strong even today. A strong bureaucracy (not democracy) was a legacy of the British rule and a tussle for power assertion could be seen in the working relationship between the political and the permanent executive in the years that followed independence.

India has seen major changes over the years, but many developmental needs in India (poverty, education, health, infrastructure, etc.,) remain unattended and despite some governmental failures in social policy and a growing private business sector that reduces the role of state in economic policy, the bureaucracy is still influential. Bureaucracy plays a subtle role in shaping policy by its advice to the higher echelons of government in drafting legislative proposals. In the process, it manages to accommodate certain interests to the exclusion of certain others, thereby providing or denying them the opportunity to benefit from policy.

The capacity of bureaucrats to embellish or alter the substance of legislation is quite significant. Their role has been particularly relevant in respect of regulatory policy that provides a good reason for certain powerful lobbies to rely on bureaucratic support to influence policy. There is no denying that civil servants have a lot of power in making and implementing policy and programmes and in shaping and interpreting many rules and regulations through delegated legislation and the use of discretionary power in executing crucial government policies, rules and laws. There is a need to understand public administration in its current neo-liberal political context. In addition to globalization and neo-liberal economic policy, popular access to increased information, recent growth in non-profit organizations and social entrepreneurship provide new approaches for furthering government initiatives. In India there has been rapid increase of judicial activism on policy matters. In addition, citizens have demanded greater openness, transparency, and accountability in the modern age. Besides, state Governments have become increasingly important in dealing with sub-national issues and have varyingly evolved capacities for new ways of doing things. It could be said that the diffusion of capacity has meant devolution of top-down policy-making practices to state and local level settings as well.

It may not, however, be far from the truth to say that during the first three decades of Independence the civil services under the leadership and support of a number of political leaders (at the Centre and in the states) were able to take up and complete many nationally important tasks and projects in the shortest possible time. These major tasks of urgency and priority included political consolidation of India by merging over 550 princely states into the Indian Union; attaining self- sufficiency in production of food grains; construction of several multi-purpose dams like Hirakud, Bhakra, Damodar Valley, for irrigation, flood control and power generation; and establishing a number of mega steel plants, e.g. at Rourkela, Bhilai, Durgapur, for rapid industrialization.

As a result of the efforts of private farmers (with government subsidies) the production of food grains in the country increased from about 50 million tonnes in 1950-51 to 259 million tonnes in 2011-12, i.e. more than five-fold. The population too increased from around 360 million in 1951 to over 1200 million in 2011, i.e. nearly three and a half times. In addition, there was tremendous growth in the production of milk, fruits and vegetables. According to the Economic Survey of India (2017-18), the country today occupies number one position in the world in the production of rice, wheat, sugarcane, cotton, fruits and vegetables. In the agriculture sector these remarkable achievements were possible because of the dedicated research activities of the Indian Council of Agricultural Research (ICAR) technical experts. They produced High Yielding Variety (HYV) of wheat and paddy seeds. Efforts were also not spared to persuade farmers to use the HYV seeds and adopt better farming methods. The required irrigation facilities were provided by building many large, medium and minor irrigation projects wherever possible. Thus, the technical knowledge of our scientific and agricultural experts along with the timeliness of the administrative services to deliver HYV seeds, fertilizer, pesticide, credit, and finally the proper coordination of all these activities through the National Agricultural Extension Blocks brought about the much needed "Green Revolution" and the "White Revolution" with a record-breaking production of food grains, milk, fruits and vegetables. Our technical and non-technical services thus proved that with mutual will and dedicated effort, goals which appeared impossible too could be achieved. India is no longer importing food grains, rather it is in a position to export a few million tonnes in a year with normal rainfall. Thus, the problem now is not of shortage of food grains, but shortage of covered storage space for the surplus food grains and the efficient and equitable distribution of the same that will help to substantially reduce hunger and poverty from India. Unfortunately, the image of the public services has gone down immensely not long after their commendable achievements in several spheres of national concern mentioned earlier. The spate of scams reported in recent years that allegedly cost thousands of crores of rupees to the public exchequer, question the honesty, efficiency and the spirit of service of many officials of the concerned ministries, departments and organizations. No doubt scams were prevalent earlier too but these were few and far between and were insignificant. Since corruption appears to be rampant today, effective measures are needed to prevent and control it.

From 1950-1990, the story of independent India can be retold as the story of the consolidation of the Administrative State, which needed to reinvent its role and responsibilities time and again with the changing contours of the political economy of the Indian state. With such an administrative overload and the rising demands of citizens of an overpopulated state, the bureaucracy took a severe beating in Indian popular imagination. It was accused (albeit unfairly at times) of inefficiency, unresponsiveness, empire building, egotism and lack of sensitivity. On a comparative note, however, it must be said that our performance cannot be matched with other more efficient public management systems like those of Singapore, South Korea or Japan, countries roughly smaller than the size of our major states. We can compare ourselves only with China perhaps, whose bureaucratic outcomes have certainly been better than India's in terms of economic growth and human development in the last 50 years, albeit under totally different political systems.

The influence of bureaucracy in implementation is well known and frequently commented upon in various evaluation studies. Manipulation and distortion of programmes and schemes during implementation have often altered and redefined the meaning of policy. Benefits have often not reached the target groups due to the wrongful exercise of discretion or identification errors generally made by higher or lower order bureaucrats.

There are a number of problems afflicting Indian civil services, like lack of professionalism and poor capacity building, inefficient incentive systems that do not appreciate outstanding civil servants, outmoded rules and procedures that restrict the civil servant from performing effectively, systemic inconsistencies in promotion, lack of adequate transparency and accountability procedures, arbitrary and whimsical transfers, insecurity in tenure and political interference which gradually lead to the erosion of values and work ethics of our public services.

Despite the above challenges, India's GDP has seen tremendous growth in the last 20 years, about 8% annually. As to specific assessments, successes exist in abundance. In continuation of the above, contribution of bureaucrats has received appreciation, such as through the Prime Minister's Award for Excellence in public administration instituted since 2006. Successful innovative practices employed at the district level to reduce poverty, strengthen human capacity, provide mass-scale access to health clinics, settle land disputes, and use information technology in disaster management have all been recorded as best practices in government which can revolutionize service delivery.

On the one hand, public administration in India has many shortcomings that cause neglect, corruption, and dysfunction and that produces, in the aggregate, societal outcomes that often barely satisfy or are scarcely manageable. On the other hand, there exist untold examples of civil servants doing the right thing and producing results in critical areas, sometimes using innovative approaches. The state of public administration continues to forge ahead on the shoulders of a largely successful business sector today, while the recurring failure of government calls into question the very essence of democracy in India from time to time.

What needs to be taken seriously is the mismatch between India's economic growth and the distributional outcomes of that growth among its citizens. Both need sustained good governance, which is always the by-product of an efficient and effective politico-administrative partnership. Interestingly wherever that has happened in any state of India, the developmental outcomes are certainly better. Inter-state comparisons in India have long been a testimony to this fact.

However, this is not to say that there have been no seminal changes in Indian administration from time to time. Though the British Indian civil service provided structural continuity to the post-independent Indian administrative service, the functions multiplied and diversified which led to a transformation of its role, intent and responsibilities. The entire task of nation building and development, led to the emergence of a massive public sector and government interventions in the economy and the social sector became a necessity in the public interest. *Despite a turn-around in recent years, public sector undertakings did not register profits on a sustainable basis for the greater part of the post-independence period, yet their collective contribution to the Indian economy even today is greater than that of the combined private sector.*

Sub-national Governments

India, since independence, has had a federal structure which now constitutes 29 states and 7 union territories. States have long assumed responsibilities for many developmental issues, and only from 1992 did constitutional amendments provide for elected local bodies in rural and urban areas, thereby establishing a constitutionally mandated three-tier government. Before that, states could shape local areas of governance through executive orders. The 1992 amendments also increased the financial and functional responsibilities of local government that provide obligatory and discretionary duties like planning for economic and social development, urban planning, land use, ecology, health, education and public works. India has a long history of intergovernmental relations (IGR) between the centre and the states. Since 1989, IGR has become increasingly competitive due to the increased presence of coalition governments in Indian politics, which require a stronger measure of political accommodation, both nationally and between the Centre and the states. *In India, prior periods of IGR that were characterized by top-down (national) coercion or negotiation within a nationwide dominant Congress party, are over, giving way to more equality, dialogue and negotiation in the relationship now and in the years to come.*

Many states in India are producing increasingly competent leaders who are redefining the economic and political map of future India. As a result of their economic and administrative successes, these state leaders have each won consecutive re-election bids. Over the past decade, voter turnout has been declining at the national level but rising at the state level. Those State Governments that have lived up to voters' expectations have been rewarded: in the 30 state elections since 2007, 50% of the incumbent chief ministers have won re-election, compared with just 25% in the preceding three decades; nearly 66% of those re-elected had delivered five years of growth that was faster than the national average.

In the 1990s, the first states to benefit from the fall of the license raj were the rich ones of the southern and western coasts, particularly Gujarat, Maharashtra, and Tamil Nadu, which already had strong industrial bases. But in the last decade, the centre of rapid growth has shifted northward and inland, to the states of Bihar, Chhattisgarh, Madhya Pradesh, Orissa, and others. The average growth rate of these northern states jumped from 2.2% in the 1990s to 9.1% over the past decade, while India's national growth rate gained just two percentage points.

The rise of the north and the BIMARU states (Bihar, Madhya Pradesh, Rajasthan and Uttar Pradesh) is nothing less than an economic miracle. For decades observers had studied the stagnant poverty there and concluded that these states were overpopulated regions and somehow socio-culturally ill-suited to economic development. Today, some of the northern states are growing faster than the national economy, and sustaining these growth levels through good initiatives in governance.

Administrative Reforms

Post-independence in 1947, the inherited Indian civil service became the All India Services, providing administrative leadership to Central and State Governments which have separate civil service cadres. The all India Services include the Indian Administrative Services (IAS), the Indian Forest Service (IFS) and the Indian Police Service (IPS). The IAS is at the top of the hierarchy.

For much of the 1945-90 period, the main thrust of administrative reforms in "development administration" was to increase the capacity of the state bureaucracy, and use traditional public administration methods to plan and execute development projects. Bureaucracy was used as an instrument of the developmentalist state. In the 1990s, a new model of "development management" found favour that mirrors a neoliberal and new public management orientation with emphasis on reducing the role of the public sector (e.g. through privatization), using incentives rather than regulations and increased customer orientation. In recent years "development governance" has emerged, which synthesizes both models and adds additional consideration that government is only one of the players in the governance process along with the private sector and civil society. Persistent social, urban, environmental, and economic problems draw attention to the need for collaboration and joint governance among sectors.

There have been two notable, high-level attempts in India for administrative reforms. The Administrative Reforms Commission-I (ARC-I) was the first post- independence committee of experts to assess the administrative machinery of the nation. ARC-I was appointed in 1966 and 20 reports were submitted with about 680 major recommendations that mostly dealt with the need for specialization in government services; unified grading structure, and the process of recruitment, conduct, discipline, and service conditions of civil servants. Most remained largely ignored during the increased political and administrative centralization of the 1970s and 1980s. In 2005, Prime Minister Manmohan Singh appointed ARC-II to suggest measures to achieve a proactive, responsive, accountable, sustainable, and efficient administration for the country at all levels of the government. ARC-II recommendations include implementation of the RTI Act and establishing a Lokpal (ombudsman), which was originally recommended in ARC-I but not implemented. Despite colossal efforts by several committees and hundreds of recommendations India's record of administrative reforms is known to be minimalist and unimpressive. This is attributable to the vested interest of the political and bureaucratic classes, fragmented electoral mandates and divided governments. Indeed, only under popular pressure ignited by Anna Hazare did the Lokpal Bill get passed in 2013. A seminal change in the Indian governance system was the adoption of structural adjustment policies and the philosophy of globalization after the 1990s. New public management was an international movement triggered by the demands of globalization, which put great pressure on the developing countries to make their governance systems capable of strengthening the competitive capacity of their respective economic systems.

A large number of such reforms are in governance with the time-tested management principles and guidelines traditionally imbibed by the private sector and are being considered equally useful for public systems. Today, the basics of good governance are being juxtaposed with New Public Management (NPM) and consequently there is an emphasis on deregulation, marketization and privatization, which is really a call for downsizing and restricting the functions of government. Other mandates are for promoting openness and transparency in governance, empowering NGOs and encouraging private public partnerships to augment socio-economic development, strengthen responsiveness and make administration more citizen friendly.

A major landmark in the Indian governance system is the promulgation of the Right to Information Act (RTI) of 2005. It initiated a new era in citizen-state relations, which also lifted the veil on administrative secrecy and the Official Secrets Act, one of the hallowed pillars of public administration of India. The success of this legislative innovation (everyday almost 5000 RTI applications are filed) would lead to greater transparency, responsiveness and accountability in the governance system, and participation of the people in administration. The RTI has emerged as a powerful tool of effective democracy and governance. In the past few years administrative reforms have remained the focus of NPM. ARC-II has brought out 15 reports which focus on specific and measurable standards of services to be provided to citizens: transparency, procedural simplification, greater responsiveness to citizen needs and effective grievance redressal systems. The government (albeit slowly) has started to work on some of the suggestions. Citizens' Charters and Service Delivery Guarantee Acts are also being legislated to make the citizens demand better service delivery standards.

The environment in which a future Indian civil servant will work will be characterized by the features of a globally competitive economy, global services, information technology and artificial intelligence. In such a milieu he will be expected to be a professional, a result-oriented and cost-effective bureaucrat with a great sense of timing and accountability. In the context of the Right to Information, accountability will be all pervasive. He will continue to perform routine law and order functions, dispense justice and work in the public interest. He will be executing development programmes but with the collaboration of the private and voluntary sectors. He will continue to aid and advise governments at the Centre and the states who would require his constant help to deliver and run effective public delivery systems. Change is the order of the day and adaptation and sensitivity are the two great qualities required of a public bureaucrat in India today. A civil servant in the new dispensation of development governance is expected to play the role of a facilitator, coordinator, advisor and motivator, not merely an executor of development programmes.

What must be stressed in today's age is the need to question the prevailing trust in the relatively higher efficiency of the private sector. In most countries the private sector is generally viewed as indifferent to the interest of the citizen except as a consumer. In no way can it replace the public sector, which despite its operational shortcomings has shown deep commitment to the welfare of the common man. Technological upgradation, computerization, privatization deregulation, debureaucratization and other structural reforms have been largely mechanical in approach superimposed on the public sector which dilutes the public philosophy of governance and in the process, the public good component and community service obligations recede into the background. In fact, accountability mechanisms, feedback, monitoring and transparency of governmental processes alone can bring a difference to the working culture prevailing in public agencies.

From the programmes of poverty alleviation, removal of inequality, illiteracy and ignorance, employment generation, management of scarce resources, meeting recurring challenges of, ecological imbalance and problems of pollution, to coping with the problems of dysfunctional and deviant behaviour such as different types of crimes, terrorism and violence endangering the unity and integrity of the nation, the civil service has trudged a long hard journey indeed in post independent India!

However, it is also unfortunately true that along the way the Indian administration has lost a great deal of its credibility. The most vital task is to restore it and this can be done by clearly defining the domains of politics and administration and playing the rules of the game. There is a pressing need to strengthen the basic administrative frame and revive and strengthen people's institutions. Decentralizing the administrative systems in terms of authority, decision-making and accountability, improving the grievance redressal machinery, enforcing discipline and productivity norms, monitoring projects and programmes'strictly and providing positive incentives for boldness, honesty and achievements —these are the priorities in administration today. Government has to display exemplary firmness and determination in dealing with matters of corruption, indiscipline, nepotism, and inordinate delay. Civil services at all levels will have to be motivated to perform and this will be possible through massive inputs of training and orientation and well thought out systems of incentives and disincentives. Administration has also to be modernized in terms of technological innovations, equipment, techniques, faster communications, better information and monitoring systems and better work environment.

Improvements in organizational systems and institutions are not only desirable but also essential. But there is the supervening need of political will and ability to fully back up and concretize the changes. Without the unflinching determination of the political leadership, the transformation of administration into an able and effective instrument of public good will merely remain wishful thinking.

The Indian State and Good Governance—Future Trends

In the post-liberalised era of the 21st century, the Indian state and administration has adjusted to seminal changes in domestic and international politics. The new state-market divide since 1991 has gradually ended monolithic state structures of the 1950-90 eras. The nation transited from the "politics of poverty" to the new "politics of prosperity", as the largest democracy and the fastest growing economy in the world. India emerges as a substantive new player in the committee of nations and a possible role model for the developing world in politics and administration.

Political Science has focused largely on democratic institutions in recent years and far less on the understanding of basic state capacity, the absence of which often undermines democracy. Democracy and good governance are separate and distinct phenomena, but worldwide empirical evidence has proved that regimes reflecting both dimensions are necessary to achieve many aspects of human security. Democracy eventually gives everyone a promise and a hope to be included in citizen entitlements. Part-IV of the Indian Constitution constitutes the core of the promise of socio-economic justice to be progressively realized through enhanced state capacity. In the post-globalized era, the Sustainable Development Goals for all governments across the globe reflect the biggest exercise in convergence in the current paradigms of democracy and good governance. These are 17 mandated goals to be met by all governments by 2030. Never before in the history of the post-Second World War era, have 193 countries been signatories to a convention to legitimize goals of good governance at a given point of time as was done in 2015 by the UN General Assembly.

The New Economic Policies of 1991 brought in a milieu of change for the Indian bureaucracy that was truly unprecedented. It lost a lot of its discretionary powers with the dismantling of the license permit raj and efforts were made to make it more accountable. New rights and new acts came in that brought the state and the citizen closer. Public goods and delivery systems had to compete in the market for consumer attention. The tasks of the bureaucracy became more focused and performance oriented as procedural and process reforms were brought in at the cutting-edge of administration. The citizen as a customer became the focus of citizen-centric reforms in administration. New flagship government programmes like National Rural Employment Guarantee Act (NREGA), which is the right to 100 days work for all adults in rural areas, or new acts like the RTI and other Public Service Guarantee Acts focused on social audit, citizen empowerment and quick redressal of citizen grievances.

Indian administration kept changing slowly but Indian democracy was changing at a surer and faster pace. A host of new acts — NREGA, Right to Education, Right to Information, Forest Rights Act, Food Security Act were passed due to the deepening of democracy and grassroots pressures from below. Sixty-seven per cent of the population were given entitlements to subsidized food grains. MNREGA (Right to work in rural areas) is the world's largest social sector programme and the Right to Education entitles the largest number of children in the school-going age to education. Between 2004 and 2012, 138 million had exited poverty thanks to sustained economic growth and stable democratic governance in India, in the last two decades. A 400-million middle class evolved during the planning era (1950-91) and it is now time for another 400 million to quit the ranks of the "poor" and enter the ranks of the middle class.

The 2019 global Multidimensional Poverty Index (MPI) from the UNDP reported that incidence of multidimensional poverty almost halved between 2005-06 and 2015-16, climbing down to 27.5%, indicating that the number of poor people in the country fell by more than 271 million within 10 years. India's progress in reducing multidimensional poverty has happened, thanks to investments in key areas. The country reduced deprivation in nutrition from 44.3% in 2005-06 to 21.2% in 2015-16. Child mortality dropped from 4.5% to 2.2%; lack of access to sanitation from 50.4% to 24.6%; people without cooking fuel from 52.9% to 26.2%; and those deprived of drinking water from 16.6% 6.2% in the same period. Despite poverty reduction across religions and caste groups, the report also found that 50% of tribals are poor, as are 33% of Dalits and 33% of Muslims. Keeping in view the ambitions of the 2030 Agenda for Sustainable Development India has to ensure that they are not left behind.

What matters are the types of investment by the State. Countries that have driven poverty reduction trends, have focused their investments on people, importantly through the provision of health, education and social protection. India has been doing that but also improving implementation of national programmes, and ensuring that they reach the last mile. These are tasks of good governance and administration.

India is a country of continental proportions and therefore some of its governmental programmes have acquired continental dimensions in their nature and scope—for example, the midday meal programme for school children is one of the world's largest school lunch programmes reaching out to millions of children. Even administration of the Kumbh Mela (once every 12 years) has been termed as the biggest management exercise in the world. So if India is to acquire a global power status the top priority is to have a world-class civil service which can transform public sector bodies or institutions in the country. Our public systems apparatus is still not equipped for its ever-growing mandates. From 1950-90, development administration was being managed with poor delivery and weak performance accountability systems. There have been some remarkable macro-achievements, and best practices here and there in public sector institutions but mediocre performances have been the norm in most sectors of Indian public administration.

As much as the 1950-90 story seems to revolve around politico-administrative regimes in the Centre, the achievements of the post-globalised era can be attributed to private sector led growth and good governance initiatives both from the centre and the states. Post-1991 reform initiatives finally seem to be bearing fruit and citizens armed with new rights have been the main catalysts for governance reform. Whether in fostering excellence in service delivery, e-governance or process reforms, it is the administration at the cutting-edge whose performance will affect the citizen most. *Ninety percent of government employees constitute*

Class III and IV employees whose pay (very low) and training (virtually non-existent) patterns need to change desperately.

Scarcity of public funds is not a debatable issue any more in India. There is a huge scope of increasing the hitherto relaxed or under taxed (we have one of the lowest per capita tax ratios in the world) revenue sources in India. Technology has to be used in an optimal manner for positive execution outcomes and incentivization of good performance should be made mandatory. New public management never really touched India in nature, depth and scope, as issues of justice, equity, citizenship or ethics remain absent from its core. It is the new social movements like the Right to Information movement and the Anna Hazare movement against corruption in recent times that have highlighted issues of ethics and accountability as never before in public life. Resurrecting a culture of caring for the citizen is the need of the hour. India needs to embark on the path to good governance by putting citizens at the centre of governance and provide them low-cost and high-quality public services. Governance should be seen as a partnership between the public servant and the citizen, where both are equal stake holders in the governance enterprise. The new Indian Public Service needs to emerge and arrive!

Chapter One

Evolution and Historical Legacies

Introduction

The Indian administrative system as it exists today is a product of two different sets of influences—the British colonial administration and the democratic ideals of a welfare state, which was constitutionally adopted in India after independence. Among India's colonial legacies, perhaps the most well-developed institution, which the British left behind, was the Indian Civil Service (ICS). This consisted of an exclusive administrative cadre, selected on merit but by mandate and training constituting the main support system of British imperial rule in India. Colonial administration in India was authoritarian, unresponsive, exclusive and paternalistic in character, qualities that the civil servants were taught to imbibe and maintain in their dealings with the public. Primarily performing regulatory functions like maintenance of law and order, collection of revenue, the administration during the British period had few developmental tasks to perform or welfare goals to achieve. The civil service was a powerful body of officials with powers of policy making and execution vested in their hands. Though the colonial government was involved in a few welfare functions (construction of roads, railways, educational institutions and hospitals, etc.), the ICS men served to some extent as an integrating force, a truly commendable role played in a country with multiple diversities such as India. They were efficient though authoritarian and paternalistic in approach.

This was the legacy which India inherited at the time of independence: a generalist civil service trained in routine ...regulatory functions and in the rigid application of rules, unused in the task of nation-building or social reconstruction and without any institutionalized system of accountability to the people. During the colonial era the foundations of a modern educational system had been laid to generate a pool of administrative personnel, and a network of communications, schools, colleges, banks, etc., came into operation and provided the basic requirements of a modern nation.

1.1 Indian Historical Legacies

Independence from British colonial rule came in 1947 and our tryst with constitutional rule started from 26th January 1950. The history of Indian administration begins from ancient times, when dynastic rulers chose administrators to assist them in the task of governing their kingdoms. However, there are seminal differences between the public administrators of the earlier eras (e.g. the Mauryan era or the Mughal period of Indian history) and the public servants of India today. The foundation of a modern civil service was laid during the British colonial rule. Public administrators in earlier eras were recruited by the king, given remuneration for tasks mandated by the king with no public status or permanency of tenure. They were like the personal servants of the king, accountable to him alone. While, public administrators in India today are recruited by independent agencies, bear a permanent tenure, are paid out of public funds and mandated to work for the public to whom they are finally and ultimately accountable since India is a democratic republic. Public bureaucrats are creatures of the law, they have to follow a code of conduct and owe their loyalty to the constitution only. They are to stay out of active 'polities' and their only political right is their right to vote. In 1953, the famous American scholar Paul Apple by had rated Indian administration as one of the best in the world in his report "Public Administration in India: Report of a Survey". More than seven decades have passed since then, and Indian administration has grown in strength and stature, having passed several tests of endurance and competence during this enormously difficult journey of nation building and consolidation of socio-economic development, during which India emerged as a major power in the committee of nations.

Indian history can be divided into four distinct periods: the Ancient (2000 BC-AD 1200), the Medieval (AD 1200-1765), the British (1765-1947), and the post-Independence period (1947 onwards). The Indian scholar cum politician Kautilya's Arthashastra compiled in 4th century BC, is the earliest treatise on the subject of public administration in the world. Its 15 books are a comprehensive treatment of public governance in which the author gives administrative advice to Chandragupta Maurya, the first ruler and founder of the Mauryan dynasty (320-185 BC). The Mauryan administration was the first administration in Indian history which was bureaucratic, run by permanent employees, hired on the basis of merit and divided into departments. King Ashoka (304-232 BC) of the same dynasty strengthened the administrative machinery and established a modern public administration. He made seminal contributions to the administration of justice, local government, and social welfare. Ashoka divided his empire into provinces, Aharas or Visayas, subdivisions and Janapadas, which were further divided into villages. With distinctive functions and work for every functionary in each rung of administration, decentralization got further extended during the Gupta administration (300-600 AD), in which almost-all functions of the government, except foreign policy was handled by the local bodies. Other important legacies of the ancient period include division of society into four castes based on occupation that initially saw a period of flexibility, but later developed into a rigid hierarchical social stratification system.

The Medieval period, saw the rise of the Mughal empire after 1526. The Mughals, who came from Central Asia, had a very centralized and militaristic form of government. The roots of several administrative institutions of present-day India may be traced back to Mughal rule. Mughal emperors through the Mansabdari System (rank-in-person system of higher bureaucracy), combined the military and civil services into 66 grades. The Mansabdari System transformed Mughal administration into a bureaucratic system with all positions into a unified hierarchy facilitating administration of personnel. The highest officer was the Wakil or Diwan (Chief Financial Officer), followed by the Bakshi (modern-day human resources head), the Qazi-ul-Qazat (Chief Justice), and the Kotwal (Chief of Police), in that order.

In 1612, the British East India Company, after winning battles against the Portuguese, established contact with the Mughal Emperor Jahangir, who permitted the company to establish trading posts and factories in the port towns of Surat (now Gujarat), Madras (now Chennai), Bombay (now Mumbai), and Calcutta (now Kolkata) in exchange for goods and merchandise from Europe. What started first as a trade agreement eventually became a precursor of British rule in India after the East India Company won major military battles at Plassey in 1757 and Buxar in 1764, defeating the Mughal emperor. They obtained revenue collection rights in the modern states of Bengal and Bihar (formerly Bengal Presidency) in 1765. The Regulating Act of 1773 was the first seminal legislation that furthered the transition of the East India Company's commercial administration into a political government in the Indian subcontinent. It laid the foundations of British rule. Finally, in 1813, the trading rights of the company were abandoned, and in 1858 the administration of the Indian continent (except for Goa and Pondicherry, which were Portuguese and French colonies, respectively) came under the British Crown (1858-1947). Of the biggest legacies of the British colonial rule is the civil service system, recommended by the Aitchison Commission (1866), which brought in the covenanted Civil Services of India. The cadre model was introduced in 1923 and the covenanted civil service reconstituted as the Indian Civil Service (ICS) became the apex cadre. Most of the top 1,000 officials were British, but by 1945, more than half were Indians. Lloyd George, Prime Minister of England (1916-22), called the ICS the "steel frame of India".

The Government of India Act of 1919 further elaborated the structure of governance by establishing a bicameral legislative body based on the parliamentary model of government, while the Government of India Act 1935 introduced the federal form that continues to be operational in India, besides the secretariat, ministries, departments and the tenure system, all of which were nurtured during the British regime. Some of the other institutional legacies of the British period are (i) a cadre-based bureaucracy, (ii) parliamentary system of government (iii) infrastructure of a modern state (roads, telegraph, railways, and the postal system), (iv) educational system with English as the medium of instruction, and (v) the introduction of a formal legal system.

1.2 The British Legacy : Structures and Features

The Civil Service in India was introduced by the East India Company and the present civil service is a modified product of successive reforms since its inception. To begin with the British Indian civil service was classified into two types-Covenanted and Uncovenanted.

The Covenanted civil servants were Englishmen constituting the graded posts who, after receiving formal education in England were sent to India. They entered into a service contract with the East India Company for a stipulated time and enjoyed privileges such as leave and pensions. The Uncovenanted civil servants were Indians who had no statutory privileges. The authority of recruitment belonged to the Directors of the East India Company.

In 1765, the East India Company increased the administrative duties and responsibilities of the civil servants from only trade-related activities to revenue and judicial administration. The Regulating Act of 1773 clearly distinguished between commercial (trade) and administrative (revenue and judicial) tasks of civil servants prohibiting them from conducting commercial activities for profit. The Pitt's India Act of 1784 recommended the filling of vacancies in the governing bodies by covenanted civil servants and also laid down the age limit for new entrants in service.

In 1805, the East India Company established a training institute for civil servants at Haileybury in England. Appointments were made through a nomination process where candidates were recommended by the Directors of the East India Company.

In 1853, a five-member committee headed by Lord Macaulay recommended that appointments to the Indian Civil Service should not be based on patronage. The committee emphasized on providing the best liberal education to candidates and recommended that the candidates should be selected through a competitive examination. The committee also proposed the need for serving a probation period before final appointments. As a result of these recommendations, a Civil Services Commission was set-up in England in 1855 which was entrusted with the responsibility of conducting the civil service exam for the covenanted service. The first competitive civil service examination was held in London in 1856.

The East India Company was removed in 1858 and the Indian administration came under the direct control of the British Crown. The powers lying with the Directors of the East India Company were then transferred to the Secretary of State in India, who became the real executive authority of the British Crown. In 1870, the British Parliament passed an Act that authorized Indians to be appointed to any office, which was earlier reserved for candidates from covenanted services.

In 1886, the Aitchison Commission headed by Sir Charles Aitchison was formed to abolish the Statutory Civil Service. It recommended a three-tier classification of civil services: Imperial, Provincial and Subordinate services. Services such as Indian Civil Service, Indian Police Service (IPS) and Indian Medical Service were included in the Imperial civil service. The Provincial services consisted of Indian Education Services, Indian Agricultural Services and Indian Veterinary Services, while the lower grades of the uncovenanted services were categorized as Subordinate service.

In August 1917, E. S. Montagu, the then Secretary of State in India, declared a new policy on increasing the association of Indians across every branch of administration. A year later in 1918, a report on constitutional changes, Royal Commission on Public Service in India by Montagu and Chelmsford, recommended that the 33% of superior posts in the Imperial service be reserved for Indians. Both of them favoured that the appointments be made without racial discrimination and that a separate competitive examination be held in India.

1.3 Indianization of Public Services

The Government of India Act of 1919 recommended that the Imperial Service be renamed as All India Service. The Act also provided safeguards against political influence in the recruitment process of the civil service. The first competitive examination in India was held in 1922 under the supervision of the Civil Service Commission of England.

In 1923, a Royal Commission on the Superior Civil Service was formed under the leadership of Lord Lee. The Lee Commission redefined the civil service into three broad categories: All India, Central and Provincial

All India Service mainly consisted of Indian Civil Service. Indian Medical Service, Indian Forest Service (IFS) and Indian Service of Engineers. The Central Service used to deal with states and foreign affairs along with railways, posts and telegraphs, customs, audits and accounts, scientific and technical departments. The Provincial Service included Indian Educational Services, Indian Agricultural Services and the Veterinary Services.

The Secretary of State retained the power of appointment and control of AIS and Central Services. Similar powers were given to the provincial government.

For fresh vacancies of the provincial service and to maintain recruitment standards, the Royal Commission under the chairmanship of Lord Lee, recommended setting up of Statutory Public Service Commission. The Statutory Public Service Commission was set up in 1926 replacing the Civil Service Commission of England. The Statutory Public Service Commission also took over the responsibility of recruitment of All India, Central and Provincial service personnel.

The Civil Services Rule of 1930 broadly classified the civil services into the following categories:

1. The All India Services
2. The Central Services
    a. Class I
    b. Class II
    c. Subordinate (ministerial, executive and outdoor duties)
    d. Inferior (peons and messengers)
3. The Provincial Services
4. The Specialist Services such as Engineering

The difference between Class I and Class II Central Services was in the matter of appointment. Class I appointments were made by the Governor General and Class II positions were appointed by a lower authority.

In 1935, the Government of India Act introduced provincial autonomy for protection of the rights and privileges of civil servants. According to this, a civil servant could not be removed by an authority below the rank of an officer who appointed him.

The First Central Pay Commission (CPC) was set-up in 1946 to report on service conditions of Class I, Class II and Subordinate Service. As per its recommendation, the Central Services were re-categorized as Class I, Class II, Class III (erstwhile Subordinate Services) and Class IV (erstwhile Inferior Services). The Specialist Services were also included in this classification; therefore post 1946 no separate Specialist Services category was made to continue. (Data: Public Service in India: A country profile, DARPG GCH-2012)

The most enduring legacy of the British rule in India was the Indian Civil Service, which was the chief instrument through which colonial authority was exercised throughout India. The consolidation of the British Empire in India would have been impossible without the contribution of the Indian Civil Service.

In the merit-based civil service it was the ranking in the competitive examination which determined the province to which a new recruit would be allotted. During 1858-1919, recruitment to the ICS was made through competitive examinations held in London.

The prescribed age limit, underwent changes from time to time, but generally moved in the range between 19 and 23 years. The competitive examination aimed at testing the proficiency of the student in certain subjects like English language, European literature, Mathematics, Sanskrit, Arabic, Moral Science, Philosophy, Logic, Natural Sciences, etc.

Efforts began at institutionalization of the training system with the setting up of the Fort William College at Calcutta in 1880. Training in Indian languages and Law was emphasized. Languages and local laws were given importance in order to bring the officials a little closer to the common people.

The idea of a central pool for drawing manpower came in 1920, on the basis of the recommendations of the Secretariat Procedure Committee (1919). The Government of India made upper division clerks of the secretariat part of an Imperial Secretariat Service and appointed a Central Staff Selection Board to supervise the recruitment process. The board consisted of three persons —an independent chairman and two members to be nominated, one each by the Home and Education departments.

In 1937, the Committee on Organization and Procedure (Maxwell Committee) recommended that the ministerial staff should be divided into two main grades, namely, assistants and clerks, the former being able to note on files and to deal with paper work, while the latter could continue with routine office work.

The staffing pattern of the Central Secretariat underwent a change as a result of the suggestions made by the Tottenham Committee (1945-46). Later, in 1950, the old Imperial Secretariat Service was replaced by the Central Secretariat Service.

Some features of the Secretariat System continue in India even today: heavy reliance on precedents, incapacity of the lower grades of officials to share responsibility and the practice of excessive record-keeping and noting.

A well-developed pay structure for civil servants had also been devised by the British. In 1918, the posts were divided into 'superior' and 'inferior' categories. A superior post was one carrying pay in excess of Rs. 1,000 a month. However, even an incumbent of an inferior post could get an 'excess' from the ninth year of his service. The total number of the superior and inferior Indian Civil Service posts under the Government of India did not exceed 84 in 1918. Promotional opportunities depended on seniority, official conduct and quality of performance. Even as early as 1834, the system of annual returns existed wherein the professional merit and conduct of the subordinate officers at work were graded by the superior officers.

However the frequency of transfers adversely affected the vitality of the officers. It was not uncommon to find three to four sub-divisional officers changing in a year.

As already mentioned, on the recommendations of the Aitchison Commission in 1887, the covenanted civil service was named the Indian Civil Service and the uncovenanted civil service was titled as the Provincial Civil Service (PCS), designated after the name of the particular province to which it belonged. The PCS was to be recruited separately in each province of India and hold the higher appointments of the existing uncovenanted service.

The lowest ranks of the uncovenanted service were constituted into a separate subordinate service. Later on, each province made its own rules regarding the recruitment of the PCS, subject to the control of the Government of India.

On the basis of the Aitchison Commission's recommendations, certain posts were transferred to the PCS, but, the government, while accepting the proposal, stipulated that promotion to higher offices of the ICS from the PCS must be by special selection and not on grounds of seniority alone. Hence, in most of the states, holders of a university degree were found to be capable enough to hold posts in the PCS and the rest of the posts were filled by promotions from the subordinate service.

From 1846, the Secretary to the Government of India in the Finance Department was nominated the *ex-officio* Accountant General of India with powers to supervise and examine Indian accounts. Another important step was the creation of a general Department of Accounts in place of separate accounts for each presidency. This brought about an integration in the system.

1.4 Revenue, District & Local Government Administration

During the Company's rule, revenue was obtained from two sources — land revenue and taxes on trade and personal property. The expenditure was classified into two heads: (i) security or defence and (ii) social and development services. The latter comprised education, public health, etc.

By far, the most important administrative innovation was the introduction of the budget system vide the Financial Resolution of 7 April 1860. Under this system, the financial estimates for each year were to *be* arranged, considered and sanctioned by the Government of India before the year commenced. It contained the anticipated income and proposed expenditure of the empire.

That the government was quite keen on reforms is also evident from the creation of reform committees in the field of revenue administration. The Resolution of 1860 provided for the creation of a Budget and Audit Committee. On the committee's recommendations, the posts of the Accountant General and Auditor General were merged into the Accountant and Auditor General's office. The committee's recommendations also led to the setting up of an Audit Board, which consisted of an Auditor General and the chief of the Military Finance Department. They were to act together in all organizational and policy matters affecting budget estimates, audit and accounts.

Another important contribution of the British was the introduction of government paper currency in 1860. The Bank of Bengal became the agent for the printing, issuing and circulation of the paper notes. In 1882, the district treasury was placed under the district collector.

A full-fledged and systematic mechanism of control was also evolved in 1919 when the Comptroller and Auditor General was made responsible to the Central Legislature. In 1926, he was given the power to inspect 'any government office of account'. In 1922, a Central Public Accounts Committee was created, consisting of both elected and official members.

It considered the Auditor General's reports on the re-appropriation amounts. Thus, through these two bodies, the Indian Legislature was to exercise control over the administration of public finance.

Under the Act of the Central Legislature of 1934, the Government of India established the Reserve Bank which began to function with effect from 1 April 1935.

The Board of Revenue, created in 1781, became the controlling authority for revenue purposes. The Board, consisting of a certain number of civil servants, acted as a link between the government and the Collectors. In 1829, Divisional Commissioners were appointed to supervise the Collectors, in four to five districts, in the exercise of their powers. They were made responsible to the Board of Revenue.

The foundations of the contemporary police administration in India were laid during the British rule, particularly after the enactment of the Indian Police Act, 1861, which created an organized system of constabulary. During the British rule, at the state level, the Inspector General of Police (IGP) exercised control over the whole police force of the provincial government. The IGP was often a member of the covenanted civil service due to which even a few ICS officers held the post of IGP. At the district level, the IGP was assisted by the Superintendent of Police (SP). A subordinate police force, comprising Inspectors/ Head Constables, Sergeants and Constables, was also created.

In fact, the Police Act of 1861 and the Code of Criminal Procedure (1861) had strengthened the position of the District Magistrate (DM) by giving him the powers of exercising general control over the district police as well as over subordinate magistracy. This over-centralization of authority in one official paved the way for administrative despotism at the district level.

It is noteworthy that the Indian Penal Code (IPC) of 1860 and the Code of Criminal Procedure (CrPC) of 1861, along with other significant legislations such as the Indian Evidence Act, constituted the legal framework of criminal justice administration that helped the police system to exercise its functions effectively.

In the earlier stages of the Company's rule, the office of the Collector combined both revenue and judicial functions. The Cornwallis Code of 1793 took away the judicial powers of the Collector laying the foundation of an independent judiciary. The code provided for a three-tier system of European judges with the Eilla and city courts at the bottom, the Provincial Court of Appeal in the middle and the *Sadar Diwani* and *Nizamat Adalat* at the top. The creation of an intermediate tier of provincial courts was intended to lessen the workload of the Governor-General. Later the intermediate tier was abolished as it slowed down the process and flow of justice and the jurisdiction of the district courts was enlarged to decentralize the administration of justice.

Another important reform was made during the time of Lord Ripon (1882-1919), who has been called the father of local self-government in India. In 1882, he introduced a new policy through a new Act. The resolution, dated 18 May, 1882, recommended the extension of the elective element in rural bodies, reduction in the size of the Official element, an elected non-official as the chairman of rural bodies, and financial decentralization. The

Decentralization Commission of 1909 examined the problem of local government in great detail. It suggested a three-tier system consisting of: (1) the village panchayat or union boards, (2) the *local tehsil* or sub-district boards, and (3) the district board. It recommended the lessening of government control over local bodies. For the cities, municipal corporations were set up in Madras in 1688 and Calcutta and Bombay in 1726.

The Montague-Chelmsford Report of 1918 on Indian constitutional reforms examined the existing system of local government in the country and concluded that local bodies were vested with greater powers and outside control was minimal. Through the Act of 1919, local self-government became a provincial and transferred subject under a responsible Indian minister. Laws were passed in every province for the growth of village panchayats. They aimed at increasing the strength of elected members to the extent of making them the immediate arbiters of policy in local affairs. The Act of 1935 introduced provincial autonomy but due to the Second World War, up till Independence, nothing more could be achieved in this realm.

1.5 The Secretariat System: Further Developments

The Central Secretariat was situated in Calcutta and was exclusively under the control of Bengal civilians till 1843. It consisted of a Secretary-General, three assistants and clerical staff. There were three departments, viz. Public, Secret and Commercial. By a resolution in 1843, four departments were set up —Military, Foreign, Home and Financial. Military affairs were managed by the Military Department; all foreign and diplomatic relations by the Foreign Department; matters of justice, education and legislation by the Home Department; and the Financial Department (though created three months earlier than the Act) looked after the financial operations, the provision of ways and means, etc. In 1855, a separate Department of Public Works was created. The portfolio system was introduced in 1858. The essence of this innovation was that a member of the Council would be appointed in charge of one or more departments of the government and he would issue orders on behalf of the Governor-General-in-Council. This practice was adopted by the Indian administrators even after Independence.

The British interest in reforms is reflected in the setting up of several commissions and committees. The Secretariat Procedure Committee recommended in 1919 a pyramidal organization for every department, with a secretary at the top, and at least two deputy secretaries. It recommended the abolition of the post of undersecretary except in the Finance Department. The idea behind these changes was to reduce administrative delays and expedite official business.

The Lewellyn Smith Committee (1920) re-examined the tenure system operating from Lord Curzon's time since 1905. It observed that the tenure of the office of secretaries and deputy secretaries should remain fixed at four years to bring about stability in the working of the secretariat. The Secretarial Committee (1935), or Wheeler Committee, studied the problem of delays in the working of the secretariat and recommended the practice of double notings to speed up the work. Further, the Maxwell Committee (1937) suggested that the secretary of the department should be responsible to the minister and that the secretary was the officer competent to guide the minister. Later, the Tottenham Committee (1945-46) reported on the organization of departments, the question of staffing and the reorganization of the entire secretariat system. It recommended that distinct duties be assigned to different grades of secretarial officers and agreed on nomenclatures for each grade.

The foregoing analysis makes it clear that under the British rule, Indian administration evolved through a series of changes and continuing innovations. The coexistence of continuity and change was an important feature of India's administrative legacy.

It is obvious that the contemporary Indian administrative system has been built on its British heritage. All India Services, civil services recruitment, administrative training, the secretariat system, office procedures, management of districts, revenue administration, police system, budgeting, accounting, auditing and a number of other structural and functional areas of Indian administration have their roots in the British rule. Though the British had their own objectives of sustaining and strengthening their imperial rule, to which the administrative system was being geared, some of the results of their organizational initiatives have proved to be useful to India even after Independence.

1.6 Departmental Organizations and their Innovations

The pre-Independence era saw the administrative organizations of the Central and the States (then called '"Provincial") governments intact. This was a factor contributing to the undisturbed transfer of power from the British to the Indian hands. The administration of the country's security, law and order, finances, communication system, educational organization and other elements of the infrastructure was made to continue as before even after independence.

After Independence on 15 August 1947, the following eighteen departments (redesignated as 'Ministries') functioned under the Government of India: (1) External Affairs and Commonwealth Relations, (2) Defence, (3) Finance, (4) Home, (5) States, (6) Legislative (Law), (7) Commerce, (8) Industries and Supplies, (9) Railways, (10) Transport, (11) Communications, (12) Labour, (13) Agriculture, (14) Food, (15) Education, (16) Health, (17) Information and Broadcasting, (18) Works, Mines and Power.

Nine decades of British rule witnessed the beginning of elementary social services like primary education, health and medicine, agricultural research, fiscal incentives for industries, etc. Legislative activity had commenced. The two World Wars introduced price and physical controls over the essential supplies including food, cloth, petrol and kerosene, etc., besides growth in armed services, war industries and supplies. In 1921, the number of departments stood at nine, which were increased to twelve in 1937. After 1919 the main administrative activities in agriculture, education, health, and labour were conducted by the provincial governments, due to decentralized initiatives under the 1919 and 1935 Government of India Acts.

The volume and variety of the administrative activities in the States have increased after Independence, the number of Secretariat departments have not grown much. The administrations in the States have changed in nature and size: in rural development, education, agriculture, health and medicine and related matters.

Usually, the ministries at the Central level have one or more departments, depending on the need for specialization. For instance, the Ministry of Personnel, Public Grievances and Pensions, as the name suggests, has three departments. The number of Ministries and their constituent departments go on increasing on both political and administrative grounds. The need to accommodate many ministries leads to proliferation of Ministries and Departments. Also, specialization calls for creation of new ministries and departments. Science and technology, Atomic Energy, Non-Conventional Energy are instances of new needs. The new economic activities undertaken by the Union Government are reflected in the departments of coal, power and non-conventional energy sources in the Ministry of Energy, departments of chemicals and petrochemicals, industrial development and public enterprises in the Ministry of Industry, departments of planning and statistics in the Ministry of Planning, and Ministries of Petroleum and Natural Gas, Programme Implementation and Steel and Mines. Nationalized banks are looked after by the Finance Ministry. Concerns for the development of Science and Technology are incorporated in the Ministries of Science and Technology and Department of Atomic Energy, Electronics and Space. The electronic media and the computers have brought about a change in methods of information, storage and retrieval, and communication. The forum of Parliament and State legislatures have brought in the Ministry of Parliamentary Affairs and increased the work of the Ministry of Law and Justice. The tremendous growth in the strength of personnel in administration has led to the creation of the new Ministry of Personnel, Public Grievances and Pensions.

Innovated organizational forms such as public corporations, government companies and joint companies have appeared on the post-Independence administrative scene, giving rise to the demand for new categories of administrators. Attached offices like the National Academy of Administration at Mussoorie and subordinate offices like the National Fire Service College at Nagpur are new off-shoots of administrative institutions. Scientific laboratories and research stations have broadened the scope of administration. Numerous advisory bodies like the Central Board of Secondary Education and the Central Labour Advisory Board evoke the participation of concerned interest groups in policy-making in those areas.

In terms of internal organization and relationships within the departments and outside, the working of the Departments have not changed much after Independence. Hierarchy, importance of the written word and the filing system have continued. Pre-Independence manuals prepared during the colonial rule still govern most of the older departments with modifications here and there. The post of Chief Secretary of provincial administration before 1947 exists today; but at the Centre, the Cabinet Secretary, de facto head of administration, is an innovation.

Another recent development is the growth of independent regulatory agencies like Telecom Regulatory Authority of India (TRAI) in telecommunication, Securities and Exchange Board of India (SEBI) in shares and stock exchanges, etc. These agencies have been set up to lend a degree of independence to quasi-judicial arbitration, rate- fixation and conflict resolution functions of the government unlike normal executive departments.

1.7 The Public Services

After Independence the Indian Civil Service was replaced by the Indian Administrative Service (IAS). A larger number of the officers in the IAS and the Indian Police Service (that replaced the Imperial Police Service) were required to replace the former services. They had to man the posts in the recently merged princely states. Much more than that, the character of the All India Services had changed when India became a democracy after Independence. The services focused now on serving the people of the country, and not the imperial masters. The ICS men were not only officials; they were a part of the colonial government. The officials of independent India—no more rulers—had to imbibe the democratic temper of its polity. This marked a change from the pre-1947 scene.

The All India Services Act, 1951, of the Indian Parliament provided for the formation of two services, the IAS and the Indian Police Service. This was an outcome of the deliberations in the Constituent Assembly of India. The Constitution contains a separate Part XIV titled 'Services under the Union and the States'. Article 312 of the Constitution relates to the All India Services.

A new All India Service, the Indian Forest Service, was constituted in July 1966, though an amendment to the All India Services Act, 1951 effected in 1963 provided for the formation of three new All India Services, viz., the Indian Service of Engineers, the Indian Forest Service and the Indian Medical and Health Service.

The personnel belonging to the Central Services work in the various departments of the Central Government. They are organized into four groups, A, B, C and D, on the basis of the pay scales of the posts in each group. The following are some of the Central Services: Central Engineering Services, Central Health Service, Central Secretariat Service, Indian Audit and Accounts Service, Indian Defence Accounts Service, Indian Foreign Service, Indian Postal Service, Indian Revenue Service, Central Legal Service, Central Information Service, Indian Statistical Service, and Indian Economic Service. Before 1947, specialist officials worked in various functional departments of the Central Government, but after Independence, different services (cadres) were formed. Statistical Service, Economic Service, Information Service and Foreign Service were some of the new cadres formed to cater to the emergent needs of the Central Government. The Indian Foreign Service attracts intelligent young graduates along with the IAS. After Independence, as the functions undertaken by the State Governments have diversified, several specialist services in Class I and II were formed. Some of these are: Forest Service, Agricultural Service, Animal Husbandry,

Prohibition and Excise, Judicial, Police, Jail, Medical, Public Health, Educational, Engineering, Accounts, Sales Tax and Industries Service. A few of these services did exist before 1947, but now their strength has gone up. Besides, Class III and IV Services are on roll.

The new public services share, to a large extent, the attributes of political impartiality, selection on merit and integrity like in the ICS and other services before Independence. The public services in free India are committed to the objectives of the Constitution. The

State Governments have their own service cadre and only a few states have their own local government bureaucratic cadre.

1.8 Public Service Commissions

To ensure impartial selection of meritorious civil servants, a Public Service Commission in India was established in 1926 with a Chairman and four members. This (Central) Public Service Commission was vested with two functions mainly: recruitment to All India and Central Services and screening of disciplinary cases. It was also to advise and assist in matters of standards of qualification and methods of examination for the civil services, so far as recruitment in India was concerned. The Commission was re-designated as the Federal Public Service Commission under the 1935 Act.

The Government of India Act, 1935, stated that each provincial government was to form a Public Service Commission independently or in groups. The functions of the Public Service Commissions after Independence have increased. The responsibilities in regard to recruitment of public employees through written test and/ or interviews are enormous in view of the large number of qualified officials the governments at the Union and the State levels require for employment. Promotions and transfers to another service are also referred to the commissions for their advice.

The Chairman and members of these Commissions are appointed by the President in the cases of the Union Commission and by the Governor in the case of a State Commission (in consultation with the council of ministers in both). It is also provided by the Constitution that nearly half of the members of each commission should have held office for ten years under the Government of India or a State Government.

It may be noted that the recommendations of the commissions to the government concerned are advisory, and not binding. It is obligatory for the commission to present its annual report to the Parliament or respective State legislatures for discussion by the members. The governments concerned have to give reasons for the non-acceptance of the Commission's recommendations.

1.9 Development Orientation

After Independence, welfare and development-oriented functions of the administration have taken precedence. This was based on the Constitution's emphasis on a democratic and egalitarian social ethos. It does not mean that during British rule the development content did not exist in administration at all. It existed but was subordinated to the Imperial motivations of the British. Railways, posts and telegraphs, roads, ports, banking and insurance, capital cities, were opened up; a foundation was laid for the future development of the country's economy. Scientific, technical and liberal education at primary, secondary and university levels began. Health and medical facilities at an elementary level were started. Agricultural research was commenced. After the First World War, fiscal incentives were given for industrial development through individual initiative.

Grass roots pressures in a democratic set up brought in a lot of welfare legislation in India after Independence. Planning has guided the economic development of the country since the beginning of the First Five Year Plan in 1951. Plans formulated by the Planning Commission aimed at the rapid all-round economic development of the country. Plans set the targets of development in different sectors including industry, agriculture, electricity, minerals, transport and communication, education, health, etc. The administration at different levels — Central, State and Local— was geared to the realization of the goals of the plans. Besides the national plan, State and District Plans were also prepared by the administration. Planned development has been the hallmark of the activities of the administration since Independence. Blueprints of post-war reconstruction plans in specific sectors like education (Sergeant Plan) and health (Bhore Plan) had been prepared by the Central Government on the eve of Independence but it was left to the governments of free India to implement these.

Rapid all-round industrial development posed a challenge-to-the administration in free India. To attain industrial self-sufficiency, basic and heavy industries like steel, machine-building, heavy-electrical machinery, extraction and processing of minerals were established. The execution of the Industrial Policy Resolution of 1948 and 1956 required industrial development through the growth of public sector as the private sector did not possess the requisite capital and technical personnel. The administration and management of the public sector industries and business called for the recruitment and training of the managerial and technical personnel in the public enterprises. The realization of the targets set before the public enterprises depended upon the efficiency, skills, innovation and hard work of the directing, managerial and administrative personnel of the public enterprises. Operating various physical and financial controls over the industry, trade and business necessitated planning and created special responsibilities for the administration. Currently, however, the government policy towards industrialization and the public enterprises is changing. A larger involvement of the private sector in the economy and gradual 'disinvestment' of government shares in public enterprises has been the preference since the 1990s.

Development administration in the rural areas has faced more difficult tasks than the administration of public enterprises. Increasing agricultural production, promoting public health and medical standards, spreading education as well as taking care of its quality, provision of civic amenities —all these and other tasks in rural areas had to be realized by providing the required economic means, technical tools and inputs. Involvement of the rural people in the transformation was sought by entrusting some of these tasks or their aspects to their political and administrative institutions.

The welfare of women, scheduled castes and tribes and other backward sections had also to be advanced by the administration in terms of the Directive Principles and Fundamental Rights mentioned in the Constitution. The achievements of the administration with regard to the above tasks may not have been uniformly satisfactory in different regions, but Indian administration has been engaged in the performance of these tasks as a response to the new social demands after Independence.

1.10 Centre-State Relations

Federalism integrates a nation by distributing governmental functions and powers between the federal, that is, the Central and the constituent State Governments. The Central Government plays an overall coordinating role.

The Constitution of India has introduced a federal political system. It has divided the country's administration into two spheres, administration of the Union (national) and of the States. The Union administration looks after the subjects in List I of the Seventh Schedule of the Constitution and the States administer the subjects enumerated in List 2. List 3 is the Concurrent list of subjects on which both the Union and the States are competent to legislate, but a Union law takes precedence over a State law on any matter in this list.

The administration of the States includes most areas of social welfare and development administration. Police, jails, land tenure and revenue, public works (except national, that is, inter-state highways, and river valleys), local government, etc., are examples of the former, while the latter includes agriculture and animal husbandry, health and medicine, and social welfare. The States administer (that is levy, collect and use) the taxes on agricultural income, estate and succession duties in respect of agricultural land, taxes on land and buildings, electricity duties, vehicle and profession taxes, etc. Some of these, for example, octroi, property tax, etc., are given over to the local bodies for levy collection and used by the State Governments through legislation.

The Union administers those subjects which are essential for national security and integrity, for the maintenance and growth of a nationwide infrastructure, and for national economic development. Some specific areas are defence, foreign affairs, atomic energy, citizenship, etc. Currency and coinage, foreign and inter-state trade and commerce, industries of national interest, banking, insurance and national finance, facilitate economic development of the country as a whole. The Union is vested with expanding financial resources. These are taxes on income other than agricultural income, customs, excise duties on manufactured and produced commodities (with some exceptions), succession and estate duties on properties other than agricultural land, etc.

The common subjects in the Concurrent List enable both the Union and the States to legislate and administer matters of special and economic significance and of legal nature implying concern to both economic and social planning, transfer of property and contracts relating to other than agricultural land, population control and family planning, trade unions and industrial labour, employment and unemployment, etc. Civil and criminal laws are of concern to both, hence, are vested in both the administrations. Education, forests and protection of wildlife have been recently transferred from the State to the Concurrent List due to growing national concern in them.

The Union Ministry in charge of subjects in the State list are engaged in coordinating the work of the States and may guide them in research, pilot projects, training and advice to the States on the concerned subjects. The remaining (residuary) subjects are vested in the Union.

Parliament adopts several laws annually; a large number of these are administered by the State administration as the Union does have its own personnel in the States, e.g. members of the IAS, the Central Services, etc. The Union Government provides financial assistance to the States as the former possesses larger financial resources and the latter fall short of these due to their growing development functions. The States call for the help of the Union forces during disturbed times. In the Planning era, even in respect to the State subjects, consultations were held between the Union and the State administrations regarding planning and progress of the plans. On matters in the Concurrent List such consultations are compulsorily held.

India's is a cooperative federation. The federal polity has to harmonize national integrity with constituent States' autonomy, necessary for a healthy federal democracy. Financially, the Union is stronger than the States, so it has to help them.

However, much has changed in Centre-State Relations after the 1990s. A real substantive economic autonomy has come to the states in the Liberalization, Privatization, Globalization (LPG) era. Now all the states compete and then cooperate in the Indian and global markets to raise funds to augment their resources for development.

Popular participation in administrative processes has assumed prominent proportions after Independence. Before Independence, it was confined to the role of the popular representatives in the local self-governing bodies. After Independence, specifically after the passage of the 73rd and the 74th amendment acts Panchayati Raj has been the most significant channel of participation of the rural people in rural development administration. Community development was the earlier phase of this popular participation. But it was dominated by the officials, so it could not evoke adequate participation of villagers in rural development. Panchayati Raj was introduced in the late fifties by a few State Governments, like Rajasthan, Andhra, Maharashtra and Gujarat. But its progress was uneven in other States. Later, West Bengal, Tripura, Andhra Pradesh and Karnataka introduced progressive measures relating to Panchayati Raj. The 73rd constitutional amendment was a land mark and has given a further boost to popular participation in rural areas by constitutionalizing the third tier of governance. Much still needs to be done to make it more meaningful and beneficial in terms of boosting livelihoods and improving the standard of life of the rural people through education, better health facilities and jobs in rural areas.

Municipal government is the mode of popular participation in civic administration. Much requires to be done to step up its efficiency. With growing urbanization civic amenities need to keep pace with urban civic demands.

Voluntary organizations can do a lot in accelerating the pace of development— both rural and urban, through their participation in the development processes and education of the people. These organizations can be a liaison between the administrative agencies and the people.

Conclusion

Elements of Continuity

There has been continuity in Indian Administration after 1947 from the pattern that existed before Independence. At the same time the political ambience and the objectives of administration have changed completely after Independence.

The most important reason for this continuity was the relatively peaceful transfer of power from the British rulers to the Indian people. Another reason was that millions of refugees migrated between the two post-partition countries, India and Pakistan, partly due to communal violence and also the option given to the sections of population to settle in either of the two countries. Indian administration got reduced in numbers as most of the Muslims and European Civil Servants resigned and left the country. Thus there were neither the resources nor the personnel to set up a new administrative machinery immediately after 1947. A stable and well-founded administrative organization comprising departments and civil services was the critical need of the hour. So, the then existing administrative framework was continued almost in its entirety after Independence.

However, India adopted its own Constitution within three years after Independence. The objectives and nature of this Constitution is altogether different from those of the constitutional acts prevailing under the British rule. India enacted a democratic constitution—periodic elections to the national Parliament and the State legislatures, adoption of the goals of a social welfare state through laws, and citizen entitlements were guaranteed through a package of rights and progressive legislation.

The liberties of the citizens, the political parties and minorities are guaranteed by the Constitution. An independent judiciary protects these rights and freedoms. The Constitution contains the ideals of a social welfare State. A federal state based on the Union (Central) and State Governments have been established by the Constitutional structure. Local governments (urban and rural) are the third tier of governance looking after the civic and developmental functions at that level. Public Service Commissions at the Union and the States levels are entrusted with the recruitment of civil servants under the Constitution.

These and other provisions of the Constitution have expanded the ambit of Public Administration in the country. Moreover, the public services are accountable to the Parliament and State legislatures. They also have to be sensitive to the aspirations and grievances of the electorate in a democracy.

The Constitution has established parliamentary democracy in the country. Before Independence the legislatures at the Centre and in the Provinces did not possess full powers and authority as under the present Constitution. During the periods of partial legislative control, 1920-35, 1937-39 and 1946-47, the public services were partially accountable to the popularly elected representatives and the ministers responsible to the public. This led to administrative continuity after Independence.

The most important change inducing factors in Indian administration has been the advent of democracy and the compulsions of development and a welfare state. The elements of stability are found in the continuity of the departmental system and the smooth induction of new public services selected on merit, with commitment to the Constitutional objectives.

The number of development and welfare departments has grown after Independence. Growth of scientific and technological knowledge and its application has also influenced the administration. However, despite such diversification of administrative structures and functions the basic problems of organization that still dominate the bureaucratic hierarchy are: predominance of formalism, presence of red tape and the existence of a large number of outmoded manuals and laws.

Various new public services have been constituted in independent India though the generalist administrator still dominates. The Indian ICS incumbents continued in office, but as a service it was replaced by the IAS. The Indian Police Service and the Indian Forest Service were the other two All India Services constituted after 1947. Besides, the Central Services man the departments of the Union government. The States also have their own services including the generalist ones and those serving various functional departments like agriculture, education, health, roads, drinking water and sanitation. Local bodies have their own personnel in some states. Public Service Commissions have been set up to ensure recruitment of personnel on merit and to advice on disciplinary cases, transfers and promotions.

The Constitutional directives seek to promote the ideals of a just social and economic order and a welfare state. Besides national planning, state and district planning have also become functional. A large public sector to bring about rapid, all-round and self-sufficient industrial development has posed a great challenge for the managerial personnel in the public enterprises.

It is said that Indian federalism is tilted towards the Centre but this was inevitable from the point of view of national security and development. Popular participation in administration, particularly of development initiatives occurs through the Panchayati Raj institutions, municipal governments, cooperatives and voluntary organizations.

Role of Civil Service Today

The role of civil service has changed significantly from the pre-Independence days to current times. This, to a large extent, has been driven by the changing domestic and international scenario and the nature of responsibilities centred on the agenda of governance of the specific period.

Prior to Independence, the main responsibility of the civil service was to maintain law and order and manage revenue administration. Civil servants immediately in the post-independence period dealt with developmental issues and hence were required to possess and continuously acquire new skills relating to development administration. In the 21st century, the present-day civil servants are responsible for trade negotiations; regulation of the private sector; effective monetary management; reduction of gender gap; elimination of social inequity; participation in international discussions; and management of Public Sector Enterprises (PSE). This has made their job highly demanding. In this context, civil servants have to be prepared to meet the new challenges and equip themselves with the necessary skills and capabilities to meet their tasks. They need to master latest technologies and adopt new modes of functioning. This requires a high degree of professionalism and competence on the part of the civil servants.

Civil servants of the pre-Independence era reported to their British masters who were not accountable to the Indian public. Today civil servants work within the boundaries of a democratic system of governance and report to elected members of a democratic government. In addition, today's environment is characterized by an ever so vigilant press, the public and alert legislatures, which make the working of civil servants all the more demanding and accountable.

Over a period of time the role of civil service has evolved from unaccountable and arbitrary styles of administration (pre-1947) to development orientation (post-1950's) and after 1990s to the imperatives of new public management in a post-globalized era. In a parliamentary system of government, the permanent executive is accountable to the political executive who in turn is accountable directly to the public. In the current era of administrative reform, the trend is towards the direct accountability of the public servant to the citizen for public service delivery through the strengthening of public accountability mechanisms.

Suggested Readings

Arora, Ramesh K., and Rajni Goyal, *Indian Public Administration: Institutions and Issues,* Delhi, New Age, 2013.

Bakshi, P. M., *The Constitution of India,* Delhi, Universal, Latest Edition.

Braibanti Ralph ed. & Joseph Spengler, *Administration and Economic Development in India,* Durham: Duke University Press, 1963

Kashyap, Subhash C., *Our Political System,* Delhi, National Book Trust, Latest Edition.

Mason, Philip, *The Men Who Ruled India,* New Delhi, Rupa, 1994.

Mishra, B. B., *The Administrative History of India,* New Delhi, OUP, 1970.

Public Service in India: A Country Profile 2012 DARPG, Ministry of Personnel, Public Grievances and Pensions GOI.

Puri B. N, *History of Indian Administration,* Munshiram Manoharlal Publishers Pvt. Limited, 1982

Ramachandran, Padma, *Public Administration in India,* Delhi, National Book Trust, 1996.

OOO

Chapter Two

Philosophical and Constitutional Framework

Introduction

The Constitution of India is a unique document. It occupies an important place not only among the constitutions of the newly independent countries of the post-Second World War period but also in the constitutional history of the world. It deals, among others with Fundamental Rights, Directive Principles of State Policy and provides the structure and powers of different levels of government and public institutions. The Preamble of the Constitution declares India to be a sovereign socialist secular democratic republic. A study of its features reveals that it is a remarkable document in size, form and content.

We have detailed provisions in our Constitution regarding the governmental machinery at the Centre and the States, their areas of jurisdiction, the judiciary, the public services, relations between the Union and the States and the rights of citizens. Another reason for our Constitution being lengthy is the vastness of the nation and the peculiar and diverse problems existing therein.

2.1 Value Premises

Like other constitutions in the world, the Constitution of India also contains a Preamble, which reflects the aims and aspiration of its citizens. The basic philosophy of our Constitution is represented in the Preamble. It is true that it is not enforceable in the courts of law. However, the Supreme Court has quoted the Preamble on several occasions while taking important judicial decisions. It reads as follows: "WE, THE PEOPLE OF INDIA, having solemnly resolved to constitute India into a SOVEREIGN SOCIALIST SECULAR DEMOCRATIC REPUBLIC and to secure to all its citizens:

JUSTICE, social, economic and political;

LIBERTY of thought, expression, belief, faith and worship;

EQUALITY of status and of opportunity, and to promote among them all;

FRATERNITY assuring the dignity of the individual and the unity and integrity of the Nation;

IN OUR CONSTITUENT ASSEMBLY, this twenty-sixth day of November, 1949, do HEREBY ADOPT, ENACT AND GIVE TO OURSELVES THIS CONSTITUTION."

Thus, the Preamble outlines the core of the system of government—its objectives, its ideals and its values. It is the responsibility of the government and administration to enforce the constitution and to create an environment in which the application of the ideals enshrined in the Preamble could be realized. The civil servant should be a "servant" of the people in its best sense and his guiding philosophy should always be the "public interest".

The word 'sovereign' means that both in domestic matters and in external affairs, India is a free nation. Further, democracy implies that the government is popularly elected and the Constitution ensures the protection of the fundamental rights of the citizens. Notably, the Indian Constitution has established a parliamentary democracy of the type established by the Federal Constitutions of Canada and Australia. The word "Republic" means a government whose head is elected by the people.

Then there are the concepts of justice, liberty, equality and fraternity. Notably, Article 38 of the Constitution states the first objective as: "The state shall strive to promote the welfare of the people by securing and protecting, as effectively as it may, a social order in which justice, social, economic and political — shall inform all the institutions of the national life." The second objective pertains to "liberty" in relation to thought, expression, belief, faith and worship. This may be viewed in the perspective of Article 25 of the Constitution which refers to the fundamental right to profess, practice and propagate any religion and also to Article 19(1) which grants the freedom of speech and expression.

The third objective pertains to "equality" of status and of opportunity. Equality, it may be emphasized, also finds expression in the fundamental right of equality enshrined in Articles 14 to 18 of the Constitution. Article 14 provides that the state shall not deny to any person equality before the law or equal protection of the law. Article 15 makes special provision for the advancement of the scheduled castes and tribes by increasing their opportunities of employment in the public service of the Union and the States by reserving posts for them in the civil services. Later Supreme Court pronouncements have extended the scope of positive discrimination to "other backward classes". Article 18 abolishes hereditary status emanating from titles.

The fourth objective of "fraternity" connotes a moral and political ideal. This idealized notion, forming a part of the motto of "Liberty, Equality, Fraternity" of the French Revolution has special relevance for a multi-racial and multi-religious country like India.

The word 'socialist' in the Preamble,

1. read with Article 39(b), would enable the Supreme Court and High Courts to uphold the constitutionality of laws of nationalization of private property;
2. read with Articles 14 and 16 of the Constitution, would enable the Supreme Court and the High Courts to deduce a fundamental right of equal pay for equal work; and
3. read with Article 14, would enable the Courts to strike down a statute which fails to achieve the socialist goal.

Interestingly, despite the centrality of Nehruvian socialism in the Preamble, a number of radical economic reforms have taken place in India since 1991 through economic liberalization, privatization and even disinvestment of the public sector. Despite these changes, the positive sign is that no attempt has been made to change the wordings of the preamble to enable any changes in the basic structure and spirit of the Indian Constitution. The roles and responsibilities of the government in accelerating equitable economic development have not been reduced as a result of the recent attempts to restructure the economy.

The word "secular" in the Preamble implies that, as far as the state is concerned, it would not support any religion out of public funds, nor would it penalize the profession and practice of any religion or the right to manage religious institutions as provided in Articles 25 and 26. There has been a spate of controversies and varying interpretations concerning the term "secular". The dispute appears to be on the issue whether the state should respect all religions equally or should dissociate itself totally from religion. While the plan of equal respect for all religions seems to be acceptable to all communities, the premise of separation of the state from religion, rooted in the European notion of a secular state, has not led to any consensus on its meaning or on its implications. The confusion continues despite a strong belief that organized religion should not be allowed to create a bias in the policies and orientations of government and administration.

It would be clear from the foregoing description that the Preamble of the Indian Constitution provides a framework of ideals and values for the Indian administration. Since the responsibility of enforcing the Constitution is that of the government, it is expected of the administrative system, which is an integral component of the executive branch of government, to facilitate the application of the ideals of liberty, equality, justice, socialism and secularism in the governance of the country. Not only must the governmental laws and politics reflect these interrelated ideals and values, but they should be manifested in the way the administrative system functions, including the attitudinal orientations and behaviour of administrators, who should strive to be neutral and unbiased at all times in the execution of laws and tracking beneficiaries of targeted governmental programmes.

2.2 Constitutionalism

The concept of constitutionalism refers to a political regime governed by or under a constitution that necessitates limited government and rule of law as opposed to arbitrary or totalitarian rule. Constitution-(s), defines the basic structure of the government and the main organs of the state— (the legislature, the executive and the judiciary), defines their powers, their responsibilities, and regulates their relationships with each other and with the citizens. Constitutional government, therefore, should necessarily be a democratic government, and a natural by-product of a written constitution. But, it is certainly conceivable that some countries (there have been many examples) may have the letter of written constitutions that are not really democratic. It can be said that they have the letter of constitutions but without the spirit of constitutionalism. Also, there are instances where there is no written constitution but democracy and constitutionalism prevail. Israel and U.K. are classic examples.

Constitutionalism normally implies that there are rules that create legislative, executive and judicial powers, but also that these rules impose limits on those powers. Constitutional limits come in a variety of forms. They can concern such things as the scope of authority (e.g. in a federal system, provincial or State Governments may have authority over health care and agriculture while the federal government's jurisdiction extends to national defence and banking); the mechanisms used in exercising the relevant power or scope of civil rights through a defined List of Rights. Constitutionalism in this inclusive sense means that government can and should be limited in its powers.

Some scholars believe that constitutional rules do not exist unless they are in some way enshrined in a written document. Others argue that constitutions can be unwritten. Constitution is not only what is written in the text but is also the practice of functioning institutions. It constantly grows and evolves. Every constitution derives meaning and content only from the manner in which and the people by whom it is operated, the effects it acquires from how it is interpreted by the courts of the land and what conventions and practices grow around its operational norms, procedures and practices.

A democratic political system provides the inputs for constitutionalism to flourish. A political system that is in conformity with the principles of constitutionalism must necessarily, inter alia, provide restraints and limitations on the exercise of powers by the organs of the State. Sovereignty belongs to the people but constitutionalism forbids the people from attempting political change through violent means. It attempts to lay down a system, of checks and balances. Separation of powers between the legislature, the executive and the judiciary is one such, device and in case of federal systems, distribution of powers between different tiers of government, is another. Arbitrary powers in the hands of any individual or any institution-even if conferred by a constitutional document negate the concept of constitutionalism.

Rule of Law is to be understood as opposed to arbitrary rule of a person or a political party. Thus, Rule of Law is an essential prerequisite for democracy. The British constitutional expert Dicey held that the 'rule of law' embraces four separate features. First, no one should be punished except for breaches of law. Second, there should be equal subjection to the law or "equality before law" Third, when law is broken, there must be a certainty of punishment. Finally, the rights and liberties of the individual should be embodied in the 'ordinary law' of the land. This would ensure that when individual rights are violated citizens can seek redressal through the judiciary.

In its broad sense, the Rule of law is a core western liberal-democratic principle, embodying ideas such as constitutionalism and limited government to which most modern states aspire. According to some scholars, the essential characteristics of Rule of law are:

1. The supremacy of law, which means that all citizens and political regimes are subject to law thereby to restrictions on the exercise of arbitrary power.
2. A practice of justice which emphasises law based on standards and the importance of procedures.
3. The exercise by Parliament of the legislative power and restrictions on the exercise of such power by the executive.
4. An independent judiciary.

It can be stated without doubt that establishment of the Rule of Law and the spirit of Constitutionalism in the administration and governance of the country was definitely in the mind and spirit of our Constitution makers.

2.3 Parliamentary Democracy

In simpler terms, parliamentary democracy stands for a form of government in which the people rule through their representatives in the parliament, chosen by adult suffrage through free and fair elections; the existence of two or more political parties is an essential postulate; fundamental rights are guaranteed; and there is a high degree of coordination between the legislature (the parliament) and the executive.

A basic feature that characterizes the parliamentary model is the presence of a double executive. The President of India is the constitutional, though titular, head of the state whereas the Prime Minister (PM) and his cabinet are the real executive. The PM and his cabinet are chosen from the majority party in the Parliament and are responsible to it for their policies and actions and remain in office as long as they enjoy the confidence of the legislature. The cabinet works as a team under the leadership of the PM For the successful implementation of policies, each member of the cabinet is individually responsible. The cabinet is also collectively responsible to the legislature. The cabinet members have to present a common front and work as a composite whole. All this operates within a system of checks and balances whereby all the three organs of the government exercise a fair measure of control over each other to check tendencies towards domination of one over the other.

The words "controlling the executive" do not imply that the Parliament is a mere watchdog over the executive. What is meant is that certain parliamentary procedures have been evolved in the course of time that make the executive accountable, responsive and responsible to the Parliament. Some tools of parliamentary control are questions, adjournment motions, no-confidence motions, calling attention notices, budget discussions and control through parliamentary committees. All these are effective instruments for securing redress from administrative errors and discussing matters of urgent public importance. The no-confidence motion, could result in even the fall of the government.

The major chunk of the Parliament's time is spent in enacting legislations. It legislates on all subjects in the Union List, the Concurrent List and, in special, circumstances, on the subjects mentioned in the State List. In addition, the residuary powers of the Union Government in respect of any matter not enumerated in any of the three lists havs been mentioned in the Constitution. Though, in the light of the increasing importance of delegated legislation, the bulk of the work related to legislation is done by civil servants. The Indian Parliament has an impressive record of legislation on a wide variety of social, political and economic matters.

Every member of the Parliament represents the segment of the population comprising his constituency. Therefore, each Member of Parliament (M.P.), in his individual capacity and the Parliament as a whole, facilitates ventilation of people's grievances, spread of popular education, and, most importantly, the integration of conflicting interests. The last mentioned function is closely linked with the norms of representative behaviour. It demands that a legislator should keep the interest of the nation above that of the masses.

It is in parliament that the grievances of the public are ventilated, a very wide range of views find expression. Parliamentarians shape the emerging legislations, and keep the public educated about the activities of the government. The televised proceedings in the Parliament are heard, read and seen by a large number of people.

Although the Indian Parliament cannot as yet be labelled as the harbinger of a new social order, it upholds ideals which can bring about a more egalitarian social order. It has been uncompromising in its opposition whenever human freedom or rights are threatened and pays special attention to weaker sections during the formulation of socio-economic policies and programmes. There is an impressive list of legislations to curb social evils like child marriage and dowry, laws related to the welfare of women, labourers, scheduled castes and scheduled tribes. Parliament has off and on passed radical social legislation but the tradition-bound Indian society refuses, on most occasions, to respond to the changing times. Therefore Parliament only sets the norm for progressive social change.

Right from the time the first Central Government was formed in 1952, the powers of the executive have been growing by leaps and bounds. Due to economic pressures, domestic disturbances, welfare imperatives and international tensions, the executive is doing a lot more work than the legislature has been able to. It appears as though the executive has taken over the legislative functions through the practice of delegated legislation. The Parliament, due to shortage of time, passes the bills in skeleton form and the majority of the provisions which actually make up the law are framed by the bureaucracy. Since the members of the Parliament do not often understand the legal technical language of laws, they may become mere tools in the hands of civil servants and the party's whip in Parliament.

In relation to the executive an undesirable trend has evolved wherein policy issues are decided to the virtual exclusion of Parliament. The General Agreement on Trade and Tariff (GATT) can be taken as an example. Despite the fact that signing treaties is an executive prerogative, where a treaty of far-reaching implications is concerned, detailed debates should and could have been held in Parliament. True, the treaty was submitted to Parliament, but the impression remains that the government could have acted in a more 'open' manner. Public apprehensions could have been laid to rest through free and open discussion. Likewise, the wastage of Parliament's precious time could have been avoided in August, 1994 had there been a better understanding between the ruling party and the opposition over the Action Taken Report (ATR) on the securities scam. Even the New Economic Policies were passed in 1991 without much debate or discussion.

Another equally dangerous trend, is that of promulgation of ordinances by the President. This gives the executive a clear power to legislate and is an encroachment on the jurisdiction of the Parliament. What is ironical is that for issuing ordinances, only the satisfaction of President is necessary. Article 123(1) of the Indian Constitution stipulates that circumstances must exist which render it necessary for the President to take immediate action. In 1993, the Centre promulgated 32 ordinances, eight more than in the previous year. In contrast, in 1963, the Nehru government had not issued a single ordinance, while 10 years later, their number was just four. An increasing recourse to ordinances tends to undermine the Parliament.

These are but a few ills that beset the Indian Parliament. However, it must be remembered that Parliament and parliamentary democracy only reflect the times and values of the era in which they operate. Parliamentary behaviour is reflective of the social conflicts of Indian society. Intemperate language, obstructionism and hijacking of certain bills by delaying tactics have demeaned parliamentary standards from time to time.

2.4 Fundamental Rights

Articles 12 to 25 deal with fundamental rights and the Constitution provides remedies against their violation by making the right to constitutional remedies a fundamental right. Fundamental rights in India operate within certain limitations. The Constitution provides for the suspension of rights such as the 'Right to Freedom' during an emergency declared by the President of India and other rights can also be amended by the Parliament. The specific rights granted by the Constitution are as follows:

1. Right to Equality (Articles 14,15,16,17 and 18);
2. Right to Freedom (Articles 19, 20, 21 and 22);
3. Right Against Exploitation (Articles 23 and 24);
4. Right of Freedom of Religion (Articles 25, 26, 27 and 28);
5. Cultural and Educational Rights (Articles 29 and 30)
6. Right to Constitutional Remedies (Act 32)

The ambit of many of these rights have been amplified by the Supreme Court in successive judgments. Fundamental rights incorporated in the Indian Constitution prescribe the parameters within which the administrative system is expected to function. Truly, the administrative system is entrusted with the legal as well as the moral responsibility of protecting and promoting the fundamental rights of the people. Not only do the people have to be treated as equal before the law, but the institutions of governance should also demonstrate a spirit of equality and justice and refrain from pursuing policies and actions that infringe such rights.

There remains the need to incessantly inculcate the positive, values of empathy, equity, justice, secularism, rule-orientation, respect for law, etc., among the civil servants at all levels. Formal training can play a useful role in this regard, though the responsibility of transforming the social psyche of the citizenry depends on the entire system of socialization. It is difficult to conceive of administrative values independent of social values Yet, the leadership role of the politico-administrative system in making the socio-economic system more favourably oriented towards the protection of fundamental rights cannot be overstressed.

2.5 Directive Principles of State Policy

Part IV of the Indian Constitution is devoted to the Directive Principles of State Policy. The principles embodied in this section are directives to the various governments and are to be followed as fundamental in the governance of the country. Yet, there is a difference between the fundamental rights and the directive principles. While the former are enforceable by the courts the latter are not. There is no judicial remedy available in case of violation of the directive principles. However, they are equally sacrosanct, as they place an ideal before the legislators of the country. Besides, they prescribe a code of conduct for administrators while discharging their responsibilities. Articles 36 to 51 of the Constitution are devoted to these principles. Some provisions in this context are as follows:

Article 38:

1. The state shall strive to promote the welfare of the people by securing and protecting a social order in which justice, social, economic and political, shall inform all the institutions of national life.
2. The state shall strive to minimize the inequalities in income and eliminate inequalities in status, facilities and opportunities amongst individuals and groups of people residing in different areas or engaged in different vocations. Article 39:

   a. The citizens, men and women, equally have the right to an adequate means of livelihood.

   b. The ownership and control of the material resources of the community are so distributed that they subserve the common good.

   c. The operation of the economic system does not result in the concentration of wealth and means of production to the common detriment.

   d. Equal pay for equal work for both men and women.

   e. The health and strength of workers, men and women and children of tender age are not abused and citizens are not forced by economic necessity to enter vocations unsuited to their age or strength.

   f. Children are to be given opportunities and facilities to develop in a healthy manner and in conditions of freedom and dignity childhood and youth are protected against exploitation and against moral and material abandonment.

Article 39A: The state shall ensure that the operation of the legal system promotes justice on the basis of equal opportunity and shall, in particular, provide free legal aid by suitable legislation or schemes in any other way so that opportunities for securing justice are not denied to any citizen by reason of economic or other disabilities Article 40: The state shall take steps to organize village Panchayats and endow them with such powers and authority as may be necessary to enable them to function as units of self-government.

Article 41: The state shall, within the limits of its economic capacity and development, make effective provision for securing the right to work, to education and to public assistance in cases of unemployment, old age, sickness and disablement and in other cases of undeserved want.

Article 42: The state shall make provision for securing just and humane conditions of work and for maternity relief.

Article 43: The state shall endeavour to secure, by suitable legislation or economic organization or in any other way, to all workers, agricultural, industrial or otherwise, work, a living wage, conditions of work ensuring a decent standard of life and full enjoyment of leisure and social and cultural opportunities and, in particular, the state shall endeavour to promote cottage, industries on an individual or cooperative basis in rural areas.

It may be mentioned that successive Constitutional amendments and interpretations and the progressive policies of the Central Government and the States have, over the years, enhanced the significance and legitimacy of the directive principles. The administrative system is expected to play a more proactive role in the implementation of these principles. Many of the Directive Principles are now 'laws' or independent 'rights' guaranteed to citizens, e.g. the right to education.

The track-record of the governance system in implementing the directive principles has been uneven. At one extreme is a principle, such as the enactment of a uniform civil code, which has been left untouched because of its religious sensitivity; on the other is a principle like promotion of Panchayati Raj which has been given substantial legitimacy through the 73rd Constitutional Amendment Act. It is clear, however, from the analysis of government plans, programmes and actions that, on most fronts, the Central as well as the State Governments have endeavoured to provide justifiability to a majority of directive principles through legal enforcement and other means. The role and responsibility of the administrative system in converting these 'voluntary' principles into ideal legal imperatives is enormous. These principles should actually become the core normative concerns of the Indian public administrators in their application of rules and laws to particular cases.

2.6 Judiciary

India's commitment to law is created in the Constitution that constituted India into a Sovereign Democratic Republic, containing a federal system with Parliamentary form of Government in the Union and the States.

The Judicial hierarchy of India starts with the Supreme Court of India at the Centre, followed by the High Courts of respective states and District Courts of the respective districts and civil and criminal courts at the lower level. The Indian Judiciary is independent of the executive and legislative branches of the Government according to the Constitution of India.

The Supreme Court of India is the highest judicial body, and aims at providing justice to all citizens. The Supreme Court of India comprises the Chief Justice and 30 other Judges appointed by the President of India. Supreme Court Judges retire upon attaining the age of 65 years. The Supreme Court handles all disputes between the Central Government and a State or between two States. The jurisdiction of the Supreme Court is divided into:

- Original jurisdiction - Subject to the provisions of Article 131 of the Indian Constitution, the Supreme Court shall, to the exclusion of any other court, have original jurisdiction in any dispute:
    - Between the Government of India (GOI) and one or more States
    - Between the GOI and any State or States on one side and one or more States on the other
    - Between two or more States
- Advisory jurisdiction - As per Article 143 of the Constitution, if at any time it appears to the President that a question of law or fact has arisen, or is likely to arise, which

is of such a nature and of such public importance that it is expedient to obtain the opinion of the Supreme Court upon it, he may refer the question to that Court for consideration and the Court may, after such hearing as it thinks fit, report to the President its opinion thereon.

- Appellate jurisdiction - The appellate jurisdiction of the Supreme Court can be invoked by a certificate granted by the High Court concerned under Article 132, 133 or 134 of the Constitution in respect of any judgement, decree or final order of a High Court in both civil and criminal cases, involving substantial questions of law as to the interpretation of the Constitution.

The Supreme Court is empowered to issue directions, orders or writs to enforce fundamental rights (right to equality, right to freedom, right against exploitation, right to freedom of religion, cultural and educational rights, right to life and right to constitutional remedies) according to Article 32 of the Indian Constitution. The Supreme Court also has the provision to accept or reject any case on its own discretion.

As per the Article 136(1) of the Constitution of India "the Supreme Court may, in its discretion, grant special leave to appeal from any judgment, decree, determination, sentence or order in any cause or matter passed or made by any court or tribunal in the territory of India." A person aggrieved by any order or judgment of High Court or of Tribunal may appeal to the Supreme Court by filing a Special Leave Petition. There are about three crore cases pending in the Supreme Court affecting about 30 crore people.

A High Court handles both civil as well as criminal cases. Most of the cases are forwarded by the district or lower courts. There are 25 High Courts in the country at present. The Judges of the High Courts are appointed by the President of India in consultation with the Chief Justice of India and the Governor of the State. The number of judges in High Courts varies and depends on the size of the States.

The High Courts are the principal civil courts of original jurisdiction in the State, and can try all offences including those punishable with death. The work of most High Courts consists of Appeals from lower courts. Each High Court has powers of superintendence over all Courts within its jurisdiction. It can call for returns from such Courts, make and issue general rules and prescribe forms to regulate their practice and proceedings.

The District Courts are established by the State Governments and fall under the administrative control of the High Court of the State. These courts are responsible for administering justice at the District level. The highest court in each district is that of the District and Sessions Judge. This is the principal court of civil jurisdiction.

In a constitutional democracy as ours, judiciary is an important organ of the state for the enforcement of rights and realization of reliefs through remedial jurisprudence. The Supreme Court of India, being the apex of the judicial administration is the main custodian of citizen rights. If a citizen is aggrieved due to failure in the performance of duty by a state agency and approaches the Supreme Court under Article 32 for the enforcement of a fundamental right, it is imperative for the apex court to act in aid of the citizen's right. Again Article 142 explicitly confers on the Supreme Court plenary powers for doing complete justice in any cause or matter before it. Hence, it is the constitutional quest for justice which empowers the Supreme Court to reach and curb injustice perpetrated by any judicial, quasi-judicial or administrative body. The role, response and commitment of the Supreme Court, therefore, is of utmost importance for the preservation, protection and promotion of human rights in our country.

Since the late 70s there has been a progressive trend of vigorous legal activism in certain areas concerning human rights. There are many instances where the Supreme Court played a creative or a catalytic role in its quest for justice that resulted in a vast expansion of the frontiers of public law and formulation of multi-dimensional legal strategies including public interest litigation (PIL) for providing access to justice as well as relief to large masses of people who were denied of their basic human rights and to whom constitutional guarantee of rights and freedom had no meaning. As a part of this enthusiastic judicial movement towards anti-poverty or people- oriented jurisprudence, the Supreme Court liberalized the traditional rule of locus standi in a series of cases in order to liberate itself from the 'shackles of procedural limitations' and thereby to enable any public-spirited individual or social activist group to invoke the jurisdiction of the court or set the machinery of justice in motion by a letter, telegram or even a postcard for enforcement of human rights, liberty and freedom of an ordinary citizen. Article 226 of the Constitution had thus been held to be capable of ventilating 'collective or common grievances as distinguished from assertion of individual rights'.

If the period between the late 70s and late 80s witnessed legal activism directed towards promotion of human rights through redressal of the plight of child labour and bonded labour, gender discrimination and injustices to women, victims of custodial violence and travesty of justice, the 90s experienced an increasing concern for legal activism towards the issues of good governance and clean environment. One of the positive achievements of legal activism has been to provide interim monetary relief to the victims of governmental action or inaction as well as administrative lawlessness.

2.7 Federalism

The political system of the Indian Constitution is based on the twin principles of parliamentary system of government and federalism though the term 'Federation' has not been used in the Constitution. A survey of our Constitution indicates that it possesses all the essential features of a federal system. While in a unitary state there is only one government, namely the national government, in a federal state, there are two sets of government the national or federal government, and the governments of the sub-national units i.e. the states.

A federal state derives its existence from the Constitution. Every power (executive, legislative or judicial) whether it belongs to the Central Government or to the state, is derived from the Constitution which is the Supreme law of the Land. Courts have the final power to interpret the Constitution and nullify any action on the part of the Federal or State Governments or their different organs which violate any of its provisions. Another important feature of a federal state is that there is a division of powers between the federal government and the governments of the states.

The Constitution of India can work as a federal system during normal times. But in times of war, insurrection or the breakdown of constitutional machinery in the states, it works more like a unitary system. A proclamation of emergency in the country automatically transforms a federal state into a unitary one.

The Indian Constitution is partly flexible and partly rigid. It is only the amendment of a few provisions of the Constitution that requires ratification by the state legislatures and even then ratification by only half of them is needed. The rest of the Constitution may be amended by a simple majority of the Union Parliament as is required for general legislation. Some examples where ratification by States is not needed are: (a) changes in the names, boundaries, area of the states and amalgamation, and separation of states (Article 4), (b) abolition or creation of the second chamber of a state legislature (Article 169), (c) administration of scheduled areas and scheduled tribes (paragraph 7 of the 5th Schedule and paragraph 21 of the 6th Schedule). Our Constitution is flexible because the Parliament can supplement the provisions of the Constitution by legislation.

The flexibility of the Constitution can also be seen from the fact that in the last seventy years, the Constitution has already been amended more than a hundred times. Centre-State relations have alternated between 'cordial' and 'turbulent' depending on the relationship between the political power at the Centre and State(s) at a particular period of time. States have in general clamored for more fiscal and taxation powers and more grants from the Centre. The erstwhile Planning Commission and the Finance Commission decided on discretionary as well as mandatory transfers to the states from the Centre. The Centre has overwhelmingly more powers under the Constitution and many instruments of interference in the affairs of states. There was progressive cooperation during the era of coalition governments at the Centre (1989-2013) and after a new government came to power in 2014 the Centre reinvented the idea of cooperative federalism, where both will be active partners in the developmental plans, processes and projects. In any case more and major items have been added to the concurrent list on which both the centre and the states can legislate.

2.8 Local Government and Administration

With about 70% of India's population residing in the rural areas, the Panchayati Raj Institution, has been the backbone of rural India since its inception. The word "Panchayat" literally means an assembly of five (panch) adults chosen by the entire village community to govern it. Panchayats are crucial for inclusive governance as they facilitate direct participation of people, ensure transparency and accountability through processes such as social audit and can prepare context specific plans to address poverty, local infrastructure and socio-economic needs. The Panchayats are set-up to formulate and administer the development programmes in villages, blocks and districts across areas in education, healthcare, public works, agriculture and social welfare.

The Constitution (73rd Amendment) Act, 1992, that came into effect in April 1993 brought about major reforms in local governance in the country. The 73rd Amendment Act, among other things provided that:

- There will be a Gram Sabha for every village or group of villages that is comprised of all the adult members registered as voters in the Panchayat area.
- Seats in Panchayats at all the three levels shall be filled by direct election. In addition, chairpersons of village Panchayats can be made members of the Panchayats at intermediate levels, and chairpersons of Panchayats at the intermediate level can be members of Panchayats at the district level.
- Members of Parliament, Members of Legislative Assembly and Members of Legislative Council should also be members of Panchayats at the intermediate or the district level.
- In all the Panchayats, seats should be reserved for Scheduled Castes and Scheduled Tribes in proportion to their population. Offices of the Chairpersons of the Panchayats at all levels shall be reserved in favour of Scheduled Castes and Scheduled Tribes in proportion to their population in the State. One third of these seats will be reserved for women.
- Every Panchayat shall have a uniform 5-year term and elections shall be held before the term of the elected members end. If the Panchayat is disbanded, elections will be compulsorily held within 6 months.
- States may, by law, endow the Panchayats with such powers and authority as may be required to enable the Panchayat to function as institutions of self- government. It is the States that have been charged with the responsibility for devolution of powers to the Panchayats.

This Act also institutionalized the Panchayati Raj Institutions (PRIs) at the village, intermediate, and district levels as the third tier of government. The Panchayati Raj system is classified as:

- Village - Gram Panchayats
- Block - Taluk Panchayats
- District - Zilla Panchayats

Currently by there are more than 2.55 lakh panchayats (including 248,263 Gram Panchayats, 6618 Block Panchayats and 595 Disrict Panchayats) in India.

2.9 Bureaucracy Democracy & Development

The role of civil service has changed significantly from the pre-independence days to the current times. This to a large extent has been driven by the changing external factors and the nature of domestic responsibilities. Prior to Independence, the main responsibility of the civil service was to maintain law and order and manage revenue administration. For an effective discharge of duties, civil servants, back then, were required to possess simple skills of regulatory administration.

In today's context, the role of the civil service is constantly evolving with changing times. In the '1950-90', period the civil servants had to essentially deal with developmental issues and hence, were required to possess and continuously acquire new skills relating to development administration. In the present post-globalized context civil servants are responsible for regulation of the private sector and the market, formulation of socio-economic and political policies; elimination of poverty; effective monetary and fiscal management; elimination of social inequities; participation in international negotiations and management of Public Sector Enterprises (PSEs). This has made the job highly challenging and requires a high degree of flexibility and competence on the part of the civil servants.

Civil servants of the pre-independence era reported to their British bosses, who in turn were not accountable to the public. Now, civil servants work within the boundaries of a democratic system, and report to elected members of the public. In addition, today's environment is characterized by an ever so vigilant press, public and alert legislatures, which make the working of civil servants all the more accountable.

Over a period of time, the role of civil service has transformed from regulatory to developmental and currently as a facilitator for the efficient delivery of public services.

The Indian Civil Service is classified into three broad categories:

- All India Services
- Central Services
- State Services

The Constitution of India has recognized the following three categories as part of the AIS:

- Indian Administrative Services (IAS) - the IAS is considered to be a support system for providing basic services to citizens and runs various development programmes.
- Indian Police Service (IPS) - the IPS is responsible for maintaining law and order and internal security of the nation.
- Indian Forest Service (IFS) - the IFo is responsible for management of the country's forest resources.

The members of All India Services are appointed by the Central Government and then assigned to the different States. The AIS is common to both; the Central and the State Governments.

Another important feature of the Constitution is that there is a special chapter that deals with civil services. This indicates a prominent place attached to services as public institutions governing India after independence. The most significant influence on the nature, structure and functioning of the Indian administration is that of the Indian democratic system. The democratic context in which the Indian administrative system functions is closely linked to the Constitution. The influence of the Constitution on public administration is broadly of two types: the formal or discernible influence that prescribes the structure of the administrative system and the informal influence which determines the role, responsibility and responsiveness of the administrative system, the character of governance and the behaviour of administrators.

2.10 Towards Ethical Governance

Ethical governance (another name for good governance) requires public officials to adhere to the principle of serving others by setting a high standard of moral conduct and by considering their jobs as a vocation. The objective is to create an atmosphere that motivates officials to respond to the challenges of government by adhering to their notion of duty and service to the community, as well as taking responsibility for the welfare of others. In order to achieve this objective, we do need to build the capacity of moral reasoning and ethical behaviour in our public service system. Without encouragement, reinforcement, resurrection and strengthening of some articles of faith (drawn from the societal values, cultural traditions, and spiritual ideals), the system of governance is never going to be ethical despite penalties for non-compliance of laws.

A breakdown of ethical standards has continued far too long without being stopped by senior administrators and ministers. It happened precisely because of the prevailing administrative and political culture that tolerated and even encouraged the corrupting practices that led to administrative abuse. Unless the politico-administrative elite are willing to accept responsibility and are interested in putting more emphasis on efficiency and probity, the culture will not change. For that environment to exist and flourish, it requires administrators and public officials to show a genuine concern for their fellow citizens, because the use of power and authority is based on certain moral connotations, which demand an unwavering commitment to serve and care for the public. This is the foundation and the basic ethics upon which depends the normal functioning and survival of a public service system.

The convergence of human development and human rights in both concept and action and the inclusion of the gender question in the agenda of human development will have far-reaching implications for public administration. Such implications would differ among countries in accordance with the varying rate of advancement in human development. As per the 2018 data, India is placed at 130 among 189 countries in the UNDP Human Development Index. The challenges before the public administration in India are stupendous and its tasks immense and multi-pronged.

Our policy makers must realize that poverty eradication is not only a development goal but also a major human rights challenge of the 21st century. For, a minimum standard of decent living, adequate nutrition, health care, education, employment and protection against calamities, are not just development goals —they are also human rights. To achieve these goals, it is not enough to formulate pro-poor economic and social policies and allocate funds for various programmes based on these policies. What seems to be more important than these exercises is to ensure proper utilization of funds so that the benefits of economic and social development percolate down, to the millions of poor in our country. There is also a need for transparency in governmental functioning. Legislative guarantees of the right to freedom of information would not be of much help unless the public functionaries are sensitized, motivated and trained to accept the change towards openness and the citizens become aware and willing to play a more pro-active role with necessary intervention of the civil society organizations. Accountability of public functionaries should be ensured at all levels of governmental system through appropriate legislative and administrative measures. It needs to be hardly emphasized that transparency and accountability would help in minimizing corruption in public life. Fortunately for India, we have a fairly open civil society and independent media. Yet, there is enough scope to institutionally strengthen our civil society organizations and the media.

It would be erroneous to contend that by playing a creative and catalytic role, our superior courts are overstepping their limits to enter the realm of the executive. A large number of recent trend-setting rulings by the apex court on public interest issues reflect executive inaction and apathy rather than judicial activism or assertiveness. Hence, the role of higher judiciary needs to be considered in the correct perspective of our constitutional jurisprudence and the state of public administration in our country. Human rights and human development cannot be realized without effective and meaningful linkages and collaboration between public service agencies and civil society organizations such as NGOs, workers and peasants' organizations, women's groups, human rights, environmental and other activist groups.

Theorists of citizenship, community, civil society and organizational humanism have helped to establish a climate in which it makes sense today to talk about a New Public Service advocated by Robert and Janet Denhardt. Though we acknowledge that differences, even substantial differences, exist in these various viewpoints, we would suggest there are also similarities that distinguish the cluster of ideas we call the New Public Service from those associated with the New Public Management and the Old Public Administration. Moreover, there are a number of practical lessons that the New Public Service suggests for those in public administration. These lessons are not mutually exclusive, rather they are mutually reinforcing. Among these ideas, we find the following the most compelling:

1. Serve Citizens, Not Customers: The public interest is the result of a dialogue about shared values rather than the aggregation of individual self- interests. Therefore, public servants do not merely respond to the demands of "customer,", but rather focus on building relationships of trust and collaboration with and among citizens.
2. Seek the Public Interest; Public administrators must contribute to building a collective, shared notion of the public interest. The goal is not to find quick solutions driven by individual choices. Rather, it is the creation of shared interests and shared responsibility.
3. Value Citizenship over Entrepreneurship: The public interest is better advanced by public servants and citizens committed to making meaningful contributions to society than by entrepreneurial managers acting as if public money were their own.
4. Think Strategically, Act Democratically: Policies and programs that meet public needs can be most effectively and responsibly achieved through collective efforts and collaborative processes.
5. Recognize that Accountability Is Not Simple: Public servants should be more attentive to certain other matters besides the market; they should also attend to statutory and constitutional law, community values, political norms, professional standards, and citizen interests.

6. Serve Rather than Steer: It is increasingly important for public servants to use shared and, value-based leadership to help citizens articulate and meet their shared interests rather than attempt to control or steer society in new directions.
7. Value People, Not Just Productivity: Public organizations and the networks in which they participate are more likely to be successful in the long run if they are operated through processes of collaboration and shared leadership based on respect for all people.

Decades ago, Herbert Kaufman (1956) suggested that, while administrative institutions are organized and operated in pursuit of different values at different times, during the period in which one idea is dominant, others are never totally neglected. Building on this idea, it makes sense to think of one normative model as prevailing at any point in time, with the other (or others) playing a somewhat lesser role within the context of the prevailing view. Currently, the New Public Management (NPM) has been established as the dominant paradigm in the field of governance and public administration. NPM talks of efficiency and effectiveness being achieved by adopting private sector techniques in public administration. In this process, there is a concern that the ideas of democratic citizenship and the public interest may be subordinated to the obsession to achieving efficiency and profit at any cost in Public Organizations.

Conclusion

We would, therefore, argue that in a democratic society, like India, a concern for democratic values should be paramount in the way we think about systems of governance. Values such as efficiency and productivity should not be lost, but should be placed in the larger context of democracy, community, and the public interest. In terms of the normative models we have examined here, the New Public Service clearly seems most consistent with the basic foundations of democracy in this country and, therefore, provides a framework within which other valuable techniques and values, might be played out. The New Public Service provides a rallying point around which we might envision a public service in India based on and fully integrated with civic discourse and the public interest.

Suggested Readings

Arora, Ramesh K. (ed) *Public Administration in India: Tradition, Trends and Transformation,* New Delhi Paragon, 2006.

Arora, Ramesh K. and Rajni Goyal, *Indian Public Administration: Institutions and Issues,* New Delhi, New Age, 2016.

Austin, Granville, *The Indian Constitution: Cornerstone of a Nation,* Oxford, Clarendon Press, 1996.

Bakshi, P. M. *The Constitution of India,* Universal, Delhi 2018

Barthwal, C. P. *Indian Administration since Independence,* Lucknow, Bharat Publishers, 2003.

Basu, D. D., *Introduction to the Constitution of India* (21st Edition), New Delhi, Prentice Hall.

Chakravarty Bidyut and Prakash Chand *Indian Administration: Evolution and Practice,* New Delhi, Sage, 2019.

Chaube, Shibani Kinkar, *Constituent Assembly of India: Springboard of Revolution,* New Delhi, Manohar 2000.

Denhardt, Robert B. and Janet V. Denhardt, *The New Public Service*, New York, M.E. Sharpe, 2007.

Dua, B.D., M. P. Singh and Rekha Saxena (eds.), *Indian judiciary and Politics: The Changing Landscape*, New Delhi, Manohar, 2006.

Hasan, Zoya, E. Sridharan and R. Sudarshan (eds.), *India's Living Constitution: Ideas, Practices, Controversies*, New Delhi, Permanent Black, 2002.

Kapur, Devesh etal (ed), *Public Institutions in India: Performance and design*, OUP, 2017.

Kashyap, S.C., *Our Political System*, New Delhi, National Book Trust, 2011.

Kirpal, B.N. et al. (eds.), *Supreme but not infallible: Essays in honor of the Supreme Court of India*, New Delhi, OUP, 2000.

Sapru, R. K., *Indian Administration, A Foundation of governance,* New Delhi, Sage 2018

Shankar, B.L. and Valerian Rodrigues,. *The Indian Parliament*, New Delhi, OUP, 2011.

Singh, M.P. and Rekha Saxena, *Indian Politics: Constitutional Foundations and Institutional Functioning*, New Delhi, Prentice Hall, 2011

Working of a democratic Constitution: The Indian Experience, OUP, 1999

OOO

Chapter Three

The Central Administrative Structure

Introduction

The Executive refers to that organ of government that executes, implements and administers the laws enacted by the legislature. Under Article 73 of the Indian constitution, the executive power of the Union extends to all matters with respect to which the Union parliament may make laws and to the exercise of all powers that accrue to the Government of India from any international treaty or agreement.

The Government of India, officially known as the Union Government, was established by the Constitution of India, and is the governing authority of the Union of 29 states and 7union territories, collectively called the Republic of India.

The three branches of government comprise the Legislature, Executive, and the Judiciary.

The head of the Indian executive is the President, who exercises his powers directly or through officers subordinate to him.

The legislative branch or the Parliament consists of the President, the directly elected lower house, the Lok Sabha (552 members) and the indirectly elected upper house, the Rajya Sabha which is a 245-member House.

The Judicial branch has the Supreme Court at its apex with 25 High Courts, and several civil, criminal and family courts at the district level.

India adopted a modified version of the British model of government by combining the parliamentary system with a federal structure. Another important departure is the replacement of monarchy by a Republican Presidency, though the two are functionally comparable in their limited and strictly nominal role. A second feature of the British model adopted by the Indian constitution is the fusion of powers between the executive and the legislature. The Union Executive is constitutive of the President in Parliament, the Prime Minister (PM) and his council of ministers who are members of Parliament. The PM is the keystone of the cabinet, which is collectively and individually responsible to the Parliament, specifically to the Lok Sabha. A third feature is the independence of the judiciary from legislative and executive control.

The Indian constitution establishes an executive at the federal level that comprises a constitutional or nominal presidency with an effective PM and his cabinet. In a parliamentary form of Government the executive power rests with the PM, the President being the Head of the State. It is the PM who exercises real powers in India and as such the elected members of the legislatures elect the Head of the State, the President.

The Union Executive consists of the President, the Vice-President, the PM and the Council of Ministers.

Article 52 says that there shall be a president who possesses executive, legislative and various other powers under the Constitution of India. His supremacy lies in protecting the supremacy of the Constitution and the law and he should devote himself to the well-being of the people of India.

The constitution provides that any person, who is a citizen of India, has completed the age of 35 years and is eligible for election as a member of Lok Sabha, is entitled to contest the election for the post of President. A person, who holds any office under the Government, is not eligible for election as a president. He is not elected directly by the people, but (according to Article 54) by the members of an electoral college consisting of (i) the elected members of both the Houses of Parliament and (ii) the elected members of the State Legislative Assemblies (but not of the Legislative Assemblies of Union Territories).

The President's term of office is five years from the date on which he enters upon his office (Article 56). He is entitled for re-election. The President may resign from his office by writing under his hand to the Vice-President of India. He can be removed from his office for violation of the constitution by the process of impeachment (Article 61).

3.1 Powers of the President

The position of the President in our polity is one of high dignity and prestige. All executive power of the Union is vested in him and is to be exercised by him either directly or through officers subordinate to him in accordance with the Constitution on the aid and advice of the Council of Ministers. 'Officers subordinate' are supposed to include Ministers (Emperor V. Srinath, AIR 1945 PC 163). All executive action of the Government of India is taken in his name. The Supreme Command of the Defence Forces is vested in him and is to be exercised in accordance with law (Articles 53 and 77). The President appoints the PM and on his advice other Ministers. All the Ministers hold office during the pleasure of the President (Article 75).

Along with the two Houses of Parliament, the President is an integral part of the Central legislature. This is in consonance with the principle that in a parliamentary system the executive is part of the legislature. The President summons the two Houses to meet, prorogues their sittings, and may dissolve the Lok Sabha (Article 85). He addresses the members of both Houses together at the beginning of the first session each year and after each General Election. All Bills after being passed by the two Houses of Parliament must receive the assent of the President in order to become law. Bills belonging to certain categories (e.g. money bills) can be introduced only with the President's recommendation (Articles 79, 85 87, 111 and 117).

When both Houses of Parliament are not in session the President can promulgate ordinances which have the same force and effect as laws passed by Parliament (Article 123). These are in the nature of interim or temporary legislation and their continuance is subject to parliamentary approval. The Supreme Court has upheld the legitimacy and validity of the

President's power to issue ordinances [A.K. Roy V. Union of India, AIR 1982 SC 710; R.K. Garg V. Union of India, AIR 1981 SC 2139].

There are certain other functions which the President is required to perform under the Constitution in relation to Parliament. He summons joint sittings of both Houses in case of final disagreement between them on a Bill. The President causes to be laid, every year, before Parliament, the Budget of the government, and certain other reports of constitutional functionaries like the Comptroller and Auditor General of India, Finance Commission, Union Public Service Commission, and the Commission for Scheduled Castes and Scheduled Tribes and Backward Classes. He may nominate not more than two members of the Anglo Indian Community to Lok Sabha, if he is of the opinion that the community is not adequately represented and 12 members for Rajya Sabha from amongst persons having special knowledge or practical experience in respect of such matters as literature, science, art and social service. Besides, judges of the Supreme Court and of the High Court, the Attorney General of India, the Comptroller and Auditor General of India, are also appointed by the President (Articles 76, 124, 148, 155 and 217).

Under Article 72, the President has the power to grant pardons, reprieves, respites or remissions of punishment or to suspend, remit or commute the sentence of any person in all cases where the punishment has been awarded by a Court Martial, is for an offence against a Union Law, or is a sentence of death. The power of the President under Article 72 is independent of the judiciary.

Despite this array of constitutionally encoded powers, the President's position is conceived as that of a constitutional head of State. It has to be remembered that Article 53 itself makes it clear that the executive power of the Union has to be exercised by the President 'in accordance with the Constitution' and the exercise of the powers of the President as the Supreme Commander of the armed forces has to be 'regulated by law' (U.N. Rao vs. Indira Gandhi, AIR 1971 S.C. 1002; Sanjeev v. State of Madras, Air 1970 S.C. 1102). Also, under Article 60, the President takes an oath 'to preserve, protect and defend the Constitution and the law' Article 74(1) requires the President to act only with the aid and advice of the Council of Ministers and that the real executive power in our system vests in the Council of Ministers (Samsher Singh v. State of Punjab, AIR 1974 SC 2192; U.N. Rao V. Indira Gandhi, AIR 1971 SC 1002; M/S Bishamber Dayal Chandra Mohan v. State of U.P. AIR 1982 S.C. 33; Ram Jawaya v. State of Punjab, AIR 1955 S.C. 544).The Constitution does not make any distinction between normal times and Emergency in the matter of the exercise of President's powers and by the 44th constitutional amendment, the position was finally put beyond all doubt and it was made clear that Emergency can be declared by the President only after receiving in writing a communication from the Union Cabinet to that effect.

Even though the Constitution makes it obligatory for the President to act on the advice of the Council of Ministers, there are some areas where the President may still have to use his own discretion. These are:

- Appointment of the PM (Article 75[1]) in a situation where no single party or alliance commands the clear support of the majority of the Lok Sabha members.

- Appointment of a PM in case of sudden death of the incumbent, where the ruling legislature party is unable to meet immediately to elect a leader, there is no settled seniority among Cabinet ministers and a name from outside the Cabinet is suggested.
- Dissolution of Lok Sabha [Article 75(2)] in case the Council of Ministers loses the confidence of the House but refuses to resign.

However, the acceptance of the advice of the Council of Ministers by the President is not axiomatic. No President can be said to be bound to accept an advice which he finds to be unconstitutional or mala fide. The President is entitled to consider it by applying his mind and holding necessary consultations with the Attorney-General and other independent experts.

Under the Proviso to Article 74 inserted in 1978 by the 44th Amendment, the President may require the Council of Ministers to reconsider their advice given to him on any matter. He shall, of course, act on the reconsidered advice. But according to Article 74(2), 'the question whether any, and if so what advice was tendered by the Ministers to the President shall not be inquired into in any court'. Of course, the Government itself is not barred from producing on its own any papers relating to the cabinet decisions and advice to the President and the Court can then look into them

When a bill is presented to the President for his assent under Article 111, he may declare that he assents to the bill or withholds assent. There is no time limit prescribed for the President giving his assent or declaring his decision to withhold it. But the President may, as soon as possible, also return the Bill, if it is not a money Bill, for reconsideration. However, if the Bill is passed, with or without amendments, and is presented to the President again, he shall not withhold his assent.

Inasmuch as giving assent to Bills is one of the functions of the President to be discharged on the advice of the Council of Ministers, it is open to him to seek clarificatory information from the PM under Article 78(b) or to send a Bill back to the Government for reconsideration under Proviso to Article 74(1). Presumably this is what was done by the President in cases of the controversial Postal Bill and the Bill seeking inter alia to provide to Members of Parliament pension after merely one year's service.

Emergency Powers of the President

Emergency Due to War or Internal Disturbance (Article 352)

This Article states that if the President is satisfied that a grave emergency exists due to which the security of India or any part thereof is threatened, whether by war or internal disturbance or armed rebellion, he may proclaim an emergency. The advice of the cabinet is to be given in writing and its duration in the first instance will be two months. Within two months, it has to be ratified by the Parliament. After it has been passed by both the Houses, it will continue as long as the President desires. However, the period cannot exceed more than six months at a time. In India, emergency under this Article has been declared three times: In 1962 and 1971 the cause was external aggression, and in 1975 it was imposed for 'internal disturbances'. The first was the longest, because it continued up till 1968, covering the Chinese as well as the Pakistani aggressions and a period following even these.

This type of emergency has the following implications:

- The life of the Lok Sabha can be extended by one year at a time by the President. The word "at a time" keeps the possibility of indefinite renewal open.
- The Parliament is empowered to frame laws on the subject mentioned in the State List.
- The President has the right to alter, vary or amend the distribution pattern of financial resources between the Centre and the States.
- The fundamental rights can be suspended

Emergency due to Failure of Constitutional Machinery in States (Article 356)

Under this Article, the President can proclaim emergency if he is satisfied on receipt of a report from the Governor or otherwise, that a situation has arisen in which the government of a state cannot be carried on in accordance with the provisions of the Constitution. The proclamation has to be approved by both the Houses in the same manner as the first kind of emergency, but by a simple majority. The proclamation, in the first instance, is applicable for two months and, after ratification by the Parliament, for six months each time but should not exceed more than three years. Emergency under this heading can have the following implications and consequences:

- The fundamental rights guaranteed under Article 19 can be suspended.
- The President can dissolve the state legislature. He can also put the state legislature in a state of suspended animation.
- The laws of the state and the budget will be passed by the Parliament. The President can delegate this power to any suitable authority, if the Parliament is unable to handle the additional workload.
- The Parliament can authorize the President to sanction expenditure from the Consolidated fund of the State.

Financial Emergency (Article 360)

According to Article 360, if the President is satisfied that a situation has arisen whereby the financial stability or credit of India or any part of it is threatened, he may proclaim a financial emergency. This emergency should also be approved by the Parliament, as in the case of the earlier two types. This is also applicable for two months in the first instance but, the Parliament, by simple majority, can increase this term.

Such an emergency can have the following effects:

- The President can issue directions to the State Governments to observe such canons of financial propriety as may be required.
- The President may order reduction of salaries and allowances of all or any class of persons serving in connection with the affairs of a state.
- A provision can be made requiring all money bills to be reserved for the consideration of the President after they are passed by the legislative assembly of the state.

Such an emergency has never been imposed in India so far.

3.2 Vice-President

Article 63 of the Indian Constitution provides for a Vice-President, who is the second highest ranking government official in the executive branch of the Central Government. Under the constitution he should have completed the age of 35 years and should be qualified for election as a member of the Council of States. The tenure of the Vice-President shall be elected by the members of an electoral college consisting of the members of both houses of the Union Parliament in accordance with the system of proportional representation by means of a single transferable vote and the voting at such an election shall be by secret ballot. Both the elected and the nominated members participate in the election.

The position of the Vice-President is one of great dignity and prestige. It was created chiefly with the intention of filling a political vacuum caused by the removal, resignation, illness, death or inability of the President in the discharge of the duties of his office. The Constitution mentions that the Vice-President shall be the ex-officio Chairman of the Council of States. His chief function is to preside over the meetings of this House.

At present, under Article 65(1), in case of a vacancy in the office of the President, the Vice-President shall act as the President until the date on which a new President is elected. This can safely be taken to mean that, even if the election of the Vice- President acting as the President is invalidated, acts done by him in the capacity of the President will not be declared void. The office also devolves on the Vice-President, as Article 65(3) says that, while acting as the President, he will have all the immunities of the President. The Second Schedule to the Constitution also provides that, while discharging the duties of the President, the Vice-President will draw on the same emoluments, allowances and privileges as the President. The Vice President can act as the President for a maximum period of six months.

3.3 Council of Ministers

Article 74 of the Constitution lays down that there shall be a Council of Ministers with the PM at the head to aid and advice the President who shall, in the exercise of his functions, act in accordance with such advice. There is no provision for the failure of constitutional machinery (as under Article 356) and direct President's rule at the Union level.

Under Article 75, the PM is appointed by the President and other Ministers are appointed by him on the advice of the PM. The Ministers hold office during the pleasure of the President. But, the Council of Ministers is collectively responsible to Lok Sabha.

The Constitution (Ninety-first Amendment) Act, 2003 inserted the following new clauses to Article 75:

(IA) The total number of Ministers, including the PM, in the Council of Ministers shall not exceed 15%, of the total number of members of the House of the People.

(IB)A member of either House of Parliament belonging to any political party who is disqualified for being a member of that House under paragraph 2 of the Tenth Schedule shall also be disqualified to be appointed as a Minister under clause (1) for duration of the period commencing from the date of his disqualification till the date on which the term of his office as such member would expire or where he contests any election to either House of Parliament before the expiry of such period, till the date on which he is declared elected, whichever is earlier.

While the Ministers are appointed by the President and said to hold office during the pleasure of the President, in actual effect, it means they are selected by the PM (the President cannot appoint anyone not recommended by the PM) and hold office at his pleasure. If the PM is unhappy or dissatisfied with any Minister, he can advise him to resign, advise the President to dismiss him or tender the resignation of his Council of Ministers and then reconstitute it after deleting the name of the Minister in question.

Our Constitution provides only for collective responsibility, which means that there cannot be 'no confidence' in a single Minister. The entire Council of Ministers is jointly responsible to the Lok Sabha for all acts of Government. Therefore, it stands or falls together. If it loses the confidence of the House, the entire Council of Ministers must resign. In India acts of the State are done in the name of the President and required to be countersigned by way of authentication not by a Minister but by a Secretary (or other authorized officers) to the Government in accordance with the rules made by the President (Article 77)

Cabinet

The Constitution speaks only of Ministers. It does not indicate any classification or categories of Ministers into Cabinet Ministers, Ministers of State, Deputy Ministers, etc. The Constitution mentions only the Council of Ministers and makes no reference to the Cabinet except in Article 352 (as amended in 1979) where Cabinet is defined as the Council consisting of Ministers of Cabinet rank. For all practical purposes, it is the Cabinet which takes policy decisions and advises the President.

3.4 The Prime Minister: Powers and Position

Parliamentary democracy in India constitutionally provides for a nominal and a real executive. They are the President and the PM respectively. This is an attempt to explain the role of the PM as the 'real chief executive' by examining his position vis-a-vis various other functionaries and institutions through whom he exercises power and fulfils his constitutional obligations.

Article 75(1) of the Indian Constitution provides that the PM shall be appointed by the President and the other ministers shall be appointed by the President on the advice of the PM. The Constitution permits a person to be appointed PM without his or her being a member of either House of Parliament at the time of appointment.

But such a person can be PM only for six months. However, we have developed a convention which requires that the President should appoint the leader of a party or a group of parties who commands majority support in the House of the People as PM.

As regards the removal of the PM by the President, Article 75(2) which conditions his continuance in office dependent on "the Pleasure of the President" has to be read with Article 75(3), which states that all the ministers are collectively responsible to the House of the people. This is taken to mean that so long as the PM is able to command majority support in the Lok Sabha, there is no threat to his continuance in office. Articles 74, 75 and 78 broadly govern the relationship between the PM and the President. The chief function of the PM (going by Article 74) is that of rendering aid and tendering advice to the President. After the 42nd Amendment of the Constitution (1976), Article 74(1) reads: 'There shall be a Council of Ministers with the PM at the head, to aid and advise the President who shall in the exercise of his functions act in accordance with such advice.' Amendment 44 (1978) added the following to the same article "provided that the President may require the Council of Ministers to reconsider such advice, either generally or otherwise, and the President shall act in accordance with the advice tendered after such reconsideration.

Article 75(2) governs another aspect of the relationship between the two. It says that 'Ministers shall hold office during the pleasure of the President.' Article 78 specifies certain duties of the PM in relation to the President. It places an obligation on the PM to convey to the President all decisions of the Council relating to the administration of affairs of the Union and proposals for legislation. Article 78, by imposing these duties on the PM, 'enables the President to exercise his right to be consulted, to encourage and to warn'.

These articles have given rise to heated controversies from time to time. In fact, as early as 1951, the first President of India had raised the question as to whether the president was always bound by the advice of the PM and his cabinet. The controversy resurfaced from time to time in the last sixty years.

With the council of ministers the concept of 'first among equals' does not appear to be appropriate in the context of the Indian PM He is not only the first among equals but the keystone of the cabinet arch. The PM represents the whole of the executive government in a way that no single member of the Council of Ministers or even the whole of the Council of Ministers can. The President appoints ministers on the advice of the PM who decides about the size of the cabinet. The PM has a free hand in the distribution of portfolios, can review such distribution, reshuffle the ministers and request any minister to resign if his services are not considered necessary.

The PM's next important role, after the formation of the cabinet, is the coordination of the cabinet activities. As the chairman of the cabinet, the PM decides when the cabinet meetings are to be held. He controls the agenda and it is for him to accept or reject proposals for discussion submitted by the ministers. All decisions of the cabinet are generally by consensus but if, on a rare occasion, voting does take place, as chairman of the cabinet, the PM has the casting vote. After the allocation of portfolios, the PM also keeps an eye on what is going in the various departments and he can intervene if he feels that things are not going on smoothly or in accordance with the goals and policies of the government. He must endeavour to see the work of the government as a whole. He should be familiar with the business of each department and should ensure their functioning in an effective manner. The PM has to make the cabinet work, arbitrate differences of view and must fit all the necessary talents together in an effective team. The style of each PM may vary, but it would be best if he provided sound guidance at the policy-making stage and then let his ministerial colleagues function with autonomy. The Prime Ministerial style must embody stress on consensus and discussion. Although the work of coordination is also done by the various cabinet committees, it is the PM who decides how this coordination should be brought about. He decides what cabinet committees there will be, appoints their chairmen and presides over some committees himself. The cabinet is thus a unified body and collective responsibility is the method by which this unity is secured. Teamwork is the hallmark of the cabinet system and the PM must strive hard to maintain unity at all costs.

The PM, by virtue of being the leader of the majority party in the Lok Sabha, is also expected to provide leadership in the House. After consultation with the cabinet, the PM advises the President to summon the Parliament and to prorogue the session. The PM is also an integral part of the process of legislation. All important bills emanate from the cabinet. Hence, no important bill can be introduced in the Lok Sabha without his consent. He also guides the bills through the various stages in the House. He, together with the Speaker, prepares a tentative programme for the Lok Sabha for each week as well as for each day.

Though, he is the leader of the majority party, the PM must also try to win the cooperation and support of the opposition. He must pay attention to the demands and grievances and reactions of the opposition. The PM has some role to play in the context of the Rajya Sabha also. The twelve members that the President appoints to the Rajya Sabha are appointed on the advice of the PM He can also act as a mediator if the Rajya Sabha and the Lok Sabha have differences of opinion.

3.5 The Parliament

The Parliament of India consists of the President and the two Houses - the Rajya Sabha (Council of states) and the Lok Sabha (House of the People). Of the three constituents of Parliament, oply the Lok Sabha is subject to dissolution. The Rajya Sabha is a permanent or continuing House and there must always be a President or a person performing the functions of the President.

Though the President of India is a constituent part of Parliament, he does not sit or participate in the discussions in either of the two Houses. The two Houses are, however, summoned by the President to meet from time to time. He can prorogue the two Houses and dissolve the Lok Sabha. Prorogation terminates the session while dissolution puts an end to the life of the House. The President's assent is essential for a Bill passed by both Houses to become law. Not only that, when both the Houses of Parliament are not in session and he is satisfied that circumstances exist which render it necessary for him to take immediate action, the President can promulgate an Ordinance having the same force and effect as a law passed by Parliament (Articles 85, 111 and 123).

Rajya Sabha:

The Rajya Sabha is, as its name indicates, the Council of States. It represents the people in an indirect way in as much as they are grouped into several components of the Union—the States and the Union Territories —and members of Rajya Sabha are elected by the elected members of the State Legislative Assemblies in accordance with the system of proportional representation by means of a single transferable vote (Article 80[4]).

Unlike the Lok Sabha, which has a fixed term but can be dissolved by the President at any time, the Rajya Sabha is a permanent body and is not subject to dissolution. While the term of an individual member of Rajya Sabha is six years, as nearly as possible, one-third of its members with the provisions made on that behalf by Parliament by law (Article 83[1]) retire, every 2 years. The Vice-President, who is elected by the members of both Houses of Parliament, is the ex-officio Chairman of Rajya Sabha, whereas the Deputy Chairman is elected by the members of the Rajya Sabha from amongst themselves (Article 64, 66 and 89).

Lok Sabha

The other House —the Lok Sabha—is the House of the people. It is directly elected by the people. Every citizen of India who is 18 years of age is entitled to vote in elections to Lok Sabha unless he is otherwise disqualified under law (Article 326). The Constitution provides that the Lok Sabha shall consist of not more than 530 members chosen by direct election from territorial constituencies in the States, and not more than 20 members to represent the Union territories, chosen in such manner as Parliament by law provides (Article 81 [1]). In addition the President may nominate not more than two members to represent the Anglo-Indian community (Article 331). The maximum strength of the House envisaged in the Constitution is thus 552.

Seats are reserved for the Scheduled Castes and Scheduled Tribes in Lok Sabha state-wise on the basis of population rations. Originally, the reservation was for 10 years but it is being extended every 10 years (Articles 330 and 334).

The term of the House in India is five years from the date appointed for its first meeting. The House may be dissolved before the expiration of its full term under certain circumstances. When a proclamation of emergency is in force the term of the Lok Sabha can be extended by the Parliament for a period not exceeding one year at a time and not exceeding in any case a period of six months after the Proclamation has ceased to operate (Article 83).

Article 111 says that when a Bill passed by the two Houses of Parliament is presented to the President, the President shall either assent to the Bill or withhold assent therefrom. He may return a Bill; if it is not a Money Bill, to the Houses for reconsideration; if the Bill is passed again with or without any amendment and presented to President for assent, he shall not withhold assent (Article 111). Another option available to the President is to seek some information or clarification or to return the Bill to the Government, i.e. the Council of Ministers, for reconsidering their advice for according assent to the Bill (Article 74 [2] and 78[b]).

Functions of Parliament

The process of legislating is the most basic function of Parliament. Under Articles 245 and 246, the Parliament can make laws for the whole or any part of India within its area of competence as defined and delimited under the distribution of legislative powers between the Union and the States vide the Seventh Schedule. In regard to the Union list, the Parliament's jurisdiction is exclusive. Both the Union and the States have concurrent power to legislate in respect of entries in the concurrent list. In case of conflict between the Union and the State laws, the former prevails (Article 245). Also the residuary powers vest in the Union Parliament (Article248 and entry 97 of the Union List).

Parliament may by law change the name, the boundaries, area, etc., of the states or establish new states (Articles 2, 3 and4), increase the number of judges of the Supreme Court or establish additional courts (Articles 124,247). Under Article 249, Parliament may legislate even on matters in the State list under 253, it may legislate for implementing a treaty or in the State list. Also, in circumstances of President's rule (Article 356) or proclamation of Emergency (Article 352), Parliament can legislate in the State field.

In the Indian political system, after a policy is laid down, a law is passed or money is sanctioned, it is the administration which is required to execute and implement. Since Parliament embodies the will of the people, it must be able to oversee the way in which public policy is carried out so as to ensure that it keeps in step with the aspirations of the people as a whole.

The various procedural devices like the system of Parliamentary Committees, Questions, Calling Attention Notices, Half-an-Hour discussions, etc., through which the parliament gets informed, also constitute very potent instruments for effecting parliamentary monitoring over administrative action.

Parliamentary surveillance over public finance —the power to levy or modify taxes and the voting of supplies and grants—is one of the most important checks against the Executive assuming arbitrary powers. No taxes can be legally levied and no expenditure incurred from the public exchequer without specific parliamentary authorization by law (Articles 114 116 and 265). The Constitution also provides for an Annual Statement of the estimated receipts and expenditure (budget) to be placed before parliament. Other means by which parliament exercises control over the public exchequer is through Public Accounts Committee, Committee on Public Undertakings, Estimates Committee and the Report on the Comptroller and Auditor General.

During debate and discussion on legislative proposals or Finance Bills, motion to consider and approve government policies, Budget, etc., members are free to express themselves and to say what is required for the public good and what modifications are required in existing policies. Nevertheless during discussions members have full liberty to criticize the administration for their past performance and suggest how they should implement policies in the future or how a particular administrative action should be carried out or implemented. The discussions are important for they indicate parliamentary mood and bring the impact of public thinking on the administrative apparatus which may otherwise remain insensitive to public sentiments and feelings.

The most well-known and effective mechanism through which members elicit information on their own is that of asking questions in the Houses of Parliament.

Another procedural device is that of the Calling Attention Notices. A member may, with the previous permission of the Speaker, call the attention of a minister to any matter of urgent public importance and request the Minister to make a statement on the subject. Members can also write to the concerned ministers and ask for the information they may need and the information is usually supplied.

Another method for the parliament to inform itself and receive necessary feedback is through the reports of various parliamentary committees. In the process of their scrutiny, the committees ask searching questions and collect extensive and valuable information from the government ministries and departments, public undertakings, etc., under examination. This procedural device has also become an important tool for eliciting information on matters of urgent public importance and has been very popular with members from both sides of the House.

Other sources of information include the mass media, political parties, interest groups and so on. Parliament has also its own institutionalized source of information, called the Parliament Library and its Research, Reference, Documentation and information Services.

Besides, parliament exercises multifarious functions, for example, in matters like the amendment of the Constitution; the impeachment of the President; removal of Supreme court and High Court judges, Comptroller and Auditor General, Chief Election commissioner, presiding Officers of the two Houses, etc.(Articles 61,124,217,148,324 and 90).

3.6 Functions of the Supreme Court

The constitutional task assigned to the judiciary is in no way less than that of the other two functionaries: legislature and the executive. Indeed, it is the role of the judiciary to carry out the constitutional intent and it is its responsibility to keep a vigilant watch over the functioning of democracy in accordance with the Constitution. The various roles and functions of the Supreme Court are discussed below.

Original Jurisdiction (Article 131)

This refers to the cases that directly originate in the Supreme Court. It has original exclusive jurisdiction in any dispute between (a) the Government of India and one or more States, (b) the Government of India and any state on one side and one or more other states on the other, (c) two or more States.

Appellate Jurisdiction (Articles 132 to 136)

This refers to the power of reviewing and revising the orders of lower courts and tribunals. This jurisdiction extends to both the civil and the criminal appeals from the High Courts under certification from these courts or, in its absence, permitted by the Supreme Court itself. Normally these appeals are in cases involving substantial question of law or interpretation of the Constitution or death penalty awarded by a High Court.

Advisory Jurisdiction

Under Article 143, the Supreme Court has been vested with the power of advisory jurisdiction. Whenever the President consults the Supreme Court, on any matter of public importance, it gives opinion to the President. The advice is not binding on the President.

Writ Jurisdiction

The Supreme Court is the guardian of the individual liberties and fundamental rights. It has the power to declare a law passed by any legislature null and void if it encroaches upon the fundamental rights guaranteed to the people by the Constitution. For the enforcement of fundamental rights, it can issue writs in the nature of Habeas Corpus, Mandamus, Certiorari, Prohibition and Quo-Warranto.

Judicial Review

Judicial review means the power of the highest court of the land to finally pronounce upon the legality or otherwise of a legislative act in so far as it conforms, or does not conform, to the provisions of the Constitution of India. The Constitution being the fundamental law of the land, every legislative enactment, whether of the Union or of the States must conform to it. The higher courts in India are endowed with powers of judicial review of legislation. But, if an Act of Parliament is set aside by the judiciary as ultra vires or violative of the Constitution, Parliament can reenact it after removing the clauses for which it was set aside. Also, Parliament may, within the limits of its constituent powers, amend the Constitution in such a manner to see that the law no longer remains unconstitutional. However, the parliament in India is not as sovereign as the British Parliament where no judicial review of legislation is permitted. At the same time, the judiciary in India is not as supreme as in the United States of America which recognizes virtually no limit on the scope of judicial review and the pronouncement of the Supreme Court in regard to the legality of a legislative measure is final. India has adopted a middle course and a compromise between the British sovereignty of Parliament and American judicial Supremacy. Since we have a written constitution and the powers and functions of every organ are defined and delimited by the Constitution, there is no question of any organ— not even parliament—being sovereign. Both Parliament and the Supreme Court are supreme in their respective spheres.

Article 32 in the Chapter on Fundamental Rights specifically confers the power of judicial review on the Supreme Court. Under this Article every citizen has the right to move the Supreme Court by appropriate proceedings for the enforcement of the rights conferred in Chapter III. The Supreme Court can hear the petition in its original jurisdiction and for the enforcement of any of the rights conferred. Under Article 226, State High Courts have been given similar powers, i.e. the power to issue to any person or authority, within its territorial jurisdiction, directions, orders, or writs.

Fundamental Rights in the Constitution make judicial review especially relevant. Article 12 guarantees fundamental rights against all State action. And 'State' under this Article has been defined to include Government and Parliament of India and the Government and the Legislature of each of the States and all local or other authorities within the territory of India or under the control of the Government.

Article 13 declares all laws inconsistent with or in derogation of the fundamental rights to be void to the extent of inconsistency. Up to 1967, the Supreme Court accepted the view that an Act amending the Constitution was not 'Law' in the definition of Article 13 (2). But, in the Golaknath case, the Supreme Court ruled by a majority judgment that an

Act amending the constitution was also 'law' under this definition and therefore subject to judicial review. The Constitution (Twenty-fourth Amendment) Act, 1971 inserted clause 13 (4) in the Constitution, laying down that an Amendment to the Constitution is not 'law' under the definition of Article 13 (2). In the Keshavananda Bharti case, the Supreme Court upheld this position.

Cases may also be brought before the Supreme Court by a State Government, or by an affected private individual or a party, claiming that in enacting a particular law, the concerned government exceeded its jurisdiction with regard to the division of powers under the Seventh Schedule. While reviewing such enactment, the Supreme Court will examine whether jurisdictional limits have been transgressed and if on that ground the law deserves to be struck down as ultra vires of the Constitution.

3.7 Judicial Activism and Public Interest Litigation

What has come to be called "Judicial Activism" was born as a corrective to inaction or failure of the executive and the legislature to provide clean, competent and citizen- friendly governance. Judicial Activism may also be looked at as a facet of Judicial review. It is the obligation of the judiciary to see that every aspect which is essential for proper implementation of the rule of law is taken care of. The obligation of the judiciary is to ensure that not only judiciary does its work, but also that every agency or instrumentality which is involved in the interpretation of law, functions effectively. Judicial activism must necessarily mean the active process of implementation of the Rule of law, essential for the preservation of a functional democracy. In the Judges Transfer Case, the seven-judge Constitution Bench of the Supreme Court held that any member of the public even if not directly involved but having 'sufficient interest' can approach the High Court under Article 226, for redressal of the grievances of the persons who cannot move the Court because of poverty, helplessness or disability or socially or economically disadvantaged position'. The Court can be approached even through a letter in such a case (S.P. Gupta vs. President of India, AIR 1982 SC 149). After this judgment, it has been open to public-minded individual citizens or social organizations to seek judicial relief in the interest of the general public.

Public Interest Litigation has come to stay in the Indian judicial system. Courts have been judiciously active in giving relief in social action litigation—ranging from issues of bonded labour to victims of custodial violence, to other cases of excesses committed by the Executive. Several issues ranging far and wide over the spectrum of daily living are being covered by such litigation.

In recent years, the Supreme Court has issued directions to control pollution, to check the evil of child prostitution, to revive a sick company to protect the livelihood of disbanded employees, to look into the danger or safety in building a dam, to provide insurance to workers in factories, to protect the Taj Mahal from environmental pollution, etc. (Subhash vs. State of Bihar, AIR1991 SC 420; Vishal vs. Union of India1990 3 SCC 318; Workers of Rohtas Industries Ltd. & Rohtas Industries Ltd. AIR 1990 SC 491; Tehri Bandh vs. State of U.P; Gaurav Jain vs. Union of India, AIR 1990 SC 292; Mehta vs. State of T.N.,AIR 1991 SC 417; M.C. Mehta vs. Union of India, AIR 1997 SC 734) However , it has been held that non-justifiable political matters cannot be brought before the court under the guise of public interest litigation. [Maharshi c. the State, AIR1990 A11.52]

The innovative judicial approach to 'Public Interest Litigation' came handy in cases of acute social injustice, economic exploitation, denial of human rights, corruption and other offences against public interest. Even hyperactivism of judiciary was justified under the powers of judicial review. It drew its strength, relevance and legitimacy from the support it elicited from the people because of their total disenchantment with the other organs of the State run by the politicians and the bureaucrats. But, the scenario has since changed. People are beginning to lose faith in the judiciary as well. Judiciary also can no more be said to be entirely free from maladies of corruption, inefficiency and misuse of authority that afflict other organs of the State.

In the ultimate analysis, orders of the courts have also to be given effect by the administration which functions under the political executive. Judiciary has to be very cautious and must ensure that a situation is not reached where its orders or directives are no more fully respected or obeyed or are found to be just unimplementable like in the 2018 Sabarimala Judgement. The courts have begun to see that in the name of public interest litigation false, frivolous, fraudulent or private interest motivated issues are not entertained. As on 31 July 2019, 3 crore cases were pending in the Supreme Court. Delay of justice may truly be construed as denial of justice, very often in the Indian context.

3.8 Judicial Reforms

The Lok Sabha passed the National Judicial Appointments Commission Bill 2014 by voice vote and the accompanying Constitution Amendment Bill by 367 roles to nil. The first Bill lays out procedures for appointing and transferring judges to the Supreme Court and the High Courts, while the second stipulates its membership and provides its constitutional protection. The political attempt to fix the current flawed system of only judges appointing other judges in the collegium system through a new system of oversight was much needed. Although the principle of judicial independence still needs to be safeguarded, this is a good example of how government and opposition can work together constructively for the sake of improved legislation. The Narendra Modi government has drawn up a proposal to set up 1800 fast-track courts (FTC) across the country to expedite delivery of justice. A detailed proposal has been made by the law ministry seeking grants from the 14th Finance Commission which allocates resources for setting up court infrastructure and for initiating judicial reforms.

Earlier, in 2000, the Central Government had allocated financial resources to the states for setting up FTCs when 1734 of them were set up. The Central grant was made available for a fixed period of five years, but was later extended till 2011. However, after the lapse of the extended deadline some of the states continued with the fast courts and at the end of March 2014, at least 976 such courts were still in operation—the highest number being in Bihar with 179, followed by UP with 153, Maharashtra 92, West Bengal 85 and Madhya Pradesh 84 among the top five. In 2019 the centre has proposed the establishment of 1800 FTCs for a period of 5 years from 2015 to 2020. However the result of FTCs have not been encouraging at all so far.

Improvement in Judge-Population Ratio

Under the directions of Supreme Court, with regard to the subordinate judiciary, there was an increase in the judge strength from 10.5 per 10 lakh people to 50 per 10 lakh people. Successive governments have made little budgetary allocations to achieve such a five-fold increase in the human resources and infrastructure of the subordinate judiciary, where the bulk of the 3.2 crore cases are pending.

3.9 Respective Powers and Functions of the Three Organs of the State

The most important function of the political system is to establish the three organs of the State —the Executive, the Legislature and the Judiciary, to demarcate their relationship of jurisdiction and authority, and to regulate their relationship with each other and with the people. In a traditional manner, it may be said that the job of the Legislature is to make laws, the executive executes and administers the laws, and the judiciary interprets laws and adjudicates disputes in accordance with the laws. The union government is divided into three distinct but interrelated branches: legislative, executive, and judicial.

The Executive and the Legislative

The scheme of the Constitution represents a real fusion of the highest executive and legislative authorities. The two are not visualized as competing centres of power but as inseparable partners or coparceners in the business of government. Strictly speaking, Parliamentary systems of government should mean Government by Parliament. But, the Parliament is a large body. It does not and cannot itself govern. The Council of Ministers may in a sense be described as the grand executive committee of Parliament charged with the responsibility of governance on behalf of the parent body.

There is, however, a clear distinction between the functions of the Executive and the functions of Parliament (Article 75). The Parliament is to deliberate, discuss, legislate, advise, criticize and ventilate public grievances. The Executive is to govern, albeit on behalf of the Parliament and the people.

While the Executive has almost unlimited right to initiate and formulate legislative and financial proposals before parliament and to give effect to approved policies unhindered by parliament, the function of Parliament is to exercise political and financial control over the Executive and to ensure parliamentary surveillance of administration.

Parliament has the power to make laws regulating the constitution, organization, jurisdiction and powers of the Courts. The Parliament is empowered to prescribe the number of judges by law (Article 124). Under our Constitution, the Parliament may by law:

1. extend the jurisdiction of High Court to, or exclude the jurisdiction of a High Court from, any Union territory;
2. establish a common High Court for two or more States or for two or more States and a Union territory, and
3. constitute a High Court for a Union territory or declare any Court in any such territory to be a High Court for all or any of the purposes of the constitution (Article 241).

A judge of the Supreme Court or any High Court can be removed from his Office by the President, only on a joint address passed by both Houses of Parliament with a special majority. Parliament is not empowered to discuss the conduct of any Judge of the Supreme Court or of a High Court in the discharge of his duties except in the case of such a motion.

Parliament may by law provide for the establishment of an administrative tribunal for the Union and a separate law made under the provision may specify the jurisdiction and powers of the tribunals. Such law may exclude the jurisdiction of all Courts, except the jurisdiction of the Supreme Court under Article 136, with respect to certain specified matters (Articles 323A and 323B). Further, the Constitution empowers Parliament to create an all India judicial service which shall not include any post inferior to that of a district judge (Articles 312[1] and [3]).

The validity of any proceedings in either House of Parliament cannot be questioned before a court of law on the ground of any alleged irregularity of procedure [Articles 122(1) and 212 (1)] [Kihoto vs. Zachilhu, AIR 1993 SC 412]. The presiding officer of each House or any other officer or Member of Parliament who is for the time being vested with the powers to regulate procedure, or enforce or carry out the decision of either House of Parliament, is not subject to the jurisdiction of the courts in exercise of those powers (Articles 122 [2] and 105[3]).

No member of Parliament is liable to any proceedings in any court in respect of anything said or any vote given by him in Parliament or any committee thereof. Also, publication of any report, paper, or proceedings of Parliament by or under authority of a House of Parliament is protected against any court proceedings (Articles 1054 [2] and 194[2]).

The Indian political system is unique in its attempt to blend the federal and the unitary and the presidential and the parliamentary. It attempts a balance between the fundamental rights of the individual on the one hand and the socio-economic interests of the people and security of the State on the other. Also, it presents a compromise between the principles of parliamentary sovereignty and judicial supremacy. The two are not visualized as competing centers of power but as inseparable partners or co-partners in the business of government.

The judiciary in India has the authority to co-ordinate with the Legislature and the Executive. Parliament has the power to make laws regulating the constitution, organization, jurisdiction and powers of the Courts. According to the constitution, Chief Justice and judges of the Supreme Court and High Courts are to be appointed by the President. They cannot be removed from office except through a process prescribed in the Constitution. The parliament may by law provide for the establishment of an administrative tribunal for each State or for two or more States.

The Parliament is not empowered to discuss the conduct of any judge of the Supreme Court or a High Court in the discharge of his duties except in the case of a motion for presenting address to the President praying for the removal of a judge. The validity of any proceedings in either House of Parliament cannot be questioned before a court of law on the ground of any alleged irregularity of procedure.

3.10 The Cabinet Secretariat: Functions

The Cabinet Secretariat (CS) is under the direct charge of the PM. The administrative head of the Secretariat is the Cabinet Secretary who is also the ex-officio Chairman of the Civil Service Board.

In the Government of India (Allocation of Business) Rules, 1961, 'Cabinet Secretariat' finds a place in the First schedule to the Rules. The subjects allotted to this secretariat are:

1. Secretarial assistance to Cabinet and Cabinet Committees
2. Rules of Business

The Cabinet Secretariat is responsible for the administration of the Government of India (Transaction of Business) Rules, 1961, and the Government of India (Allocation of Business) Rules, 1961, facilitating smooth transaction of business in Ministries/ Departments of the Government by ensuring adherence to these rules. The Secretariat assists in decision making in Government by ensuring inter-ministerial coordination, ironing out differences amongst Ministries/Departments and evolving consensus through the instrumentality of the standing /adhoc committees of secretaries. Through this mechanism new policy initiatives are also promoted.

The Cabinet Secretariat ensures that the President, the Vice President and the Ministers are kept informed of the major activities of the government's management of major crisis situations in the country and coordinating activities of various ministries in such a situation is also one of the functions of the Cabinet Secretariat.

The secretarial assistance provided by the Cabinet Secretariat to the Cabinet and Cabinet committees, includes:

- Convening of the meetings of the cabinet on the orders of the PM.
- Preparation and circulation of the agenda.
- Circulating papers related to the cases on the agenda.
- Preparing a record of discussions taken.
- Circulation of the record after obtaining the approval of the PM.
- Watching implementation of the decisions taken by the Cabinet.

While each Ministry is responsible for acting on its own for expeditious implementation of Government policies plans and programmes, where inter-ministerial cooperation is involved they often seek the assistance of the Cabinet Secretariat. The inter-ministerial problems are dealt with in the meetings of the Committees of Secretaries (COS). Committees are constituted for discussing specific matters and proposals emanating from various secretaries to the Government and meetings are held under the chairmanship of the cabinet secretary. These committees have been able to break bottlenecks or secure mutually supporting inter-ministerial action.

The discussions of the COS takes place on the basis of a paper formulated by the principle department concerned and the Department with a different point of view, if any, providing a supplementary note. The decisions or recommendations of the COS are unanimous. These proceedings are also circulated to and are followed up by the departments. There are other important functions which it discharges, viz.,

1. Monitoring
2. Coordination
3. Promoting new policy initiatives.

In addition, the following cases are brought to the Central Secretariat on which it is expected to provide assistance and information to the cabinet:

- Cases involving legislation including the issuing of ordinances
- Messages of the president to the Parliament
- Proposals to summon, prorogue or dissolve the Lok Sabha
- Cases involving negotiations with foreign countries on treaties or agreements
- Proposals for sending delegations of persons or groups abroad
- Appointments of public committees of enquiry and consideration of their reports
- Cases involving financial implications
- Ministerial proposals to the cabinet for decision and direction
- Cases of disagreements among ministries
- Cases which the president or the prime minister may, by discretion, require to be put before the cabinet

The progress of implementation of the centrally sponsored schemes is sometimes reviewed by the cabinet secretary and necessary suggestions are issued by him to the state government to improve the effectiveness and efficiency of execution of the schemes. For example, the Direct Benefit Transfer (DBT) scheme has been shifted in 2015 to Cabinet Secretariat and its implementation is being monitored by the Prime Minister's Office (PMO) so that its benefits reach out to individual beneficiaries directly.

The Role of the CS could be seen in operation in the case of disaster caused by Cyclone Phailin in October 2013 in Odisha when the cabinet secretary took special interest in the restoration of connectivity or telecom services. An important function of the CS is to not only communicate to the ministry concerned the decision of the cabinet or the cabinet committees and follow up its implementation but also to perform inter-ministerial coordination that involves matters relating to delay, differences and coordination of policies.

In recent years, the rise of the Prime Minister's Secretariat has become centralized, owing to the formation of a large secretariat with many whole time and a host of full-time service officers in-charge of different subjects. This has caused unnecessary centralization of power and reduction of the powers of the ministers and departmental secretaries. The Central Secretariat, originally conceived for securing coordination should not itself become – a de-coordinating agency. It should serve the cabinet and its committees.

The Cabinet Secretariat is seen as a useful mechanism by the departments for promoting inter-ministerial coordination since the cabinet secretary is also the head of the civil services.

The secretaries felt it necessary to keep the cabinet secretary informed of developments from time to time. The Transaction of Business Rules also require them to keep the cabinet secretary informed of developments every now and then, especially if there are any departures from these rules.

3.11 Cabinet Committees

As it is very difficult for the PM to convene the entire cabinet for each and every issue, a system of cabinet committees has been introduced to facilitate the smooth functioning of the government. Committee is a device for increasing the output of an organization. Introduction of a system of cabinet committees reduces the work burden of the entire cabinet.

They provide necessary information to the cabinet to take a decision on a particular matter. The system also safeguards the principles of collective responsibility. It also vastly increases the effectiveness of the control of the political executive over the bureaucracy.

Cabinet committees are necessary to perform functions devolved on them by the cabinet. Another advantage of the cabinet committees is that they facilitate effective co-ordination among the members of the cabinet.

There are two types of cabinet committees: Standing and Ad hoc. As the name itself indicates ad hoc committees are formed to settle some specific problems and once the task is finished the committee ceases to exist.

But standing committees yield real power and are of great importance in the political system. A cabinet committee is headed by a cabinet Minister and under exceptional circumstances we also see the PM heading a cabinet committee.

The cabinet makes use of the committee system to facilitate decision-making in specific areas. The Business Rules provide for the constitution of standing committees of the cabinet to ensure speedy decisions on vital questions of political and economic significance and other matters of importance as also to effect coordination in well- defined fields of administration. These committees change according to the requirements of the situation and occasionally ad hoc committees are appointed.

The number of such committees has been changing from time to time. However, the membership of the cabinet committees normally varies from three to eight. The chairmanship is shared between the PM and the Home Minister. Of these the most powerful is the Political Affairs Committee, consisting as it does of the senior most ministers. It functions as a super cabinet in providing direction to the government.

In June 2019, the list of Cabinet Committees stands as follows:

1. *Cabinet committee on Political Affairs* (*CCPA*) : CCPA was set up in May 2014 and is chaired by the PM. It is also known as 'Super cabinet' as it is the most important of all. It deals with all policy matters pertaining to domestic and foreign affairs. Besides the PM, 12 cabinet ministers are members of the CCPA.

   It deals with issues related to Centre-state relations, consider economic and political issues from a wider perspective and analyse policy matters concerning foreign affairs with no security implications.

2. *Appointments Committee of the Cabinet (ACC):* ACC is composed of the PM (who is the chairman) and the Minister of Home Affairs. The Establishment Officer's division processes all proposals for senior appointments in the GOI that require approval of the ACC under the GOI Transactions of Business Rules, 1961. These include board-level appointments in Public Sector Undertakings (PSUs) and appointments to the posts at the level of joint secretary. In addition, all appointments by promotion that require ACC approval are processed through the Establishment Officer's division.
3. *Cabinet Committee on Economic Affairs (CCEA):* CCEA is one of the standing committees of the cabinet constituted by GOI. It comprises the PM (chairman) and 11 other Cabinet Ministers.

   Some of the major functions of the CCEA are: reviewing economic trends and evolving an economic policy framework for the country; coordinating policies and activities in the economic field including foreign investment; reviewing progress of activities in rural development and fixation of prices of agriculture products; reviewing performance of Public Sector Undertakings and price controls of industrial raw materials and products and disinvestments: facilitating finalization factual reports on the accomplishments of the ministries, agencies and PSUs involved in projects for evaluation.
4. *Cabinet Committee on Parliamentary Affairs:* The cabinet Committee of Parliamentary Affairs, headed by the home minister is mandated to recommend the dates of Parliament sessions. It has 11 members, including 3 special invitees. It also watches the progress of government business in Parliament and gives such directions as may be necessary from time to time in order to secure smooth and efficient conduct of such business.

   Its main function is to ensure smooth and efficient conduct of government business in Parliament and review legislation undertaken by state legislatures from an all-India point of view.
5. *Cabinet Committee on Accommodation (CCA):* The CCA is chaired by the minister of home affairs. Besides the home minister, 3 cabinet ministers are part of this committee. It mainly deals with accommodation problems of the ministers and top positions in the GoI.

   It forms the guidelines for the out-of-turn allotment of government accommodation and also takes decision on allotment of government accommodation to non-eligible persons and organisations
6. *Cabinet Committee on Security (CCS):* The CCS of the government decides on India's defence expenditure, matters of national security and makes significant appointments. CCS is chaired by the PM and comprises of the minister of defence, the minister of finance, minister of home affairs, and the minister of external affairs.
7. *Cabinet Committee on Investment and Growth (CIG)*: The committee's function is to suggest policies conducive to investments and growth. It is chaired by the Prime Minister and has 5 other Cabinet Ministers as members.

8. *Cabinet Committee on Employment and Skill Development*: Its main function is to figure out ways to create more job opportunities with a focus on skill development. It is chaired by the Prime Minister and has 10 other Ministers as Members of this committee.

In addition to these 8 cabinet committees, there are ad hoc committees which may be set up by the prime minister to deal with problems of national importance.

The cabinet committees are instruments to organize coordination in clearly defined fields of administration and relieve the cabinet of their burden of work. The flexibility in membership of these committees enable interested Ministers to exchange views, and arrive at agreed solutions without involving the cabinet, thus, reducing pressure of work upon the latter. Also, there is considerable sharing of work, with the result that many matters which could otherwise travel up to the cabinet for decision-making are settled at the level of cabinet committees. This ensures continuous coordination on vital economic and political issues, and speedy decision-making when required. Any matter which calls for a cabinet decision may come directly to the appropriate committee before the cabinet takes a decision. The cabinet may often merely accept the decision already taken by the cabinet committees. However, despite the fact that some cabinet committees have often exercised real authority, these committees have not been uniformly or consistently effective. They do not cover all important areas of government or functioning. They can take up a matter only when it is referred to by the Minister concerned or by the cabinet, Lastly, they do not meet regularly, which is absolutely necessary if sustained attention is to be given to complex problems and progress in implementation of important policies and programmes is to be kept under constant review.

3.12 Role of the Cabinet Secretary

The office of the cabinet secretary and its functions has evolved over a period of time. The incumbent is the senior most civil servant who presides over the committees of secretaries. These committees examine inter-ministry matters, and issue notices that concern the Government as a whole. The cabinet refers certain matters to them as well. The committees, however, recommend a decision to the concerned ministry; they do not decide.

The cabinet secretary directly handles all senior appointments in the Government. From the early 1950s, the practice followed is that the cabinet secretary usually does not prepare papers for the cabinet or its committees, nor does he take upon himself the responsibility for a comprehensive scrutiny of the agenda papers for the cabinet. All that he does is to ensure that the notes are self-contained and that appropriate details for discussion are provided, occasionally seeking clarification or raising points for modification with the ministry concerned.

The cabinet secretary is present in all meetings of the cabinet and its committees. He is responsible for preparing the agenda, priorities of items and allocation of subjects to cabinet committees. The PM approves these. In these matters the cabinet secretary has to exercise his judgments taking into account the national priorities and what is considered important by the ministries. The cabinet minutes are prepared by the cabinet secretary and decisions communicated to the ministries by him.

The cabinet secretary has to play varied roles. He must keep track of urgent social, economic and political problems, or bottlenecks in the implementation of Government programmes, on issues that the PM should know urgently and matters requiring his decisions. The cabinet secretary must use his discretion in all these matters and keep himself up-to-date with relevant inputs. As there are no fixed sources for such data, the interpersonal skills of the incumbent and the confidence he evokes are two important requirements of the Cabinet secretary's post.

3.13 Prime Minister's Office (PMO)

The PM as the head of the Government plays a crucial role in the politico administrative system of the country. To fulfill his responsibility he is assisted by the PMO, which is a staff agency providing secretarial assistance and crucial advice to the PM. It is an extra constitutional body and enjoys the status of a department of the Government of India under the Allocation of Business rules 1961. PMO came into existence in 1947 by replacing the secretary to the Governor General (Personal) and since 1977 came to be known as the PM's office. PMO is headed by the PM and administered by the Principal Secretary. Additionally it consists of one or two additional secretaries, 3-5 joint secretaries and a number of directors, Deputy secretaries/undersecretaries.

The office houses the PM and a few selected officers of the Indian Administrative Service who work with him to manage and coordinate the government and his office. The PM through his office coordinates with all ministers in the union cabinet, minister of independent charges, governors and ministers of State Governments.

The PMO provides secretarial assistance to the PM. It is headed by the Principal Secretary to the PM. The PMO includes an anti-corruption unit and a public wing dealing with grievances.

The subject matter of files required to be submitted to the PM depends on whether he is holding direct charge of a Ministry or whether there is a cabinet Minister or Minister of State (Independent Charge) incharge of the Ministry.

In the case of the latter, matters are dealt with by the cabinet Minister/Minister of State incharge only of important policy issues, and on other issues which the Minister concerned feels should be submitted to the PM for orders or information, are received in the PMO.

In cases where the PM is the Minister-in-charge, all matters requiring Ministerial approval not delegated to the Minister of State/Deputy Minister, if any, are submitted for orders: The PM has traditionally been the Minister-in-charge of the Department of Space, Atomic energy, and Ministry of Personnel, Public Grievances and Pensions.

Some of the important matters that require the PM's personal attention and are included in the work agenda of the PM are:

- Important defence-related issues;

- Decorations, both civilian and defence, where Presidential approval is required;
- Proposals for appointment of Indian Heads of Missions abroad and requests for grant of agreement for foreign Heads of Missions posted to India.
- All important decisions relating to the Cabinet Secretariat;
- Appointments to State Administrative Tribunals and the Central Administrative Tribunal, UPSC, Election Commission, appointment of members of statutory/ constitutional committees, Commissions attached to various Ministries.
- All policy matters relating to the administration of the Civil Services and administrative reforms;
- Special packages announced by the PM for States are monitored in the PMO and periodical reports submitted to PM; and
- All judicial appointments for which Presidential approval is required. Parliament questions relating to the ministries and departments of which PM is the minister-in-charge are answered by someone nominated for the purpose or by the PM himself. The Prime Minister's National Relief Fund (PMNRF) and the National Defence Fund (NDF) are operated directly from the PMO.

At present PMO has more than 400 people working in it. It has a large establishment and every ministry/ department of the Central Government is represented in the PMO. Due to the authority wielded by the PMO it has been criticized with epithets such as "Super cabinet", "Super Ministry", the "Government of the Government of India", etc. The organizational hierarchy is flexible and the size and composition of the office may vary with the change in the political leadership. Officers on special duty may be appointed to look after specific affairs, while technocrats, subject specialists, press advisors and political advisors may be given various assignments. Every PMO mirrors the personality of the incumbent PM, his needs, his prioritized agendas. Two other bodies have developed within the PMO. They are the Strategic Management Group (SMG) and the PM's Economic Advisory Committee (EAC).Through these bodies, the PMO virtually monitors the progress of various ministries but may also directly monitor completion of government sanctioned projects of high investment value.

Due to the enlarging scope of functions performed by the PM, PMO has become a power center operating like the PM's think tank. The power and prestige enjoyed by the PMO since independence reflected the power and prestige enjoyed by respective PMs.

Under the present circumstances PMO should be a highly professional body and should reflect the increasing complexity of governance in India today. The PM cannot deal with economic and political complexities at home and abroad without a score of specialized advisors. He should keep a critical watch over the performance of his ministers to ensure a proper image of his government and should also display equal vigilance to ensure that the officials in the PMO do not misuse their position and power. Both the Cabinet Secretariat and the PMO perform the role of coordination but differently. PMO has to coordinate with the PM's team of ministers to enable the PM to discharge his responsibilities as the chief

Executive. It is the job of the Cabinet Secretariat to coordinate the work of the Council of Ministers. Due to the over-powering influence of the PMO, ministers are largely dependent on it for endorsements rather than on the Cabinet Secretariat.

With Narendra Modi emerging as the unchallenged leader of his party and perhaps the main architect of the 2014 and 2019 Lok Sabha poll victories, his PMO was naturally expected to be a powerful one. It is claimed to be the strongest PMO since Mrs Gandhi's. The PMO is been made a mechanism of exercising control and establishing the PM's authority over ministries.

Prime Minister Modi has made it clear that power in the government would vest in the PMO. He relies more on bureaucracy than his cabinet. An empowered PMO is the idea which is not dependent on ministers for policy initative and direction. The NITI Aayog is the brain child of the PM for policy initiatives and starting a new phase of union-state cooperative relations. The PMO in Modi's period reflects the image of an efficient and effective organisation which is constantly engaged not only in grievance redressal but also in directing, supervising and monitoring different plans and projects. It also asks different organisations to initiate different policy initiatives.

It may therefore be concluded that the PMO which started initially as a small organization to assist the prime minister has developed into one of the most powerful centres of power in India.

3.14 Central Secretariat

The Central Secretariat occupies a key position in Indian administration. The Secretariat refers to the conglomeration of various ministries/departments of the Central Government. The Secretariat works as a single unit with collective responsibility as in the case of the council of Ministers. Under existing rules each Secretariat department is required to consult any other department that may be interested or concerned before disposing of a case. Secretaries thus, are secretaries to the Government as a whole and not to any particular minister.

The Secretariat assists the ministers in the formulation of governmental policies. Firstly, ministers finalize policies on the basis of adequate data, precedents and other relevant information. The Secretariat makes these available to the minister, thus, enabling him to formulate policies. Secondly, the Secretariat assists ministers in their legislative work too. The Secretariat prepares legislative drafts to be introduced in the legislature. Thirdly, it engages in the collection of relevant information for answering parliamentary questions, and, also, for various parliamentary committees. Fourthly, it carries out a detailed scrutiny of a problem bringing an overall comprehensive viewpoint on it, getting approval, if required, from other lateral agencies like the Ministry of Law and the Ministry of Finance, and also, consulting other governmental bodies. Fifthly, it functions as the main channel of communication between the government and other concerned agencies. Lastly, the Secretariat also ensures that field offices execute the policies and decisions of the Government with efficiency and economy.

Functions of the Central Secretariat

The Central Secretariat system in India is based on two principles:

Split System

Secretariat system in India is based on the principle of separation of policy making function from that of policy execution. Under the scheme of separation (i.e. split system) the Secretariat should be concerned only with making and should not indulge itself in policy execution. Policy execution should be left to executive agencies which are located outside the Secretariat organization.

Tenure System

Under the tenure system of staffing, every official will be deputed to the Central Secretariat and has to work there for a fixed period and should return back to his parent cadre after the expiry of the time limit. It was introduced in India in 1905 by Lord Curzon because he believed that India may be governed from Shimla or Kolkata but is administered from the plains.

The Central Secretariat is a policy-making body of the government and is not, to undertake works of execution, unless necessitated by the lack of official agencies to perform certain tasks. The Central Secretariat normally performs the following functions:

1. Assisting the minister in the discharge of his policy-making and parliamentary functions.
2. Framing legislation, rules and principles of procedure.
3. Sectoral planning and programme formulation.
   a. Budgeting and control of expenditure in respect of activities of the Ministry/ department.
   b. Securing administrative and financial approval to operational programmes and their subsequent modifications.
   c. Supervision and control over the execution of policies and programmes by the executive departments or semi- autonomous field agencies.
   d. Initiating steps to develop greater personnel and organizational competence both in the ministry/department and its executive agencies.
   e. Assisting in increasing coordination at the central level.

Structure of the Secretariat

The Central Secretariat is a collection of various ministries and departments. A ministry is responsible for the formulation of the policy of government within its sphere of responsibility as well as for the execution and review of that policy. A ministry, for the purpose of internal organization, is divided into the following subgroups with an officer in charge of each of them.

Department	Secretary/Additional/Special Secretary
Wing Division Branch Section	Additional/Joint Secretary Deputy Secretary Under Secretary Section Officer

The lowest of these units is a section in charge of a Section Officer and consists of a number of assistants, clerks, typists and peons, and deals with the work relating to the subject allotted to it. It is also referred to as the office. Two sections constitute the branch that is under the charge of an Under Secretary, also known as the branch officer. Two branches ordinarily form a division that is normally headed by a deputy secretary. When the column of work in a ministry exceeds the manageable charge of a secretary, one or more wings are established with a joint secretary in charge of each wing. At the top of the hierarchy comes the department which is headed by the secretary himself or in some cases by an additional/ special secretary. In some cases, a department may be as autonomous as a ministry and equivalent to it in rank.

Ministries

The distinction between department and 'ministry' may be explained by referring to 'ministry' as the minister's charge and department, as the secretary's charge. Although a ministry stands for the minister's charge, its administrative divisions are not uniform. A ministry may not have a department: or may have one or more than one department in which it is formally divided. There are ministers of state in some ministries, some of whom hold independent charge of a department. Many ministries have one or more special purpose entities, boards, departmental undertakings, government owned enterprises, agencies etc-attached to them.

While a department may be referred to as the secretary's charge, all secretaries, although they get the same salary, are not necessarily of equal 'rank'. A ministry may have two or more secretaries, each in charge of a specified segment of the ministry's work, or of a department in it, but there is, in addition, one secretary who is head of, and represents, the entire ministry. Although all of them are secretaries, the former are subordinate to the latter who, in addition to his own work, coordinates the work of these secretaries of departments/segments of work within the ministry.

Functions of Different Grades of Officers of the Secretariat

At present the grades of officers in the Central Secretariat are as follows:

- Secretary
- Additional Secretary
- Joint Secretary
- Deputy Secretary
- Under Secretary

The first three grades constitute what in administrative parlance may be called 'Top Management' while the grades of Deputy Secretary and Under Secretary, are referred to as the 'Middle Management'. The Secretary is the administrative head of the ministry/ department and the principal adviser to the minister. He represents his ministry/department before the committees of Parliament.

He is supposed to keep himself fully informed of the work of his ministry/ department by demanding weekly summaries on the nature of cases disposed of by lower levels. Where the charge of a Secretary is too large, he may be assisted by a Joint or Additional Secretary who formally functions as Secretary in relation to the subject allotted to him in the ministry/ department. The function of the latter is to relieve the Secretary of a bloc of work and to deal, where necessary, direct with the minister. The Secretary, however, is invariably kept informed on all these direct dealings with the minister, for he is not formally relieved of his responsibility as head of the ministry/ department.

The Deputy Secretary is an officer who, as his designation implies, acts on behalf of Secretary. He should dispose of as many cases as possible on his own. Only on more important cases he should seek the Secretary's instruction either by referring to him in writing or discussing with him orally.

The Under Secretary should dispose of minor cases on his own. He should submit more important matters to the Deputy Secretary in such a form that the latter is able to deal with them quickly.

It must be stressed here that the functionaries at these different levels are supposed to perform their functions, keeping in mind the interests of the Government of India as a whole. The Secretary, in other words, is the Secretary to the Government of India, not to his minister alone. This is true of lower levels as well.

3.15 Departments

The work of the Government of India is distributed into different ministries/ departments. A department has also been defined in the General Financial Rules as follows:

- A department is responsible for formulation of policies of the government in relation to business allocated to it and also for the execution and review of those policies.
- For the efficient disposal of business allotted to it, a department is divided into Wings, Divisions, Branches and Sections.
- A department is normally headed by a secretary to the Government of India who acts as the administrative head of the department and principal adviser of the minister on all matters of policy and administration within the department.
- The work in a department is normally divided into wings with a Special Secretary/ Additional Secretary/Joint Secretary in charge of each wing. Such a functionary is normally vested with the maximum measure of independent functioning and responsibility in respect of the business falling within his wing subject to the overall responsibility of the Secretary for the administration of the department as a whole.
- A wing is normally comprised of a number of divisions, each functioning under the charge of an officer of the level of Director/Joint Director/Deputy Secretary. A

division may have several branches each under the charge of an Under Secretary or an equivalent officer.

- A section is generally the lowest organizational unit in a department with a well-defined area of cases (including noting and drafting), which is generally done by assistants and clerks who are also known as the dealing hands.
- While the above represents the commonly adopted pattern of organization of a department there are certain variations, the most notable among them being the Desk Officer System. In this system the work of a department at the lowest level is organized into distinct functional desks each manned by two desk functionaries of appropriate ranks, e.g. Under Secretary or Section Officer. Each desk functionary handles the cases himself and is provided adequate stenographic and clerical assistance.
- The Secretary is the administrative head of a department and in a Department, the structure may comprise Special Secretaries, Additional Secretaries, Joint Secretaries, Directors, Deputy Secretaries, Under Secretaries and Section Officers.

Reform Proposals

Reform Commissions have repeatedly argued for the winding up of several largely redundant and superfluous ministries in order to cut cost and red tape, and the restructuring of others so as to create greater synergies, and reduce overlap and turf wars. It has been calculated (Times of India, 19th February 2013), that even a mid-level bureaucrat costs the exchequer Rs. 2 lakh month, which is taxpayer's money.

Over time, the compulsions of coalition, vote banks and patronage have led to the mushrooming of ministries (coal and mines were, for instance, split into coal and mines); small divisions, which were manned by joint secretaries, were spun off into full-fledged ministries.

While new ministries were created, several old ones that had outlived their purpose because of structural economic changes continued to chug along unproductively and at taxpayers' expense. With steel production largely now in the private sector—as opposed to a time when there was just the public sector and Tata Steel—where is the need for a steel ministry?

The process began with the United Front governments in the 1990s and continued through NDA and UPA terms. The present government's "minimum government, maximum governance" promise could usher in a restructuring of ministries. In contrast, commerce department is severely short-staffed and is looking for officers who can be part of intense negotiations for trade deals and at the World Trade Organization.

Similarly, the ministry of external affairs is short of diplomats who can push India's case with global bodies and in foreign countries. For instance, apart from the ministry of agriculture, there are separate departments or ministries dealing with inputs such as fertilizers, chemicals and water, in addition to procurement (handled by department of food) and another one for food processing.

Similarly, ministries of oil, power coal, renewable energy and water resources are linked to the energy sector. While merger of ministries will help improve delivery of government service, the task may not be easy.

3.16 Executive Agencies

In India there are various types of administrative agencies which are meant to carry out the policies of the government as decided upon in the Secretariat. Such agencies are called executive agencies and can be grouped into various categories.

Under the Secretariat there are a network of agencies which are responsible for the execution of the government policies. With the steady expansion in, and increasing complexity of, the governmental functions, the executive agencies have been variously organized to suit the requirements of the job.

Executive Agencies and the Secretariat

The existence of the Secretariat as an entity separate from the executive agencies is based on the belief that the task of policy-making needs to be separated from that of its execution. Development administration must necessarily move towards decentralization which means that effective power and authority must be possessed by the executive agencies. Though the number of executive agencies have steadily risen over the years, there has not been an increase in their power corresponding to their responsibilities, it is common knowledge that Secretariat performs a lot of policy-executing tasks of an original nature, which could readily be passed on to the executive agencies. However, what needs to be noted is that the relation between the Central Secretariat and the executive agencies have been quite strained and tension ridden instead of gradually becoming cooperative and amiable. There are six principal patterns of relationship developed at the Central level between the Secretariat and the executive agencies. These may briefly be discussed here:

1. There is complete merger between the ministry and heads of executive departments. The examples are the Railway Board and the Ministry of Communications. This pattern is most suitable for organizations undertaking work of an operational or commercial nature.
2. In the second pattern, a senior officer of the ministry concurrently operates as head of the executing department. In this way he becomes responsible both for formulation of policies and for its implementation with the assistance of the common office located in the Ministry. The Additional Secretary in the Department of Agriculture is the Director-General of Food. The main disadvantage of this pattern is that the system completely blurs the functions of the Secretariat and the head of an executive department.
3. The Minister's Office is merged in the office of the executive department. The common office serves both the secretariat offices and the officers of the executive office. The advantages of this arrangement are that any administrative proposal is examined only once, thus, expediting the disposal of cases, and, secondly it results in sizeable economy in office maintenance.

4. The ministry and the executive department continues to have separate offices with separate officers but have common files and common file bureau, all located in the organization of the executive agency. This pattern has significant advantages but it does not do away with the problems of separate offices with duplicate staff and double scrutiny. A good example is the Ministry of Defence and the Air Force Headquarters.
5. The ministry and the executive departments continue to have separate offices and separates files but the head of the Executive office is given an ex-officio Secretariat status. Thus, the Textile Commissioner is the ex-officio Joint Secretary in the Ministry of Commerce. This pattern has some advantages. Under this arrangement, there is considerable saving of time as well as paper work, as every matter does not travel up to the Secretariat for finalization. Also, the accepted policy is implemented in a more efficient manner as the head of the office, because of his Secretariat status, has full awareness of the background in which the policy was framed. Its major drawback, however, is that it goes against the fundamental principle of the Secretariat system, namely, policy-making must remain separated from policy implementation.
6. Both the Ministry and the executive agency have separate and distinct offices and files of their own, and consultation between them occurs through self-contained letters. This is the standard pattern both at the Centre and in the States. This pattern is based on the dichotomy between staff and line. The ministry is Staff: the executive office is Line. An example is the Directorate General of All India Radio in relation to the Ministry of information and Broadcasting. In other words, in this pattern, a wider perspective is brought to bear on the examination of proposals. It is also always desirable to have a specialist's scheme scrutinized by a layman. This arrangement provides for a division of work between the Secretariat and the executive agencies. The former concentrates on policy-making and the latter on the execution of the policy. The disadvantage of this arrangement is that, this scheme is processed twice in two different offices. This involves duplication of work and causes delay.

Each pattern thus has advantages as well as disadvantages. No hard and fast rules can be laid down regarding the pattern of relationship which could be appropriate to a particular sphere of governmental activity. The pattern has to be so tailored as to suit the nature of activities or the past experience of the organization. Nevertheless, neither absolute separation nor absolute merger of both is normally desirable.

The machinery of government has at its top the political executive. Below the political executive sprawls the administrative machinery, which is a three-tier machinery in the Government of India. Indian administration is based on the doctrine of policy/administration dichotomy and as such immediately below the political executive comes the policy making organ, called the Secretariat. This term refers to the complex of ministries and departments in the Government of India, the defining characteristic being their location immediately below the minister. The Secretariat is the extended personality of the minister engaged in policy-making and related activities like drafting of necessary legislation to be placed before parliament for enactment, preparation of the ministry's budget, etc. The secretary is assisted by an array of officers of the rank of Additional Secretaries, Joint Secretaries, Directors,

Deputy Secretaries, Under Secretaries and other clerical personnel, the exact number being fixed according to the perception of administrative requirements and therefore changeable.

Below this policy-making organ of government there exist executive agencies that are variously organized to suit the requirements of the government. The functions of a modern state are vast and varied, necessitating designing of new forms of organization. The expansion of public enterprises led to the setting up of the company and corporation forms of organization. To handle activities involving research, training and dissemination of information, registered societies under the Societies Registration Act have been established. In short, the executive agencies in the Government of India have been principally organized in the following six forms:

1. Attached Office (e.g. Central Public Works Department)
2. Subordinate Office (e.g. Sardar Patel National Police Academy)
3. Departmental Undertaking (e.g. The Indian Railways)
4. A company under the Companies Act (e.g. Hindustan Copper Ltd.)
5. A corporation (e.g. Industrial Finance Corporation of India)
6. A Society under the Societies Registration Act (e.g. Council of Scientific and Industrial Research)

The common forms of organization of the executive agencies are the attached office and the subordinate office. An attached office is the repository of technical knowledge and information. Since policy making must necessarily be based on technical knowledge, the attached office makes the necessary input available to the policy makers. Its second function is to issue executive directions to the lowest tier of administration which is charged with the responsibility of detailed implementation of policies and programmers finalized at the higher levels. The subordinate office that is at the lowest tier functions as a field establishment or as agency responsible for the detailed execution of the policies of government. In 1998 the Government of India had 118 attached offices. Ordinarily, a subordinate office operates under the executive control of the attached office but this is not always the case. A subordinate office may function directly under the Secretariat. One must equally note that some ministries have no attached and subordinate offices under them.

The higher positions in the Secretariat are generally manned by members of the All India Services (Indian Administrative Service, Indian Police Service, and Indian Forest Service) particularly by the Indian Administrative Services. Members of the IAS decline in number as one goes down the hierarchy: personnel from other services also man the positions below the top, although many from such services are also getting appointed as secretaries. Members of the technical services are mostly found in the attached offices and subordinates offices of the Government of India.

After the Second World War extensive use has been made of some new types of agencies to perform complex functions undertaken by governments all over the world. In India, too there has been a proliferation of new agencies and organizations since Independence. Numerous boards, commissions, corporations and companies have been established, both by the Central and State Governments, for performing functions like conducting elections and service examinations, regulating trade, commerce, transport and communication and rendering financial assistance.

These bodies can be classified in two different types: First, classification according to the nature of their authority: and second, classification on the basis of their legal status. We can divide these bodies into three categories according to the nature of their authority, that is to say (i) Whether a board/commission is purely advisory which will include boards like Small-Scale Industries Board (ii) Whether a board/commission combines policy making and administrative directions, like the erstwhile Planning Commission and (iii) Whether a board/commission not only makes policy and gives administrative directions but also executes the policies, like the Railway Board or the Atomic Energy Commission.

On the basis of their legal status these bodies can be classified into three categories. In the first category we can place constitutional commissions like the Election Commission, the Union Public Service Commission, the Finance Commission, the National Commission for Scheduled Castes and Scheduled Tribes, the Commissioner for Linguistic Minorities. The second category could be those Boards/Commissions which are created by an Act of parliament and known as statutory bodies like the University Grants Commission, the Central Board of Direct Taxes, the Central Board of Excise and Customs, National Commission for Minorities, the National Commission for Backward Classes, the National Commission for women. The third category could include such boards/ commissions which have been created by an executive order or by a resolution of the Union Government and could be termed as attached boards or commissions placed directly under the control of relevant ministries. In this category we may place the, National Commission for Safai Karamcharies, Central Social Welfare Board, Staff Selection Commission, the All India Handloom Board, etc. Yet another basis of classification could be the consideration whether a board or commission is a substitute for the ministry or department or an agency under it. The example of such substructure boards are the Railway Board, the Atomic Energy Commission, etc. These bodies could be suitably called administrative boards or commissions.

A board is a multi-headed extra departmental organization. It typically consists of a group of individuals, mainly specialists, who are collectively assigned the responsibility for carrying out certain governmental functions. A board prefers a single head when quasi-legislative and quasi-judicial functions have to be performed. Under a Board type of organization, it is possible to pool together the knowledge and experience of several individuals.

A commission type of organization as distinct from the customary departmental type is invoked for the performance of a function requiring expert, specialist knowledge. It is a form of organization designed to facilitate collective deliberation by a group of experts who are able to pool their knowledge and experience to arrive at informed and objective decisions. When decisions are collectively made, such a method of arriving at decisions is described as a corporate mode of functioning or decision-making. The body thus acting corporately is described as a board. Incidentally, it should be remembered that boards may also bear such designation as councils, corporations, companies, authorities, and so on; and, of course, a board may also be styled simply as a board.

When a commission consisting of experts meets to deliberate on issues, professional and technical criteria receive necessary emphasis. When several heads combine for deliberation, biases are cancelled out and objectivity is ensured. Since a commission functions outside the mould of normal governmental machinery, greater flexibility and innovativeness of approach is possible.

3.17 Reforms in Central Administration (June 2014 Onwards)

A general perception of PM Narendra Modi's style of governance is that administrative efficiency being his hallmark, his entire emphasis would be on timely implementation of laws and policies leading to effective delivery of public goods and services.

Narendra Modi started in June 2014 by forming a prime ministerial cabinet with 52 portfolios in the hands of 45 ministers. He rationalized the Council of Ministers by merging cognate ministries and sought to downsize it. He disbanded nearly 50 groups of ministers (GOMs) and empowered GOMs started by Shri Atal Bihari Vajpayee as a device of removing inter-ministerial differences and conflicts which were expanded to 78 in the second UPA government.

Alongside the ministries kept in his own hands, Modi allocated 'all policy issues' relating to the government to himself. The PM's Office (PMO) and the Cabinet Secretariat have again swung into action in decision making in not only big issues but also down to the issue of approving the appointment of personal secretaries of ministers. The PM has appointed his Principal Secretary that required a statutory amendment for which he got an ordinance issued. Ministers are within the age group of 38 and 74; these posts have not been given strictly to MPs who have crossed the age of 75. Ministers have been asked not to appoint their Personal Secretaries from kith and kin. Officials have been asked to declare their assets and properties.

In Modi's second tenure, there are 24 cabinet ministers, 24 ministers of state and 9 have been given the minister of state with independent charge rank. An important feature of Modi's style is co-opting the senior bureaucracy and police as part of his very own team who will put the delivery systems in place. While the government has termed the reshuffle of 50 mid-ranking bureaucrats as 'routine administrative transfers' the buzz in various ministries is that the transfers have been done keeping in mind various factors which may include efficiency of a bureaucrat as well.

In a bid to tone up decision making and enforcing accountability, government officials have been told to act only on written orders from superiors, be it ministers or their staff. An advisory issued as part of an office memorandum at the behest of the PMO in November 2014 directed officials to carry out oral orders of seniors only after getting written confirmation. In case the orders are 'not in accordance with the norms, rules, regulations or procedures' the officials should inform the secretary or the head of department where the officer concerned is working. The instruction from the PMO are the latest in a series of advisories on improving the overall decision-making progress. PM Narendra Modi will have the final word on matters relating to Lokpal, CVC, cadre allocation among IAS/IPS probationers, RTI and anti-corruption policy, as per delegation of powers made between various divisions of the Ministry of personnel, public grievances and pensions. According to a note detailing the work and final authority for disposal of matters handled by the Ministry, all cabinet notes concerning DOPT will require the final approval of the PM, who will also clear posting and transfer of officers of joint secretary level and above. The PM will also decide on cases of persons found involved in subversive activities, besides approving policies relating to retirement age, representation of minorities and policy issues regarding reservation in government jobs. Apart from deciding disciplinary cases against IAS and Grade-I CSS officers, the PM will approve matters relating to central Lokpal legislation, making CVC a statutory body and policy issues relating to Right to Information. The PM will be the final authority for constitution of a new All India Service, and will decide policy matters relating to review of cases of IAS officers for continuance in service beyond 50 years of age or after completion of 30 years of service.

Besides fixed tenure for civil servants, the current government is working to *institutionalize lateral entry* from academia and the private sector into some senior government positions. This is a long overdue reform with far reaching potential to change the way bureaucracy works and move from a closed to an open system for recruiting civil servants to improve the quality of governance. Domain competence and a combination of relevant knowledge and skills are an essential requirement in governance. These attributes are not always present in a cadre of generalists, moreover one that is recruited increasingly through reserved quotas which limit competition. The Second ARC envisaged a shift from a career-based approach to a post-based approach in the top tier of government jobs. Civil servants ought to compete with domain experts from outside government for senior positions. However the PM has also given the signal of weeding out "corrupt" officers, while increasing the retirement age of civil servants. Work monitoring with strict punishment for corruption and ample recognition for meritorious civil servants are on the anvil.

The Narendra Modi government proposes to cut the duration of induction training for IAS officers from existing 103 weeks to just 75 weeks. Based on the recommendations of the Kiran Aggarwal Committee, the time period of the IAS professional course (Phase I) is sought to be brought down by 5 weeks and district training by a whole 21 weeks. Citing the rising median age of entry (28 years) by when most have significant work experience and which makes reduced training period for increased potential years of service, and better access and delivery of information and knowledge due to advent of information technology.

Addressing more than 80 secretaries at a high tea at his residence in November 2014, setting the tone of his administration PM Modi assured them that there would no political interference in decision making. His assurance came in view of a Supreme Court order doing away with Section 6 of the Delhi Police Establishment Act which forbade investigating agencies from lodging FIRs against officers of the rank of Joint Secretary and above without prior clearance.

Repeal of Old Obsolete Laws

PM Narendra Modi constituted the Ramanujam committee to identify all obsolete and archaic laws with a view to weeding them out systematically. The panel to be chaired by the secretary in the PMO, R. Ramanujam, and comprising former secretary, legislative department, V.K. Bhasin, will examine all Acts recommended for repeal by the Committee on Review of Administrative Laws appointed in 1998 by the Atal Bihari Vajpayee government. The PM has expressed concern that out of the 1382 Acts recommended for repeal by the earlier committee, only 415 have been repealed so far. Modi repeatedly believes that archaic laws only hamper governance by creating avoidable confusion. The Law Commission has already submitted a list of 72 laws to the Centre that need to be repealed immediately —the oldest being the Bengal Districts Act of 1836 that provides for creation of districts.

Continuity of Old Welfare Schemes

Most of the welfare schemes of the earlier UPA government: flagship schemes like MNREGA, National Rural Health Mission, Right to Education or Right to Food Acts have neither been repealed or discontinued despite proposals to target them better have come from the new government. However, PM Modi has announced his intention to step up expenditures to reflect his grand vision for India. This vision includes elimination of abject poverty, electricity for all, Swachh Bharat by 2019, 100 smart cities and expanded road and rail networks. Implementation of this vision requires resources. Streamlining existing schemes as also replacing them by new ones are essential steps towards garnering these resources. While increased revenues will follow as the economy picks up, there are inevitable time lags. So some programmes have to be pruned here and now. This alone justifies the proposal to confine NREGA to 200 poorest districts. The Home Ministry has come out in full support of the Aadhar Scheme for authentication of beneficiaries for all government schemes.

But the compelling reason for limiting NREGA consists precisely in the fact that it has drawbacks that an alternative policy of cash transfers does not have. By opting to retain and complete the Aadhar project and launching the Jan Dhan Yojna (enabling every citizen to open a bank account), which would together provide the necessary infrastructure, the PM would seem to have cleared the way for an eventual move to a system of direct cash transfers to beneficiaries as a poverty alleviation measure. That makes pruning NREGA as the instrument of shifting income to the poor an eminently reasonable interim step.

Replacement of Planning Commission

The PM has indicated a greater role for states by replacing the Planning Commission. The new entity (Niti Aayog) which has replaced the Planning Commission is likely to have members that include economists, representatives from the social sector, government, industry and academics. The panel will advise the government on the approach to reforms and is expected to function as a dispute resolution forum for states. A federalist direction was echoed in urging every MP to develop model villages through their MPLAD funds before the next elections. With the PM keen on 'cooperative federalism', some CMs could be part of the new body. The PM's idea of making states equal partners in growth is a step in the right direction. Earlier Planning Commission used to act as an interface between the Centre and the States.

Therefore the successor of Planning Commission will work as a think tank for the government against the backdrop of new economic realities that will have a 'bottom-up approach' instead of a centralized planning model of the Nehruvian era. States are also expected to have a major say in the new entity as the government is of the view that the mandate of the Finance Commission is limited and the Inter State Council is moribund.

3.18 Government Spending on Central Government Employees

(Thirtieth Report of Director General of Employment & Training, Ministry of Labour & Employment, Govt of India) Presented on 4th May, 2012)

India's Central or Federal government has spent around Rs 3,64,613 to 2.5 crore (68 billion) on 2.5 million employees between 2006 and 2011. And here's the clincher: the total number of Government employees has actually come down from 2.8 million in 2005-06 to 2.5 million in 2009-10.

Now the Rs 3,64,613 crore excludes incentives, which amounted to Rs 25,697 crore in the same period. Railways, Home and Defence Ministries had the highest salary expenditure. All ministries saw a drop in 'basic' or base pay after the implementation of the Sixth Pay Commission.

Here is a look at the total number of Central Government employees and the total remuneration they received over the last few years:

1. As per the result of Census Enquiries, the total regular employment under Central Government as on 31st March 2009 was 30.99 lakh as against 31.12 lakh on 31st March 2008. The employment has, thus, recorded a decline of 0.42% in 2009 over 2008.
2. Employment in Ministry of Railways was the highest (44.74%) followed by the Ministry of Home Affairs (24.14%), Defence (11.77%), Communications and IT (7.06%), and Finance (3.49%). Other ministries/departments collectively shared the rest 9% of the total Central Government employment.
3. Out of 30.99 lakh regular employees, 3.11 lakh were women. The proportion of women in the total employment is almost static, around 10%in the year2009, 2008 and 2006.
4. About 95%of regular Central Government employees were Non- Gazetted. The overall ratio of Gazetted to Non-Gazetted employees was 1:19. In case of Ministry of Railways, however, this ratio was 1:114.
5. Amongst regular Central Government employees, 63% were holding Group-" C" posts and 26% were in Group-"D" posts. About 8% were holding Group-"B" posts whereas employees holding Group- "A" posts were only about 3%.
6. About 90% of regular Central Government employees were found in the Grade pay of Rs. 1800 to Rs. 5400 which mainly consists of Group "B", Group "C" and Group "D" posts. OnlyO.16% employees were in the highest scale, i.e. HAG + Apex & Cabinet Secretary level.
7. Amongst regular Central Government employees, 18% were working at offices located in 'X' class cities and 29% in "Y' class cities. The percentage of employees in all the cities/areas other than class X and Y cities was 53%.

8. Amongst states and Union Territory Administrations, the highest number of regular Central Government employees was in the state of Uttar Pradesh(9.51%) followed by Maharashtra (9.06%), West Bengal (8.54%), Delhi (6.55%), Andhra Pradesh (5.97%), Tamil Nadu (4.79%) and Madhya Pradesh (4.07%), In the remaining States/ UTs the proportion was less than 4%.

3.19 Second Administrative Reforms Commission-13th Report (Extracts)

1. Recasting the Allocation of Business Rules

There is need to recast the Allocation of Business Rules to make them more focused on the goals and outcomes of each Ministry/ Department in order to shift the emphasis from a detailed listing of activities/ subjects of each ministry/department to a broader perspective. The Allocation of Business Rules should first provide a statement of the mission of the department followed by a list of subjects and functions.

There is need to bring greater uniformity in the description of the roles and functions of various ministries/department. Instead of naming the individual PSUs and autonomous organizations under each ministry, the Rules should merely have a generic entry to the effect that all PSUs and Autonomous Organizations whose functioning is directly related to subject(s) of the concerned Ministry would be under its jurisdiction.

2. Rationalising the Functions of Government

Government at all levels should be guided by the principle of subsidiarity. There is need to carry out a detailed analysis of the functions/activities in each ministry/department. This should be followed by restructuring which may include decentralization, delegation or hiving off activities.

3. Rationalising and Reorganising the Ministries and Departments

The concept of a ministry would have to be redefined. A ministry would mean a group of departments whose functions and subjects are closely related and is assigned to a First or Coordinating Minister for the purpose of providing overall leadership and coordination. Individual departments of any combination of these could be headed by the coordination (or First) Minister, other Cabinet Minister(s), Minister(s) of States.

The structure of the Government of India should be rationalized by grouping together closely related subjects in order to reduce the number of Ministries.

4. Reorganization of Ministries

Each Department should lay down a detailed scheme of delegation at all levels so that the decision-making takes place at the most appropriate level. It should be laid down in the Manual of Office Procedure so that every Ministry should prescribe a scheme of delegation for its officers.

The scheme of delegation should be updated periodically and should also be 'audited' at regular intervals. The audit should ensure that the delegated authority is actually exercised by the delegate. The number of levels through which a file passes for a decision should not exceed three. For addressing cross-cutting issues the secretary of the concerned Department should have the flexibility to create interdisciplinary teams.

The Department should build an electronic database of decisions that are likely to be used as precedents. Thereafter, such database should be periodically reviewed and where necessary, changes in rules introduced in order to codify them.

5. Focus on Policy Analysis

Ministries/Departments should concentrate on the following:

1. Policy analysis, planning, policy making and strategic decisions
2. Budgeting and Parliamentary work
3. Monitoring of implementation through systems and procedures
4. Appointments of key personnel
5. Coordination
6. Evaluation

Attached and subordinate offices, should serve as the executive agencies of the ministries and concentrate on the implementation of Government policies and programmes.

6. Policy Evaluation

Each Department should introduce a system of policy evaluation to be carried out at the end of prescribed periods. All relevant policies should be updated on the findings of such evaluations.

7. Creation of Effective Executive Agencies

Each Union Government Ministry should scrutinize the functions/ activities of the ministry to confirm whether these activities functions are critical to the mission of the Department and can only be carried out by government agencies.

Each agency, whether a new body or an existing departmental undertaking/ agency/ board/special purpose body, etc., that is to function as an executive agency, must be autonomous or semi autonomous and professionally managed under a mandate. Such executive agencies could be structured as a department, board, commission, company, society, etc.

The right balance between autonomy and accountability needs to be struck while designing the institutional framework of executive agencies. This could be achieved through well-designed performance agreements, Memorandum of Understanding (MOU), contracts, etc. However, preparing and enforcing such performance contracts requires considerable upgradation of capacity in the concerned government departments.

8. Coordination Mechanisms

There is need to ensure that the existing coordination mechanisms like the Group of

Ministers and Committee of Secretaries function effectively and help in early resolution of issues. Selective, but effective use of GOMs with clear mandate and prescribed time limits would be helpful.

Unresolved issues concerning States which require inter- Ministerial coordination in the Government of India, should be placed before the Committee of secretaries (COSs) and then to the Union Cabinet for resolution.

9. Creating an Effective Regulatory Framework

Setting up a Regulator should be preceded by a detailed review to decide whether the policy regime in the concerned sector is such that a Regulator would be better placed to deliver the policy objectives of the department concerned.

In addition to the statutory framework which underpins the interface between the government and the regulator, each ministry/department should evolve a Management Statement outlining the objectives and roles of each regulator and the guidelines governing their interaction with the government. This would guide both the government department and the regulator.

There is need for greater uniformity in the terms of appointment, tenure and removal of various regulatory authorities considering these have been set up with broadly similar objectives and functions and should enjoy the same degree of autonomy. The initial process of appointment of Chairmen and Board Members should be transparent, credible and fair.

There is need to achieve greater uniformity in the structure of a Regulator. The existing coordination mechanisms such as the Committee of Secretaries/Cabinet Committees, assisted by Secretary (coordination) could easily ensure that the institutional framework for all Regulators follow, by and large, a uniform pattern.

Conclusion

No one can deny that PM Narendra Modi has changed the narrative of administration and governance in seminal ways. As PM, he wanted to demonstrate a few things early, that the PMO was back to wielding ultimate political authority and since he would brook no indiscipline or inertia in public service delivery, a new work ethics in administration and governance would be the order of the day. After the introduction of his Cabinet came the first indication of policy priorities that would determine the trajectory of this government's future tenure.

His formula for change is exactly to create a mechanism of delivery that works, focuses on simple goals that are stated clearly and is reinforced by repeated implementation. The modality employed provides reasons from within rather than the use of force. For instance, in the Modi scheme of things, corruption is stifled by creating disincentives rather than exposing it. PM Modi's defining contribution to date will be to dramatically improve execution at all levels of the government. Tangible evidence has emerged from the Cabinet Secretariat's Project Monitoring Group, which is attempting to debottleneck hundreds of stalled projects. It is vigorously engaged with officials from central ministries, the states and businesses. The Project Monitoring Group is digitizing on a common platform 60 clearances from 20 ministries required for setting up an industry in India—25 at the Centre and 35 in the States.

The self-stated goal of the PM of the world's largest democracy, has been to construct a new vocabulary of governance where it is equated with clearly stated national objectives and purposes matched by effective implementation and public service delivery.

Suggested Readings

Avasthy, A., *Central Administration*, New Delhi, Tata McGraw-Hill, 1980.

Ghosh, Soma, *An Independent and Accountable Judiciary: Pillar of Democracy*, Kolkata, Pragatishil Prokashak, 2005.

Jain, H.M., *The Union Executive*, Allahabad, Chaitanya Publishing House, 1969.

Jain, U.C. and Jeevan Nair, *Judiciary in India*, Jaipur, Pointer, 2000.

Jha Rajani Ranjan, *"Prime Minister's Office: The Fulcrum of Indian Administration"* Indian Journal of Public Administration, Sage, 2019, pp13-27

Kapur, Devesh et al, *Public Institutions in India: Performance and Design*, OUP, 2017.

Kashyap, Subhash C.(ed.), *Indian Polity-Retrospect and Prospect,* Delhi 1989

Our Parliament, New Delhi, N.B.T., 2004.

—*Framing of India's Constitution- A Study*, New Delhi, Universal, 2004.

—*Our Constitution*, New Delhi, N.B.T., 2005.

Maheshwari; S.R., *Indian Administration*, New Delhi, Orient Longman, 2005.

Report of the National Commission to Review the Working of the Constitution (NCRWC Report), New Delhi, 2002.

Shakdher, S.L., *Glimpses of the Working of Parliament,* New Delhi, Metropolitan, 1977.

Singh, Hoshiar and Pankaj Singh, *Indian Administration*, New Delhi, Pearson, 2014.

Singh, M.P., and Rekha Saxena, *Indian Politics: Constitutional Foundations and Institutional Functioning*, Delhi, PHI, 2012.

OOO

Chapter Four

The Administrative Machinery of the States

States of India: Why Diversity Matters

Introduction

India has been rightly called a quasi-federal state due to the preponderance of legislative, executive and taxation powers constitutionally vested in the Union parliament and the Central Government. The major developmental responsibilities are, however, in the State List in the constitution—social services, land, labor, health, agriculture, roads, irrigation, local government, distribution of water, justice and police, etc. It has been an old refrain of the states that their fiscal powers do not match their developmental responsibilities. India has 29 states and 7 union territories. It is only after the 1992 constitutional amendments that the three-tiered governance system was introduced and states came to share many of their original powers with the local self-governments. The states in India differ widely on their growth patterns, (in agriculture, industry and in the service sectors) their human development records, and their governance performances both in comparison to each other as also in comparison to the Centre. Till 1967 it was the Congress party which was in a ruling majority in most of the states of India, but the picture has changed hugely since then. It is the states of India and their regional parties who have truly ushered in a multi-party system in India. They also deliver a bewildering variety of administrative and policy outcomes since no policy is ever implemented with the same outcome in the 29 states of India. State growth rates, human development or policy outcomes do influence substantively the macro outcomes. When any state does well in any domain, it becomes a role model for that sector to follow in the rest of India. Today in the post-globalized era, states have much more access to independent sources of funds raised from the market besides mandatory transfers from the Finance commission. Since the 1990s the states have had more autonomy in the making or the execution of public policy than in the planning era. Centre-State relations had become increasingly cooperative due to the sustained presence of coalition governments in Indian politics (1989-2013), which required a stronger measure of political accommodation, between the Centre and the States. In India, the period prior to 1989 was characterized by top-down (national) coercion or negotiation within a nationwide dominant Congress party. Today there is more equality, dialogue and negotiation in Centre-State relations since all regional parties have shared power with the Centre in coalition government-(s) till the general election of 2019.

If there is one political development that needs to be watched it is that many states are producing increasingly competent leaders who are remaking the economic and political map of future India. As a result of their economic or governance successes, these state leaders have won consecutive re-election bids. In 2014 India had six chief ministers who had returned to office for at least three terms in a row, a feat unheard of in earlier generations. In the 30 state elections between 2007 and 2014, 50% of the incumbent chief ministers had won re-elections, compared with just 25% in the preceding three decades, nearly 66% of those re-elected had delivered five years of growth that was faster than the national average.

In the 1990s, the first states to benefit from the New Economic Policies were the rich ones of southern and western India, particularly Gujarat, Maharashtra and Tamil Nadu, which already had strong industrial bases. But since 2000, the center of rapid growth has shifted northwards to the states of Bihar, Chhatisgarh, Madhya Pradesh, Orissa and others (the erstwhile BIMARU States). The average growth rate of these states jumped from 2.2% in the 1990s to 9.1% over the past decade, while India's national growth rate moved from an average of 5% to 7% in the same period. These states have sustained these growth levels through good initiatives in governance.

India's annual GDP growth averaged 8.45%, in the five-year phase of 2004-05 to 2008-09. Historically, the backward states with a poor economy were Orissa plus the BIMARU quartet (Bihar, Madhya Pradesh, Rajasthan, Uttar Pradesh), of which three have been sub-divided. Five of India's eight poorest states have become miracle economies, defined internationally as those with over 7% growth. The best news comes from Bihar, historically one of the most backward states. From 2004-05 to 2008-09, Bihar averaged 11.03% growth annually. It was virtually India's fastest growing state, at par with Gujarat (11.05%).

Other poor states have also done well. Uttarakhand (9.31%), Orissa (8.74%), Jharkhand (8.45%) and Chhatisgarh (7.35%), have all grown faster than the standard miracle benchmark of 7%. Orissa's performance is remarkable, since 10 years ago it had the worst fiscal indicators among all states.

Uttar Pradesh's growth rate has risen slowly to 6.29% annually. This falls short of the miracle benchmark of 7%, but not by much. Uttar Pradesh has benefited from overall buoyancy in the Indian economy. Something similar can be said of Chhattisgarh, Rajasthan and Madhya Pradesh, which have averaged over 6% per annum. Of the eight historically poor states, Bihar, Uttarakhand, Orissa and Jharkhand have grown as fast as or faster than the all India average of 8.49%. The economic gap between some poor and rich states is shrinking dramatically. This is surely one of the biggest achievements of the beginning decades of 21st~-century India.

The census has good news on literacy. The census says literacy has improved from 64.84% in 2001 to 74.04% in 2011, up by 9.2%. So, in the two decades since 1991, literacy has risen 21.83 points. Clearly, literacy has accelerated in the reform era, most of all in the poorest states.

In Bihar, long the worst performer, literacy shot up from 47% to 63.82%, up by 16.82%. Big gains came in other poor, backward states—Uttar Pradesh (11.45%), Jharkhand (16.07%), Orissa (10.37%) and Assam (9.93%). So poor states gained almost 30 percentage points in the two decades of economic reform.

South India has long been India's leader in literacy. Orissa, Chhattisgarh, Madhya Pradesh and even Uttar Pradesh have overtaken Andhra Pradesh in literacy, and Jharkhand is virtually at par. Female literacy has shot up much faster than male literacy. Phenomenal gains in female literacy have been recorded in the last decade in Bihar (19.76%), Uttar Pradesh (16.28%), Jharkhand (15.893%) and Orissa (13.39%).

The Centre's social spending (mainly on education and health) was just 1.28% of GDP in 1992-93, but has moved up over the last two decades to 7.27% of GDP. Much of this is wasted because State Governments are unwilling to check absenteeism or non-performance among teachers and health staff, who are protected by powerful trade unions. Yet the sheer mass of spending has helped improve literacy sharply.

However, the impact on health seems far less than on literacy. Family health surveys reveal very high levels of anaemia and malnutrition. Critics have noted that infant mortality fell substantially from 110 to 80 deaths per thousand births between 1981 and 1991. But afterwards, the pace of improvement almost halved, so that a reduction from 80 to 50 per thousand took two decades.

Why did infant mortality fall exceptionally fast in 1981-91? This was possibly because child immunization improved seriously in that decade, a low-cost strategy that had a huge and immediate impact on deaths. However, that impact later tapered off at the all-India level. It continues to have an impact in some poor states. In sum, the reform era has sparked an explosive growth of social spending, which has led to much larger declines in illiteracy and infant mortality.

India's 29 states vary enormously with Uttar Pradesh having 200 million people, Maharashtra and West Bengal around 90-100 million each, but smaller states such as Sikkim, Arunachal and Mizoram hovering between 0.5-1.5 million. To argue, that more jobs will automatically be created or that the attendance of teachers and doctors will suddenly improve or that upgrades in delivery of public services will be dramatic in smaller states is an exaggeration. Further, the distribution of good versus bad governance appears to be evenly spread across small and large states.

If one looks specifically at the new states created after 2000 and compares sample economic indicators, the evidence is again very mixed. The energy sector affects the daily life of citizens, rich and poor, like none other. In 2011, the debt owed by state utilities as percentage of state GDP was: MP (8%) versus Chhattisgarh (5%) and UP (43%) versus Uttarakhand (1%). The projected gap between average cost and average revenue, which is the key driver of high financial losses, for 2013-17 is estimated to be: Bihar and Jharkhand both around 42%, MP and Chhatisgarh both around 20%, Uttar Pradesh (24%) and Uttarakhand (5%).

If the average spent on education per enrolled child is mapped against learning outcomes, small states like Jharkhand, Chhattisgarh and large states like MP, Rajasthan and UP all figure at the bottom end of the spectrum. On the top are Andhra Pradesh and Goa, a big and a small state. Likewise, money spent on healthcare per person per annum is the highest in a small state like Kerala (Rs. 3700) but also the lowest in another small state Jharkhand (Rs.

500). A big state, Gujarat, is the only one that offers 24x7 power to all its 18,000 villages. Karnataka, another big state, brilliantly digitized the land records of 6 million farmers and thus made transactions speedier.

A smaller state does not necessarily mean smaller government. On the contrary, in the short term the cost of governance will increase as one will duplicate a lot of the existing infrastructure and resources in the new state. One should look at what is the most effective size of government that could deliver the growth and development goals of a state.

What is required is another States Reorganization Commission to look at comprehensive data of economic performance across several such metrics in different states. Identity cannot and must not become a substitute for the principles of economics and good governance. India is the world's most heterogeneous country with several linguistic, religious, caste and sub-caste divisions. Strong states and a strong Centre are not mutually exclusive to each other. Rather, they can reinforce each other to ensure superior political and economic outcomes.

Bihar, Orissa, Uttar Pradesh, Madhya Pradesh and Rajasthan, make up 40% of India's population and produce only 25% of the national output, while India's five richest states of Gujarat, Haryana, Maharashtra, Punjab and Tamil Nadu, with around 25% of the population produce 40% of the national output. These records are a testimony to the fact that size and GDP growth may not have the direct causal relationship that one would like to establish. International Monetary Fund research indicates that the richest states (such as Punjab) grew three-four times faster than the poorest states (such as Bihar and Uttar Pradesh) between 1970 and 2005. Interestingly, the Gini coefficient of per capita consumption is also the highest for Tamil Nadu and Maharashtra (between 0.35 and 0.4%), which indicates extreme variations (intrastate) even in the richest states, as also in the poorer states.

A team of NGOs from 10 states led by the Centre for Budget and Governance Accountability (CBGA) conducted a detailed study of the budget-formulating process of each state by meeting officials and legislators, as also studying all budget-related documents. A checklist of eight parameters was used to give scores. These were: availability of budget documents, completeness of information, facilitating its understanding, timeliness, audit and performance assessment, scope for legislative scrutiny, budgeting for disadvantaged sections and fiscal decentralization. The results show that most of the states observed scored well in making budget related documents available and in completeness of information. However, there was wide divergence observed on other parameters. Most states had low scores on practices relating to fiscal decentralization—the average was just 23%, with Assam scoring the maximum (31%) and Madhya Pradesh scoring the least (14%).

On the matter of availability of budget documents, most states had high scores with Gujarat getting 87% and Rajasthan 80%. Even the least scoring state, Uttar Pradesh, had 64%. On completeness of information Gujarat, Chhattisgarh and Maharashtra had high scores while Rajasthan fell behind with the lowest score of 56%. How much effort do the State Governments make in helping common people understand the budget documents? Rajasthan and Maharashtra put out easy to understand documents which included discussion and comments. So they got about 70% on this count. MP and Chhattisgarh scored less than 40% on this parameter.

Surprisingly, most states had below-par scores on audit and performance review. Only MP with a score of 67%, followed by Chhattisgarh (55%), had respectable scores. Jharkhand had the lowest score at 23%. This parameter reviewed timely audit of accounts, performance reviews including Five-Year Plan reviews and publication of these documents. (Centre for Budget and Governance Accountability Analysis Summary 2014)

States where poverty has reduced significantly include Kerala, West Bengal, Punjab, Andhra Pradesh and Tamil Nadu. It has come down best in Assam, Jammu and Kashmir, Bihar, Madhya Pradesh and Rajasthan. The BIMARU states have grown substantively but poverty levels have not come down correspondingly. Poverty can best be handled where effective governmental power rests on a broad political base, rulers have minimized the hold of upper classes, successfully organized the middle and lower strata into an effective power bloc and then used this power to channel resources to the poor (Kohli and Singh 2013). South Indian states are definitely better administered—with higher human development indicators than their peers in the north. Kerala's performance in human development is much applauded but Tamil Nadu's performance is even better, both its growth and achievements in administering education, health care and Public Distribution System (PDS) has been one of the best in India. That higher growth rates do not bring down poverty automatically (e.g. BIMARU states) or lead to better human development outcomes (Punjab, Haryana, Maharashtra or Gujarat) has been amply proved in the experience of Indian states in the post-reform era. Interestingly, the education and health outcomes of some of the North-eastern states are better than the national average, e.g. Mizoram, Meghalaya and Nagaland have literacy rates above 90%. The Central Government initiated various health programmes and these have been implemented efficiently in all these three states.

Some states in India are demographically and geographically larger than many nation states globally. Social indicators at the macro level (India's HDI Index 2018 is 130 out of 188 nations) often disguise micro deprivations at the state or district level, e.g. women born in UP are expected to live 20 years less than in Kerala. A child in Orissa is five times less likely to survive than a girl in Manipur. A girl in Bihar is half as likely to be literate as a girl in Himachal Pradesh.

In education and health, states account for nearly 90% of total government expenditure. It is the State Governments rather than the Central that have been the key unit of social policy in India. What matters in social development is political will, political competition, civil society activism and an established administrative machinery to deliver public and social services to the people. The 'new rights' approach has led to the enactment of many new rights in India in the post-reform era. How the benefits of these rights reach the people will depend entirely on the efficiency and effectiveness of sub national, district and local government units of administration in different states of India. Therefore the Right to Education, the Right to Food, MNREGA or the National Rural Health Mission are all differently administered in different states with different outcomes. In sum, the evidence of small versus larger states is extremely mixed; there is little causal relationship between size and many economic indicators. Instead the fundamentals of good governance namely a strong predictable policy framework, conducive business environment for private sector investment, good law and order, and justice system, strong institutional mechanisms, and robust human development must be sought and established. Developmental performance of Indian states depends on several dimensions —economic growth, distribution of that growth, poverty alleviation and quality of governance.

4.1 The State Governmental Machinery

A parliamentary system of Government with a constitutional Head and with ministerial responsibility to the popular House of the Legislature is the pattern of government at the state level. The real executive power is exercised by the Ministers. "Satisfaction" of the Governor means the satisfaction of the Council of Ministers. [Ram Jawaya Kapur v. State of Punjab, AIR 1955 SC 549; Shamsher Singh v. State of Punjab, AIR 1974 SC 2193]

Several states enjoy special status and have certain special provisions applicable to only each one of them separately, e.g. States of Maharashtra and Gujarat (Article 371), Nagaland (371 A), Assam (371 B), Manipur (371 C), Andhra Pradesh (371 D & 371 E), Sikkim (371 F), Mizoram (371 G), Arunachal Pradesh (371 H) and Goa (371 I). There are important reasons why states occupy an important role in the governmental system of the country.

- The states are the agencies for execution of planned programmes. Most subjects that constitute the ingredients of development administration are within the exclusive jurisdiction of the states.
- The State Governments act in many cases as the agents of the Union in discharging their functions.
- Maintenance of law and order is a very important state function which constitutes a vital part of regulatory administration.

4.2 The Governor

Article 155 stipulates that the Governor of a state shall be appointed by the President of India and shall hold office during the pleasure of the President. Subject to this provision, he shall hold office for a term of five years from the date on which he assumes office. Since he holds office during the pleasure of the President, no process of impeachment or any other method of removal is prescribed by the Constitution.

The qualifications for this post are that the person should be a citizen of India and should have completed 35 years of age. He should not be a member of the Union or state legislatures and, if he is, his seat in the House falls vacant on the date on which he enters the office as Governor. He shall not hold any other office of profit. His emoluments, allowances and privileges may be determined by parliamentary laws.

The powers exercised by the Governor can be divided under two broad categories: (1) those exercised with the aid and advice of the Chief Minister and his council of ministers and (2) discretionary powers.

Powers Exercised on the Aid and Advice of the Chief Minister and his Council

Article 154 states that the executive powers of the state shall be vested in the Governor and shall be exercised by him either directly or through officers subordinate to him in accordance with the Constitution. The word 'subordinates' includes all the ministers and the Chief Minister. His executive powers are co-extensive with the legislative powers of the state legislature. It covers all the subjects on which the state legislature can enact laws.

The Governor is required to frame rules of business allocating work to different ministers.

He appoints the council of ministers for the state, the Advocate General and the members of the State Public Service Commission. He appoints one member of the Anglo-Indian community to the legislative assembly wherever necessary. He also appoints a few members in the State Legislative Council, if there is one, in the state. These persons should be eminent in the fields of arts, science, literature, social sciences.

However, the most important legislative power is that of issuing ordinances. They are issued by him with the advice of the President or the Chief Minister and his ministers. He can promulgate an ordinance under Article 213 (1), only when the state legislature is not in session in order to meet an emergency which requires immediate action. Every such ordinance will be laid before the state legislature and shall cease to operate at the expiry of six weeks from the reassembly of the legislature or if, before the expiration of that period, a resolution that disapproves it is passed by the state legislature. There are three circumstances when the Governor cannot promulgate an ordinance without prior instructions from the President: (1) if a bill containing the same provisions would require the prior sanction of the President before its introduction; (2) if he would have deemed it necessary to reserve a bill containing the same provision for the consideration of the President; and (3) if an Act under the same provision would have been reserved for the consideration of the President and would have received his assent.

The notorious misuse of ordinance making powers of the governor was highlighted in D.C. Wadhava versus State of Bihar [(1987) ISCC 378]. In Bihar, between 1967 and 1981, 256 ordinances were promulgated by the Governor. In other words, in 11 years, on an average, for every one Act of the legislature there were 12 ordinances of the Governor. In Bihar, some ordinances had a life of 13 to 14 years. This can happen because there is no bar in the Constitution on the number of times the Governor can promulgate the same ordinance.

The Governor of a state also has the power to grant pardons, reprieves, respites or remissions of punishment or to suspend, remit or commute the sentence of any person convicted of any offence against any law relating to a matter to which the executive power of the state extends. He can also grant amnesty. There is a difference between the pardon granted by the President under Article 72 and by the Governor under Article 161. The President has an exclusive power to grant pardon in cases where the sentence is a sentence of death. Secondly, the President can pardon punishments or sentences inflicted by a court martial. The Governor has no such powers.

Discretionary Powers of the Governor

Article 163 makes the Governor the sole judge in matters in which he is required to act in his discretion. Article 163 (1) says:

There shall be a Council of Ministers with the Chief Minister (CM) at the head to aid and advise the Governor in the exercise of his functions, except in so far as he is by or under this Constitution required to exercise his functions or any of them in his discretion. If any question arises whether any matter is or is not a matter as respect to which the Governor is by or under this Constitution required to act in his discretion, the decision of the Governor in his discretion shall be final and the validity of anything done by the Governor shall not be called in question on the ground that he ought or ought not to have acted in his discretion.

The question whether any, and, if so, what advice was tendered by ministers to the Governor shall not be inquired into in any court.

- Article 166(3) which states that the Governor can make rules of business except in cases where he can act in his discretion,
- Article 200 which says that the Governor can reserve a bill for the consideration of the President,
- Article 356(1) which provides that the Governor can make a report about the failure of the constitutional machinery in the state,
- Article 239(2) which gives him certain functions when appointed as Administrator of a Union Territory,
- Article 239(2) which bestows on him the power to make rules, and
- The Sixth Schedule, which gives the Governor of Assam two discretionary powers; the first deals with disputes between the Government of Assam and an autonomous Tribal District Council with respect to the sharing of royalties that accrue from the lease of mining rights within the autonomous district and the second relates to the manner in which the Governor may apply certain special administrative provisions in the Constitution with respect to tribal areas in Assam vis-a-vispaxticulai tribal areas.

Besides, the Governor has certain special responsibilities to discharge according to the directives issued by the President under Articles 371(2); 371A (1) (b), 371 (C), etc. He does not have to consult the C.M. or his council of ministers.

Appointment of a Chief Minister

When there is a party in the state legislature with a clear majority, the Governor has no discretion because he has only to invite the leader of that party to become the Chief Minister. In case there is no party with an absolute majority in the state legislature, should he invite the leader of the single largest party?

How, then, is the Governor to make his choice? For this purpose, the Governors have generally employed three methods: List system, parade system and list-cum-parade system. Under the first method, he can ask the contenders to provide a list of their supporters and to enquire from each member on the list about his choice. If the balance is held by the independents he must enquire from each independent his verdict. The parade system is the physical verification of the list in the Assembly. He must summon the session of the Assembly and ask the contenders to show their strength on the floor of the House. In case he uses both the methods, it is known as the list-cum-parade method.

Dismissal of the Chief Minister and the Council of Ministers

The Chief Minister (CM) and his ministers, according to Article 164(1), hold office during the pleasure of the Governor. Yet, they are not totally at the mercy of the Governor because Clause (1) of Article 164 must be read together with Clause (2) of the same article. It says that the council of ministers is collectively responsible to the state legislature. It also includes the Chief Minister ostensibly because he is the head of this council. This means that so long as the ministry enjoys the confidence of the legislature, it can hold office.

What happens when a Chief Minister and his party are reduced to a minority in the legislature through defections? The Governor, in this case, can ask the CM to prove his strength on the floor of the House. He can also make a report to the President under Article 356 regarding failure of constitutional machinery in his state. What is to be emphasized here is that dismissal should take place only after a clear cut verdict by the Assembly. It other words, Article 164(1) should come into force when Article 164(2) have been fully observed. A situation may arise when a defeated ministry refuses to resign even after a vote of no-confidence has been passed against it. In such circumstances, the Governor is entitled to dismiss the ministry and install a new ministry in the state. Defeat of the government on important policy matters, for instance the budget, also amounts to a vote of no-confidence against the government and creates grounds for intervention by the Governor and, in all probability, would lead to the dismissal of the government.

The power to dismiss the CM of a state is not a discretionary one in reality and may have serious repercussions on the Governor's career itself, as was proved in April 1994 in the case of Goa. On 2 April 1994, Governor Bhanu Pratap Singh dismissed the CM of the state, following serious differences of opinion with the latter on a variety of issues, despite the fact that the CM had the support of 23 MLAs out of the 38 members of the Goa State Assembly. The Governor administered the oath of office to the CM's closest rival Ravi Naik without taking the approval of the Centre. Thereafter, the Governor himself was unceremoniously dismissed on 3rd April 1994.

Reservation of Bills for Reconsideration by the President

In the process of legislation, the Governor does not have a total veto power but can only stall legislation. Under Article 200, the Governor can reserve a bill passed by the legislature for reconsideration of the President. A bill can be reserved under the following circumstances: (i) if the bill is unconstitutional, (ii) if it is against the larger interest of the country, (iii) if it is in direct opposition to the Directive Principles of State Policy, (iv) if the bill passed by the state legislature is of grave national importance, (v) if it endangers the position of the High Court and (vi) if the bill, deals with the compulsory acquisition of property under Article 31(3). It is interesting to note that under Article 201, when the Governor sends a bill to the President for reconsideration, the President has to declare whether he is giving or withholding his assent. In cases of non-money bills, the President, if he is not giving his assent, can ask the Governor to send the bill back to the House or Houses as the case may be. The House or Houses will reconsider this bill, sent by the President, within a period of six months from the date of receipt of such a message and, if it is again passed by the House or Houses, with or without amendment, it shall be presented again to the President for his consideration.

Use of Article 356

Under Article 356, the President can declare a state of emergency in a state on receipt of a report from the Governor of the state, or otherwise if a situation has arisen in which the government of the state cannot operate in accordance with the provisions of the Constitution. An important aspect of this article is that emergency can be imposed on a state even without the Governor's report. For this, the reason(s) could be: (a) breakdown of law and order machinery; (b) political instability as a result of defections; (c) paralysis of the parliamentary process, for instance, when the Chief Minister does not resign, even after losing the majority; (d) corruption, maladministration, separatist activity and terrorism; (e) popular agitation against the ministry; (f) loss of public confidence in the majority; (g) no coalition government is set up; and (h) voluntary courting of it by a state to override a peculiar or particular problem.

Such an emergency can have the following effects: (a) the President can assume to himself all or any of the functions of the government of the state other than the High Court, (b) declare that the powers of the legislature of the state shall be exercisable by or under the authority of the Parliament, and (c) make provisions necessary or desirable for giving effect to the objects of the proclamation.

Every such proclamation must be laid before each House of the Parliament and will cease to exist at the expiration of two months unless it has been approved by both chambers of the Parliament before this term expires. If, during these two months, the Lok Sabha is dissolved and the Rajya Sabha has approved it, then, the proclamation shall cease to operate on expiration of thirty days from the date on which the Lok Sabha first sits after its reconstitution, unless it is approved by the Lok Sabha before the expiration of this term. A proclamation so approved shall, unless revoked, cease to operate on the expiration of a period of six months from the date of issue of the proclamation. Unless revoked, its life can be extended by six months each, several times, but in no case beyond three years.

If we examine the 123 cases (till 2014) of the imposition of the President's rule in states since the starting of the constitution, a large number would appear to be controversial. In fact, discretion not backed by objectivity and rationality is bound to create controversies.

Some recent cases of Governor's actions highlighted the controversial role played by them in the states. In 1998, UP Governor Romesh Bhandari installed a government headed by J. Pal, dismissing the Kalyan Singh government. In September 1998, S.S. Bhandari, the Governor of Bihar, recommended the imposition of President's rule in Bihar on the ground that "the Bihar government symbolizes the most malignant and uncouth level of functioning in Indian politics" but the president saw no evidence of a Constitutional breakdown in Bihar. In 2000, Bihar Governor Vinod Pandey swore in JD (U) leader Nitish Kumar as Chief Minister after the elections even though he did not have adequate members to prove his majority in the Assembly. On 30 June 2001, Tamil Nadu Chief Minister Jayalalitha ordered the arrest of the former Chief Minister M. Karunanidhi when the DMK was supporting the NDA government at the Centre. On 1 July 2001, the Union cabinet recommended to the President to withdraw his pleasure from the Tamil Nadu Governor Fathima Bibi as they felt that the Governor failed to fulfill her Constitutional obligations of office. On 2 February 2005, the Goa Governor dismissed the 32-month old government of Manohar Parrikar-led BJP coalition, even when the government won a controversial vote of confidence. Though the Governor asked for the confidence vote report, he did not wait for the speaker's report and dismissed the government. In Jharkhand, BJP emerged as the single largest party in the 2005 assembly election along with its partner NDA. But the Congress Party at the Centre supported Shibu Soren and the Governor rejected the BJP's claim to form the government and swore in JMM leader Shibu Soren as Chief Minister.

Even though there are a number of criticisms and problems with regard to the role of Governor, it would not be feasible or desirable to formulate comprehensive guidelines for the exercise of the discretionary powers of the Governor. Under such circumstances, the Governors should be able to deal with situations according to their best judgement, keeping in view the laws and conventions of the Parliamentary system of India and the Constitution of the country.

It has been held that generally the Governor cannot act "except in accordance with the advice of his ministers". [Sanjeevi vs State of Madras, AIR 1970 SC 1102; IIP. Service Commission vs Suresh, AIR 1987 sc 1953; Sunit Kumar vs Government of West Bengal, AIR 1950 Cal. 274]

There are certain areas where the Governor may have to use his own wisdom and discretion, e.g. in (a) appointing a new Chief Minister in a situation where no single party or leader commands majority support; (b) dismissing a Ministry which refuses to resign even after losing majority support in the House or after being defeated on a no confidence motion; (c) dissolution of the Assembly on the advice of the Chief Minister who has lost majority support; (d) determining the royalty for mineral licenses to District Councils in case of tribal areas of Assam, under the Sixth Schedule; (e) advising the President of the failure of the constitutional machinery and to impose President's rule; and (f) giving or withholding assent to Bills, returning a Bill for reconsideration of the House/s or reserving it for the consideration of the President.

When a Chief Minister of UP was dismissed by the Governor after a group of members withdrew their support and the Governor appointed another person as the Chief Minister without a majority test on the floor of the House and the High Court ordered the reinstatement of the former Chief Minister, the Supreme Court ordered a special session of the State Assembly to have a composite floor test between the two contending claimants of Chief Ministership. [Jagdambika Pal vs Union of India, AIR 1998 SC 998]

Can Governors be trusted to remain within the ambit of the Constitution? The Constituent Assembly had toyed with the idea of activating Governors by making the post a responsible activist institution. But the idea of elected Governors was abandoned so that directly 'elected' Governors would not vie for prominence against indirectly selected Chief Ministers.

Except during the Nehru era, the Governor's office had become a political office. During the Indira Gandhi era, many Governors ran amok holding a Congress brief for the party in power in New Delhi rather than objectively discharging their constitutional powers and responsibilities.

The Bhagwan Sahay Committee (1971) sustained this charge; and the Sarkaria Commission (1988) openly stated that "the role of the Governor has emerged as one of the key issues in Union-State relations". Unfortunately none of the recommendations of the Sarkaria report on the Governor has been followed. An important recommendation was that the people from the party in power should not be appointed to the office of Governor. The Constitution Review Commission also recommended the same. But it was not put into practice by any of the Central Governments that ruled the country over the past 60 years.

What is needed is more neutral, less political and in that context less-activist Governors. Since the Governor is appointed by the President on the advice of the PM, such posts should be within the scrutiny of Parliament. The Narendra Modi government had advised the UP A appointed governors to resign (June 2014). Amidst mixed reactions, five governors had put in their papers. Initially some had questioned the propriety of the Home Ministry's move, but gradually there appears to be general compliance. A constitutional office therefore seems to have acquired a political character. The Supreme Court ruling in Bommai Case (1988) adding a restrictive clause to the use of Art. 356 has defined the status of the Governor in the constitution. He is meant to be a representative of the President, not a mere agent of the President. A PIL filed by the BJP leader BP Singhal on 2 May 2004, challenged the removal of the Governors of Uttar Pradesh, Gujarat, Haryana and Goa, and elicited a ruling by a five-judge Constitution Bench headed by the then Chief Justice of India, KG Balakrishnan. The Bench observed, "change in government at the Centre is not a ground for removal of governors holding office to make way for others favoured by the new government."

Despite all that has happened earlier neither the Congress nor the BJP appear to be motivated for any constructive initiative to change the unhealthy precedents of the past which would insulate the governor's post from such intense politicization in the future.

4.3 The Chief Minister

Article 164(1) maintains that the CM holds office at the pleasure of the Governor. This article must be read with Article 164(2), which says that the ministers, including the CM, are responsible to the Legislative Assembly of the state. This has several implications. It is normally taken to mean that so long as the CM enjoys the support and confidence of the Assembly, he cannot be removed by the Governor. Dismissal, in this sense, could occur only if the CM loses his support or the ministry is defeated on a major policy issue on the floor of the Assembly leading to a no-confidence motion. However, what happens in practice is that the removal of a CM is rarely the decision of the Governor. The latter acts only as an agent of the Union Government and, therefore, it is the Union Government which generally removes a Chief Minister from office. This usually happens when the CM of a state refuses to follow the directions of the Centre and, when the party ruling in the state is other than the one at the Centre. This is done through the provision of Article 356.

In a parliamentary set-up, the council of ministers, headed by the CM, is the de facto executive of the State Government. In the appointment of a CM, although the Governor has some discretion in certain cases, in the constitution of the council of ministers, he has none. Usually, all the ministers are the choice of the CM and the Governor is expected to formally approve the names recommended by the former. The ministers are responsible to the Legislative Assembly of the state and not to the Governor.

The Constitution (Ninety-first Amendment) Act, 2003 inserted the following new clauses to Article 164:

(IA) The total number of Ministers, including the Chief Minister, in the Council of Ministers in a State shall not exceed fifteen percent of the total number of members of the Legislative Assembly of that state;

Provided further that where the total number of Ministers, including the Chief Minister, in the Council of Ministers in any State at the commencement of the Constitution (Nine-first Amendment) Act, 2003, exceeds the said fifteen percent, of the number specified in the first proviso, as the case may be, then the total number of Ministers in that state shall be brought in conformity with the provisions of this clause within six months from such date as the President may by public notification appoint.

(IB) A member of the Legislative Assembly of a State or either House of the Legislature of State having Legislative Council belonging to any political party who is disqualified for being a member of that House under Paragraph 2 of the Tenth Schedule shall also be disqualified to be appointed as a Minister under clause (1) for duration of the period commencing from the date of his disqualification till the date on which the term of his office would expire or where he would contest any election to the Legislative Assembly of a State or either House of the Legislature of a State having Legislative Council, as the case may be, before the expiry of such period, till the date on which he is declared elected, whichever is earlier.

Chief Minister and The Council

At the state level, the council of ministers is a three-tier body with the cabinet at the apex. The cabinet is a small body of ministers that holds the most important portfolios. In case of differences of opinion in the cabinet, the CM has to iron them out and hold the cabinet together.

The minister and the secretary of the department concerned supervise the execution of the decisions of the cabinet. The CM evaluates the performance of the various executive agencies and takes corrective action wherever necessary.

The Chief Minister's Secretariat

In the face of the growing responsibilities of the CM, there was a need for providing him with intensive administrative assistance. Such assistance is provided by the Chief Minister's Secretariat, which is accountable only to him. This organization ensures that the CM's directives are implemented by various state and district agencies. It is headed by a secretary belonging to the selection/ super-time scale of the I.A.S., who is assisted by deputy secretaries OSDs, deputy directors, assistant secretaries, accounts officers, Statistical assistants and the Superintendent of Police (Vigilance). The CM's Secretariat looks after the functions related to the tours and correspondence of the CM, redressal of public grievances, management of the CM's benevolent funds, implementation of the CM's assurances and monitoring.

The Secretary to the CM, while providing administrative assistance to the CM, keeps confidential documents and correspondence, accompanies the CM on important tours, takes follow-up action on cabinet decisions, apprises the CM of major developments and issues, helps him in the conduct of assembly work and supervises the staff of the CM's Secretariat. Moreover, he writes informal notes on all important files going to the Chief Minister to facilitate his making decisions.

The post of the Secretary to the Chief Minister (in some states, he is called Principal Secretary to the Chief Minister), has acquired enormous status and influence in recent times. The rationale behind this phenomenon is the assumption that the Secretary to the Chief Minister is the alter ego of his boss, i.e. the Chief Minister.

4.4 The State Council of Ministers

The position of the council of ministers in the states is quite similar to that of the council of ministers at the Union level. The 'real' governance of the state is carried on by the council of ministers headed by the Chief Minister, The conventions that apply in a parliamentary model also apply to the state council of ministers.

Although, in theory, the position of the Chief Minister in the cabinet is that of primus inter pares, in practice, he is the Captain of the 'cabinet-ship' and all ministers look up to him for direction and leadership. He holds the cabinet together as a team. All important decisions in the cabinet are taken by him and a member who does not agree with him generally has to resign. He is also responsible for the appointment of ministers, distribution of portfolios and their dismissal. In theory, although the ministers are responsible to the Legislative Assembly, in fact they are responsible, chiefly, to the Chief Minister.

This is an age-old norm of the cabinet government that all the ministers sink or swim together. They must voice the same opinion before the state legislature. In cabinet meetings, they can differ from each other but any public exposure of these differences is considered undesirable. In maintaining this solidarity, several factors play a role, the most important ones being the personal standing of the Chief Minister (his personality, qualities of leadership, decision-making style, etc.,) the size of the cabinet (if small, it is easier to hold together) and the strength of the Chief Minister's party in the State Assembly (in case, he is heading a coalition ministry, he may find it difficult to hold it together). A decision, once taken, is the decision of the cabinet.

The council of ministers of a state takes all important policy decisions that concern the governance of the state. It also oversees the implementation of these decisions. Each cabinet minister is the head of one or more departments. Thus, the ministers not only are the political heads but, by virtue of their being responsible for all actions of the department, assume the overall politico-administrative leadership and role.

Below the political leadership is the administrative leadership which is held by the secretary of a department who, in most cases, belongs to the IAS. Below the secretariat level organization is the directorate administration. A directorate is generally headed by a specialist, though in a number of cases, a generalist (IAS) officer may head a directorate. The council of ministers is responsible for the functioning of all the government departments as well as the relatively autonomous corporations and agencies which are non-departmental in form.

Broadly, the council of ministers of a state deals with the following matters:

1. Any matter that the state Governor may refer to it under Clause (i) of Article 167 of the Constitution of India.
2. Any matter referred to it for consideration by the Chief Minister.
3. Proposals for fresh legislation or for amendments in the existing laws.
4. Important policy matters, including changes in the existing policies.
5. Matters concerning the state revenue, expenditure, investment and audit of accounts.
6. Proposals for budget, supplementary demands and advances from the Contingency Fund.
7. Important structural changes in the state administrative system.
8. State service rules.
9. Appeals made by government servants to the Governor against the orders issued by the State Government on disciplinary matters.
10. Union-state relations,
11. Interstate relations.
12. Any other matter which, in the view of the council of ministers, deserves its attention and warrants any decisions or action under the Constitution and the existing laws.

In addition, the council of ministers is responsible for rendering advice to the Governor on all important state administrative matters.

4.5 The Chief Secretary : Role and Functions

The Chief Secretary is the administrative head of state administration in India. He is, in many ways, the counterpart, at the state level, of the Cabinet Secretary. As the chief coordinator of the state secretariat and other administrative departments and as head of the civil service, he is the pivot of the state governance system. His role in policy formulation, formal and informal, is substantial and so is his supervisory role in the policy implementation apparatus.

Until 1973, the Chief Secretary was not necessarily the senior most civil servant of the state. In 1973 the post of the Chief Secretary was upgraded and, presently it is regarded as the most prestigious and influential post in the state civil service structure. It is generally held by one of the senior most officers of the IAS. His status is equal to that of a Secretary to the GOI.

The incumbent to the post of Chief Secretary is chosen by the Chief Minister of the state. The CM may consult the cabinet or a few of his ministerial colleagues on this matter but, the final decision is his.

Though the Chief Secretary is at the apex of the administrative hierarchy of a state, the-Indian Constitution does not list his powers and functions. His functions are defined in the Rules of Business, which each State Government frames for itself. These are amended from time to time. Some of the functions, however, have also evolved through custom and conventions.

The Chief Secretary of a state acts as the ex-officio Secretary to the Council of Ministers and, in that capacity, he is known as the Secretary to the Cabinet.

The Chief Secretary decides whether the memo submitted by a particular department, regarding the case to be discussed, is adequately furnished with relevant facts and data. He is also responsible for the preparation of the agenda papers. In his capacity as the ex-officio Secretary to the Council, he attends all the cabinet meetings and also of the sub-committees of the cabinet. He arranges the recording of the decisions taken in the cabinet meetings and forwards a copy to the Governor, the CM and the council of ministers.

The Chief Secretary, while attending the meetings of the cabinet, may be asked to express his views on important matters. He acts as the main source of information and advice to the CM and other ministers. As the Secretary to the Council, he attends all the meetings of the cabinet.

When a decision is arrived at by the cabinet, it is the task of the secretary of the concerned department to implement that particular decision. Here, the Chief Secretary plays an effective supervisory role, as the most important cases of the various departments are sent to the Chief Secretary for final decision or for onward transmission to the CM or the concerned ministers. All important cases that involve adoption of new schemes have to be approved by the Chief Secretary. At the state level, the Chief Secretary is generally the administrative head of a few departments, the most important among them being General Administration, Personnel, Administrative Reforms and Planning. There is no uniformity among the various states in regard to the administrative departments directly under the charge of the Chief Secretary. However, as a rule, only those departments which have a crucial role in the coordination and supervision of state administrative departments/ agencies are given the status.

Accordingly, in a number of states, the Chief-Secretary functions today as the Personnel Secretary. In that capacity, his role involves the following functions:

1. He is responsible for personnel matters of the state cadre officers of the IAS, the highest state service, and any other service described in the Rules of Business of the state.

He deals with all matters related to vacancies, appointments, transfers, placements, seniority, promotions and retirement of personnel of the higher civil services. He also plays a crucial role in the promotion of state service officers to the IAS. All matters pertaining to determination of seniority of the above- mentioned officers are sent to him for consideration.

2. His approval is sought for amendments in service rules.
3. He is also generally consulted by the Chief Minister while making appointments to the posts of chairman and members of the State Public Service Commission.
4. As Personnel Secretary, the Chief Secretary has to ensure that conduct rules are followed strictly by the state civil servants. Hence, cases regarding disciplinary action against all the services mentioned under his charge are brought up before him. The decisions of the Chief Secretary on disciplinary proceedings against All India Service officers, heads of departments and other state civil service officers are generally endorsed by the Chief Minister.
5. He also writes the Annual Confidential Reports (ACRs) or performance appraisal reports (APRs) of the officers of All India Services posted in his state.
6. Some states have the office of the Lok Ayukta to examine complaints made by citizens against defaulting officers. The CM may consult the Chief Secretary while appointing the Lok Ayukta. The annual reports of the Lok Ayukta are routed through the Chief Secretary, before being sent through the proper channel to the legislative assembly of the state.
7. He can intervene in matters involving staff welfare and service conditions of State Government officials.
8. He is the overall in charge of training and career management of the civil servants of the state.

It may be mentioned that in most of the states in India, the Chief Secretary functions as the Secretary, General Administration. This department is responsible for taking care of the general administrative matters of different State Government departments and provides miscellaneous facilities to the departments and officers. This can be done effectively under the leadership of the senior most civil servant, whose judgement and authority are trusted and accepted. The role of the Chief Secretary regarding general administration involves a number of tasks.

1. During visits of dignitaries to the state, he looks after all the necessary arrangements.
2. He chairs an expert body which decides on granting awards, honours and distinctions.
3. He deals with matters related to interstate disputes.
4. The Chief Secretary can initiate changes in Rules of Business but, the final decision in this respect rests with the cabinet.
5. Cases that concern grants-in-aid to NGOs engaged in social and cultural development are routed through him to the CM.

6. All matters related to housing accommodation, and government buildings fall under his jurisdiction.

These responsibilities of the Chief Secretary affect all the departments and, therefore, the role of the Chief Secretary as head of the General Administration Department is of substantial significance.

The last, but by far the most important, function of the Chief Secretary is to coordinate the activities of the entire State Government machinery.

Centre-State and Interstate Coordination

The Chief Secretary is a major channel of communication between the Centre and the State Governments. In matters like planning, financial and personnel management, the activities of the two are closely interlinked. For this purpose, he keeps regular contacts with the Central level functionaries such as the Cabinet Secretary, the Home Secretary, the Personnel Secretary and the Planning Secretary through both formal and informal channels. His contacts with these senior officers help him to secure financial and other resources for the state such as allocation of food grains, power, water, etc.

Conferences are called and councils are set up by the Central Government for the purpose of bringing about greater coordination. The following are examples of such conferences and councils:

1. The Chief Secretaries Conference
2. Zonal Councils

The success and prestige enjoyed by a Chief Secretary depends, to a large extent, upon his equation and relationship with the varied sets of people and institutions that form his work environment. On the one side, there are the Chief Minister, ministers, MPs and MLAs, and, on the other, there is a network of administrative functionaries. His position, therefore, depends upon his sagacity, capacity and dynamism in handling the members of his role-set in an effective manner.

4.6 State Secretariat

At the Union level, each state has a secretariat of its own which is the highest echelon of the state administrative structure that offers locus for the exercise of authority by the State Government. The expression "secretariat" is used to refer to the complex of departments whose political heads are ministers while the administrative heads are Secretaries to the Government, The entire administrative machinery of the state is divided into several departments. The secretariat is a conglomeration of all these departments. The ministers are in charge of these departments and are answerable to the legislature for the activities therein. Several career civil servants are posted below the ministers in each department, who carry out the orders of their political bosses, advise them and help them by providing necessary information required for facing the legislature and its committees.

A secretariat department is different from an executive department. The latter is the executive organization of the government and has at its top a functionary, generally known as the head of the department. The Agriculture Department in the secretariat, for instance, is headed by the Secretary, Agriculture, but has the Director of Agriculture as its head of the department. The latter is subordinate to the former. Not all secretariat departments have 'executive departments' attached to them, as some of them are engaged in an advisory and controlling capacity. Departments of Finance, Personnel, Planning, Administrative Reforms, Law, etc., come under this category.

The head of the department is generally a specialist and the secretary is a generalist civil servant, though there are a number of executive departments which are headed by generalists and, conversely, a few (in fact, very few) secretariat departments are headed by specialists. The number of secretariat departments is usually more than the number of secretaries. The normal practice is to entrust more than one department to the charge of one secretary though, in the case of major departments like Finance and Home, the secretaries have only single charge.

A secretariat department has been defined as an organizational unit that consists of a Secretary to the Government, together with a part of the secretariat under his administrative control to which responsibility for the performance of specified functions has been assigned under the Rules of Business framed for this purpose. As mentioned already, the secretariat is divided into a number of departments. The exact number of departments varies from state to state. Most states have 30 to 40 departments. But there are a few departments which are common to all states, viz. General Administration, Personnel, Home, Finance, Agriculture, Public Works, Industries, Irrigation, Health, Education, Law, Medical, Planning, Information, Rural Development, Transport, Revenue, etc.

Amalgamations, bifurcations, trifurcations and again mergers are a continuous process of departmentalization in India at the Union as well as the state levels. Unlike in the USA, where such adjustments cannot be made without legislative approval, in India, the political executive is at liberty to design and redesign its administrative system.

The basic pattern of organization in departments is broadly similar. The secretary is the official head and he is assisted by one or more additional/joint/special/ deputy and under/ assistant secretaries, depending upon the size of the department. Nomenclatures of these officials differ from state to state. Usually the hierarchy comprises secretary, special secretary, deputy secretary and assistant secretaries, while in some states there are also joint secretaries who are above the rank of deputy secretaries. In Rajasthan, the designation of special secretary is given to an IAS officer who is of selection scale, while in Maharashtra it is accorded to very senior IAS officer (s) in the super-time scale. Such differences are very common in the cross-state context. Further, a number of deputy and assistant secretaries belong to a state secretariat service.

Functions of the Secretariat

The broad functions of the secretariat in the Indian states may be mentioned briefly here.

- The secretariat helps the ministers in their individual and collective capacity to formulate policies on all matters of state administration. It is the main coordinating agency for state administration.

- It serves as a "think-tank" and "brain-trust" of the State Government. Since each policy is based on a body of data, the secretariat is a sort of databank engaged in collecting information, classifying it, analyzing it and supplying it promptly when most needed.
- It gives directions and guidance to the directorates and field organizations for the implementation of government policies.
- It also undertakes quasi-legislative work, as it helps the ministers in drafting legislation, framing rules and regulations and also formulates principles of procedures and financial control.
- It is also the spokesman of the State Government. The Central and other State Governments have to contact it first and not the state organizations directly. Within this broad framework of functions, the State Governments have their own list of duties to be performed by the secretariat.

General administrative matters include the following:

1. All matters of general policy.
2. Interdepartmental coordination.
3. Matters pertaining to the framing of legal enactments or rules or amendments to the existing ones and cases involving interpretation or relaxation of existing rules or orders.
4. Correspondence with the Union government and other State Governments and governments of union territories.
5. All matters pertaining to the preparation and adoption of new plan schemes and important modifications in the existing schemes.
6. Inspecting reports and tour notes recorded by the heads of departments.
7. Holding all-India conferences and important conferences at the state level.
8. Answering questions before the Public Accounts Committee, Estimates Committee, and other Parliamentary and Assembly questions.
9. Appeals and revisions within the powers of the State Government.

Financial matters may be summed up as:

1. Scrutiny and approval of departmental budget estimates, major appropriation of accounts, surrender of funds and supplementary grants.
2. All proposals involving new items of expenditure.
3. Financial sanction not within the competence of the heads of departments.
4. Sanction of expenditure out of the Contingency Fund.
5. Write off cases beyond the powers of heads of departments and cases of audit objections regarding the offices of heads of departments and the secretariat.

Service matters within the ambit of the secretariat are as follows:

1. Approval of service rules and their amendments.
2. Matters relating to senior appointments, promotions, transfers and cases of disciplinary proceedings against gazetted officers.
3. Initial appointment of officers belonging to the state service.
4. Creation of posts, their extension and continuance, re-employment, resignations, special pay and allowances and pensions not within the authority of heads of departments.

These functions just discussed are generally common to all the state secretariats.

Problems

The organization of the secretariat has always been a challenging task. The problems of rational grouping, allocation of subjects, improving the process of decision-making have always received the attention of the state administrative reforms committees. Some of the problems as pointed out by these committees and experienced by the practitioners and observers are:

1. Whenever a new government is formed, more so during quick succession, the regrouping and reorientation becomes a problem. The secretariat, more than any other segment of the bureaucracy, receives the first shock of political changes in the government. It has to adapt promptly to the aspirations and needs of every new government.
2. The tenure system of staffing, which ensures recycling of personnel between the line and staff positions, does not operate rhythmically. Resultantly, several senior civil servants continue to rotate between the Central and State secretariats and thus remain largely unexposed to fieldwork and the realities of administration.
3. The ideal relationship between the minister, the secretariat and the executive departments would be one wherein the minister represents the will of the people, the secretariat acts as the brain and the head, and the executive departments act as the "thinking hands" of the government. But, this ideal is followed more in its breach than in its practice.
4. Lastly, there is the problem of "over-administration". Since Independence, due to the proliferation of the State Government activities, the number of government departments have increased remarkably. The need for a bigger administrative apparatus was felt with the diversification of the functions of the government and a natural corollary was the expansion of the secretariat activities.

Though there has been a continuing debate on the utility or futility of the state secretariat, experience underscores the point that the secretariat formulates and moderates policies in tune with the broader environmental imperatives; coordinates the approaches to governance so that they are properly synchronized; smoothens the Center-State relations; maintains financial discipline and control; formulates and monitors planning; regulates the personnel policy and administration; supervises the implementation of government polices and decisions; and even maintains a close linkage with the district administration. The secretariat is the nerve-centre of the politico-administrative system of a State and its utility is not likely to be minimized.

4.7 Directorates: Meaning and Organization

The Secretariat is concerned with the setting of the broader policies and goals of the State Government while the responsibility for achieving those goals and executing those policies rests with the heads of the executive departments. The executive agencies are as a rule located outside the Secretariat and constitute distinct organizational entities. A popular label to identify an executive agency is "Directorate". In a large number of cases, the heads of the executive agencies are known as directors. Many examples of this could be cited: director of agriculture, director of animal husbandry, director of education, director of social welfare, director of transport, director of public health, director of town planning, and so on.

However, other nomenclatures are also used to refer to the heads of the executive departments. Thus, the executive head of the department of police is known as the Inspector/ Director General of Police; that of the jail department, the Inspector- General of jails; that of the forest department, the chief conservator of forests; that of the cooperative department, the registrar of cooperative societies; that of the sales tax department, the commissioner of sales tax; that of the irrigation department, the chief engineer (irrigation); and so forth. In other words, although in a large number of cases, the heads of the executive departments are called Directors, they are also known by other names.

Organization of Directorates at the State and Sub-State Levels

Apart from the state level, the executive agencies also function at the sub-state levels. While the policy must be formulated at one Centre (the state headquarters presently, the state headquarters is signified by Secretariat and Directorates), its execution must necessarily take place in the field. Therefore, the Directorates must make a conscious effort at achieving a vertical penetration down to the grassroots level. When this is done, lesser Directorates emerge at the regional level: the state level executive department establishes offices in the regions; a region is simply a territorial unit below the state but above the district level. When this process progresses further down the line, the district, block and village level field agencies of a Directorate emerge.

At the state level, the headship would normally be with a 'full' director who would be assisted by a group of lesser directors: additional directors, senior joint directors, joint directors, deputy directors, assistant directors, and other functionaries. Of course, as would be understood, depending upon the workload of a department, the number of levels of hierarchy at the headquarters could be larger or smaller. The regional level set up of an executive department, would usually be headed by an officer of a lower rank, a senior joint director in this case. It could indeed even be a person of simply a position like joint director or even lower level, which would again depend on the workload and other factors. Many district level offices of the executive departments are headed by deputy or even assistant directors. Again, many factors will combine to determine the rank of the officer who may head the district level set up.

At the level immediately below the district (block level), each development department is represented by an extension officer who is a part of the extension team functioning under the block development officer. Thus, to take an example, there would be an agriculture extension officer in each block, representing the state level directorate of agriculture. At the village level, as is well-known, there exist the multi-purpose extension functionaries known as the village level workers (VLWs).

4.8 Types of Executive Agencies

With a steady increase in the functions of government, the executive agencies have grown in number as well as variety. The two most familiarly known executive agencies are the attached offices and the subordinate offices. But with the emergence of a large public sector in the country, other types of executive agencies have also developed. Of these, the public corporation (e.g. Life Insurance Corporation of India) and the government company (e.g. Steel Authority of India Ltd.) remain the most outstanding examples. There are other types of executive agencies too. What needs to be remembered is that with the growing governmental functions, a variety of organizational patterns have been evolved to suit the requirements of the varied range of functions, which the government is increasingly taking on.

4.9 Role of Attached and Subordinate Offices

Let us now briefly see what are Attached and Subordinate Offices, which, as we have stated above, are the two most important forms of executive agencies. The Manual of Office describes these as:

> *"Where the execution of policies of government requires decentralisation of executive direction and the establishment of field agencies, a Ministry has under its domain, the subsidiary offices, which are Attached and Subordinate Offices. The Attached Offices are responsible for providing executive direction required for the implementation of the policies laid down by the Ministry to which they are attached. They also serve as repository of technical information and advice to the Ministry on technical aspects of the questions dealt with by them. The Subordinate Offices function as field establishments or as the agencies responsible for the detailed execution of the decisions of government. They generally function under the direction of an Attached Office..."*

Thus, the Attached Offices have in essence a two-fold function. First, they furnish technical data and advice to the Ministry to which they are attached. (Ministry is the policy-making body, but this policy-making exercise must be based on technical information and advice. It is the Attached Office, which supplies this assistance to the ministry). The second function of the Attached Office is to provide executive directions to the agencies, which are responsible for implementing the policies of government.

As contrasted with the Attached Office, a Subordinate Office functions as the field establishment or as the agency responsible for the detailed execution of the policies and programmes of the government. As a rule, it functions under an Attached Office.

4.10 Factors Shaping the Secretariat-Directorate Relationship

The Secretariat and the Directorate constitute two arms of the governmental machinery. Unless they achieve a certain measure of coordination and cooperation, the ability of the machinery to deliver public goods is hampered. Two sets of factors have played a dominant role in shaping the Secretariat-Directorate relationship at the state level. Of these, one concerns the functioning of the Secretariat at a practical plane. The second is concerned with the expansion that has lately come about in the Secretariat—its role, personnel, number of administrative units and so on. Of course, the two factors are closely interrelated; it is to facilitate academic understanding of the matter that these are being dealt with separately here. It may be noted, it is these very factors that—as they work themselves out—generate situations, which tend to build up tension in the Secretariat-Directorate relationship.

The institution of Secretariat has attracted considerable criticism. One cannot perhaps find fault with the Secretariat as a concept, for at a conceptual plane it is meant to encourage division of labour (between policy making and policy executing agencies) and specialisation, which results from such compartmentalisation of work. Again, at a conceptual level, the idea of Secretariat is meant to promote delegation of authority from policy making to policy execution level. By implication, it discourages centralization and concentration.

However, in practice, these advantages of the Secretariat system have failed to fully materialize. There is a large divergence between what is held to be valid in theory and what is achieved in practice. The manner of functioning of the Secretariat and its overbearing attitude have generated tensions in the Secretariat-Directorate relationship and adversely affected the advantages commonly ascribed to the Secretariat System.

The substantive points of criticism against the Secretariat, which have a bearing on its relationship with the executive departments, can be discussed:

1. Firstly, Secretariat has an expansionist attitude; it has arrogated functions to itself, which do not belong to it. It does not confine itself to policy making; instead the Secretariat often engages in matters of an executive nature as well. This encroachment has materially weakened the authority of the executive agencies. Secondly, the Secretariat hesitates to delegate adequately to the Executive Agencies. As a result of this, the execution of policies is delayed. Besides, the initiatives of the Executive Agencies are cramped through the need for repeated consultations with, and approvals from, the Secretariat. Thirdly, Scrutiny, in the Secretariat, of proposals submitted by the heads of the Executive Departments begins at the clerical level. This procedure is dilatory. Besides, it undermines the authority of the heads. As is well-known, the proposals of the heads of the departments are based on proposals received from the district and regional level officers and are submitted to the Secretariat after a detailed scrutiny in the Attached Offices. If, therefore, these proposals are to be subjected to further

scrutiny, it leads to unnecessary duplication and delay. Lastly more substantively, the very idea of the generalist administrators (who staff the Secretariat) overseeing, superintending and evaluating the work of specialists and technocrats (who staff the Executive Agencies) is out of place in the modern technological age. It is all the more untenable that the Secretariat should scrutinize the proposals and schemes emanating from the attached offices, since the lay generalists have possibly nothing to contribute in such an exercise.

The above-noted situations, coupled with the fact that Secretariat has come to be identified with the real power structure in the governmental system have unduly inflated the influence and authority of the Secretariat and aggravated tensions between the Secretariat and the Executive Departments. The importance of the Secretariat has further enhanced since, as previously noted, it delves into the questions not only of policy (which constitute its legitimate sphere) but also those of execution. It has thus expanded its functional area through large, unauthorized encroachments in the executive sphere. This is, quite obviously, at the expense of the executive offices and only further adds to tension between the Secretariat and the Executive Agencies. Another situation, which must be noted in this regard, is the easy access, which Secretariat officers enjoy with the political executive. There is no gain saying the fact, that this, in its own way, contributes to the existing tensions between the Secretariat and Attached Offices.

Concurrent Appointment of Secretary as the Head of the Executive Agency

We have referred to the ex-officio Secretariat System earlier. Under this, an appropriate secretariat status is conferred upon the head of the Executive Department. The reverse is also done; namely a Secretary is concurrently appointed as head of the Attached Office. In this way, a single functionary is made responsible for both, policy formulation as well as policy implementation with the assistance of a common office located in the Secretariat. Some examples of this could be cited from the Central Government; Joint Secretary in the Department of Labour and Employment (Ministry of Labour, Employment and Rehabilitation) is concurrently the Director-General of Employment and Training. Similarly, Additional Secretary in the Department of Food (Ministry of Food and Agriculture) is also the Director-General of Food.

The advantage of this system is clear enough; namely, it helps to eliminate the distance between the Secretariat and the Attached Office. But, at the same time, the system blurs the distinction between the Secretariat and the Head of the Department.

A comprehensive projection of the system throughout the country could only take place if the view is held that the Secretariat as such has no longer a role apart from that of the executive head.

Directorate is an executive agency charged with the role of translating the policies framed at the Secretariat level into concrete action. Directorates establish intermediate level administrative set up—between the headquarters and the districts—which coordinate and supervise field operations. The intermediate set up is called the regional administration. The Board of Revenue is an organization at the headquarters to deal with issues like revenue administration of the state. It is an autonomous body with a distinct and separate existence from most of the State Government machinery.

In the possible patterns of relationship between the Secretariat and the Directorate, the two agencies remain locked in a process of constant interaction. Therefore, the relational patterns, which are generated, would be many. As the quest for greater efficiency in government forges ahead, administrative experiments ensue in its wake. This leads to modifications and alterations in particular patterns and abandonment of others. The old gives place to the new; the process is ongoing.

4.11 Second ARC - 15th Report (Extracts)

State Administration:

Size of the Council of Ministers

The size of the Council of Ministers in the States needs to be reduced further considering the needs of an efficient government. For this purpose the maximum size of the Council of Ministers may be fixed in a range between 10% and 15% of the strength of their Legislative Assemblies. In the larger State (where membership of the Assembly is more than 200) such maximum percentage should be 10% where as in the medium (where the strength of the Assembly is between 80 and 200) and the smaller States (where the strength of the Assembly is below 80) it may be 12% and 15% respectively. There is need to arrive at a national consensus on this issue through deliberations/discussions with the States at the Interstate Council.

Rationalizing the Number of Secretariat Departments

The number of Secretariat Departments in the States should be further rationalized on the following basis:

- The existing departments covering interrelated subjects, activities and functions should be merged.
- Need for synergy between the activities of various departments; devolution of a large number of functions to the Panchayati Raj institution and urban local bodies.
- The role of Secretaries to be redefined; to be divested of non-essential responsibilities and executive work and larger delegation of power to the executive departments/ agencies.
- Need for streamlining the decision-making process.

Executive Agencies

The State Government should scrutinize the functions/ activities of each department to confirm whether these activities/functions are critical to the mission of the department and can only be carried out by government agencies. There is need for a right balance between autonomy and accountability while designing the institutional framework of executive agencies. This could be achieved through well-designed performance agreements, Memorandum of Understanding (MoU), contract, etc. However, preparing and enforcing such performance contracts requires considerable upgradation of capacity in the concerned governmental departments. Agencies dealing with subjects where major functions and activities have devolved on local governments would need to concentrate on monitoring and supervision, ensuring standards and quality, guiding local governments on technical matters, training personnel, giving feedback to the government on implementation and performance and advising on changes that are needed in plans and programmes.

Appointment and Security of Tenure at the Senior Levels in the State Government

The proposed State Civil Service Authority should deal with matters that are concerned with appointment and tenure of senior officers of all ranks in the State Governments. Till the time that such an Authority is constituted, the following mechanism may be adopted for appointment of the Chief Secretary and Principal Conservator of Forests in the States:

1. There should be a collegium to recommend a panel of names to the Chief Minister/ Cabinet for these two posts. For the post of Chief Secretary, this collegium may consist of (a) a Minister nominated by the Chief Minister, (b) the Leader of the Opposition in the State Legislative Assembly and (c) the incumbent Chief Secretary. For the selection to the post of Principal Chief Conservator of Forests the collegiums may consist of the Minister In-charge of Forests, (b) the Leader of Opposition in the State Legislative Assembly and (c) the Chief Secretary.
2. There should be a fixed tenure of at least two years for both these posts.
3. The selection for the post of Chief Secretary and Principal Chief Conservator of Forests should be widened to include all officers above a specified seniority (e.g. 30 years). All officers with seniority higher than a prescribed limit should be eligible to be a part of the panel.

Expenditure Management

The State Governments need to take steps to ensure that projects and programmes are included in the budget only after well-considered deliberations and processes. The practice of announcing projects and schemes on an ad hoc basis needs to be done away with.

The State should take priority steps to improve their expenditure profile by finalizing the detailed project reports of schemes in the preceding year and (b) ensure that the financial sanctions are given to the departments in the first two months of the current financial year. The States should conduct a zero-base review of programmes and schemes that are more than five years old and that involve large sums of public money (say over 50 crores).

There should be prudent and realistic economic assumptions in formulation of budget estimates. At the end of every financial year, the gap between the estimates and the actual should be analyzed so that the underlying economic assumptions could be suitably calibrated for the future. There should be interaction between the State Government and stakeholders including industry associations, think tanks, etc., in budget formulation. In order to make such consultations effective and meaningful, steps should be taken to (a) provide information access to citizens and (b) educate citizens and leaders of society on budget making and its implications.

State Governments should shift to multi-year budgeting and give the estimates of revenue and expenditure for a period of four years in addition to the year to which the budget pertains. This should be done on a roll-on basis. In order to remove prejudice against non-plan expenditure, the State should take steps to provide for maintenance of the asset in the project cost itself and ensure its maintenance for at least five years after it is acquired. This action should go hand in hand with recovery of adequate user charges.

Conclusion

The most important public discourse in Indian democracy today is the debate bordering around interstate inequalities and the paradox of differentiated citizenship entitlements in a country that makes a constitutional promise of equality and social justice to all its citizens. A resident of Jammu and Kashmir, Manipur, Nagaland or Bihar may get quite a different access to basic public goods than a resident of Tamil Nadu, Kerala or Himachal Pradesh. The Human Development Reports of different states in India give a bewildering picture of this interstate disparity in citizen entitlements. Citizens as ultimate consumers, clients or user groups have a right to know and be guaranteed a minimum access to public goods and services. The Right to Public Service Guarantee Acts (first enacted by-Madhya Pradesh) now passed by 20 states of India with five declared intents: (a) assurance of the service (b) service within a stipulated time frame (c) holding designated officers accountable (d) a system of penalty for denial of service, are some good governance initiatives taken by various states of India.

In a federal system, good governance is a partnership between the Centre and the States. After 1991 the contribution of states to good governance initiatives has become significant and noticeable. Madhya Pradesh and Chhattisgarh have made significant innovations in decentralization, education and health delivery; Maharashtra was a pioneer in Employment Guarantees (precursor to MNREGA), Kerala accomplished major successes in land reforms and education, Andhra Pradesh in e-governance, Mizoram and Himachal Pradesh in communication and education and Rajasthan deserves laurels for pioneering the Right to Information Movement. Indeed best practices in good governance in different sectoral areas of public service delivery have been reported in all states.

Suggested Readings

Ahluwalia, M. S., "*Economic Performance of States in Post-Reform Period*," EPW (2000): pp. 1637-48.

Chatterjee, Sibranjan, *Governor's Role in the Indian Constitution*, New Delhi, Mittal Publications, 1992.

Dasgupta, Monica, *et al*., "*How might India's public health system be strengthened? Lessons from Tamil Nadu*," EPW 45 no. 10 (2010): pp. 46-60.

Dreze, Jean and Amartya Sen *(eds.), Indian Development: Selected Regional Perspectives*, Delhi, OUP, 1986.

Gupta Bhuvanesh, *State Administration in India*, RBSA Publishers 2012.

Harris, John, "Do Political regimes matter? *Poverty reduction and regime differences across India*," *in Changing Paths: International Development and the New Politics of Inclusion*, eds. Mick Moore and Peter Hontzager Ann Arbor, University of Michigan Press, 2003.

Kapoor, Gyan, *The Chief Minister as Administrator*, Jaipur, Arihant, 1992.

Kashyap, Anirban, *Governor's Role in Indian Constitution*, New Delhi, Lancers,1993

Kohli, Atul and Prerna Singh, *Routledge Handbook of Indian Politics*, UK, Routledge, 2013.

Kohli, Atul, *Poverty Amid Plenty in the New India: Politics, Economics and Inequality*, UK, Cambridge University Press, 2012.

Maheshwari, S. R., *State Administration in India*, New Delhi, Macmillan, 1979.

Mathur, P. L., *Role of Governor in Non-Congress States*, Jaipur, Rawat Publications, 1988.

Padhi, A.P. (ed.), *State Administration in India*, New Delhi, Uppal, 1988.

Panagariya, Arvind, *India: The Emerging Giant*, New York, OUP, 2008.

Rao, M.G. and Nirvikar Singh *Political Economy of Federalism in India*, Delhi, OUP, 2005.

Rao, M.G., R. Shand and K. Kalirajan, "*Convergence of Incomes across Indian States: A Divergent View*," EPW 34 no. 13 (1999).

Sarkaria Commission Report, 1988. Available at: http://interstatecouncil.nic.inSARCOMM.htim

Second Administrative Reforms Commission Report, 2005. Available at: http://arc.gov.in

Sogani, Meena, *The Chief Secretary in India*, New Delhi, Associated Press, 1984.

Sorabji, Soli, *et al.*, *The Governor: Sage or Saboteur* New Delhi, Roli Books, 1985.

OOO

Chapter Five

District Administration

Introduction

The policies and programmes adopted by the Central and State Governments are actually implemented by the district administration in the Indian federal system. The district administration's role as an implementing agency remains pivotal. It is considered to be the main pillar on which Indian Administration rests. It acts as an important source of State income by collecting land revenues. Moreover, it acts as a representative of the State Government that carries out the general tasks of administration. Acting as the District Election Officer, on behalf of the Election Commission the, District Collector conducts elections of different bodies, such as Parliament, the State Assembly and the urban and rural bodies.

The collector is a functionary with several responsibilities. The administration of the district is carried on by the collector in accordance with the directives from the State Government. The staff of the district machinery has to act, under the leadership of the collector, conforming to the policies, programmes and decisions made by the State Government. In addition to this, the district administration has to execute plans, policies and programmes of the Central Government whenever asked for. So it can be called an "executive body" to perform the duties as assigned by the State Government and also by the Central Government from time to time. However, the district administration is not autonomous in framing its policies but acts as the agent or representative of the State Government at the local level.

Public Administration performs functions, which are vital to citizen's lives such as maintenance of law and order, supply of essential commodities, provision of housing and sustainable livelihoods. In India, efficiency of the administration means in effect the efficacy of the district administration, because it is the district administration that comes into direct contact with the people. As the captain of the team of district officials, the collector has to coordinate the different departmental units to implement government policies and programmes as effectively as possible.

Currently we have 712 districts in India. The formation or reorganization of a new district is the subject matter of state administration.

5.1 District Administration: Functions and Role

Since the British period, the pivot of administration was the district and the principal task of the district administration was the maintenance of law and order and the collection of revenues.

The district is further divided into levels at division, sub-division, tehsil, pargana and village. Mainly the structure of administration at the district level consists of district (as a whole), sub-division (revenue division), tehsil (consisting of 200 – 600 villages), pargana (a circle in Punjab and Maarashtra, pargana in Uttar Pradesh and firka in Tamil Nadu) and village (lowest unit for all administrative and fiscal purposes). The representative of the government in the village is the patwari (a government official who keeps records regarding the ownership of land) who is considered to be 'eyes and ears' of the collector. He holds an important position in the lower level of bureaucracy. The DC through the Zila Parishads, blocks and gram panchayats carries out development programmes.

In addition to the DC, there are many other functionaries at the district level which include Superintendent of Police (SP), chief medical officer, district and sessions judge, executive engineer, district education officer; district food and supply officer, district social welfare officer; district development officer (DDO) and a host of other officers. These officers keep the DC informed of their activities and report any serious matters connected with law and order to him.

After Independence, the district administration has undergone a radical change and consequently, the structure and tasks of district administration have also correspondingly changed. The two major factors responsible for the change are democracy and development, which were the declared goals of governance in post- Independent India.

The goal of every successive government in post-Independent India has been to bring about improvement in the standards of living of the people. The Collector today is more a servant of the public than a representative of the government as in the colonial past and the main focus of attention has shifted from law and order (regulatory) to the welfare (development administration) of the people.

The office of the District Collector admirably survived the changing times: from colonialism to Independence, the planning era, and beyond to the post-globalized era today. Since Independence, his role has become increasingly versatile. The main factors that influence the role of the Collector in India today are supremacy of the Constitution, democratic practice and precedents, attempts at decentralization, increased developmental responsibilities of different political parties ruling in the States, changing Centre-State relations, rise of new social movements and civil society activism in post-globalized India.

The Collector belongs to the Indian Administrative Service and is appointed under the Land Revenue Code and vested with powers under the various Central and State laws either by express provisions or by delegation. He is allotted a State cadre in accordance with the existing scheme of the IAS. He is known by various names —the District Collector, District Officer, District Magistrate or the Deputy Commissioner in some states. The IAS consists of direct recruits and those promoted from the State Civil Services.

The social composition of the IAS also underwent a change over the years. Earlier the Collectors belonged to the upper strata of society, now, due to the spread of education and reservation of seats, a more egalitarian composition has emerged. Some of the Collectors belong to the low-income groups and hence, a greater degree of empathy and understanding for the underprivileged sections could be expected of them. It is this change in the composition of the IAS, which has the greatest potential for the eventual democratization of the civil service ethos.

While the mindset of the bureaucracy towards the public underwent a change with the ushering in of democracy, changing political and administrative realities also changed the position of the Collector. The emergence of technical departments like labour, agriculture, cooperatives, etc., together with a host of executive officers who man these departments led to a perceptible decline in the Collector's generalist authority. Some of the technical departments are headed by specialists and are relatively independent of the Collector. Democratic decentralization as it emerged after 1992 has also curtailed his powers. The Zila Parishads, particularly, have emerged as separate centres of power, largely independent of the Collector after the passage of the 73rd Amendment to the Constitution.

Several other factors such as the Collector being overworked, frequent breakdown of law and order machinery, large size of the districts, problems of coordination with the police, changes in revenue administration besides the presence of technical departments with specialist heads also play a role in determining the extent of the shrinkage in his position. However/it can be said that though his influence is waning, his area of functions have not correspondingly been reduced. He is the most important functionary at the apex of the district administration. However, his functions change in relative importance as well as in scale from state to state depending on the administrative ethos and the politico-administrative culture of that state.

Basically, he has three major functions namely revenue, magisterial and developmental.

Revenue Functions

This is still the primary task of the Collector. As the head of the revenue administration of the district, his foremost task is the assessment and collection of land revenue. Taxes due to the government may be of several types, such as irrigation dues, income-tax dues, agricultural dues, canal dues or *taqavi* loans.

The irrigation department makes out demand lists of irrigation dues each season and sends them to the Collector who is then responsible for the recovery of these loans. Although income tax is in the Central List, collection of arrears is yet another responsibility of the Collector. Others include court fees payable in connection with various judicial proceedings, taxes levied in the shape of revenue stamps on documents such as sale and transfer deeds, agreements of various kinds and other receipts. Excise duties on various commodities such as liquor, drugs, petrol, etc., are levied by the District Excise Officer working under the Collector.

Agricultural loans (taqavi or tagai) are distributed by the Collector and his staff, relief works are taken up in the district, seeds distributed, cattle and agricultural implements supplied, land revenue and rents remitted or suspended.

Land acquisition is another major responsibility of the Collector. Due to various development projects, housing schemes, slum clearance, etc., land has to be acquired for public purposes. The Collector is responsible for this acquisition. The district treasury comes under the control of the Collector. The Collector is responsible for general supervision, physical verification at regular intervals, checking, certifying and communicating the exact balances as found to exist directly to the Accountant General at his inspection.

In addition, an important function as a revenue officer is the preparation as well as maintenance of land records. This includes survey of land and settlement operations, and execution of land reform laws. He is the manager of government estates in the district, government land, forests, waterways, etc. Lastly, he also hears appeals in revenue cases against the orders of the lower courts.

The revenue work is a colossal task in itself and, therefore, the Collector has a whole hierarchy of staff to assist him. The general pattern in most of the states is that there are Sub-Divisional Officers, Naibs, Tehsildars, Patwaris, Kanungos and Girdawars.

Magisterial Functions

In his capacity as a District Magistrate (DM), he is responsible for the maintenance of law and order in his district. His position in this context assumes greater significance looking into the social political and communal tensions that may threaten the law and order situation in a district. Terrorism, communalism, Naxalism, smuggling and other economic offences have often been additional burdens.

Three elements are involved here —the police, the judiciary and the jails. The police force in the district, with the Superintendent of Police (SP) at its head, is kept under the control and supervision of the DM. Although the actual internal administration of the police is discharged through its own departmental line and, for purposes of disciplinary and technical supervision, the SP is responsible to the Director General of Police, the operational control of the police force comes under the direct charge of the DM.

In the 1970s, a debate was generated which relates to the relationship between the SP and the DM. The problem is how to reconcile the general supervision exercised by the Collector with the freedom required by the SP in his day-to-day working.

Relationship with Police

Relationship between the DM and the district SP has always been problematic. After Independence, the police has resented its subordinate role in matters of law and order administration with respect to the DM. The SP in practice is the head of criminal administration and the real head of the police force in the district. A practice has been evolved by which the DM and the SP submit joint report on incidents of police firing and other matters affecting law and order.

Police excesses are increasingly becoming a source of embarrassment to governments. Senior police personnel are sometime unable to impose discipline and the DM has to bear the brunt of lapses of the police. There are public attacks on the police for its excesses and, on most occasions, the government parries the problem by holding inquiries. But there is no doubt that there is little control of the DM over the police. The senior police officers, such as IG, DIG and SSP, have started resenting the authority of the DM in law and order matters. After the autonomy of the police in the district was accepted by the government, the subordinate staff in the police force started taking advantage of the politician-criminal nexus and challenged, in practice, the authority of their own superiors.

For example often after clash between two communities the DM of an area has used Section 144 of Code of Criminal Procedure prohibiting unlawful assembly of people and carrying of weapons in order to restore normalcy.

Today, tensions can be generated when supervision could be mistaken for interference. In metropolitan cities like Kolkata, Mumbai, Delhi and Chennai, since 1978, the responsibility for law and order vests with the Police Commissioner and the DM has no say in this regard.

The Directive Principles of State Policy, as prescribed by Article 50 of the Constitution, separates the judiciary from the executive. Due to this separation, the entire range of judicial proceedings, civil as well as criminal, is now the sole responsibility of the judiciary under the control of the High Court of the state. The judges hear appeals against the magistracy, including the DM. A verdict or judgment by the DM is in most cases appealable to the district judge. There we have the supremacy of law.

The DM acts in many ways as an agent of the judiciary. The execution of writs of the civil and criminal courts, including criminal writs from courts outside the district, is normally done through the magisterial element of the district administration. He can hear cases under the "preventive" section of the Code of Criminal Procedure and exercise powers under Section 144 in case of disturbance to peace within his jurisdiction. He supervises the subordinate magistracy, orders magisterial postings during festivals and has powers under several acts like Trade Mark Act, Sugar Factories Control Act, Entertainment Tax Act, Press Act, etc. The responsibility for the speedy disposal of cases rests with the Sessions Judge.

The district jail is under the general control of the DM. He can visit the jail from time to time to see that all is well and ensure the expeditious disposal of cases of under trial prisoners. He deals with problems such as the grant of superior classes to prisoners, premature release of prisoners, release of prisoners on parole, mercy petition of prisoners, etc.

Developmental Role

Formerly, the District Collector's office used to be the coordinating agency in overall charge of every important official activity in the district. After Independence, several departments were set up at the district level. Some of these are technical in nature and headed by specialists. Some such departments are public health, public works, agriculture, irrigation and education. The problem is that, although these departments function in the district, they are not under the supervision of the Collector. They are, administratively and technically, responsible to their respective heads of departments in the state secretariat. That problem becomes serious in view of the fact that several departmental agencies, with their own bureaucratic and specialist hierarchies, have been made in charge of development activities. These departments have their own programmes of development, which they conduct on their own without the interference of the Collector. This has weakened the Collector's role as a coordinating agency. The need to strengthen his role in this context is particularly strong because on this role depends the success of district planning considerably. As all plans take the district as the major operational unit, the coordinating role of the Collector becomes vital in ensuring that the various departments do not work at cross-purposes During emergencies and crises, the Collector's effectiveness and versatility is tested severely, e.g. during floods, he has to organize rescue operations, take steps to check epidemics, call for the army for help and supply food items. During external aggression, he is armed with several powers under the Defence of India Rules. The Collector enforces civil defence measures, is responsible for the protection of vital installations, and performs a host of other crucial functions.

The developmental role of the Collector became a focal point after the initiation of development planning in India. It was felt that the great influence that the Collector wielded in the district should be harnessed to the task of development. Rural development was an essential precondition for the establishment of a welfare state and several programmes for the benefit of the poor beginning with the Community Development Programme in 1952 were introduced. In the 1960s, several schemes of rural development were started. These related to health, education, employment, and improvement of housing conditions and some special programmes for rural women, children and youth. These programmes aimed at eradicating poverty and improving the living standards of the poor.

In this task of development, the emphasis was on his leadership role in the extension and development activity. It may be mentioned here that the situation is not the same in all states. The Collector, as the District Development Officer, must see that:

1. Technical assistance is made available to extension officers by the concerned departments of the State Government;
2. Adequate precaution of loans advanced by the State Government to Panchayat Samitis;
3. Panchayats and Panchayat Samitis are provided with necessary assistance in the early recovery of their dues, whether as tax or on account of loans; and
4. Whether priorities as fixed in the plans are being adhered to and the general pattern of work is in conformity with the policies laid down by the State or Central Government.

The developmental role of the Collector is evidenced in his position as the ex-officio chairman of the District Rural Development Agency (DRDA). This is a society registered under the Indian Societies Registration Act and is responsible for the implementation of rural development programmes. Several types of schemes are implemented by DRDA under the broad framework of the Integrated Rural Development Programme (IRDP). Firstly, there are the area-based schemes such as Desert Development Programme (DDP) and the Drought Prone Area Programme (DPAP). Secondly, there are individual beneficiary schemes. Some of them aim at the benefit of the poorest of the poor, some such as Training the Rural Youth for Self Employment (TRYSEM) and the National Rural Employment Programme (NREP) aim at providing more employment to the rural youth. Others such as Development of Women and Children in Rural Areas (DWCRA) aim at the welfare of women alone. Lastly, there are schemes such as the Samagra Gram Vikas Programme and various schemes for tribal development, which are also area based.

The Collector, with the assistance of the district-level staff, is responsible for the implementation of these schemes. He also performs developmental roles in his formal capacity as the head of the District Industries Centre, chairman of the district-level Bankers Coordination Committee, Chairman of the City Monitoring Committee, etc.

The role of the Collector at the district level in rural development has to be viewed in terms of his position in and relationship with the Zila Parishad, Panchayat Samitis and Gram Panchayats. It was suggested that the Collector be made the chairman of the Zila Parishad. The contention behind this was that the Collector, by virtue of his eminent position and authority in the district, could give guidance to the Zila Parishad. Unfortunately, it did not notice any contradictions that would arise, if the Collector were to head an elective institutional setup.

There emerged different patterns of relations between the Zila Parishad and the Collector. In some states, the Collector was made the chairman and the member of the Zila Parishad; in some he was a member of the Zila Parishad and chairman of certain committees. In Rajasthan, Orissa and Himachal Pradesh, the Collector is a member of the Zila Parishad (in Rajasthan he has no voting right) and chairman of several standing committees whereby he exercises considerable authority. Lastly, in some states, such as in Maharashtra and West Bengal, he is excluded from the Zila Parishad and he only has some powers pertaining to general supervision and control.

Practical experience also shows that it is not advisable to keep the Collector out of the Parishad and out of development activities. Many State Governments had tried to dispense with the services of the Collector in the field of development but he bounced back, time and again, on the development scene. However, the Constitutional enactments on Panchayati Raj by various states in 1993 and early 1994 have in any case reduced the burden of the Collector with regard to development activities.

Miscellaneous Functions of the Collector

A few other important functions of the Collector are given below:

- Functions as the District Census Officer responsible for the conduct of census operations once in 10 years.
- Acts as the Chief Returning Officer for elections to Parliamentary and State Legislative Assembly constituencies and coordinates the election work at the district.
- Supervises the working of the municipalities in the district.
- Ensures that there is no shortage of essential commodities and food supplies.
- Undertakes regular tours of the district, meeting people, and generally acting as the intermediary between the government and the people.

Another reason for the aforementioned development could be the gradual process in the form of assertion of people's will. But in the post-Independence period, as in the past, the approach adopted was paternalistic in nature. The position of the District Magistrate could only be restored in case of its reinforcement of democratic ethos, which paved the way for responsiveness. Another feature which reinforced this kind of thinking was the need felt for planning from below, in which the institutions at the grassroots have an important place. Thus, it was realized that PRIs would help facilitate the smooth process of district administration, of course under the Collector's leadership.

Over the years, development administration has acquired deep roots, as opposed to traditional administration. The roles of the Collector and the DM have also undergone a huge change. Although strong arguments were advanced for delinking him from development, his eminent position could not really be challenged.

5.2 The District Collector in Governance Today: Challenges

The post of District Collector (DC) has been the most important feature of field administration in India for the last 200 years. The role and responsibility of DC has undergone considerable changes since the adoption of the Indian Constitution on January 26, 1950. The DC assumed the role of social benefactor and nation-builder apart from regulator of peace and order and collector of revenue. However, these days the role is more of a facilitator and a development agent rather than that of a mere revenue collector. It is clear that in future the role of the Collector has to go beyond that of a "good administrator" in the traditional sense to include the requisite skills and motivation required to be a catalyst of development activities at the district level.

Despite differences in the actual working of Collectors in different parts of the country, and the changes in their roles and functions over a period of time, the Collector's role is still considered the most important and challenging at the cutting- edge level of governance, where societal expectations from his post are still very high and demanding.

A present day DC faces many challenges in discharging his duties through independent decision-making based on equity, fairness and rule of law. His decisions are often influenced by the agenda of the political bosses, and coalition governments have contributed in making the local leaders rather powerful and important players in the governance process. Untimely transfer of government officials is used as a threat to ensure compliance. The local MLA has become a super local administrator with authority to direct local officers, not excluding the DM. Good governance has become a casualty of political interference and bureaucratic pliability. Politicians and people perceive bureaucracy as inflexible, inward-looking, and insensitive to policy outcomes. Bureaucrats lampoon politicians as short-sighted, partisan, power-hungry and corrupt. In such an atmosphere, it is futile to expect that civil servants would all remain committed to the cause they were meant to serve with diligence, objectivity and impartiality.

A democracy is run by a politico-administrative regime. Political interference and patronage should be reduced and civil servants enjoying it or striving to acquire it should be isolated. The topmost priority has to be to insulate government servants from political interference. Objectivity and transparency in recruitment, postings, transfers and disciplinary action, must be the pre-requisites of good personnel administration. Likewise, it is important to link promotion to performance. The Second Administrative Reforms Commission has made a number of good suggestions in this regard. The recent government directive to all administrators to act only on written orders is a good step to insulate top civil servants from the tyranny of oral "directives" from political bosses.

India is a country where 65% of people still live in rural areas. Unless we reform governance from the village level upwards, there can be no real reform at the national level. Apart from the maintenance of law and order, district planning is an equally important part of the work of a DC. Today socio-economic planning has to take into account the fast changing social circumstances. We had a major shift in administration through the 73rd and 74th Constitutional Amendments. Though as per the new administrative and development environment, PRIs/ULBs are the third tier of government, they do not totally remove the Collector's responsibility in matters of local development. The role of the Collector has only been transformed into a more powerful one of facilitator and a person who is responsible for intersectoral coordination of various activities. It is incumbent upon the DC to work in tandem and with dedication with all the three tiers of public representatives. They must learn to win the admiration and respect of various PRI representatives first before being able to guide them.

Over the last decade, the tenure of a DC in the district has been reduced significantly. The situation has become so bad that some of the DCs have had less than three months' tenure and often the average tenure is less than a year. Considering the variety of tasks and responsibilities of a DC, it is an injustice to the local population to appoint their chief executive for such short tenures. Frequent transfers demoralize officers, whereby motivation and commitment levels drop drastically. To check the above anomaly, there are suggestions for a guaranteed tenure for every post. For promotion and selection, separate bodies should be set up and any rejection of their recommendations should be put in the public domain.

The enactment of the Right to Information Act (RTI), 2005, heralded a new era of hope for an open, transparent and accountable governance system in India. It marks the beginning of a new set of relationships between the government and the various segments of the society. RTI can prove to be a 'boon' or a 'bane' depending on how it is implemented at the district and lower levels of administration. Deepening the reach, utility and impact of RTI becomes all the more challenging at the cutting-edge levels of governance.

Good governance is not merely about more efficient management of organizations, it is also about humane and ethical management. DCs should treat spreading of social justice as their personal obligation to society. Such a commitment is vital to the success of our strategy of promoting "Inclusive Growth". As government moves away from running industries and controlling economic activity, to managing public service delivery, it must pay greater attention to improving its human face. In sectors like education, health and employment generation, the challenge is one of effective and equitable delivery of public services. We must also use the Public Private Partnerships (PPP), in the social sector to reach the needy and the vulnerable.

The plurality of organizations and departments at the district level has created problems. There is the Collector, rural development agencies, the police, revenue officers, and the judiciary—all of whom should ideally function as a team. District administration, in order to be effective, must have a unity of purpose and singularity of approach which is often found missing.

Though the Collector's role in the development process has been over-emphasized, in recent years, we have seen that due to the frequent breakdown in the law and order situation in the districts, the Collector has less and less time for development administration. Besides, his role in this sphere is being reduced in a number of states and the Chief Executive Officer of the Zila Parishad is emerging as the predominant functionary in development administration. The Panchayati Raj Acts of 1993 and 1994 of various states are clearly indicative of the diminishing role of the Collector in development administration.

Besides, his judicial functions have been transferred to the judicial officers and, time and again, the police urge that law and order is its prerogative. In some states like Bihar, his revenue functions are being transferred to Panchayats.

Despite the recent measures to reduce the responsibilities of the DC, this key actor of Indian administration continues to suffer from role-overload as never before. His knowledge, skill sets and practical competence in the ultimate help him to strike a balance among his multifarious responsibilities. A DC's position has also undergone many changes after the advent of globalization and decentralization.

In the age of globalization, the role of the state is being redefined in many sectors. In many manufacturing and service sectors the government is moving from being a provider of goods and services to being a regulator and facilitator ensuring fair play and adherence to standards of integrity and efficiency. The objective of welfare administration has also shifted from welfare maximization to people empowerment through a rights-based approach. At the district level, the DC is expected to act as a facilitator in the developmental process rather than being a director and regulator reminiscent of the pre-globalized era. In the redefined role of the Government, the cutting edge of a Government function is at the district and lower levels and the efficiency of district administration determines the effectiveness of the policies of the Government, e.g. NREGA initiated by the Central Government has become successful in some states whereas it has failed to achieve the desired results in many other states.

The Collector is an intersectoral functionary who is the source of strength for local administration and whose objectives have changed in the wake of the passage of the 73rd and the 74th amendments. The role of the collector has been transformed into a more powerful one of coordinator, facilitator and a person who is responsible for intersectoral coordination of various activities that characterize the work of our grass roots administration. The test of a good administrator is his ability to work with the people and not above them—to inspire people and not regulate their affairs, to release their latent creativity and not restrict their freedom. Decentralization is not merely a political imperative but as much a managerial necessity given the large size of population in our states. Even a district in our country is similar to a province in some countries. It is therefore a managerial imperative to strengthen the middle management level in our country system for effective delivery of public services and this has to be at the level of a collector. Due to decentralization, the traditional forms of administrative structures at the local level have been expanded to include NGOs, civil societies, pressure groups, markets and the people themselves. In this changing scenario, the DC has to be a coordinator of and facilitator between these agencies to ensure overall development.

India is a country that is characterized by imbalanced development between the regions and the people. The major challenge for the district administration is to ensure faster economic growth and improvement of human development indicators at the district level. In order to be ethically neutral in the context of inequality, district administration has to be partisan—partisan towards the poor, the weaker sections, the minorities, women, scheduled castes and tribes, and all such disadvantaged people who need the support of district administration. For the process of globalization to be successful, it has to be inclusive. This will mean every section of society must be able to benefit from the process of reform. It requires immediate attention to issues like agriculture, rural development, health, education, infrastructure, with particular focus on the weaker sections ensuring communal harmony at all costs. Globalization has opened new opportunities for the people and the district administrator has to identify the areas of strength in the district and market them effectively to benefit from the globalization process. District administration can reduce the influence of intermediaries between local producers and consumers and the international market through the use of computers and the Internet.

There are various factors responsible for the decline in authority and increase in responsibility of the DC. The judicial power available with erstwhile IAS officers are gone with the separation of judicial and executive functions as per the revised Criminal Procedure Code in 1973. The developmental authority of the Collector has been taken over by other district bodies like the DRDA. The Zila Parishads, Panchayat Samitis and Gram Panchayats are now exercising more important roles in sanctioning funds in the district which are headed by political representatives. In NREGA the real authority is with the Gram Sabha and the Panchayats. In sanctioning district planning funds (under schemes like Sectoral Decentralized Planning, Backward Area Sub-Plan, etc.,) the District Level Planning and Development Committees are supposed to sanction the funds. Now the Gram Sabhas select the BPL and Indira Awas Yojna beneficiaries. Similarly, in many of the District Level Coordination and

Monitoring Committees like District Twenty Point Programme Committee, District Grievances Committee, etc., political representatives head the Committees. Unlike the past when there were only the MPs, Ministers and MLAs wielding political authority in the district, now there are additional representatives of the Zila Parishad, Panchayat Samiti, Gram Panchayats, non-official members of various State/District level Committees, etc., with varying degrees of authority. The district officer has to deal with all the 'new' bosses with whom he must discuss, and at times persuade or cajole to get that done. Apart from the vertical commands of the administrative hierarchy, there are the additional-commands of the elected representatives. The local pressure groups also interfere and assert their authority which has eroded the finality of the decision of the officer on the field. Panchayati Raj has led to the emergence of a new class of district level politicians who have come to command considerable patronage and power, over the State Government, thus superseding the position of the DC in the state administrative system.

But this declining position of the DC does not automatically mean a decline in his responsibility or answerability. The DC is now more of a coordinator and leader of the team who is accountable for almost everything happening in the district. As the local politicians realize the importance of good governance for winning elections, the political masters look upon the DCs for effective public service delivery but without assigning too much power to them. For an ordinary citizen, it is the DC who is considered as a messiah for resolving all his grievances even though they might pertain to different departments—whether directly under the control of the Collector (e.g. Revenue) or not (e.g. PWD). In all the spheres where the power/authority to sanction funds/schemes have been formally transferred to other authorities (like PRIs/Gram Sabhas) even now the DC is responsible for leading the development story and is responsible both for good and bad performances especially in cases where the PRI representatives behave in a partisan way.

Moreover, some additional responsibilities have been added in the last decade or so to the already overloaded schedule of the DC as the chairperson of various new Committees of line departments, like ATMA (of Agriculture Department), Horticulture Technology Mission (of Horticulture Development), NRHM (of Health Department), etc. Though in charge of these programmes, the Collector has no formal disciplinary authority over the line department officials and has only coordinating or persuasive authority to get work done. The prevailing system of making the head of the office solely responsible for any failure is also not always fair because the lower order officials do not have adequate powers though they might actually be blamed for implementation failures at the grass roots.

Besides, the concentrated command and authority of an IAS officer has decreased gradually. The DM has been increasingly feeling that though he is responsible for law and order, he is not in actual command of the police. Moreover, other factors have also enhanced the accountability and responsiveness of the DC in the present governance set-up—like increasingly proactive judicial activism, growing prevalence of citizens' charters, enhanced e-governance, and a probing media. Similarly, the Right to Information Act has added newer responsibilities.

However, the above description does not mean that the above trends are necessarily problematic in making bureaucracies work or that increased accountability leads to implementation paralysis. They are part and parcel of the changing nature of administrative governance in the 21st century. There has to be a proper match between the authority and responsibility of a DC to enable him to discharge his duties efficiently, effectively and accountably without fear, favour or bias.

The recommendations from the 2nd ARC Report are extremely important and pertinent. The relevant extracts are as follows:

5.3 2nd ARC-15th Report (extracts): Redefining the Collector's Role

The Collector needs to focus on core functions —land and revenue, law and order, public distribution and civil supplies.

The commission reiterates its recommendations regarding the Land Title Management System made in its eleventh Report on e-governance. It should be one of the primary duties of the DC to perform the task envisaged in the aforesaid recommendations. There is a need to strengthen the compliance machinery at the district level to enforce provisions of the RTI Act and to reduce the element of delay and subjectivity in the functioning of lower level formations of the government. This should be done by creating a special RTI Cell in the office of the Collector, whose functions should be reviewed by the Collector at regular periods.

Officers may be posted as DM early in their career, but in complex and problem-prone districts an IAS officer should be posted as DM only on completion of 10-12 years of service. Steps should be taken to ensure that the Collector plays an effective coordination role in activities and programmes of other departments at the district level.

Modernizing the Office of the DC

The following steps should be taken to modernize the office of the DC:-

1. Management Information System (MIS) should be set-up in the office of the Collector for effective monitoring and evaluation of programmes/projects under his direct control.
2. A computerized District Grievance Cell should also be set up in the Collectorate.
3. An exclusive Vigilance Cell should be set up at the district level under an overall supervision of the DC.
4. A forum should be established at the district level to interact with civil society groups and media on important public issues.
5. Immediate steps should be taken to introduce process re-engineering and increased use of information technology.

Innovations and best practice initiated by officers should be documented adequately and institutionalized through changes in rules/laws wherever required.

District Administration: Functional and Structural Reforms

There should be integrated governing structure at the district level in the form of the "District Council" with representation from both urban and rural areas. The Council will act as the "District Government".

The DC should have a dual role in this government structure. He should work as the Chief Officer of the District Council and should be fully accountable to the District Council on all local matters. The District Officer would also be fully accountable so the State Government on all regulatory/ other matters to be delegated to the District Government.

Conclusion

Why District Administration Is Still So Crucial?

The district has been a basic and crucial territorial administrative unit in India throughout its administrative history. It assumed great significance during British times and has continued to remain important. The Deputy Commissioner or District Collector selected from the IAS cadre is the administrative head at the district level. Over the last century the role of the DC has changed considerably and this has most recently been documented by the Second Administrative Reforms Commission (SARC) (GoI, 2009, pp. 60-63) From revenue collection and maintenance of law and order under the British regime, the DC's powers have expanded manifold in Independent India, especially in the area of implementation of various rural development programmes. With the formal introduction of Panchayati Raj system in the 1950s and the Constitutional status given to Panchayati Raj Institutions (PRI) in 1993, the importance of DC was expected to subside. Contrary to expectations, the DC found a new role as a link between the PRIs and the state, alongside discharging his traditional duties. If the recommendations of the ARC-II are heeded its powers will only grow further with the formation of 'district government', with the DC as the chief of a council involving PRIs (Recommendation 13 in GoI 2009). Thus while new and smaller states have the potential to bring in more funds from the Centre, the efficiency of district administration is also important to ensure that the funds are well implemented at the district and sub-district levels.

There has been a continuous increase in the number of districts in Independent India due to political and administrative reasons. *The number of districts doubled from just over 300 in 1951 to 640 on January 1, 2010 to 712 in 2019.* 'Heavy' states like Delhi formed new districts to reduce the population served by each district while 'remote' states like Arunachal Pradesh formed new districts to reduce the size of the area administered by each district. Many districts were formed purely on political considerations.

The proponents of small districts argue that smaller district size reduces the workload of district administration enabling it to focus on its core responsibilities, thus improving governance and development. Assessing the size-development relationship is tough due to limited uniform data available on development indicators. Poverty estimates from the National Sample Survey Data are computed primarily at the state level. Some states have their own human development reports with district rankings according to HDI scores but one cannot compare district HDI scores across states. The Backward Regions Grant Fund (BRGF) set up in 2007 listed 250 districts as backward primarily on agricultural productivity, health, educational and physical infrastructure parameters. We can use Census 2011 details on district area, population and urbanization statistics for only 640 districts. The 250 backward districts of 2007 correspond to 246 backward districts in 2001 as some new districts were created in between, which we adjust with the parent districts. Delhi, Goa and the Union Territories have no backward districts.

District size does matter, especially in terms of area size. Large area districts are difficult to administer and hamper governance and development. Creating smaller districts from the large area districts is then, a policy option. While many have argued in favour of status-quo as bigger districts could be suitably managed by bigger staff and that there was a cost attached with new district creation, the consensus view suggests that new districts could be created when the size becomes 'unwieldy'.

District administration is and will remain the pivot around which our entire administrative system moves and rests. Therefore, strengthening district administration along region-specific needs is absolutely mandatory for administrative reforms to succeed. Some creative innovations have been done in certain states and the Second Administrative Reforms Commission's suggestions can also act as a catalyst for future reform in different states of India.

Suggested Readings

Dhariwal, Suneel and M. C. Sharma (eds.), *District level Administration and Role of Collector,* Jaipur, Alekh Publishers, 2007.

Hooja, Rakesh and Sunil Dutt (eds.), *District Administration: Redefining the development role,* New Delhi, Kanishka Publishers, 2008.

Nawani, N. P., *District Administration — Theory and Practice,* Publication Division Ministry of Information and Broadcasting, GOI, 2006.

State and District Administration, 15th Report of the Second Administrative Reforms Commission, Department of Administrative Reforms and Public Grievances in the Ministry of Personnel, Public Grievances and Pension, 2009

Tummala, K. K., *Public Administration in India,* Delhi, Allied Publishers Limited, 1996

OOO

Chapter Six

Rural Local Government

Introduction

One of the key challenges of good governance in today's India lies in the strengthening of local governments in both rural and urban areas. While we have averaged over 6% growth rate in the last two decades, the vast majority of our population, still have minimal or no access to education, health services, clean drinking water, adequate nutrition and electricity. Effective and empowered local governments, comprising panchayats, municipalities, autonomous district and regional councils and other similar structures of governance could truly build up an entire edifice of Indian democracy which would bring the State and the citizen closer through greater accountability in the delivery of public services at the local level.

Before or after Independence, Mahatma Gandhi's vision of a direct democracy through self-sufficient autonomous village republics did not find many supporters (e.g. the Chairman of the Drafting Committee of our Constitution Dr. B.R. Ambedkar's suspicion of traditional panchayats is well known). Had it not been for the president of the Constituent Assembly, Dr. Rajendra Prasad, Article 40 would not have been inserted in the Indian Constitution. Rajendra Prasad wanted a mention of Panchayats in the Constitution and consequently an amendment proposed by the well-known Gandhian K. Santhanam led to the insertion of Article 40 in the Directive Principles of State Policy, which stated that the State shall take steps to organize village panchayats and endow them with such power and authority as may be necessary to enable them to function as units of self-government.

The next two decades registered uneven progress in decentralization, which the report of the Committee on Panchayati Raj Institutions 1978 (the Ashoka Mehta Committee) categorized into three phases: those of ascendancy (1959-64), stagnation (1965-69) and decline (1969-71). The Ashok Mehta Committee was the first to address the issue of strengthening the panchayats across the country. It stated that panchayats should emerge as a system of democratic local government, discharging regulatory developmental and municipal functions. As a means, the Committee said that panchayats would continue to discharge obligations entrusted to it by the National and State Governments in spheres not yet transferred to its exclusive jurisdiction. The committee concurred with the predominant view of those who responded to its call for suggestions and recommended constitutional status to be given to the panchayats. In 1989, Rajiv Gandhi suggested the constitutionalisation of local governments as a key to the strengthening of democracy at the grass roots.

The 73rd and 74th amendments could be piloted through the Union legislature by a minority government largely because of the recommendations of a Joint Select Committee before its introduction in Parliament. These amendments brought about some standardization particularly with respect to the establishment of rural LGs at three levels: conduct of regular elections, reservation of seats and the establishment of independent authorities mandated in the amendments such as the State finance and election commissions.

6.1 The Constitutional Setting and the 73rd Amendment

Until the passage of the 73rd and 74th constitutional amendments, the states were the only subnational units officially recognized by the Indian Constitution. The Constitution grants individual states considerable legislative autonomy. Schedule Seven of the Constitution explicitly demarcates the respective legislative domains of the State legislatures and the national parliament. The functional areas over which the national parliament has exclusive domain are specified in List I, also called the "Union List". Items on this list include among other things, defense, foreign affairs, currency, income taxes, interstate commerce, and key infrastructure. On the other hand, State legislatures have exclusive authority to enact legislation dealing with the items in List II, known as the "State List". Included in this list are items such as law and order, public health, agriculture, wealth taxes, land tenure and land reforms, and most notably in the current context, functions of local governments. List III, the "Concurrent List" includes items such as electricity, newspapers, education, price controls, etc., over which the national parliament and the State legislatures share jurisdiction.

With local government being a State subject in Schedule Seven of the Constitution, any legislation reforming the structure of local government has to, ultimately, be enacted at the State level. The first task of the states was therefore to pass conformity acts, which either introduced new legislation or amended existing legislation, to bring the State laws into line with the provisions of the amendment. Under the amendments, states had a year, from the date the amendment went into effect, to do so.

Of the mandatory provisions of the Panchayati Raj Act, the most critical are those that strengthen the structure of representative democracy and political representation at the local level.

The key mandatory provisions are:

- The establishment in every state (except those with populations below 2 million) of rural local bodies (panchayats) at the village, intermediate and district levels (Article 243B).
- Direct elections to all seats in the panchayats at all levels (Article 243C).
- Compulsory elections to panchayats every five years with the elections being held before the end of the term of the incumbent panchayat. In the event that a panchayat is dissolved prematurely, elections must be held within six months, with the newly elected members serving out the remainder of the five year term (Article 243E).
- Mandatory reservation of seats in all panchayats at all levels for Dalits and Adivasis in proportion to their share of the panchayat population (Article 243D).
- Mandatory reservation of one-third of all seats in all panchayats at all levels for women, with the reservation for women applying to the seats reserved for Dalits and Adivasis as well (Article 243D).

- Indirect elections to the position of panchayat chairperson at the intermediate and district levels (Article 243C).
- Mandatory reservation of the position of panchayat chairperson at all levels for Dalits and Adivasis in proportion to their share in the State population (Article 243D).
- Mandatory reservation of one-third of the positions of panchayat chairperson at all three levels for women (Article 243D).
- In addition, the act mandates the Constitution of two state-level commissions: an independent election commission to supervise and manage elections to local bodies, much as the Election Commission of India manages State assembly and parliamentary elections (Article 243K); and a State finance commission, established every five years, to review the financial position of local bodies and recommend the principles that should govern the allocation of funds and taxation authority to local bodies (Article 2431).

Among the *discretionary* provisions, the two central ones, which in the opinion of many observers lie at the core of the amendment, call upon the states to:

- Endow the Gram Sabha —the electorate of a village panchayat—with powers and functions at the village level (Article 243A).
- Devolve powers and authority to panchayats so as to enable them to function as institutions of self-government. In particular, the provision calls for devolution of powers and responsibilities for the preparation of plans and implementation of schemes for development and social justice dealing with an impressively wide range of items, which are listed in a new schedule, Schedule XI, of the Constitution (Article 243G).
- A further discretionary provision (Article 243H), authorizes States to pass legislation aimed at increasing the financial resources available to rural local bodies by increasing the latter[7] s statutory taxation powers and by providing for grants-in-aid from the State Government.

Two other points need to be mentioned. The first is that while, for the most part, the 74th Amendment Act deals with urban local bodies, a key article contained in that amendment applies to rural local bodies as well. The article in question, Article 243ZD, mandates the constitution of District Planning Committees to consolidate the plans prepared by both rural and urban local bodies.

The second point is that the provisions of the 73rd Amendment did not apply to what is known as Scheduled Areas, constitutionally recognized areas of the country with large Adivasi populations. The amendment did, however, contain a provision reserving the right of parliament to extend the amendments' provisions regarding local bodies to Scheduled Areas at a later date without the need for a further constitutional amendment. Parallel provisions regarding local governments in

Scheduled Areas were ultimately enacted through the Provisions of the Panchayats Act of 1996 (Extension to the Scheduled Areas).

6.2 Programme Implementation-Need for Grass-root Convergence

There is a marked shift in the Indian Government's approach towards development in the 21st century. Instead of relying on prosperity to enhance the living standards of citizens, the approach considers the acquisition of minimum levels of education, health, employment and nutrition as basic entitlements, and recognizes the key role of the State in providing them to every needy citizen in the country. In essence, the shift is towards universalization of rights and entitlements to all citizens.

There is also added emphasis on promoting balanced development so that all regions in the country have a fair opportunity to develop evenly. This equity- promoting role demands that greater resources be allocated to the backward regions and rural areas to remove gaps in the provision of basic services to equalize human development levels in all parts of the country. As a result, large investments will flow to those districts of the country which are classified as backward. Admittedly, these are the districts where it is difficult to implement development programmes effectively because of poor governance structures, low organizational capacity, weak infrastructure and unequal power structures. If the programmes can be implemented in these backward regions, with a modicum of success, it would usher in the mainstreaming of development in the poorest parts of the country. Therefore it comes as no surprise that the Naxalite prone districts, also known as the Red corridor of the Indian state, exemplify such backward districts.

There is also a fundamental change in how government programmes are funded and executed. Increasingly, key programmes are being funded by the Union Government and executed by State Governments. This ensures that on the one hand, no entitlement programme is made to suffer due to resource constraint and, on the other, funds are available with greater regularity to implementing districts, blocks and Panchayati Raj Institutions so that programme outcomes can be harmoniously achieved with local participation, ownership, initiative and supervision irrespective of diverse political regimes in different parts of the country.

Since these flagship programmes are bound by the common objective of delivering citizen entitlements on a universal scale, it is necessary that they converge at the grass roots and their individual planning systems are integrated harmoniously. Such integration would ensure common implementation framework for all the schemes.

Above all, well-coordinated administrative and institutional arrangements are essential for the success of these programmes. In their design, these programmes provide for a multi-tier structure of administrative and institutional arrangements for implementation and monitoring with specified roles and responsibilities. The agencies involved are the respective ministries of the Union Government, departments of the State Governments and the local governments. The pattern of implementation and monitoring is both elaborate and complex. The requirement for the successful execution of the programmes is both vertical coordination of different tiers of governments, and horizontal coordination across departments for execution of the programmes through the local government.

6.3 Extension of Panchayati Raj in Scheduled Areas (PESA-the Provisions of the Panchayats [Extension to the Scheduled Areas] Act)

Through an Act of Parliament passed in 1996, the provisions of the 73rd Amendment, with some modifications, were extended to the tribal areas under Schedule V in the States of Andhra Pradesh, Bihar, Gujarat, Himachal Pradesh, Maharashtra, Madhya Pradesh, Orissa and Rajasthan. Subsequently, Chhattisgarh and Jharkhand were constituted as separate States. Almost all of Chhatisgarh and Jharkhand continue to have Schedule V status.

The main constitutional issue is whether PESA 1996 is to be implemented as such in Schedule V areas or treated merely as enabling model legislation. The main objective of PESA was to enable tribal society to assume control over their livelihoods, conserve and manage natural resources and protect their traditional rights. All States have enacted legislation as provided for in the Central Act. Notwithstanding the legislation, the implementation Act states that much has been diluted at the cost of tribals. Critical issues such as access to natural resources, especially the definition and rights over minor forest products such as bamboo, remain unresolved and in general the intentions of the PESA have not been realized in any serious measure in any of the States with large tribal populations. Capacity building efforts aimed at Panchayati Raj Institutions (PRI) are especially weak in these States.

6.4 Role of Elected Women Representatives

Article 243 constitutes mandatory provisions regarding the constitution, composition, election procedures, resource allocation and functions of Panchayats and urban local bodies (ULB), some of which are nothing short of revolutionary, such as the reservation of elected positions for women, Scheduled Castes and Scheduled Tribes. Others, in combination, ensure their continued existence and provide safeguards against dissolution or supersession, assure independent elections by State Election Commissions and direct the allocation of resources by independent State Finance Commissions—in all, providing a secure foundation for their existence and functioning. The provision for reservation of seats for women, SC and ST representatives makes it even more representative of the general population than higher levels of governments have been so far.

The provisions that were left to the discretion of the State Governments, however, allow for a substantial variation in the structure and functioning. Important among them are the specifications for the links to be established (or not) between the three tiers of Panchayats, the extent of reservation for various groups in the positions of Chairpersons and Vice-Chairpersons, seat reservations for other backward castes, and most significantly, the powers, responsibilities and (concomitant) resources to be transferred to panchayats. Variation of these aspects across States results in very different patterns of functioning and outcomes in terms of both democratic participation and development. Moreover, the pace and trajectory of progress in realizing the full potential of the Constitutional provisions differs across States. A periodic stock-taking of the situation in different States and Union territories is therefore useful and necessary for further policy and action intervention on the part of both the Central and State Governments.

6.5 Centrally Sponsored Schemes (CSS) and Activity Mapping

A substantial portion of resources for local development is provided by the Central Government through its various Schemes, and in the last few years, a number of significant schemes have been introduced in the social sectors. These include, *inter alia*, the Mahatma Gandhi Rural Employment Guarantee Act, Sarva Shiksha Abhiyan, National Rural Health Mission, Central Rural Sanitation Programme which channel funds for employment, sectoral development and basic services in rural areas. The design of these programs, particularly the structure and procedures prescribed for implementation at the district level and below has important implications for the roles and functioning of local governments, particularly as they relate to some of the functions listed for transfer to Panchayats in the Eleventh Schedule. Therefore it may be necessary to investigate the design and functioning of some of the 'flagship' programs and assess the space and roles accorded to Panchayats and the implications for their identity as local governments.

The design of these schemes provides a varying degree in the nature of space for Panchayat involvement; MNREGA was found to have recourse to greatest reliance on Panchayats. The Panchayats have largely been involved in 'agency functions' of implementation; their roles and responsibilities in planning for these central schemes could be enlarged. The degree of involvement has varied based on the specifications available in the scheme guidelines as also the extent of devolution of functions, functionaries and funds the States have enacted.

Following a conference of Ministers of Panchayati Raj and Rural Development convened by the Ministry of Rural Development, GOI, a Committee had been set up to develop a framework that could provide guidance for detailed devolution of powers to Panchayats. One of the key recommendations of the Committee was a template for 'activity mapping', which yielded itself to breaking down subjects to activities and determining the level to which every activity could be devolved utilizing the principle of 'subsidiarity'. During subsequent consultations between Governments at the Centre and the States, the importance of adopting the activity mapping exercise had been stressed and mutually accepted. All States have, however, unilaterally determined paths for devolution of functions and funds. The Central Finance Commission awards have substantially bolstered the allocations to local governments. Most States have also received, and varyingly acted upon the recommendations of State Finance Commissions. As a result, there are increased resources available to Panchayats and some States like Punjab and Haryana have substantially increased the financial sanction limits for Panchayats. States such as Gujarat and Maharashtra have had a cadre of Panchayat Officials/functionaries (variously called) since more than three decades. Karnataka has created a cadre of technical personnel for Panchayats. Kerala has re-designated the chief functionaries at district and below as Secretaries of the corresponding Panchayats thereby ascribing executive status to its elected Panchayats. The matter of creating a cadre of technical service personnel is under active consideration in the Government of Rajasthan. Punjab and Haryana have reorganized their rural medical services, rural veterinary services, as also elementary school education systems. Himachal Pradesh has empanelled technical personnel on whom the Panchayats could draw upon. Andhra Pradesh is actively considering a similar arrangement in the State. Many States have also empowered the Panchayats with some controlling powers over functionaries working at their levels.

6.6 State Governments and PRIs

The States have to increase the share of transfers to PRIs from State Governments as "untied grants" by: (a) consolidating State Schemes with broad Rural Development objectives into "untied grants", as Kerala has done; (b) making these grants a share of State revenues, (c) explicitly defining (through State legislation) formulae to allocate grants to PRI levels; and (d) transfer collection of village taxes, such as land revenue and irrigation tax to the PRIs. The formula of transfer should not only give weightage to population and poverty but also to efficiency, for increasing the sources of revenues of PRIs through own and assigned taxes and increasing their capacity to collect.

State Governments should put in place and implement a comprehensive training and capacity-building programme for elected representatives of the local self- government institutions and Panchayati Raj Institutions. Such training programmes should preferably be completed with universal coverage within one year of the elections to these bodies. The Central Government should facilitate such programmes through monetary and other support.

The States could be afforded the option of doing away with one of the Panchayat levels, after the implications for efficiency, equity and participation have been studied.

Panchayats are often too large; the Kerala Panchayats cover about 23,000 people and the Orissa and West Bengal Panchayats some 15 to 20 villages. Smaller bodies need to be formed for operational purposes. It is suggested that for each function of the Gram Panchayat, the Gram Sabha be a forum where people can volunteer or be selected to be part of the Committee looking after a specific function, e.g. Health, Anganwadi, lights, water, etc. A member of the Gram Panchayat can be identified for each of these Committees for good quality service delivery that leads to development and excellence. This is absolutely necessary since every Gram Panchayat receives Rs. 25 lakh a year for development works.

6.7 Performance Across States

Most commentators would concur that it is difficult to generalize across states in an attempt to ascertain the impact of Panchayati Raj reforms. A small group of six states arc often identified as more progressive in implementing conformity legislation governing the flow of funds and transfer of powers to panchayats. They include states that have maintained functioning panchayat bodies since the 1950s, most notably Maharashtra and Gujarat, and others that have made steady progress in measures to strengthen panchayats such as Kerala, Karnataka, Madhya Pradesh, and West Bengal. At the other end of the spectrum are states where little progress has taken place over two decades, which results in poorly functioning and under-financed Panchayati Raj institutions. These include states such as Bihar, and Jammu and Kashmir, which delayed holding elections to panchayat bodies for many years, and Orissa and Uttar Pradesh, where political instability have undermined local bodies, despite some degree of policy commitment.

Commitment to deepening the reform process expressed through political will, supportive legislation, and State administrative support is an indispensable condition for progress and is present to varying degrees in the six leading states. Conducive structural conditions are also important for institutional reforms to succeed, and it is evident that a less obvious class and caste polarisation offers better conditions for Panchayati Raj institutions to function effectively.

The three states that introduced the most far-reaching reforms since the introduction of the constitutional amendments — Kerala, Madhya Pradesh and West Bengal —were controlled by political parties with a leadership that showed a strong commitment to empowering panchayats. In Kerala, the People's Planning Campaign was predicated on a high level of popular mobilization that was made possible by high levels of literacy and professional support, and a mass social movement. In Madhya Pradesh, the Congress government led by Chief Minister Digvijay Singh introduced a series of reforms to strengthen district governments and the role of Gram Sabhas in planning and priority setting. The Communist Party of India (CPM, [Marxist]) government in West Bengal consciously used Panchayati Raj as a means of to accomplish its land-reforms agenda and strengthen its political support in rural areas with a significant degree of success.

6.8 Political Decentralization and Democracy

Vastly increased numbers of elected representatives have provided new opportunities for political representation at the local level, especially for women and marginalized social groups. Rates of political participation have also increased, which is reflected in active campaigning (usually on a non-party basis for gram panchayats), high levels of voter turnout, and heightened engagement with local officials and elected representatives. This in turn has helped to invigorate local democracy.

The Gram Sabhas, however, continue to function imperfectly in most states since they have limited powers and only meet on ad hoc agenda, largely at the initiative of local bureaucrats, to ratify the beneficiaries for Central or State Government social sector programmes. Attendance in Gram Sabha meetings is generally poor as substantive issues are rarely discussed, with the result that they do not provide an effective platform for deliberation of local policy options and programme priorities. For these reasons popular oversight is weak and the accountability of elected representatives cannot be assured.

Constitutional provision for reserved seats for women and scheduled castes and tribes distinguishes the current phase of Panchayati Raj reforms from earlier initiatives. On the one hand, seat reservations have provided underprivileged groups with increased visibility and an opportunity to influence local affairs. There are many instances where women have managed to generate modest local development dividends by marshalling financial resources and lobbying bureaucrats and politicians at higher levels. On the other hand, elite dominance continues to prevail in most panchayats with the result that traditional caste leaders and landed elites dominate decision making by proxy or manipulation influencing decision making to control resources. Outspoken scheduled caste and female representatives have often had to contend with violence, ostracism or non-cooperation from dominant interests.

Evidence from West Bengal and Kerala indicate that rates of participation in local bodies have increased for women and scheduled castes and tribes, but, without a clear and visible impact on local expenditure priorities, service-delivery outcomes, or rates of poverty. In other states, seat reservations have increased formal representation in panchayat bodies for women and scheduled castes and tribes, but in the absence of comparative data the overall impact of affirmative action is difficult to discern. Women have made some headway in gram panchayats by using reserved seats as a vantage point to shape local development priorities. Scattered evidence suggests that individual women panchayat leaders have registered significant success in securing government resources for sanitation and street lighting (as health and safety issues are prioritized by women), local infrastructure in the form of village roads and community buildings (such as schools and childcare centres), and ensuring that public servants such as school teachers carry out their designated responsibilities. These modest but important gains demonstrate the ability of women to use the elected office for the benefit of the community and strengthen their legitimacy as elected representatives (Stephen and Sekaran 2001).

At the same time, elected women representatives often face considerable opposition in seeking to carry out the duties of office in a responsible manner from male relatives who resent their public role and from vested interests who are opposed to affirmative action. Intimidatory tactics and the lack of incentives and resources for effective development work dissuade many women from standing for elected office, especially in unreserved seats. (Vijayalakshmi and Chandrashekhar 2000).

To ascertain the impact of the Panchayati Raj reforms on scheduled castes and tribes is difficult in the absence of meticulous research. Seat reservations in proportion with their numbers in the population have provided men and women from scheduled castes and tribes a guaranteed level of representation and share of leadership positions. Some elected presidents from these communities have been able to use their new-found authority significantly by bringing in more funds and challenging caste discrimination in Panchayat matters. But high-caste leaders resent this intrusion on traditional patterns of leadership and have used a combination of threats and co-option to undermine the authority of panchayat representatives elected in reserved seats.

There are instances where scheduled caste leaders have been able to make effective use of these committees to block inappropriate decisions or challenge the authority of the dominant castes.

Available evidence indicates that the increased numerical presence of women and men from the scheduled castes and tribes in panchayat institutions have not automatically translated into sustained pro-poor development outcomes, at least not at a significant level. This tends to reflect the limited resources at the disposal of panchayats and the limited power they possess to determine local expenditure priorities. Moreover, the resources available for social welfare programmes are spread very thinly with the result that only a handful of individuals receive these benefits each year in the average gram panchayat. Without a much greater devolution of financial resources, the potential development impact of decentralization will remain limited; a marked effect on poverty levels at the local levels is therefore highly unlikely under such restrictive conditions. Similarly, the fact that health and education remain subject to highly centralized forms of provision means that elected representatives have little influence over service delivery at the local level.

6.9 Financial Devolution

Financial devolution has progressed to a very limited extent as resource flows are determined by the implementation guidelines for State and Central Government anti-poverty schemes. The scope for local revenue mobilization is very restricted that results in too much dependence on fund flows from higher echelons of government. Elected representatives, especially in gram panchayats, exercise minimal influence over local expenditure priorities. In practice, the recommendations of State finance commissions governing panchayat finances are often ignored by their respective State Governments usually on the grounds of resource constraints. Most State Governments in India are experiencing fiscal deficits and are reluctant to devolve greater expenditure autonomy to local governments. The budget for capital expenditure is very limited since recurrent salary costs absorb the lion's share of resources and the bureaucracy is very resistant to reform.

Political commitment alone cannot ensure well-functioning Panchayati Raj institutions in the absence of transfer of sufficient powers, responsibilities, and resources to the lower tiers of government. Across states there has been extremely uneven progress on fiscal devolution. For the most part, development resources are tied into programmes determined by State and Central Governments and subject to narrowly specified spending parameters and end uses. The role of panchayats in these programmes is generally restricted to identification of beneficiaries for subsidized housing schemes (Indira Awas Yojana) and employment generation (Sampoorna Grameen Rozgar Yojana), subject to ratification by the Gram Sabha. Small amounts of untied funds are provided for local development purposes mainly in the form of small-scale infrastructure like village roads and community buildings. Gram panchayats are empowered to raise modest resources through local property taxes but these are difficult to collect and only a small proportion of their funds are raised through this source.

Only two states have devolved resources on a significant scale to panchayat bodies, namely, West Bengal and Kerala, both under left-dominated political coalitions. West Bengal has witnessed the most sustained attempt of any state in the country over a period spanning twenty-five years to devolve powers and responsibilities to panchayats. This has been accompanied and in turn fortified by an ambitious land- reforms programme to provide sharecroppers with security of tenure and ownership rights. Under the People's Campaign for Decentralised Planning in Kerala, the extent of fiscal devolution was much greater and faster with nearly 40% of state development resources devolved to panchayats in the period 2001-12.

6.10 Administrative Decentralization—Role of Gram Sabhas

The role of local officials is largely confined to the implementation of development programmes. Health and education programmes are formulated by line ministries at the state level with responsibility for implementation assigned to bureaucrats in local government jurisdictions. Elected representatives have minimal influence over local development priorities and exercise limited oversight over line department officials.

No state in India has managed to make significant progress on staff transfers to local governments or to ensure effective oversight by elected representatives over local officials. Bureaucrats in local governments, especially gram panchayat secretaries, continue to exercise considerable influence over elected representatives as they are privy to information contained in government orders that may not be readily accessible to elected representatives who lack an understanding of official procedures or basic literacy skills.

Of late, however, as a result of several initiatives of the Central Government— in partnership with State Governments —a view has emerged which favours the strengthening of Gram Sabhas as the bedrock of democracy at the grass-roots level.

Gram Sabha is not only an institution articulating the needs and aspirations of the community but is also a method of mobilizing community participation. While Gram Sabhas check against abuse of powers by the panchayat, they can assist the very same panchayats to implement development programmes. Gram Sabhas are supposed to act as watchdogs to protect community interests and common property resources.

To make Panchayati Raj Institutions an effective bedrock of democracy, Gram Sabha should be given a greater role in managing financial resources given to panchayats in addition to the routine functions. Further, PRIs particularly Gram Sabhas can facilitate the governance structure in the country as Gram Sabha could be an effective forum where elected representatives of panchayats and higher tier of government can explain their plan of action/development strategies and get spontaneous feedback on implementation of the programmes. The higher tier of panchayats as well as State Governments may depute an official to attend the Gram Sabha meeting, to record Gram Sabha's views and to report to the appropriate level of government to take remedial measures wherever necessary. The Gram Sabha, if regularly held, can become an effective forum of accountability not only for elected gram panchayat members but also for the elected representatives of the higher tiers where they could be compelled to explain their past performance and future action plan for development of the people. The existence of Gram Sabha/panchayats help in the process of social audit. Gram Sabha can evaluate the work carried out by panchayats and judge their quality, effectiveness and conformity with accepted norms. PRIs can also ensure wide publicity for their activities among the people through the Gram Sabha. Activities of various NGOs/CBOs working at the village level can be effectively monitored by insisting on their close cooperation with the Gram Sabha.

Agenda of Gram Sabha meetings must transcend the presently limited jurisdiction of Gram Panchayats. At present, Gram Sabhas attract only the potential "beneficiaries". The States/UTs must devolve more powers upon panchayats, particularly gram panchayats and remove provisions which undermine Gram Panchayats/Gram Sabhas. Gram Sabhas also have to learn to define their own agenda and seek local solutions. Further, States could extend powers enjoyed by Gram Sabhas in Scheduled areas to the Gram Sabhas in non-scheduled areas to make them the real fulcrum of the Panchayati Raj system.

6.11 Devolution Index

In the Budget Speech of 1999-2000, the Finance Minister had announced that to ensure that funds under wage employment programmes are spent with active involvement of the elected PRIs, 80% of the funds would be released to implementing agencies as per normal procedure, the remaining 20% will be released as an incentive only if the State has put in place elected and empowered PRIs in the State.

Pursuant to this, the Ministry of Rural Development has evolved a Panchayati Raj Devolution Index which consists of five parameters viz.:

1. Constitutional and Political Devolution (PD)
2. Administrative Devolution (AD)
3. Financial Devolution (FID)
4. Functional Devolution (FUD)
5. Devolution to Gram Sabhas (DGS)

The Devolution Index (DI) can be computed on the basis of the following methodology:

DI = (PD+AD+FID+FUD+EGS)/5

The DI would help us to know the extent of devolution of three F's, i.e. Functions, Functionaries and Funds and administrative devolution to the PRIs in the States.

Union Ministry of Panchayati Raj : Initiatives

As far as the union Ministry of Panchayati Raj (created in 2004) is concerned, it has been playing the role of a motivator, guide and supporter for the implementation of the Amendment Act in states and union territories. It has the primary objective of ensuring the compliance of the provisions of Part IX of the Constitution, provisions regarding the district planning committees as per Article 243ZD and Panchayat Extension to Scheduled Areas Act (PESA), 1996.

Today, there are more than 2.55 lakh panchayats in the country, which include 248,263 gram panchayats, 6,618 block panchayats and 595 district panchyats. There are more than 30 lakh panchayat representatives which also include nearly 14.37 lakh elected women representatives. 'Panchayat' is a state subject and MoPR promotes Panchayati Raj through its schemes, advocacy with states, and by creating and sharing knowledge about Panchayati Raj.

Further, since majority of elected three million representatives in the panchayats lack adequate knowledge and experience about working of panchayats, orientation and training for them on large scale are needed. MoPR is trying to help the state governments financially and otherwise to improve and expand requisite raining programmes for these representatives and officers of panchayats.

Rashtriya Gram Swaraj Abhiyan (RGSA): A new restructured scheme, namely RGSA, to help PRIs to develop governance capabilities to deliver on the sustainable development goals (SDGs) was announced in 2016. RGSA has the following sub-scheme: (a) capacity building

(b) MMP on e-panchayat, (c) ATM services in panchayat bhawans and (d) incentivization of panchayats.

Besides, the FFC award (for the period of 2015-20) has created an opportunity for convergent plans at the local level and leadership by panchayats in providing basic amenities and services to the people. The thrust of the new scheme will be on the lines of the Gramoday se Bharat Uday programme which focuses on social empowerment, economic empowerment and enabled gram sabhas through, convergence of resources at the panchayat level. MoPR has supported states to develop state-specific guidelines for GPDP which converge all the resources over which the panchayats have command e.g. FFC, MGNREGA and Swachh Bharat funds.

Initiatives, undertaken by the MoPR for capacity building include support for training of all stakeholders of local governance; support for building training capability, infrastructure and human resources, providing computers and e-governance tools for information and governance support for strengthening Panchayati Raj everywhere. Supportive material and guidelines have been prepared and disseminated to the states and training institutions including in PESA villages.

e-Panchayat Initiatives: The MoPR is also working with the state governments for automating nearly 2.5 lakh panchayats across the country, benefitting approximately 30 lakh elected members and about 10 lakh PRI functionaries and improving local governance at grassroots level. In this regard, e-panchayat is one of the Mission Mode Projects (MMPs) under the Digital India programme of GoI. The project seeks to completely transform the functioning of PRIs, making them more transparent, accountable and effective as organs of decentralized self-governing institutions. This will make democracy truly decentralized. The states are also being provided financial support for manpower, computers and capacity building for the implementation of e-panchayat through the ministry's umbrella scheme, RGSA.

The state legislatures are to decide on the nature of devolution to the panchayats, including the 29 matters set out in the Eleventh Schedule. Thus, states play a critical role in building panchayat capacities and in creating an appropriate framework for accountability and transparency.

Fifteenth Finance Commission

Under the FFC award for the period 2015-20, grants to the tune of Rs. 200,292.20 crore are being devolved to gram panchayats in the country, constituted under Part IZ of the Constitution for 26 states to ensure stable flow of resources at regular intervals which will augment resources available with them to discharge their statutorily assigned functions.

To facilitate better monitoring of the release and utilization of grants, including FFC grants, an online system (MIS) has been developed. PRIA Soft (web-based panchayat accounting software) and Plan Plus (web-based participatory planning software) have also been developed by the ministry for adoption by the states. The 15th FC has been constituted on 27 November 2017 to strengthen cooperative federalism and protect fiscal stability.

6.12 Panchayati Raj: A Review

Local Government (LG) empowerment in India has not been consistent across states with only a few examples of accelerated devolution (Karnataka, West Bengal, Madhya Pradesh and Kerala). States have had varied experiences with democratic decentralization even after the passage of the 73rd and 74th Constitution Amendment Acts.

It wouldn't be wrong to say that none have been consistent in their pursuit of decentralization. Most states have gone through brief periods of support in terms of devolution of functions, funds and functionaries to LGs, alternating with longer periods when support has been low and rhetoric replaced action.

In almost all states, even after activity mapping exercises there is considerable overlap between the functions of different levels of LGs. In no state are LGs given tax responsibilities with which they can address their functional commitments. Most State Government fund transfers are tied down to specific governmental schemes where LGs do not function as anything more than agents of the State Government.

Even more humiliating for LGs is the fact that not having separate civil services or the flexibility to secure manpower and capacity, they are left to depend on the states for their staff, training and development. Thus local functionaries spend a greater part of their time negotiating with higher officers in the bureaucracy rather than carry out their core responsibilities.

In the context of rural India where 70% of our population lives, it is still widely believed that the district level bureaucracy stands between the people and gram swaraj. The district collector is still considered the head of the district administration and along with the superintendent of police, the district forest officer, the executive engineer and the director of the district rural development agency (DRDA) constitute its oligarchic power centre.

The members of legislative assemblies occupy an important position in a district's political set up and the district panchayat and municipal presidents are considered much lower in the political hierarchy. A further problem arises when Central Governments persistently believe that constitutionally mandated LGs are incapable or too political to be effective equitable agents of development and contract out public service delivery to department sponsored user groups, contractor NGOs, and artificially boosted community-based organizations (CBOs). In doing so, they loosely equate these bodies with LGs. The basis of their faith on government sponsored CBOs and user groups lie on the belief that they are apolitical, less corrupt, more efficient and have greater capacity to perform. This, however, has not been proved by research. There is little evidence to show that such groups are insulated from all those evils that are supposed to bedevil Panchayati Raj Institutions (PRIs).

Paradoxically, it is often debated whether the Union Government can drive decentralization efforts better than individual states. In recent years, India's economic resurgence has resulted in greater latitude for the Central Government to spend money, and observers point out to the increasing level of funds that the Centre spends in areas that pertain to the functional domain desired for the LGs. In the Tenth and Eleventh plan periods, new schemes such as the National Rural Health Mission, the Jawaharlal Nehru

National Urban Renewal Mission (JNNURM) and the Backward Regions Grant Fund (BRGF) have been launched and others such as the Sarva Shiksha Abhiyan, the Accelerated Rural Water Supply Programme and the Pradhan Mantri Gram Sadak Yojana have been revamped. Legislation such as the Mahatma Gandhi National Rural Employment Guarantee Act, the Disaster Management Act and the Rights of Forest Dwellers Act have given greater powers and responsibilities to LGs. Thus the Centre can design schemes and laws in a pro-LG manner and influence states to move down the path of more devolution of powers and responsibilities to LGs. Even if paradoxical, decentralization can therefore be driven through Central Acts of Parliament. The total member of centrally sponsored schemes in 2012-13 was 120 with a total allocation of 130,000 crore.

Can true decentralization be catalysed through well-meaning local bureaucracy driven efforts? There is need to change the whole paradigm of local government capacity; from a low value, supply driven one to an effective, demand and knowledge driven one. Only then can we rapidly reach out to large numbers of elected representatives, who need information and guidance, by using a carefully designed basket of user-friendly technologies. But in order to achieve this, the political elites must understand that the 3.2 million elected representatives of LGs are a valuable and responsive human resource, that there is now a sub-optimal utilization of the enormous potential that exists within the LG structure. Secondly, the governments at the state level must realize that there is no clearly discernible functional space for LGs and that the State Governments have been unable to satisfactorily respond to the huge demand for knowledge and training at the grass roots for governance support. It is necessary to realize that devolution by itself will accelerate capacity building by making it demand driven. If one really gives LGs clear roles and holds them accountable for these, they will have an incentive to seek out the capacity support they need.

How does one plan for local needs? How does one bring errant officials to book? All these require a sound and effective training system for panchayat leaders and officials, and a skill exchange platform for social networking among the local bodies. Pointing to the large number of poor and illiterate members elected to LGs, most believe that capacity building should precede devolution. The National Capacity Building Framework prepared by the Ministry of Panchayati Raj estimated that over 30,000 well-trained resource persons are required for delivering a quality training programme for elected representatives to PRIs. About Rs. 2400 crore is required for the hardware to provide satellite assisted training and about Rs. 900 crore annually to meet the revenue cost of training. Currently the Ministry of Rural Development provides Rs. 67 crore for strengthening state institutes of rural development of which about Rs. 15 crore lapses annually. The Ministry of Panchayati Raj provides Rs. 293 crore for the same purpose and half the amount remains unutilized by States (Ministry of Panchayati Raj Annual Reports 2010-12).

Seminal changes in our local governance structures through constitutional amendments were sought to be made by the Union Parliament to bring in true democracy and effective local public service delivery systems at the grass roots two decades ago. Both these mandates have not been made truly operational in letter and spirit by the states through follow up legislation and practice as yet. Any deviation from these key principles would mean a deviation from the original intent of our parliamentarians who drafted and passed these Acts. The 73rd and 74th amendments were meant to design parameters that create the right incentive for local bodies to function in a responsible and accountable mariner. First, under the new dispensation, states were to create proper incentives for LGs to function the way they ought to. It was hoped that LGs did not have to deal institutionally with higher political functionaries or matching fiscal resources, they would have the incentive to seek the capacity they need to perform effectively. Citizens were expected to be more vigilant and seek performance, particularly if they perceive that it is their taxes that are being utilized to deliver the expected services. Most importantly, a good LG based democracy requires the elected representatives to be accountable to the local people alone and not to the higher levels of bureaucracy and State Governments.

The 73rd and 74th Amendments left the question of association of MPs and MLAs to be tackled at the level of States. Accepted at that time as a political compromise, this needs to be looked at afresh from the angle of constitutional propriety and clean and people friendly governance. If the aim of PRIs was to reduce the unhealthy role of MPs and MLAs, the decision of some of the States to include them in PRIs with or without votes does not seem to be justified. MPs and MLAs must appreciate that their role is that of law makers and policy setters at the Union level for the whole of India and at the State level for the State as a whole. Local matters must be left to be handled at local levels by the representatives of the people elected to the local bodies. Also, executive functions have to be left to executive agencies at concerned levels. Schemes like the MP and MLA LADS — Local Area Development Schemes with some 3000 crores of public money involved each year — are an affront to the constitutional principles of distribution of powers between the Union and the States and separation of executive and legislative functions. Also, these schemes make the financially bankrupt PRIs look insignificant and powerless with each MP and MLA having large funds at their disposal for spending on local area schemes which are most legitimately the concern of PRIs under the 73rd and 74th Amendments. Even if largely suggestive and illustrative, the 11th and 12th Schedules to the Constitution become irrelevant if members of the Union Parliament and of State legislatures exercise executive powers in matters of local development otherwise supposedly reserved for Panchayats and Nagarpalikas.

In the North-East States, local traditional institutions of Government need to be modernized with gender justice for women and used as institutions of governance. Overlapping jurisdiction of State Government, Autonomous District Councils (ADCs) and traditional systems of governance and the problems thereof must be removed and jurisdictions of each clearly defined. Greater autonomy should be provided to ADCs by amending the Sixth Schedule. Problems with regard to participation of non-tribals in ADCs need to be addressed. Issues in judicial administration are due to multiple overlapping jurisdictions of the traditional institutions, ADCs and the subordinate judiciary and the emerging conflict between human rights and tribal rights and between conservation laws and tribal rights should be analyzed and resolved.

Conclusion

In the aftermath of the 73rd and 74th Amendments, some degree of standardization has been brought into the structure of LGs across India. This is because the Constitution has defined some aspects of the structure in mandatory terms, whereas flexibility is given to states in others. However, questions are often asked whether the constitutional amendment route through the instrumentality of the Union parliament is the best way of strengthening LGs in India. At least two reports, have suggested amendments to Part IX and IX-A of the Constitution, mainly to bring about a better definition of the scope of powers and responsibilities of LGs, as also their fiscal domain. It is suggested that further changes in the constitutional structure are required because even after two decades since these two amendments were introduced, there are no truly empowered LGs. The current structure leaves plenty of arguments for the enemies of devolution (the higher politico-administrative elite) to indulge in the rhetoric of devolution while not empowering LGs under an umbrella of rules, regulations and guidelines. On the other hand, the advocates of "no-change" argue that considerable progress has been achieved and what is required is not newer Central legislation or constitutional amendment; but greater devolution of functions, funds and functionaries to the LGs by the State Governments through their own legislative powers.

Therefore in conclusion, it can be argued that substantive decentralization efforts in India have been driven much more by constitutional amendment, parliamentary legislation and Central Government schemes than the efforts of State Governments though there have always been some exceptions to this rule, e.g. states like Kerala, West Bengal, Madhya Pradesh and Karnataka have initiated legislation and efforts to truly devolve more powers funds and responsibilities to LGs in their respective states. In fact, better performing states not only set the norm and the standards of optimal performance but also help to build a culture of self-sufficiency, independence and accountability in the delivery of public goods and services at the local level.

It would be ideal if, we get a directory of best practices from local bodies themselves since there is complete ignorance among the general public about their functional achievements in rural and urban governments.

Suggested Readings

Annual Reports of the Ministry of Panchayati Raj, GOI.

Baviskar, B. S., and George Mathew (eds.), *Inclusion and Exclusion in Local Governance: Field Studies from Rural India,* New Delhi, Sage, 2009.

Behar, Amitabh and Yogesh Kumar, *Decentralisation in Madhya Pradesh, India: From Panchayati Raj to Gram Swaraj* (1995-2001), Working Paper 170, London, Overseas Development Institute, 2002.

Buch, Nirmala, *Reservation for Women in Panchayats: A Sop in Disguise?,* Economic and Political Weekly, Vol. 44, No. 40 (2009), pp. 8-10

Crook, Richard C. and Alan S. Sverrisson, *Decentralisation and Poverty-Alleviation in Developing Countries: A Comparative Analysis or, is West Bengal Unique?* Working Paper 130, Brighton, Institute of Development Studies, 2001.

Crook, Richard C. and James Manor (eds.), *Democracy and Decentralisation in South Asia and West Africa: Participation, Accountability, and Performance,* UK, Cambridge University Press, 1998.

DeSouza, Peter R., "Decentralisation and Local Government: The "Second Wind" of Democracy in India," in *India's Constitution: Ideas, Practices, Controversies,* eds. Zoya Hasan, E. Sridharan, and R. Sudarshan, New Delhi, Permanent Black, 2002, pp. 370-404.

Isaac, T.M. Thomas and Richard W. Franke, *Local Democracy and Development: People's Campaign for Decentralized Planning in Kerala,* New Delhi, Leftword, 2000.

Jain, S. P. (ed.), *Emerging Institutions for Decentralised Rural Development, 2 Vols.,* Hyderabad, National Institute for Rural Devèlopment, 2001 and 2002.

Jayal, Niraja Gopal, *Local Governance in India: Decentralization and beyond,* New Delhi, OUP, 2007.

Johnson, Craig, *Decentralisation in India: Poverty, Politics and Panchayati Raj* ODI Working Paper No. 199. London, Overseas Development Institute, 2003.

Kumar, Girish, *Local Democracy in India,* New Delhi, Sage, 2006

Mathew, George, *"Panchayati Raj in India—An Overview," Institute of Social Sciences,* 2000, pp. 3-22.

Raghunandan, T. R., *Decentralisation and Local Governments: The Indian Experience,* Orient Black Swan, New Delhi, 2012.

Robinson, Mark and Gordon White, *The Democratic Development State: The Politics of Institutional Design,* UK, Oxford University Press, 1998.

Stephen, F. and N. Raja Sekaran, *Sheep and Lambs: An Empirical Study of Women in Local Self- Governance in Karnataka,* Bangalore, SEARCH, 2001.

Vijayalakshmi, V. and B. K. Chandrashekhar, *Gender Inequality, Differences, and Identities: Women and Local Governance in Karnataka,* Working Paper 72, Bangalore, Institute of Social and Economic Change, 2000.

ooo

Chapter Seven

Urban Local Governance

Introduction

As per the 2011 census, only 31.2% (377 million) of India's population was classified as urban. Urbanization is an irreversible trend in developing countries. Poverty and lack of employment opportunities in the rural areas lead to migration from rural to urban areas; industrialization has also accelerated the growth of new towns; better means of transport have facilitated migration and, above all, cities provide a better quality of life, in terms of educational and health facilities.

The urban scene in India presents a series of paradoxes —growth and decay, poverty and affluence, slums and skyscrapers, illiteracy and educational excellence, particularistic groups and universalistic associations. The urban centres are characterized by interplay of multi-level socio-political and economic forces, which, cumulatively, have added to the complexity of city life. This complexity poses enormous challenges to the administrators involved in managing regulatory as well as development affairs in urban areas.

India's Urban Population

- 377 million urban population is 31.2% of the total population, i.e. the second largest urban population in the world
- Net addition of population in urban areas was 70 million in 1991-2001 decade with decadal growth of 31.2%.
- 27 million plus cities (35 urban agglomerations).
- 5000 census urban areas.
- In India about 14% of urban population—53 million people —stay in the three 10 million plus urban agglomerations (Delhi, Kolkata and Mumbai).
- About 9% or 32 million stay in cities of population sizes ranging between 5 and 10 million.
- A whopping 27% the total urban population, i.e. about 101 million people dwell in cities between a population size of half a million and 5 million.
- The bulk of urban Indians —181 million or 50% — stay in small towns with less than half a million population (5 lakh).
- Census 2011 recorded 1.3 crore urban slum households

In order to understand the contemporary process of urbanization in India, let's study the census definition of urban areas. The census definition of an 'urban area' is:

All the places with municipal corporations, municipalities, cantonment boards, or notified area committees, etc., that is 'statutory towns'; and all other places that satisfy the following criteria:

1. a minimum population of 5,000;
2. at least 75% of the male working population engaged in non-agricultural pursuits and a density of at least 400 persons/sq. km.

Places fulfilling the criteria above are known as non-statutory or 'census towns'. The 'urban' thus covers a wide spectrum: from mega cities to medium towns and from municipal agglomerations to town panchayats. Therefore, what is urban in India is a widely distributed collection of cities, towns and urbanized villages.

7.1 Urban Infrastructure:

The provision of infrastructure facilities required to support such a large concentration of population lags far behind the pace of urbanization in India. All cities in India do not necessarily have assured water supply, sewerage facilities, developed land, housing, transportation and other facilities. Several studies have indicated that large segments of urban population do not have access to basic services —drinking water, sanitation, basic health services and education. These deficiencies have serious health impacts on the urban poor. Primary urban infrastructure such as water supply and sewerage are not available outside the municipal limits.

The data available from the census 2011 indicates that the percentage of urban households with access to safe drinking water has gone up to 90%. Nearly 74% of the urban households are served by piped water supply. Approximately 11% of the urban households have no access to toilet facilities within their premises and are forced to use open spaces. Nearly 33% of the households have no access to sewerage facilities within the premises. In million-plus cities, nearly 40% of households, or 17.4% of total urban households in India live in slums. The five metros —Mumbai, Delhi, Chennai, Hyderabad and Kolkata—make up 50% of the slums in India. The total solid waste generated is 1,15,000 MTD and almost all of it is disposed of without any scientific treatment. Non-scientific discharge of waste leads to pollution, environmental degradation and health risks. In industrial areas of many cities, municipal solid waste gets mixed up with hazardous wastes, posing a serious environmental threat. Public transport constitutes only 22% of urban transport.

There is an urgent need to evolve policy guidelines that address these issues. This calls for larger investments in water supply and sewerage, transport and communications, housing and community facilities, all within a coordinated framework of economic and spatial planning in existing and evolving urban conglomerations. Urban development falls under the jurisdiction of the respective State Governments under the Indian Constitution. Therefore, legislation governing various aspects of urban development and the implementation of various development programmes, implementation of the 74th Constitutional Amendment Act (CAA) promulgated in 1992, urban reforms in general, vary across states. The 74th CAA is briefly discussed with its implications for urban governance.

7.2 The 74th Constitutional Amendment Act (CAA)

The 74th Constitutional Amendment Act (CAA) was passed in 1992 to accord formal recognition to Urban Local Bodies (ULBs) in the Constitution and make them more autonomous and participatory. It provided powers to ULBs to function as 'independent institutions of self-government[7] and directed states to devolve specific functions (18) to ULBs under Schedule XII (Art 243 W). ULBs were also empowered to collect taxes and states were required to set up State Finance Commissions (SFCs) to review and make recommendations regarding distribution of taxes, revenue-sharing, grant-in- aid system, issues of local autonomy between the state and ULBs. This amendment also provided for having an elected council for each ULB (with reservation for women); constitution of ward committees; creation of a district/metropolitan planning committee and establishment of funds at the ULB level to handle receipts and disbursements. Although most states have amended their municipal laws in accordance with the 74th CAA, the extent of devolution/ decentralization to ULBs has been uneven across the states.

The Act introduces a new part, namely Part IXA, and consists of Articles 243P to 243ZG in the Constitution. It adds a new Twelfth Schedule which contains 18 functional items for ULB jurisdiction. It deals with issues related to municipalities such as their structure and composition, reservation of seats, elections, powers and functions, finances, and some miscellaneous provisions. The 74th Amendment Act thus gives a constitutional status to the municipalities. The provisions of the Act apply to the states as well as the union territories. However, in relation to the latter, the President can make certain reservations and modifications. The provisions do not apply to the Scheduled Areas and Tribal Areas governed by Article 244(1) and (2) of the Constitution.

Together with the various forms of urban local government existing at present, the Act also provides for setting up of Nagar Panchayats. A Nagar Panchayat will be constituted for a transitional area. Such an area is basically rural in character, which over a period of time is likely to develop urban characteristics. Hence, this urban local body would have to perform both rural and urban functions.

Each state/UT will have to constitute a State Election Commission (SEC), headed by a State Election Commissioner appointed by the Governor of the state. The superintendence, direction and control of the preparation of the electoral rolls and the conduct of all elections to the municipalities shall be vested in the SEC. Several states have already appointed such commissions.

In order that the financial position of the municipalities is reviewed periodically, it has been laid down that a SFC will have to be constituted by the Governor of the state within one year from the commencement of the 74th CAA, and, thereafter, at the expiry of every five years. The composition, qualifications and manner of appointment of the members of the SFC will be determined by the state legislature.

7.3 Urban Government: Structural Patterns

The following eight types of urban local bodies exist for administration of urban areas:
Municipal Corporation

Municipal corporations are set up only in big cities. The 74th CAA provides that different types of urban bodies would be specified by the Governor of the state, taking into account the density of the population therein, revenue generated by the local body, etc. Corporations are created by an Act of the state legislature or of the Parliament in case of a union territory.

The municipal corporation is a popular body that provides representation to the city's population. Most of its members are directly elected on the basis of adult franchise. It does not have a sovereign status or inherent powers. It exercises only those functions, which are allocated to it by the State Government. An important feature of a corporation is that there is a statutory separation of the legislative (or the deliberative) wing and the executive wing. The Mayor heads the council of a corporation and its standing committees constitute the deliberative wing, which take decisions. The Municipal Commissioner is the executive authority, responsible for enforcing these decisions. Collectively, the council, headed by the Mayor, the standing committees and the Municipal Commissioner make up the corporation.

The council of the corporation consists of councillors who function for a period of five years. The composition of the municipal bodies have also undergone a change since the the 74th CAA. It lays down that all the seats shall be filled by direct elections for which the municipal area would be divided into wards. Each seat shall represent a ward in the municipality. Apart from the seats filled by direct elections, some seats may be filled by nominations of persons with special knowledge or experience of municipal administration, but such members would not enjoy any voting rights. Besides the members of Parliament, members of the state legislature will also be voting members in a municipality.

The Act also gives details regarding the reservation of one-third seats for SC/ ST, women and backward classes. The 74th Constitutional Amendment Act does not specify the manner and procedure of election of the chairperson. It has been left to the state legislature. It may either be by direct elections or from amongst the elected members of the municipality concerned.

The chairperson in a corporation is the Mayor, who is supported by a Deputy Mayor. The Mayor is elected in most of the states generally for a one-year renewable term. He can be removed from his office by a no-confidence motion of the council. He is the "first citizen" of the city but is not the real executive. The Mayor presides over the meetings of the council. In some states, he is authorized to constitute committees/make appointments to the lower grade positions, supervise and inspect the working of various units and represent the corporation on national and social occasions. As the size of a corporation is generally large, several committees are set up to facilitate its working. The committees such as those dealing with finance, public works, etc., are common to all the corporations.

The Municipal Commissioner is the chief executive officer of the corporation. He is at the apex of the municipal hierarchy and is the key officer controlling the administrative machinery of the corporation. The State Government appoints him. In the case of a union territory, the Central Government makes the appointment. Generally, officers belonging to the Indian Administrative Service are appointed to this post though, at the state level, even a state service officer may be appointed. Since a municipal commissioner is the pivot of municipal administration, he performs varied tasks. He executes or implements the decisions of the council and its committees. All municipal records are in his custody; he prepares the budget estimates, makes appointments to certain categories of posts and can enter into contracts on behalf of the corporation.

Municipal bodies are performing the traditional civic functions of municipalities. However, the 74th CAA lays down that municipalities would go beyond the mere provisions of civic amenities. Now, they are expected to play a crucial role in the formulation of plans for local development and the implementation of development projects and programmes, including those specially designed for urban poverty alleviation.

An illustrative list of functions that may be entrusted to the municipalities has been incorporated in the Twelfth Schedule of the Constitution. A state legislature would be free to select from this list or add to this list while stipulating the functions to be performed by municipalities.

Municipal Council / Committee / Municipality

A municipal council is a statutory body created by an Act of the state legislature and the criteria for setting it up vary from state to state. Broadly, these are: population, size, sources of income, industrial/commercial future and prospects of the city. Even within a state, the criteria may differ. A city, which is industrially advanced, may have a municipality despite its low population. The size of a municipality is determined by the State Government, but the minimum number of councillors should be five. The size increases with the increase in population. Their tenure, under the 74th CAA, 1992, is five years.

A municipal council consists of elected, co-opted and associate members. For the elected seats, elections are held on the basis of adult suffrage and secret ballot and for this purpose the city is divided into wards. Seats are reserved for SC/ST, women and backward classes. Nominated members and members with voting rights are the same as for the municipal corporation. The councillors can be removed by the municipal council, by the citizens of the ward or by the State Government, according to the prescribed procedure. In order to lessen the workload of the council, several sub-committees are set up such as the Ward Committee to manage the affairs of a ward and committees dealing with subjects like buildings, vehicles, works, finance, lease, etc.

The municipal council elects, from amongst its members, a President for a period of five years. The council also elects one or two Vice-Presidents —one senior and one junior— who are removable by the council itself. The President plays a pivotal role in municipal administration and enjoys real deliberative and executive powers. He presides over the meetings of the council, guides the deliberations and gets the decisions implemented. He is the administrative head of all the officers of the municipality, is the custodian of municipal records, approves all financial matters before they are placed in the council and represents the council on national and social occasions. He enjoys special extraordinary powers, under which he can order the immediate execution or suspension of any work.

The State Government also appoints an Executive Officer in the municipal council for the conduct of general administrative work. He exercises general control and supervision over the municipal office, can transfer clerical employees, prepares the municipal budget, keeps an eye on expenditure, is responsible for the collection of taxes and fees and takes measures for recovering municipal arrears and dues. He can be removed by the council or by the State Government.

As already pointed out, the functions of the municipal council are broadly similar to those of a municipal corporation. When a city that has a municipal council is given a municipal corporation, the latter takes up the functions of the former.

Notified Area Committee (NAC)

The Notified Area Committee is set up for an area which does not yet fulfill all the conditions necessary for the constitution of a municipality but which the State Government otherwise considers important. Generally, it is created in an area which is fast developing and where new industries are being set up. It is not created by statute but by a notification in the government gazette and, hence, the name 'notified area'. The State Government constitutes a committee called the Notified Area Committee (NAC) to administer this area. All the members of this committee are nominated by the State Government and there are no elected members.

Its chairman is also appointed by the State Government. The criteria for establishing this committee differ from state to state. As all the members of the NAC are appointed by the government, it is clearly a violation of the democratic principle. In a number of states, there are demands for abolishing these committees and setting up municipalities in their place so that the local people can solve their problems themselves.

Town Area Committee (TAC)

It is a semi-municipal authority, constituted for small towns. Such committees exist in several states. The TAC is constituted and governed by an Act of the state legislature and its composition and functions are specified. Its membership differs from state to state. The committee may be partly elected, partly nominated or wholly elected or wholly nominated. The committee is assigned a limited number of functions, such as street lighting, drainage, roads, conservancy, etc. The District Collector, in some states, has been given control and powers of surveillance over a TAC. Following the recommendations of the Rural Urban Relationship Committee (1966) that the smaller TACs be merged with the Panchayati Raj bodies, lately, Madhya Pradesh and Haryana have merged their TACs with Panchayati Raj institutions.

Township

Several large-sized public enterprises have been set up in India. A few examples are: the steel plants at Rourkela, Bhilai, Jamshedpur, Bharat Heavy Electricals Limited near Bhopal and Hindustan Aeronautics near Bangalore. Near the plants, housing colonies have been built for the staff and workers. Since these industries are a source of employment, people from urban as well as rural areas are drawn to them and, resultantly, small townships evolve around them. Among the well-known examples are the townships of Jugsalai and Adityapur near Jamshedpur. These townships are administered by the municipal corporation or council within whose boundary they fall. For administering them, the corporations/councils appoint a Town Administrator, who is assisted by a few engineers and technicians. It is not an elected body. The townships are well planned and contain facilities like water, electricity, roads, drainage, markets, parks, etc. The expenditure on these services is shared by the industry concerned.

Cantonment Board

While all other institutions of urban governance are administered by the State Government, these are the only bodies which are centrally administered by the Defence Ministry. When a military station is established in an area, the military personnel move in and, to provide them with facilities of everyday life, a sizeable civilian population also joins the developing area. Soon, colonies, markets, etc., develop near such military stations. For administering these areas, cantonment boards are created. There are 63 cantonment boards in India which are grouped into three classes:

1. Class I cantonment in which the civilian population exceeds 10,000.
2. Class II cantonment in which the civilian population is between 2,500 and 10,000.
3. Class III cantonment in which the civilian population is less than 2,500.

The board consists of both elected and nominated members. The officer commanding the station is the President of the board. An elected member holds office for three years, while the nominated members continue as long as they hold the office in that station. A Class I cantonment consists of: (i) the officer commanding the station, (ii) a first class magistrate nominated by the district magistrate, (iii) a Health Officer, (iv) and Executive Engineer, (v) four military officers, nominated by the officer commanding the station, and (vi) seven members elected by the people of the cantonment. The board performs obligatory functions such as lighting, streets, drainage, cleaning of streets, markets, planting of trees, supply of water, registering births and deaths, protection against fire, establishment of schools and hospitals, public vaccination, etc. Some of the discretionary functions are: construction of public works and wells and provision of public transport.

It is set up under the provisions of the Cantonments Act of 2006—a legislation enacted by the Central Government which repealed the Cantonments Act of 1924. The new Act was enacted with a view to impart greater democratization improve the financial base and make provisions for developmental activities in the Cantonment areas.

The executive officer of the Cantonment Board is appointed by the President of India. He implements all the decisions of the board and belongs to the Central cadre established for the purpose.

Port Trusts

The port trusts are established in the port areas like Mumbai, Kolkata, Chennai and other port towns for 2 purposes: (a) to manage and protect the ports and (b) to provide civic amenities like those of a municipality. A port trust is created by an Act of Parliament. It consists of both elected and nominated members.

Special Purpose Agencies

In addition to these seven area-based urban bodies there are special purpose agencies. These agencies are set up as government departments or as statutory bodies under separate Acts of the State Government. Some such agencies are housing boards, pollution control boards, water supply and sewerage boards. Such bodies are set up, even though other municipal agencies exist for the same area, since there are certain activities which require expertise, concentrated attention and special skills which the municipal bodies do not possess. Besides, the municipal bodies are already overburdened and they lack the requisite administrative machinery and the necessary resources in order to deal with problems arising out of rapid urbanization. These are function based and not area based. Some of these bodies are (a) Town improvement trusts (b) urban development authorities (c) water supply and sewerage boards (d) housing boards (e) pollution control boards (f) electricity supply boards (g) city transport boards.

These functional local bodies are established as Statutory bodies by an act of state legislature or as departments by an executive resolution. They function as autonomous bodies and are not subordinate agencies of the local municipal bodies.

Responsibility of Municipalities

Legislatures of states have been conferred the power (Article 243W) to confer on the municipalities all such powers as may be necessary to enable them to function as institutions of self-government. They may be given the responsibility of:

1. Preparing plans for economic development and social justice;
2. Implementing schemes of e.g. poverty alleviation; and
3. Implementing matters contained in the Twelfth Schedule which contains 18 items.

However, major functions that the municipal bodies handle are (a) public health and sanitation, (b) water supply and drainage, (c) public works and roads, (d) primary education. The usual practice is to divide the state functions into various sub-functions and delegate some of these to the municipalities.

State Finance Commissions

The legislature of a state may by law authorize a municipality to levy, collect and appropriate taxes, duties, tools and fees. It can also assign to a municipality various taxes, duties and so on collected by the state government. Further grants-in-aid may be assigned to the municipalities from the state consolidated fund.

The SFC appointed under Article 243-I under Panchayat Finance Commission shall also review the financial position of the municipalities and make recommendations to the governor on the following:

1. The principles which should govern
    a. the distribution between the state and the municipalities of the net proceeds of the taxes, duties, tools and fees to be levied by the state and the allocation between the municipalities at all levels;

   b. the determination of the taxes, duties, tolls and fees which may be assigned to the municipalities; and
   c. the grants-in-aid to the municipalities from the Consolidated Fund of the state
2. The measures needed to improve the financial position of the municipalities
3. Any other matter that may be referred to FC by the governor

The Finance Commission appointed under Article 280 would also make recommendation with regard to the measures needed to augment the Consolidated Fund of a State to supplement the resources of the municipalities in the state on the basis of the recommendations made by the state.

Constitution of District and Metropolitan Committees

The 74th Amendment also provides for creation of the following:

- District Planning Committee (243ZD), which shall prepare and forward the development plan to the state government
- Metropolitan Planning Committee (243ZE), which shall prepare a development plan for the whole metropolitan area and forward to the state government

The composition of the committees and the manner in which chairpersons are to be chosen and seats are to be filled are to be provided by a law to be made by the state legislature. But it has been laid down that

- in case of the District Planning Committee, at least four-fifth of the members shall be elected by the elected members of the district-level panchayat and of municipalities in the district from amongst themselves. Their proportion would be in accordance with the ratio of urban and rural population of the district; and
- in case of Metropolitan Planning Committee, at least two-thirds of the members of the committee shall be elected by the members of the municipalities and chairpersons of the panchayats in the metropolitan area form amongst themselves.

With respect to functions that are to be performed by the district committee and Metropolitan Planning Committee (to prepare a development plan for the whole metropolitan area), the state legislature would by law make provisions including functions relating to planning and coordination for the metropolitan area.

7.4 Personnel Administration in Urban Bodies

There are three types of municipal personnel systems in the Indian states and union territories.

1. **The Separate Personnel System:** In this system, each local authority has the power to appoint its own personnel. Such personnel are administered and controlled by the local authority and are not transferable to any other unit. It is the most widely prevalent system.
2. **The Unified Personnel System:** Under this system/all or some local bodies form a single career service for the entire state, from which officers and other employees are posted in various units and are also transferable within the state. The service is

administered by the State Government. This system is prevalent in Andhra Pradesh, Tamil Nadu, Uttar Pradesh, Rajasthan and Madhya Pradesh.

3. **The Integrated Personnel System:** Under this pattern, personnel of the local bodies and those of the State Government form a part of the same service. All or some categories of personnel of the local bodies may be drawn from this service. The local civil service is absorbed into the state civil service. The State Government can transfer them from the urban body to other departments. This system continues in Odisha, Bihar, Karnataka, Punjab and Haryana, etc. Therefore in India, all the three systems operate in various states. The separate personnel system is found in West Bengal and Gujarat. The integrated personnel system operates in almost all the states, though in a limited form. For instance, the Municipal Commissioner in a corporation or the Secretary of an improvement trust are almost always members of the Indian Administrative Service or of the state service. Other senior positions, both administrative and technical, are also filled by senior officers of the state services. Some may, however, belong to the municipal service or may be deputed from other services to the local bodies.

7.5 Global Cities

The opening up of the Indian economy after the advent of globalization has led to the creation of 'global cities'. For example, in 1991, of the 20 largest cities in the world, 3 were from India and by 2001, 6 largest cities out of 20 were from India. In 1991 there were 23 million plus cities in India and their number increased to 40 in 2001 and are expected to go up to 70 in 2021. In 1991, 26% of the Indian population were living in urban areas which has increased to 33% in 2001 and is expected to go up to 40% by 2021. These cities became the hub of industrial and economic activities and attractive destinations for foreign direct investment. It has become a major challenge for civic agencies especially in larger cities to provide internationally competitive infrastructural facilities to attract FDI flows. As Indian markets are being opened to international markets, decentralizsation became inevitable to make the local bodies accountable to the stake holders. Larger cities became the hub of economic activities because they were able to provide basic infrastructure required for overall development. It has resulted in the need to devolve power and authority to the lower tier of the government, i.e. municipal bodies to provide infrastructural facilities within city limits.

7.6 Jawaharlal Nehru National Urban Renewal Mission

Jawaharlal Nehru National Urban Renewal Mission (JNNURM) was the Centre's flagship massive city-modernization scheme, the first of its kind since Independence to be launched by the GOI under the Ministry of Urban Development. It allocated a total investment of over $20 billion over seven years. The scheme was officially inaugurated on 3 December 2005 meant to improve the quality of life and infrastructure in the cities. It was launched in 2005 for a seven-year period (up to March 2012) to encourage cities to initiate steps for bringing phased improvements in their civic service delivery levels. The government further extended the tenure of the mission for two years, i.e. from April 2012 to March 31, 2014.

JNNURM aimed at creating economically productive, efficient, equitable and responsive cities by a strategy of upgrading the social and economic infrastructure in cities, provision of Basic Services to Urban Poor (BSUP) and wide-ranging urban sector reforms to strengthen municipal governance in accordance with the 74th CAA, 1992. JNNURM primarily incorporated two sub-missions into its program:

- The Sub-Mission for Urban Infrastructure and Governance administered by the Ministry of Urban Development, with a focus on water supply and sanitation, solid waste management, road network, urban transport and redevelopment of old city areas.
- The Sub-Mission for Basic Services to the Urban Poor (BSUP) administered by the Ministry of Housing and Urban Poverty Alleviation with a focus on integrated development of slums.

In addition to this, it had two further components:

- The Sub-Mission for Urban Infrastructure Development Scheme for Small and Medium Towns (UIDSSMT) administered by the Ministry of Urban Development, with a focus on subsuming the schemes of Integrated Development of Small and Medium Towns (IDSMT) and Accelerated Urban Water Supply Programme (AUWSP) which aim at planned urban infrastructural improvement in towns and cities under its purview.
- The Sub-Mission for Integrated Housing and Slum Development Programme (IHSDP) administered by the Ministry of Housing and Urban Poverty Alleviation (MHUPA) was envisaged and brought into effect in 1993-94 in accordance with providing the entire population with safe and adequate water supply facilities. The program was mainly implemented in towns with populations less than 20,000 as per the 1991 census.
- JNNURM was launched in 2005. It was a reform-driven, fast-track programme to ensure planned development of cities/towns with focus of efficiency in urban infrastructure/service delivery mechanisms and through community participation and enhanced accountability of ULBs/ para-para-statal agencies towards citizens. Under priority has been accorded in sanctioning of projects for water supply, sewerage and drainage sectors. Also projects have been sanctioned for urban transport sector which include construction of roads, flyovers, bus rapid transport system. The Mission has already sanctioned projects for 65 select cities across the country. Out of these 65 cities, 35 cities are with a million plus population and other 30 cities are either state capitals or cities of heritage and tourist importance, totaling 55 mission cities under UIG.

Some Recent Programmes of Urban Governance

Union Ministry of Urban Development

The Ministry of Urban Development has the responsibility of broad policy formulation and monitoring of programmes in the area of urban development. Urban development is a state subject but the GoI plays a coordinating and monitoring role and also supports urban development through centrally sponsored schemes. The ministry addresses various issues of the urban sector through policy guidelines, legislative guidance and sectoral programmes.

Smart Cities Mission

The Smart Cities Mission was launched by the central government in 2015. Smart Cities Mission is based on the idea of development of the entire urban ecosystem on the principles of complete and integrated planning.

The mission is operated as a centrally sponsored scheme. The central government has announced the list of first 20 urban areas that will be developed as smart cities. They are Ahmedabad, Belagavi (Belgaum), Bhopal, Bhubaneshwar, Chennai, Coimbatore, Davanagere, Guwahati, Indore, Jabalpur, Jaipur, Kakinada, Kochi, Ludhiana, New Delhi, Pune, Solapur, Surat, Udaipur and Vishakhapatnam. The money will be released for the Mission from the centre, and states would be part of this exercise. GoI selected 27more cities for conversion as smart cities.

In the approach of the Smart Cities Mission, the objective is to promote cities that provide core infrastructure and give a decent quality of life to its citizens, a clean and sustainable environment and application of 'smart' solutions. 'The focus is on sustainable and inclusive development and the idea is to look at compact areas, create a replicable model which will act like a lighthouse to other aspiring cities'. The core infrastructure elements in a smart city would include (a) adequate water supply; (b) assured electricity supply; (c) sanitation, including solid waste management; (d) efficient urban mobility and public transport; (e) affordable housing, especially for the poor; (f) robust IT connectivity and digitalization; (g) good governance, especially e-governance and citizen participation; (h) sustainable environment; (i) safety and security of citizens, particularly women, children and the elderly; and (j) health and education.

Atal Mission for Rejuvenation and Urban Transformation

The Atal Mission for Rejuvenation and Urban Transformation (AMRUT) was launched in 2015. The objective of the Mission is to improve basic urban infrastructure in 500 cities / towns which would be known as Mission cities/towns. The Mission is being operated as a centrally sponsored scheme. It aims to cover all cities and towns with a population of over one lakh with notified municipalities, including Cantonment Boards (civilian areas) and certain other cities such as capital towns, some cities on stem of main rivers and tourist and hill destinations.

The purpose of AMRUT is to (a) ensure that every household has access to a tap with assured supply of water and a sewerage connection; (b) increase the amenity value of cities by developing greenery and well maintained open spaces (e.g., parks); and (c) reduce pollution by switching to public transport or constructing facilities for non-motorized transport (e.g., walking and cycling). AMRUT makes states equal partners in planning and implementation of projects, thus actualizing the spirit of cooperative federalism. As of now, 497 cities/towns have been selected under this mission.

7.7 Reforms in Urban Governance: Policy Recommendations

In the past decade, public and private investments have been changing city landscapes. Consideration of urban issues within the government has seen the gradual improvement of cities, with or without the JNNURM. The improvements have been through both people's own investments in housing and basic infrastructure at the local level and also ULB or State Government investments in core as well as settlement-level infrastructure. Improvement in coverage of water supply and sanitation through taps has occurred due to the ULB initiatives. At the city level, availability of covered or underground drainage in the slums is severely lagging behind. Improvement in this infrastructure has not been as rapid as some others. Improvements for the bottom half of the urban poor are slower than for the remaining population. There are two reasons for this. In the metropolitan cities, improvements for those living in slums is slow because of lack of tenure security in the non-notified slums. Second, the poor are concentrated in the non-metropolitan cities, which do not even have capacity to extend basic services, leave aside address questions of poverty.

A Citizens' Group (Public Affairs Centre, Bangalore, 2009) report shows that there have been arbitrary changes in land use to accommodate prime or fashionable projects, while informal housing and economic activity running against planning restrictions have not been permitted.

In practice, however, one finds greater bias on improving the efficiency in the functioning of the overall city economy and meeting the infrastructural deficiencies at the macro-level rather than addressing the issues of distributional inadequacy and improving the access of the poor to these. A section of the poor, who can satisfy the norms of selection through possession of voter I-cards, ration cards, etc., below a minimum threshold, would benefit from urban amenities. The slum colonies that are being taken up under integrated housing projects, essentially through relocation, are those that are occupying critical areas affecting the efficiency of the city.

The shift of emphasis from the provision of basic amenities for the poor to integrated multi-storied housing projects inevitably brings in real estate developers and enables them to corner a large part of the slum land that is used for commercial purposes. Needless to mention that the number of slum dwellers that would be rehabilitated through government programmes would go up to a couple of millions but would still be far short of the figure of 24.7 million (urban ews housing shortage) needed as estimated by the Ministry of Housing and Urban Poverty Alleviation at the beginning of the Eleventh Five-Year Plan to meet the needs of the urban poor.

Despite JNNURM providing vital assistance to states for urban renewal the phenomenon of large-scale underutilization of the JNNURM funds and inability of the smaller ULBs to prepare draft plans and generate matching resources can only be addressed by paying urgent attention to urban governance reforms, building capabilities at the ULB level and developing professional management capabilities of city governments especially those in the economically backward states. Efforts should be taken to make special provisions for unconditional general grants addressed towards their infrastructure and housing needs till the time they develop the capacities to receive project funding. This will certainly help in making the growth process more inclusive, where the urban poor would be partners in the developmental process, and ensure equitable and sustainable urban growth.

Deficiencies in urban governance and especially in JNNURM span a range of areas. The key institutional problems are: (i) the multiplicity of organizations engaged in governing and service delivery; (ii) lack of coordination among them in relation to territorial functions; (iii) ever-expanding boundaries and often boundaries demarcated in an ad hoc manner creating further confusion in defining the jurisdictions and functions of existing institutions; (iv) lack of functional and financial powers of the ULB for it to function as a true third tier of government, for example, State Governments holding on to functional powers through parastatals and state-level departments; (v) lack of adequate decentralization, for example, by not forming ward committees as mandated by the 74th CAA, and dysfunctional ward committees wherever formed; (vi) lack of community participation and stakeholder involvement in key city/local-level decisions; (vii) inadequate monitoring of service delivery; (viii) lack of an enabling legislative framework to fill in institutional lacunae; and (ix) lack of transparency in the utilization of funds and negotiating contracts relating to Public-Private Participation (PPP) agreements.

Given that the implementation of reforms requires substantial changes in the way the states and the cities are functioning, and the lack of enthusiasm shown by the states in implementing the 74th CAA, progress on urban reforms have been slow. The progress is slowest in implementing reforms that would devolve powers to the ULBs, involve community participation in decision making and usher in institutional coordination. The cities are floundering in implementing administrative and structural reforms. Progress is also slow with regard, to the cost recovery of O&M (operations and maintenance) charges for water supply and Sewage Management. Many cities have, however, taken to promoting Public-Private Partnerships for certain services. It is heartening to see that a number of cities have earmarked funds in their budgets for deployment towards services for the poor, but the progress in earmarking land for low-income housing programmes is deficient. Finally, many cities have begun reforms on e-governance, but case studies highlight that setting up an e-governance portal is as difficult as undertaking other reforms.

Conclusion

The success of the SMART cities or AMRUT concepts are dependent on the administrative capabilities of the states and the cities. Better performing states are likely to continue to perform well. The JNNURM has, however, given them additional impetus to increase urban investments in infrastructure and low-income housing. It also needs to be understood that a move towards good governance or inclusive cities requires far more than just the JNNURM reforms.

Financial problems will remain unless the fiscal system is reworked to give the cities their dues. This would require an equitable tax sharing formula to be worked out between the Central, State, and Local governments, and ensuring that the taxes are shared as a right of the cities and not as charity transfers or as transfers attached to conditionalities. This would require a change in legislation as well as institutions. The cities do not have the powers to decide their own tax sources and tax rates.

There is a massive informal sector in the cities. Their properties and activities are not within the local tax net. Sometimes, the slum-dwellers want to pay property tax as this provides them with some assurance of security of tenure. The city governments do not, however, wish to do that, primarily due to the fear that land rights will have to be surrendered to the slum-dwellers. The local government officials need to change their attitude towards informal sector households and enterprises. Autonomy of the cities from the State Government remains a crucial question/The State Governments have kept the powers to themselves through a variety of mechanisms, notwithstanding the 74th CAA.

The ULBs are still dependent on the State Government for finances. The State Government decides the boundaries of the city government and also declares a settlement to be urban. The considerations vary from state to state and are ad hoc. The concerned bodies are not consulted in decisions concerning tax rates and sources or in those relating to the city's boundaries (amalgamation of the local governments or separation of local governments). The State Governments continue to hold the power to sanction the development plans and master plans and thereby the control of land allocations, activities, and development within the city. The cities are to a substantial degree dependent on the State Governments for the executive heads.

The first recommendation emerging from the experience of cities is that the states and the cities should be given greater flexibility in implementing the reforms. The Central Government could ask the states and cities to prioritize reforms based on their own assessment of the issues that confront them and ask them to set their own deadlines for achieving the reforms.

The financial sustainability of the cities can become a reality only when the cities receive their due share of public finances. In all probability, the JNNURM reforms were a small step in that direction but the long-term requirement is for a new paradigm of urban governance in India.

The higher challenge for policy makers then is to address the changing demographics of India. India's urban population is already touching 30% and growing every year. The government allocates its urban citizens only one-sixth of the per capita spending allocated for rural citizens, spending on the urban poor is roughly one-tenth of that on the rural poor. If by 2050, more than 70% of India lives in urban agglomerations, new policies and new governance structures will be needed to meet the needs and aspirations of the urban populace.

Suggested Readings

Batra, Lalit, *A Review of Urbanisation and Urban Policy in Post-Independent India,* CSLG Working Paper Series, CSLG/WP/09/05, Centre for the Study of Law and Governance, Jawaharlal Nehru University, 2009.

Chand, Vikram K., *Public Service Delivery in India: Understanding the Reform Process,* New Delhi, OUP, 2010.

Datta, Abhijit, "Strategies for Municipal Decentralization in India: Functions, Finances and Autonomy/' in *Accountability and Decentralization in Urban Governance,* National Workshop organised by the National Foundation for India, New Delhi, 7 October 1994 (Publication No. 2/95).

Jain, A.K., *Urban Planning and Governance,* Delhi, Bookwell, 2010.

Kundu, A., *"Pattern of Urbanisation with Special Reference to Small and Medium Towns in India" in Sectoral Issues in the Indian Economy,* ed. G.K. Chadha, New Delhi, Har-Anand Publications, 1994.

Kundu, Amitabh, *Trends and Processes of Urbanisation in India,* Urbanisation and Emerging Population Issues-6, Human Settlements Group, IIED, Population and Development Branch, UNFPA, 2011.

Mahadevia, D. (ed.), *Inside the Transforming Urban Asia: Processes, Policies and Public Actions,* New Delhi, Concept, 2008.

Ministry of Housing and Urban Poverty Alleviation, *National Urban Housing and Habitat Policy,* 2007.

Ministry of Housing and Urban Poverty Alleviation, *Report of the Committee on Slum Census/ Statistics,* 2008.

Overview: Jawaharlal Nehru National Urban Renewal Mission available at http://jnnurm.nic.in/ overview. pdf

Provisional Population Total Paper 2, Volume 1 of 2011 *Rural Urban Distribution,* India Series 1, Census of India.

Rao, P. S. N., *Urban Governance and Management: Indian Initiatives,* Delhi, Kanishka Publications, 2006.

Report on Indian Urban Infrastructure and Services, High Powered Expert Committee, Ministry of Urban Development, 2011.

Shaw, Annapurna, "Urban Policy in Post-Independent India: An Appraisal/' *The Economic and Political Weekly,* January 27,1996: pp. 224-28.

Sivarama, Krishnan K.C., Amitabh Kundu and B. N. Singh, *Handbook of Urbanization in India,* New Delhi, Oxford University Press, 2005.

The Future of Urbanisation - Spread and Shape in Selected States, Report of the Study supported by HDFC, IDFC, IL&FS, Centre for Policy Research 2001.

OOO

Chapter Eight

Law and Order Administration

Introduction

As the coercive arm of the state, the police is called upon to maintain civil order and play a role in ensuring the rule of law and providing security to the citizens. Undoubtedly, the role of the police in India is extremely difficult and sensitive in view of the fact that we have adopted democracy as a form of government, amidst a multicultural and multiethnic population. In view of the recurring violence, extensive social conflicts, and serious threats of terrorist activities, the role of the police is an important factor in the stability of the country. The legal assurances of equality and dignity to the minorities and weaker sections of the society are also dependent upon the unbiased functioning of the police.

Though the Constitution of India mandates 'Public Order' as a subject in the State List, the Code of Criminal Procedure (CrPC) and Indian Penal Code (IPC) are subjects in the Concurrent List. There are certain provisions in the Constitution which empower the Central Government to intervene or perform special functions in matters related to law and order. It is the duty of the Centre to protect the states against internal disturbances and to ensure that the governance of every state is carried on in accordance with the provisions of the Constitution (Article 355). As per List 1 of the 7th Schedule, the Parliament has exclusive powers to make laws with respect to:

- the armed forces of the Union, which includes the Central Para-Military Forces (Entry 2A);
- The Central Bureau of Investigation (CBI) and Intelligence Bureau (IB) (Entry 8);
- The Union agencies and institutions for training of police officers, promotion of special studies or research, scientific and technical assistance in the investigation or detection of crime (Entry 65);
- All-India Services (Entry 70); and
- Extension of the powers and jurisdiction of members of one state police force to another with the consent of that state or to outside railway areas (Entry 80).

The Union Ministry for Home Affairs controls the nationwide Indian Police Service, most of the paramilitary forces, and the internal intelligence bureaus. The Police is a civil authority subordinate to the Executive, represented in the Union Government by the PM and in the States by the Chief Minister, and their respective Councils of Ministers. Prominent among the Union police forces are the Central Bureau of Investigation (CBI), Border Security Force (BSF), Central Reserve Police Force (CRPF), Central Industrial Security Force (CISF) and the Indo-Tibetan Border

Police (ITBP). Each of these forces is headed by a Director/Director-General with the status of a three-star General in the Army. The CBI is controlled by the Department of Personnel of the Union Government headed by a Minister of State who reports to the PM. The other forces are controlled by the Union Ministry of Home Affairs headed by a Cabinet Minister.

The rapid growth of the internal intelligence bureaus and the increased use of paramilitary forces against separatist insurgencies and communal unrest have given the Union Home Ministry increasing day-to-day control over law and order operations. Centrally controlled paramilitary forces are deployed throughout India and the Army has also been deployed for internal security duty in Kashmir and the Northeast.

The Union Ministry for Home Affairs controls most of the paramilitary forces, the internal intelligence bureaus, and the nationwide police service; it provides training for senior police officers for the state-organized police forces. It also establishes and maintains institutions for research and training of scientific aids to investigation.

The Central Police organization today includes the Assam Rifles, BSF, CRPF, CISF, RAF, and ITBF. In addition, there exist a number of Bureaus like the National Crime Records Bureau, and a number of Forensic Science Laboratories. Moreover, India is a permanent member of the International Police Organisation (INTERPOL) and has been taking active part in its various conferences, symposia and meetings.

The Central Government coordinates the activities of various state police organizations and provides financial assistance for the modernization of state police forces.

8.1 Role of Central Agencies in Maintenance of Law and Order

Makers of the Indian Constitution did not envisage any central machinery for the maintenance of law and order: The states are in sole charge of public order and the protection of central property in the states is the responsibility of state governments (centre is vested with the power to give guidance and assistance to the states). 'Police' and the 'public order' are subjects under the State List. The only fetter on state autonomy in this regard emanates from centre's directive power. A few important central agencies having responsibility for law and order and police administration are discussed:

Union Ministry of Home Affairs

Under the federal structure, the Constitution imposes certain responsibilities in regard to the police on the central government. The latter, through the Ministry of Home Affairs, monitors trends and developments in the law and order situation and matters relating to communal harmony and internal security of the country. The ministry provides assistance to the states as and when needed. It has the total responsibility for the administration of law and order of union territories.

The Ministry of Home Affairs is also the cadre controlling authority for the IPS, Delhi, Andaman and Nicobar Islands Police Service (DANIPS), and Delhi, Andaman and Nicobar Islands Civil Service (DANICS). Police I division of the ministry is the cadre controlling authority in respect of the IPS; whereas, the union territories division is the controlling authority for DANIPS and DANICS and the All India Services officers posted and working in the AGMUT (Arunchal Pradesh, Goa, Mizoram and Union Territories) Cadre.

Central Armed Police Forces

The Central Armed Police Forces (CAPF) refers to union nomenclature of five security forces in India under the authority of Ministry of Home Affairs. They are the Border Security Force (BSF), Central Reserve Police Force (CRPF), Central Industrial Security Force (CISF) Indo- Tibetan Border Police (ITBP) and Sashastra Seema Bal (SSB).

Each of these, BSF, CRPF, ITBP, CISF and SSB – has its own cadre of officers, but they are headed by the IPS officers. The higher echelons in these organizations, including the head of the organizations, designated as director general, is reserved by the Ministry of Home Affairs for IPS officers.

As far as recruitment of the forces is concerned, it is conducted mainly in three modes.

Gazetted officers in CAPFs are recruited through CAPF (assistant commandants) examination conducted by UPSC. They are appointed as assistant commandants and are gazetted officers, generally referred as DAGOs (directly appointed gazetted officers). DEGOs (departmental entry gazetted officers) are the ones who have been promoted through departmental examination conducted internally for subordinate officers. Subordinate officers such as sub-inspectors are recruited through competitive examination conducted by Staff Selection Commission and they are referred as DASOs (directly appointed subordinate officers). DESOs (departmental entry subordinate officers) are the ones who have been promoted through departmental examination conducted internally for constables, head constables and assistant sub-inspectors.

8.2 Police Wing at the State Level

In most of the states and union territories, the pattern of organization of the police wing is as follows:

- State police is headed by an IPS officer in the rank of DGP who is assisted by two or more additional DGPs.
- State forces are organized into zones which consist of two or more ranges, and each zone is headed by an inspector general of police.
- Further, ranges consist of several districts, and each range is headed by a deputy inspector general of police.
- District of more importance is headed by a Senior Superintendent of Police, while other districts are headed by a superintendent of police. In case SSP is heading the district, s/he is assisted by one or more superintendents of police. If superintendent of police is heading the district, then s/he is assisted by one or more additional superintendents of police.
- Each district is divided into subdivisions or circles and will be under the command of a DSP.

- Each subdivision is made up of several police stations under the command of an inspector of police, who, in turn, is assisted by sub-inspector (and above) they are the only officers who can file a charge sheet in the court.

Recruitment and Training

Each state and union territory administration has its own system of recruitment and training. The recruitment process differs according to the level of the position, and direct entry (where an applicant does not have to start at the lowest level) is possible. The educational requirements increase with recruitment for higher posts.

Assistant Commissioners of Police (ASPs) are recruited every year by the UPSC through an extremely competitive examination and are appointed into the IPS. IPS Officers are then assigned to a state police force. Superintendents of police undergo rigorous training for 44 weeks. The training programme also involves external invitees such as lawyers and management consultants. At the end of probation, they undergo an orientation training of few weeks at the assigned state's police academy.

Lower, non-managerial positions are selected by the state or central government and are trained at Police Recruit Schools. The duration of training for inspectors is roughly a year, and for constables is nearly nine months. The training staff for these are drawn from the police force itself. Police are trained in basic law, self-protection, weapon handling and so on. From recruit stations, best recruits are taken into special forces where they undergo special training.

The basic unit of law and administration is the police thana headed by the SHO who in his duties is assisted by a complement of inspectors, sub-inspectors, head constables and constables. The SP or SSP, in-charge of the district police, is an important functionary in the police hierarchy. Officers in charge of sub-units within a district such as subdivisions, circles and police stations are subordinated to the SSP/SP.

SP/SSP, in some states, works under the overall supervision of the DM and looks through the problems of law and order and of administration of crime in the district. He is empowered to take all sorts of preventive measures if a breach of peace is apprehended in the district. He advises the DM to impose prohibitory orders and even curfew. In the event of breach of law, s/he makes adequate police arrangements to meet the situation.

8.3 Indian Police Service (IPS)

At the time of independence, India inherited from the British two All-India Services — the Indian Civil Service (ICS) and the Indian Police (IP). These were subsequently renamed as the Indian Administrative Service (IAS) and the Indian Police Service (IPS) respectively. These services were constituted under Article 312 of the Constitution of India and legislation was framed to govern them. Recruitment of officers to the IPS is done by the Central Government on the basis of a competitive examination conducted by the Union Public Service Commission (UPSC) annually.

After selection, the officers receive their professional training in the National Police Academy, Hyderabad. The IPS cadre is controlled by the Ministry of Home Affairs of the

Government of India. The officers selected to the IPS are allotted to the various state cadres. They join as Assistant Superintendents of Police and remain on probation for a period of two years, after which they are confirmed. It is the IPS officers who man the senior posts in the police forces of all States/Union Territories and in Central Police Organisations. All matters relating to postings, transfers or promotions of IPS officers in the states are handled exclusively by the State Governments, while similar administrative control is exercised by the Central Government in respect to officers working under the Central Government.

8.4 Police Legislation and Administration

The Police Act of 1861 remains the central piece of legislation that governs all aspects of policing in India. Much of police work is also administered by the IPC, the CrPC and the Indian Evidence Act 1872.

The advent of Indian Independence transformed the political system, but the Police Act of 1861 was not repudiated. Political control over the police remained intact. Implanting mechanisms to assure accountability of the police to the public it serves did not become a priority, as it should have been in a democratic order. To this day, the police system in India remains accountable only to its civilian political executive, not to the masses.

The 29 State Governments have primary responsibility for maintaining law and order. However, the Central Government provides guidance and support through use of national paramilitary forces and in law has ultimate responsibility for protecting the fundamental rights guaranteed under the Constitution.

The bulk of the Indian Police is comprised of forces in the State. Each State has its own force headed by a Director-General of Police (DGP) who is equivalent in rank to his counterpart in the Union Government. A number of Additional Directors- General or Inspectors-General of Police (IGP) who look after various portfolios, such as Personnel, Law and Order, Intelligence, Crime, Armed Police, Training, and Technical Services are located at the State Police Headquarters and report directly to the DGP. Major cities in a State are headed by a Commissioner of Police (CP) who, again, reports to the DGP. Areas outside these cities in a State are divided into districts of varying size. Each district is headed by a Superintendent of Police (SP) and supervised by a Deputy Inspector-General (DIG) whose jurisdiction is called a Range, composed of a group of three or four districts.

The administration of prisons in India is the sole responsibility of the States. All prisons are managed by State Governments or by the Union Territory administration. The Central Government is largely concerned with policy formulation and planning services. In each State, the head of prison administration is an Inspector-General of police.

The rank and administrative structure of the Police organizations are based on a vertical pyramid. The state forces which largely function under the Police Act of 1861 are headed by a Director General of Police, who is responsible to the State Government for the administration of the police force throughout the state and also for giving advice on police matters. The states are divided into districts, which are headed by Superintendents of Police. A group of districts form a range, which is looked after by a Deputy Inspector General of

Police. In some bigger states, there are police Zones comprising two or more ranges, headed by officers in the rank of Inspector General of Police.

The police station is the basic and key unit of police administration. It is the crime investigation center and under the CrPC all crimes have to be recorded here from where all preventive, detective and law and order work of the police are carried on. The main characteristic of district police administration is the system of dual-control. The legal framework under which police functions is the Police Act of 1861. Section 4 of this Act vests the police administration of the district in the District Superintendent of Police; subject to the " general control and direction" of the District Magistrate. As a result of this provision the district police has been closely associated with the District Magistrate, who functions as the Chief Executive in the district. In several state manuals, the District Magistrate is referred to as the Head of the criminal administration in the district. This has resulted in the exercise of dual control over the work of the police.

In the metropolitan cities, i.e. Delhi, Kolkata, Chennai, and Mumbai as well as some big cities like Hyderabad, Ahmedabad, Baroda, Bangalore, Pune, Nagpur, the city police is placed under Commissioners of Police. They are empowered to exercise regulatory, licensing and even magisterial powers. Unlike districts, the chain of command here is one.

All states have criminal investigation departments, intelligence departments, and training and modernization wings. Policing on the railways within the states is the responsibility of the State Governments for which they have government railway police.

Although, under the Constitution, 'police' and 'public order' are included in the State List, the CBI and the IB are listed in the Union List in the 7th Schedule of Article 246. Also included in the Union List are subjects such as the training of police officers, scientific or technical assistance in the investigation or detection of crime, and extension of powers and jurisdiction of members of the police force of any state to, any area outside the state. The Central Government thus has very clear responsibility for coordination amongst states, in investigation by the CBI, police training and scientific investigation and intelligence gathering. For assisting the Central Government in coordinating the efforts in the field of training, research and modernization of police forces, there is a Bureau of Police Research and Development (BPR&D) which undertakes systematic studies of police problems and is responsible for promoting the application of science and technology to the police work, improving and development of training programs for police forces in the Centre and the States. Under entry 2 and 2-A in list 1 of Seventh Schedule of the Constitution, for assistance to states and guarding borders, the Centre maintains armed forces, such as BSF, CRPF, etc.

Recruitment into police organizations, both at the central as well as state levels, is made in three ranks namely (1) Constable, (2) Sub-Inspector and (3) Assistant Commandant and Deputy Superintendent of Police. Recruitment and training of IPS officers, who are supposed to provide leadership to police forces both in states and central police organizations, are done by the Government of India.

8.5 Police Administration: A Critique

The organizational structure of the Indian police has remained virtually unchanged from 1861. Although new ranks have been created, financial powers enhanced and training curriculum modified to suit the variety of enhanced tasks, the institutional features are the same. The police are organized provincially, made accountable indirectly through the home minister, and continue to execute the orders of the politico-administrative regime.

Apart from these historical legacies there are other additional institutional features that have been crucial in affecting police performance.

Armed Policing

Use of the armed police has become a recurring feature of the Indian police system to deal with law and order problems. Indeed, the Indian police has always prioritized law and order maintenance over crime prevention in its functions. Every successive government has funded the phenomenal growth of armed police and paramilitary forces in the country on grounds of escalating violence, terrorism, and threats to stability of the Indian state. Many specialized police units have been created to deal with communal problems (RAF), for providing security to important people (NSG and SPG) and for preventing cross-border smuggling and terrorism (BSF). There are also separate armed police forces to protect railway properties (Railway Protection Force), to police the Himalayan region (ITBP) and to provide security to the public sector industries (CISF). A women's battalion in the CRPF has also been created to deal with the increasing number of female agitators. Furthermore, every state has an armed police contingent. Additionally, every district police also maintains a large contingent of an armed unit from within its workforce. These armed police forces are only meant for Law and order' duties and their personnel cannot be used for crime investigation or service functions. Thus, both at the central and provincial levels armed police units far outnumber the ones engaged in crime control tasks.

Armed police is outside the purview of civilian ratings and the Central Government has deployed them in many 'disturbed' areas of the country affecting sensitive issues like elections, communal problems or public dissent, often overriding the objections of State Governments.

Armed police have discretionary powers that are not always exercised keeping in mind the rights of freedom and liberty of the citizens in a democracy.

Dual Control : DM vs SP

The second issue pertains to the system of dual control over the police. Section 4 of the Police Act states that at the district level the police and the Superintendent of Police(SP) will 'function under the general control and direction' of the District Magistrate (DM). The office of the collector cum district magistrate belonging to the IAS is an older institution than the police. Accordingly, the Police Act sought to maintain the hegemony of this office. But this has made the SP subordinate to the DM for law and order functions and also to the DGP for internal management of the district police. The DMs have been given powers to initiate the confidential reports of the SP, inspect police stations, approve postings of the subordinate officers made by the SP, and have control over sanction of prosecution.

Furthermore, the DGP is under the control of the Home Ministry. Thus, the police, and the IPS cadre are controlled by the IAS officers whose salary structure and powers have been considerably enhanced to reflect their superiority. Considering that these officers are selected from the same examination system administered by the UPSC, the enmity between the two can be personal as well as professional. The DGP is the senior most police officer and second only in importance to the chief secretary. Yet, the home secretary can thwart the policies and recommendations of the police chief. The IAS has become the most powerful administrative regime in the country. Accordingly, proposals and attempts to remove this dual control have been strongly opposed by the IAS fraternity. Indeed, it has been suggested that a reason for non- acceptance of the National Police Commission report was the recommendation to abolish the control by the civilian bureaucrats and replace it with an independent security commission (National Police Commission Report). The demand for operational autonomy has been voiced by the police establishment for a very long time now.

Politicization of the Police

After Independence, the functions of the government have multiplied. The British rulers were largely concerned with the collection of revenue, maintenance of order, and administration of law, the present day governmental responsibilities include providing food and shelter, education, health and welfare, gainful employment, community development, improving agriculture, banking, marketing, communications and public sector undertakings. Almost every aspect of internal social, economic, and political development is the concern of national and state elected governments. Consequently, public dissatisfaction with the quality of life issues whether directed at the failure to provide food at reasonable prices, affordable education, health, infrastructure, or even subsidies to stabilize the market are now directed at the government. Police as the coercive arm of the law have to bear the brunt of the public dissatisfaction against public policies reflected through a trend of agitationist politics.

Volatile social, economic, religious, and political conditions leading to recurring intra-state conflicts have forced modern Indian police to lay more stress on order maintenance than 'due process of law'. Furthermore, even if the existing police institution is not entirely mal-intentioned, it is generally perceived to be serving the interests of the propertied and ruling classes. This makes public cooperation difficult which is so essential for democratic policing. Sixty years of democratic India has seen considerable politicization of the police forces.

The National Police Commission Report has commented harshly on this interference in police work and cited several instances of unwarranted and blatant political misuse of the police organization (GOI 1979).

The day-to-day political interference in the work of police officers has reinforced the public impression that police are unable to discharge their duties properly because politicians do not let them function impartially, and in true public interest. The large scale transfers and postings of all ranks of officers on political considerations and the inability of the police leadership to discipline officers who are politically connected present evidence of a police force that is ruled by political expediency rather than any established procedures and norms.

Whether it is taking action against the politicians involved in criminal acts, or making arrests of anti-social elements or controlling order maintenance problems, the supervisory officers have to tread very carefully. Their judgments are contested by politicians who attempt to make political capital out of every incident.

New Challenges

The role of the police is not well defined in Manuals and has, generally been expanding. The colonial model was designed for the maintenance of the interest of the ruling class and keeping the sovereignty of the British. Independence brought many new challenges — that of social conflicts, terrorism, communal disturbances, and special needs of the minority and weaker sections. The tendency of the state to control unwanted behaviour by criminalizing it has invariably expanded the areas of police action. Thus, laws abolishing untouchability, dowry, child labour, trafficking of women, and misuse of the Internet have expanded police powers. The expansion in armed units has already been described. New units in the name of 'protection of weaker sections', 'Harijan', 'women' and even 'tourist police' have been created within state police organizations. These have been done without taking into account the capabilities and efficiency of the police institutions. On the other hand, the police has also successfully thwarted attempts to open its operations for scrutiny or accountability to the rights of citizens.

The growth in the activities of an emerging democratic state has been paralleled by the expansion of the bureaucratic machine. In particular, the expansion of the IPS has only been second to that of the IAS. They have expanded their rank and structure (from inspector-general to director-general), enhanced their promotional avenues, garnered many resources, and enlarged their perks. The IPS cadre command all the senior posts related to internal security and enforcement of criminal laws in the country. Not only all the para-military forces like the BSF, CRPF, ITBP, and others, but also the intelligence gathering and investigating agencies like the IB, RAW, and the CBI are commanded by IPS officers on deputation. Furthermore, organizations like the Institute of Forensic Sciences, research establishments like the Bureau of Police Research and Development and large prisons (like Tihar Jail in Delhi) are also controlled by the IPS. In many states the IPS officers have also prevailed upon the governments to create ex-cadre posts in public relations, publishing, and even public sector industries. The expansion has given the IPS a vast say in the administration of the country that was perhaps not envisaged in the original constitutional design.

Corruption

Pervasive corruption and brutality flourishes because of the police organizational culture that evolved through several kinds of practices, beliefs, and value systems. The British for the purpose of establishing their Raj assiduously built the colonial feudal repressive sub-culture of the Indian police. The police were meant to suppress any dissent against British rule,a situation that gave unlimited power to police officers. Consequently, corruption and brutality became endemic and rampant in the police department. Every rank, from the lowest constable, the village watchman, to the highest ranking DGP became prone to corruption. The investigating officers extort money from complainants, witnesses, and naturally the accused. The constable extorts money from hawkers, footpath dwellers, truck and bus drivers, etc. Regular extortions in every police station (so-called hafta) are also common. Corrupt practices are now part of the Indian police system and are found in every mode of its duty and operations.

Nature of Police duties

Let us take the nature of duties that have been thrust on the police in recent times. Provision of security to a large number of persons who are 'very important' and vulnerable, watching over land sites under dispute, resolving disturbances in educational institutions and hospitals and in communal conflicts — all these form a part of their duties today .The police is part of the social and legal system, the penal institutions and voluntary organizations. More and more crimes against women and against members of the Scheduled Castes and tribes are being brought to notice. Political agitations such as jathas, processions, satyagrahs and bandhs require police presence. Several 'new' offences like smuggling and dealing in drugs are also widespread. Every religion has festivals that frequently coincide and the police has to be vigilant to prevent communal trouble. All these new and extra demands have their effect on the quality of police work. The Rule of Law requires police officers to do their work within the framework of the law and with objectivity. Quite often, this is thwarted by political forces.

In 2005 the Central Government set up a Police Act Drafting Committee (PADC), commonly known as the Soli Sorabjee Committee tasked to draft a new model Police Act. The PADC was mandated to take into account the changing role and responsibilities of the police and the challenges before it and draft a model act that could guide states while adopting their own legislation. The PADC submitted its Model Police Act, 2006.

8.6 Supreme Court Directives

In an important public interest case on police reforms, Supreme Court of India gave seven important directives to the Union government and states. The judgement was delivered on 22 September 2006 (Prakash Singh v. Union of India, https:indiankanoon.org). The Court in the said judgement directed the Union Government and State Governments to set up mechanisms as directed by December 31, 2006, and file affidavits of compliance by January 3, 2007.

Supreme Court Directives Inter-alia were:

- The State Governments were directed to constitute a State Security Commission in every State to ensure that the State Government does not exercise unwarranted influence or pressure on the State police and for laying down the broad policy guidelines so that the State police always act according to the laws of the land and the Constitution of the country. This watchdog body shall be headed by the Chief Minister or Home Minister as Chairman and have the DGPof the State as its ex-officio Secretary. The other members of the Commission shall be chosen in such a manner that it is able to function independent of Government control. The recommendations of this Commission shall be binding on the State Government. The functions of the

State Security Commission would include laying down the broad policies and giving directions for the performance of the preventive tasks and service oriented functions of the police, evaluation of the performance of the State police and preparing a report thereon for being placed before the State legislature.

- The Director General of Police of the State shall be selected by the State Government from amongst the three senior-most officers of the Department who have been empanelled for promotion to that rank by the UPSC on the basis of their length of service, very good record and range of experience heading the police force. Once he has been selected for the job, he should have a minimum tenure of at least two years irrespective of his date of superannuation.
- Police Officers on operational duties in the field like the Inspector General of Police in-charge of Zone, Deputy Inspector General of Police in-charge of Range, Superintendent of Police in-charge of district and Station House Officer in-charge of a Police Station shall also have a prescribed minimum tenure of two years unless it is found necessary to remove them prematurely following disciplinary proceedings against them.
- There shall be a Police Establishment Board in each State which shall decide all transfers, postings, promotions and other service related matters of officers of and below the rank of Deputy Superintendent of Police. The Establishment Board shall be a departmental body comprising the Director General of Police and four other senior officers of the Department. The State Government may interfere with the decision of the Board in exceptional cases only after recording its reasons for doing so. The Board shall also be authorized to make appropriate recommendations to the State Government regarding the posting and transfers of officers of and above the rank of Superintendent of Police, and the Government is expected to give due weight to these recommendations and shall normally accept it. It shall also function as a forum of appeal for disposing of representations from officers of the rank of Superintendent of Police and above regarding their promotion, transfer, disciplinary proceedings or their being subjected to illegal or irregular orders and generally reviewing the function of the police in the State.
- The Central Government shall set up a National Security Commission at the Union level to prepare a panel for being placed before the appropriate Appointing Authority for selection and placement of Chiefs of the Central Police Organizations (CPO), who should also be given a minimum tenure of two years. The Commission would also review measures from time to time to upgrade the effectiveness of these forces, improve the service conditions of its personnel, ensure that there is proper coordination between them and that the forces are generally utilized for the purposes for which they were raised and make recommendations on their behalf. The National Security Commission could be headed by the Union Home Minister and comprise heads of the CPOs and a couple of security experts as members with the Union Home Secretary as its Secretary.

- There shall be a Police Complaints Authority at the district level to look into complaints against police officers of and up to the rank of Deputy Superintendent of Police. Similarly, there should be another Police Complaints Authority at the State level to look into complaints against- officers of the rank of Superintendent of Police and above. The district level authority may be headed by a retired District Judge while the State level authority may be headed by a retired Judge of the High Court/ Supreme Court. The head of the State level complaints authority shall be chosen by the State Government out of a panel of names proposed by the Chief Justice; the head of the district level complaints authority may also be chosen out of a panel of names proposed by the Chief Justice or a Judge of the High Court nominated by him. The panel may include members from amongst retired civil servants, police officers from any other department, or from the civil society.
- The investigating police shall be separated from the law and order police to ensure speedier investigation, better expertise and improved police public relations.

The deadline of 31st December 2006 was fixed initially by the Supreme Court for compliance of these directives. Later, the Supreme Court, by an Order dated 16.05.2008, set up this Committee (hereinafter referred to as "the committee") to monitor the implementation of the above directives by the state Governments.

Terms of reference of the Committee

The terms of the committee's work were set out in the aforementioned order as follows:

1. To examine the affidavits filed by the different States and the Union Territories in compliance to the Court's directions with reference to the ground realities.
2. Advise the respondents wherever the implementation is falling short of the Court's orders, after considering the respondents' stated difficulties in implementation.
3. Bring to the notice of the Court any genuine problem the respondents may be having in view of the specific conditions prevailing in a State or Union Territory.
4. Examine the new legislations enacted by different States regarding the police to see whether these are in compliance with the letter and spirit of this Court's directions.
5. Apprise the Court about unnecessary objections or delays on the part of any respondent so that appropriate follow-up action could be taken against that respondent.
6. Submit a status report in compliance to this Court every six months.

On 31 October 2006, Government of India circulated a draft Model Police Act to states for consideration and appropriate action. The purpose was to improve (i) functional autonomy, (ii) professionalism, (iii) service conditions and (iv) accountability. Since then, a number of states have enacted/amended their police acts.

Conclusion

With India's police to population ratio at 130 (per 1,00,000 people) it is well below the UN recommended figure of 222. This means that while a significant portion of tax payers' money is used to keep VIPs safe there are very few police men on the ground to serve the common man.

Institutions are important in the life of a nation. The police institution is obviously one that is important in the democratic system of the country. The security and well- being of the citizen is dependent upon the police. Yet, the police institution in India is in a pathetic state: disorganized, inefficient, corrupt, and partisan in its operations. It is unable to perform in accordance with the expectations of a democratic society. The fault lies in the design and inability to adapt to the changing circumstances that have emerged after Independence. It has failed to deal with social conflicts and prevent growing violence. The force has become heavily politicized and its leadership has been reduced to tools of compliance.

A reform can only come from the pressure exerted by the public and other institutions. The judiciary, National Human Rights Commission, the media, academic community and several kinds of civil society groups have an interest in reforming the police. At present, some of these institutions and citizen groups like the People's Union for Democratic Rights, the People's Union for Civil Liberties, Majdoor Kisan Sangharsh Samiti have achieved some success. These have forced the government to be accountable for its policies and actions.

Besides whatever else that needs to be done, one problem that needs to be addressed urgently is with regard to the systemic deficiency of the police force, i.e. about the poor skill quality of constables who are officially estimated to make 87% of the police personnel. This vital aspect has been flagged by the government-appointed Soli Sorabjee Committee Report, which submitted an updated draft of the Police Bill in 2006 shortly after the Supreme Court judgment mandating police reforms.

The draft bill dedicated a whole chapter to what it called the "primary rank in civil police". It proposed a big jump in the status of constables, who are generally matriculates depending more on brawn than brain to do their policing duties.

Given the need for "better-educated persons to exercise discretionary powers in dealing with people and investigating cases", the Sorabjee Committee suggested that the rank of constable be replaced with that of "civil police officer" (CPO). The proposed change in nomenclature is part of a larger scheme spelt out by it for instilling a greater degree of professionalism in the rank and file.

The government, on its part has made little progress in adopting the Sorabjee draft as the "Model Police Act" that it was supposed to be. This was despite several meetings it held with the states on issues that included the police reforms issue. But the agenda for government meetings were not the only Sorabjee report but also the 2007 report of the Administrative Reforms Commission (ARC), which had come up with an altogether different prescription for upgrading what it called "the cutting edge functionaries" of the police.

The Second ARC said that the existing system of constabulary should be phased out and that all future recruitments at the lower end should be at the level of the assistant sub-inspector (ASI), who would be a graduate. As a corollary, the ARC suggested that some of the chores currently performed by constables —"non-core functions" such as delivery of court summons or verification of antecedents for passport applications —could be outsourced to other agencies.

While opinion is divided on which approach to constabulary is more feasible, the government cannot pretend to be earnest about its attempts to restore law and order unless it displays the resolve to take up such long-term reforms.

It should get down to implementing either the Sorabjee recommendation of introducing CPOs or the ARC proposal of making the ASI the bottom layer of the police hierarchy. The commitment, devotion and accountability of the police has to be only to the Rule of Law. The supervision and control has to be such that it ensures that the police inculcates and internalizes a public service oriented approach. The role and functions of the police need to be redefined in a new Police Act which ensures that the police is made accountable essentially and primarily to the law of the land and its people. The Police Act of 1861 is an anachronism that needs to be repealed and repudiated in a democracy.

The primary objective of the police remains the maintenance of law and order rather than crime prevention. The modern day mandate of police forces everywhere in the world is to provide a public good that prevents crime and protects victims. Understaffed, undertrained and underpaid, the Indian Police needs many of the technological capabilities necessary to perform quality investigations. All of these contribute to the low conviction rates that discredit both the police and the courts in every branch of the criminal justice system. Revamping the lower order police cadre and training officers in professional skills can have positive effects both on public satisfaction with the police and the quality of police work.

Suggested Readings

Bajpai, G.S., *Victim in the Criminal Justice Process: Perspective on Police and Judiciary*, Delhi, Uppal, 1997.

Bawa, P.S., *System of Policing*, Delhi, Rupa, 1995.

Begum, S. Mehartaj, *District Police Administration: A Case Study*, Delhi, Anmol, 1996.

Ghosh, S. K., *The Betrayal of the Police*, Delhi, Ashish, 1991.

Ghosh, S.K. and K.F. Rustamji (eds.), *Encyclopaedia of Police in India*, 3 Vols., Delhi, Ashish, 1997.

Government of India, Report of the National Police Commission, 8 vols., Delhi, Ministry of Home * Affairs, 1981.

Guha Roy, Jayatilak (ed), *Policing in Twenty first century*, New Delhi, 11PA, 1999.

Jha, Sudhir Kumar, *Raj to Swaraj: Changing Contours of Police*, Delhi, Lancer Publishers, 1995.

Kapur, Devesh etal, Rethinking Public Institutions in India, OUP, 2017.

Mathur, Krishna Mohan, *Indian Police: Role and Challenges*, Delhi, Gyan, 1994.

Minocha, O.P. and Jaytilak Guha Roy, *Recruitment Policy and Programmes for State Police Organisations*, Delhi, IIPA, 1998.

National Symposia on Human Resource Management at Constabulary Level and Human Rights Imperatives in Day to Day Policing, 1996, Proceedings, Hyderabad, Sardar Vallabhabhai Patel National Police Academy.

Saxena, Anil K., *Professionalism in Indian Police*, Delhi, APH Publishing, 1997.

Sen, Sankar, *Indian Police Today*, Delhi, Ashish, 1994.

OOO

Chapter Nine

Disaster Management

Introduction

India has been exposed to natural disasters throughout its long recorded history. Cyclones, floods, earthquakes and droughts have recurred from time to time causing massive devastation. About 60% of the Indian landmass is prone to earthquakes and droughts of various intensities, and over 40 million hectares is prone to seasonal floods. This not only results in loss of thousands of lives, but also large-scale destruction of private and public assets.

The Government of India (GOI) has now brought about a paradigm shift in its approach to disaster management, from being relief centric to one with greater emphasis on preparedness, prevention and mitigation. This approach proceeds from the conviction that development cannot be sustained unless disaster mitigation is built into development policy. Another cornerstone of the approach is that mitigation has to be interdisciplinary, encompassing all sectors of the development process. Disaster Management should occupy a prime place in the policy framework as it is the poorest citizens who are worst affected by calamities and disasters.

Disaster Management is a multidisciplinary concern in which a wide range of issues that range from forecasting, warning, search and rescue, relief, reconstruction and rehabilitation are included. It is multi-sectoral as it involves administrators, scientists, planners, volunteers and communities. The aim is to plan the pre-disaster, on disaster and post-disaster periods. All these activities are complementary and supplementary to each other and there is a critical need for coordinating these activities.

Natural disasters directly impact economies, agriculture, food security, water, sanitation, environment and health. We have also to study the social and psychological dimensions of disasters to evolve appropriate strategies for mitigation.

9.1 Types of Disasters

Due to the increasing frequency of natural and man-made disasters and their severe impact on individuals, society, economy, natural resources and the environment, GOI constituted a High Powered Committee (HPC) on Disaster Management in August 1999 to prepare comprehensive plans for National, State and District levels. The HPC stressed on the need for a comprehensive and holistic approach towards dealing with all kinds of disasters. From a compartmentalized response-oriented approach, a coordinated, holistic and participatory approach has been recommended. HPC categorized disasters into the following five sub-groups depending on generic (origin) considerations and various departments/ministries dealing with their various aspects:

Water and Climate Related Disasters

Floods, cyclones, tornadoes and hurricanes, hailstorm, cloud burst, heat wave and cold wave, snow avalanches, droughts, sea erosion and thunder and lightning.

Geologically Related Disasters

Landslides and Mudflows, Earthquakes, Dam Failures/Dam Bursts and Mine Fires

Chemical, Industrial and Nuclear Related Disasters

Chemical, industrial and nuclear disasters occur due to an accident, negligence, damage or incompetence.

Accident Related Disasters

Forest Fires, Urban Fires, Mines Flooding, Oil Spill, Major Building Collapse, Serial Bomb Blasts, Festival related disasters, Electrical disasters and Fires, Air, Road and Rail Accidents, Boat Capsizing and Village Fire have been included in this subgroup by HPC.

Biologically Related Disasters

Epidemics, Pest Attacks, Cattle epidemics and Food poisoning. Natural disasters are natural phenomena, while man-made disasters are events which, either intentionally or by accident cause severe threats to public health and well-being. Since their occurrence is unpredictable, man-made disasters pose an especially challenging threat that must be dealt with thorough vigilance, proper preparedness and response.

9.2 Institutional and Policy Framework

- The institutional and policy mechanisms for carrying out response, relief and rehabilitation are now well-established. These mechanisms relate generally to post-disaster relief and rehabilitation measures.
- At the national level, the Ministry of Home Affairs is the nodal Ministry for all matters concerning disaster management. The Central Relief Commissioner (CRC) in the Ministry of Home Affairs is the nodal officer who coordinates, relief operations for natural disasters. The CRC receives information relating to forecasting/ warning of a natural calamity from India Meteorological Department (IMD) or from Central Water Commission of Ministry of Water Resources on a continuing basis.

Each Ministry/Department/Organization nominates their nodal officer to the Crisis Management Group chaired by CRC. The nodal officer is responsible for preparing sectoral Action Plan/Emergency Support Function Plan for managing disasters.

National Crisis Management Committee (NCMC): Cabinet Secretary, who is the highest executive officer, heads the NCMC. Secretaries of all the concerned Ministries/ Departments as well as organizations are the members of the Committee. The NCMC gives direction to the Crisis Management Group as deemed necessary.

Crisis Management Group: The Central Relief Commissioner in the Ministry of Home Affairs is the Chairman of the CMG, consisting of senior officers (called nodal officers) from various concerned Ministries. The CMG's functions include the annual review of contingency plans formulated by various Ministries/ Departments/Organizations in their respective sectors; measures required for dealing with natural disasters; coordinate the activities of the Central Ministries and the State Governments in relation to disaster preparedness and relief; and to obtain information from the nodal officers on measures relating to above. Control Room (Emergency Operation Room): An Emergency Operations Center (Control Room) exists in the nodal Ministry of Home Affairs, which functions round the clock, to assist the Central Relief Commissioner in the discharge of his duties. The activities of the Control Room include collection and transmission of information concerning natural calamity and relief, keeping close contact with governments of the affected States, interaction with other Central Ministries/ Departments/Organizations in connection with relief, maintaining records containing all relevant information relating to action points and contact points in Central Ministries, etc., keeping up-to-date details of all concerned officers at the Central and State levels.

Contingency Action Plan: A National Contingency Action Plan (CAP) for dealing with contingencies arising in the wake of natural disasters has been formulated by the GOI and it has been periodically updated. It facilitates the launch of relief operations without delay. The CAP identifies the initiatives required to be taken by various Central Ministries/ Departments in the wake of natural calamities, sets down the procedure and determines the focal points in the administrative machinery.

Funding mechanisms: The policy and the funding mechanisms for provision of relief assistance to those affected by natural calamities are clearly laid down. These are reviewed by the Finance Commission appointed by the GOI every five years. The Finance Commission makes recommendations regarding the division of tax and non-tax revenues between the Central and the State Governments and also regarding policy for provision of relief assistance and their share of expenditure thereon. A Calamity Relief Fund (CRF) has been set up in the State as per the recommendations of the Eleventh Finance Commission (Centre contribute 75% whereas State 25%). State can get assistance through National Calamity Contingency Fund (NCCF) and also through the Prime Minister's Fund. At the State level, response, relief and rehabilitation are handled by Departments of Relief and Rehabilitation. The State Crisis Management Committee is set up under the Chairmanship of the Chief Secretary in the State. All the concerned Departments and organizations of the State and Central Government Departments located in the State are represented in this Committee.

- The key level for disaster relief operations is the district which prepares district plans and monitors calamities for relief. A district level coordination and relief committee is constituted and is headed by the collector as Chairman. This Committee may include both governmental and non-governmental responsibilities.

9.3 Disaster Management in India

In India, natural disasters like floods, cyclones and droughts occur repeatedly in different parts of the country. Many districts of India are prone to multiple hazards and face different disasters around the year. Earthquake, hailstorms, avalanches, and landslides also occur in some parts of India but the impact depends on the magnitude of the event and the vulnerability of the location.

In India, the human and economic losses from disasters are high in comparison to many other developing nations. According to an estimate by the World Bank direct losses from natural disasters are up to 2% of India's GDP. More importantly, the impact of most of the disasters is disproportionately high on the poor.

The Hyogo Framework of Action (HFA) that was approved in 2005 by the UN to which India is a signatory, advocates mainstreaming disaster risk reduction into socio-economic development planning and activities by adopting five priorities for action through a five-fold process, viz.:

1. Political process requiring countries to develop policies, legislative and institutional frameworks for disaster risk reduction and commit resources for their prevention, mitigation and preparedness.
2. Technical process which calls for application of science and technology for assessment, identification and monitoring of disasters and enhancing early warning systems.
3. Socio-educational process aiming at increasing citizen's understanding and skills to build a culture of safety and resilience at all levels.
4. Development process seeking to integrate disaster risk in all relevant sectors of development planning and programmes.
5. Humanitarian process that requires factoring disaster risk reduction in disaster response and recovery.

GOI started work on some of these ideas as early as August 1999 when a High Powered Committee (HPC) on Disaster Management was constituted under the Chairmanship of Shri J.C. Pant, former Secretary of Agriculture to the GOI along with experts and officials, to suggest measures to bring about institutional reforms in the field of disaster management. Keeping in view our federal structure, the Committee was also mandated to prepare comprehensive plans for National, State and District levels. Soon after its formation, the scope of the Committee was enlarged to include man-made disasters like chemical, industrial, nuclear and others.

The turning point in the thinking on disaster management was the Indian Ocean Tsunami of 26th December 2004. This disaster struck the country in more than seven states which highlighted the gaps in early warning, coordination and the management of disasters. In an All Party Meeting held on 9th January 2005, the need for national level legislation for management of natural and man-made disasters was highlighted. Consequent to this meeting, GOI decided to enact a law on disaster management to provide for a requisite institutional mechanism for drawing up and monitoring the implementation of the disaster management plans, ensuring measures by various wings of the Government for prevention and mitigation of disasters and for undertaking a holistic, coordinated and prompt response to any disaster situation. Accordingly a Bill was introduced in the Rajya Sabha on 11th May 2005.

The Disaster Management Act, 2005 lays down institutional, legal financial and coordination mechanisms at the Central, State, District and Local levels. These institutions are not parallel structures and will work in close harmony. The new institutional framework is expected to ensure implementation of the national desire for a paradigm shift in DM from a relief-centric approach to a proactive regime that lays greater emphasis on preparedness, prevention and mitigation.

With the enactment of Disaster Management Act 2005 the National Disaster Management Authority (NDMA) was established under the Chairmanship of the Prime Minister. The Act also provides for the establishment of State Disaster Management Authorities (SDMA) and District Disaster Management Authorities (DDMA). Therefore, the Disaster Management architecture for the country has now been provided with legal backing and with clear allocation of responsibility to specific government bodies. The Acts also provide for budget allocation for disaster risk reduction and for response. With this framework in place it is now up to the Central and the State Governments to utilize these provisions effectively to reduce the impact of disasters on the people and the nation's resources and assets.

9.4 New Institutions

The National Policy on Disaster Management prepared by the NDMA, GOI, and approved by the Cabinet in 2009 was formulated with the vision to build a safe and disaster resilient India by developing a holistic, proactive, multi-disaster oriented and technology-driven strategy through a culture of prevention, mitigation and response. The National Policy envisaged a paradigm shift from the hitherto reactive post-disaster relief-centric regime to a more proactive and enabling environment of strengthened disaster preparedness, mitigation and improved emergency response capacities of all stakeholder groups. Mandated by the enactment of the Disaster Management Act 2005, institutional mechanisms like the NDMA chaired by the PM of India at the national level, SDMAs chaired by the Chief Ministers of the respective State Governments at the state level and District Disaster Management Authorities DDMAs chaired by the respective District Collectors and co-chaired by the Sabha patis of the Zilla Parishads at the district level were established. However, in many cases, these institutions are not active and operational except a few honorable exceptions. Similarly, even though the Disaster Management Act 2005 stipulated the setting up of the Disaster Response Fund and the Disaster Mitigation Fund at national, state and district levels, only the National and State Disaster Response Funds have become operational till now. The increasing frequency and damage to property, assets and infrastructure caused by disasters like the Uttarakhand flood in 2013 or the Kashmir flood 2014 makes it imperative that the provisions of the Disaster Management Act 2005 are enforced in letter and spirit.

In the event of a sudden disaster, the restoration of disrupted services, the effective and efficient delivery of services to the disaster-affected communities and the setting up of a transparent mechanism of ensuring that the disaster-affected people receive the relief entitlements which are intended for them have to be necessarily integral components of good governance at the district, state and national levels. With the good practice examples of deployment of information technology innovations like biometrics and smart cards in humanitarian assistance in recent disasters in some of the countries affected by disasters, our administrative machinery has to explore ways of ensuring efficiency and effectiveness in the delivery of services, minimizing inordinate delays, red tape and extraneous pressures of excluding real victims and accommodating false claimants. Private sector bodies, Community Based Organizations and Non-Governmental Organizations can play the role of watchdogs in creating a level playing field for the victims affected by disasters. Wherever expedient and unavoidable, justice has to be ensured by resorting to the instruments of good governance like Right to Information and legal options like Public Interest Litigation.

9.5 Systemic Inefficiencies

The Eleventh Five Year Plan document made a strategic and pioneering shift towards mainstreaming disaster management in development planning and made several strong suggestions in this direction. The Finance Ministry of the GOI prescribed radical changes in 2009 in the formats for submission of plan proposals from Ministries and Departments of the GOI and State Governments. The formats incorporated self- certification by the proposing officials to the effect that the proposals have factored in the disaster risk and vulnerability of the concerned geographical area. However, the continuing increase in the damage and destruction of property, assets and public infrastructure makes it necessary to carry out random audits of such proposals in areas affected by disasters and to fix accountability for the financial loss on erring officials. This has become necessary to streamline the process of mainstreaming disaster risk reduction in development planning. It is also unfortunate that most of the mitigation projects proposed in the 12th Five Year Plan have remained non-starters.

9.6 Capacity building

Capacity building of various stakeholder groups is one of the most formidable challenges in a large nation facing high risk from multiple disasters. Training, public awareness, research and education in disaster management must reach out to communities for strengthening disaster preparedness, prevention, mitigation, emergency response, disaster resilient reconstruction and recovery at local levels. It is necessary to involve civil society organizations, community-based organizations, corporate sector entities, local administration' officials, elected representatives and professionals in these activities. The experience of Andhra Pradesh and Karnataka in the 2009 floods when 7.5 lakh houses and 5.5 lakh houses respectively were washed away, should compel public functionaries to ensure that all mass housing schemes like Indira Awas Yojana in the rural areas and Rajiv Awas Yojana in urban and peri-urban areas must comply with disaster resilience features so that we are not reconstructing risk in disaster-prone areas. The approach document of the 12th Five Year Plan has observed that "a major weakness of the Indira Awaas Yojana (IAY) has been the quality of housing. There have been complaints about weak foundations, poor roofing materials and incomplete constructions. There is a clear need for developing and popularising innovative, location-specific technologies, materials, designs and methods through a network of institutions, which could result in low-cost, environment friendly and disaster resistant houses as per local cultural preferences. Better systems for monitoring of the programme are also required."

9.7 Financing Post-Disaster Recovery

The responsibility for disaster funding in the aftermath of a natural catastrophe is shared by the Central and State Governments. While the affected state manages the relief and reconstruction efforts, the Central Government provides financial support. Originally, the Central Government financed catastrophe relief efforts through margin money allocated to the states from the successive Finance Commissions. However, the general experience under this system was that actual calamity expenditures consistently outpaced underlying budget expectations. Under the Ninth Finance Commission, the government revised the system and created a Calamity Relief Fund (CRF) from which states can draw upon under emergencies. The additional funds will be provided by the centre from National Calamity Contingency Fund (NCCF), after the submission of memorandum (damage assessment report) by the States to the Center. The 13th Finance Commission has merged CRF and NCCF into one fund called National Disaster Response Fund (NDRF). All these funds could be utilized only for the immediate relief given to the affected and immediate temporary recovery of critical installations. There is no provision or dedicated fund available for long-term recovery.

National Disaster Management Act 2005 has made provision for constitution of two funds viz. National Disaster Response Fund and National Disaster Mitigation Fund. The NDRF, as specified in the Act, would be used for meeting any threatening disaster situation or disaster. The Response Fund would be available with the National Executive Committee, who would use it towards meeting the expenses for emergency response, relief and rehabilitation according to the guidelines laid down by the Government, in consultation with the National Authority. The National Disaster Mitigation Fund has been provided exclusively for the purpose of mitigation and would be used only for mitigation projects. The corpus of the fund would be provided by the Central Government after due appropriation made by Parliament, by law.

The Act has also made provisions for similar funds at the State and district levels. The State Disaster Response Fund shall be available with the State Executive Committee for emergency response, relief and rehabilitation at the State level, while the State Disaster Mitigation Fund shall be made available to the State Disaster Management Authority for mitigation projects.

All these provisions of disaster funding are limited to immediate and intermediate disaster recovery. Long-term recovery funding is an unaddressed issue. After so many disasters in the country, India has just gone for a few long-term recovery programmes with the objective to 'build back better' by incorporating mitigation into reconstruction programmes such as in the case of the Maharashtra Latur earthquake (1994), Andhra Pradesh Cyclone (1997), Orissa Cyclone (1999), Gujarat earthquake (2001), Tsunami (2004), Leh cloud burst (2010) and Sikkim earthquake (2011). Many recent catastrophic disasters remained unattended for long-term recovery (Bihar, Orissa and Assam successive floods, Karnataka and Andhra floods 2008, Bengal Cyclone 2010).

9.8 National Disaster Response Force

Three successive national calamities in quick succession—the Orissa Super Cyclone (1999) with 10,000 casualties, Gujarat Earthquake (2001) with 20,000 casualties and the Tsunami in 2004 with 12,000 casualties brought about a realization of the need to have a specialist response, mechanism at the National level to effectively respond to disasters. Until 2001 the responsibility for the management of disasters was that of the Agriculture Ministry alone (whose approach was essentially relief centric) till it was transferred to the Ministry of Home Affairs (MHA) in June 2002. The MHA constituted a steering committee in 2003 under the Chairmanship of the Union Home Secretary to address the need to effectively manage disasters. The Committee recommended the conversion of two battalions each of Border Security Force (BSF) Central Reserve Police Force (CRPF) Central Industrial Security Force (CISF) and Indo Tibetan Border Police (ITBP) as Disaster Response Battalions. Later, the enactment of the Disaster Management Act 2005 brought about a seminal change in disaster management in the country. This Act has made the statutory provision for the constitution of the NDRF. The new vision of the Act was to develop a proactive multi-hazard and technology-driven strategy for Disaster Management. The paradigm shift was a change from relief centric to pre-emptive strategies of Disaster Management in India.

Composition of NDRF

At present NDRF consists of ten battalions (of 1149 personnel each) from the paramilitary forces. The force is gradually emerging as the most visible and vibrant multi-disciplinary, multi-skilled and high-tech stand-alone force which has successfully handled both man-made and natural disasters in almost 75 response operations in the country in a short period of time (2007-13) including a highly acclaimed performance in the Orissa Super Cyclone 2013 and the Kashmir Floods of 2014. NDRF battalions are located at ten different locations based on the vulnerability profile of our country and to cut down the response time for their deployment. This force as per the Disaster Management Act 2005 would be under the superintendence, direction and control of NDMA, the open policy-making body on Disaster Management in the country. NDMA provided the much needed impetus to establish the NDRF as a truly specialist force by according highest priority to ensure a state-of-the-art training and equipment for the Force.

Each battalion has 18 self-contained specialist search and secure teams of 44 personnel each including engineers, technicians, electricians, dog squads and paramedics. The ten battalions contain 180 teams, the total strength of NDRF is about 11,590 personnel. With inclusion of 2 more battalions in 2011-12 and by further expansion of 2 more battalions (already sanctioned) the NDRF has acquired the unique distinction of being the single largest dedicated disaster response force in the world. The response time of this force has been reduced to the minimum on account of the concept of proactive availability of this Force to the states and also the concept of pre-positioning the force in threatening disaster scenarios (e.g. in the recent 2013 Orissa Super Cyclone). It is indeed very encouraging that within a short span of less than a decade NDRF is not only the most trusted face of NDMA but has acquired the reputation of a "specialist force" capable of responding to any natural disaster or emergencies with competence and professionalism.

In the NDMA's vision of Disaster Response Mechanism, NDRF is at the apex as a dedicated specialist force trained and equipped as per international standards. At the state level, State Disaster Response Force (SDRF) is being constituted and trained on the lines of NDRF and at the district level personnel of Civil Defense and Home Guards are being trained to be included in the statutory mandated three-tier disaster response mechanism in the country.

In addition to its mandated tasks, NDRF has significantly engaged itself in capacity-building programmes in communities in several states. Since its inception, NDRF personnel have trained and sensitized about 30 lakh people under these programmes. The target groups are villagers, local people, school children and volunteers selected by the state administration. 300 Block exercises on cyclones, industrial disasters, urban flooding, etc., have been organized by NDRF battalions in different parts of India.

Training

One of the key factors contributing towards a high degree of professionalism of NDRF has been the NDMA's vision to train this force as per international standards. As a sequel to this vision, the trainers of this force have acquired training under the aegis of some of the best known Institutions, namely, ADPC Bangkok, USAID PEER Programme, Swiss Development Cooperation Bern, Advance Search & Rescue Training Centre-Florida, Civil Defence Academy-Singapore, DRDE-Gwalior, CME- Pune and BARC-Mumbai.

In the initial years one of the major problems faced by this Force was non availability of manpower as personnel of NDRF were being deployed regularly for routine Law and Order duties, thereby adversely affecting the training programmes of the Force. In a landmark development, Shri M.K. Narayanan, the then National Security Advisor, in a meeting of the NDMA with Hon'ble Prime Minister on 25th October 2007, highlighted the importance and need of NDRF being made a dedicated force exclusively for disaster-related activities only. Acceptance of this suggestion by the then PM paved the way for notification of NDRF Rules on 14th February 2008, making NDRF a dedicated force for Disaster Response related duties only under the unified command of the Director General NDRF.

Achievements

As regards the response mechanism, the concept of "proactive availability" of this Force to the State and also the concept of "pre-positioning" this Force in threatening disaster scenarios paid maximum dividends during various calamities. The first major disaster for NDRF was the Kosi Flood in 2008. In line with the above mentioned two concepts, NDRF Forces were moved to Bihar immediately after the breach in Kosi barrage was noticed on 19th August 2008. The situation was handled by the NDMA on a war footing by airlifting 153 high-speed motorized boats with 780 flood rescue trained personnel drawn from three different Battalions to the five flood-affected districts with utmost promptitude. As a result, over

1 lakh affected people were rescued during the initial stage. The prompt and professional response of NDRF was highly appreciated by the Chief Minister of Bihar. In the Assam floods in 2012, NDRF rescued over 32,200 flood marooned people.

Besides the professionalism shown during rescue operations in floods and cyclones, NDRF has also acquired considerable expertise in Collapsed Structure Search and Rescue (CSSR) operations. This expertise was exhibited in a commendable response operation by the NDRF during a six storey building collapse at Bellary (Karnataka) in January 2010. In a meticulously planned round-the-clock operation lasting 7 days, the NDRF rescued 20 trapped live victims and retrieved 29 bodies. Similarly, in a multi-storey factory building collapse at Jalandhar (Punjab) in April 2012, the NDRF successfully rescued 12 live victims trapped under a huge pile of rubble and also recovered 19 dead bodies.

One of the most notable achievements of the NDRF has been the work done by this force during the triple disaster (Earthquake, Tsunami and Radiation leakage) in Japan in March 2011, which was significantly the first mission of this Force abroad. The outstanding work done by the Force in Japan attracted great appreciation from the Japanese Government, the people and the media.

> *Significantly; during the last seven years, NDRF has been deployed on more than 150 occasions in various parts of the country wherein it has saved/rescued around 2,67,000 lives and retrieved 772 untraceable bodies, (http://www.ndma.gov.in).*

9.9 CAG Reports - Critical Gaps in Manpower Management

- Deficiency of personnel given the volume of work
- Shortage of Manpower in NDRF Headquarters
- Shortage of Medical Staff

Training System

- Specialized Training: Presently at various Government and Private Institutes in ad hoc manner (insufficient slots for NDRF).
- National Institute of Disaster Management: Yet to establish comprehensive training needs of NDRF.

Infrastructure

- NDRF Headquarters: Temporarily accommodated at Civil Defence Building.
- NDRF Battalions Office: Training, residential and storage accommodation not established at all locational sites.

Other Concerns

- Non-procurement of remaining equipment such as satellite phones, etc.
- Idling of equipment such as ultrasound machines, VSAT-mounted vehicles, etc.
- Need for Approval of Standard Operating Procedures for Deployment.

The NDMA was set up as the most important organizational entity at the national level for the purpose of putting in place an effective system of disaster management. In the seven years since its inception the NDMA has had some achievements to its credit. About 17 guidelines have been issued on subjects ranging from earthquakes and cyclones to chemical and biological disasters. The NDRF has been deployed several times for search and rescue operations in disaster-affected areas of the country—be it heavy floods, cyclones or earthquakes. The Disaster Management Act 2005 clearly distinguishes between "general response" and "specialist response". Immediate emergency response to a disaster situation can come successfully from well-equipped agencies with comprehensive response capabilities acquired through technical and professional training alone.

The NDRF even though created from existing central armed police forces, has developed into a specialized and highly skilled disaster response force. It has successfully been deployed and has significant achievements to its credit. No doubt police, central armed police forces and the armed force will continue to play an important role in search and rescue operations. In a huge country like India, the NDRF, even with the strength of 12 battalions, cannot cope with the number of crises. Yet, it can play a critical role for the purpose of specialist response. Indeed it is the only visible face of NDMA during periods of crises and certainly a one of a kind force in disaster management in the world.

9.10 Disaster Management - Lessons learnt from Phailin 2013

The Orissa super cyclone Phailin 2013 has been termed as the biggest disaster management exercise in history. 8.73 lakh people were evacuated through a calibrated approach to disaster management, otherwise found wanting in earlier efforts. This timely prediction of wind velocity by the Indian Meteorological Department, quick response to early warning of Phailin[7] s potential to cause havoc, timely evacuation of nearly 8 lakh people from the littoral districts of Odisha and Andhra Pradesh, besides well-organized provisions to cater to the emergency needs of those rescued from the killer cyclone are optimistic signs that the country's disaster management authorities have been able to get their act together. Such an effort was entirely lacking in the wake of July 2013's disastrous cloud burst in Uttarakhand of the same year. About 3000 NDRF were deployed to rescue 1000 people stranded in various districts. NDRF teams cleared 865 km of road and removed 20 electric poles besides engaging 55 teams in rescue work in Odisha, Andhra Pradesh and West Bengal.

The "very severe" cyclonic storm had its landfall at Gopalpur port at about 9 pm on 12 October 2013. Winds with a speed of 200 kmph swept the port town in Ganjam district and nearby places. The city of Berhampur, the headquarters of Ganjam district, and adjoining places were worst hit. The sea came in very close in Gopalpur, destroying the boats of fishermen, while the wind blew their huts away. Huge trees were uprooted, electric and telephone poles ripped away, houses collapsed, mobile towers were crushed, and power stations destroyed. Road communications were disrupted with trees falling across them. The destruction was near total in Ganjam district, and parts of Puri district also bore extensive signs of devastation. The other badly affected districts were Nayagarh, Jagatsinghpur and Khurda. Largely, Phailin's might was experienced by 13 districts in the state.

Flash floods occurred in the northern districts of Balasore, Bhadrak, Mayurbhanj and Jaipur. The administrations of these four districts evacuated 1,12,241 people from villages in flood-hit areas to safer places. In all, the cyclone and floods affected around 1.2 crore people in 16,487 villages, or 2015 Gram Panchayats and 43 urban local bodies, spread over 148 blocks in the state. Phailin and the floods damaged about 4,00,000 houses and 1182 power transformers in 17 districts.

The preparation for Phailin was initiated with the objective of "zero casualties". The massive evacuation operation, which finally involved moving 10,95,794 people to safe ground, undoubtedly reduced the loss of lives. Till 16 October, only 28 human casualties had been reported from the affected districts —21 due to Phailin and seven due to floods.

Despite some drawbacks, it is undeniable that the Odisha state administration was quite effective and efficient both before and after the cyclonic storm. The Press Trust of India (PYI) reported on 15 October that Margareta Wahlstorm, Special Representative of the UN Secretary General for Disaster Risk Reduction, has commented that Odisha's handling of the very severe cyclone was a "landmark success story in disaster management" and "a successful case study globally". Wahlstorm lauded the efforts of the administrative machinery and told the Times of India, Bhubaneswar, "We are very impressed. We have plans to use it as a model for other cities and countries to follow as part of our global efforts on disaster risk reduction."

The guiding principle in disaster management is the 4 R's- rescue, relief, rehabilitation, and reconstruction. But the success of the evacuation in Odisha has added a new "R" to this formula—relocation, at least temporarily. A lot now remains to be done in reconstructing and rebuilding infrastructure and livelihoods.

Phailin would have exacted a high price in terms of human lives along with the trail of destruction it left behind if the state administration had not been able to effectively contain hazards and deal with its aftermath. Accurate weather forecasting, effective planning, and the dedication shown by the administrative machinery helped make it an almost "zero casualty" natural disaster. Given that the super cyclone in Odisha, claimed nearly 10,000 lives earlier in 1999, this was a remarkable achievement and a trail blazer in the future of disaster management efforts in India.

Again Odisha was hit by the severe Cyclone Fani in May 2019 in which 10 lakh people were evacuated in temporary shelters and only 12 people were reportedly killed. Though this was a severe cyclone, the losses and casualities were less and the fact that Odisha had put together a good disaster management framework was amply proved.

Conclusion

Half the battle against heavy odds are won when a coordinated plan, backed by relevant metrological information, is put into effective action as was the case in the Odisha cyclone (a role model for Disaster Management efforts) and when this kind of coordinated effort is missing, failure would be inevitable as was the case in Uttarakhand 2013. These two cases are important studies in contrast in disaster management in the same year of 2013.

Suggested Readings

Dash, Satya Prakash, "How Odisha Managed the Phailin Disaster/' *The Economic and Political Weekly,* XLVIII no. 44 (Nov. 2, 2013).

Disaster Management in India, Ministry of Home Affairs, Government of India, New Delhi, 2014.

National Disaster Management Guidelines on Incident Response System, National Disaster Management Authority, Government of India, New Delhi, 2010.

Parasuram, S., *India Disasters Report: Towards a Policy Initiative,* New Delhi, Oxford University Press, 2000.

Paul, Bimal Kanti, *Environmental Hazards and Disasters: Contexts, Perspectives and Management*, India, John Wiley, 2011.

Report of the Task Force - A Review of the Disaster Management Act 2005, Ministry of Home Affairs, GOI, March 2013.

Sahni Pardeep, Alka Dhameja Uma Medury *Disaster Mitigation-Experiences and Reflections,* New Delhi, PHI 2001.

Sahni Pardeep, Madhavi Malalgoda Ariyabandhu *Disaster Risk Reduction in South Asia*, New Delhi, PHI 2003.

Yojna: issue on Disaster Management, March 2012

ooo

Chapter Ten

Centre State Relations

Introduction

Every federation works on the principle of a clear-cut division of legislative, administrative and financial powers between the constituent units of a federation. The Indian Constitution has clearly demarcated the line between the legislative, administrative and financial areas of the union and the states. This division ensures that the partners to the federation should enjoy their respective spheres of autonomy within their well-defined jurisdiction. However, centre-state relations in India is not to be treated only in terms of separation of powers between the centre and the states. On the other hand, in consonance with the concept of cooperative federalism, there are many areas of cooperation and coordination between the Union and the States both within the constitution as well as in the practice of centre-state relations.

Despite a clear-cut constitutional distribution of legislative, administrative and financial distribution of powers, the fact remains that there is a bias in favour of the Centre in the sense that it enjoys preponderance of powers vis-a-vis the States. There is no dual citizenship, no right to secede given to Indian states, there is a single unified judiciary and the civil service system is fairly integrated.

Though there is a strong unitary bias and the exceptions from a classical federal scheme are many, the Constitution introduces a federal system as the basic structure of government of the country. A federal system that postulates distribution of powers and functions between the federation and the units proceeds on two lines:

1. The territory over which the Federation and Units shall, respectively, have their jurisdiction.
2. The subjects to which their respective jurisdiction shall extend.

Administrative centralization has also been reflected in bureaucratic and judicial institutions. The Indian bureaucracy is provided constitutional recognition. The Central and State level tiers of the "public services" are given shape through the provisions of Part XIV of the Constitution. Since each political layer of government requires its own administrative apparatus, any bureaucracy in a federation will have a federal character. In particular, State Governments must be able to appoint and dismiss bureaucrats to implement state-level policies. This is certainly the case in India, where there is a central bureaucracy as well as an independent bureaucracy in each state. However, the key component of the bureaucracy is the Indian Administrative Service (IAS), whose members are chosen by a centralized process trained together, and then assigned to particular states. This structure was designed as a compromise between the desire to have an effective apparatus at the state level, and the fear of promoting regional loyalties over national ones. This compromise has been problematic since conflicts arise between state and central politicians (the latter acting through IAS members assigned to the Central Government) in directing state-level IAS bureaucrats.

At the national and state levels, the judiciary constitutes a distinct branch of government, though the legislative branch influences appointments. At the local level, IAS members are vested with some judicial authority. The Supreme Court stands at the top of the Indian Judicial hierarchy. The President, in consultation with the PM, appoints its Justices. Its powers include broad original and appellate jurisdiction and the right to pronounce on the constitutionality of laws passed by Parliament. In practice, there has been conflict between the Supreme Court and the legislature/ executive over the scope of these powers, and their boundaries remain subject to contestation.

10.1 Legislative Relations

Legislation provides the framework for governmental decisions and equips the government with the powers to implement policy. Our constitution provides that every state shall have at least one house, viz. the legislative assembly chosen by direct election on the basis of adult suffrage from territorial constituencies. Any state can create a second house, viz. legislative council if it so desires. This can be done by a resolution of the assembly passed by a special majority followed by an Act of Parliament. By the same process, the existing legislative council can be abolished also. At present, only Bihar, Maharashtra, Karnataka, U.P. and Jammu and Kashmir have two houses.

The Constitution (VI Schedule) adopts a three-fold distribution of legislative powers by placing them in any of the three lists, namely, Union List, State List and Concurrent List.

Articles 245 to 255 in Part XI deal with the legislative relations between the Centre and the States. The union list has at present 100 subjects (originally 97) of national importance like Defence, Atomic Energy, Foreign Affairs, War and Peace, Citizenship, Railways, Income-tax, Excise, etc., over which the Parliament has an exclusive authority to formulate laws.

The State List includes 61 subjects (originally 66) of importance to the States such as Public order, Police, Local Government, Public health, Agriculture, etc., over which the State has an exclusive legislative authority.

The Concurrent List contains 52 subjects (originally 47) of mutual relevance over which both Parliament and State legislatures can legislate but in case of conflict the Union law will prevail. These include Criminal law and procedure, Family laws, Inter-State Trade Commerce and Communication, Electricity, Economic and Social Planning, Education, Stamp duties, and so on. Residual powers are vested in the Parliament.

However, the Union government can legislate on any subject included in the State list, under some specific circumstances:

1. If the Rajya Sabha recommends by a two-third majority that such legislation is in national interest;
2. If two or more States mutually agree that such a legislation should be made for them;
3. In order to implement treaties or international agreements or connections; and

4. During the proclamation of emergency made by the President of India, on account of internal disturbance or external aggression, the Parliament acquires the authority to make laws on all the subjects mentioned in the State List. However, all such laws made by the Parliament become ineffective six months after the Proclamation of Emergency ceases to operate.
5. In case of emergency due to the failure of the constitutional machinery in States, the President of India can authorize the Parliament to exercise the powers of the State Legislature. All such laws also cease to operate within six months after the Proclamation of Emergency comes to an end.

Article 200 of the Constitution empowers the Governor to reserve a bill passed by the State legislature for consideration by the President of India. This provision has led to a considerable degree of resentment among the State Governments, especially due to inordinate delays in communicating the Centre's decision to the States on the bills so reserved.

Articles 245 and 246 demarcate the legislative domain, subject to the controlling principle of the supremacy of the Union, which is the basis of the entire system.

The Concurrent List gives power to two legislatures, the Union as well as the States, to legislate on the same subject. In case of conflict or inconsistency, the rule of repugnancy, as contained in Article 254 comes into play. Under this rule, if there is any discrepancy between the State and the Centre over a subject in the Concurrent List, the Union law takes precedence over the state law.

Article 200 of the Constitution grants the Union an executive power to intervene in the legislative process of a State. A bill presented to the Governor for his assent may be reserved for consideration by the Union executive with its power to either approve it or disallow it.

However, in India this has been a major irritant in Union-State relations as is amply documented by the Sarkaria Commission Report (1988). The Report shows that out of 15 State legislations so reserved between 10.11.1969 and 7.6.1984, the Union Government withheld its assent in 9 cases. In 6 cases, decision was taken after one and a half years, in 5 cases after three years, in three cases after six years and in 1 case after twelve years. The Commission recommended that normally the Governor must abide by the advice of the Council of Ministers. In its views, the discretion of reservation of a State legislation by the Governor should be exercised in "rare and exceptional cases" when such a legislation is "patently unconstitutional". The commission also recommended that a State bill so reserved should be disposed off within four months from the date of its receipt. This practice of reservation of state bills has continued to the present time with occasional controversies when divergent parties are in power in New Delhi and the concerned state. The M.M. Punchhi

Commission on Centre-State Relations (2010) has recommended the disposal of a bill so reserved within six months.

Parliament may make laws for the whole or any part of India. The Legislature of a State may make laws for the whole or any part of the State. Any State law would be void if it has extra-territorial operation (Kochuni vs. State of Madras, AIR 1960 SC 1080) unless sufficient nexus can be shown to exist between the object and the State (State of Bombay v. RMDC, AIR 1957 SC 699; Tata Iron & Steel Co. v. State of Bihar; AIR 1958 SC 452). Laws made by Parliament, however, cannot be questioned on grounds of extra-territorial operation (Article 245).

Amendments in the three lists have been effected by the third, sixth, seventh, fifteenth, thirty-second, forty-second and forty-sixth amendments. But the largest number of changes were made by the seventh and the forty-second amendments.

The Union List, the longest of the three lists, consists of important subjects like Defence, Foreign Affairs, Railways, Communication, Banking and Currency, etc., subjects which are of common interest to the Union and with respect to which uniformity of legislation throughout the Union is essential. Subjects that allow for diversity of interest and treatment are included in the State List and matters in which uniformity of legislation throughout the Union is desirable, but not essential, are included in the Concurrent List. Although the State is given exclusive powers over the subjects in the State List, there are two exceptions to this general rule. Under Article 249, if the Rajya Sabha declares by a Resolution supported by two-thirds of the members present and voting that it is necessary or expedient in the national interest that Parliament should make laws with respect to any matter enumerated in the State List, Parliament is competent to make laws on that matter for the whole or any part of India. Such a resolution remains valid for a year; it can be extended by another year by a subsequent resolution. Any law passed under this provision would cease to be in force within six months after the end of the year.

Again under Article 250, Parliament is empowered to make laws on any item included in the State List for the whole or any part of India while a Proclamation of Emergency is in operation. The maximum duration of validity of such laws will be six months after the expiry of the Emergency.

In case of inconsistency between laws made by Parliament under Articles 249 and 250 and laws made by State Legislatures, the law made by Parliament shall prevail, and the State law shall be inoperative to the extent of repugnancy while the law made by Parliament remains in effect (Article 251).

If two or more State Legislatures consider it desirable that any of the matters within their exclusive legislative competence should be regulated by parliamentary legislation and pass resolutions to that effect, Parliament can undertake necessary legislation. However, the legislation so passed has effect only in the State which had requested and those others which may adopt it afterwards by resolutions passed on that behalf (Article 252). Some of the entries in the Union List themselves empower the Parliament to take over to itself, by making the requisite declaration by law, certain spheres and subjects from the State field (Seventh Schedule, e.g. entries 7, 23, 24, 27, 52, 54, 56, 62, 63, 64 and 67).

These changes are not to be treated as amendments to the Constitution and can be effected if the Parliament passes a Bill by a simple majority on the recommendation of the President. Such a Bill is required to be referred to the legislatures of the State concerned for expressing their views thereon, within the time allowed for the purpose. However, this reference in practice, does not restrict the jurisdiction of Parliament. Parliament has been empowered to abolish or create a Legislative Council in a State by a simple procedure not involving a constitutional amendment. It can be done by an Act of Parliament, if the Legislative Assembly of the State passes a resolution to that effect by a special majority (Article 169).

The relationship between the Union and the States in India represents a compromise between a normal division of powers under which States enjoy autonomy within their own spheres and need for national integrity and a strong Union under exceptional circumstances. The arrangement has come to be understood under what is sometimes called a system of cooperative federalism.

The problems that have attracted attention in the field of Union-State relations have less to do with the structure or the rationale of the Concurrent List than with the manner in which the Union has exercised its powers. Union-State relations should be studied in the context of the political regime that prevailed in the country over the last half century. The first four decades of the Republic was characterized by single party dominance at the centre.

Under the Constitution, the Governor of a State is authorized to issue ordinances, when the State Legislature is not in session. Though, it is expected that the Governor will issue such ordinances only with the approval of the State Council of Ministers, but under certain circumstances, he can issue these ordinances only with the prior approval of the President of India.

1. If the ordinance deals with the subject regarding which laws can be introduced in the state legislature only with the prior approval of the President.
2. If a bill has been reserved for the opinion of the President, an ordinance on the same subject can be issued only with prior approval of the President.
3. Ordinance on a subject on which a law passed by the state legislature is not valid without the approval of the President.

The term 'concurrent' is a misnomer if one takes into account the overriding powers of the Union, particularly in view of the concentration of fiscal and economic powers at the Union level and States' virtual dependence on the Union in discharging only such functions which are leftover by and are permitted and tolerated by the latter. This makes for excessive centralization, which is not conducive to democratic aspirations and can be articulated in our kind of uneven society in a decentralized framework. Besides the list of subjects over which lately the Panchayati Raj institutions are enabled to have jurisdiction cannot become operationally relevant unless the States are adequately empowered to make their choices in a relatively autonomous manner with matching financial autonomy and are in a position to make resources available to the Panchayats in a coordinated manner.

It is clear that though the Centre and the States have been assigned independent legislative spheres the Centre reserves the right to interfere in the sphere reserved for the States.

10.2 Administrative Relations

Federal polity involves the setting up of dual governments and division of powers.

But the success and strength of the federal polity depends upon maximum cooperation and co-ordination between the Centre and the States.

The executive power of the Union extends only through those matters which are mentioned in the Union List and over which the Parliament has legislative powers. In addition, the Union can exercise administrative control over the state through the following methods:

- Articles 255 to 256 seek to regulate administrative relations between the Union and the States. The Constitution of India seeks to achieve a smooth working relationship between the two levels. It provides that the executive powers of the State Government are to be exercised in such a way as to ensure compliance with the laws made by Parliament.
- Article 257 provides that the executive power of every State shall be so exercised as not to impede the exercise of the executive power of the Union and the Union may issue necessary directions in that regard and for protection of railways and maintenance of means of communication of national or military importance. Any expenditure incurred by the State for the purpose of fulfilling Central directives is to be reimbursed by the Centre to the States.
- Under Article 258 the President may, with the consent of the State Government, entrust functions to that Government or its officers in relation to any matter to which the executive power of the Union extends.
- Under Article 258 A the Governor of a State may, with the consent of the Union Government, entrust functions to that Government or to its offices in relation to any matter to which the executive power of the State extends.
- Article 261 directs that full faith and credit shall be given to public acts, records and judicial proceedings of the Union and the States in all parts of the Indian territory, which adds a lot to the smooth working of the Union-State relations.
- Under Article 262 Parliamentary control over inter-State rivers and provisions for adjudication of inter-State water disputes have taken away a host of possibilities of friction between the Union and the States themselves.
- Article 263 empowers the President to establish an inter-State council to inquire into and advise upon inter-State disputes, between the Union and the States and make recommendations for better co-ordination of policy and action.
- In Article 356 emergency provisions contained in Part XVIII of the Constitution are one of the most important provisions with profound influence on the development of India's federal polity. Article 356 provides that if the President is satisfied that a situation has arisen in which the governance of a State cannot be carried out in accordance with the provisions of the Constitution, he may by proclamation impose

an emergency resulting in the imposition of President's rule. In the Constituent Assembly, Dr. Ambedkar referred to these provisions as 'safety valves' and expressed the hope that there would be no occasion to use them. Ironically, this came to be one of the most 'overused' provisions of the constitution.

10.3 Financial Relations

No system of federation can be successful unless both the Union and the States have at their disposal adequate financial resources to enable them to discharge their respective responsibilities under the Constitution. The Indian Constitution has made elaborate provisions, relating to the distribution of the taxes as well as non-tax revenues and the power of borrowing, supplemented by provisions for grants-in- aid by the Union to the States. It is to be noted that the Indian Constitution makes a distinction between the legislative power to levy a tax and power to appropriate the proceeds of a tax so levied.

The legislative power to make a law for imposing a tax is divided as between the Union and States by means of specific entries in the Union and State Legislative Lists in Schedule VIII. Thus, while the States Legislature has the power to levy an estate duty in respect of agricultural lands, the power to levy an estate duty in respect of non-agricultural land belongs to the Parliament. Similarly, it is the State Legislature which is competent to levy a tax on agricultural income, while Parliament has the power to levy income tax on all incomes other than agricultural income.

The distribution of the tax-revenue between the Union and the States stands as follows:

1. Taxes belonging to the Union exclusively: Customs, corporation tax, taxes on capital value of assets of individuals and companies, surcharge on income tax, fees in respect of matters in the Union List.
2. Taxes belonging to the States exclusively: Land revenue, stamp duty except in documents included in the Union List, succession duty, estate duty, and income tax on agricultural land, taxes on passengers and goods carried on inland waterways, taxes on lands and buildings, mineral rights. Taxes on animals and boats, on road vehicles, on advertisements, on consumption of electricity, on luxuries and amusements, etc. (This is being supplemented by GST).
3. Duties levied by the Union but collected and appropriated by the States: Stamp duties on bills of exchange, etc., and excise duties on medical and toilet preparations containing alcohol (Article 268).
4. Taxes levied as well as collected by the union, but assigned to the States within which they are leviable: Duties on succession to property other than agricultural land; estate duty in respect of property other than agricultural land; terminal taxes on goods or passengers carried by railway, air or sea; taxes on railway fares and freights, and so on.
5. Taxes levied and collected by the Union and distributed between Union and the States: Certain taxes shall be levied as well as collected by the Union, but their proceeds shall be divided between the Union and the States in a certain proportion, in order to effect on equitable division of the financial resources. These are:

- Taxes on income other than on agricultural income (Art 270).
- Duties of excise as are included in the Union List, excepting medicinal and toilet preparations may also be distributed, if Parliament by law so provides (Article 272-).

Non-Tax Revenue

Important sources of Non-Tax revenues of the Union are the receipts from Railways, Posts and Telegraphs; Broadcasting; Opium; Currency and Mint; Industrial Commercial Undertakings of the Central Government relating to the subjects over which the union has the jurisdiction.

Similarly for the States the sources are: Forests, Irrigation and Commercial Enterprises and Industrial Undertakings such as soap, sandalwood, iron and steel in Karnataka, Paper in M.P. milk supply in Mumbai, deep sea fishing and silk in West Bengal.

Grants-in-Aid

The above mentioned sources are not adequate for the States to carry out the development programmes and the Constitution provides that grants-in-aid shall be made in each year by the Union to such States that the Parliament may determine to be in need of assistance; particularly for the promotion of welfare of tribal areas, including special grants to Assam (Article 275).

Articles 270, 273, 275 and 280 provide for the constitution of a Finance Commission to recommend to the President certain measures relating to the distribution of financial resources between the Union and the States, for instance, the percentage of the net proceeds of income tax which should be assigned by the Union to the States and the manner in which the assigned share shall be distributed among the States (Article 280).

By way of safeguarding the interests of the States in the Union, taxes which are divisible according to the foregoing provisions, it is provided by the Constitution (Article 274) that no bill or amendment which varies the rate of any tax or duty in which the States are interested or affects the principles on which moneys are distributable according to the foregoing provision of the Constitution or imposes any surcharge on any such tax or duty for the purposes of the Union shall be introduced or moved in Parliament except on the recommendations of the President.

As in the case of legislative and administrative spheres, so in financial matters, the normal relation between the Union and the States (under Articles 268-279) is liable to be modified in different kinds of emergencies.

1. While a Proclamation of Emergency (Article 352[1]) is in operation, the President may by order direct that, for a period not extending beyond the expiration of the financial year in which the Proclamation ceases to operate, all or any of the provisions relating to the divisions of the taxes between the Union and the States and grants-in-aid shall be suspended (Art 354). As a result, if the President makes any such order, the States will be left to their narrow resources from the revenues under the State List, without any augmentation by contributions from the Union.

2. In case of Financial Emergency (Article 360[1]) declared by the President, it shall be competent for the Union to give directions to the States
   a. To observe such cannons of financial propriety and other safeguards as may be specified.
   b. To reduce the salaries and allowances of all persons serving in connection with the affairs of the States, including High Court Judges;
   c. To reserve for the consideration of the President all money and financial bills, after they are passed by the Legislature of the State (Article 360).

A major problem, faced in a system with multiple fiscal authorities, is integration of financial policies, which is an objective in a planned economy. Another problem arises due to the imbalance of financial resources between the Centre and the States. The difference in levels of economic development leads to imbalance between different States in terms of income and wealth disparities. This inter-State imbalance creates a perennial source of tension with the Centre.

The most important problem for all the State Governments is the shortage of financial sources within the present structure of Centre-State relations. On the one hand, the financial requirements of the states have vastly increased, and on the other hand, the Centre has been gradually encroaching on financial powers and cornering for itself a major share of the total national resources. Another tendency noticed has been the increasing indebtedness of the States to the Centre for various developmental purposes. The states are finding themselves unable to repay the installments or interests on the debts without further central assistance.

The Seventh Schedule of the Constitution vests the taxing powers both in the Union List and the State List. But there is a contradiction between the elastic sources of revenue earmarked for the Centre and the expansive developmental expenditure of the States.

Resources and needs are reviewed periodically by a Finance Commission, which recommends the requisite changes, derived on the basis of experience and resources, to be made in the distribution of finances between the Union and the States. This is a unique feature of the Indian Constitution, in fact, by providing for the establishment of the Finance Commission for the purpose of allocating and readjusting the receipts from certain sources, the Constitution has made an original contribution in this extremely complicated aspect of federal relationships. The Union and States are mutually dependent and this coordinate nature has given stability to the working of the Indian federation.

Every State wants more resources, and a larger share of the divisible pool. The Finance Commission is mandated to do justice between the Centre and the States, and between a State and a State.

10.4 Distribution of Competence

- Distribution of powers is essentially based on the notion of territoriality and specification of subjects accordingly. There are subjects like industry, mines and minerals, which find place in both the lists. To find an answer to this, one has to look into the types of competence available in the federal scheme of India. Broadly, there are three types of competence: one, on which the respective sets of government have exclusive and distinct competence. It is rarely seen that on items like defence, foreign affairs, etc., delegation of authority is made by the Union Government. Two, on items like industry, mines and minerals, the State Government has exclusive but limited competence. On these subjects, its competence is subjected to the regulation by the Union Government in order to serve the larger public and national interests.

- There are items of concurrent jurisdiction (List three) on which each unit of the federation enjoys exclusive but concurring competence. In the event of conflict, it is usually the Union law that prevails over States' laws. On matters of non-enumerated items, the Union Government has been vested with residuary powers of legislation.
- So far as the distribution of executive authority is concerned, it generally follows the scheme of distribution of the legislative powers. In other words, executive powers of the Union and State Governments are co-extensive with their respective legislative competence. In the case of a State Government, its executive authority over a legislative field has been subjected to the qualificatory restriction of the 'doctrine of territorial nexus'.
- As regards matters included in the concurrent Legislative List (i.e. List III), the executive function shall ordinarily remain with the states, but subject to the provisions of the constitution or of any law of Parliament conferring such function expressly upon the Union.
- This includes Union's powers to give directions to the State Governments; ensuring due compliance with Union laws; ensuring exercise of executive power of the State in such a manner as not to interfere with the Union's executive power; "to ensure the construction and maintenance of the means of communication of national or military importance by the state; to ensure protection of railways within the state; to ensure drawing and execution of schemes specified in the directions to be essential for the welfare of the Scheduled Tribes in the states; securing adequate provision by the state for instruction in mother tongue at the primary stage; ensuring development of Hindi language in the state; and above all, "to ensure that the government of a state is carried on in accordance with the provisions of the constitution". Also, during an emergency of any type, the Union Government may regulate through its power of issuing directions the manner in which the executive power of the State has to be exercised. In other words, the State has been assigned certain obligatory duties under the Federal Constitution of India.
- The Centre-State administrative relationship is based on the principle of division [Jurisdictional partitioning of control and execution of decisions over a subject matter], coordination and cooperation in policy and planning. In many areas, while Centre retains its exclusive legislative competence, it, however, delegates powers of ancillary legislation and exclusive executive competence to take decisions independently to the States. The Centre administers directly only on the matters

pertaining to defence, foreign affairs including passports, communications (post and telegraphs, telephones), the union list taxes, and industrial regulation. On rest of the enumeration in the Union lists, the administrative function is exercised by the States 'under statutory or executive delegation'.

- Executive powers of Union and State Governments are coterminous with their legislative jurisdictions. The Constitution of India envisages what may be called "cooperative federalism" inasmuch as Article 256 stipulates that the executive power of the State "shall be so exercised as to ensure compliance with the laws made by Parliament". This Article goes on to say that "the executive power of the Union shall extend to the giving of such directions to a State as may, appear to the Government of India to be necessary for that purpose".
- Power to enter into any international treaties or conventions is a power of the Union executive. However, Article 253 of the Constitution requires a parliamentary legislation for giving effect to these agreements. This provision of the Constitution has acquired a somewhat controversial dimension in the context of globalization. For example, the Union of India signed the WTO treaty in 1995, which entailed obligations for the federating States even in their exclusive jurisdictions, e.g. agriculture. The states of Punjab, Rajasthan, Orissa and Tamil Nadu in fact filed cases in the Supreme Court precisely on this issue, which subsequently were withdrawn presumably after suitable assurances from the Union Government for such occasions in the future. Article 253 was also in the eye of a political storm in 2007 in the context of Indo-US nuclear civilian deal in the Parliament where the opposition, especially the communist allies of the Congress-led coalition government in New Delhi and state units of left parties were up in arms for parliamentary approval of the treaty. In all probability, the Union of India would be more cautious in the exercise of its executive treaty making power in view of possible responses and reactions from the Parliament as well as from State Governments.
- The office of the Governor has become perhaps the most contentious issue in Union-State relations. Controversies have arisen on the question of partisan appointment of the Governor by the party in power at the Centre and patently political role of the incumbent to appease the powers that be, in New Delhi.
- The emergency power of the Union to take over the Government of a State under Article 356 on the recommendation of the Governor or otherwise is also controversial. This power has been one of the most grossly misused emergency powers for partisan considerations by all parties in power in New Delhi in the past. A classic example of this abuse was the dismissal of 9 Congress State Governments and dissolution of their respective Assemblies by the Janata Party Government at the Centre in 1977, and the dissolution of exactly 9 State Governments led by the Janata Party and other opposition parties by Prime Minister Indira Gandhi when she returned to power in 1980. In 1983, Indira Gandhi, under pressure of the Opposition, appointed the Sarkaria Commission on Centre-State relations. Several political parties and State

Governments in their submissions to this Commission demanded repeal of this provision or at least bringing it under greater constitutional limitations.

- The constitution details the essential features of the Union-State administrative relations, and raises no walls of separation between them. There is no rigid pattern of allocation of responsibilities. The Union Parliament may confer powers, and may impose duties under laws pertaining to the Union list. The President may entrust functions to the State Governments "in relation to any matter, to which the executive power of the Union extends... The state executive functions can, notwithstanding anything, be entrusted either conditionally or unconditionally" to the Central Government. In actual practice the States exercise a large measure of executive authority even within the administrative field of the Union government.

10.5 Sarkaria Commission: Major Recommendations:

- There should be an amendment in Articles 355 and 356 to enable the Centre to bring specific trouble-torn areas under its rule for a limited period.
- The Commission has proposed "localising emergency provisions" under Articles 355 and 356, contending that localised areas —either a district or parts of a district—be brought under Governor's rule instead of the whole state. Such an emergency provision should, however, not be for a duration of more than three months.
- The Commission supports the right to give sanction for the prosecution of ministers against the advice of the State Governments.
- To make an amendment in the Communal Violence Bill to allow deployment of Central forces without the state's consent for a short period. It was proposed that State consent should not become a hurdle in deployment of central forces in a communal conflagration. However, such deployment should only be for a week and post-facto consent should be taken from the state.
- The Commission in its Report did not recommend the abolition of Article 356 but strongly urged the federal functionaries to exercise this power with due restraint expected by framers of the Constitution. It also laid down some guidelines for the Governor, and by implication for the President and the Union Cabinet. But the Supreme Court departed from tradition and made President's rule subject to judicial review in S. R. Bommai and others vs. Union of India and others (1994).

10.6 Judicial Opinions

Courts have generally been protective of the federal structure of the Constitution, especially in more recent decades. The courts have done this at least in four ways. First, as early as in Hargovind Pant vs. Raghukul Tilak and others (1979), the Supreme Court gave an essentially federal, as distinguished from central, interpretation of the role of the Governor. It observed that the Governor "is an independent constitutional office which is not subject to the control of the Government of India." Second, in S.R. Bommai and others vs. Union of India and others (1994), the Supreme Court reserved its earlier decisions in a number of cases previously decided wherein it had consistently maintained that the determination under Article 356 of the Constitution (whether a constitutional machinery in a State had broken down or not) was a "political decision" best left in the hands of the Union executive. The Court now maintained that the satisfaction of the President in the matter was "subjective" but "not entirely absolute" and must be exercised on some palpable material or evidence in the public domain. Third, in the foregoing judgement as well as in Keshavananda Bharti vs. Union of India (1973) and Minerva Mills vs. Union of India (1980), the Supreme Court established the doctrine of the unamendability of the 'basic structure' of the Constitution, of which federalism is illustratively declared to be a part. Fourth the Supreme Court in settling Union-State legislative jurisdictional disputes over the years has acted in as balanced a manner as possible. Typical of the court's adjudication in this regard is its judgement in the State of West Bengal vs. Kesoram Industries Ltd. (2004). This case related to constitutional allocation of legislative and taxation powers between the Union and the States as regards coal, tea, brick-field, and minor minerals in which entries in the State List are subject to Union's power of regulation and development in public or national interest. The court prescribed the norm of accommodation of competing legislative and taxing claims of both orders of governments as far as possible. It ruled that "the Union's power to regulate and control does not result in depriving the states of their power to levy tax or fee within their legislative competence without treading upon the field of regulation and control."

10.7 Intergovernmental Fiscal Relations: Features

Today states get about 42% of central taxes. Their demand is for a 50% transfer of central taxes. Till recently Finance Commission accounted for two thirds of total fiscal transfers, the remaining was through Planning Commission and the Central ministries. India has developed explicit as well as implicit channels for managing intergovernmental fiscal relations, and for making vertical transfers, particularly from the Centre to the States and Union Territories. This section reviews constitutional tax and expenditure assignments, the role of the Finance Commission, Niti Aayog and Central ministries in making intergovernmental fiscal transfers, and the nature and associated problems of sub-national borrowing. It will be seen that India's intergovernmental fiscal transfer system till recently was complicated by the existence of multiple channels, particularly the Planning Commission, which was charged with drawing up and implementing five-year economic development plans. Furthermore, while the bulk of transfers are general-purpose formulaic, transfers, there is also a complex mix of specific purpose transfers, sometimes with ad hoc matching requirements, and often determined through political bargaining.

Expenditure and Tax Assignments

Economic theories of government are based on the idea that public (non-rival and non-exclusive) goods are not well provided by the market mechanism. In addition, governments are not perfectly informed but intrinsically required to maintain macroeconomic stability at home and not jeopardise international trade and relations. The major subjects assigned to the states comprise public order, public health, agriculture, irrigation, land rights, fisheries and industries and minor minerals. The States also assume a significant role for subjects in the Concurrent List, such as education and transportation, social security and social insurance.

The assignment of tax powers in India is based on a principle of separation, i.e. tax categories are exclusively assigned either to the Centre or to the States. Most broad-based (in principle though not in practice) taxes have been assigned to the Centre, including taxes on income and wealth from non-agricultural sources, corporation tax, taxes on production (excluding those on alcoholic liquors) and customs duty. A long list of taxes is assigned to the states. However, only the tax on the sale and purchase of goods has been significant for state revenues. This narrow and ineffective tax base is largely a result of political economy factors that have eroded or prevented the use of taxes on agricultural land or incomes by State Governments. The centre has also been assigned all residual powers, so that taxes not mentioned in any of the lists automatically fall into its domain.

The tax assignment system has some problematic features. The separation of income tax powers between the Centre and the States based on whether the source of income is agriculture or non-agriculture has opened up avenues for both avoidance and evasion of the personal income tax. Second, even though in a legal sense taxes on production (central manufacturing excises) and sale (state sales taxes) are separate, they tax the same base, causing overlapping and leaving less tax room to the latter. Finally, the states are allowed to levy taxes on the sale and purchase of goods (entry 54 in the State list) but not services.

The realized outcome of the Indian assignments of tax and expenditure authority, their particular history of implementation, and the response of different levels of government and tax payers to the assignment has been a substantial vertical fiscal imbalance. The states on an average raised about 40% of government revenues, but incurred about 60% of expenditures. Transfers from the Centre made up the balance—though perverse fiscal incentives for the States in this system have, in fact, increased the imbalance. In fact, the ability of the States to finance their current expenditures from their own sources of revenue has seen a long-run decline, from 69% in 1955-56 to 52% in 2002-03. In terms of total expenditure (including capital spending), the states were even more dependent on the Centre, with only 40% of their overall spending being covered by their own revenue receipts in 2009-10.

Finance Commission Transfers

The Constitution recognized that its assignment of tax powers and expenditure functions would create imbalances between expenditure 'needs' and abilities to raise revenue. The imbalances could be both vertical, among different levels of government, and horizontal, among different units within a sub-central level. Therefore, the Constitution originally provided for the sharing of the proceeds of certain centrally levied taxes (e.g. non-corporate income tax, Article 270; and Union excise duty, Article 272) with .the states, as well as grants to the states from the Consolidated Fund of India. Recent constitutional changes in this scheme have simplified this sharing arrangement, replacing it with an overall share of the Consolidated Fund. The shares of the Centre and the States, and their allocation among different states are determined by the Finance Commission, which is also a constitutional creation, and is appointed by the President of India every five years (or earlier if needed). In addition to tax devolution, the Finance Commission is also required to recommend grants to the states in need of assistance under Article 275. Finance Commission transfers are, thus, all unconditional in nature.

The Finance Commissions' approach to federal transfers has consisted of (i) assessment of overall budgetary requirements of the Centre and States to determine the volume of resources available for transfer with the Centre during the period of recommendation, (ii) projecting of States' own revenues and non-plan current expenditures, (iii) determining and distributing the States' share of the consolidated fund of the Centre, and (iv) filling gaps between projected expenditures and revenues after tax devolution with grants.

Over the last 60 years, 14 Finance Commissions have made recommendations to the Central Government and barring a few exceptions, these have been accepted. In this process, the Commissions have developed an elaborate methodology for dealing with horizontal as well as vertical fiscal imbalances. In particular, the formula for tax devolution is quite complicated, as a result of attempts to capture simultaneously disparate (and even contradictory) factors such as poverty, 'backwardness', tax effort, fiscal discipline, and population control efforts. The result has been that the impact of Finance Commission transfers on horizontal equity (equalizing fiscal capacity across states) has been somewhat limited. Despite the ad hoc nature of the tax-sharing formula, its persistence reflects the nature of precedent that has grown around the Finance Commission, even though it is not a permanent body.

Grants recommended by the Finance Commissions have typically been determined on the basis of projected gaps between non-plan current expenditures and post- tax devolution revenues. As with tax sharing, these grants have generally been unconditional, although some of the Commissions (particularly after the Sixth) also attempted to enhance outlays on specified services in the States by making close- ended specific purpose non-matching grants. In either case, however, the incentive problems with this "gap-filling" approach are obvious. Some of the Commissions did attempt to take account of normative growth rates of revenues and expenditures in projections, but these attempts were selective and relatively unimportant.

Despite the Finance Commissions' success in establishing guidelines and stability for Centre-State tax sharing, their methodology and processes have been often criticized. The main criticisms are: (i) the scope of the Finance Commissions through the Presidential terms of reference have been too restricted; and (ii) the design of their transfer schemes have reduced State Government incentives for fiscal discipline (through 'gap-filling' transfers), while doing relatively little to reduce inter-State inequities. Therefore one can argue that there is still an opportunity to improve this aspect of India's IGFR system.

Central Ministry Transfers

Finally, various ministries give grants to their counterparts in the states for specified projects, either wholly funded by the centre (central sector projects) or requiring the states to share a proportion of the cost (centrally sponsored schemes). Both these categories are reported together as central schemes. The ostensible rationale for these programmes is financing activities with a high degree of inter-state spillovers, or which are merit goods (e.g., poverty alleviation and family planning), but they are often driven by pork-barrel objectives. These projects WEREe monitored by the erstwhile Planning Commission, and coordinated with the overall state plans but both monitoring and coordination are relatively ineffective.

There are over hundred such schemes, and several attempts in the past to consolidate them into broad sectoral programmes have not been successful. These programmes have provided the Central Government with an instrument to actively influence states' spending, replacing the pre-1969 plan transfers in this role. The proliferation of schemes may also have increased the size and control of the bureaucracy.

While the specific purposes and matching requirements of Central and centrally sponsored schemes make them potentially an important channel for dealing with spillovers, as noted, the implementation of these schemes has been problematic, with issues such as lack of transparency, poor selection of projects, and ineffective monitoring. Nevertheless, the discretionary aspect of these intergovernmental transfers have made them attractive to Central ministries, and, their relative importance in overall transfers have increased.

Loans and Guarantees

In addition to explicit transfers, intergovernmental loans, to the extent that they are subsidized, also constitute implicit transfers to states. Ideally, borrowing should be to finance investment, but State Governments have increasingly used borrowing to meet current expenditure needs (now approaching 50%). State Governments can only borrow from the market with Central Government approval if they are indebted to the Centre, and this constraint binds all the states. Central loans now constitute about 60% of the states' indebtedness, with another 22% being market borrowing, and the remainder made up of pension funds, shares of rural small savings, and required holdings of State Government bonds by commercial banks. While these sources of finance are limited, the states have been able to soften their budget constraints further by off-budget borrowing or non-payment by their public sector enterprises (PSEs). For example, the State Electricity Boards (SEBs) have been tardy in paying the National Thermal Power Corporation, a central PSE.

Other sources of softness in State Government budget constraints include Central Government guarantees of loans made to State Government PSEs by external agencies, and central forgiveness of past loans made to State Governments, presumably to gain political advantage. Even in the case of attempts to impose conditions on state borrowing that would encourage fiscal reforms, the Centre has not been able to harden budget constraints. In particular, in 1999-2000, eleven states signed Memorandum of Understanding (MOUs) with the Centre, promising fiscal reforms in exchange for ways and means advances (essentially, overdrafts) on tax devolution and grants due to them. In some cases, however, the Centre has had to convert these advances into three-year loans. The Reserve Bank of India (RBI) reports stopping payments to three states (Reserve Bank of India, 2001), but there is a political difficulty of not bailing out states that are both, poor and populous.

Since the 1990s, India has struggled with high fiscal deficits and the states have contributed significantly to this problem after 1997-98. Several states have also followed the

Centre's lead in passing Fiscal Responsibility and Budget Management Acts to set targets for deficit reduction, and recently the Ministry of Finance has released a report outlining a roadmap for achieving deficit reduction targets. Improvements in financial information, budgeting practices, regulatory norms and monitoring are all required here, as well as changes in the institutional rules. Some reform is already taking place, including statutory or administrative borrowing ceilings, guarantee redemption funds, explicit restructuring and write-offs, and market-based borrowing mechanisms such as auctions conducted by the Reserve Bank of India.

Another approach to the states' indebtedness and continued high fiscal deficits has been to tie some portion of intergovernmental transfers to state-level fiscal reforms. The Eleventh Finance Commission worked out a scheme by pooling 15% of revenue deficit grants and adding an equal amount to it to create an incentive fund to be allocated among the states based on fulfillment of targets of growth of tax and non-tax revenues and expenditures on salaries, interest payments and subsidies, as set in the fiscal restructuring plan detailed by the Commission. The incentive fund has been allocated to the states according to their population shares. A state will get its full amount if it fulfills the specified targets of the monitorable measure (revenue deficit as a percentage of total revenue receipts of the states) evolved for the purpose, with graduated rewards for partial fulfillment. However, the potential problems with this scheme include the relatively small size of the incentive fund, biases in the monitorable measure against smaller and poorer states, conflicts with other fiscal incentive programmes, and opportunities for moving deficits off budget to manipulate the programme outcomes.

10.8 Agencies for Federalism

A few non-statutory and statutory bodies (through constitutional prescriptions or parliamentary legislation) have been established for one purpose or the other of common interest for the Union and the states. Apart from extra-constitutional agencies, such as the NITI Aayog, set up by the union government which further the coordination of state policy and smoothen differences between the states, the Indian Constitution establishes the Finance Commission (under Article 280) for facilitating intergovernmental financial cooperation and Inter State Council or ISC (under Article 263) for investigating and discussing subjects of common interests between and among states and the Union. Administrative coordination between the states and the Union is also being promoted by the constitutional provision under Article 312 for All India Services are common to both the Union and the states. Recently the Goods and Services Tax Council (GSTC) has been set up on 16 September 2016 under Article 279A for improving tax compliance and effecting governance of cooperative federalism.

10.9 NITI Aayog

NITI Aayog was created through a union cabinet resolution on 1 January 2015 in place of the Planning Commission. The NITI Aayog's task to serve as a directional think tank' of the government providing the governments at the centre and the states with strategic and technical advice on key policy matters including economic issues of national and international importance.

As per the policy statement of the government, NITI Aayog will create a knowledge, innovation and entrepreneurial support system through a collaborative community of national and international experts, practitioners and partners. It will offer a platform for resolution of inter-sectoral and inter-departmental issues in order to accelerate the implementation of the development agenda. Noting that progress is not possible without all states advancing in unison, Prime Minister Modi called upon chief ministers to work with the Centre to forge a model for cooperative federalism; whereby the Centre and the states can come together to resolve differences. Through the mechanism of the NITI Aayog, India would move away from 'one-size-fits-all' schemes and forge a better match between various schemes and the needs of states. One of the objectives of and NITI Aayog will be to ensure that the interests of national security are incorporated in economic strategy and policy.

Organization of the NITI Aayog

The NITI Aayog comprises the following:

1. The Prime Minister is the ex officio Chair Person
    - Vice chairperson – a full-time member of eminence;
    - Members-two full-time experts;
    - Part-time members-maximum of two from leading universities, research organizations and other relevant institutions in an ex officio capacity. Part-time members will be on a rotational basis;
    - Ex officio members-maximum of four members of the Union Council of Ministers to be nominated by the prime minister;
    - Chief executive officer-to be appointed by the prime minister for a fixed tenure, in the rank of secretary to the GoI; and
    - Secretariat, as deemed necessary.
2. Governing council comprising the chief ministers of all the states and union territories with legislatures and lieutenant governors of other union territories.
3. Regional councils will be formed to address specific issues and contingencies impacting more than one state or a region. These will be formed for a specified tenure.
4. Experts, specialists and practitioners with relevant domain knowledge as special invitees nominated by the prime minister.

In addition, the NITI Aayog will monitor and evaluate the implementation of programmes and focus on technology upgradation and capacity building. The NITI Aayog will aim to accomplish the following objectives and opportunities:

- An administrative paradigm in which the government is an 'enabler' rather than a 'provider of first and last resort'.
- Progress from 'food security' to focus on a mix of agricultural production as well as actual returns that farmers get from their produce.

- Ensure that India is an active player in the debates and deliberations on the global commons.
- Ensure that the economically vibrant middle class remains engaged, and its potential is fully realized.
- Leverage India's pool of entrepreneurial scientific and intellectual human capital.
- Incorporate the significant geo-economic and geo-political strength of the Non-Resident Indian community
- Use urbanization as an opportunity to create a wholesome and secure habit through the use of modern technology.
- Use technology to reduce opacity and potential for misadventure in governance.

The NITI Aayog aims to enable India to better face complex, challenges, through the following:

- Leveraging of India's demographic dividend and realization of the potential of youth, men and women, trough education skill development, elimination of gender bias and employment.
- Elimination of poverty and the chance for every Indian to live a life of dignity and self-respect.
- Redressal of inequalities based on gender bias, caste and economic disparities.
- Integrate villages institutionally into the development progress.
- Policy support to more than 50 million small businesses, which are a major source of employment creation safeguarding of our environmental and ecological assets.

The NITI Aayog is quite different from the Planning Commission. Two key activities of the commission had been to prepare and implement the Five Year Plans and to allocate financial resources to states. However, neither of these activities from a part of the mandate of NITI Aayog. The 12th Five Year Plan which ended on 31st March 2017 was India's last Five Year Plan.

The 14th Finance Commission raised the shares of states in the divisible pool from 32% to 42% leaving no additional funds for allocation to states through NITI Aayog. Likewise, the annual resource allocation exercise that brought state chief ministers to the doorstep of the Planning Commission does not exist anymore. The Planning Commission is now abolished.

It is observed that among the many functions the NITI Aayog performs three stand out notably: (a) promotion of cooperative and competitive federalism, (b) assisting the central government in policy making and (c) serving as the central government's think tank.

The governing council of NITI Aayog on 8 February 2015 appointed three subgroups of chief ministers to advise central government on the subjects of 'Centrally Sponsored Schemes', Skill Development' and 'Swachh Bharat Mission'. It also set up two task forces at the Aayog on 'Agricultural Development' and 'Elimination of Poverty', with parallel task force on each subject constituted in the states and union territories. The NITI Aayog is also in the process of bringing out the 15-year Vision, 7-year Strategy, and 3-year Action plan documents with regard to the implementation of the United Nations Sustainable Development Goals by 2030.

Prime Minister Narendra Modi approved the reconstitution of the policy think tank of the government, NITI Aayog, ahead of its first meeting in the National Democratic Alliance's second term.

In a statement issued by the Cabinet Secretariat, Rajiv Kumar continues as vice chairman in the reconstituted body, and VK Saraswat, Ramesh Chand and VK Paul as full-time members.

Mr. Bibek Debroy will continue to work in his capacity as chairman of the Economic Advisory council to the Prime Minister.

As per the Cabinet Secretariat statement, PM Modi, who is also the chairperson of the Niti Aayog, appointed home minister Amit Shah, defence minister Rajnath Singh, finance minister Nirmala Sitharaman and agriculture minister Narendra Singh Tomar as ex-officio members.

The prime minister also appointed road transport minister Nitin Gadkari, commerce & industry and railway minister Piyush Goyal, social justice minister Thawar Chand Gehlot and statistics & programme implementation minister Rao Inderjit Singh as special invitees to the panel.

Niti Aayog CEO Amitabh Kant, who was given an extension till June 30, 2019 will continue in his role till the end of his tenure.

The fifth meeting of the Governing Council of Niti Aayog was held under the chairmanship of the Prime Minister at Rashtrapati Bhawan on June 15, 2019. It was attended by the Governor of Jammu & Kashmir, 26 Chief Ministers and the Lieutenant Governor of Andaman & Nicobar Islands, apart from Union Ministers, who are ex-officio members and special invitees. Vice Chairman, Members, CEO and senior officers of NITI Aayog also attended the meeting.

The Prime Minister emphasized that this was the meeting of Team India and said that States should recognise their core competence, and work towards raising GDP targets right from the district level.

The major points of focus of the Aayog was spelt out by the PM. In his words:

- NITI Aayog has key role to play in fulfilling the mantra of Sabkas Saaath, Sabka Vikas, Sabka Vishwas.
- Goal to make India a 5 trillion dollar economy by 2024, is challenging, but achievable, with the concerted efforts of States.
- Export sector vital for boosting income and employment; States should focus on export promotion.
- Newly created Jal Shakti Ministry will help provide an integrated approach to water; States can also integrate various efforts towards water conservation and management.

- We are now moving towards a governance system characterized by Performance, Transparency and Delivery.

With a view to seeing that NITI Aayog plays an effective intergovernmental policy making and conflict resolution role among and between the Union and state governments, it is important for the union government to ensure that NITI Aayog be given statutory status and powers in promoting intergovernmental bargains, resolving issues and coordinating policies between the Union and the states in the spirit of cooperative federalism.

The cabinet resolution lays down only the broad framework for the Aayog. The effectiveness of the NITI Aayog in transforming India will depend upon the clarity in the functions assigned, the status and power given and the quality of the people who will steer the institution.

The abolition of the Planning commission paves the way for restoring the role of the Finance Commission to assess the total requirements of the states in the revenue account without making a distinction between plan and non-plan spending. However, the Finance Commission does not have a comparative advantage in recommending specific purpose transfers unless it is made a permanent body. The constitutional provision does not require it to be a temporary body – Article 280 simply states the commission should be appointed every five years.

One point is clear here. It may be argued that the NITI Aayog will entail neither a reduction in the amount of resources available to the states, nor any increase in the centre's control over state plans, since it will be open to the states to tie up with investors, (both domestic and foreign), to work out investment projects of any description and any amount.

10.10 Inter State Council (ISC)

Accepting the recommendations of the first commission on centre-state relations, (the Sarkaria Commission which submitted its report in January 1988), the GoI constituted an ISC under Article 263 on 28 May 1990.

The composition of the council as per the presidential order dated 28 May 1990 is as follows:

1. PM as the chairman
2. Chief ministers of all states
3. Chief ministers of union territories having a legislative assembly and Administrators of union territories not having a legislative assembly
4. Six ministers of cabinet rank in the Union Council of Ministers to be nominated by the prime minister

The Punchhi Commission on centre-state relations (2010) recommended functional independence and quasi-judicial status for the ISC. It also recommended that ISC should be made a vibrant negotiating forum for policy development and conflict resolution.

The Constitution of India empowers the President of India to establish a constitutional body for inquiring into and advising upon inter-state disputes under Art 263 (a) and for achieving better coordination of policy and action under Article 263 (b) and (c), regarding subjects of common interest to some or all of the states, or the Union and one or more of the states.

However, the following issues may not be brought up before the Council:

1. Any issue which can be resolved at the official/ministerial level
2. Any issue which has to be dealt with by the ND, the National Integration Council (NIC), and the Finance Commission
3. Any issue which is sub judice or is under consideration in either House of Parliament
4. Any other issue the discussion of which may, in the opinion of the chairman, create discord between the states or otherwise be against the public interest or against the interests of the sovereignty or integrity of India, the security of the state, friendly relations with foreign state or public order

It maybe mentioned that there is no provision that makes it mandatory for the Council to hold its meetings on regular basis with a constitutionally specified frequency. Ten members, including the chairman, form the quorum for a meeting of the Council. The union government on 1 November 2017 reconstituted the ISC, the mandate of which is to investigate and advise on disputes between states, with PM Narendra Modi being its chairman and six union ministers and chief ministers of all states and union territories having legislative assemblies. Eight other union ministers have been made permanent invitees to the council. They represent Ministers of commerce, Food, Food Processing Industries, Tribal Affairs, HRD, Petroleum, Railways and Home. In another notification, the government reconstituted the standing committee of the ISC under the chairmanship of the Home Minister. Four union ministers and seven chief ministers are members of the new standing committee of the council. The job of the standing committee will be to monitor the implementation of decisions taken on the recommendations of the council and consider any other matter referred to it by the council.

The power of the president to set up ISC may be exercised not only for advising upon disputes but also for the purpose of investigating and discussing subjects in which some or all of the states of the Union and one or more of the states have a common interest. In exercise of this power, the president has already constituted the Central Council of Health, the Central Council of Local Self-Government, the Central Council of Indian Medicine and the Central Council of Homeopathy. In this connection, it should be mentioned that advisory bodies to advice on inter-state matters have also been established under statutory authority.

The ISC is the only constitutional body to deal with federal disputes in a comprehensive manner. It has a high potential to strengthen vertical and horizontal cooperation in Indian federalism. However, this potential remained untapped.

10.11 Goods and Services Tax Council (GSTC)

On 8 September 2016, the Constitution (101st Amendment) Act, 2016, received the assent of the President of India for the introduction of GST in the country (the notification for bringing into force Article 279A (1) with effect from 12 September 2016 was issued on 10 September 2016. On 12 September 2016, the union cabinet approved the creation of GSTC and its secretariat, and, on 16 September 2016, the GSTC was set up under Article 279A of the Indian Constitution. GSTC is an institutional mechanism comprising a chairperson (union finance minister) and one member nominee from each state government as members. Nominee ministers from the state governments have been given power to choose 'one amongst themselves' a vice chairperson of the council 'for such period as they may decide', allowing rotation if needed. One-half of the total number of members of the GSTC is the determined quorum as its meetings, and every decision is to be taken by a majority of not less than three-fourth of the weighted votes-central government has one-third weightage of the votes cast and state governments taken together, two-third-members present and voting at the meeting. As the GSTC is mandated to be guided by the need for a harmonized structure of goods and services tax and for the development of harmonized national market for goods and service, the Council has to recommend the following:

1. the taxes, cesses and surcharges levied by the Union, the States and the local bodies which may be subsumed in the goods and services tax;
2. the goods and services that may be subjected to, or exempted from goods and services tax;
3. model Goods and Services Tax Laws, principles of levy, appointment of Goods and Services Tax levied on supplies in the course of inter-State trade or commerce under Article 269A and the principles that govern the place of supply;
4. the threshold limit of turnover below which goods and services may be exempted from goods and services tax;
5. the rates, including floor rates, with bands of goods and services tax;
6. any special rate or rates for a specific period, to raise additional resources during any natural calamity or disaster;.
7. special provision with respect to the States of Arunachal Pradesh, Assam, Jammu and Kashmir, Manipur, Mizoram, Nagaland, Sikkim, Tripura, Himachal Pradesh and Uttarakhand; and
8. any other matter relating to the goods and services tax, to be decided by the GST Council.

GSTC has the mandate to recommend to the legislature the full implications of the GST on (a) tax structure, (b) tax incidence, (c) tax consumption, (d) tax payment, (e) compliance, (f) credit utilization and (g) reporting, and it also has in its zone of consideration business-process implications in terms of (i) pricing of product and services, (ii) supply chain operations, (iii) realistic accounting and (iv) e-governance. After receipt of the GSTC recommendations, legislative action will follow in the Parliament of India.

It is said that 'adoption of the goods and services tax would create a seamless common market'. The GST would subsume and eliminate the previous cascade of 17 central and state taxes and 23 cesses, leading to efficiency gains and lowering of retail prices.

It may be mentioned here that the GSTC has been constituted as a fully discursive body in the spirit of cooperative federalism. It is not merely a forum of compensation-seekers, but an apex recommendatory constitutional entity. The voting pattern of the GSTC is such that the states will play a major role with a two-third share, and though the central government with a one-thirds share has veto power, decisions will be taken by a three-fourth majority.

10.12 Judicial Tribunals

While Article 131 provides for the judicial determination of disputes between states by vesting the Supreme Court with exclusive jurisdiction in the matter, Article 262 provides for the adjudication of one class of disputes by an extra judicial tribunal. Under the Article, the Parliament has enacted the Inter-State Water Disputes Act, 1956, to provide for adjudication of disputes relating to waters of inter-state rivers and river valleys. Under the aforesaid Act, the union government has constituted several water dispute Tribunals.

In the context of the water disputes involving one or more states, the National Commission to Review the Working of the Constitution (NCRWC) 2002 made certain suggestions. First, it observed that it was not necessary to exclude inter-state water disputes from the original jurisdiction of the Supreme Court under Article 131. Second, the NCRWC has recommended that appropriate parliamentary legislation should be made for repealing the River Boards Act, 1956, and replacing it by another comprehensive enactment under Entry 56 of List 1. Third, the NCRWC is of the view that as water disputes are important, they should be heard and disposed by a bench not less than three judges and if necessary, a bench of five judges of the Supreme Cour for the final disposal of the suit.

On 18 December 2016, the Centre decided to set up a single, permanent tribunal to adjudicate all inter-state river water disputes subsuming existing tribunals in order to resolve grievances of states in a speedy manner.

10.13 Intergovernmental Relations: Policy Imperatives

Several institutional developments and policy imperatives stand out in a review of India's Intergovernmental Relations system, and represent new opportunities and challenges. India has taken major strides in decentralizing government by creating a tier of local government that has constitutional status, and that requires another layer of intergovernmental transfer. At the same time, market-oriented economic reforms have weakened traditional hierarchical mechanisms of fiscal control, and require new institutional approaches. These include reforms in several areas, particularly in the tax system, in this new era of redefining boundaries between government and market, where regional inequalities still remain a major concern.

A key change brought about by the 73rd and 74th amendments was a reduction of State Government discretion concerning elections to rural local government bodies. Direct elections to local bodies must be held every five years. This is a positive step to the extent that it provides more refined incentives, subject to the caveat of effective monitoring and transparency being achievable. Local government reform also has changed the nature of tax and expenditure assignments to local governments, and instituted a system of formal state-local transfers modeled on the component of the existing Centre-State system that is governed by the Finance Commission. While there are some serious issues with the new assignments, including problems of local capacity and efficiency of raising and spending money, we focus here on the new transfer system.

The new State Finance Commissions (SFCs) have struggled to formulate the principles for sharing or assigning state taxes, toils, and fees and for making grants- in-aid. Lack of political will at the state level and the states' own fiscal problems have together restricted progress in this dimension. On the other hand, the current situation with respect to local governments seems no worse than the previous one of ad hoc and discretionary transfers and control of local bodies by State Governments, the new constitutional structures create a space within which local governments may become effective over time.

One way out of this impasse may be for states to give local governments greater effective taxing powers, and to improve their collection capabilities.

The evidence from several studies suggests growing inequality among the Indian states in the past three decades, with the rate increasing since the 1990s. Differences in infrastructure and institutions that seem to explain interstate differences have been persistent. Finance Commission transfers, Planning Commission transfers or Central ministry transfers did not make a substantial dent in regional inequalities in India. Growing regional inequality is a concern, particularly because it can threaten political stability. Liberalization has meant a reduction in Central Government control of industrial investment and other aspects of regional economic policy, leaving the intergovernmental transfer system in the spotlight.

The issues that created tensions and conflicts between the Centre and the States are: (1) Mode of appointment and dismissal of governors (2) Discriminatory and partisan role of governors (3) Imposition of President's Rule for partisan interests (4) Deployment of Central forces in the states to maintain law and order (5) Reservation of state bills for the consideration of the President (6) Discrimination in financial allocations to the states and sharing of finances (7) Management of All India services (8) Encroachment by the Centre on the State List (9) Mineral and forest rich states are often poor because they have no power to manage their resources.

What are possible reforms that can be made in the transfer system, if growing regional disparities are a concern, and can they be politically feasible? Centre-State relations remain an area of contestation—India had 14 states in 1957, the number rose to 17 by 1971, 23 by 1981, 28 by 2001 and 29 by 2014. One example of the political feasibility in the process of institutional reform comes from the case of tax-sharing arrangements. The Constitution specified certain categories of centrally collected taxes that were to be shared with the States, according to criteria to be determined by the Finance Commission. In particular, personal income taxes were a major component of tax transfers from the Centre to the States, which received 87.5% of such tax revenues. However, income tax surcharges were kept entirely by the Centre. Commentators have suggested that there were obvious incentive problems with such arrangements, and the Tenth Finance Commission recommended alternative arrangements whereby a proportion of overall central tax revenues would be devolved to the States. This required bargaining and agreement among the Centre and the States, as well as a constitutional amendment, but this was all accomplished by 2000. However, following the acceptance of the recommendations of the Fourteenth Finance Commission, the centre has increased the share of central taxes flowing directly to the states from 32 to 42 per cent. This historic shift, although not free of implementation issues, along with the Goods and Services Tax (GST, once it becomes operational), will markedly shift India's fiscal federalism in ways that are likely to significantly remake India's fiscal federalism in ways that are likely to significantly remake India's political economy. But, if further fiscal decentralization to the third tier (local governments) does not occur, the Indian body politic will have an expansive middle bugle and weakened head and feet.

Conclusion

The Supreme Court, in its judgement in the case of State of West Bengal vs. Union of India (1963), had held that the Indian Constitution did not propound the principle of absolute federalism. Though the states have a subordinate position, yet the functional balance is in favour of the supremacy of the Union.

The nature of federalism in India during the coalition era (1989-2013) was transformed. Political considerations seem to overshadow the administrative and financial facets of the Union-State relations in India. The states having the governments of those parties that formed part of the central coalition seemed to have no conflict with the Centre. Their grievances were subdued and the general perception was that they got special consideration and support in matters of resources distributed by the Centre. One heard sometimes that the Centre was being partial against the states having governments of the opposition parties. However, when one notices the allocations of the Central plan fund released by the then Planning Commission on an annual basis, it appears that there is no such glaring discrimination.

An important issue that crops up from time to time, relates to development programmes initiated and funded by the Central Government on a uniform basis throughout the country. Most of the flagship programmes such as MNREGA, Sarva Shiksha Abhiyan and the National Rural Health Mission represent the initiatives of the Central Government without adequately consulting the states on the problems likely to be confronted by them in their implementation. The process of consultation between the Centre and the States concerning massive national programmes of socioeconomic development ought to be regular and systematic and the states should not feel that they are sidelined when important policy decisions are made by the Central Government. A more collaborative relationship between the two alone will strengthen the spirit of federalism.

A sound approach to federalism in India also requires continuing meaningful interactions between the Centre and the States and among States themselves. There are a number of critical issues that require a concerted effort through serious dialogues, the most important being the river water disputes occasionally emerging as issues of friction. There have been a few success stories, e.g. concerning the Krishna River the role of the tribunal for adjudication on river water disputes has been eminently useful. Occasionally, there is demand that the major rivers be declared national assets and the subject of distribution of water should fall within the ambit of the Union government. Even if this principle is accepted, it will be desirable to involve all the states concerned to protect the federal as well as state interests in water management. It is high time that the Inter-state River Water Disputes Act 1956 is made an effective instrument to solve the pending inter-state water disputes pertaining to Godavari, Narmada, Cauveri and other rivers that are our true national assets.

Union-State relations and intergovernmental relations in India have largely conformed to the model of cooperative federalism by and large, some irritants and tension areas notwithstanding. Using its larger resource and expenditure capacities the Union had initiated Centrally Sponsored Schemes (CSS) with the consent of State Governments in all major policy areas. State Governments have, however, been complaining about fiscal domination of the Centre over the States and demanding redistribution of powers and revenue resources. But neither the Sarkaria Commission on Centre-State Relations nor the National Commission for Review of the Constitution (NCRWC) or the M.M. Punchhi Commission on Centre-State Relations has recommended any substantial review in this arrangement.

A paradigm shift in economic policies which subsequently impacted on Centre- State relations leading to a growing federalization of the Indian polity are the visible trends after 1991. Federalization has accentuated the tendency towards political as well as economic regionalism. With increased levels of decentralized planning after the 73rd and 74th amendments being put in practice, the public investment in the economy has considerably gone down. This has opened up opportunities for economically more developed States to chart out their own strategies of development in collaboration with the private sector, but backward States have been put to disadvantage on account of lack of their own resources and declining public investment on the part of the federal Government. However, private sector investment has also risen in backward regions. Since the early 1990S, there has been a growing increase in regional economic disparities among states.

Scholarly studies also reveal that during August 1991 to March 2000 the states of Andhra Pradesh, Gujarat, Haryana, Karnataka, Kerala, Punjab, and Tamil Nadu got proposals of private capital investment to the tune of 66.7% as against only 27.4% received by the states of Assam, Bihar, Madhya Pradesh, Orissa, Rajasthan, Uttar Pradesh, and West Bengal. Difference in regard to foreign direct investment (FDI) are even more glaring. In the phase of globalization, only five states—Andhra Pradesh, Gujarat, Karnataka, Maharashtra, and Tamil Nadu—got a disproportionately large (75%) of FDI investment in India.

Structural arrangements and clearly defined norms and procedures embodied in the Constitution have provided the guidelines for Indian federalism but it is in the operating dynamics of Centre-State relations that one can see the true nature of Indian federalism being played out at three levels, viz. political, constitutional and procedural. The political or politico-constitutional pendulum of Indian federal system has been relentlessly swinging towards a strong Centre for the last five decades and India has become what K. Santhanam called "Centre Paramount Federation" in view of the paramount need to maintain the unity and integrity of India. Appointment and the role of governors, allocation of resources from the Centre to the States, deployment of the Central Police Forces and imposition of President's rule in the States are some of the main irritants in Centre-State relations at the procedural level.

After nearly seventy years of Indian Independence, one must redefine the mechanisms and practices of Union-State relations and give it a proper constitutional form by carrying out required adjustments. The Union List needs to be deleted considerably to augment the State List. The State List needs revision and replenishment. The Concurrent List should orient and must provide areas of commonality. If conflicts between the Union and the States are to be avoided, the states must be made financially self-sufficient in resources.

With the rationalization of the party system and some visible changes in the attitudes and behaviour patterns of Central and State functionaries, the framework of political power in India has now become more federalized than ever before. State Governments now are more autonomous and less insecure of central intervention at every step. The planning process has also become less centralized both on account of coalitional governments and economic liberalization and the resultant deregulation of the private sector as also disinvestment of Public Sector Undertakings. However, monetary and fiscal processes still continue to be highly centralized. The State Governments continue to be resentful about Centre's fiscal dominance. It is in these areas that India could do with a greater openness to the forces of federalization and economic liberalization.

There is an overwhelming consensus that the Finance Commission and the ISC are the two constitutional bodies which have the potential to strengthen federalism in India. The NITI Aayog is also specifically designed to promote cooperative federalism. The strength of a federal system of government lies in the harmonious, efficient and effective operation of Centre-State relations. Unfortunately healthy working relationships between the Centre and State Governments have, often been undermined due to misuse of constitutional authority by both the Congress as well as non-Congress governments against the State Governments in the past. In a federal state of continental dimensions like India, the lessons from Centre-State relations must be learnt on a continuous basis from past experiences and fresh efforts have to be made time and again which will set healthy precedents for a cooperative relationship between the Centre and the States in the years to come.

Suggested Readings

Commission on Centre-State Relations Report, Part 1 1988 Government of India Press, Nasik, Chair: Justice R.S. Sarkaria.

Dua, B. D. and M. P. Singh (eds.), *Indian Federalism in the New Millennium*, New Delhi, Manohar, 2003.

Rao, M. Govinda and Nirvikar Singh, *Political Economy of Federalism in India*, New Delhi, OUP, 2005.

Report of the Fourtheenth Finance Commission – 2015-2020, GOI

Saez, Lawrence, *Federations without a Centre: The Impact of Political and Economic Reform on India's Federal System*, New Delhi, Sage, 2002.

Sharma, C.K. *Intergovernmental Coordination Mechanisms in India, South Asia Journal of Socio-political studies* 15, no. 2 (2015) : 48

Singh, M. P. and Rekha Saxena, *India at the Polls: Parliamentary Elections in the Federal Phase,* Delhi, Orient Longman, 2003.

Singh, M. P., "From Hegemony to Multi-Level Federalism? India's Parliamentary-Federal System/' *The Indian Journal of Social Science*, vol. 5 no. 3 (July-September).

ООО

Chapter Eleven

Public Finance Management

Introduction

Public Finance management is a core component of public systems management in all countries. In India, financial administration constitutes the functions of generation, regulation, and distribution of public monies in order to sustain the political economy of the country. Thus, financial administration is a significant subsystem of the administrative system in India.

Budget is the heart of financial administration. It is a government document containing a preliminary approval plan of public revenue and expenditure.

Budget is something more than a mere estimate of public revenues and expenditures. It is one of the instruments for the expression of a government's policies and plays an important role in the economy of a state. Through a budget, citizens are benefited from various plans and programmes of the government. The budget policy of the government aims at removal of poverty, unemployment, social, and economic inequalities in society. By imposing graded taxation upon articles of consumption, it can encourage investment, and thus, promote a nation's economic growth. By taxing the rich, it can mitigate economic inequality. The signs of a welfare state are reflected in a budget which has a heavy outlay on social services. Budget, thus, is an instrument of socio-economic change and a comprehensive expression of public policy.

Budget also acts as an allocator of public goods and social resources. It is the government which allocates society's resources by mandating that taxes be collected and then by deciding where those taxes should be spent. Services and goods that cannot be divided or assigned a cost to individuals—public goods—will not be provided by a profit-driven market. Where price is not a good indicator of the value of a service, the private sector is unlikely to provide the service. Similarly, goods and service provisions where extraordinary risks are involved will not find free enterprise operating except in partnership with the public sector. In all such cases, the government is expected to see that certain resources are allocated to provide those services. In this way, the budget acts as an allocator of social resources.

Therefore, the budget is a multi-faceted tool: for an economist it is an instrument to influence the economy; the politician uses it for defending or attacking the government; the administrator uses it as a framework for coordination and imposing financial discipline throughout the administrative system.

Public Finance Management (PFM) deals with all aspects of resource mobilization and expenditure management in government. Fiscal Responsibility and Budget Management (FRBM) Act, 2003, is an Act providing for the responsibility of Central Government to ensure inter-generational equity in fiscal management and long term macro-economic stability. FRBM Act, 2003, stipulates that in each financial year the Central Government shall lay in the Statements of fiscal policy along with the Annual Financial Statement and Budget Demands for Grants before both Houses of Parliament. These are as follows:

- The medium-term fiscal policy statement: A statement mentioning the three year rolling targets for indicators such as the revenue deficit, fiscal deficit, tax to GDP ratio and total outstanding debt at the end of the year.
- The fiscal policy strategy statement: A statement outlining the strategic fiscal priorities of the Government for the ensuing year.
- The macro-economic framework: A statement containing an assessment of the growth prospects of the economy.

Preparation of the Annual Budget in the GOI follows both the top-down and bottom-up approaches while the guidelines and instructions are issued by the Ministry of Finance.

The Budget Cycle commences towards the end of September of a particular year and lasts till May of the next financial year. The first step starts with the Ministries' or Departments' review of the existing Expenditure Budget and prioritizing the activities and schemes. As per the instructions of the Ministry of Finance, no demand should normally be made in the budget without completion of a pre-budget scrutiny of a project/ scheme. However, in the budgetary system unrealistic budget estimates, delay in implementation of projects, dispersed pattern, ad hoc project announcements and emphasis on compliance with processes rather than on outcomes, have often been observed.

This has led to a situation where the Ministries/Departments are not in a position to make a correct assessment of fund requirements or assess ground realities. Various reform measures have been proposed in the past to move away from the emphasis on compliance aspects of the annual budget rather than measurement of actual outcomes. The first significant step in this direction was taken by the First ARC in the form of a performance budget. A performance budget is a technique of presenting government operations in terms of functions, programmes, activities and projects. The First ARC recommended three steps for conducting a performance budgeting exercise:

1. Establishing a functional programme classification of government operations
2. The system of accounting and financial management should be in accord with this classification
3. Evolving suitable norms, work units of performance and unit costs, under each programme and activity for their reporting and evaluation

Performance budgets were initially presented for a few Departments on a supplementary basis and later were extended to all Ministries.

The Ministry of Finance introduced zero-based budgeting in 1986, and recommended that all Ministries/Departments of the Government adopt it. In contrast to traditional budgeting where variances are measured against past years, zero-based budgeting requires the analysis and approval of each and every line item. However, due to lack of capability building initiatives, the concept did not become popular.

Later in 2005, an outcome-based budgeting system was introduced. The Department of Expenditure and the Planning Commission had jointly prepared the first ever Outcome Budget for the year 2005-2006, which was presented to the Parliament on August 25, 2005. Thereafter, a series of detailed guidelines were issued to all Ministries/Departments on preparation of Outcome Budget and Performance Budget by individual Ministries. Outcome Budget has become an integral part of the budgeting process since 2005-06.

The outcome budget and the performance budget were merged and placed in one combined document. Thus, while the annual financial statement and outcome budget would be for the ensuing financial year, the performance budget would present the picture of actual achievement performance of the previous financial year.

With the introduction of the outcome budget in 2005-06, it was claimed that the budgetary process had moved beyond the traditional line-item system of budgeting to clearly defined outcomes of all government programmes. In fact, the outcome budget of 2007-08 states in its preface.

"The Outcome Budget is an endeavour of the Government to convert the 'Outlays' into 'Outcomes' by planning the expenditure, fixing appropriate targets, quantifying the deliverables in each scheme and bring to the knowledge of all the 'Outcomes' of the Budget outlays provided for each scheme/programme. Thus, the 'Outcome Budget' is an effort of the Government to be accountable and transparent to the people."

However, critics have pointed out that if one looks at the outcome budgets prepared by various departments, the measurement of outputs and outcomes seems to have been somewhat mixed up. What actually happens is that departments, while preparing their outcome budgets, merely reproduce the output targets as outcomes, and more often than not, the general intent of the programs are presented as outcomes. The outcome budgets, as prepared by departments, do not clearly present the fiscal year goals that could provide a sense of performance measures, economy of resource use, efficiency in operation, and effectiveness in results. As they are presented now, the outcome budgets, notwithstanding the objectives articulated in the explanatory memorandum, have an uncanny resemblance to the all-too-familiar performance budgets of earlier periods.

Despite its flawed design and implementation, the effort deserves to be complimented because it has set the agenda for evaluating budgetary spending. As we mentioned earlier, the way performance is designed should be the determining factor in a system of outcome budgeting.

11.1 Budgetary Process—Agencies/Actors

Parliament

The Parliament of India may be taken as the lead actor in the budgetary process of the country. In accordance with the norms of parliamentary democracy, parliament is entrusted with the primary responsibility of acting as the custodian of finances in the country. By way of discharging its responsibilities as a fund-raising and fund-granting agency, it exercises almost absolute control over the budget of India through its powers of levy, abolish, or decrease of any tax or other budgetary allocations. Indeed, such a commanding position to the Parliament has been accorded by the Indian Constitution itself. Hence, under Article 112 of the Constitution, the President has been vested with the responsibility of causing to be laid, the 'annual financial statement', the constitutional terminology for budget, before the houses of Parliament. However, of the two houses of Parliament, it is the lower house or the Lok Sabha that holds absolute control over the budgetary process with just nominal role assigned to the upper house or the Rajya Sabha.

As the core unit of the executive entrusted with the task of managing the budget, the Ministry of Finance may arguably be taken as the nodal agency of the budgetary process in India. For instance, right from estimating the final figures of the revenues and expenditures of the government for presentation before the parliament, the ministry is vested with the task of ultimately ensuring that the finances of the country are managed properly. The major contours of the functioning of the ministry are discerned from its structural divisions in the three departments, that is, Department of Economic Affairs, Department of Revenue, and Department of Expenditure.

An important actor in the budgetary process of democratic societies is the institution of independent audit. In India, such a function is discharged by the constitutional authority, called the Comptroller and Auditor General (CAG) of India. Under the provisions of Article 148 of the Constitution, the CAG conducts such an audit on behalf of the parliament to investigate and report on the legality and efficiency of all the financial transactions carried out by the government departments. The role of CAG in the budgetary process of India has been a by product of the parliamentary democratic system of governance provided for under the Constitution where an independent agency comments on the financial propriety of public expenditure.

Finally, the parliamentary committees constitute the last set of actors playing a significant role in the budgetary process of the country. The role of these committees exposes the inadequacy of the control exercised by the parliament over the finances of the government due to paucity of time and lack of expertise. Previously, there used to be only two committees, that is, the Estimates Committee and the Public Accounts Committee of Parliament to discharge the necessary functions of legislative control. But, in recent times, with the creation of the departmentally related standing committees of Parliament, the role of the Parliament in the functioning of the various departments of the government has become more comprehensive and focused. Nonetheless, the role of these committees is distinct in relation to the budgetary process. The Estimates Committee, for instance, suggests economies in estimates of expenditures of various government departments in order to make them more realistic and economical. On the contrary, the Public Accounts Committee carries out a post mortem of the appropriation accounts in the light of the audit report of the CAG. In the process, it attracts the attention of the legislature to financial irregularities, if any, and suggests remedial measures for the same. In distinction with others, the departmentally related standing committees carry out not just financial control over the concerned departments but also scrutinize their overall functioning from time to time.

In brief, the major actors or agencies in the budgetary process of India are numerous and varied, owing to the variety of functions each of them is supposed to perform. Such functions may be classified in three groups with each having their critical value in the smooth functioning of the budgetary system. Hence, while the broad functions of parliament as the fund-granting agency are well-established, the role of its executive and sub-agencies, such as the Ministry of Finance, as the proposer of financial estimates is also accepted. What is, however, unique to India is apparently its elaborate system of legislative control over the budget through the mechanism of its own committees as well as the institution of an independent audit. Indeed the successful functioning of the public finance management system in India is credited to the reasonably satisfactory role played by these actors in the budgetary process of the country.

11.2 Parliamentary Control

Financial administration is executed through: (a) the legislative, (b) the executive, (c) the Finance Department, (d) the audit, and (e) the parliamentary committees.

The importance given to public sector and planning led to rapid increase in the expenditure of the government in India in the post-Independence period. It is imperative for the institutions like the Parliament and State Legislatures to scrutinize the expenditure by the executive for proper accountability of public money. The enormous increase in public expenditure in recent times led to the formation of an effective control mechanism by the Parliament. The Constitution has provided mechanism for effective parliamentary control over public finances.

The financial system consists of two components—revenue and expenditure.

1. As regards revenue, it is expressly laid down by our Constitution (Article 265) that no tax shall be levied or collected except by authority of law. The result is that the Executive cannot impose any tax without legislative sanction.
2. The second principle is that Lok Sabha has the exclusive control of the Money Bills.
3. The demand for grants must come from the government. Neither the Lok Sabha, nor a State Assembly may vote a grant except on a demand for grant from the government.
4. As regards expenditure, the pivot of parliamentary control is the Consolidated Fund of India. This is the reservoir into which all the revenues received by the GOI as well as all loans raised by it are paid and the constitution provides that no moneys shall be appropriated out of the Consolidated Fund of India except in accordance with law (Article 266[3]).-This law means an Act of Appropriation passed in conformity with Article 114.

While an Act of Appropriation ensures that there cannot be any expenditure of the public revenues without the sanction of Parliament, Parliament's control over the expenditure cannot be complete unless it is able to ensure economy in the volume of expenditure. On this point, however, reconciliation has to be made between two conflicting principles, namely, the need, for parliamentary control and the responsibility of the Government in power for the administration of its policies.

Effective parliamentary control over the administration of the country involves scrutiny into the details of government accounts and expenditure, but the parliament itself may not be a suitable body to probe into such minute points of detail, for it generally lacks the time or the expertise for such detailed examination. The parliament in India, in order to exercise effective control over the general and financial administration of the country has set up a number of committees of the House.

1. The Public Accounts Committee (PAC)
2. The Estimates Committee
3. The Committee on Public Undertakings

These three committees exercise detailed and substantial control and the Committee on Assurances undertake a scrutiny of promises, assurances, undertakings, etc., given by ministers.

11.3 Public Accounts Committee (PAC)

The Public Accounts Committee, constituted by both the Houses of Parliament, is a powerful organ to complete the accountability of the government in the matter of finance. While scrutinizing the Appropriation Accounts and the Audit Report submitted by the CAG, the Committee has to satisfy itself: that due economy has been exercised in the financial transactions of the government; and that high standards of public morality have been observed in all matters of finance. The PAC consists of 15 members from the Lok Sabha and 7 members from the Rajya Sabha It shall be the duty of the PAC to examine:

1. in the light of the report of the CAG, the statement of accounts showing the income and expenditure of State Corporations, trading and manufacturing schemes and projects, together with the balance sheet and statements of profit and loss accounts, which the President may have required to be prepared or are prepared under the provisions of the Statutory rules regulating financing of a particular corporation, trading concern or project.
2. the statement of accounts showing the income and expenditure of autonomous bodies the audit of which may be conducted by the CAG, either under the directions of the President or by a statute of Parliament; and
3. the report of the CAG in cases where the President may have required him to conduct an audit of any receipts or to examine the accounts of stores and stocks.

The main function of the PAC is to examine the report of the CAG in order to ascertain whether the money granted by the Parliament has been spent by the Government within the scope of the demands. The examination of the committee extends beyond the formalities of the expenditure to its wisdom, faithfulness and economy. It is the duty of the Committee, among other things, to draw the attention of the Parliament to cases of improper, wasteful expenditure, frauds or irregularities, malpractices, misappropriation, etc.

The Committee may send for persons, papers and records. The conclusions of the Committee are submitted to the Parliament in the form of a report. To enable intensive examination the committee takes resort to the practice of consulting study groups, dealing with specified departments such as, Defence, Railways, etc. These study groups submit their reports to the Committee. The Committee in turn considers them and makes recommendations to the government in anticipation of the final report, which is placed before the House. A convention has evolved that the recommendations of the Committee are normally accepted by the Government. If, however, the government feels that a particular recommendation is not acceptable to it on certain grounds, it requests a reconsideration of the recommendation. If, however, a specific issue defies any solution in this way and the Committee and government continue to take different positions, the final arbiter is the Parliament.

At best, the PAC probe relates to transactions completed and damage done. It conducts post-mortem examination of public accounts. However, it must be remembered that auditing is done after the work is completed and nothing can be changed at that point of time.

The recommendations by the Committee are used as a guide for both the future estimates and future policies. However, regular, recurrence and ever changing pattern of official neglect or default brought to light, year after year, does suggest that the value of the PAC's deliberations is limited.

11.4 The Estimates Committee

Parliamentary control over financial administration is further strengthened by the Estimates Committee. Although the parliament discusses the estimates for a fairly adequate period, it has neither the time nor the flexibility to probe into the details and technical aspects of the estimates. Therefore, before the estimates are presented to the parliament, they are projected to scrutiny by this independent financial committee.

The Estimates Committee is a standing committee, and is set up every year from amongst the members of the Lok Sabha according to the principle of proportional representation by means of single transferable vote. Its functions are laid down in the Rules of Procedure and Conduct of Business in the Lok Sabha. It consists of members from Lok Sabha only. The Chairman is appointed by the Speaker and if Deputy Speaker happens to be a member of the committee, he automatically becomes the chairman.

The most important function of the committee is to suggest economies in expenditure. The Committee is strictly not concerned with the policy of the government. Its business is to ensure that within the framework of the policy laid down by the government and the House, only the minimum expenditure needed for the purpose of fulfilling the objectives of the government would be incurred. The report contains three types of recommendations:

1. For improving the organization.
2. For securing the economy.
3. For providing guidance in the presentation of estimates.

The Estimates Committee is performing useful work in highlighting the various acts of omission and commission of the government. In its various reports submitted from time to time the committee suggested various reforms in financial as well as administrative systems.

The Estimates Committee is performing a useful role in the Indian administrative system. It keeps the machinery of administration under parliamentary scrutiny, which is a very healthy feature. It acts as a standing committee on administrative improvement by highlighting the shortcomings and mistakes of public organizations. Its role is quite significant as the Government accepts almost all its recommendations.

11.5 Committee on Public Undertakings

Since 1964, the Committee on Public Undertakings (COPU) has taken over the work relating to autonomous public Enterprises from the two financial committees. The Committee's major functions include the examination of reports and accounts of public undertakings; examination of reports, if any, of the CAG or the public undertakings; to examine whether the public undertakings are being managed in accordance with sound business principles and prudent commercial practices; and to discharge other functions assigned to it by the Speaker from time to time. The Committee undertakes its studies of individual public undertakings by rotation.

Strengthening Parliamentary Committees

The two Parliamentary Committees PAC and COPU are able to examine only a few paras and reviews out of large number of audit reports submitted to them, which defeats the very purpose of parliamentary financial control and the accountability of Executive that the Parliament is required to enforce. For example, during 2007-08 out of 16 Reports submitted to the Parliament containing 1209 paras, the number of paras/reviews selected for examination was 76, out of which, only 16 could be discussed by the PAC. In States there is a huge backlog of work before the PAC.

In order to strengthen parliamentary control over the executive it is necessary to devise a system which envisages that PAC examines all the reports submitted by CAG and submits its recommendations to the Legislature within a time limit. This is possible if the volume of CAG's Audit reports is reduced and only matters of critical importance are included in the Audit Reports. (Other financial irregularities noticed during audit need to be settled with the concerned ministries/departments through forums such as Audit Committees which need to be devised in consultation with Ministry of Finance). For PAC to function effectively and its members to develop specialization, the life of PAC should be made co-extensive with the life of Parliament/State legislature with one-third of members retiring every year. It is to be taken for consideration whether PAC should be given a Constitutional status with clearly defined mandate, duties and functions.

11.6 Role of Ministry of Finance

The financial control by the executive could be exercised when estimates are prepared and expenditure is incurred. The heads of subordinate agencies scrutinize expenditure proposals enacting from within in terms of their need and spending capacity. This process moves upward to the heads of departments who are expected to moderate the estimates in the light of accepted policies of the government and needs of programmes. Under the cabinet system, the central financial agency is entrusted with the responsibility of consolidating the estimates of the various departments. While discharging this function, the central budget may be able to modify departmental estimates through scrutiny and advice in terms of national policies and priorities, norms of expenditure and constraints of resources. The powers and influence of the central budget agency may vary from country to country. In India, the central budget agency is the Ministry of Finance.

Besides, the finance ministry sends its own finance officers to each ministry (except railway and defence), who exercise control over expenditure through scrutiny and examination of the legality, accuracy and propriety of expenditure. They also advise the departmental heads upon the financial implications of their schemes and plans and furnish reports on the financial administration of the ministry to which they are attached to the finance ministry.

The departmental control of expenditure takes place through an elaborate system of returns and reports frequently submitted by officers at various levels to their superior officers and ultimately to the head of the department. The accounts are to be maintained in a prescribed manner. Vouchers are to be certified according to rules. Payment is to be made in accordance with the prescribed procedure. The disbursing officers maintain the record of all accounts which are examined by the controlling officer.

The controlling officer prepares a statement and sends it to the head of the department. On the basis of the return received by him, the head of the department prepares an account showing the complete expenditure out of the grant at his disposal up to the end of the preceding month and submits the same to the office of the Accountant-General. *The NDA government at the Centre took a decision to end the practice of presenting the Annual Railway Budget starting from financial year 2018. It is now merged with the Union Budget. The government also decided to supplant the plan /non plan division of expenditure in Budget.*

11.7 The Comptroller and Auditor General of India

The Comptroller and Auditor General (CAG) of India is appointed by the President and shall only be removed from office in like manner and on the like grounds as a Judge of the Supreme Court.

The CAG of India derives his/her position and authority from the Constitution of India. Article 149 of the Constitution prescribes: "The Comptroller and Auditor-General shall perform such duties and exercise such powers in relation to the accounts of the Union and of the States and of any other authority or body as may be prescribed by or under any law made by Parliament". In pursuance of the Constitution, the Parliament established the law defining duties, powers and conditions of service of the CAG of India. The CAG is responsible for auditing the functioning of Central and State Governments including all government-owned companies, public sector undertakings and other autonomous bodies funded by public resources.

The duty of CAG of India includes auditing of all expenditure from the Consolidated Fund of the Centre, States and UTs. The objective is to ensure the money shown in the accounts as disbursed were legally available for and applicable to the service they have been associated with. The CAG submits a number of audit reports relating to Central and State Governments to the Parliament and the State legislature. These audit reports are examined by the Public Accounts Committees (PAC). The CAG of India is also the head of the Indian Audit and Accounts Department. In addition, CAG also executes performance and compliance audits of various functions and departments of the Central and State Governments.

One of the primary functions of audit is to see that provisions of law, rules and regulations are properly applied while incurring expenditure or collecting revenue. In order to regulate usage of money, elaborate rules and regulations have been drawn by government. While audit notices systematic violation of law, rules and regulations by departmental officers it is unable to take an effective action to prevent them.

The institution of CAG today faces consider able challenge to put an effective mechanism in place which ensures accountability for the usage of the entire range of public funds and resources by the central and state governments. In this era of economic liberalization government operations have become increasingly complex, public expenditure has multiplied with substantial portion of expenditure being incurred by autonomous bodies, grant-in-aid institutions and not-for-profit bodies with no clear accountability structure. A big amount of central government's expenditure is on centrally sponsored schemes, whose implementation is the responsibility of state governments. The bulk of the money is spent through non-government actors and it becomes a difficult task to track whether public money has reached the targeted beneficiaries. Government has also embarked on new areas of activities such as public-private partnership, leaving loopholes in the arrangement, which allows evasion of audit. A good part of government's transactions have been computerised-they are prone to cyber attacks and computer frauds.

The Office of the CAG is highly centralized with all powers concentrated in the headquarters and more particularly in the person holding the office of CAG. Delegation to field officers who do all the audit work is rare. India is perhaps the only federal country of the world where there is no statutory recognition to the head of audit who conducts audit of state government transactions.

The organizational structure of the Office of CAG is not in consonance with the scheme of federal arrangement as envisaged in the Constitution. While every state has a separate legislature, governor, high court and a public service commission, there is no provision for a separate audit chief for the states enjoying constitutional or legal status. Under the existing arrangement, the accountants general (AG)/ principal accountants general (Pr AG) are responsible for auditing the finances of the states and functioning as subordinate offices of the CAG.

Lack of legal status for the state AG seriously impairs his functioning. He is not able to deal effectively with the Public Accounts Committee (PAC) of the Legislature, nor is he able to take up issues of critical importance with the state government without clearance from the headquarters.

There also exists justification for a Pr AG to be given the power of finalization of state audit reports and its presentation to legislature, within the broad policy framework laid down by the CAG.

The accounts-keeping of State Government companies are in a chaotic state. Out of about 900 State Government companies the Annual Accounts of about 700 companies is in arrears sometimes for periods as long as ten to twelve years. The Companies Act stipulates that the Annual Accounts of these companies should get audited by Statutory auditors and CAG within six months, i.e. the close of every financial year viz. 30th September. Similar is the situation with large number of autonomous bodies, which receive substantial grants from government every year. Many of them do not submit their Annual Accounts in time for audit. In numerous cases, accounts when prepared do not follow the accounting standards, contain serious mistakes and when pointed out, the concerned organizations refuse to rectify the errors. And yet they continue to get government grants every year. Should not CAG be empowered to take legal action against management of such defaulting organizations, so that tax payers are assured that no misuse and misappropriation of public funds take place year after year?

Every Year, CAG presents about 40-50 reports for central government to parliament and another 90-100 reports for state governments (including UTs with legislatures). They deal with the entire gamut of the government's functioning such as lapses in defence deals and mega contracts, evasion of taxes, poor outcome of development schemes and malfeasance on the part of public officials causing loss to exchequer. It is not possible for any individual to go through such voluminous material, and satisfy himself about the findings presented therein

The situation in our country needs to be remedied by conferring legal power to Audit Officers to enable them to implement their findings by making suitable provisions in the C&AG's Act on the lines enjoyed by State audit institutions of other countries. The Act should entrust Audit Officers with the following powers: (a) powers to summon the concerned officers before it for evidence on oath; (b) in cases of default, after giving due opportunity, they be required to make up for the loss; (c) in case the official does not make up for the loss and the default or neglect is established, a report be made to the superior authority of the department where the officer is working for taking disciplinary action under the Civil Services Conduct Rules; (e) where action of public official involves criminal liability, the public prosecutor be informed either by Audit official or by the Department to which he belongs for initiating criminal action under the Penal code. For discharging this quasi-judicial function the powers similar to those available under Commission of Enquiry Act be vested with the Accountant General/Principal Director of Audit who are heads of department by making suitable legal provision to that effect.

The CAG report on the 2G Spectrum allocation provided a credible basis both for the CBI investigation and the hearings of the Public Accounts Committee (PAC) of the Parliament. CAG report on multiple irregularities related to Commonwealth Games Coalgate and Air India raised issues about systemic correction needed in the government departments regarding awarding of various kinds of contracts. There were also reports in the

CAG regarding the working of the Civil Aviation and Petroleum Ministries on the purchase of aircrafts and cost over runs on production sharing contracts. As the principle auditor of the country, it is the obligatory duty of the CAG to point out the deviations and irregularities as he perceives and it is for the concerned ministry or institution to reply, respond, correct and initiate follow up action wherever appropriate. Finally it is important to remember that CAG is an examining agency and not an investigative one with sweeping powers as in some other democracies.

The total strength of the Audit and Accounts Department is about 46,000, which comprises of about 700 Group A officers belonging to the IA&AS and 15,000 Group B officers known as audit/accounts officers. The balance 30,000 (around 70%) comprises ministerial staff who work as auditors, accountants, data entry operators and clerks.

Professionalism in the audit department can be brought by overhauling personnel management by inducting computer specialists, engineers, scientists and economists in its senior cadre, as well as hire domain experts and specialists for a short-term consultancy assignment for undertaking performance audit task, a practice extensively followed by the UK, the USA, Sweden and other developed countries. This will bring greater credibility to the audit reports and command respect of the auditee institutions.

11.8 Cash vs. Accrual-Based System of Accounting

In June 2011, the GOI announced that it is moving to an accrual based system of accounting. All this time, the Government accounts were being prepared on a cash- based accounting system. The major flaw of the cash-based accounting system was that it did not give an accurate picture of the Government's financial position as it lacked an adequate framework for accounting of assets and liabilities as capital expenditure is reflected in the books of accounts only in the year of a sale or purchase. It also does not depict a clear picture of Government liabilities arising as a result of the difference between commitments and payments made.

The Government Accounting Standards Advisory Board (GASAB) of the CAG is working on a detailed plan. An accrual-based system of accounting will report revenue in the year in which it is earned and expenses in the year in which they are incurred. Such a system is expected to make the financial reporting more meaningful and transparent. (DARPG, GOI)

11.9 Central Plan Scheme Monitoring System

The Central Plan Scheme Monitoring System (CPSMS) has been developed by the Controller General of Accounts (CGA). The CPSMS is an online management and decision support system that helps the GOI in tracking and monitoring funds. The system helps to calculate the utilization of funds at different levels on a real-time basis. There are over 1,000 Centrally Sponsored and Central Sector Schemes being implemented through the different Ministries of the GOI. Given the diversity in the implementation hierarchy the number of implementing units and the geographical reach of these schemes, it has been a challenge to have meaningful information on these schemes.

The need for a central monitoring, evaluation and accounting system for the Plan Schemes has been widely acknowledged. This not only effects the monitoring of the Plan Schemes but also has implications for financial management in the public sector.

The Economic Survey (2007-08) emphasized the need of output and outcome monitoring and creating knowledge-based expertise for effective financial monitoring of the Plan Schemes. Subsequently, the Finance Minister in his Budget Speech (2008-09) announced the setting of the Central Plan Schemes Monitoring System towards establishment of a comprehensive Decision Support System and Management Information System.

The CPSMS web-based application was implemented by the CGA. All Ministries/ Departments have to register the details of agencies receiving grants from the Central Government of India and this helps in maintaining a comprehensive database of agencies.

The CPSMS has been capturing the fund disbursement information of several government initiatives such as' the National Rural Health Mission, National Rural Employment Guarantee Act and Prime Minister's Gram Sadak Yojana.

Once fully implemented, the system would provide a platform to Secretaries, Additional Secretaries of the Administrative Departments and the District Collectors to monitor deployment and utilization of funds under the various schemes at different levels. The CPSMS has also been linked with the Core Banking Solution of all Public Sector banks and major private banks.

The CPSMS helps in creating an efficient internal control system to track fraud and theft. It also acts as an online portal for providing information to citizens on the fund allocation of the Government.

11.10 2nd ARC Report (Extracts) Flow of Funds

- Decide on the guiding principles for the flow of sanctions from the Central Ministries/ Departments to the implementing agencies in the States

Financial Information System

- Introduce a new robust financial information system that provides real time information on government expenditure at all levels and also to the public

Accrual System of Accounting:

- Build a task force to analyze and predict the cost and benefits of introducing accrual based accounting
- Implement an accrual based accounting system initially across a few departments for a period of 2-3 years to examine the tangible benefits

Internal Audit:

- Create an office of Chief Internal Audit in selected Ministries/Departments to oversee Internal Audit. The Chief Internal Auditor should be directly responsible to the Secretary of the Department
- Formation of the audit committee comprising a Chairperson and two members to oversee internal as well as external audit

Conclusion

The underlying theme for a good system of public financial management is the maintenance of financial discipline and prudence while simultaneously ensuring prompt and efficient utilization of resources to achieve the goals of different government agencies. Towards this end, accountability needs to shift from compliance with procedures to a much greater focus on results and outcomes. Tools of modern financial management like information technology and financial information system need to be used to improve accountability combined with accurate budgeting and realistic economic goals.

An assessment of the role and utility of the CAG, points to two very diverse opinions. On the one hand, there are some who believe that he plays a very useful constitutional role. On the other, there is Paul Appleby's criticism whose contention was that this office is an inheritance from colonial rule, and that the CAG is responsible for a widespread and paralyzing unwillingness to decide and act. Auditors do not know and are not expected to know very much about good administration, and thus, auditing is a necessary but highly pedestrian function with a narrow perspective and very limited utility. Appleby goes one step further and observes that a deputy secretary in the department knows more about the problems in his department than does the CAG and that too many reports of the CAG are mere substitutions of hindsight for the kind of judgement possible and necessary at the time of action.

The CAG has recently been accused of overreach, particularly when audit widens its horizons and attempts to examine 'efficiency' or 'cost effectiveness' or 'propriety' in a meticulous manner. However, given the fact that the policy process and the incurring of public expenditure are interrelated, it is in tune with the spirit of the constitution to go beyond just the regulatory auditing.

In the past few years, the quality of CAG reports has improved; they have become more up-to-date and are being issued on matters of current public interest to highlight cases of gross financial irregularities and corruption.

The Second Administrative Reforms Commission therefore argued that the CAG should offer constructive suggestions for strengthening government operations and thus become reform-oriented by suggesting certain best practices. It must identify systemic problems and should look at itself as an agency for change and improvement rather than primarily as an instrument for the detection of irregularities.

Public financial management is clearly governed by certain well-defined principles based on governmental economic priorities (drawn on public demands and needs) and the ideological compulsions of the ruling party. In all democracies the economic agenda of the government is indirectly set by the public. Budget making therefore becomes a complex public accountability exercise where the government has to balance multiple demands with scarce resources. The efficient management of public resources to ensure prompt citizen access to public goods and entitlements is the biggest challenge faced by governments in India. Crores of public funds (tax payer's money) are spent on the public governance system and government schemes targeted for the public in different social sectors. CAG has pointed out that much of government expenditure is ill-spent or not spent for the purposes sanctioned. Therefore, accountability for public money spent is the single most important issue of public governance in India today.

Suggested Readings

Arora, Ramesh K. and Rajni Goyal, *Indian Public Administration*, New Delhi, New Age, 2016.

Centre for Budget and Governance Accountability Annual Reports

Chandrashekhar R. K., *The Comptroller and Auditor General of India*, Vol. II, New Delhi, APH, 1990.

Chelliah, Raja J., *Fiscal Policy in underdeveloped countries with special reference to India*, Vol 31, Routledge, 2010.

Goel, S. L., *Public Financial Administration*, New Delhi, Deep and Deep, 2004.

Hansen, James A. and Sanjay Kathuria (eds.), *India: A Financial System for the Twenty First Century*, New Delhi, Oxford University Press, 1999.

Kumar, V, *The comptroller and Auditor general: A thematic history* (1990 - 2007) New Delhi, APH 2008

Mahajan Sanjeev Kumar and Anupama Puri Mahajan, *Financial Administration in India* and New Delhi, PHI, 2014.

Mathur, B.P. Mathur, *Government Accountability and Public Audit*, New Delhi, Uppal Publishing House, 2007.

Prasad, Eswar S. and Raghuram G. Rajan, *"Next Generation Financial Reforms in India," Finance and Development*, 45 September 9, 2008.

Rao, M. Govind, *"The Fiscal Situation and a Reform Agenda for the New Government," Economic and Political Weekly*, XLIV no. 25 June 20, 2009.

Reddy, Y.V., *"Monetary and Financial Sector Reforms in India: A Practitioner's Perspective," in India's Emerging Economy: Performance and Prospects in the 1990s and Beyond*, ed. Kaushik Basu, New Delhi, Oxford University Press, 2004.

Sarapa, A., *Public Finance in India*, New Delhi, Kanishka, 2004.

The comptroller and Auditor General : Reform the Institution to Enforce Government's Accountability", IJPA Journal – 64(3) 442-453 sage, 2018

ooo

Chapter Twelve

Public Sector Enterprises

Introduction

There are about 1400 public enterprises at the Centre, State and Local levels organized principally in the form of government agencies, statutory corporations, departmental enterprises, commissions, boards, companies and port trusts. These employ about 6 million personnel. Public Sector Enterprises (PSEs) are organizations where more than half of the paid-up share capital is held by the Central or a State Government. Public Sector includes all activities funded out of government budget and accounts for two fifth of total government investment and contributes a quarter of GDP. There are about 300 Central Public Sector Enterprises in total.

After Independence, through various Industrial Policy Resolutions, an attempt has been made to demarcate the role of the public enterprises in the country. Successive governments in Independent India have made policy statements starting from 1948.

In India, like in most developing countries, the 1960s and 70s were characterized by interventions by the State in the market, and the public sector was encouraged to grow at a rapid pace.

Even though the Indian public sector attracted the best human resources in the last five decades, they have been plagued by multiple problems —poor performance, lack of competitiveness and low productivity. This was entirely due to management structures characterized by multiple principles and goals which forced them into a bureaucratic rather than commercial mode of functioning, characteristics of which were lack of autonomy and performance accountability.

The post-1991 period has witnessed significant changes in the public sector policies of the government. The areas reserved for public sector were reduced.

By 2010, five items were taken out in which the private sector was allowed to operate and only three are currently earmarked for exclusive public sector domain including (a) atomic energy, (b) minerals specified in the 1953 schedule and (c) rail transport.

The Central Public Sector Enterprises (CPSEs) were expected to look for internal resources and borrowings and concentrate on improvement in operations and efficiency on commercial lines of operation aimed at earning profit.

In pursuance of the Industrial Policy Statement of 24.7.1991, detailed guidelines on composition of Board of Directors were issued by the Department of Public Enterprises (DPE) in March 1992. These guidelines inter-alia provided that at least one-third of the Directors on the Board of a CPSE should be non-official Directors. The Navaratna and Miniratna schemes that were evolved by the Government in 1997 provided that these

CPSEs should set up Audit Committees based on the SEBI (Stock Exchange Board of India) guidelines. Further instructions were issued by DPE in November 2001 stating that at least half of the Board of listed CPSEs with executive Chairmen should have independent directors.

The PSEs are categorized into four schedules, namely 'A', 'B', 'C' and 'D'. The pay scales of chief executives and full-time functional Directors of CPSEs are linked with the schedule of the concerned enterprise.

The initial categorization of CPSEs in the mid-sixties was made on the basis of their importance to the economy and complexities of their problems. Over the years, the DPE has evolved norms for the purpose of categorization/ recategorization of CPSEs. Categorization is based on quantitative factors like investment, capital employed, net sales, profit, number of employees and qualitative factors like national importance, complexity of problems, level of technology, prospects for expansion, diversification of activities, and competition from other sectors. In addition, criteria relating to the strategic importance of CPSEs are also taken into account. The present procedure involves consideration of the proposals in the administrative ministry concerned and the DPEs, which consults the Public Enterprises Selection Board. As on 31.1.2010 there were 59 Schedule 'A', 70 Schedule 'B', 45 Schedule 'C, 6 Schedule 'D' and 67 uncategorized PSEs.

Since Independence the Indian government did make several efforts to bring about development of the core sector of the economy by setting up PSEs. The role of the PSEs was earlier limited to basic heavy and core industries which were considered of strategic importance. The government had to set up these PSEs because the nation was in the initial stages of development and private enterprise could not afford massive investments that the core sector called for.

With the introduction of economic reforms and liberalization since 1991, the Government initiated a systemic shift to a more open economy with greater reliance on market forces and a larger role of the private sector, including foreign investment. As a result, the PSEs met with competition from domestic private sector companies as well as multinational companies. To sustain in a growing competitive scenario Indian PSEs have undertaken several steps to perform and operate at par with the private sector by adopting state-of-the-art technology, focusing on improving productivity, giving performance-related pay, welfare facilities and other benefits to employees, establishing brands and increasing efforts towards cost effectiveness of their enterprises.

12.1 Public Sector Enterprises (PSEs) in India: Forms

The PSEs in India are basically categorized under four broad types based on their ownership structure. These include departmental undertakings, statutory corporations, government-owned companies and autonomous bodies set up as registered societies.

- **Departmental Undertakings:** Departmental undertakings are primarily meant to provide essential services such as railways. They function under the control of respective ministries of GOI. A departmental undertaking structure is considered suitable for activities the government aims to keep in its control in view of the public interest.

- **Statutory Corporations:** Statutory corporations came into existence by Special Acts of the Parliament. The Act defines the powers and functions, rules and regulations governing the employees and the relationship of the corporation with other government departments, e.g. Airport Authority of India, Food Corporation of India and Industrial Finance Corporation of India.
- **Government-owned companies:** Government-owned or controlled companies refer to companies in which 51% or more of the paid-up capital is held by the Central or any State Government (partly or wholly by both). It is registered under the Indian Companies Act and is fully governed by the provisions of this Act, e.g. Steel Authority of India, Coal India Limited or Hindustan Copper Ltd.
- **Autonomous bodies:** Autonomous bodies are set up whenever it is felt that certain functions need to be discharged outside the governmental set up with some amount of independence and flexibility without day-to-day interference from the governmental machinery. These bodies are set up by the concerned ministries or their departments and are funded through grants-in-aid, either fully or partially, depending on the extent to which such institutes generate internal resources of their own. These grants are regulated by the Ministry of Finance (MoF) through their instructions. They are mostly registered as societies under the 'Societies Registration Act' and in certain cases they have been set up as statutory institutions under the provisions contained in various Acts, e.g. Indian Council of Agricultural Research, Council of Scientific and Industrial Research.

Out of the total 300 operating CPSEs, a majority of 158 CPSEs are profit-making enterprises. There are also approximately 837 State Public Enterprises having 18.7 lakh employees

12.2 CPSE's Role in the Economy

The CPSEs investment has a multiplier effect on the economy. During the first five-year plan (1950-51 to 1955-56) there were only 5 CPSEs with a total financial investment (including equity plus long-term loans) of 290 million, whereas in November 2011, there were 248 CPSEs (including 220 operating and 28 CPSEs that were yet to commence commercial operations and excluding seven insurance companies) with a total financial investment of ?6,668.5 billion as on March 31, 2011.

CPSEs continue to hold control across several industries, despite the initiation of several sectors for private investment. They continue to have complete monopoly in nuclear power generation. Other leading areas of dominance are coal (over 80%), crude oil (over 70%), refineries (over 55%) and wired lines (over 80%).

The CPSEs also contribute substantively to the Central Exchequer. The Central Exchequer derives income from CPSEs through two main sources namely investments in the CPSEs and earns returns in the form of dividend and interest and through various taxes and duties levied.

A major chunk of revenue derived by the Central exchequer is through various taxes and duties. Excise duties and corporate taxes, on an average accounted for around 40% and 25% of the total contribution to Central exchequer respectively during the five-year period of 2007 to 2012. During the same period, corporate tax and dividend tax were the fastest-growing sources, which can be primarily attributed to the higher corporate and dividend taxes paid during this period.

Performance of CPSEs

The government has awarded the status of 'Maharatna' 'Navratna', ' Miniratna - Category I' and 'Miniratna - Category IF to certain CPSEs after their assessment, based on certain select criteria. These CPSEs have been granted operational and financial autonomy in order to equip them to react proactively to market forces with enhanced powers.

In 2010, the government established the higher *Maharatna* category, which raises a company's investment ceiling from Rs. 1,000 crore to Rs. 5,000 crore. The *Maharatna* firms can now decide on investments of up to 15 per cent of their net worth in a project while the Navaratna companies could invest up to Rs. 1,000 crore without explicit government approval. Two categories of Miniratanas afford less extensive financial autonomy. As on 13 Sept 2017 there are 8 Maharatnas, 16 Navaratnas and 74 Miniratnas

Disinvestment of government equity in CPSEs began since 1991-92. However, during recent years, it has gained increasing importance in order to enhance the competitiveness of PSEs. The disinvestment process is carried out in various ways including strategic sale to private entities and auction to private entities among others.

All the CPSEs which divested in 2011 and 2012 chose the public offering route. In 2010, more than 90% of the disinvestment was carried out through the former means and the rest was through CPSE-to-CPSE sales. The Memorandum of Understanding (MOU) as applicable to CPSEs is a negotiated document between the management of the company and the government, specifying clearly the objectives of the agreement and the obligations of both the parties involved. Performance evaluation is done based on the comparison between the government and the CPSE. It constitutes of both financial and non-financial parameters with different weights assigned to the different parameters.

The MOU system that commenced with just four CPSEs signing MOU in 1987 increased its coverage to 202 CPSEs in 2011, out of which 43 CPSEs could not submit MoU performance evaluation reports during this period.

The share for number of companies with an "Excellent" and "Very Good" rating went down from 45% and 36% in 2007 to 42% and 26% respectively in 2011. The share of CPSEs with a "Good" rating climbed up by 2.4% in 2011 over 2007. The share of CPSE in the "Fair" rating category witnessed the highest growth by 9.2% during the same period. There were no companies under the "Poor" rating category during 2007 and 2008. However, it increased from 1 in 2009 to 2 in 2011. During 2011, out of a total 220 operating CPSEs, a majority of 158 CPSEs (70%) were profit making and 62 CPSEs incurred losses.

The number of sick CPSEs also came down to 49 as of March 31, 2014, from 105 as of March 31, 2011. GOI had set up the Board for Reconstruction of Public Sector Enterprises (BRPSE) in December 2004 to advise on the strategies, measures and schemes related to strengthening, modernizing, reviving and restructuring of the PSEs.

Out of the 64 CPSEs registered with the Board for Industrial and Financial Reconstruction (BIFR) up to June 30, 2011, the BIFR had disposed of 48 cases either through sanctioning revival schemes (15 cases), or declaring "no longer sick" (two cases), or dropping due to net worth turning positive (five cases), or dismissing the cases as non-maintainable (four cases), or deregistering the BIFR/others (two cases) or recommending winding up (19 cases), or winding up notice issued (one case). The BIFR was planning to take further view on 16 cases of CPSEs.

12.3 Issues and Problems before PSEs

In the history of planning in India, over the last six decades, there has been a definite shift in the assigned role of public enterprises in the country through various Five Year Plans from "attaining the commanding heights" in the national economy and "easing out private sector" to a restricted role in the era of liberalization and globalization. It has been a perennial problem for the policy makers to set the role of the public sector in the Indian economy and it would continue to be so.

Furthermore, the objectives of public sector have been defined but goals are not very systematically decided in each case. Even the objectives at the macro level have been mixed-up with a number of propositions, sometimes contradictory in nature.

Whether the public sector should extend to a wide variety of economic activities or remain confined to a selected few only, is a very crucial decision. Similarly, whether the economy of the country should be open to private sector or be confined only to the public sector monopoly, or both, or should it be given a competitive share in open market becomes another crucial political decision. The problem is consistently persisting in the Indian polity, more particularly from the recent past.

The organization and management of the PSEs has been on "trial and error"' ever since Independence. Initially, the enterprises were organized as departmental undertakings owing to their simplicity of operations and management. Then came a time when the government company form was most prevalent. Following the developments in the international field, particularly in England, the corporate form was adopted in India too in 1991. A host of corporations were created, both sectoral and multipurpose. Lastly, joint ventures came in the scene from the 1990s in the post-globalized era.

The constitution of management boards is the other major problem, which merits attention. Here, the government burdens the governing boards with civil servants, undermining the principle of autonomy of the enterprises. The management board tilts the balance of decision making on policy matters greatly in government favour, thus reducing the enterprise to more or less, a government department.

The personnel management of the public sector is beset with a plethora of problems which were mostly responsible for their inefficient and uneconomic performance. The recruitment to public enterprises is done by individual enterprises through a central personnel agency for a group of enterprises in a given sector that follows general guidelines of the government in the matter of reservations, etc. While compensation for top managers is usually high in most of the enterprises with innumerable perks, other amenities and benefits, it is progressively lower in the middle and lower level cadres. The performance appraisal in most of the public enterprises is done only as the annual recording of character rolls. This results in low standards of performance and the efficiency of the enterprises goes down progressively. The prime requirement of a majority of the enterprises is sound and scientific financial management as they lack financial discipline and professionalism.

A number of agencies are involved in the planning and control of financial management of public enterprises in the country, viz. Board of Management, Administrative Ministry, Ministry of Finance, Bureau of Public Enterprises, Planning Commission, Director General of Technical Development and Public Investment Board.

With a view to ensure increased productivity, worker's participation in management (WPM) was launched for the larger benefit of the enterprise, the employees and the community; to give workers a better understanding of their role in the production process; and to satisfy their demands for self-expression leading to better industrial relations. The process of WPM involves four main steps, viz. information sharing, joint consultations, joint decision-making and self-management. The workers are involved at all these levels to take the decisions in the best interest of the enterprise.

With regard to workers' participating at various levels including board level, it is beset with a number of problems relating to selection of employees to be represented on the Board of Management.

Autonomy in the case of public enterprises does not imply 'full freedom' to act as desired by the individual enterprise management. The PSEs are accountable to Parliament through the concerned minister and therefore cannot act freely. At the same time the public enterprises should be accorded sufficient autonomy to run their operations on business lines. It facilitates quick decision-making and encourages initiative.

12.4 Accountability and Control

There is no need to justify the rationale of control over public enterprises as it is ingrained in the word 'public'. In India, three types of controls are exercised in this regard, namely Parliamentary control, Ministerial control and Audit control.

The parliamentary control over public enterprises is needed for fulfilling the constitutional responsibility of the parliament in respect to these enterprises like protection of capital invested, safeguarding public interest in running of these enterprises, formulating general policy in regard to public enterprise operations, maintaining uniformity in such policies, along with monitoring and implementing such policies, effecting control over 'state capitalism' and civil servants, approving statutes regulating the public enterprises and appointing committees like Committee on Public Undertakings and other ad hoc committees.

From the very inception of a public enterprise, the minister is associated in one way or the other with its operations and management. In the Indian context, ministerial control is more real than is admitted. The ministers have been following a variety of methods to effect control over public enterprises. It can be both formal and informal taking explicit or implicit directives like consultations, discussions, or other informal contacts, etc.

Effective audit control is imperative in case of public enterprises, as the investments made in them belong to the people. Constitutionally, the CAG of India is empowered to exercise audit control over public enterprises. A separate comprehensive Power and Conditions of service Act, 1971, was passed by the Indian Parliament to regulate the duties and powers of CAG. Under the Act, the audit of public enterprises in India is not restricted to finance and compliance audit only but it extends to efficiency, economy and effectiveness of operations as well. It covers propriety audit also which scrutinizes the management decisions involving expenditure.

Besides the CAG, the internal audit is performed by the enterprise itself to scrutinize the financial expenditure and to ensure the financial canons.

12.5 Causes for the Decline of the Public Sector and Need for its Restructuring

At the global level, a compelling combination of circumstances leading to restructuring of economies included successful global economic performance of Japan and Asian Tigers in the 80s and 90s, based on a global approach to production and competition and development of technologies, which changed the very concept of productivity and led to a serious thinking among policy makers in India about the viability of the public sector in Independent India. Under these circumstances, the public sector policies could hardly afford to remain immune from mainstream development, as they have invariably been a critical and an integral part of most economies. The insular, state interventionist public sector policies of 60s, 70s and 80s in India could no longer be sustained in any meaningful way, except on the premises of efficiency and competitiveness.

Since 1980s, privatization has become a buzzword in global economies. Taking a cue from UK and the USA, other countries of the world have also attempted privatization in different forms. In India efforts to privatize parts of the public sector were initiated by the Indira Gandhi government and later on accentuated by the Rajiv Gandhi government. A great impetus has taken place since 1991 with the government's enunciation of New Economic Policies.

Privatization means transfer of management control of a government enterprise to the private company either with sale of a portion of total equity or by lease strategic sale which means the same. Disinvestment means divesting a portion of government equity in a government enterprise to retail investors, mutual funds, employees of the unit, etc., to raise funds. It does not involve transfer of management.

The policy of the Government on disinvestment has evolved over a period since the 1990s. It started with selling of minority shares in 1991-92 and continues today with emphasis on strategic sale. Before the year 2000, the government had primarily sold minority shares in public sector companies. The price realized through the sale of shares, even in blue chip companies like IOC, BPCL, HPCL, GAIL and VSNL was low. On the other hand, the prices realized through strategic disinvestments have been high.

Fears expressed by employees of the public sector on disinvestments seem grossly exaggerated. Of a total workforce of about 350 million in the country, the public sector employees are about 2 million. During the last ten years, without any privatization or strategic disinvestments, this workforce has been reduced from 2.3 million to 1.7 million, on account of economic pressures. Some of the companies are now in the process of restructuring and adopting VRS (Voluntary Retirement Scheme). These companies are giving VRS to the employees, which are normally higher than the Government Voluntary Retirement Scheme.

The New Industrial Policy announced in 1991 envisaged disinvestments of part of the government shareholding in the case of selected PSEs to provide financial discipline and improve the performance of the public enterprises. In pursuit of this, beginning from 1991-92, disinvestment of government equity have been completed in about 50 central PSUs. In the process an amount of 20,000 crore has been realized.

Strategic Sale

Sale of a portion or whole of Government equity along with transfer of management control is called Strategic Sale. The equity sold is generally less than 25% if the recent experience starting from Modern Foods to VSNL, IBP and IPCL are the indications. At the same time, each one has seen management control transferred to the party that bid for and bought the government equity. The advantages with strategic sale are: (a) It attracts investment, (b) The strategic partner with management control will invest further for diversification and technological improvement, (c) Market perception will improve as it is no longer a government company, (d) Shareholder value will increase, (e) With the improvement in the functioning of the company, personnel welfare benefits will also be guaranteed.

Based on the recommendations of the Arjun Sen Gupta Committee on PSEs the pattern of public enterprises in India can take one of the following forms: (a) Complete privatization (b) Partial privatization (c) Privatization of the management (d) Creating competitive conditions (e) Deregulation (f) Delicensing and (g) Disinvestments and other liberalization measures. As a consequence, they must also follow the trend of the overall economic policy, which, in the current context, is heavily tilted towards functional autonomy, marketization and cost effectiveness.

12.6 The Public Sector: Role and Future Trajectory

In the years of its commanding role, a certain level of efficiency was assumed on the part of the public sector, which was expected to generate resources, which would be made available to other sectors. However, this did not happen to the extent required. On the other hand, there is no doubt in the minds of informed observers of the Indian economy that although the public sector is still playing an important and critical role in the economic development of the country, the current benefits from it are not (and have not been) commensurate with the investments made. Investment on the public sector is of the order of about $50 to 70 billion with 1.57 lakh crore pumped into loss-making enterprises. The return on this investment has varied from a poor 2% to 5% in the last few years.

Considering that the investment funds must have come out of savings which are being serviced by the government at about 12%, a return of *2%* to 5% would appear to be too paltry to enable servicing of the equity as well as the loan content of the investment adequately. Quite obviously, the government is using budgetary resources (or further savings) to service both equity and debt.

It must be considered fair for any nation to expect a reasonable return from public investment. Consequently, the categorical need for restructuring such investments is clearly unavoidable, based on a closer re-look at their initial objectives, their current structure and their likely future, despite the fact that in the past this was avoided for various reasons of public policy that are invalid and, therefore, no longer avoidable in the light of the new policy of plugging the Indian economy into the global market on the premises of its efficiency and competitiveness.

Therefore, there was a need on the part of the government for making use of both the strategies, i.e. (i) outright Sale and (ii) to fashion an administrative interface between itself and the enterprise that optimized their commercial performance by tackling the problems highlighted above.

12.7 New Policies: Impacts of Liberalization

Opening up of Public Sector to Competition: The areas, which were earlier reserved under the monopoly of public sector, have been changed. Seventeen industries reserved for public enterprises under the Industrial Policy Resolution of 1956 have been reduced to six and even out of these six, some private organizations have already been allowed to operate in coal and lignite.

Raising of Resources, Disinvestments and Rehabilitation of Sick Units: As a part of the policy announced to raise resources, encourage wider participation and promote greater accountability, the GOI has offered disinvestments in selected public enterprises. A large number of public enterprises were earlier allowed equity participation by the financial institutions and the general public.

The PSUs, which are chronically sick and unlikely to turn around, are being referred to the Board for Industrial and Financial Reconstruction (BIFR) for the formulation of revival/rehabilitation schemes.

Corporate Governance

The concept of corporate governance has generated a great deal of interest and public debate. Corporate governance is intended primarily to ensure transparency in management of the enterprise and encompasses the entire functioning of the company. Keeping in view relevant laws, instructions and procedures, the DPE brought out the 'Guidelines on Corporate Governance' for CPSEs in June 2007.

CPSEs have been, furthermore, categorized into two groups for purpose of Corporate Governance, namely (a) those listed in the Stock Exchange and (b) those not listed in the

Stock Exchanges. So far as the listed CPSEs are concerned, they have to follow the **Securities and Exchange Board of India** (SEBI) guidelines on Corporate Governance. They may, in addition, follow those provisions of the

Guidelines brought out by the DPE which do not exist in the SEBI guidelines and also do not contradict provisions in the SEBI guidelines. The non-listed CPSEs are to follow the DPE guidelines on Corporate Governance, although these are voluntary in nature. These guidelines are under implementation by the CPSEs.

12.8 Operational Excellence Initiatives Adopted by CPSEs

The CPSEs continue to have a significant share in several sectors/industries on account of their continued efforts towards achieving competitiveness and excellence to operate at par vis-a-vis their private sector counterparts. We attempt to highlight some of the key operational best practices embraced by CPSEs in their quest towards maintaining market share as well as being corporate citizens. For purpose of analysis these initiatives have been grounded in to the following categories:

- Corporate Governance
- Organization Development/Human Resources Management

Corporate Governance: Illustrative Examples

Most established codes of Corporate Governance for state owned enterprises (SoE), including the OECD Guidelines on Corporate Governance of SoEs envisage a proactive role of the organization in (a) Ensuring equitable treatment of shareholders (b) Recognizing, respecting and reporting on relations with all key stakeholders (c) Maintaining high standards of transparency and disclosure and (d) Having requisite systems and practices for its Board of Directors to effectively discharge its role of guiding and monitoring the SoE.

- Most CPSEs in India would compare favorably when it comes to adoption of the above measures.
- Having an active policy for communication with all shareholders for ensuring dissemination of information on key business decisions.
- Ensuring representation of minority shareholders on the board of Directors for assuring them that their interests are taken into consideration
- Having internal code of business conduct and ethics for ensuring ethical and transparent process in managing the affairs of the enterprise.
- ONGC is one of the organizations which has been following these guidelines even when it was voluntary for the companies to comply with these guidelines. As a part of Corporate Governance initiatives, ONGC has inducted 4 independent directors on its board along with formation of various board level committees, viz. Audit and Ethics Committee, Remuneration Committee, Health Safety and Environment Committee, etc.
- NTPC has been following Corporate Governance guidelines issued by the DPE. As part of the initiative, it has inducted 9 independent directors in its Board along

with formation of audit committee, remuneration committee, shareholder grievance committee, etc. The organization has also formulated policies including whistle blower policy, ethical code of conduct, succession planning, etc.

Organization Development/Human Resource Management/Examples

There is an increasing realization that development of quality human resources is critical for sustainable performance of the CPSEs. Accordingly, in pursuance of attracting and retaining quality talent, the Government/most of the CPSEs have taken requisite initiatives including the following:

- Adopting contractual recruitment in key management positions with market- linked compensation including variable pay.
- Organizing/ arranging training programs, aimed at capacity building and augmentation of skill sets of the employees.
- Having a succession planning policy aimed at identifying employees with leadership potential and accordingly grooming them to fit into the envisaged leadership roles.
- The Government has taken an initiative in forming a committee under Justice M. Jaganadha Rao for recommending a suitable pay structure for CPSEs. Key recommendations of this committee include:
- Executive compensation package should be independent of that proposed for Government servants and should progressively be aligned with their counterparts in the private sector.
- Recommended pay package can be implemented only by profitable CPSEs and may be considered in various stages for ensuring that the post-implementation profitability is not significantly impacted.
- Performance-linked pay can be implemented only if the enterprise has a performance management system in place, has entered into an MoU with its parent department/ ministry and have inducted independent directors on their board.
- Annual increments can be paid based on performance of individual as determined by the performance appraisal system and the ability of the CPSE to pay.
- Oil India Limited (OIL) has in place a "Performance Management System" (PMS) with the objective to achieve enhanced work standards, identify knowledge and skills required, provide feedback on performance, identify Training & Development (T&D) needs, provide objective performance evaluation for promotions, and grant of incentives and inputs for succession planning. This system is used to track: (i) performance of its employees against Key Result Area (KRAs) linked to the overall objective of the organization and (ii) identify development needs of individuals.
- SAIL has organized Training programs aimed at continuously updating technologies, skills, attitudinal changes, career growth and leadership development for its employees. Further, for the transfer and absorption of advanced and new technologies, a good number of qualified technologists and specialists of SAIL plants are deputed every

year for training abroad in countries like USA, Russia, Germany, UK, Japan, Austria, Australia, etc.

Professionalization of Boards

The guidelines issued by the DPE in 1992 provide for induction of outside professionals on the Boards of CPSEs as part-time non-official Directors. The number of such Directors, moreover, has to be at least l/3rd of the actual strength of the Board. In the case of listed CPSEs headed by an executive Chairman, the number of non- official Directors (Independent Directors) should be at least half the strength of the Board. The guidelines also provide that the number of Government Directors on the Boards should be not more than one-sixth of the actual strength of the Board subject to a maximum of two. Apart from this, there should be some functional Directors on each Board whose number should not exceed 50% of the actual strength of the Board. The proposals for appointment of non-official Directors are initiated by the concerned Administrative Ministries/Departments. In so far as Navratna and Miniratna CPSEs are concerned, the selection of non-official Directors is made by the Search Committee consisting of Chairman (PESB), Secretary (DPE), Secretary of the administrative Ministry/Department of the CPSE, Chief Executive of the concerned CPSE and non-official Members. In the case of remaining CPSEs (other than Navratna/Miniratna (CPSEs), Public Enterprises Selection Board (PESB) makes the selection of non-official Directors. The concerned Administrative Ministry/ Department appoints the non-official Directors on the basis of recommendations of Search Committee/PESB after obtaining the approval of competent authority, i.e. Appointments Committee of Cabinet (ACC).

12.9 Autonomy in Public Sector

During the last few years, there has been a demand for greater autonomy to the public enterprises. It has been argued that Article 12 of the Constitution, where the public sector units are treated as 'authorities' under the 'State', has put a lot of constraints on them.

The government has barred its officers and staff from using the infrastructure or facilities of the state-owned companies and asked administrative ministries to repatriate PSU staff working with them. The measures are aimed at providing greater autonomy to the state-owned companies by keeping administrative ministries at a professional distance. The government is of view that it is important to separate the functions of the ministry and its public undertakings, given the government's disinvestment programme. No PSU official should be involved in such decision making process barring the chairman and his appointed staff. The DPE, the nodal agency for all state-owned companies, has also come out with guidelines restricting officials of the administrative ministry from participating in retail issues. The same is applicable to PSU employees who are involved in the decision-making process.

India created a new category for its highly efficient state-run firms, called 'Maharatnas' to extend mu h greater autonomy to its management and flexibility in areas like mergers, acquisitions and recruitment.

The main objective of the Maharatna scheme is to empower the mega CPSEs to expand their operations and emerge as global giants. The proposed higher category will act as an incentive for other 'Navratnas', provide brand value and facilitate the delegation of enhanced powers to CPSEs. Currently, there are 16 Navratnas among state-run firms. For a company to be accorded Maharatna status, it would first have to be a Navratna, besides being listed on stock exchanges with public shareholding as prescribed by the SEBI. The firm should also have attained an average annual turnover of Rs. 20,000 crore with an average annual net worth of Rs. 10,000 crore in the past three years before it is accorded such status. It should also have posted annual net profit of more than Rs. 5,000 crore ($1 billion) during the past three years and enjoyed a significant global presence.

The procedure for grant of Maharatna status as well as their review is proposed to be similar to that undertaken for the grant of Navratna status. Now there are seven Maharatna companies, ONGC, INDIAN OIL, GAIL, BHEL, NTPC, CIL AND SAIL.

Bharat Petroleum Corporation Limited (BPCL)

Some of the special powers held by Maharatna companies include:

- Make equity investment to establish joint ventures and subsidiaries in India or abroad.
- Execute mergers in India or abroad subject to a ceiling of 15% of its net worth up to an absolute ceiling of 5,000 crore ($1 billion)
- Powers of the Board on recruitment.

The government had introduced the Navratna scheme in 1997 to identify state- run firms that had comparative advantage over others and needed autonomy and support to become global giants. The boards of these Navratna companies have been delegated powers in areas such as capital expenditure, investment in joint ventures or subsidiaries, mergers and human resource management. Over the years some Navratna companies have grown significantly and have considerably large operations. The proposed higher category (of Maharatna) will act as an incentive for other Navratna companies, provide brand value and facilitate delegation of enhanced powers to CPSEs. Considering the diversity of forms, nature and levels of performance of PSEs, a gradual and flexible approach for implementing corporate government practices is desirable. The formulation of a clear and stable policy environment would create conditions for exercising such enhanced powers. The ownership rights of the government should be exercised with caution so that the capacity of PEs to function along commercial lines is not impaired, even while they meet the public policy objectives of the government. The government should limit its role to policy formulation and laying down strategic objectives. The government's influence over the public enterprise should be exercised through a transparent board nomination process.

Besides complying with the legal requirements, the board should focus on developing a work culture based on the understanding of the expectations of various stakeholders. Formulating and enforcing a code of ethics and conduct is another area that deserves attention of the board. This code should encompass areas that include conflict of interest, responsiveness to workers concern for value of public assets, non-abuse of official position and continuous improvement through professionalism.

Appropriate performance measurement indicators should be developed in the public sector. The government must require both outcome indicators (measures of effectiveness, in terms of the contribution of the relevant PE outputs to achievement of both commercial and social outcomes) and output indicators (measure of efficiency, in terms of the price, quantity and quality of the final output).

Seeing the global scenario it is obvious that good corporate governance practice indoctrinates the essential vision in companies, i.e. long-term structures and processes, to make decisions that ensure growth with sustainability. Particularly, we need companies that can be profitable as well as achieve the social and economic value for society.

Although the employee strength in CPSEs has reduced over the years, aggregate emoluments have increased from Rs. 0.5 lakh crores in 2006 to around Rs. 0.8 crores in 2009 with increasing salary levels. Based on the growth witnessed in market capitalization of the listed CPSEs it can be observed that they have emerged as major wealth creators for investors/stakeholders. As on March 31, 2009, market capitalization of 41 listed companies accounted for 26.4% of the BSE market capitalization compared to 21.8% of the same in 2008. On account of progressive liberalization in India's overseas investment policy, FDI outflows witnessed significant increase with total outflows through investment in joint ventures/wholly- owned subsidiaries increasing from USD 6 billion in 2006 to around USD 18.6 billion in 2009.

CPSE's contribution in outbound investment has also been significant primarily on account of investments made by ONGC Videsh Ltd. (wholly owned subsidiary of ONGC) involved in overseas exploration and production activities. Other key CPSEs with significant outbound investment include Indian OIL Corporation, GAIL, BHEL, NTPC, RITES, etc. In addition to significant contributions towards the growth of the Indian economy, most of the CPSEs have been able to ensure viable operations on a self-sustainable basis, which is evident from the decline in budgetary support in terms of loans and equity from the Government over the years.

Red tape, risk aversion, administered pricing systems, inability to hire the best talent because of poor compensation, political interference, and corruption are among the many reasons that cause PSUs to under-perform. Is it possible to preserve the public ownership structure and at the same time increase the market viability of PSEs? Is it pragmatic to believe that we can create a culture of innovation and high performance and make PSUs autonomous, accountable and cost effective?

To guarantee that the Indian economy continues to scale new heights and emerge as an economic superpower, it is imperative for the PSEs to continue to demonstrate global competitiveness and achieve market leadership. However, to make these CPSEs now emerge as global leaders in their respective areas, requisite interventions need to be made by the government.

12.10 Priority Intervention: Areas

- There is a need to segregate ownership and governance of commercially run CPSEs. All key strategic and operational decisions pertaining to the PSEs should be delegated to the Board of Directors, which should comprise eminent professionals and have minimum representation from the Government.

- While Government should not intervene in the day-to-day management of the CPSEs, in its role as promoter/shareholder it should closely monitor the overall performance including creation of shareholder value in the respective enterprises. The key pre-requisites include: (a) clearly defined institutional framework within the Government led by a nodal agency/ department with representation from concerned ministries/ department which would monitor the performance of all PSUs at pre-specified intervals and be empowered to take remedial action in case of significant concerns and (b) well-defined processes and templates for collection, collation and analysis of necessary information from the PSUs for purposes of performance evaluation.
- While the principles underlying some of the above interventions are already reflected in the existing guidelines for managing PSUs in India, there is an urgent need for implementing them in a time-bound manner so that Indian PSUs can be key beneficiaries from emerging economic opportunities both in India and the global market. Public funds invested in the market need to match public outcomes.

Conclusion

India has two categories of PSEs. One set is administered by the Union Government and is, by and large, professionally managed. The other category, owned by the State Governments, is run by bureaucrats and is rife with political interference. In the post-1991 period the profits of the public sector (Central) enterprises have gone up significantly per annum, so that they have risen, e.g. from Rs. 2368 crore in 1990-01 to Rs. 53,169 crore in 2003-04 or about 22 times. The relatively successful performance of the CPSUs can be accounted for by their professional management and autonomy and the lack of these in the State Government managed ones.

Less is known about the state public sector undertakings, which comprise state government companies as well as statutory corporations. The former includes state road transport corporations, state financial corporations, state electricity generation and distribution companies and numerous others in sectors from water to warehousing. The latter, i.e. statutory corporations, usually comprise Electricity Regulatory Commissions.

Left-leaning states like Kerala and West Bengal seem to live up to their reputations when it comes to the number of SPSUs. Kerala has the largest number of working SPSUs (113) while West Bengal has the fourth largest number (after Karnataka and Gujarat). About a quarter of the 1,173 SPSUs across the 16 largest states are "non-functioning" enterprises.

Unsurprisingly, in aggregate, state PSUs suffer large losses with the electricity sector being the principal culprit. In 2015-16, the total losses of PSUs in the 16 largest states amounted to Rs 62,931.21 crore with losses in state PSUs in UP alone accounting for Rs 17,790 crore.

The Modi government identified over a dozen blue-chip public sector companies to provide increased managerial autonomy and plans have been made for a second exchange-traded fund (ETF).

Sources said the idea of a second ETF was proposed by rating agencies to the Department of Economic Affairs recently and it is being "considered seriously", although unlike the first such fund, the new one will be 'energy light'. An ETF is a basket of stocks that is traded on stock exchanges and the first one launched during the 2013 fiscal was seen to have a heavy presence of energy PSUs.

The government also set up a Disinvestment Commission under G V Ramakrishna in August 1996 for deriving a long-term disinvestment program in order to modernize and upgrade the PSEs and also to ensure that disinvestment does not lead to private monopoly.

For disinvestment of PSUs, the government followed different methods such as Initial Public Offering (IPO), strategic sale, sale to foreigners, management-employment buyouts, etc. In the initial phase (1991-92 to 1998-99), the government followed IPO as a means of disinvestment, and strategic sales method was adopted in the later period. The prominent companies that have disinvested through strategic sale in the recent past include Modern foods, BALCO, CMC, VSNL, IBM, ITDC Hotels, IPCL, Maruti Udyog Ltd., and HZL.

On the basis of certain selected indicators, it is noticed that PSEs performed better in the post-reform period compared to the pre-reform period. The interesting point to be noticed here is that the sources of finance to CPSEs have undergone a major change. In the early years of establishment, most of the funding to these enterprises was in the form of budgetary support. In the post-reform period, the share of budgetary support declined to around 1% and the share of internal resource mobilization increased to 55% in recent times. Further, overstaffing had also reduced with the implementation of voluntary retirement schemes. The profitability of PSEs showed improvement and made them raise resources internally suggesting that the performance of PSEs have improved in response to the liberalization measures.

Suggested Readings

Central Public Sector Enterprises: Leading Companies of India, Department of Public Enterprises, GOI, Shipra Publishers, 2010.

Department of Public Enterprises, Ministry of Heavy Industries and Public Enterprises, GOI, Annual Reports 2010-13.

Dhameja, Nand and K. S. Sastry, *Public Sector Restructuring and Privatization,* Delhi, Kanishka, 2002.

Empowering Public Sector Enterprises in India: Proceedings of Chief Executive, Department of Public Enterprises GOI, Shipra Publishers, 2007.

Gangadhar, V. and S. Kavitha, *Disinvestment of Central PSEs: An Appraisal,* Ambala, the Associated, 2007.

Saksena, K. D., *Economic Reforms: The Indian Experience,* Delhi, Shipra Publishers, 2005.

ooo

Chapter Thirteen

Civil Services in India

Introduction

The role of civil service has changed significantly from the pre-Independence days to current times. This to a large extent has been driven by the changing domestic environment and the nature of responsibilities bearing on civil servants. Prior to Independence, the main responsibility of the civil service was to maintain law and order and manage revenue administration. For an effective discharge of duties, civil servants, back then, were required to possess simple regulatory skills of administration.

After Independence, the role kept evolving as the civil service became more and more development oriented. Today, in the post-globalized era the civil servant has to keep acquiring new skills to deal with both developmental and regulatory issues, to mediate between the state, citizen and the market and to cope with the new demands of a neo-liberal economy and polity. The present-day civil servants are responsible for trade negotiations; regulation of the private sector; formulation of socio-economic policies; implementation of new goals like the Sustainable Development Goals; development of rural areas; combating inflation; effective monetary management; elimination of social inequities; participation in global trade negotiations and management of Public Sector Enterprises (PSE). This has made the job highly demanding and requires a great degree of flexibility and competence on the part of the civil servants.

Civil servants of the pre-Independence era reported to senior bosses who were appointed by Governors, who in turn were not accountable to the public. These days, civil servants work within the boundaries of a democratic system of governance and report to elected members of the public. In addition, today's environment is characterized by an ever so vigilant press, the public and alert legislatures, which make the working of civil servants all the more demanding. Over a period of time, the role of civil service has transformed from regulatory to developmental and now to facilitating the efficient delivery of public services.

It would be interesting to mention here that India does not as yet possess an overarching and comprehensive Civil Service Law, though we do have an enabling provision in the constitution to do so. We have the All India Services Act 1951 enacted by Parliament to regulate the recruitment and service conditions for the All India Services (AIS) common to the Union and the States. However, for the lower ranking civil servants who constitute over 90% of the government employees there is no parliamentary legal framework at all. Some of the states, however, have enacted state civil services Acts for their own employees.

This is surprising despite Articles 308 and 309 which give a vision to Parliament and State legislatures and the power to legislate on the recruitment and conditions of service of persons appointed to the public services. Though no overarching law on personnel matters exists till now, a number of rules have been made from time to time by the union and the State Governments which govern and regulate the civil services in India.

However, a great need was felt from time to time for such a law. It is good to note that the GOI plans to enact a civil service law. The Draft Civil Services Bill 2009 is poised to become a law. The purpose of the Bill is stated to be as follows:

"To provide a statutory basis for the regulation of the civil services in India, as enshrined in Article 309 and Article 312 of the Constitution of India, to regulate the appointment and conditions of the service of civil servants, to lay down the fundamental values of civil services, the civil services Code of Ethics, Civil Services Authority for facilitating review and to develop civil services as a professional, neutral, merit based and accountable instrument for promoting good governance and better delivery of services to the citizens."

The move to enact a comprehensive civil service law is a very good one. Drafted properly, it can provide a clear and unified framework within which the civil service can carry out its distinctive roles and responsibilities. It should establish the core principles and values creating a distinctive culture and ethos of the civil service. It becomes a mission statement of what is expected of civil servants towards better performance and accountability. Finally, a civil service law can also provide the basis for bringing about necessary reform in the civil service.

Currently, the civil service is classified into three broad categories:

- All India Services
- Central Services
- State Services

13.1 All India Services (AIS)

There are three All India Services. They are:

- Indian Administrative Services (IAS): the IAS is considered the backbone of our development administration and public service delivery system.
- Indian Police Service (IPS): the IPS is responsible for maintaining law and order and internal security of the nation.
- Indian Forest Service (IFS): is responsible for management of the country's forest resources.

The members of the AIS are appointed by the Central Government and then assigned to the different States. The AIS is common to both—the Central and the State Governments. The cadre strength of IAS, IPS and IFS are 6396, 4802 and 3131 officers respectively.

13.2 Central Services

Central Services are under the control of the Central Government. The Central Services are generally appointed to serve in areas such as foreign affairs, defence, taxation, engineering, accounts and communication. The Central Services are classified into A, B, C and D Groups according to the rank and responsibilities. Based on functionality, the Central Services are also classified as technical and non-technical services. The technical services include areas such as civil engineering, electrical engineering, mechanical engineering and non-technical services include audit, income tax and post and telegraph.

13.3 State Services

State Services are under the control of the State Governments and 33% of the posts in AIS are filled by the promotion from State Services. State Services are also classified as Group A, B, C and D according to the rank, and responsibilities. The State Services are responsible for handling government activities at the State level.

Apart from the above three-tier classification, all posts of Group A and few posts of Group B are also recognized as gazetted officers, whereas the rest, including Group B, Group C and Group D, form the non-gazetted officers. Any civil servant appointed by the President of India or by the Governor of a State and included in the Indian Gazetted List or the State Gazetted List is called a gazetted officer.

13.4 History and Evolution of the Civil Service

The Civil Service in India was introduced by the British East India Company and the present civil service is a modified version of successive reforms. The East India Company designed a grading system of posts to build a hierarchical civil service structure.

The civil service was classified into two types —Covenanted and Uncovenanted.

- Covenanted civil servants were Englishmen who had received formal education in England and were sent to India. They had also entered into a covenant with the East India Company for a stipulated time and enjoyed privileges such as leave and pensions.
- The Uncovenanted civil servants were made up of Indians and had no special privileges. The authority of recruitment was with the members of the Directors of the East India Company.

In 1765, the East India Company was granted the name 'Diwan' by the Moghuls and the administrative duties and responsibilities of the civil servants were increased from only trade-related activities to include revenue and judicial administration. The Regulating Act of 1773 clearly demarcated the commercial (trade) and administrative (revenue and judicial) tasks and prohibited civil servants from conducting private trade and also from accepting gifts. The Pitt's India Act of 1784 recommended filling of vacancies in the governing bodies, by covenanted civil servants and also laid down the age limits for new entrants in service

In 1805, the East India Company established a training institute for civil servants at Haileybury in England. At that point of time, the appointments were made through a nomination procedure where candidates were recommended by the Directors of the East India Company. A strong need was felt to replace the patronage enjoyed by the Directors of the East India Company in the recruitment process. It was also considered necessary to initiate a system of competitive examinations. As a result, the privileges and the rights of the Directors of the East India Company to nominate candidates for civil service were withdrawn.

In 1853, a five-member committee headed by Lord Macaulay was set-up which recommended that appointments to the Indian Civil Service should not be based on, "patronage". The committee emphasized on providing the best liberal education to candidates and recommended that the candidates should be selected through a competitive examination. The committee also proposed the need for serving a probation period before final appointments. As a result of these recommendations, a Civil Service Commission was set-up in England in 1855 and was entrusted with the responsibility of conducting the civil service exam for the Covenanted service. The first competitive civil service examination was held in London in 1856.

The East India Company was removed in 1858 and the Indian Administration came under the direct control of the British Crown.

The powers lying with the Directors of the East India Company were now transferred to the Secretary of State in India, who was the exercising authority of the British Crown. In 1870, the British Parliament passed an Act that authorized Indians to be appointed at any office, which was earlier reserved for candidates from covenanted services.

The Statutory Civil Service framed in 1879 emphasized reserving one-fifth of covenanted civil service posts for Indians subject to an approval from the Secretary of State. In 1886, a commission headed by Sir Charles Aitchison was formed to abolish the Statutory Civil Service and recommended a three-tier classification—Imperial, Provincial and Subordinate. Services such as Indian Civil Service, Indian Police Service (IPS) and Indian Medical Service were included in the Imperial civil service. The Provincial services consisted of Indian Education Services, Indian Agricultural Services and Indian Veterinary Services, while the lower grades of the uncovenanted services were included in the Subordinate service.

In August 1917, E. S. Montagu, the then Secretary of State in India, declared a new policy on increasing the association of Indians across every branch of administration. A year later in 1918, a report on constitutional changes by Montagu and Chelmsford recommended that 33% of superior posts in the Imperial service be reserved for Indians. Both of them favoured that the appointments be made without racial discrimination and that a separate competitive examination be held in India.

The GOI Act of 1919 recommended that the Imperial Service be renamed as All India Service (AIS). The Act also provided a safeguard against political influence in the recruitment process of civil service. The first competitive examination in India was held in 1922 under the supervision of the Civil Service Commission of England.

In 1923, a Royal Commission was formed under the leadership of Lord Lee. The Commission redefined the civil service into three broad categories —All India, Central and Provincial.

- All India Service mainly consisted of IAS, IPS, Indian Medical and Health Service, IFS and Indian Service of Engineers.
- The Central Service dealt with States and foreign affairs along with State railways, posts and telegraphs, customs, audits and accounts, scientific and technical departments.

- The Provincial Service included Indian Educational Services, Indian Agricultural Services and the Veterinary Services.

The Secretary of State retained the power of appointment and control of AIS and Central Services. The provincial government was given the power to make appointments for fresh vacancies of the Provincial Service.

In order to maintain the recruitment standards, the Royal Commission under the chairmanship of Lord Lee, recommended setting up of the Statutory Public Service Commission. The Statutory Public Service Commission was set up in 1926 and took over the process of conducting the civil service examination from the Civil Service Commission of England. The Statutory Public Service Commission was also entrusted with the responsibility for the recruitment of All India, Central and Provincial service personnel.

In 1935, the GOI Act introduced provincial autonomy for the protection of the rights and privileges of civil servants. According to the Act, a civil servant could not be removed by an authority below the rank of an officer who appointed him.

The First Central Pay Commission (CPC) was set up in 1946 to report on the conditions of service of Class I, Class II and Subordinate Services. As per its recommendation, the Central Services were re-categorized as Class I, Class II, Class III (erstwhile Subordinate Services) and Class IV (erstwhile Inferior Services). The Specialist Services were also drawn into this classification, with the result that post- 1946 no separate Specialist Services category existed.

13.5 Recruitment

Role of Nodal Agencies

Personnel Administration: Nodal Bodies

The Ministry of Personnel, Public Grievances and Pensions is the nodal Ministry in the GOI especially in matters of recruitment, training, career development, staff welfare, administrative reforms and post-retirement dispensation. The Ministry of Personnel, Public Grievances and Pensions is under the charge of the PM of India and assisted by a Minister of State. The Ministry comprises three departments, namely:

- Department of Personnel and Training (DOPT)
- Department of Administrative Reform and Public Grievances (DARPG)
- Department of Pensions and Pensioners' Welfare (DPPW)

Department of Personnel and Training (DOPT): The DOPT is the nodal agency of the Central Government for issues related to personnel matters such as recruitment, training, career development and staff welfare. To handle these, DOPT has ten separate divisions and each division is under the supervision of an officer at the level of Joint Secretary or above. Each division has clearly defined roles and responsibilities. Some of the major divisions are listed below:

- Establishment Office: It is responsible for all appointments on the Board of

Management of PSEs (such as Chairman, Managing Director and Director) Statutory Commissions, Tribunals, Railways, Banks and. Financial Institutions.

- Establishment Division: It takes care of the personnel and human resource management policies for the Central Government employees including policy formulation, policy management and advisory services regarding leave, pay and allowances
- Administrative Tribunal: It handles cases of employees aggrieved by Government decisions and relating to service matters which were previously dealt with by Courts.
- Central Secretariat: It is the Cadre Controlling Authority in respect of the three Central Secretariat Services
- Retraining and Redeployment: It is responsible for conducting re-training and re-deployment of surplus Central Government employees.
- Vigilance: It drives initiatives on eradication of corruption and coordinates the activities of various Ministries/Departments on this issue.
- Training: It administers induction training to recruits of the IAS, AIS and Central Services. The Training Division has also been coordinating the implementation of the National Training Policy

Department of Administrative Reforms and Public Grievances (DARPG): The DARPG is the nodal agency primarily for administrative reforms and redressal of public grievances relating to the States and Central Government. The Department endeavours to document and publicize successful good governance practices through publications, and after international exchange and cooperation to promote public service reforms. The objectives of the DARPG have been laid out as:

- Promoting administrative reforms in government policies, structures and processes.
- Promoting reforms through e-governance.
- Formulation of policy and coordination of issues relating to redressal of grievances.
- Dissemination of governance knowledge and best practices.

Department of Pensions and Pensioners' Welfare (DPPW): The Department is the nodal Department for formulation of policies relating to pension and other retirement benefits of Central Government employees covered under the Pension Rules of 1972. It provides a forum for the redressal of pensioner's grievances.

As per the New Pension Scheme, the pensionary matters of all Central Government employees who joined on or after January 1, 2004, are being dealt with by the Ministry of Finance (Department of Financial Services). The Department has taken several steps over the years to ease the process of pension administration system and provide convenience for the welfare of the pensioners. The Department launched a pensioners' portal in March 2007 to facilitate the information on pension matters and to address grievances online.

Article 309 of the Indian Constitution empowers the Parliament or the State Legislature to make laws to regulate the recruitment and conditions of service of persons appointed to public services and posts in connection with the affairs of the Union or the States, as the case may be. It also authorizes the President or the Governor to make rules for the above purposes until revision on their behalf is made by or under an Act of Parliament or the State Legislature.

The Union Public Service Commission (UPSC)

The UPSC has been established under Article 315 of the Constitution of India and comprises a Chairman and a team of members. The UPSC handles the recruitment of AIS, Group A Central Services and Group B gazetted posts in Ministries/Departments of the Central Government. The Commission also conducts the examination for recruitment of Commissioned Officers in the Defence forces. Some UTs also avail the services of the UPSC for recruitment to the posts under the UTs. As per Article 320 of the Indian Constitution, the function of the UPSC includes recruitment for all civil services and civil posts by:

- Written examination with or without a viva voce examination or interview to supplement them
- Interview
- Promotion
- Advising the Government on disciplinary matters relating to government servants holding civil posts

Within the constitutionally mandated range of UPSC's functions, three areas stand out: recruitment, promotions, and advice in disciplinary matters.

According to the UPSC's Citizens Charter, its functions include: (i) recruitment by conduct of competitive examinations; (ii) recruitment by selection through interviews; (iii) advising on the suitability of officers for appointment, promotion as well as transfer-on-deputation; (iv) advising the government on all matters relating to recruitment to various services and posts; framing and amendment of recruitment rules; (v.) disciplinary cases relating to different civil services; (in) miscellaneous matters relating to grant of extraordinary pensions, reimbursement of legal expenses etc.,; (vii) advising the government on any matter referred to it by the President of India; and (viii) on the request of a Governor of a state, to serve all or any of the needs of a state relating to recruitment with the approval of the President of India (UPSC 2010).

UPSC holds 12 regular examinations including four for defence services. Procedurally, while UPSC's secretariat prepares the groundwork, the critical stages in each area (interview panel/committee meeting final advice on penalty) are invariably headed or handled by a Member of UPSC.

Other than the main Civil Services Examination (CSE) UPSC holds recruitment examinations for entry level posts to organized Group A services such as the engineering, health, economic, statistical, and forest services and to central police forces, in addition to post-school and post-college recruitment to the officer cadres of the armed forces. It also has the responsibility for holding a limited departmental competitive examination for selecting section officers to different secretariat positions in the Central Government from amongst serving officials. Without calling into question the importance of ensuring proper selection to government posts at any level, why UPSC has to continue doing this exercise when the direct recruitment to these positions has been handed over to the Staff Selection Commission (SSC) is an enigma. There is enough evidence in UPSC's annual reports that points to the preponderance of recruitment work that could be effectively removed from its ambit so as to allow it to concentrate on more important matters.

The 2nd ARC has observed that UPSC has been encumbered with routine administrative matters at the cost of its broader mandate which is to advise the government on the principles of recruitment and promotion (Gol 2008:121). It is necessary that the balance be restored by entrusting the more crucial and less mundane selection decisions to UPSC. The rest can be hived off, either to bodies such as the Staff Selection Commission (SSC), or to the government departments themselves, with suitable oversight provisions as recommended by the 2nd ARC with regard to departmental promotion committees (Gol 2008: 122).

By revitalizing the recruitment system through reforms a small beginning can be made towards improving the larger personnel management system of government. Simultaneously, it is for the government and the larger policy community to ponder over the negative externalities generated in the entire governance system by overloading UPSC with routine work and reducing its ability to assume its rightful constitutional role. It is mandatory that UPSC be involved in more important personnel decisions made by government in a more direct fashion. This can be done only if its energies are released from tiresome routine work that can be done equally effectively by other agencies and instead applied to the more important tasks at hand.

The recruitment at the State Government level is carried out by the State Public Service Commissions (SPSC). Each State in India has its own Public Service Commission with experienced members from Central or State Governments. The members of the SPSC are appointed by the Governor and can only be removed by the President of India. The SPSC submits an annual report on its work to the Governor of the State.

The recruitment of Group C (non-technical) and Group B (non-gazetted: both technical and non-technical) posts in various Ministries /Departments of GOI has been mandated to the Staff Selection Commission (SSC). The SSC has a nationwide network of nine regional/sub-regional offices located at Allahabad, Bengaluru, Chennai, Guwahati, Kolkata, Mumbai, New Delhi, Chandigarh and Raipur.

Central Staffing Scheme (CSS)

The Central Staffing Scheme (CSS) provides a systematic arrangement for the selection and appointment of officers to senior administrative posts at the Centre, excluding posts which are specifically encadred within the organized Group A services or filled by recruitment through the UPSC. Some posts of Deputy Secretary and Under Secretary under the Central Government are shown as members, without specifying individual posts, in the cadre strength of the CSS. These posts are filled in accordance with the rules of the Central Secretariat Service, and when so filled, stand outside the CSS. Appointments to all other posts of the rank of Under Secretary and above in the GOI are filled under the CSS, by borrowing officers from the AIS and participating Group A services.

The CSS has been set-up to support the Centre's need for fresh inputs at senior levels in policy planning, formulation of policy and implementation of' programmes from 36 participating services including the AIS and other organized Group A Services.

The Railway employees are classified as gazetted (Group A and B) and non- gazetted (Group C and D) grades. The appointments of Group A employees, are mainly done through the UPSC. The recruitment to railway posts at Group C and D level takes place through the Railway Recruitment Boards (RRB) that have been constituted throughout the country.

The selection and placement of personnel in the posts of Chairman, Managing Director or Chairman-cum-Managing Director and functional Directors of Central PSEs is managed by the Public Enterprises Selection Board (PE.SB). The PESB is comprised of the Chairman and three Members. The PESB maintains the Board structure of Central PSEs, updates the description of open posts in consultation with the Administrative Ministry of the CPSE, invites applications, shortlists applicants for selection interview and sends recommendations for appointment to the Administrative Ministry.

Eligibility for All India Civil Services

Candidates appearing for the all India civil services examination must hold a degree of any University incorporated by an Act of the Central or State Legislature in India or other educational institutions established by an Act of Parliament or declared to be deemed as a University under Section-3 of the University Grants Commission Act, 1956.

The UPSC, sometime around 1979, divided the original single written examination into three parts: Part I, the preliminary; Part II, the main; and Part III, an oral examination. The preliminary examination is an aptitude test consisting of two objective tests at high level, general studies, and one optional (chosen from among specialized subjects of the candidate's choice). Based on the results of Part I, candidates are chosen to appear for the main (Part II) written test (in essay format). This part consists of the following: one examination in general essay, 4 papers in general studies, special subjects chosen out of a long list of subjects (normally offered in universities). The standard of these examinations is set at slightly less than the master's level but a little higher than the bachelor's level (which is commonly known as the honors level). These examinations are meant "to assess overall intellectual traits and the depth of understanding . . . rather than merely the range of ... information and memory." Candidates who are successful in Part II written examinations are given the Part III oral examination. The cumulative score decides the ranking of the selected candidates who are picked from the top to fill the available positions. Note that the aptitude test scores do not count.

Annually, besides the general merit category (open to candidates belonging to all communities), a certain quota of the positions considered "reserved" must be filled by candidates belonging to SC, ST, and Other Backward Classes (OBCs). Given their inability to compete within the general merit category and the constitutional dictates of encouraging these "classes," it was thought that they should be allowed more chances at the examinations.

It should be noted that other than those selected by examination, there are promotions to the two AIS from state cadres.

In what is considered to be one of the most rigorous contests in the world, 500,000 of the brightest in India write a year-long multi-stage examination competing for just 80 seats in the Indian Administrative service—half of which are reserved. The percentage of success is just 0.02% roughly the same as the IIT entrance examination. What is indeed heartening to note from the above figures is that the civil service has been the preferred destination of the best and the brightest in successive generations in post-Independent India.

13.6 Training – National Training Policy 2012

The Department of Personnel and Training (DOPT) is the nodal agency of GOI responsible for matters related to training of civil servants. The National Training Policy (NTP) was formulated in 1996 for the training of civil servants. Due to the emerging challenges in civil service, the institutional mechanism of training has been redesigned. Accordingly, the NTP 2012, was formulated in consultation with all Ministries/Departments of GOI. The Government has approved and directed the NTP 2012 to all Ministries/Departments.

Training has usually been based on the duties that are to be performed in a particular post. While moving towards a competency-based approach, it is necessary to classify the distinct types of posts and to indicate the competencies required in such posts. Once the competencies are laid down, an individual's development can be more objectively linked to the competencies needed for the current or future jobs.

The training plan of each Ministry/Department/Organization needs to address the gap between the existing and the required competencies and provide opportunities to the employees to develop their competencies.

The objective of training is to develop a professional, impartial and efficient civil service that is responsive to the needs of the citizens. All civil servants are provided with training to equip themselves with the competencies for their current or future jobs. Such training occurs:

- At the time of their entry into service, and
- At appropriate intervals in the course of their careers.

As per the NTP 2012, every Ministry/Department needs to create a training cell to classify all posts with clear job description and required competencies. Based on these requirements, Cadre Training Plans (CTP) are developed to link the training and development of competencies to the career progression of individuals. These Cadre Training Plans are prepared with the guidance of training institutes.

The Trainer Development Programme has been one of the most successful instances of transfer of learning resulting in the development of a cadre of trainers. The Sixth CTP has proposed major incentives such as a 30% Training Allowance, rent-free accommodation, etc., for Central Training Institutions for Group A officers, in recognition of the importance of this function and to attract a wider range of officers to this function. It is recommended that State Governments provide similar incentives to the faculty of the State Training Institutions.

Foreign training fills a crucial gap in the training system. Since 2001, the scheme of

Domestic Funding for Foreign Training has become the main source under which officers are now sent for foreign training.

The NTP of 1996 had recommended that 1.5% of the salary budget be set aside by each Department to be used solely for the purpose of training. Given the increase in the need for training for moving to a competency-based system, it is recommended in NTP 2012 that each Ministry/Department set aside at least 2.5% of its salary budget for training.

As the officers of the IAS and State Civil Services play an important role in the administrative set up at all levels, they need to be familiarized with grassroots institutions of rural and urban governance. The IAS Probationers/Officer Trainees are given hands-on experience of grassroot level administration in PRI, Urban Local Bodies by placing them as Executive Officers of Gram Panchayats/Municipalities for a suitable duration.

For monitoring the implementation of the NTP and taking appropriate steps to facilitate such implementation, a Committee chaired by the Secretary, Ministry of Personnel, Public Grievances and Pensions and consisting of the Secretaries of the Departments of Urban Development and Rural Development, Administrative Reforms and Public Grievances, the Director of the Lal Bahadur Shastri National Academy of Administration (LBSNAA) and three Representatives each of the 2 State and Central Training Institutions (on a 2-year rotational basis) with Joint Secretary (Training) as the Member Secretary has been formed. This Committee meets bi-annually.

Ministries are scaling up their training activity and National Flagship Programmes such as the Mahatma Gandhi National Rural Employment Guarantee Programme, National Rural Health Mission, and Sarva Shiksha Abhiyan have been allocated large amounts for capacity building.

Distance and e-learning provide unparalleled opportunities for meeting the training needs of large number of civil servants dispersed across the country in different cities, towns and villages. The Training Division has taken a major step in this direction by tying up with the Indira Gandhi National Open University to facilitate distance learning in a wide range of subjects and courses.

In-Service Training Programmes

Under the present system of in-service training for IAS Officers and officers working under the CSS, every officer is required to attend a one-week training programme each year in a bloc of two years. For the year 2012-13, all officers whose allotment year (batch) was between 1982 and 2002 and born on or after April 1, 1956, were eligible for one-week training. The eligibility to attend the in-service training programme is subjected to the following conditions:

- The officer has to attend one 1-week in-service training programme each year in a block of two years.
- All officers who have attended the Mid-Career Training programme are also eligible to opt for the 1-week in-service training programme.

- All officers who are posted abroad are exempted from the in-service training programmes, only for the period of their posting abroad.

All the eligible officers have to attend training programmes in accordance with the slots given to them unless they are specifically exempted or slotted for mid-career training.

The Officers have to opt for those training programmes that are relevant for their current job as well as the kind of assignments they are likely to hold in future. Several one-week training programmes are conducted by the State Administrative Training Institutions, Central Training Institutes, Indian Institute of Management (IIM) Bangalore, ASCI Hyderabad and other autonomous institutions. While slotting an officer for training, the Training Division takes into account the job profile and the past training, apart from the options indicated by the officer. Officers eligible for training are slotted by the Training Division, DOPT, to programmes in accordance with their options. The DOPT pays a consolidated fee to the institutes conducting these programmes. No course fee is payable either by the State Government or Ministry/ Department or by the participants.

Mid-Career Training Programme

A career-linked and mandatory Mid-Career Training Programme for IAS officers was started in January 2007 with an objective of improving the next level competencies at certain identified stages of their careers. The successful completion of Phase III, Phase IV and Phase V of the Mid-Career Training Programme is a pre-requisite for the promotion to Junior Administrative Grade, Super Time Scale and Increment after 28th year of service, respectively. The minimum residual service required to undergo the mandatory Mid-Career Training Programme has been fixed at three years.

In order to strike a balance between the implementation of the mandatory provisions of the IAS (Pay) rules/and the difficulties faced by the Cadre Controlling Authorities, each officer is allowed three chances to complete each phase of the Mid-Career Training Programme. All phases of the: mandatory Mid-Career Training Programme are compulsory to attend by all officers. Postponement of participation is allowed after the prior approval of the DOPT.

All Group-A civil servants have to undergo a two-year induction training. The training period comprises a foundation course and a professional course. The foundation course is spread over a period of 15 weeks and is conducted at the Lal Bahadur Shastri National Academy of Administration (LBSNAA), Mussoorie.

Each of the services has its own training school. The IAS officers were originally trained in New Delhi (the capital of India and the administrative hub) and Shimla. But both were merged into the newly created Lal Bahadur Shashtri National Academy of Administration {the academy) in 1959 in Mussoorie. The IPS officers are trained in Hyderabad, and personnel in other central services are trained at different individual schools.

The Mussoorie academy serves as a foundation course for all direct recruits to the AIS (including the Indian Forest Service) and central services (Group A) as a professional training course for IAS, and as training for promotees from state cadres to IAS. The foundation course runs for 15 weeks, providing basic understanding of the Constitution of India and also of the political, socio-economic, and legal framework. It is also intended to establish an esprit de corps among all services that would facilitate later coordination among them.

After foundation course training, the IAS officers are further trained in two phases. Phase I consists of training in their profession for 26 weeks. During the first 9 weeks, they are sent on a nationwide tour and are also attached to the three armed forces, public sector undertakings (those indulging in commercial activity of the government), private sector units, municipal bodies, volunteer agencies, and so on. The rest of their time is spent in classrooms learning professional skills needed during the first 10 years of tenure. This is followed by 52 weeks of district training, which is expected to enable the recruits to shoulder the government in the district later. On completion, the recruits return to the academy for Phase II training, where they share and consolidate their training.

About 2.15 crore government employees are currently working in India. This includes both Central and State government employees excluding the defense personnel. There are four classes of employees at the central level, viz. Group A, B, C and D. Group C and D employees provide support services to officers of Group A and B services, which are 29 in number and of which the first 12 fall within the scope of the Group A and are considered to be the top most central services. For Group A personnel, recruitment is done by the UPSC and the foundation training is imparted by LBSNAA, Mussoorie.

13.7 Promotion

Performance appraisal is a joint effort between the employee and the reporting officer who initially sets the targets and the goals. The performance management system has to be designed in accordance with the overall strategic framework of the Department. Rewarding the employees for their performance and acknowledging their contributions can result in overall performance improvement of the organization. A civil servant's performance appraisal is captured in -two ways:

- Closed system of Annual Confidential Report (ACR), and
- Performance appraisal with openness

The ACR is the traditional approach of absolute/relative grading or evaluating officers in terms of achieving the targets. It is typically conducted at the end of a set period, usually a calendar year. The significant feature of this method is the complete secrecy of the exercise, both in process and results, unless the rules specifically mention otherwise. Adverse remarks are communicated to the officer reported upon.

The performance appraisal with openness is an improvement over the ACR. It is transparent and involves the officer at different levels. The performance appraisal process starts with the goal setting exercise, followed by an interim performance review and a final assessment in the end. Finally, performance excellence is decided by a number (grades of 1-10) to be assigned by the reporting officer.

The performance of a Government servant is assessed annually through the Confidential Report, which is an important document providing the basic and vital inputs for assessing the performance of the Government servant and his/her suitability for career advancement on occasions such as confirmation, promotion, selection for deputation and selection for foreign assignment. Performance appraisal through confidential reports is a tool for human resource development in order to enable a Government servant to realize his/her true potential.

The promotion guidelines for the members of the Indian Administrative Service to the higher scales are:

- Senior Time Scale: An officer is eligible for appointment to Senior Time Scale on completing four years of service: A Committee consisting of the Chief Secretary and two officers of least Supertime Scale level of the State Government evaluate the performance of the eligible officers for deciding their suitability for promotion to posts in the Senior Time Scale.
- Junior Administrative Grade: An officer is eligible for appointment to this on completing nine years of service. This grade is non-functional and admissible without any screening. This is applicable to all the officers of the Senior Time Scale, except in cases where any disciplinary/criminal proceedings are pending against the officer.
- Selection Grade: An officer is eligible for appointment to Selection Grade on completion of 13 years of service. A committee comprising the Chief Secretary and two officers of the concerned State Government, in the Supertime Scale or above, screens the eligible members of the Service for promotion in this grade.
- Supertime Scale: The members of the Service who complete 16 years of service are eligible for appointment to the Supertime Scale. The Screening Committee comprises the Chief Secretary as Chairman and two officers working in the' grade of Principal Secretary within the State Government concerned.
- Principal Secretary to the Government: One is eligible to this on completion of 25 years of service. The Screening Committee comprises the Chief Secretary as Chairman and one senior-most officer each working in the grades of Chief Secretary to the Government and Principal Secretary to the Government-, respectively in the cadre.
- Chief Secretary: The consideration for promotion in this grade consists of all the members who complete 30 years of service. The Screening Committee comprise the Chief Secretary concerned, one officer working in this grade, in the cadre, and another officer of the cadre serving in GOI in the same grade.

Each Committee decides its own method and procedure for objective assessment of the suitability of the candidate to be considered for promotion. Merit has to be recognized and rewarded. Based on the hard work, good conduct and result-oriented performance as reflected in the ACR and based on strict and rigorous selection process, promotions are made. The ACRs are the basic inputs on the basis of which assessment is to be made by each Committee.

The Fifth Pay Commission recommended Assured Career Progression Scheme (ACPS) for the general employees in the Government. The scheme of ACPS recommended time-bound promotions for the services.

- Group A - 4, 8 and 13 year of service
- Group B - 8 and 16 years of service
- Group C- 10 and 20 years of service
- Group D -12 and 24 years' of service

The Government accepted this recommendation in a modified manner and introduced the ACPS for Groups B, C and D and isolated posts in Group A where two financial upgradations were to be provided on completion of 12 and 24 years of service. The financial upgradations were to be in the next higher grade in the existing hierarchy. The benefits of pay fixation were to be given at the time of financial upgradations but there was no change in the designation. This created uneven benefits to employees in different organizations that had lower intermediary grades.

The Sixth CPC recommended continuing the concept of ACPS with following modifications:

- The scheme to be available to all posts belonging to Group A.
- Benefit of pay fixation to be available at the time of financial upgradations.
- The grade pay to be changed at the time of financial upgradation.
- Financial upgradation to be available whenever a person has spent 12 years of service in the same grade. However, only two financial upgradations are possible in the entire career.

This scheme with aforesaid modifications is called modified ACPS to ensure suitable progression uniformly to all the employees in the Central Government.

In case of promotions from lower group to Group A, the mode of promotion happens to be "selection by merit". The benchmark prescribed is "good" and only those officers who obtain the said benchmark are promoted in the order of merit as per grading obtained. The Departmental Promotion Committee determines the merit of those being assessed for promotion with reference to the prescribed benchmark and accordingly grades the officers as fit and unfit. Those officers graded fit by the Departmental Promotion Committee are included in the selection panel list.

13.8 Civil service code of Conduct: Political Rights

The goal of this code of conduct is to establish norms of conduct for the civil service and inform citizens about the conduct that civil servants need to have for the purpose of improving the quality of the civil service.

Based on the recommendations of the Committee on Prevention of Corruption (1964) headed by Shri K. Santhanam, the conduct rules for government servants were revised with a view to maintaining integrity in the public services. The Central Civil Services (Conduct) Rules, 1964 were notified laying down the code of conduct for Central government employees. The Commission recommended that every government servant shall at all times:

1. Maintain absolute integrity.

2. Maintain devotion to duty.
3. Do nothing which is unbecoming of a government servant.
4. Every Government servant holding a supervisory post shall take all possible steps to ensure the integrity and devotion to duty of all government servants for the time being under his control and authority.
5. No government servant shall, in the performance of his official duties, or in the exercise of powers conferred on him, act otherwise than in best judgement except when he is acting under the direction of his official superior.
6. The direction of the official superior shall ordinarily be in writing. Oral direction to subordinates shall be avoided, as possible. Where the issue of oral direction becomes unavoidable, the official superior shall confirm it in writing immediately thereafter.

This, the codes of conduct are guidelines for civil servants to make them accountable to the people and for performing their duties with devotion and integrity.

Political Rights of Civil servants

Civil servants in India have the right to vote and form associations, but they are debarred from indulging in political activities. They can neither become members of a political party nor be a beneficiary to its funds. The objective behind this is to keep the civil services neutral and unbiased in public service delivery. Whatever political party comes into power, civil servants have to be loyal to the government and to the objectives of the Constitution. Thus, civil servants have the right to vote and the right to form organizations for fulfilling their professional objectives, but can not take part in active politics.

Civil Services Neutrality

Neutrality is the hallmark of the civil services in India. A civil servant should not identify himself with political parties and preserve his neutrality in matters of public policy. They are required to serve every government in power. Civil servants not only implement policies and decisions by the political masters but they also advise them on policy-making. They can play this role better only when they observe complete neutrality in political matters.

Civil Service Activism

Civil service activism is about the exceptional role of a civil servant played sometimes in the public interest. It includes regular meetings with the people, solving their grievances and assisting them as competently as possible. Sometimes he may initiate innovative reform programmes to educate and reach out to the public. He can be a friend, philosopher and guide of the masses. It is also about taking strict action even against the policies of the government if required to protect the interest of the people. Steps taken by T. N. Seshan for electoral reforms and those for police reforms initiated by Kiran Bedi are good examples of civil service activism.

13.9 Recruitment, Training, Promotion: A Review

The professional standards that define the skills, qualities and qualifications for the public services, and the candidates aspiring for these, broadly form the competency framework in administration. These are the benchmarks for the standard by which he or she is supposed to perform and also directly or indirectly contribute to the public organization. These standards need to be applied at all levels in the career of an individual starting from recruitment. Some of these competencies, especially those relating to knowledge and attitude are expected to be developed in the regular course of professional capacity building. Individuals are expected to develop and master these competencies through education on the job and overall work experience.

Interestingly in India, which has a long history of bureaucratic administration, there is still no extant framework for the recruitment, training and promotion of civil servants which is explicit to the employers or the civil servants.

The UPSC that recruits personnel for the higher civil services in India works on preconceived notions on how to match the needs of the various government departments which it recruits and the tests it administers for the purpose. On UPSC website there is no mention of the competency requirements for different jobs. However, it lists out the syllabus requirement for different written examinations, but there is nothing that links the syllabus to the competencies necessary for different posts (functions).

Similarly, the Lal Bahadur Shastri National Academy of Administration (LBSNAA) trains civil servants on the basis of an unwritten understanding of what the competency requirements are at different levels. However, even after 50 years of existence, it has no explicit competency framework regarding the officers it trains. The subjects and the broad syllabus of each subject to be covered in the professional training of IAS officers are specified by statute, namely the First Schedule to the Indian Administrative Service Regulation, 1955 (Probationers Final Examination). In effect the syllabus and marks specified by the First Schedule have been functioning as a broad narrative framework within which LBSNAA has been regularly updating the syllabus, and fixing the total number of marks for each subject. This syllabus is somehow expected to develop the competencies of the probationers.

Every ten years or so a syllabus review committee is constituted to revise the syllabus in view of the changes in the external environment. The Report of the Syllabus Review Committee for Induction Training (Dr. R. V. Vaidyanathan Ayyar Committee, June 2007), the most recent of such committees, was an extremely comprehensive one and recommended that training should lay more emphasis on the following skills and competencies:

- Leadership, conflict resolution, team building.
- Negotiation, communication, interpersonal skills, etc.

It went on to recommend the inculcation and development of personal_values and attitudes such as: "Integrity, work ethic and self-confidence" and professional values and attitudes such as:

"Professional integrity, commitment to Constitutional values, principles of good governance, outcome orientation".

None of these committees focused on identifying competencies in a scientific manner, nor did the terms of reference expect them to do so.

Like all training institutions, the LBSNAA aims at development of appropriate knowledge, skills and attitudes. However, what is appropriate is arrived at not on the basis of competencies which have been systematically mapped, but on the practical experience of the practitioner faculty which manages the training. In recent years, however, training at LBSNAA has come to focus on the training needs appropriate to the positions that officers are expected to occupy in the next few years. While some Training Needs Assessment (TNA) work has been done for the mid-career training programmes, similar exercises have so far not been completed for the induction training.

When it comes to promotions, the departmental promotion committees base their recommendations on the grades earned by officers in their Annual Confidential Reports/ Performance Appraisal Reports over the past 5-10 years but nothing about the specific competencies necessary for the job for which the performance is assessed. The revised format of the Performance Appraisal Report for IAS officers is an improvement in terms of the more specific and longer list of attributes that are required to be assessed by the superior.

One thing which is clear is that competencies with respect to different assignments need to be identified and codified. If we are to proceed in a systematic manner, this must begin with documentation of the job descriptions and responsibilities of different sets of employees. These need to be mapped against the job/tasks that employees are expected to do. The initial recruitment process should test the candidate for the competencies appropriate to the job that education and experience would have provided.

Once the candidate is selected, the training institutions are expected to fine tune the competencies already found in the recruit and develop those which are specific to the job, to which the recruit may not have been exposed earlier. Post-induction training, the officer through practice and experience is expected to develop and master these competencies.

At the time of promotion or for taking up of different assignments, the competencies already developed and assessed become the basis for selection for the next assignment. Before taking up the new assignment which could involve a different job description and set of responsibilities, the competencies appropriate to the new job need to be developed through in situ and institutional training. For the IAS, the Mid-Career Training Programmes are stages when competencies can be assessed, the gaps identified and remedial training recommended and facilitated. This would involve development of an Assessment Centre at the LBSNAA.

The DOPT along with United Nations Development Programme (UNDP), LBSNAA and the National Institute of Administrative Research (NIAR) have conceived a project for developing competency frameworks of the All India Services and Central Services. A beginning has been made by the National Conference on Human Resource Management: Towards Competency-based Performance Management for the Civil Service organized by the DoPT and the UNDP in New Delhi on 29—30 November 2011. NIAR along with LBSNAA is likely to work on the competency framework for the IAS.

Finally, we must understand that in the post-globalized era India cannot complete with a hopelessly archaic, centralized, process-driven civil service, which do not respond to the needs and challenges of the changing era and needs of its billion plus citizens. We need better public policies and far more effective and responsive public delivery systems. Several countries in the world have already built efficient, competent and user friendly public services. Effective public systems management is the hallmark of good governance. We need to reform and change with continuity. The continuing features could include the centrality of merit as a value in the management of the civil service and its a-political character within a structure of democratic government and ministerial control of administration. A performance culture has to be additionally built into the civil service.

13.10 Politico-Administrative Relations

In the post-Independence period, India adopted a written constitution, which embodies certain principles intended to determine the ends and purposes of the polity as well as of the social order the constitution was designed to establish. Apart from the preamble and the directive principles of state policy, the 25th Amendment 1971 inserted a new Article, 31C, intended to give effect to a socialistic economic order. A civil servant in India is required to take an oath of loyalty to the constitution, to commit himself through that oath to the Preamble, the Fundamental Rights and the directive principles which envisage the establishment of an egalitarian social order. In view of the socio-economic goals of the constitution there naturally arose a pressing need for commitment on the part of the civil service.

However, the practical problems involved in the question of commitment are far more complex. Indian politics could not build the egalitarian social order necessary to sustain a modern administration suited to carry out the social objectives of the constitution. As many commentators have pointed out, it would in fact be unrealistic to expect that the extent and depth of the commitment of the civil service in India would differ in any marked respect from that of Indian society in general where social equality has over the ages remained a subject to be preached, but hardly to be practiced.

Soon after Independence, the minister-civil servant relationship had to move towards certain norms. Since, the rule of law lacked roots in the Indian soil, it was not very surprising to find that elected representatives and the civil servants did not show marked behavioural differences from the general social ethos. Thus ministers often forgot to bear in mind that according to the principles of parliamentary democracy they were as much servants of the state as were civil servants, and the civil servants, were not their personal servants, but like them, servants of the state. Over the years the search for a compliant civil service continued, committed not only to the ideals enshrined in the Constitution, but also to the ruling party.

In reality, the matters of high moment that interest ministers are appointments, transfers, promotions, licenses and permits. These are not matters in which heartfelt commitment to the lofty aims of government are directly relevant. What is desired is commitment to the ministers personally.

Such ministerial behaviour could of course be attributed basically to a tradition- bound caste and status-ridden society which lacks the capacity, for organized and collective resistance to corruption. While its declared political goal was parliamentary democracy, which emphasized the primacy of the party in parliament exercising power with responsibility, a radical and power-motivated wing of the Congress in India attempted to act on the Soviet model which gives primacy to the party executive outside the legislature. It was generally believed that the call for a "committed bureaucracy" from many top Congress leaders including the PM herself during Mrs. Gandhi's regime could be traced to shortcomings in the implementation of development plans and the resultant social unrest.

It is true that the social background of the administrative elite after Independence was such that they tended to overlook the demands of mass democracy, where, as a result of education, achievement or income, new classes emerge which endeavour to supplant old social and behavioural norms. But the rule-oriented bureaucrat tends to view even new and unique situations of socio political nature as falling within the realm of administration. This is precisely what happened under the post-73rd constitution amendment Panchayati Raj scheme, which could not provide a solid institutional base for democracy as an alternative to bureaucracy. The stratified leadership of the panchayats were often too busy battling with each other to take any effective collective decisions thus ensuring the continuance of bureaucratic control. Since the Panchayati Raj model acted as a mere funnel to facilitate the downward filtration of political interests, especially for electoral purposes, it is the administration that continues to dominate the rural scene and act in a routine manner independently of what might be called the normative goals of politics. In view of the weak institutional base of democratic politics especially at lower levels, the bureaucracy remains the virtual arbitrator between different social groups. The general trend of political development since Independence has been that the ruling party at the centre could not but let the higher bureaucracy share power with it in its own interest and for the sake of its own security. It ensured some kind of balance in the power structure of the country on the basis of an identity of interest between the political and the administrative elite being slightly favourable to the latter.

Thus it seems axiomatic that the bureaucratic apparatus of a state cannot be intelligently analyzed without relating it to the political context. The notion of a just and responsible administration in a democracy demands that bureaucracy act in the public interest. However, the interpretation of what public interest means in a given administrative situation has very often been a point of debate between administrators and politicians.

The administrator tends to look at administrative problems, particularly in relation to development and public interest from a rule-oriented angle. He blames the political leadership for introducing irrational criteria in the implementation of schemes for rational development and for twisting administrative matters to prevent decisions purely on merit. What he calls "political interference" is a constant irritant threatening to demoralize the whole bureaucracy. Politicians on the other hand seem always to emphasize their authority as the representatives of the public assuming they are the best custodians of the public interest. Politicians have found it profitable to get into every aspect of execution and indulge in rampant corruption, while the civil service is left to write something that passes off as policy. The roles sometimes did get reversed in the post-Independence context.

Thus, we can see that the administrative responsibility of the political executive is bound with the notion of a public interest that is to be protected by administrators acting as a kind of neutral arbitrator between the state and citizenry. Administrative responsibility in a modern democratic state rests on two criteria —technical knowledge and popular support. Clearly certain public problems demand technical solutions, which do not automatically guarantee political responsibility. Popular support must be assessed through legislative communications, public opinion polls and responses of affected groups. The citizen is thus viewed as the ultimate source of administrative power not only because it is axiomatic in a democracy but also because he is a rational consumer of public goods and services.

In the context of prevailing politico-administrative relations it would be unfair to comment upon the falling standards of bureaucratic performance without simultaneously acknowledging the fact that the restructuring of the bureaucratic instrument is primarily a political task. Conceding the fact that the Indian bureaucracy enjoys a great deal of autonomy as an initiator and implementer of developmental schemes it should also be made clear that its mandate is limited, and that qualitative transformation is essentially a political task. Bureaucracies are not especially prone to innovation and change, political rulers should be and often are more responsive to societal demands. Therefore if we are to assume that conditions in modernizing politics do not favour a rigid application of the concept of a neutral or depoliticized bureaucracy, that civil servants are unlikely to retain a passive neutrality for long, and further that pressures for politicization are bound to increase in all governmental systems irrespective of their ideologies (since the fortunes of political leaders are likely to be linked with bureaucratic performance) the question arises whether time is not ripe for the construction of a new normative model on which the politico-administrative relationship of developmental democracies like India could gradually evolve.

The central problem of development in developing societies is the problem of balancing public policies with a constant rising level of differentiated group demands. Sustained political growth is thus the central problem of modernization and ability to deal with continuous change is the crucial test of this growth. In shouldering these demands the main partner of the Indian State has been the bureaucracy. Adult franchise, mass education and other developments in the new technologies of transport and communication have resulted in extensive social mobilization and the sudden entry of new populations into political participation in India in the last few decades. This has also resulted in an explosion of rising public demands much more than the existent politico-bureaucratic apparatus can effectively cope with. The problems of a growing democracy in India are partly administrative and partly political. The Indian bureaucracy can be criticized for its professional dysfunctionalities but these criticisms could best be termed procedural and not substantive. The real problem lies in coping with demands, which are strictly political or which in the process of an administrative solution have become so. The political executive needs to understand that every single enforcement action by any top civil servant will necessarily have a repercussion for it to get its desired objective or be effective. That must not become a convenient scapegoat for the political executive to suspend or even transfer inconvenient officers. Constitutional protection of the All India Services under Act 311 is essential for our democracy. *In this respect the new transfer rules following Supreme Court directives 2013 and the passage of the Whistle blowers Protection Act 2013 are both welcome developments.*

The bureaucracy in post-Independent India has helped to maintain the framework of a unified polity as well as the capacity to absorb varied demands and to regulate them as effectively as they could in the general political atmosphere of scarcity. Not only were they important instruments for unification and centralization, but they enabled the ruling elites maintain a certain degree of continuity in policy making. In addition, they also served as important instruments for mobilization of resources: revenues, manpower and political support.

The bureaucracies have also performed crucial functions in regulating social change. They regulated potential conflicts between the major groups of society, assured them of continuous service and upheld their rights, irrespective of momentary changes in their power relations. They have helped to accommodate various groups to the framework of the centralized polity and to its basic institutions and norms. In this way the Indian bureaucracy has, on the whole, tried to enhance the ability of our political system to deal with major challenges. In the process, however, the bureaucracy has become a relatively narrow and yet very strong pressure group, which often obstructs schemes of economic development, which threaten its own level of income, power and influence.

In all developing societies like India where meeting the tasks of development is the bureaucracy's main priority, we need to evolve an effectiveness model, whose only yardstick for success measurement should be its ability to cope with differentiated group demands.

However, I would like to state that the entire issue of politico-administrative confrontation in India is more cosmetic, than real. There are several commonalities between the political and administrative elite in India.. Both are power elites who share a joint belief in incremental social change and adoption of suppressive policies to lower the level of particular public demands as and when such demands become a threat to system maintenance.

It has been increasingly felt that we need to focus on how democratic governance works to sharpen the efficacy of public accountability mechanisms. Academics have focused largely on democratic politics in recent years but far less on the understanding of public institutional capacity, the absence of which often undermines democracy. The challenge for democracies is therefore not simply to strengthen downward electoral accountability so that vote seeking politicians have an incentive to pay attention to citizen needs. It is equally important to endow the public governance systems with the capacity, technical skills and resources so that elected leaders can deliver things that most citizens want: food and nutrition, education, basic health care and sustainable livelihoods. Recognizing the need for both democracy and development, the challenge of developing societies like India is to make democratic governance work through effective politico-administrative regimes ensuring good public service delivery systems that truly impact the lives of citizens.

But, it would do well to remember that the nature of democratic politics is to continuously widen the social base of political participation and it is in this process that new political demands may often defy a piecemeal political approach or a purely administrative solution. In a pluralist democracy like India, which section of the public interest or which social groups the politico-administrative elite will serve have often been the bone of contention between both. It is all very well to say that the bureaucrats should be committed to the goals of our constitution, which actually boils down to the lowest common denominator of public interest, which again in an actual administrative situation is a vague yardstick of action. What really happens in the administration of development (in the prevailing atmosphere of scarcity), is that bureaucrats in the use of their discretionary power may often differ with politicians as to who should be the beneficiaries of development and frequently bureaucrats may be asked to bend rules for the politicians' need to distribute favour to their clients.

In 2013 the Supreme Court directed the Central Government to safeguard civil servants from political pressure by giving them a fixed tenure. The government has amended the rules governing IAS, IPS and IFS officers to assure them at least two years in a given posting. Every state will have to make appointments of cadre officers on the recommendation of a Civil Services Board set up by it under the Chief Secretary. The competent authority may reject the recommendation of the board, but the reasons thereof must be recorded.

According to the amendments effected to the IAS/ IPS/ IFS cadre rules, a cadre officer appointed to any cadre post shall hold the office for at least two years unless in the meantime, he/she is promoted, retired or sent on deputation outside the state or training exceeding two months. The fixed tenure may be specified by the State Government in the case of cadre officer appointed to non-cadre posts.

The Board shall examine cases of premature transfers, consider for transfer before fixed tenure based on circumstances it thinks fit, and recommend to the competent authority names of officers for premature transfer with reasons to be recorded in writing.

The Board can seek justification from the administrative department of the concerned state for premature transfers, obtain comments or views of the officer proposed to be transferred, and not recommend premature transfer unless satisfied with the reasons. The Board shall also submit a quarterly report to the Centre giving details of officers recommended to be transferred before the minimum tenure and the reasons thereof.

As more and more pressure increases for a wider diffusion of the benefits of development the political and the administrative elite in India will have to work towards a value consensus on which they want to build up our future polity. This will involve fundamental questions like Development for whom (which social groups are to be its principal beneficiaries) and how (the means to be adopted in the progressively wider diffusion of social benefits) and lastly but most importantly, as to when and how force is to be used to contain political demands on the system in the ultimate resort. These involve crucial questions on ends and means which our politico-administrative system cannot afford to evade for long.

No political system can survive bureaucratic incapacity for long and ours is no exception. It is only when our political elite, in sheer political expediency if not in political wisdom, face up to the challenges and dilemmas of development and governance with the seriousness it deserves, that the bureaucracy will not lag far behind in emulating their political masters, in what is, and should be a truly "committed" joint endeavour. Many in the civil services break the law, and collude with the political executive and the common weal is dammed in the process. *Yet, every single day, all across the country, away from the media glare, there are many doing good work and holding the country together in circumstances in which no corporate sector executive or even members of the hallowed defence forces would like to work in.* The time has come to begin exploring the limits of control that the political executive needs to have over the permanent executive. The political executive must learn to have good officers around them, which alone makes for impartial honest advice. There is need to protect our constitutional democracy whose lynchpin is the permanent executive working in tandem with the political executive not necessarily subservient to the latter.

13.11 Performance of Civil Service: A Review (1950-to the present)

Civil services are comprised of permanent government servants essential to carry on the numerous governmental activities in different areas. Further, these services are considered even more necessary in a democracy where the political executive may change after periodic elections, and the permanent civil services remain to provide continuity and stability in the country's governance.

The performance and achievements of the public servants in the first three decades of Independence can be rated to be of very high order. Immediately after partition, the country faced the difficult task of rehabilitating millions of displaced persons from Pakistan. The public services of the Central and State Governments as also the All India Services rose to the occasion and restored normalcy in the country very speedily. The 500-plus Indian native states too were merged into the Indian Union in less than two years, thanks to the strong political leadership of Sardar Patel, the then Home Minister of India, and due to the dynamism and drive shown by the senior public servants of that time.

After the immediate post-partition problems, socio-economic development tasks through Five Year Plans became the main focus of attention of the Public Services. Being the implementation agencies of the Five Year Developmental Plans, Public Services played a crucial role in their success. Their commendable performance in the agricultural sector particularly in increasing food grain production from around 50 million tons in. 1951 to over 210 million tons by 2003-04 is a story of high achievement. With a billion plus population now India is not only able to feed it, there are times it is in a position to export surplus food grain to other countries. A vast number of public servants of the State and the Central agricultural services, including research scientists, producers of HYV seeds, agriculture extension officers, and administrators at the Block and District levels, displayed their capability, commitment and missionary zeal in bringing about the "Green Revolution" and freeing the country from the constant fear of famine and starvation deaths. Similarly, public servants connected with other allied activities in the food sector like fisheries, animal husbandry, poultry, dairy farming, and horticulture, etc., spared no efforts in raising the levels of production in their respective fields. Presently as the world's second largest producer of fruits and with 90 million tons of vegetable production, India ranks as the world's highest vegetable producer. Milk production too went up from around 17 million tons in 1951-52 to about 91 million tons (over five times) in 2004-05. This is another success story which ushered in the "White Revolution".

However, due to our rising population and uncertainty of monsoons the vigour and dynamism shown on the agricultural front in the earlier years need to be repeated to avoid any food crisis in the future. In fact, there is need for a second "Green Revolution".

There were other commendable achievements of the public services in India in the non-agricultural sector also. These would include construction of many huge multipurpose river dams like Hirakud, Bhakranangal, Nagarjuna Sagar, Damodar Valley, etc., for irrigation, flood control and power generation. These immensely helped in agricultural and industrial developments. Further, all major rivers of the country like Ganga, Yamuna, Brahmaputra, Mahanadi, Krishna, Godavari and Narmada, etc., were bridged at several places to facilitate all-weather road transportation throughout the country. Several railway lines connecting major cities, ports, mines and industrial areas were doubled and electrified to enhance and speed up the movement of goods and passenger traffic. New major ports like Paradeep, Haldia, Kandla and New Bombay were built and some others were widened and deepened to facilitate entry of bigger ships into the harbours. Basic industries of large capacities, like steel making, aluminum, zinc, copper, cement, chemical, and oil refineries were built in the public sector. Most of these major projects were executed generally within deadlines and in a cost-effective manner, which reflected efficiency and a sense of economy on the part of the public servants.

Thus strong foundations were laid during the planning era (1st to 7th Plan) from 1951 to 1990, by the public servants of those years to enable India to attain great economic height and strength in subsequent Five Year Plan periods.

13.12 Problems in Civil Services Today

Unfortunately, in the last three decades or so, the quality of public services has considerably come down. This is further visible at the grassroots or what is known as the cutting-edge level where the common man comes directly in contact with the public officials. At such various delivery points of public services, corruption, delay, harassment and uncivil behaviour towards the common citizen has reached an intolerable level. Hence people, by and large, view public servants (barring some exceptions) to be corrupt, unhelpful and unresponsive. These so-called "civil servants" are regarded to be neither "civil" nor good "servants" in performance of their public duties.

One unfortunate aspect of law enforcement in our administrative system that breeds corruption is that unduly large powers have been vested in the lower level functionaries like the patwaris and kanungos with regard to land records; the Police SHO with regard to criminal laws; the Junior Engineers of electricity, telephone, municipal bodies; and other host of inspectors like weights and measures, food adulteration, sales tax and factory inspectors, etc., to enforce laws relating to their respective areas of work. They are the grassroots level public servants with powers to set the laws in motion against any person. There are often complaints that people are falsely accused of violation of laws by these petty officials only to extract illegal money. Sadly there is little effective supervision to curb their widespread and open malpractices. Instead politicians make use of them for their own political ends and in return give them protection against any departmental action.

Of the several ills that have been afflicting the public services since long, widespread corruption is the most serious. According to the Transparency International's 2018

Corruption Prevention Index (CPI) India scored only 2.5 out of 10 on corruption prevention, in simple terms India is one of the most corrupt countries in the world. The spread of corruption is so widespread that in most government offices no work is expedited unless constantly chased from office to office and from seat to seat with the use of "speed money" by the applicants. According to a survey conducted by the Delhi-based Centre for Media Studies (CMS) in 2010, as many as 62% of the citizens think that corruption, is real and they have had first-hand experience of paying a bribe or using a contact to get a job done in a public office. People have little option but to comply with the illegitimate demands of petty public officials to get ration cards, telephone connections, passports, birth and death certificates, sales tax and income tax clearance certificates, motor driving licences, approval of building plans, conversion of lease-holds to freeholds, registration of legal documents, etc. "Speed money" has to be paid to avoid hours of unnecessary waiting in government offices.

While in earlier days corruption was, by and large, confined to the lower non- gazetted staff, in the course of time, particularly from the early 80s, it has spread to all categories and to all levels of public servants. The culture of corruption is now all-pervasive and has, so to say, become a part of life. To prevent people taking law into their own hands it is necessary to find effective legal ways to compel public officials to perform their duties transparently and honestly. They have to be made accountable for their acts of commission and omission. The enactment of the Right to Information Act 2005 may serve this purpose to some extent if properly and effectively implemented. The intention behind this Act as stated in its opening para is also: "to contain corruption and to hold governments and their instrumentalities accountable to the governed."

The many ills and shortcomings of the public services in India are now fairly well known. Most of these had also been identified by a number of Reform Committees and Commissions in the past with useful recommendations for corrective measures. The two important bodies among them were the Santhanam Committee in 1964 and the Administrative Reforms Commission (1966-1970) headed by Shri Morarji Desai that worked on the problems of corruption. The latter Commission covered the entire gamut of administration in its 20 reports. They made many practical suggestions to improve the quality and performance of public services. The Central Pay Commissions have also dealt with the shortcomings of the public services in their reports on each occasion.

Many of these faults and shortcomings have aggravated during the last three decades. Instead of appointing anymore commissions and committees for administrative reforms it would perhaps be better to implement the many practical measures already suggested by the earlier bodies.

The Draft Public Service Bill 2006 has recognized that "a politically neutral, professional, accountable and efficient public service is an essential instrument for promotion of good governance." The Bill also highlights the values that should guide the public servants in their functioning. These include allegiance to the Constitution, to function in an apolitical manner; to provide services for the betterment of the public at large and to foster socio-economic development; to ensure that public money is used with utmost economy and care. The Bill also provides for a Central Public Service Authority to ensure justice and fair play for the public servants.

Public Servants to Population Ratio

Long reviled for being bloated, India's Central and State Governments (taken together) in fact have just a fifth as many public servants as the United States, relative to population. Data compiled from multiple sources, including a 2008 official survey, Right to Information applications, media reports and the 2011 census, show that *India has 1,622.8 government servants for every 100,000 residents*. In stark contrast, the U.S. has 7,681 for the same. The Central Government, with 3.1 million employees, thus has 257 serving every 100,000 population, against the U.S. federal government's 840. Though people keep complaining the government is too big, the figures show that it is in fact not bloated at all in ratio to the population.

The highest ratios of public servants to population among the Indian States are in the conflict-torn or border regions, where the Central Government has made special funding available for enhancing employment in an effort to contain discontent. Thus, Mizoram has 3,950.27 public servants, Nagaland 3,920.62 and Jammu and Kashmir 3,585.96 (per lakh population). Barring Sikkim, with 6,394.89 public servants per 100,000 no State comes close to the international levels. (Data: Institute of Conflict Management, New Delhi).

For the most part though, India's relatively backward states have low numbers of public servants. This means enough staff members are not available for the provision of education, health and social services needed to address the worst kinds of poverty. Bihar has just 457.60 per 100,000, Madhya Pradesh 826.47, Uttar Pradesh has 801.67, Orissa 1,191.97 and Chhattisgarh 1,174.62 (per lakh).

This is not to suggest that there is a causal link between poverty and low levels of public servants: Gujarat has just 826.47 per 100,000 and Punjab 1,263.34. The data could explain, though, why even well-off States like these have found it tough to ensure universal primary education and eradicating poverty.

Census of Central Government Employees 2018	
Total Central Government Employees:	31.16 lakhs
Railways:	45.32%
MO Home:	22.20%
Defence Civil:	11.35%
Communication and IT:	7.7%
Finance:	3.62%
Other Ministries and Departments:	9.76%
Regular Employees:	3.20 lakh
Total Women Employees:	10.26%
Non-Gazzetted Employees:	96%
Regular Employees: Group C:	57.80
Group D	30.62%
Group B:	8.63%
Group A:	2.95%

13.13 Mandate for the Public Services

India, as emphasized earlier has still a long way to go in improving the economic conditions and quality of life of its billion plus population. Promoting excellence in the public services therefore, is of vital importance to the country. The known faults and shortcomings of the public services need to be tackled promptly but in a balanced and rational way so that the morale of public services does not suffer. India is known for its bright and talented human resources and can indeed become a strong economic power in the near future if its public servants function honestly, efficiently and in a citizen-friendly way. A firm political will and commitment to a well-defined anti-corruption agenda is required. This would accordingly be the opportune time to implement many important administrative reforms and make the civil services in India fit instruments of public service and good governance in the 21st century.

Excellence in public services can be achieved by a host of measures such as:

- The right type of candidates be recruited through a merit-based selection by an impartial statutory or constitutional body.
- Civil servants are promoted to higher grades on the basis of measurable objective criteria in a transparent manner;
- Civil servants are assured of security of tenure in key official posts.
- Civil servants are held accountable for performance through spelt out performance targets for which they are given sufficient autonomy;
- Civil servants are paid adequate remuneration and allowances to enable them to perform public service without sense of deprivation;
- Excellent work done by civil servants may be recognized through suitable institutional arrangements.
- Adequately tailored training programmes are conducted to upgrade the relevant skills and domain knowledge of civil servants;
- Corrupt civil servants are dismissed forthwith and post-decisional hearing is given to defend themselves in a departmental proceeding or a criminal trial. In the 21st century, civil service must also innovate to solve problems of the people in a period of rapid change. The good governance debate in the context of globalization and liberalization is an ongoing debate in India since the 1990s. Indian administration is responding to the challenges of managing the largest democracy in the world through a framework of socio-economic planning, negotiating with the needs of a changing federal structure and evolving appropriate policy interventions. The administrators are increasingly becoming facilitators in this transformational process of empowerment through conscious policies of civil service reform.

Conclusion

Governments today and in the future in India will undergo enormous social and economic transformations, profoundly affecting the work of public administration. Innovative ways of steering society will require us to consider new standards of assessing administrative performance, including not only the traditional legal and political standards, but also the market and economic criteria and finally the democratic and social criteria associated with the proposed New Public Service (see last chapter). While it is imperative to maintain a concern for legal, political, and economic criteria, it is of overwhelming importance that we place at the centre of our work a concept of the public service based on and fully integrated with citizen discourse and the public interest.

Today public administration in India relates to the whole of society and to the changed political economy, after liberalization. Thus assuming its overwhelming importance, a question may now be asked: What is the criteria of successful administration in today's changing India? The norms of an administrative system are both old and new. Traditional norms —efficacy, economy, good management and public interest—are well-established measures of judging the success of any administrative system. To these, can be added, continuing socio-economic progress, maintenance of good delivery systems, economic regulation and striving for equity and justice. Inequality is still a big political and human rights issue in India. Widespread inequalities provide the breeding ground for social ferment, dissent and alienation. The effective public administrator will continue to be the 'rational calculator' of different ways of implementing public policies. He will have to learn to satisfy conflicting public demands and understand the continual need of improving public services with fixed resources. With the increasing diversification of tasks there is no room for the amateur in administration now. What is needed is a specialist or a professional civil servant who has acquired the requisite professional training and is truly dedicated and committed to the goals and objectives of this service.

Public administration in India will have to face a host of challenges and pressures that will put its adaptability and performance capacity to a severe test. If man is to survive in the face of nuclear threats, overpopulation, environmental pollution, rapid technological change coupled with increasing societal turbulence, public administration will also have to learn to decentralize, democratize and humanize itself. To be a good and effective civil servant one will need to be more responsive and responsible. The key to responsiveness is organizational adaptability to change. The process of social, economic and political change will continue to accelerate making it vitally important that organizations adapt. Organization leaders must learn to anticipate social, economic and political change and to creatively work on it. There will be conditions under which the patterns of change will require organizational growth. But there will be equally as many and perhaps more situations, in which these change processes will require organizational decline, cut back and devolution. The good administrator will be adept at scanning the political, economic and social horizons and lead the processes of adaptation to growth or decline. Change in the 21st century is more likely to be the result of imaginative policies and difficult economic, political and social choices than the mere application of technological solutions to administrative problems.

Suggested Readings

Arora, Ramesh K. and Rajni Goyal, *Indian Public Administration: Institution and Issues*, New Delhi, New Age, 2016.

Census of Central Government Employees, Ministry of Labour and Employment, 2009.

Chaturvedi, T. N., .and S. Maheshwari, *Administrative Reforms*, New Delhi, Indian Institute of Public Administration, 1984.

Das, S. K., *Building a World Class Civil Service for Twenty-First Century* India New Delhi, OUP, 2010.

______ *The Civil Services in India*, OUP 2013

Government of India 2009 a, February. Citizen Centric Administration: The Heart of Governance, Second ARC, GOI, New Delhi

Hanumanthaiya, K, *A Brief Survey: The ARC and Its Work*, New Delhi, GOI Press, 1970.

Public Service in India: A Country Profile 2012 DARPG, GOI.

Reports of the Second ARC 2005-09 (15 Reports) DARPG, GOI.

Shukla, J. D., *Indianisation of All-India Services and Its Impact on Administration*, New Delhi, Allied Publishers, 1982.

Tangirala, M. P., "*UPSC: Civil Services Examination and Beyond*. The Indian Journal of Public Administration, 56 no. 4 (2010): pp. 920-32.

Tummala, K. K., *The Ambiguity of Ideology and Administrative Reform*, New Delhi, Allied Publishers, 1979.

----- *Public Administration in India*, New Delhi, Allied Publishers, 1994.

OOO

Chapter Fourteen

Corruption and Public Accountability

Introduction

Corruption, both petty and large, can be either the cause or the effect of poor governance. Large-scale corruption occurs because discretionary decision making in some areas is used to the advantage of a few. Corruption undermines the legitimacy of the system in the eyes of the public because public governance is maintained out of public funding and therefore the public have a right to know what government does with their money. Corruption surfaces in many forms, all of which erodes the confidence of the citizen in the quality of governance. They range from petty corruption associated with getting permissions that should be routinely available, to large-scale corruption associated with faulty procedures used for acquiring large contracts. However, public awareness of corruption as a social problem has increased much more today. This is in part because of greater awareness and increased transparency (e.g. with the Right to Information Act) and also the operation of a vigilant media. Many economic reforms after 91, such as the abolition of industrial licensing and import licensing have actually ended corruption in areas where it was earlier widely prevalent. However, rapid economic growth has caused sharp increase in the value of scarce resources, e.g. minerals, spectrum, or land, and as long as these are allocated on the basis of discretion exercised in a non-transparent manner, the likelihood of corruption increases. It is the lack of reforms in these areas to reflect the needs of the situation that is the real source of the problem.

We must aim at reducing corruption through further simplification of procedures for delivery of public services introducing greater transparency in public procurement processes. Mechanisms must be strengthened for dealing with corruption through institutions such as the Lokpal and the Lokayuktas. Corruption associated with government contracts can be minimized by restructuring government procurement processes. An Expert Committee has recommended enactment of a National Public Procurement Act in line with international practices in many countries. The Government has announced its intention to put a suitable law in place along these lines as soon as possible. Removal of corruption in the interface between the aam aadmi and the government should be the government's top priority. It is vital that systems for delivery of public services should be made citizen-friendly and time-bound. This requires reforms in the implementing agencies, including in the State Governments where most of the public services are delivered at the grassroots level. Information and Communication Technology (ICT) can play a major role in achieving these results. A citizen's charter which lays down the quality standards in delivery of services will help greatly. Perceptions of public services and quality of governance can be measured and evaluated by independent institutions in terms of citizens' report cards or social audits through surveys focusing on levels of satisfaction from public services as perceived by citizens. Public Services Guarantee Acts passed by several states are a welcome initiative.

The most cited causes of corruption include:

1. the absence of rules, regulations, policies and legislation;
2. weak systems of enforcement;
3. weak systems of oversight (i.e. the absence of a watchdog institution);
4. lack of accountability;
5. lack of transparency;
6. lack of checks and balances in the system (e.g. institutional weaknesses in the legislative and judicial systems);
7. lack of integrity;
8. monopoly of power;
9. high degree of discretion;
10. low salaries;
11. high rewards compared to risks; and
12. low detection rate.

Therefore, the antidote to corruption should follow from the causes. First, there is an issue of reforming the civil services, including codes of conduct, salaries, entry and promotions and laws against corruption that are credible. Second, this implies the existence of independent anti-corruption bodies. Third, the monopoly in providing public services can be ended by enabling private sector delivery, since many such public goods and services are no longer instances of market failure. Fourth, public procurement needs to become much more transparent. Fifth, countervailing pressure must be created by civil society, which in turn, requires awareness and dissemination of information. Only a few of these pre-conditions have been met so far in India.

India is currently ranked 80th on the Corruption Perception Index out of the 180 countries surveyed by Transparency International (CPI 2017).

14.1 Legal and Institutional Structures

There are a host of laws against corruption in India. The All India Service Act of 1951 empowers the GOI to formulate rules for laying down the conditions of services for the persons appointed to the civil services after consultation with State Governments. The Indian Penal Code regulates the moral behavior of the civil servants. The All India Service Conduct Rules of 1968 and the Central Services Conduct Rules of 1968, which emphasize focusing on "service content" as their core functional domain, laid down the rules for civil services. A clear mention has been made about using authority for no other purpose than public welfare. The Conference of the Chief Ministers, held in 1996, emphasized on the initiation of change in policy stressing the Charters of Citizen's Rights, accountability of public, servants, and transparency in administration. This was followed by a "workshop" held on November 20, 1996, in which all Chief Secretaries of States participated to prepare a roadmap to ensure the implementation of decisions taken during this workshop. The major outcomes had been translated through promulgation of the Charter of Ethics and the Civil Service Code on the basis of equality, secularism, impartiality, social justice, and the rule of law. The main conclusions are that civil service loyalty should be only towards the public in accordance with the rule of law, working with a focus on citizen-centered administration that stresses transparency in administration and the Citizen's Charter for all service institutions. According to the Service Conduct Rules established in 2000, it is mandatory for the members of Central and All India Services to be responsive to the common man. The following reform areas are included: (1) developing effective and transparent systems of governance; (2) ensuring integrity in civil services; (3) promoting a code of conduct that is in line with the existing relevant international standards; (4) regular, training of officials to ensure proper understanding of their responsibilities and ethical roles governing their activities; and (5) making civil services more professional and competent. The Anti-Corruption Act of 1986 also substantiated the other efforts taken by the government to combat corruption. The important amendments enacted after independence in the Act in the years 1950, 1958, 1961, 1971, 1988, 1993, and 2000 certainly validate the seriousness of the Indian government to tackle the issue of ethics among government officials.

More recently, the Right to Information Act of 2005 (RTI) provides guidelines for the political regime to ensure access to information by citizens from the public authority to promote transparency and accountability. It emphasizes that democracy requires informed citizenry and transparency of information, which is vital to its functioning and is a means of holding government and instrumentalities accountable to the governed. There is a change of the mindset required from concealing information to sharing information. At the same time, this has also made civil servants more accountable, committed, and performance oriented.

The institutions responsible for controlling the conduct of civil servants in performing their duties as servants for the public have a strong legacy. Constitutional Articles 309 to 311 are related to the disciplinary procedure for civil servants and dictate the imposition of penalties according to violation of the law by the civil servants. The impositions are categorized as minor and major punishments. Apart from this, there is also a system of writing Confidential Reports, which present impartial evaluations of the performances of the subordinates. If cases of inefficiency and abuse are reported in the Confidential Report, it could also lead to the subordinates' demotion, detainment, suspension, or even termination.

Lokayukta and the Lokpal are important institutions to check the misuse of the enormous power granted to approximately 8 million civil servants in India, There are independent agencies, such as the Central Bureau of Investigation, the Central Vigilance Commission, and the Anti-Corruption Department, to maintain the integrity of the officers and officials.

Administrative solutions could be many, but they require policy leverage to translate the solutions into action. The Indian government through democratic institutions has been enacting legislation, thus creating an ambience for effective policy-making since independence. Hence, it will be pertinent to look at recent policy perspectives initiated by the government to uphold public service ethics.

14.2 Policy Initiatives: Role of CVC

Central Vigilance Commission (CVC) is a nodal apex Indian governmental body created in 1964 on the recommendations of the Santhanam committee to address the malaise of corrupt practices in government, civil services and public sector undertakings. CVC is an autonomous body, charged with monitoring and vigilance activity under the Central Government of India, advising various authorities in Central Government organizations in planning, executing, reviewing and reforming their vigilance work.

The Chief Vigilance Officers are extended hands of the CVC to implement the guidelines of government and CVC to ensure transparency, accountability, equity and integrity in functioning of departmental organizations and Central Government PSU's

A major initiative was taken by the Central Vigilance Commission towards improving Vigilance administration by leveraging technology vide circular dated 22nd November 2006 through which it has been emphasized that compliance be made by all Govt, departments/organizations/agencies over which the commission has jurisdiction with regard to providing complete information on their websites regarding the laws, rules and procedures governing the issue of licenses, permissions, clearances, etc., and also adhere to good governance through e-governance by implementing e-payments, e-billing, e-procurement and reverse auction, e-auction, up loading of contract documents as well as award details, vendor registration for tracking of their bill status & online Inspection Management System, etc.

The RTI of 2005 has given a much needed impetus to rebuild the public trust. It has also been instrumental in curbing corruption, which has been an issue of great concern for the government. In this light, the Indian government responded by structuring necessary institutions. The government constituted the Central Information Commission (CIC) with a chief information commissioner and four information commissioners. E-technology has facilitated a more transparent mechanism, and all decisions of CIC are being posted on the web site (http://cic.gov.in). The states have also constituted State Information Commissions with state chief information commissioners as the ultimate authority in the respective states. This has been instrumental in dealing with the systemic malaise of corruption because the Indian system is yet to respond to the call for a culture of openness. Until recent times, the culture of secrecy was more prevalent in the domain of public services. The Second Administrative Reforms Commission has made very important recommendations pertaining to effective implementation of this act. For instance, it has recommended that the National Coordination Committee be set up under the chairmanship of the chief information commissioner with the nodal Union Ministry, the state information commissioners, and representatives of states as members. Another fundamental recommendation includes provisions of applying it to the non-governmental bodies. Digitalization is preferred to expedite the quick disposal of cases. The growing number of applicants is a positive indication in the direction of applying the concept of good governance. This is an important intervention to ensure directly the accountability of each individual civil servant in delivering the public services.

The Information Technology Act of 2000 aims to provide the legal infrastructure for e-commerce in India and would have a major effect for e-businesses and the new economy in India. It was amended by the Information Technology (Amendment) Act of 2008. The enactment of this act is now changing the mode of governance from manual to digital, although there still are areas where this makeover is not complete. E-governance is facilitated through this act. By and large, all departments have been computerized, and government has taken the extra, initiative to promote web-based administration. As a result, in the coming years, a more transparent and ethical- based governance might emerge. There are several examples in which information technology has been used to detect and curb corrupt practices. The most notable is the Bhoomi (land) project in the southern state of Karnataka. Before digitization, farmers in Karnataka had to depend on village accountants (VAs) to manage their land records. The VAs abused their powers and were often unavailable when the farmers needed their services. Farmers had to wait anywhere between 3 and 30 days and pay bribes ranging from Rs. 100 to Rs. 2,500 to obtain certificates for getting loans, pension verification, and so on. Under the Bhoomi project, the Government of Karnataka set up kiosks that automated 20 million land records, allowing the farmers to access their documents within a time bound period by a small fee of 15.

The role of civil society has surfaced more prominently in the last couple of years. Citizen-voices are now being heard, and many forums have come together to deprecate the corrupt practices. The decade of the 1990s witnessed civil society initiatives to improve governance. It would be pertinent to refer to movements, such as the *Report Card Survey of Public Affairs Centre, Bangalore;* Jan Sunwai *by* Majdoor Kisan Shakti Sangathan, *Rajasthan;* Parivartan, *a programme for the safety of women and children by the New Delhi Police; the Campaign for Electoral Reforms and Citizens' Charter by Lok Satta, Hyderabad; and the Campaign for Effective Municipal Decentralization by CIVIC, Bangalore. Most recently the campaign India Against Corruption* was mobilizing the citizens to come forward to register their vote to fight against corruption. This phenomenon of collective voices in the coming years may have a cleansing effect on the conduct of public servants. The recent phenomena that moved everyone to come together to fight corruption initiated by Anna Hazare on April 4, 2011, has opened new vistas of change.

The Second Administrative Reforms Commission constituted under the chairmanship of M. Veerappa Molly in 2005 laid down the roadmap of reinvigorating the civil services in India. Among others, the commission was asked to make recommendations on ethics in governance and steps to ensure the effective administration at the state, district, and local levels. In the Fourth Report submitted by this commission on "Ethics in Governance", the commission has laid down the duties and responsibilities with structured and interlocking accountability in which the government servant can be held accountable for his or her actions.

At various levels of government functionaries, there are Departmental Enquiry Committees, which are set up by the respective departments to look into the complaints received against civil servants. There is also a system of judicial review, although it is not predominantly applied in the Indian system, to check the accountability of civil servants; however, the increasing judicial activism in recent times has forced the government to re-examine some of the issues of integrity that have been of wider interest. Furthermore, from the perspective of providing protection to the civil servants against any intentional damage to their prestige, administrative tribunals provide the, legal remedy to control such injustices done to any civil servant.

14.3 Grievance Redressal Mechanisms (Post-1990s)

The concept of Citizen's Charter has been introduced to address and resolve the problems encountered by citizens while receiving a public service. A Citizen's Charter helps in ensuring that public agencies are providing services to the citizens and are maintaining the minimum standards and norms of service quality. The main objective behind introducing Citizen's Charter is to ensure transparency in all government dealings that helps build trust and confidence towards the administration. There is a strong need to introduce legislation to ensure time-bound delivery of public services and a grievance redressal structure that can take care of complaints regarding public service delivery.

The first directive of the Central Government to incorporate Citizen's Charters across all Ministries/Departments was given in 1996. The DARPG took the responsibility of coordination, formulation and implementation of Citizen's Charters in all Ministries/ Departments. A website on Citizen's Charters has been developed and launched by the: DARPG to provide information to all Ministries/Departments. Regional seminars have been conducted that provide a platform for sharing of experiences in formulation and implementation of Citizen's Charters at the State and National level.

The focus on citizen centricity has led the GOI to develop a new mechanism for public service delivery called Sevottam. The word Sevottam has been derived from two Hindi words —"seva" and "uttam" that mean "Service Excellence". Sevottam is a quality management frame work for public service delivery organizations to systematically assess and improve the quality of services delivered to the citizens.

There are seven basic tenets that each Ministry/Department has to follow in order to implement the Sevottam model:

- Define service and identify clients
- Set standards and norms for each service
- Develop capability to meet the standards
- Perform to achieve the standards
- Monitor performance against the set standards
- Evaluate impact through an independent mechanism
- Continuous improvement based on monitoring and evaluation

The Sevottam framework was created by the DARPG in 2005. The Sevottam framework includes identification of services to be delivered by setting service norms according to the expectations of citizens and deciding the metrics for quality management and improvement using processes such as business process redesign and information technology. The DARPG has also formed a dedicated team for initiating the process of implementation of Sevottam in all Departments of the GOI. The GOI has taken several initiatives to facilitate timely redressal of public grievances. In 1988, the Directorate of Public Grievances was set up as a part of the Cabinet Secretariat for handling grievances pertaining to 20 Central Government Organizations. The DARPG was entrusted with the responsibility for formulating the policy and the guidelines for institutionalizing public grievances redressal mechanisms in India. According to these guidelines, all Ministries/Departments are required to put in place internal machinery for redressing grievances and designate a Director of Grievance in every office. It has also been recommended that the Departments should acknowledge each grievance within three days of receipt and should fix the timeframe for its disposal.

The DARPG along with the National Informatics Centre (NIC) has also developed an online portal for the citizens to post public grievances, The public grievances portal developed by the DARPG and NIC has two interfaces, a Public Grievances Lodging and Monitoring system for citizens to post complaints and a Centralized Public Grievances Redress and Monitoring System (CPGRAMS) for Ministries / Departments and other organizations to monitor and to address grievances.

CPGRAMS is an online web-enabled system developed with an objective of speedy redress and effective monitoring of grievances by Ministries/Departments of the Central Government.

- CPGRAMS facilitates the online lodging of grievances by citizens to the concerned Ministries/Departments/Organizations which can be linked to their official web site.
- CPGRAMS also facilitates the Ministries/Departments/ Organizations to enter the grievances received locally in their offices and to forward the same to their subordinate organizations online for ultimate redress.
- CPGRAMS helps in producing monitoring reports and queries as per the requirement of Ministries/Departments/Organizations for effective monitoring for pending grievances.
- CPGRAMS also helps generate automated letters such as acknowledgement and final reply letters, for official correspondence with complainants.

In 2009, about 54% of the grievances received were disposed. This number rose significantly to 92% in 2010, when out of a total of 1,26,890 receipts, 115414 were disposed.

14.4 The Public Interest Disclosure and Protection to Persons Making the Disclosures Act, 2013

The GOI has undertaken a variety of initiatives to instill transparency and accountability. To ensure that these initiatives are not misused and serve the desired purpose, the Government introduced the Public Interest Disclosure and Protection to Person's Making the Disclosures Act in 2013. The Act seeks to establish a mechanism to receive complaints relating to disclosure on any allegation of corruption against any public servant and to inquire into such disclosure and to provide adequate safeguards against victimization of the person making such complaint.

The Act was renamed as the Whistle blowers Protection Act in 2013. The Bill protects whistle blowers and states that any person can make a public interest disclosure before the Competent Authority (Central Vigilance Commission or any other authority as notified by the Central Government, the State Vigilance Commissioner, any officer of a State Government or any other authority as notified by the State Government). The Competent Authority, on receipt of a public interest disclosure makes an inquiry. In case the Competent Authority is of the opinion that the disclosure requires to be investigated, it shall seek comments, or explanation or a report from the Head of the Department of the organization. While seeking explanations, the Competent Authority and the Head of the Department of the organization concerned shall not reveal the identity of the complainant or the public servants The Central Government needs to ensure that no person or a public servant who has made a disclosure under this Act is victimized by initiation of any proceedings.

The Act lays down penalties for different offences. Any organization or official, who knowingly does not submit or submits incomplete information to the Competent Authority, shall be fined up to Rs. 250 for each day till the report is submitted. The total penalty amount however cannot exceed Rs. 50,000. Any person or officer who reveals the identity of the complainant will be penalized through imprisonment for a term which, may extend up to three years-and a fine which may extend, up to Rs. 50,000. The Act also prescribes penalties for making false complaints through imprisonment for up to two years and a maximum fine of Rs. 30,000.

14.5 The Lokpal and Lokayuktas (L&L) Act 2014

This Act was passed by the Parliament in December 2013, and got Presidential assent on 1 January 2014. It aims to prevent and control corruption through the setting up of an independent and empowered body at the central level, called the Lokpal that would receive complaints relating to corruption against most categories of public servants and ensure that these are properly investigated and, where warranted, effectively prosecuted. All this is envisaged in a time-bound manner, with the help of special courts set up for the purpose. The Act also makes it incumbent for each state to pass, within a year, a law setting up a body of Lokayuktas at the state level, but leaves it to the states to work out the details.

The legislation envisages that the Lokpal would receive complaints of corruption against the PM, ministers, Member of Parliament (MPs), officers of the Central Government (all levels), and against functionaries of any entity that is wholly or partly financed by the government with an annual income above a specified limit, and also, all entities receiving donations from foreign sources in excess of 10 lakh per year.

The Act states that on receipt of a complaint against any public servant, except for officers from groups A, B, C or D, the Lokpal will order a preliminary inquiry against the public servant. The inquiry may be done by its own inquiry wing, provided for this purpose, or the Lokpal may direct the Central Bureau of Investigation (CBI) or any other agency to do the preliminary inquiry. The preliminary inquiry has to ordinarily be completed within 60 to 90 days and a report has to be submitted to the Lokpal. For complaints against public servants belonging to group A, B, C or D, the Lokpal will refer the complaints to the Central Vigilance Commission (CVC) for preliminary inquiry. After the completion of preliminary inquiry, the CVC will submit its report to the Lokpal in respect of public servants belonging to group A or B, while in cases of public servants belonging to group C or D, the CVC will proceed in accordance with the provisions of the CVC Act, 2003.

Upon receiving the report of the preliminary inquiry (for groups A and B officers and other public servants, including ministers and MPs), the Lokpal will give an opportunity to the public servant to be heard, and if it decides that there exists a prima facie case, then it can order an investigation by the CBI (or any other agency) or order departmental proceedings against the concerned public servant. The investigation has to be ordinarily completed within six months, extendable to one year, and a report has to be submitted to the appropriate court having jurisdiction, with a copy being sent to the Lokpal.

Every investigation report must be considered by a bench consisting of not less than three members of the Lokpal and, after obtaining the comments of the public functionary, the Lokpal may grant sanction to its own prosecution wing, or to the investigating agency, to file a charge sheet before the special court, or direct filing of a closure report, or direct initiation of departmental proceedings against the concerned public servant.

Apart from providing the Lokpal with its own prosecution wing, the bill provides for amending the Delhi Special Police Establishment Act, 1946 to set up a Directorate of Prosecution headed by a Director of Prosecution under the overall control of the CBI director.

For the purpose of deciding cases arising out of the Prevention of Corruption Act (PCA), 1988, the bill provides for setting up of special courts. All trials in the special courts have to be ordinarily completed within one year, extendable to two years for reasons to be recorded in writing.

Lokpal and Lokayuktas Act of 2014 can be said to be a positive step forward. If the Lokpal and Lokayuktas Act is properly implemented, it should provide a significant deterrent to corruption, especially the high level of corruption at the higher levels of government that seem to have become widespread in India. Of course, in order to achieve that, it has to be ensured that the right people are appointed to the post of Lokpal. Also, the people and the agencies assisting them are provided adequate and appropriate human and financial resources, that there is political will, especially among the top political and bureaucratic leadership, to make this institution succeed.

The Lokpal, set to be headed by Justice Pinaki Chandra Ghose, will have two former high court chief justices – Justices Abilasha Kumari and Dilip Babasaheb Bhosale – as judicial members along with three non-judicial members.

It is important to address a crucial question; Is the office of the Lokpal independent of the government and others whom it is mandated to scrutinise?

This question is important because the government, regard-less of the party in power, has a tendency to interfere in autonomous institutions that are set up to ensure transparency and accountability of governance. For example, the Central Bureau of Investigation (CBI) has long borne the brunt of such meddling, so much so that it has been called a "caged parrot". In recent times, the Reserve Bank of India has also faced similar challenges.

There are four aspects that need to be considered while examining the issue of independence. First, the 2013 Lokpal Act provides for a selection committee comprising the Prime Minister, the Lok Sabha Speaker, The Leader of Opposition (LoP), the Chief Justice of India and an eminent jurist. This is supposed to be baipartisan in representation to ensure that the Lokpal is not beholden to any particular group and can function independently. However, in the absence of a formal LoP being declared (as is the present case), the panel has had no representation from the Opposition. In 2014, amendments to address this issue were introduced, and subsequently approved by the Parliamentary Standing Committee. However, they have not been passed in Parliament. This must be rectified. Second, there is a lack of clarity on the interplay and hierarchy between the Lokpal, the CBI and the Central Vigilance Commission (CVC).

14.6 Other Measures

The CAG of India is the supreme audit authority in the country. Accountants Generals (AGs) offices can be found in all state headquarters (AGs are independent of State Governments and are accountable only to the CAG.) Public expenses management reportedly suffers from poor monitoring, poor targeting and corrupt practices. The Public Procurement Bill 2012 gives CAG power to audit the accounts of public-private partnership (PPP) projects, which is seen as the government' s effort to improve compliance between the UNCAC (United Nations Convention against Corruption) and domestic laws in India.

Right to public services legislation: Right to Public Services legislation, which has been enacted in 20 states of India, guarantees time bound delivery of services for various public services rendered by the Government to citizens and provides mechanisms for punishing the errant public servant who is deficient in providing the service stipulated under the statute. Right to Service legislation is meant to reduce corruption among the government officials and to increase transparency and public accountability.

India is a signatory to the United Nations Convention against Corruption (UNCAC) since 2005 (ratified 2011). The Convention covers a wide range of acts of corruption and also proposes certain preventive policies.

The Department of Personnel & Training (DOPT): Based on the above UNCAC resolution, the nodal Ministry dealing with anti-corruption issues has formed a committee which in consultation with ASSOCHAM, FICCI, SEBI, PSU, CVOs, etc., and all the stakeholders will attempt to bring a culture of transparency and integrity particularly in the private sector to ensure confidence among the people/ common man.

A committee headed by the Chairman of Central Board of Direct Taxes (CBDT) has been constituted to examine ways to strengthen laws to curb generation of black money in India, its illegal transfer abroad and its recovery.

The Companies Act, 2013 contains certain provisions to regulate fraud by corporations, including increased penalties for frauds, giving more powers to Serious Frauds Investigation Office, mandatory responsibility to auditors to reveal fraud and increased responsibilities to independent directors. The Companies Act, 2013 also provides for mandatory vigil mechanisms which allow directors and employees to report concerns and whistleblower protection mechanisms for every listed company and other companies which accept deposits from the public or have taken loans more than 50 crore rupees from banks and financial institutions.

Conclusion

Corruption is a social malaise and cannot be fought by the government alone. Integrity in governance can never be ensured by punitive action alone. That is a slow process of change with no radical transformation guaranteed. The fight against corruption has to become a mass movement, spearheaded by the people who are affected most. The culture of integrity has to come from within, from an ethics internalized by education of every citizen who constitute the society and the nation.

Looking at the multiple dimensions of corruption, the challenge lies in turning corruption from a low-risk high-return activity to a high-risk low-return enterprise. Tackling the inadequacies of the legal machinery, reform of the supply side of delivery, civil service reform, procurement reform, independent anti-corruption bodies and strengthening the demand side of governance are among some of the suggested remedies.

Suggested Readings

Arora, R. K. and T. Saxena (eds.), *Excellence, Ethics and the World of Management*, Jaipur, Alekh Publishers, 2009.

Dwivedi, O. P., "Ethics and Value of Public Responsibility and Accountability/' *International Review of Administrative Sciences*, 51, (1985): pp. 64-6.

Godbole, M.G., *Good Governance Never on India's Radar*, New Delhi, Rupa Publishing House, 2014.

Guhan, S. and P. Samuel *Corruption in India: Agenda for Action*. New Delhi, Vision Books, 1997.

Johri, Amrita, Anjali Bharadwaj and Shekhar Singh "*The Lokpal Act of 2014: An Assessment*," EPW, XLIX no. 5. (2014): pp. 10-13.

Pathak, R. and R. Prasad, *Role of e-governance in Tackling Corruption: The Indian Experience. Paper presented at the Network of Asia-Pacific Schools and Institutes of Public Administration and Governance (NAPSIPAG)* Annual Conference, 5-7 December 2005. Beijing, PRC, 2005.

Public Service in India: A Country Profile, DARPG, GOI, 2012.

Quah, J. S. T., "*Curbing Corruption in India: An Impossible Dream*?" Asian Journal of Political Science, 16 no. 3 (2008): pp. 240-59.

Samuel, Paul (ed.), *Fighting Corruption: The Way Forward*, New Delhi, Academic Foundation, 2013.

Second ARC, Right to Information: Master Key to Good Governance. Section ARC, GOI, 2006.

__ *Citizen Centric Administration: The Heart of Governance*. Second ARC, GOI, 2009.

Singh, Sujata, *Reforms in Governance: Six Decades of Administrative Reforms*, New Delhi, Indian Institute of Public Administration, 2009.

ooo

Chapter Fifteen

Ethics in Governance

Introduction

Ethics in governance refers to generally accepted moral principles and rules of conduct informing both the legal framework and institutions of governance, which determine the nature of operational values to be practiced by the politico-administrative regime in any country.

The importance of practicing ethics and morality in public life has always been recognized as a value addition in the lives of statesman and civil servants as public figures. What has added special significance to the ethical conduct of civil servants in public dealings is the increasing realization that since power corrupts, the discretionary powers of administrators need to be watched and guarded. Accountability of public powers is an ethical imperative in democracies. Ethics can be considered a form of self-accountability or an inner check on their own conduct by public administrators.

Administrative ethics is important because an administration functions in a political environment and administrators cannot be entirely divorced from politics. The essence of ethical governance in today's times is the practice of good governance. Bringing in transparency and accountability have been the major ethical standards that are demanded from good governance.

In India after Independence, administration could no longer be minimalist or regulatory akin to the colonial era of Indian history. Social change was aspired through a political regime committed to a welfare state ideology which was to be worked through the political machinery of a democratic, parliamentary and federal state system. India consciously and deliberately opted for development administration as its principal tool to bring about the goals of nation-building and socio-economic progress. All this had to be accomplished in the changed political milieu where the public administrators had to gradually transit from being the "masters'" of the people to being their "servants".

India, after Independence, continued with the parliamentary model, which the British had introduced during the Colonial rule. This model is based on the Weberian concept of 'neutral competence' which India inherited with the ICS tradition of a neutral bureaucracy. Max Weber espouses a model of bureaucracy which is based on merit, the rule of law and is therefore the most rational way of exercising authority over others. Bureaucratic behavior is neutral apolitical and unbiased in their treatment of clientele.

Over the years in post-Independent India the civil service, finds itself in a deep crisis of values. Even the best in the administrative field may fall prey to corrupt practices. Fortunately, there have been civil servants who have had the courage to stand up and fight for the values they cherish and the principles they uphold, though they are a vanishing tribe today. Even more dangerous is the attempt to alter social perceptions and values and to pose these as the new social paradigms of a modernizing era. Ethical non-accountability and insensitiveness have become all-pervading in the administrative culture of contemporary India. That this factor has started affecting the very core of democratic governance is well-illustrated in the functioning of the administrative processes where petty corruption affects the citizens routinely in their daily lives.

The credibility and capability of a government in power largely depends on the quality of the public service both in matters of policy-making and policy implementation.

15.1 Need for Professional Code

Every profession needs to develop its working code of ethics. Such a code presupposes the prevalence of an inherent sense of pride and strong intra-departmental bonding, a wide sharing of a common set of values, a confidence that the profession has a capacity for self-regulation to ensure technical proficiency, moral integrity, discipline and a fair amount of autonomy.

Apart from the issues outlined above, recent efforts for administrative reforms in India have also been influenced by international experience in the field of public administration and civil service reforms such as:

- Changing role of government from the regulator to the facilitator, with an emphasis on refocusing on the needs of citizens.
- The systematic identification of regulatory constraints to the timely delivery of services to the people, followed by efforts for simplified procedures and decentralization to cut through the multiple layers of governance and ensure efficient service delivery to the doorstep of citizens.
- Customer orientation and emphasis on quality and standards of service, as symbolized in Citizen Charters and Service Guarantee Acts.
- Reviewing administrative structures, by distinguishing between the core responsibilities from policy and the managerial aspects of implementation.
- Firm steps to control corruption through a variety of measures including establishment of independent agencies, to pursue preventive vigilance and exemplary prosecution.

Corruption is a recurrent evil in all societies. It is, therefore, common to all countries, irrespective of their stages of development. However its nature, volume, and dimensions differ largely from state to state. To explain corruption as a global phenomenon may offer some consolation but no solution. A plethora of panacea has been prescribed in many quarters but none have been effective in completely weeding out corruption. The ultimate remedy is generating ethical values which can be internalized by the bulk of government employees at the workplace.

Our recent economic reforms provide a new context to the subject of values and morality in our public life. China which embarked on the course of liberalization in 1978 has brought in spectacular growth but it has destroyed the Spartan values of Maoist communism and is said to be in the grip of rampant corruption. In Russia, too, in the wake of the collapse of communism and disintegration of the erstwhile Soviet Union in 1991 there was an upsurge in crime, violence, theft and murder that Moscow came to be known as the crime capital of the world. In India, the post-liberalization period has been marked by innumerable scams right under the nose of the Reserve Bank of India.

In the West the discussion about the role of ethics, values, morality and religion in the realm of governance has been carefully by-passed. It was thought that in public interest statecraft had to be kept out of party politics, patronage, and unethical behavior. Ethics and morality were seen as subjective factors, mostly emotive, and in the personal realm. The Weberian model of bureaucracy required neutral and unbiased conduct in the application of rules and regulations in public affairs and governance.

There is no doubt that the intention to keep politics and religion out of administration was wise in order to bring equality of treatment and to control patronage and corruption; but the end product was that it withered out even morality and ethics from the domain of governance. The movement led by the US scholars, in effect, overlooked the fact that even their own democratic society was founded on the principle of human dignity and societal values which were drawn from various moral principles of Christianity. Even such fundamental rights as equality of treatment, justice for all, the rule of law, and even political rights —all derived their source from societal ethics, morality, and religious precepts.

Then, what should good governance be based on?

15.2 Ethics and Public Service

Its importance can be gleaned from the fact that it prevents corruption, creates the atmosphere for delivering efficient and effective public services, helps to avoid and control situations of conflict of interests, assists in managing the proper use of government resources, and brings transparency in procurements, awarding contracts and selecting consultants. As we all know that in the world today, corruption is the biggest impediment to good governance and protection of the common good; its prevention is more important than its prosecution because prosecutions are delayed for years while preventive measures reduce the need to use drastic measures, disciplinary action, prosecution and punishment.

The effects of corruption are not only corrosive in any organization, but are also the main obstacle for the rule of law, fairness, national development, and weakens the perception of legitimacy and trust in the political and governing process. We should also realize that major problems of corruption and mismanagement generally start at the higher level simply because it is there that stakes are high. That is why ethical leadership is crucial otherwise its absence breeds cynicism and generates tolerance of hypocrisy, greed, and self-indulgence in the lower levels of the bureaucratic hierarchy.

Although ethical indolence in public offices may result partly from the absence of deterrence, it is also partly from the increasing tendency to moral relativism or the decline in moral teaching and training. In order to improve ethical behaviour in government organizations, it is necessary to strengthen the feeling among public servants that it is their professional duty and responsibility to serve the public, above all else. No matter how many laws are passed, codes of conduct promulgated, and threats of disciplinary action made, these cannot force public officials to behave ethically. Instead, a better option is to inculcate in them the sense of public duty, patriotism, professionalism and reinforcing the idea that the man at the top must lead by example.

Thus, ethical governance requires public officials who adhere to the principle of serving others by setting a high standard of moral conduct and by considering their jobs as a vocation. The objective is to create an atmosphere that motivates officials to respond to the challenges of their job by adhering to the notion of duty and service to the nation, as well as taking responsibility for public welfare. Without resurrecting and reinforcing some articles of faith (drawn from the social values, cultural traditions, and spiritual ideals), the system of governance is never going to possess moral authority; and ultimately, we shall end by making all kinds of anti- corruption laws and yet tolerate a high level of corruption.

To be first and foremost servants of the public with a sense of duty is the most essential virtue for public servants. This concept can be viewed from two dimensions: the religious and the secular. Historically, religion has played a crucial role in upholding the virtue of social and public service because all religions exhort their people that serving others is serving humanity. One can look up to Buddha, Christ, and Gandhi as examples of such individuals who devoted their lives to the principles of individual self-sacrifice, compassion and justice, while striving for the highest moral duty of serving others. However, by the 1970s, many countries gave employees the right to strike and bargain collectively, which resulted in the acquisition of political power by the staff unions. Unions brought to the fore the concept of "job" in place of "service", by discarding the concept of duty to serve. More recently, in 2005, the International Institute of Administrative Sciences (Brussels) brought out a report on administering global governance, The World We Could Win, which listed the following major public service values: access to justice, adherence to due process and to the rule of law, respect for human rights, respect for democratic values, care for the need of the poorest and vulnerable groups, tolerance, diversity, protection of the environment, sustainability of outcomes, and public service professionalism.

On the other hand, the concept of ethical governance requires public servants to act according to certain principles, such as: (a) responsibility cannot be disclaimed because disclaimers are not self-validating; (b) responsibility cannot be evaded by diluting the gravity of their actions or by pleading special or trying circumstances, or personal events which forced them to disown the consequences of their actions; (c) responsibility cannot be deflected by stating that someone else should have taken the action; and (d) command responsibility never disappears which means that once an order has been issued, the responsibility will rest with the officer although the person might have moved to another position.

Thus, the critical issue before us is: how can we rebalance the relationship between Parliament and government so that the chain of accountability is restored by undertaking certain specific actions such as controlling partisan political involvement in the administration of public programmes, improving sufficient oversight by senior public servants, restricting the avoidance of compliance with established policies and legislation, and ensuring that ministers and senior officials are duty-bound to acknowledge the responsibility for any mismanagement that might occur? Without some specific measures of deterrence such as a higher level of professionalism, building character, and enhancing personal ethics/ spirituality, good governance may remain a distant Utopia.

15.3 Public Service as a Vocation:

It draws on the doctrine of vocation (or calling) and the concept of service, relates to the sense of mission which a public official is supposed to undertake, to serve the public, perform duties and fulfill obligations. It also includes the concept of "paying back" a debt to the society which an individual may have born or lived in. Thus the concept stresses the "service" dimension in government employment. It involves a notion of duty and service to members of the public, as well as undertaking the responsibility for their welfare; and it means that public servants "must always be thinking ahead of the community, on behalf of the community". However, the concept of public service vocation should not be equated with any specific political ideology or even religion because it is reconciled with the notion of a secularism of public morality.

Both the duty to serve and responsibility to care ought to be seen as integral parts of public service vocation because these two include not only the required ethical behaviour (accomplishment of a job entrusted in a most professional manner), but also exhibit positive attributes such as trust, fairness, conduct beyond the call of duty. Hence, standards and requisites of performance should include the limitation on the power of a public servant as well as an equal emphasis on the positive side of what he or she "ought to do".

15.4 The Ethical Approach to Public Administration

A training course on public service ethics and responsibility should be made compulsory for all administrators. When designing such a course, it should be approached from three dimensions: (a) classical, (b) legal, and (c) cultural. The classical approach emphasizes drawing from the philosophical and religious traditions of a nation to internalize some universal values. The legal approach focuses on laws, rules and regulations, and legal constraints on individuals to regulate their administrative power and authority. The cultural approach aims at sensitizing public servants to the social need to act as guardians of the state so that its resources are appropriately used and carefully protected; for this they might act somewhat as Plato's philosopher kings. For ethical public servants, one important challenge they are facing now is how to control if not reverse the tide of an 'ethical deficit' in many nations. The term 'ethical deficit' means that the public in those nations would not hesitate to pay an "extra sum" in order to receive service that it deserves from an official; and to avoid unnecessary delay in receiving the service, being unable to fight excessive and dilatory bureaucratic rules and procedures.

All these factors (systematic corruption, weak moral leadership, and increase in moral relativism) have caused irreparable ethical deficit in many professions including the public service. Ethical conduct begins with ethical leadership, at all levels of the organization. What leaders say and do influences all employees, and when their decisions are based on ethical principles, those values become 'living values' of the organization as their actions encourage the creation of transparency and accountability. Eventually, such values also become the shared values of all.

15.5 Restoring the Oversight Responsibility of Governance and Accountability to Parliament

Despite the complexity of modern government, ministerial responsibility previously served as a Viable central pillar of parliamentary democracy holding the executive accountable for the direction and management of government programmes and policies. The New Public Management paradigm dominated by its protagonists forced the executive to believe in adopting the private sector techniques to bring in profit in governance performance rather than on responsible and ethical governance; thereby no effort was made to restore Parliament's capacity to oversee government's direction of the public service and its programmes. A seminal way in which accountability should be restored in a government is through strong, ethical leadership and changing the culture of administration such that the concept of the duty to serve the public is fully internalized by the public servants.

15.6 The Issue of Corruption

Amorality has vitiated the public service ethos in India. It is difficult to comprehend that a country that had a plethora of ancient discourses on maintaining the highest standards of morality in the public and private lives of rulers have accepted nonconformity to morality in its functioning.

Most of the demands for bribery are for timely delivery of services, while the remaining are made to protect the self or protect business interests. Paradoxically, most bribes are given as a token for rendering services that otherwise are mandatory for officials to perform. This closely relates to the sharp erosion of ethics, to the extent that even the rendering of the regular services that constitute the working domain of most of the public servants have been severely affected by corruption. This has led to the complete lack of public trust in the governmental system, a situation that is becoming graver with time.

The decline of public ethics is substantiated by the fact that 91% of bribes are accepted by government officials. This clearly depicts the unaccountability of public officials in general and further predisposes them to immoral acts with routine insensitivity.

To strategize efforts to deal with pervasive corruption in the Indian system of governance, there is a need to work out a complete strategy at every level of its functioning. This involves the refurbished role of educational institutions in sticking to the norms of morality, the social call for negating any act of taking and giving bribes of which a pattern is already depicted, introducing a speedy castigatory process of imposing a severe penalty if found guilty of wrongdoing, bringing out electoral reforms that would set the platform for facilitating the election of people with impeccable integrity, and inoculating values among the public servants.

The year 2011 will go down as a memorable period in Indian history because the massive all India campaign against corruption has sown the seeds of a need for an ethics-laden administration. The mass mobilization by Anna Hazare finally led to the passage of the Lokpal bill to eradicate corruption from all levels of administration. Despite disagreements concise steps to explore the latent dimensions of eliminating corruption to restore an ethics-centered administration are required. Some ongoing efforts are as follows:

- The culture of transparency in public dealings and providing information could not take its roots even after the enactment of a strong legislation (RTI of 2005). There are two important prerequisites to instill a change of mindset in civil servants at large: (1) the information about misuse or abuse of authority by any public servant along with the punitive action against such individuals must be put on a Web site, and (2) a special "training" in behavior modification for public servants to adapt to the present scenario must be provided by the public institutions.
- Democracy that has been the strength of the Indian system must be followed in principle and spirit. Citizens are the epicenter of any democracy; administration therefore must be citizen centric. The elected representatives must be more sensitive to public demands, and this is of national importance. The technological tools have made it easy for any public institution to connect to people to find out public opinion. It is perceived that the absence of such a mechanism has resulted in ego wars between governments and the governed. The role of a civil society should be better recognized in a democracy.

The foundations of ethical practices can be built-in only by reforming the educational sector. In this respect, the GOI has enacted the Right of Children to Free and Compulsory Education Act of 2009, which came into force on April 1, 2010, to ensure quality education for children. Among many important decisions, it has notified respective State Governments to establish State Commissions for Protection of Child Rights, which shall constitute Right to Education Protection Authority to perform the functions specified in the act. With the advent of this act, education has become the fundamental right of every child between ages 6 and 14 years. Interestingly, India has become one of the 135 countries to provide free school education. Several other provisions regarding improvement of school infrastructure, teacher-student ratio, and faculty have been made in the Act. India has suffered on the grounds of not making education accessible to every child, and this has resulted in many anomalies in society that eventually also eroded values. It is hoped that this reform in the school sector will now bring about grassroots change.

The government has decided to draft a Judicial Accountability Bill 2012 to revamp the Indian judiciary. The improvement of the system of justice delivery will recommence the faith in non-partisan action by delineating politics from its ambit. With this, many structural changes will also be introduced and efficacy will inevitably improve by sticking to the e-tools. Web connectivity has already been introduced in the judiciary, but with this change it will become more intensive and penetrative. A proposal has recently been put forth to introduce an Indian Judicial Services (IJS) a similar structure as that of the Indian Administrative

Service (IAS) with the aim of revamping the judicial system in the hope of attracting young talent.

The civil services should nurture India's spirit of harmony, tolerance, and respect for diversity; imbue integrity, professionalism, and dedication; facilitate impartial implementation of the rule of law; maintain political neutrality; further cost-effective and efficient services and a culture of continuous improvement; and enable citizens to organize and express their needs and compel public services to respond to them. The training curriculum focuses on the core to make civil servants aware of the entire system of administration and public welfare; on the behavioral aspects, it relates to the reorientation of mindsets of the civil servants to sensitize them to the problems of citizens. Last but not the least, field training is also given to the incumbents so that they can have practical exposure. The Second Administrative Reforms Commission in 2005 also emphasized integrated training and refocused on the importance of public administration in understanding administrative dynamics. Major training techniques for ethics include sensitivity-T-group training (most popular) in organizational behavior and laboratory group training for refreshers. Audiovisual techniques using CDs designed by management gurus are the latest trend in the training curricula of civil servants.

It is heartening, therefore, to note that the Draft Civil Services Bill, 2009, proposes a set of values for the civil services and civil servants. They are:

1. democratic values;
2. patriotism, upholding national pride and allegiance to the Constitution and the law of the nation;
3. sovereignty;
4. accountability, objectivity, impartiality, honesty, diligence, courtesy, transparency, compassion, courage, perseverance. self-discipline, loyalty, and faith;
5. spirit of service and self-sacrifice;
6. empathy towards weaker sections and respect for human rights;
7. absolute integrity; and
8. professionalism

The Draft Bill (2009), in Chapter IV, provides for the preparation of a Civil Services Code of Conduct and Ethics which shall contain provisions for imposing restrictions on civil servants/issuing directions on:

1. employment of near relatives of civil servants in companies or firms;
2. taking part in politics or elections;
3. connection with press or radio;
4. criticism of Government;
5. evidence before committees;
6. unauthorized communication of information;
7. subscriptions, gifts, dowry;

8. public demonstration in honour of civil servants;
9. private trade or employment;
10. investment, lending, and borrowing;
11. insolvency and habitual indebtedness;
12. movable, immovable, and valuable property;
13. observance of cultural norms;
14. restrictions regarding marriage; and
15. consumption of intoxicating drinks and drugs.

These are special obligations expected of civil servants and, therefore, it is necessary that civil service values should reflect them. Civil service values can be classified into the following four categories in terms of relationships and behaviours:

1. with the government, legislature, and political system;
2. with the community;
3. in the way the civil servants' work; and
4. in the workplace.

We need to recognize that the governmental system in India provides a model of accountability in which public interest is very clearly articulated. It is the government and the ministers who determine the public interest in terms of policies and programme priorities, and civil servants, within the requirement of the constitutional and legal framework, advise on and implement their decisions. Therefore, the civil service has a particular responsibility for the public interest in upholding the law and ensuring that proper procedures are followed.

The civil service needs to serve the community by ensuring that the entitlements and services provided to it under law and government policy are delivered effectively, fairly, courteously, and professionally. This means that civil servants should be professional and effective in the delivery of services. Responsiveness also means that while a civil servant cannot make exceptions in individual cases where these are not sanctioned by law, and while the civil servant must ensure equality of access for all citizens, he/she should try to be responsive as he/she administers entitlements or provides services and to avoid unnecessary rigidity.

Civil servants need to be scrupulous in the way they use the community's resources including money, goods and services, vehicles, office equipment, telecommunications, and information technology infrastructure. It is necessary that civil servants have the highest quality of and ethical standards in the way they work.

It is essential that the civil service law should describe expected values and standards of behavior in a statement for the civil servants in a clear and concise manner. The statement should become a part of the civil servant's terms and conditions of employment. In respect of breaches of values and provisions in the Civil Services Code of Conduct and Ethics, the Draft Civil Service Bill (2009) provides that the Controlling Authority and the Disciplinary Authority, as the case may be, should impose the following sanctions on a civil servant:

1. censure;
2. withholding of promotions;
3. recovery from pay of the whole or part of pecuniary loss caused to the Government;
4. withholding of increments;
5. reducing to lower time scale of pay, grade, or post;
6. compulsory retirement;
7. removal from service; and
8. dismissal from service.

The Bill also provides that the Civil Service Code of Conduct and Ethics should describe the procedure for determining the breach of the Code; the functions, powers, and limitations on the powers of these authorities; and the procedure for appeal. These provisions are adequate for dealing with breaches of values and the provisions in the Civil Services Code of Conduct and Ethics. In addition, it is suggested that the Civil Services Authorities should be given the responsibility of evaluating the extent to which the ministries/departments incorporate and uphold these values and principles, and the adequacy of systems and procedures to ensure compliance with the Civil Services Code of Conduct and Ethics.

15.7 Challenges for Ethical Governance

The ethical domain in public services faces some fundamental challenges from outside and within. The depletion of ethical values in recent decades is an increasing area of concern for the government. The insensitivity of the political system with regard to respecting the people's voice while drafting laws and their later implementation has further complicated the situation over the years. Most of the civil society movements (e.g. one led by Jayaprakash Narayan in the 1970s or the more recent Anna Hazare) have been highlighting the need to be sensitive to public needs and assertions. The kind of insensitivity shown by elected representatives on fundamental issues has given rise to a debate on what democracy truly represents. Therefore, the foremost challenge is to introduce mechanisms to get public feedback before the enactment of any law. Further, the dynamism is changing because of the difference in the pace of technological induction and the social transformation with which a system is responding.

Despite several civil service reforms, laws, and acts promoting ethics, the traditional bureaucratic mindset is yet to see a major transformation. The enactment of new acts in recent times in India, such as the RTI, the Right to Education Act, the Information and Technology Act, and now the Lokpal Act, may not lead to the anticipated change very quickly but certainly a beginning has been made.

The recent upsurge in the number of corruption episodes that were exposed in India has highlighted the need for internalizing a core set of values and ethics for public service. There are many ways of bridging the gap between administration and citizens, which causes which a trust deficit. However, the intentions of the government are clear and are supported by judicial activism; hence, India may soon look forward to evolving administrative procedures that are simple and easy to digitize, leading to more understandable policy designs and invariably invigorating ethics in public conduct. The young aspirants to civil services are more tolerant of the ethnicity of different sections of society, are more professional, and are ready to share information. This positive undercurrent that is far more visible in the present scenario will reshape the ethics of our public service. The guiding ethos for the evolving system of civil services should be reflected in the everlasting statement of Mahatma Gandhi, who said that politics without principles, wealth without work, commerce without morality, education without character, pleasure without consciousness, science without humanity, and worship without sacrifice are detrimental for any civil society. Anna Hazare's movement has recently reaffirmed the faith in non-violence and has given a new hope to young India to fight corruption at two different levels —one at the governmental level and another at the personal level—by not accepting and giving any bribe for services rendered.

India is currently ranked 81st out of 180 countries on the Corruption Perception Index surveyed by Transparency International (CPI 2017). In India corruption has been attributed to many causes, the most cited ones have been: (a) existence of an over-regulatory state (b) low public sector salaries (c) high electoral costs (d) lack of governmental accountability (e) dilatory laws, government rules and procedures (f) leadership deficits and administrative under-performance (g) lack of political will for radical reform. According to the Service Conduct Rules revalidated in 2000, it is mandatory for the members of the Central and All India Services to be citizen responsive and sensitive. The major outcomes of the Chief Ministers Conference in 1996 has been translated through promulgation of the Charter of Ethics and the Civil Service Code on the basis of equality, secularism impartiality, social justice and the rule of law. The following thrust areas for reform have been spelt out: (1) developing an effective and transparent system of governance; (2) promoting a code of conduct that is in consonance with global standards; (3) ensuring integrity in personnel performance; and (4) training civil servants to be competent professionals. The fact that the Anti-Corruption Act has been repeatedly amended amply proves the sincere intent of the Indian government to inculcate the value of ethical governance among its civil servants.

Indeed, Singapore and Hong Kong which are ranked very high on ethical standards in governance have both followed a three-pronged approach in order to maintain the integrity of the civil services. It is an approach of ethical leadership, ethical training and ethics legislation, e.g. in Hong Kong anyone aggrieved with a government decision has access to a full range of avenues to seek redress: the media, interest groups/specific redressal mechanisms, the legislature, and the courts. Besides these, there exists the Independent Commission against Corruption, the Audit Commission and the office of the Ombudsman.

The Second Administrative Reforms Commission's Fourth Report on "Ethics in Governance" discusses the following measures:

> *(a) electoral reforms (b) discontinuation of discretionary funds at the disposal of legislators (c) public service values towards which all public servants should be defined and made applicable to all tiers of government. Any transgression of these values should*

be treated as misconduct, inviting punishment (d) ethical framework for judiciary (e) liability of corrupt public servants to pay damages (f) promoting competition and simplifying transactions in government (g) using information technology (h) protecting whistle-blowers (i) reducing discretionary powers of civil servants

Conclusion

The 73rd and 74th Constitutional Amendments, which empowered the local institutions of governance, are now delivering results by bringing governance to the doorstep of the people. The devolution of power has strengthened the core of ethics in local governance. It is easier for the people to keep a watch and monitor the activities of local public officials than the distant officials of the Central Government.

The Right to Information Act of 2005 was a step in the right direction to combat the unethical practices of civil servants. It has fundamentally altered the relationship between the state and the citizen. The citizen is now legally empowered with information of the failures and misdeeds of politicians or public officials to act on them.

The positive role played by the electronic media in having raised awareness levels of the citizenry through various operations is helping the common man to understand the mechanisms of corruption. E-tools have helped the common man to raise his voice against the malpractices of public servants who no longer seem invincible simply because they are a part of the steel frame.

The enactment of the Lokpal Act was a milestone in setting ethical standards for the bureaucracy. With the commencement of this Act and others in the near future, the entire politico-administrative system would, make a giant step towards public accountability. An ethically regulated society can be created only when it develops a politico-administrative system that is sensitive, responsive, and accountable. To create such a system, ethics needs to be relocated at the core of administrative activity.

Suggested Readings

Arora R. K. and T. Saxena (eds.), *Excellence, Ethics and World of Management*, Jaipur, Alekh Publishers, 2009.

Brownman, James, "*Ethics in Government: A National Survey of Public Administrators,*" Public Administrative Review, xxxxx no. 3 (1990).

Das, S. K., *Building a World Class Civil Service for Twenty-First Century* India, New Delhi, OUP, 2010.

Desai, A., *India Corruption and Bribery Report*. Accessed August 21, 2011. www.corruptioninindia. org.

Dwivedi, O. P., "Ethics and Values of Public Responsibility and Accountability/' *International Review of Administrative Sciences*, 51 (1985): pp. 64-66.

Dwivedi, O. P., "*Public Service Ethics in a Globalized World: The Duty to Serve and Responsibility to Care*/' IJPA, LVII no. 1 (2011): pp. 1-14.

Guhan, S. and P. Samuel, *Corruption in India: Agenda for Action*. New Delhi, Vision Books, 1997.

Pathak, R. and R. Prasad, *Role of E-Governance in Tackling Corruption: The Indian Experience. Paper Presented at the Network of Asia-Pacific Schools and Institutes of Public Administration and Governance (NAPSIPAG)* Annual Conference, 5-7 December 2005, Beijing, PRC.

Patts, Steven, "*Ethics in Public Service: An Idea Whose Time Has Come," in Public Sector Ethics: Finding and Implementing Values*, eds. Noel Preston and Charles Sampford, New York, Routledge, 1998.

Second Administrative Reforms Commission, Unlocking Human Capital: Entitlements and Governance - A Case Study, New Delhi, GOI.

Sharma, S., *"Reassessing Indian Administrative Culture Premises" in Administrative Culture Premises and Perspective*, eds. C.M. Jain and A. Hingar Jaipur, India, RBSA Publishers, pp. 139-48.

Thompson, Dennis F., "*Paradox of Government Ethics,*" *Public Administration Review*, Lll no. 3 (May-June 1992)

OOO

Chapter Sixteen

Human Rights in Administration

Introduction

The first global declaration endorsing a set of human rights came in the form of the Universal Declaration of Human Rights (UDHR) adopted by the UN General Assembly in 1948. The declaration recognizes that human beings are inherently entitled to certain rights and global justice can be established only if the human dignity of the entire world's people is respected and honoured. The declaration recognizes freedom of speech, freedom of belief, freedom from fear and freedom from want as the highest aspirations of mankind. The declaration consists of 30 articles which have been elaborated in subsequent international treaties, regional human rights instruments, national constitutions and laws. The International Bill of Human Rights, which consists of the Universal Declaration of Human Rights (UDHR) the International Covenant on Economic, Social and Cultural Rights, and the International Covenant on Civil and Political Rights and its two Protocols, took on the force of international law in 1976. Subsequently, the Vienna Declaration and Plan of action were adopted in 1993. This declaration established the interdependence of democracy, economic development, and human rights; conceptualized as being indivisible, interdependent, and inter-related. The declaration created the post of the United Nations High Commissioner for Human Rights. India is also a signatory to the Vienna declaration.

The main framework for protecting human rights in India is provided by the *Protection of Human Rights Act, 1993.* This has been enacted pursuant to the directive under Article 51 of the Constitution and also the commitments taken at the Vienna conference. It defines human right as the right relating to liberty, equality and dignity of the individual guaranteed by the Indian Constitution as embodied in the fundamental rights and the International covenants (International Covenant on Civil and Political Rights and the Internal Covenant on Economic, Social and Cultural Rights) adopted by the General Assembly of the United Nations on the 16th of December 1966, and enforceable by courts in India. The Act provides for the constitution of a National Human Rights Commission, State Human Rights Commissions and Human Rights Courts for better protection of human rights in India.

Dr. B. R. Ambedkar, who was one of the main architects of the Indian Constitution, cherished the ideals of human dignity and human development. It was a significant historical coincidence that around the time the Constituent Assembly of Independent India was deliberating upon the Draft Constitution, the UN General Assembly was also drafting the UDHR. It was, therefore, quite natural that the ethos of our national liberation movement and the world community's concern for human rights were manifested in the framing of our Constitution. Hence, apart from the perambulatory promises of '*Justice, Liberty, Equality and Fraternity*,' the traditional civil and political rights or the first generation of human rights were incorporated as Fundamental Rights in Part III of the Constitution, while the second generation of human rights, that is social, economic and cultural rights were included in Part IV as Directive Principles of State Policy. Even the third generation of human rights, that is group rights, found partial expression in some of the constitutional provisions, such as abolition of the practice of untouchability (Article 17), prohibition of employment of children in factories or mines or in any other hazardous employment (Article 24), affirmative State action for the advancement of women and children (Article 15) and appointment of a National Commission for Scheduled Castes and Scheduled Tribes (Article 338) and appointment of a Commission to investigate the conditions of socially and educationally backward classes (Article 340). In pursuance with these constitutional provisions a number of legislations have been enacted by the Central and State Governments from time to time.

The exclusion of certain basic human rights such as the right to food, right to shelter, right to work and right to medical care from Part III of the Constitution, embodying justiciable Fundamental Rights has been criticized by scholars and activists. Such exclusion, however, has to be viewed in the historical backdrop of the time when the Constitution was framed. Perhaps, keeping in view the then socio-economic conditions of the Indian society (post two hundred years of colonial exploitation) the founding fathers of our Constitution might have thought that the inclusion of these second generation rights as guaranteed rights would be futile, since the nascent Indian state would lack the resource capacity to enforce socio-economic rights immediately after Independence. Therefore, it was considered prudent to include them as Directive Principles of State Policy with a mandate (vide Art 37) that though non-justiciable, it shall be the duty of the State to apply these principles in making laws.

In the last 50 years, the Supreme Court has extended the ambit and scope of human rights keeping in view international conventions, declarations and resolutions relating to human rights and fundamental freedoms. The definition of human rights provided in Section 2(d) of the Protection of Human Rights Act, 1993 covers, only a limited scope of human rights. There are proposals that the definition of human rights should be amended and extended in such a way so that it may cover those human rights and fundamental freedoms which have been declared by the Supreme Court as a fundamental right/human right under the Constitution, e.g. the right to development, rights of women, right to protect ecology and environmental protection, etc.

In terms of human development indicators, the South Asian region has a dismal record. The Millennium Development Goals Report 2012 has estimated that mounting food prices are likely to push as many as 100 million people in absolute poverty, mostly in "Sub-Saharan Africa and Southern Asia, already regions with the largest number of people living in extreme poverty". According to the 2012 Global Hunger Index (GHI) Report, Sub-Saharan Africa and South Asia share the highest regional Hunger Index scores, making poverty and hunger levels in these regions "alarming". This fact is further corroborated by the Multidimensional Poverty Index (MPI), developed by the Oxford Poverty and Human Development Initiative in collaboration with UNDP, according to which 8 Indian states including Bihar, Uttar Pradesh, West Bengal, "together account for more poor people than in the 26 poorest African Nations combined" (*Times of India,* 12 July 2010). India's human development index is 130 out of 189 countries counted according to the UNDP Report 2018. India has one third of the world's poor, the largest number of malnourished children and illiterates, and one of the worst public health systems in the world.

While it is widely recognized that no social phenomenon is as antithetical to human rights as poverty, there are several other socio-economic inequalities that exist, which prevent people from living capacitated lives. These inequities often reflect themselves in what the political scientist Johan Galtung, famously described as "structural violence", which is a reference to a form of violence based on the systematic ways in which the existence of certain social structures or institutions harm people by preventing them from meeting their basic needs. Institutionalized casteism, sexism, or communalism are just some examples of structural violence embedded in Indian society which leads to systematic overt and covert violation of human rights on a recurring basis.

16.1 National Human Rights Commission (NHRC)

NHRC established in 1993 is required to inquire into violation of human rights, or abetment or negligence in the prevention of such violation, by a public servant; intervene in any proceeding involving any allegation of violation of human rights pending before a court with the approval of such court; visit any jail on any other institution under the control of the State Government, where persons are detained or lodged for purposes of treatment, reformation or protection to study the living condition of the inmates and make recommendations thereon; review the safeguards under the Constitution or any existing law for the protection of human rights and recommend measures for their effective implementation; review the factors, including acts of terrorism that inhibit the enjoyment of human rights and recommend appropriate remedial measures; study treaties and other international instruments on human rights and make recommendations for their effective implementation; undertake and promote research in the field of human rights; spread human rights literacy among various sections of society and promote awareness of the safeguards available for the protection of these rights through various media organs; and encourage the efforts of non-governmental organizations and institutions working in the field of human rights.

The NHRC takes up cases either on its own initiative or on the basis of complaints received. It has all the powers of a civil court trying a suit under the Code of Civil Procedure, 1908, particularly with regard to summoning witnesses and examining them on oath; receiving evidence on affidavits; requisitioning any public record or its copy from any court or office and issuing commissions for the examination of witnesses or documents. The Commission has its own investigating staff headed by a Director General of Police for investigation into complaints of human rights violations. Under the Act, it is open to the Commission to utilize the services of any officer or investigation agency of the Central Government or any State Government. The Commission has also associated non-governmental organizations in many cases.

The NHRC can recommend to the concerned government to initiate action against the guilty; it can recommend grant of immediate relief to the victim or his family; and it can also approach the Supreme Court or High Courts for orders that they may deem necessary.

The concerned government is required to indicate the action taken on the Commission's recommendations within one month in general cases and three months in cases concerning the armed forces.

The NHRC, in its journey of over 25 years, has relentlessly endeavoured to be at the vanguard of the battle to curb violations of human rights, across the country and create an enabling environment for the realization of social and economic justice. In furtherance of its task to better protect and promote human rights, it has realized that violations in the sphere of human rights in economic, social and cultural areas are widespread in India. The struggle for the promotion and protection of human rights inevitably requires the elimination of aberrations that, over time, fragment society and create a level inequality.

Efforts are thus essential for continuous active engagement in the protection and promotion of the rights of the weaker sections of the society through various programmes such as social and educational empowerment, labour welfare, supplementary and continuing education, rehabilitation for the physically and mentally challenged, sustainable livelihoods and women's empowerment, among a host of other remedial measures.

While human rights institutions like the NHRC have a significant role in the promotion and protection of human rights in all spheres including social, economic, political and cultural, these can at best work as catalysts in assisting in efforts towards protecting and promoting human rights of the most vulnerable groups. The contributions of civil society actors and the state are just as crucial.

The autonomy of the Commission derives, *inter alia*, from the method of appointing its Chairperson and Members, their fixity of tenure, and statutory guarantees thereto, the status they have been accorded and. the manner in which the staff is responsible to the Commission—including its investigative agency are appointed and conduct themselves.

The Chairperson and Members of the Commission are appointed by the President on the basis of recommendations of a Committee comprising the PM as the Chairperson, the Speaker of Lok Sabha, the Home Minister, the leader of the opposition in the Lok Sabha and Rajya Sabha and the Deputy Chairman of the Rajya Sabha as Members.

The Commission's purview covers the entire range of civil and political, as well as economic, social and cultural rights. Areas facing terrorism and insurgency, custodial death, rape and torture, reform of the police, prisons, and other institutions such as juvenile homes, mental hospitals and shelters for women have been given special attention by the NHRC. The Commission has urged the provision of primary health facilities to ensure maternal and child welfare, basic needs such as drinking water, food and nutrition, and highlighted fundamental questions of equity and justice for the less privileged, namely the Scheduled Castes and Scheduled Tribes and the prevention of atrocities perpetrated against them. Rights of the disabled; access to public services; displacement of populations, especially of tribes, by developmental projects; food scarcity; rights of the children on various needs and issues; rights of women subjected to violence, sexual harassment and discrimination; and rights of minorities have been the focus of the Commission's action.

The NHRC has evolved and helped to introduce a new culture of governance by involving NGOs, educational and training institutions and individual activists in its efforts to protect and promote human rights particularly with respect to efforts to deal with child prostitution, child labour, bonded labour, problems of the mentally disabled, prison reforms and rehabilitation of persons displaced by the construction of so-called development projects. Being an important corrective institution of governance, the Commission has set art example to other institutions of governance by inculcating and strengthening a new culture of accountability in governance.

However, the NHRC is handicapped on several accounts. Firstly, out of 29 states, State Human Rights Commissions have not so far been set up in 8 states. Secondly, Human Rights Courts at the district level, as envisaged in the PoHR Act 1993, have been set up in only 5 states. Thirdly, the NHRC is only an investigative and recommendatory body with no powers of prosecution. It also has no powers to inquire into abuses by the armed forces.

Ever since its constitution in 1993, the NHRC has been discharging a role complementary to that of the Supreme Court of India by performing those tasks which by their very nature the NHRC can perform better, e.g. the Supreme Court has referred a number of important matters to the Commission for monitoring. The coordination between these institutions has considerably improved the mechanism for the protection of human rights in the country, which is primarily a state responsibility. Since its establishment, the NHRC has made inquiry and investigation into a large number of complaints of the violation of human rights. It has made recommendations to the concerned Governments and appropriate authorities for necessary action. It has submitted annual and special reports to the Central Government.

16.2 Towards Humane Governance: Role of Judiciary

Wherever the Executive failed in enforcing Directive Principles of State Policy (DPSP), the judiciary stepped in. The advent of Public Interest Litigation (PIL) jurisdiction under Article 32 coupled with liberal interpretation of various Articles like Art. 14, 19, 21, 32 and 226 has ushered in a new era in modern India, where Judiciary is not only seen as the guardian of the Constitution but also as the guardian of the poor and the marginalized sections of society.

In *Consumer Education & Research Centre, V. Union of India AIR 1995,* Honorable Supreme Court elaborated on the theme of social justice envisioned in the Preamble to the Constitution and Part IV. The Court held that social justice is the arch of the

Constitution which ensures life to be meaningful and liveable with human dignity. Social justice is a dynamic device to mitigate the suffering of the poor, the Dalits, various tribes and the deprived sections of the society and to elevate them to a level where they can live a life of dignity. The aim of social justice is to attain a substantial degree of social, economic and political equality.

Further, the Supreme Court has given an extended meaning to Art 142 (power to do complete justice) giving an extension to its own powers to give relief. It has been expanding the horizons of Art. 12 (meaning of 'state') primarily to inject a respect for human rights in India's corporate structure. The idea that Fundamental Rights are but a means to achieve the goals indicated in the Directive Principles and must be construed in the light of the same has been advocated by the Supreme Court time and again. The biggest beneficiary of this approach has been Art. 21. By reading Art. 21 with the Directive Principles the Supreme Court has derived a bundle of rights from there. To name a few of these:

- *The right to live with human dignity. (Bandhua Mukti Morcha v. Union of India AIR 1984)*
- *Right to free legal aid. (M.H. Hoskot v. State of Maharashtra AIR 1978)*
- Right to life includes the right to enjoy pollution free water, air and environment *(Subhash Kumar v. State of Bihar AIR 1991)*
- Right to health and social justice has been held as a fundamental right of workers. This right has been derived from Art. 21 read with Art 39 (e), 41, 43 and 48A. *(Consumer Education v. Union of India Air 1995).*
- Right to Shelter included in Right to life. (*Chameli Singh v. State of UP AIR 1996)*
- Right to Education. Derived from Art.21 read with Art. 41 & 45 *(Unnikrishnan v. State ofA.P. AIR 1993)*
- Right to life includes "right to livelihood". The Supreme Court has taken recourse to art. 39(a) to interpret Art. 21 to include this right. (*Olga Tellis v. Bombay Municipal Corporation)*
- *Right to access roads for hilly areas. (State of Himachal Pradesh v. Umed Ram AIR 1986)*

These are a few examples of various rights intricately connected with the mandate of social justice, which our Judiciary has evolved and invoked. In brief, read with various Directive Principles, Art 21 has emerged as a multi-dimensional Fundamental Right. Art 14 and Art 39(d), read together, have led to the emergence of the principle of equal pay for equal work.

Further, the Directive Principles are now regarded as a dependable index of "public purpose" by our judiciary. If a law is enacted to implement the socioeconomic policy envisaged in the DPSP, then it must be regarded as one for public purpose. Thus, the Wealth Tax Act was held to be valid by Supreme Court to prevent concentration of wealth in a few hands. Likewise, acquisition of agricultural land above the ceiling and its distribution among the landless has been held to be valid. Similarly, Supreme Court recognized the difference between formal and substantive equality and upheld, in various cases, affirmative actions taken by governments for Backward Classes.

In recent decisions of the Supreme Court, one can find extensive reference to Human rights. "*Today human rights jurisprudence in India has Constitutional Status*", said Justice Krishna Iyer, in *Sunil Batra (no. 2) v. Delhi Administration, AIR 980 SC 1579.* In *Prem Shankar v. Delhi Administration AIR 1982 SC149,* Krishna Iyer said that in interpreting constitutional and statutory provisions the Court should not forget the core principle found in the Universal Declaration of Human Rights, 1948. This approach will go a long way in inculcating a sense of accountability in public authorities discharging public duties towards the people and particularly towards the human rights of the marginalized. In this way, our Judiciary has played a key role in enforcing social justice and made our legal system more accessible and responsive to the diverse needs, of various sections of society like women, unorganized labour, Dalits and the disabled.

Since 1970 there has been a progressive trend of vigorous legalism in certain areas concerning human rights. There are many instances where the Supreme Court played a creative or a catalytic role in its quest for humane governance which resulted in a vast expansion of the frontiers of public law and formulation of multi-dimensional legal strategies including public interest litigation (PIL) for providing access to justice as well as relief to large masses of people who were denied of their basic human rights and to whom constitutional guarantee of rights and freedom had no meaning. As a part of this judicial trajectory towards anti-poverty or citizen-centric jurisprudence, the Supreme Court liberalized the traditional rule of *locus standi* in a series of cases in order to liberate itself from the shackles of procedural limitations and thereby to enable any public-spirited individual or social activist group to invoke the jurisdiction of the court or set the machinery of justice in motion by a letter, telegram or even a postcard for enforcement of human rights, liberty and freedom of any Indian citizen.

The late 70s and 80s witnessed legal activism directed towards redressal of the plight of child and bonded labour, injustices to women and victims of custodial violence or denial of justice. The 90s experienced an increasing concern of legal activism towards the issues of good governance and clean environment. One of the positive achievements of such activism has been to provide interim monetary relief to the victims of governmental action or inaction as well as administrative arbitrariness or misuse of power.

In *Saheli V. Commissioner of Police, Delhi,* the Supreme Court directed the Delhi Administration to pay Rs. 75,000/- as damage to the parents of a child, who died in police custody after being beaten and assaulted by police officials. The Delhi Administration was further directed to take appropriate steps to recover the amount or part thereof from the officer or officers who would be found responsible. These landmark directives of the apex court were a glaring instance of judicial creativity or innovativeness. For, under the common law system which we follow the concept of individual accountability does not exist in public law pertaining to liability in tort. Our Supreme Court has in fact, borrowed this concept from the Continental Law System operative in France, Germany and some other continental countries and innovatively applied it in our legal system to ensure accountability of an individual public functionary for abuse of authority or violation of citizen rights.

Judicial activism has proceeded further in the reduction of the area of immunity and extension of the area of liability of public servants. In Nilabati Behera (Smt.) V. State of Orissa, the Supreme Court, while ordering the State of Orissa to pay a sum of Rs. 1,50,000/- as compensation to the mother of the victim of custodial death, explicitly held: "The defence of sovereign immunity being inapplicable, and alien to the concept of guarantee of fundamental rights, there can be no question of such a defence being available in the constitutional remedy". The court further held that the purpose of public law is not only to civilize public power but also to assure the citizen that they live under a legal system which aims to protect their interests and preserve their rights, and hence, "the payment of compensation in such cases is not to be understood, as it is generally understood in a civil action for damages under the private law but in the broader sense of providing relief by an order of making 'monetary amends', under the public law for the wrong done due to breach of public duty, of not protecting the fundamental rights of the citizen."

In *N. Nagendra Rao & Co. V. State of A.P.,* the Supreme Court further clarified the legal position concerning the applicability of the doctrine of sovereign immunity. As the court held: "The demarcating line between sovereign and non-sovereign powers for which no rational basis survives has largely disappeared. Therefore, barring functions such as administration of justice, maintenance of law and order and repression of crimes, etc., which are among the primary and inalienable functions of a constitutional Government, the State cannot claim any immunity".

16.3 Other Human Rights Issues

The right to a speedy trial has been recognized by the Supreme Court as a part of protection available under Article 21 of the Constitution. Unfortunately, all such pronouncements have remained on paper with pendency of cases reaching a figure of 3 crore. Of these nearly 70% are criminal cases and the balance are civil cases. *There is no country in the world where litigation goes on for as long a period as in India.*

There are only 10-12 judges for every million people in India, while advanced countries have more than 50 judges per million. And in those countries, hardly 7 to 10% of the cases go to trial. The rest are settled out of court. A related and important aspect pertains to updating the old and outdated laws. A commission appointed by the Central Government has pointed out that over 1200 central laws were outdated and either needed to be repealed altogether or amended suitably. It is a travesty that most State Governments have not even started an exercise to identify laws which have outlived their utility.

The most striking feature of the Indian judicial system is the large number of under trials at any given time. The estimated number of under trials in the country is about 2,00,000. The Supreme Court has given a series of interim orders to give relief to under trials. These included those who had served more than the maximum sentence that could have been given had they been convicted, and were to be discharged and proceedings against them to be quashed; bail on personal recognizance if they fulfilled certain conditions (this decision was set aside by a Constitution Bench of the Supreme Court in April 2002); releasing all prisoners against whom no charge sheets had been filed for two years; all prisoners who were unable to hire counsel had a right to legal aid; all women and children in protective custody, whether victims or witnesses, to be released on personal bonds; the state cannot avoid its constitutional obligation to provide speedy trials to the accused by pleading financial or administrative inability and so on.

For want of adequate manpower and supervision in jails, and neglected police investigations and follow-ups, the under trails have to languish in jails for years making it difficult for the accused to furnish bail. The proportion of under trial prisoners was more than 80% of the total prison population in seven states (GOI Report 2006-07). According to the National Crime Records Bureau, Uttar Pradesh had the maximum number of under trials

(54,062) at the end of 2018. Bihar was next with 23,417, with Madhya Pradesh, Maharashtra and West Bengal making up the top five.

The Committee on Reforms of the Criminal Justice System (Justice B.S. Malimath Committee), in its report submitted in March 2003, made wide-ranging recommendations to deal with the two problems—huge pendency of cases and poor rate of conviction—which have plagued the Indian criminal justice system (GOI 2003). According to the committee, two areas which need special attention for improving the quality of justice are prescribing required qualifications for judges and the quality of training being imparted in judicial academies. The committee also dealt with the widely prevalent practice of perjury in criminal cases. Like so many reports of other committees, this report too has been languishing without any perceptible action for a long time.

16.4 Administration of 'New Rights'

Since the 1990s a number of legislative and administrative measures to confer rights on the citizens —Right to Information, Right to Education, Right to Employment and Right to Food have taken place. The Right to Information Act has become an effective tool to make public authorities and government accountable to the people and fight corruption by disclosure. The Act has changed the power equation between Indian citizens and the government. It has forced local authorities, State Governments and Central Government to disclose information to them earlier denied. The Act has led to some remarkable disclosures of information in the public domain. However the working of the Act has not been smooth. In many states, several positions of Information Commissioners are vacant, consequently thousands of cases are pending. In cases where the departments concerned should have *suo moto* offered information to the citizens, misleading, confusing, incomplete, delayed and wrong information has been given. However, there is a lack of proper implementation mechanism for the implementation of penal orders passed by the Information Commissioners. Punitive action against officers who fail to carry out orders of Information Commissioners and appeal authorities is ignored. The state information commissioners do not use their powers to compel the government to follow their acts. Lastly many activists who brought up cases under the Information Act were killed. All these have taken a heavy toll on the effectiveness of the Act.

The Right to Education Act was enacted in 2009 to ensure free and compulsory education to all children between 6 to 14 years of age. The Union Government which has enacted the law has left the implementation entirely to the states. But the administration from state secretariat to the level of local government is mired in utter confusion and piecemeal actions rather than a comprehensive integrated action has been the norm. A survey showed that 25% of quota for poor students has not been filled as stipulated under RTE even in state schools. The Act, meant to be student friendly, has banned any terminal examination till the 8th standard. It is widely reported that this has led to students not taking their studies seriously till middle school. The Act has laid down high standards of infrastructure facilities for schools like well-appointed buildings, classrooms, office rooms, toilets, drinking water facility, good student-teacher ratio, etc. The worst culprits in this respect are government, municipal and local schools, 90% of them do not comply with the 10 infrastructure parameters under RTE Act. Before imposing the Act governments should have built the infrastructure first in government schools. The Act should have made a sound beginning of educational reform. Lastly, there is no adequate administrative machinery in the Education departments of the states to monitor the implementation of the Act.

The Mahatma Gandhi National Rural Employment Guarantee Act 2005 (MNREGA) promises 100 days of work each year to every rural household. It is the largest social welfare programme in the world. Though a Central Act, its implementation is entirely in the hands of the states. Several flaws have been noticed in the implementation of the Act like the delay in payment (15 to 90 days) of wages amount to almost 25% of wage payments made across the country and the poor quality of assets created. The weakness in the implementation is often due to the poor administrative structure of implementation. MNREGA, it is argued, created problems for agricultural economy by artificially jacking up wage rates and making it difficult to get labour since it is diverted to easy work under MNREGA scheme. Other complaints of large-scale leakages and corruption have also come to light in the implementation of the MNREGA programme.

The Food Security Act 2013 sought to provide 5 kg of food grains, per person per month covering 75% of rural population and 50% of urban population, i.e. 67% of India's total population would be entitled to wheat at Rs. 2/- per kg., coarse gram at Re 1/- per kg and rice at Rs.3/- per kg. This Act again has serious problems in implementation. The cost of ensuring food security would place enormous fiscal burden on the economy. Rising fiscal deficit will add to inflationary spiral. Government efforts to procure and store foodgrains would need to be augmented specially in states where PDS system is not working properly. Entrusting food security to such a system would lead to leakages and corruption. Therefore merely enacting rights will not be citizen empowering unless an appropriate implementation mechanism has been put in place by the states.

16.5 Good Governance as a Human Right

The Key dimensions of good governance are accountability, a legal framework for development, information and transparency. Human rights values become non- negotiable for good states. The human rights approach stresses that states and state institutions are only instruments for protecting, promoting and securing human rights for all.

The Universal Declaration of Human Rights (UDHR), especially Article 21, provides a good starting point. The characteristics of good governance derive from, or are related to UDHR and include:

- Government officials must be accountable for their actions through clearly formulated and transparent processes, and more particularly the legitimacy of a government must be regularly established through a well-defined open process of public choice.
- The safety and security of citizens must be assured , the rule of law must prevail and citizens must be protected from arbitrary or capricious actions by public authorities
- Everyone has the right to an adequate standard of living and the necessities of life, which should be provided for the benefit of all citizens in an equitable manner.

- Freedom of association and expression of opinion must be permitted and information must be readily available to ensure accountability

The true test of good governance is the degree to which it delivers, protects and ensures human rights-civil, cultural, social, economic, and political. The actual meaning of good governance for a common man is guaranteed right to food, education, health, adequate housing, justice and personal security. The purpose of good governance is not only to provide basic amenities to the people but a life with assured human dignity. The main attributes of good governance are participation, rule of law, transparency, responsiveness, equity, inclusiveness and accountability.

Conclusion

It took us two world wars to realize and accept that peace and freedom are indivisible and can be achieved only if we respect the inherent dignity of every individual and are committed to establishing social, political and economic orders that are fair and just for all. The Universal Declaration of Human Rights may not be legally binding on nations but as part of customary international law, it does affect the conscience of nations and subject them to moral pressure to work towards securing rights and justice for their people. Similarly the Millennium Development Goals were a landmark Charter of Governance which was adopted by 189 member states in 2000. The eight goals are a human rights centric minimum agenda of good governance to be pursued by all signatory states.

For a country like India whose commitment to this objective is amply visible in its public policies since 2001, the actual attainment of an envisioned just state has not been easy. To start with, probably no other country in the world has to reckon with as many potentially divisive forces, besides differences in economic status and educational attainment. Then there are people with physical and age-related disabilities, those rendered homeless due to internal conflicts, natural disasters, industrialization and such other reasons, whose rights need to be specially protected. Economic development and rapid urbanization have contributed their own sets of vulnerable population groups —the migrants, the slum dwellers, the industrial labourers, and those affected by deterioration of the environment. *So when India talks of securing human rights and social justice for all it is not about a small, manageable, largely homogenous citizenry. It is actually talking about securing the rights of more than a billion people, immensely heterogeneous in their diversity and often having interests that appear to be in direct conflict with another citizen group, very diverse in many matters.*

India's track record in this area is typically that of a student who has made significant achievement but has miles to go. So, while our women today are definitely on a steady path to empowerment, a lot many of our children are still deprived of even basic education, and are forced into employment even while they are minors. Our mechanisms and institutions for providing long-term and sustainable care to the elderly and the disabled are still very sketchy. While the government is taking rapid strides in the area of ensuring inclusive growth, caste and region-based differences will persist. Despite these, we can take pride in the fact that our framework for securing human rights and establishing a just social order is a very strong one. The judiciary has proved this time and again. Organizations like the National Commission for Protection of Child Rights, the many NGOs working in these areas and also our Central and State Governments have brought in relevant and meaningful legislations and are striving to implement the same.

As for the issue of resources, the Indian Supreme Court considered the question of how courts should respond to the often routine objection of state parties that they do not have adequate funds to ensure that basic fundamental rights are enforced. In the Ratlam Municipality case, the Supreme Court decried the perverse expenditure logic of the state departments in any matter concerning the enforcement of human rights.

There have been hundreds of cases relating to the enforcement of Fundamental Rights through Public Interest Litigations. For instance, in the People's Union for Civil Liberties case, which is a petition that has affected millions of people throughout India, the Supreme Court directed *a Mid-day meal for school children, the giving of highly subsidized grain to the poor and an employment scheme for the unemployed.* Similarly, in the Unikrishnan case, the Supreme Court said that education was a Fundamental Right and it was the duty of the State to provide free and compulsory education for all children.

In fact despite the best intentions of public policy, implementation of government schemes and programmes have been very weak due to inefficient and incompetent public delivery systems. Therefore, thanks to the deepening of democracy, civil society movements and judicial decisions, the Indian state was forced to adopt a new approach to development—the Rights-based approach. One after, another new Rights came to be guaranteed and made justifiable to the Indian citizen—the Right to Work in rural areas, the Right to Education, the Right to Information, the Right to Food, etc. All these are now guaranteed socio-economic rights for which there is legal remedy against bureaucratic non-performance, inactivity, malintention or apathy.

Our policy makers must realize that poverty eradication is not, only a development goal but also a major human rights challenge of the 21st century. A minimum standard of decent living, adequate nutrition, health care, education, employment and protection against calamities, are not just development goals they are also human rights. To achieve these goals, it is not enough to formulate pro-poor economic and social policies and allocate funds for various programmes based on these policies. What seems to be much more important than these exercises is to ensure proper utilization of earmarked funds, so that the benefits of economic and social development percolate down to the millions of poor people in this country.

There is also need for transparency in governmental functioning. Our experiences with the law on the Right to Information, reveal that legislative guarantee of the right to freedom of information would not be of much help unless the public functionaries are sensitized, motivated and trained to accept the change towards openness and citizens become aware and willing to play a more pro-active role with necessary intervention of the civil society organizations. Yet the Right to Information (RTI) has certainly changed state-citizen relations as never before. Nearly 40 lakh RTI applications are filed every year and many of them are used for enforcing human rights or other citizen entitlements.

Accountability of public functionaries should be ensured at all levels of the governmental system through appropriate legislative and administrative measures. It needs to be hardly emphasized that transparency and accountability would help in minimizing corruption in public life. E-governance and the passage of the Right to Public Service Guarantee Acts in more than half the states of India are all steps in the right direction. The creation of a Lokpal and Lokayuktas in states will also help to enforce public accountability with new vigour to fight corruption and abuse of public power in administrative decisions. The area of "discretionary" power to be exercised by government servants will thus be considerably reduced and the constitutionalised 'Rule of Law' made finally to prevail.

Public scrutiny and state accountability are complementary to each other. Fortunately for India, we have a fairly open civil society and independent media to help the citizen in highlighting bureaucratic abuse of power and violation of citizen rights and entitlements. It would be erroneous to contend that by playing a creative and catalytic role, our superior courts are overstepping their limits to enter the realm of the executive. A large number of recent trendsetting rulings by the apex court on public interest issues reflect judicial activism in order to fight executive inaction and apathy. Hence, the role of higher judiciary needs to be considered in the correct perspective of our constitutional jurisprudence and the practice of administrative power and discretion in our country.

Human rights and human development cannot be realized without effective and meaningful linkages between public service agencies, civil society organizations, NGOs, labour and women's groups, human rights, environmental and other activist groups. In the contemporary context of globalization and economic liberalization, partnership between government and industry not only in the economic sector but also in the social sector needs to be enhanced.

In addition, to minimizing the state propensity for violation of human rights, the system of policing and police administration should be restructured in such a manner as to ensure professional autonomy along with accountability to ordinary citizens. Since "policing" is a state subject the recommendations of the National Police Commission as well as the NHRC on police reforms deserve serious consideration by State Governments. Likewise, reforms in prison administration should also receive adequate attention of the State Governments.

Last but not the least, the NHRC should be strengthened with more statutory powers and adequate logistic support to enable it to discharge its duties and responsibilities more effectively as a key institution for the protection and promotion of human rights in India.

Although India has ratified the International Convention Against Torture in 1977, incidents of custodial death and acts of torture still continue. There have also been a number of rape cases (including custodial rape) that have come to light in recent years, which became landmark events for a change in public laws. The Rameeza Bee case, the Mathura rape case, the Nirbhaya case in Delhi and lastly the Manorama Devi case forced the Indian Government to review the Armed Forces Special Powers Act and anti-rape laws.

Despite the Bonded Labour (Regulation and Abolition) Act the amended Industrial Disputes Act, and the Trade Union Act, child labour and other violations of labour laws still persist. The biggest bane of the Indian legal system are the draconian preventive detention laws like Armed Forces Special Powers Act, the Maintenance of Internal Security Act and the Essential Services Maintenance Act which can and have been reportedly abused in cases of human rights violations..

Lastly in the post-globalized era new human rights violations are being reported: contractualization of labour, banning of trade union activity in the private sector, rights violations in Special Economic Zones by MNCs are all examples of the indirect/ implicit defense of "private purpose" by the state at the expense of the "public". Good governance is truly another name for human rights-based citizen-centric governance.

To make development work we need: - A consolidated package of specific requirements that include honest government, open legislative and transparent regulatory systems, properly trained and remunerated officials and a vigorous commitment by leaders to fight corruption at all levels.

- An effective and impartial legal and justice system, with protection of positive support for rights and freedom of various kinds, a well organised financial system, effective social safety nets and essential social programmes.
- Education and knowledge institutions that offer access to all at every level. There must also be a real commitment to extend the coverage of health services, family planning and clean water and sewerage system to all (Amartya Sen, 1999)

Suggested Readings

Agarwal, B., *Field of One's Own: Gender and Land Rights in South Asia*, New York, Cambridge University Press, 1994.

Bannerjee, Sumanta, *"Human Rights in India in the Global Context,"* EPW, 38 no.5, (Feb. 1, 2003).

Baxi, Upendra, *ITie Future of Human Rights*, New Delhi, OUP, 2002.

Dev, Arjun, et. al., *Human Rights: A Source Book*, NCERT, 1996.

Gonsalves, Colin, *Kaliyug: The Decline of Human Rights Law in the Period of Globalization*, New Delhi, Human Rights Law Network, 2011.

Kumar, Vijay, *The Supreme Court of India: Policy Formulator or Active Protector*? Delhi, Manak Publications Pvt. Ltd., 2012.

Mohanty, M. (ed.), *Class, Caste, Gender*, Delhi, Sage, 2004.

Motilal, Shashi and Bijayalaxmi Nanda, *Human Rights, Gender and Environment*, Delhi, Allied Publishers, 2006.

Rao, Anupama (ed.), *Gender and Caste: Issues in Contemporary Indian Feminism*, Delhi, Kali for Women, 2003.

Sen, Amartya, *Development as Freedom*, New Delhi, OUP, 1999

OOO

Chapter Seventeen

Citizens and Administration

Introduction

Citizen-administration relations are important because the support and consent of the governed is a prerequisite for the success of a democratic government. The state and the administration have significant responsibilities for providing major amenities such as education, health, employment opportunities; improved means of transport and infrastructure, etc., to its citizens. In public administration two noticeable trends have emerged in recent times. First, there has been an expansion in the size, powers and activities of the public bureaucracy. Secondly, in the wake of the spread of general education and public awareness, there has been a rise in the expectations of the people from the administration.

There are several ways in which citizens interact with the administrative agencies in everyday life. Mohit Bhattacharya (2008) illustrates five categories of such interactions. These could be in the form of:

1. **Clients:** In this form, citizens seek to obtain benefits or services from governmental agencies. For example, patients visit a government hospital for a medical checkup or send their children to government schools.
2. **Regulatee:** As regulatee, the public interacts with many government agencies like the police, income tax authorities, licensing authorities etc.
3. **Litigants:** As litigants, the public may move to the court, eg. when the motor vehicles authority may be delaying the issuance of a car license.
4. **Participants:** In this form people become direct participants in decision-making in public agencies at different levels. For example; parents become members of a school's guardians' committee, an irrigation project associates the farmers with the different decision-making processes of the project.
5. **Cutting-edge encounters:** In this form people approach the agencies which are responsible for day today primary services and facilities to the public. For example, people approach municipal employees for water, electricity, and sanitation facilities.
6. **Protesters:** People often interact with government agencies on public policy as protesters, opposing the injustice in government policies or actions. For example, people oppose the construction of nuclear power facilities in their locality.

Thus citizens in day to day life constantly interact with the administration. The purposes of contact may be varied, for example, it may be for getting basic services like water, electricity and health services or it may be for getting a driving license or an income tax return from the income tax department. When people do not get services on time or are harassed by public authorities, they seek redressal of their grievance from the court and when they do not see justice coming from any side, they resort to protests against the government. Based the these interactions, citizens form their opinion about public authorities or agencies.

17.1 Citizen's Perceptions about the Administration

Though ideally speaking, the interaction between citizens and the administration should be trustworthy and purposeful, in reality, it may be plagued by conflicts and disappointments. Discontent amongst the citizens due to the wide disparity between the performance of administration and popular expectations have become a part of life of the Indian citizen. The general feeling which persists is that the policies are cumbersome, or the processes of administration are unjust. Yet another important problem is deterioration in the standards of honesty and integrity in both, politics and administration due to corruption. Rigid observance of rules and regulations, non-acknowledgement of complaints, inordinate delays in the disposal of various matters account for the lack of public faith in administration.

A number of research studies have been undertaken to examine the relationship between the citizens and administration in India. Some such important ones include studies on 'Police Administration' by Davis H. Baley (1969), 'Rural Development' by Rakesh Hooja (1978) 'Urban Government' by V. Jagannadhan (1978) and 'India's Public Services' (Samuel Paul 2006). The findings of these studies reveal interesting information on citizens' perceptions about public administration in India. The general perceptions of the people on administration that emerge out of these studies include:

1. Inordinate delays in getting things done.
2. Favouritism in administration.
3. Need for middlemen (brokers) or 'speed money' to hasten services.
4. Unhelpful attitude of the officials especially lower level functionaries.
5. Citizens' ignorance about procedures leads to their exploitation.
6. Discrimination in administration; the rich having access to administration and the general tendency of officials to avoid the poor and underplay their needs and interests (Bhattacharya 2008).

A recent study (ARC 2009) by the Centre for Media Studies (CMS) shows that a majority of citizens are not satisfied with the delivery of public services. In seven out of the eleven departments covered in the study, less than one-third of citizens were satisfied with the services delivered. In fact, in most need-based services such as the police, judiciary and municipalities, (which enjoy a greater discretion of power), not even 20 per cent of the households were satisfied with the services. Even in essential services such as the Public Distribution System (PDS), hospitals, electricity and water supplies, a mere 30-40 per cent of the households were happy with the services (Second Administrative Reforms Commission 2009).

The Second Administrative Commission in its 12th Report on *Citizen-Centric Administration in India* observes:

1. Wooden, inflexible, self-perpetuating and inward looking attitude of civil servants

2. Lack of accountability of civil servants
3. Red-tapism
4. Ineffective implementation of laws and rules
5. Low levels of awareness of the rights and duties of citizens

Thus, the reason for the administration not being citizen-centric can be attributed to the attitude and work of some government servants, the deficiencies in the existing institutional structures and the lack of awareness about rights and duties on the part of the citizens.

The poor image of the government in the minds of large sections of the population points towards an inefficient and ineffective administration. This highlights the need for substantially reforming our governance systems. The main focus of such reform should be on making citizens central to all government activities and reorganizing the government to effectively address their concerns.

17.2 The Right to Information (RTI)

The Right to Information (RTI) Act of 2005, which came into effect on October 12, 2005, is one of the most radical in the world. It attempts to bring about transparency and accountability in all three organs of government: legislature, executive, and judiciary. Since its enactment, the RTI Act has been extensively used in all states of India, including rural and urban areas. In 2017-18, forty lakh cases were filed seeking information on various issues from public agencies. In fact, it has become so popular that governmental attempts to amend this law and make access to information more difficult, has been fiercely opposed by civil society groups and the public at large.

17.3 RTI Act of 2005: Major Provisions

The RTI Act of 2005 (hailed globally as an example of best practice) is comprehensive, which includes provisions for independent appeals, proactive disclosure, and penalties for non-compliance. Its major features are discussed in this section.

The RTI Act of 2005 confers a constitutional right to citizens, and the word "information" is broader in ambit than just records or documents. Information includes permission for the inspection of public works. It also covers information relating to a private body that can be accessed by a public authority under any other law in force for the time being (Section 2(0). The list of information to be proactively published by public bodies is also fairly large. Public authorities have been asked to publish the allocated budget of each agency; proposed expenditures; the manner of execution of subsidy programs; recipients of concessions, permits, and licenses; and facts taken into consideration while formulating policies. Public information officers (PIOs)/ assistant PIOs are to be appointed in all administrative units/ offices as may be necessary to provide information to persons requesting it. The act lays down the time limit as 30 days (Section 7) for normal applications and 40 days where a third- party submission is called for (Section 11(3)). It is interesting to note that these time limits are reduced to a mere 48 hours where the information sought "concerns the life-and liberty of a person" (an innovation by global standards). The application fee is to be reasonable (currently

Rs. 10), and no fee is to be charged to persons who are below the "poverty line" as determined by the government. When a public authority fails to comply with time limits under the act, the information shall be provided free of charge. The act provides for the establishment of a Central Information Commission (CIC) at the Centre and State Information Commissions (SICs) in all states, comprising a chief information commissioner and other information commissioners. The information commissions can make any order required to bring about compliance with the law, including release of documents, appointment of PIOs, and publication of specified information. A central CIC will be appointed by a committee consisting of the PM, the leader of the opposition, and a union minister nominated by the PM. Every PIO can be penalized Rs. 250 per day up to a maximum of Rs. 25,000 for not accepting applications; for delaying information release without reasonable cause; and for providing incomplete, incorrect, and misleading information. The act exempts cabinet papers, information covering a wide range of central intelligence and security agencies, and information that is more than 20 years old. Appellants need to be informed of the reasons for the rejection of the case, the period within which an appeal can be made, and the particulars of the appellate authority to which they can appeal. Appellants can lodge a complaint with the CIC/SIC as the case may be if they were

- Unable to submit request to PIO/APIO
- Refused access to information
- Not given a response within the stipulated time limit
- Required to pay an unreasonable fee
- Given incomplete, misleading, or false information
- To require information on any other matter relating to access to records

The RTI Act defines information in a very broad manner so that the citizens can have access to many items. Information means any material in any form, including records, documents, memos, e-mails, opinions, advice, press releases, circulars, orders, logbooks, contracts, reports, papers, samples, models, data material, and information relating to any private body that can be accessed by a public authority under any other law for the time being in force.

"Public authority" under the act means any authority or body recognized by the constitution or law made by parliament or any state legislature. Some categories of information that can be exempted from disclosure are related to:

- Information which would affect the security, strategic, scientific or economic interest of the state, or conduct of international relations.
- Any information, the disclosure of which may constitute contempt of court.
- Any information, the disclosure of which would cause a breach of privilege of parliament or state legislature.
- Any information, including commercial confidence, trade secrets, or intellectual property, the disclosure of which would harm the competitive position of the third party.

- Cabinet papers and deliberations of the Council of Ministers and their secretaries. Notwithstanding anything in the Official Secrets Act of 1923, a public authority may allow access to information, if public interest in disclosure outweighs "the harm" to the protected interests.

Since 2006, amendments are being contemplated in the act. However, the outcry and disagreement within (and outside) the ruling coalition in the Central Government led to the proposals being dropped. The Department of Personnel and Training (the nodal agency in charge of implementation of the act) has said that it is considering amendments to the act, but it will act only when a public consensus emerges. There was a proposal to exempt "file noting" and examination papers of the Union Public Service Commission from disclosure. Thereis another proposal to prohibit frivolous and vexatious applications. Activists hold that all the existing problems can be remedied through changes in the rules, training of the staff, and better record management by public authorities. A change in the act should not be contemplated.

Inclusions and Exemption

Although the ambit of the act includes only public authorities (Central, State, or Local), it also includes bodies substantially financed by the government, which has also been interpreted to mean private bodies or NGOs. "Information" has been defined to include information relating to any private body that can be accessed by a public authority under any other law in force for the time being. The role of the CIC has been to continuously increase the ambit of RTI. All public authorities have been asked to publish all relevant facts while formulating important policies or announcing decisions that affect the public and provide reasons for administrative or quasi-judicial decisions to affected persons. Exemptions under 10 categories are provided under the Act (Section 8(1)). These may be overridden in the public interest. Only in the case of infringement of copyright vesting in a person other than the state does there exist absolute exemption (Section 9). Under provisions of Sections 8(1), 9, and 18, intelligence and security organizations listed in the Second Schedule do not come under the purview of the act unless these are allegations on corruption and human rights violations. The first appeal lies with the officer who is senior in rank to the central public information officer (CPIO)/state public information officer (SPIO) in each public authority (Section 19(1)). A second appeal lies with the CIC or the SIC (Section 19(3)). There is a bar on jurisdiction of courts (Section 23). However, because the RTI is a constitutional right, the citizens have a right-to go to a high court or the Supreme Court.

17.4 RTI - Coverage

The RTI has certainly been used extensively in India. It has begun to permeate almost every sphere of governance. Different stratum of citizenry (individually or collectively) have used it for seeking redress of personal grievances or seeking access to entitlements or enforcing rights, thereby enabling the average citizen to make informed choices. A large number of poor have used it through NGOs and civil society groups to fight injustice; to seek access to entitlements, such as food, housing, wages, and employment; and to fight corruption in remote areas of the country. Public administration is a huge monolith in India, and the act, by helping to breach the walls of India's power structures, its veils of secrecy, has given the citizen a new dignity and respect in the eyes of the bureaucracy. Civil liberties and human rights activists are using principles of the RTI to ensure transparency and accountability of the police and custodial institutions. People displaced by dams and special economic zones, communities affected by polluting industries, and forest dwellers evicted by new industries have all used the RTI in their battle for lost land, homes, or livelihoods. As movements and groups make their questions more focused and the public body or agency is forced to part with information, it can be expected that public bureaucracies and governments in India at all levels will become more sensitized to people's issues. The fact that public servants are paid out of public funds places the issue of public accountability at the heart of public administration. When we assess the effect of RTI, we need to primarily look at its effect on public authorities, the information commissions, and ordinary citizens.

The RTI Act of 2005 entitles citizens to a Right to Information from public authorities. Public authorities are obligated to provide information through their PIOs. To enable people to know from which authorities to access information, an exhaustive list of public authorities must be prepared by Central and State Governments. Ministries and departments are mandated to identify public authorities falling under their jurisdiction, including public sector undertakings (PSUs) and NGOs substantially financed by the government. The Department of Personnel and Training (DOP&T) under the Union Ministry of Personnel, Public Grievances, and Pensions is the nodal ministry in the implementation of the act. Furthermore, the entry for each public authority should list the details of all public authorities subordinate to it, reaching down to the lowest levels in the institutional hierarchy. All these details should be made available on the web sites of the respective public authorities in a hierarchical form. There are several CIC/SIC rulings on what constitutes "public authority". There has been a debate on expanding the definition of public authorities to include members of parliament in so far as local area development funds at their disposal are concerned. It has also been suggested that the RTI Act should extend to private bodies performing public functions or dealing with public money and trusts. Although the act applies to all the three organs of the State, namely the executive, the legislative, and the judiciary, there have been cases in which the judiciary has taken a stand that it does not fall within the ambit of the RTI Act. In a recent case, Subhash Chandra Agrawal vs. Supreme Court of India the appellant sought information on whether judges of the Supreme Court should make a declaration of their assets to the chief justice of India (CJI) in line with the resolution dated May 7, 2007, passed by the erstwhile judges of the Supreme Court. The CPIO of the Supreme Court contended that the RTI Act applies only to the executive government, and the Supreme Court of India, being a constitutional body, is outside the purview of the RTI Act. The full bench of the commission that heard the matter stated that the term "public authority", as defined under Section 2(h) of the RTI Act, to mean any authority, body, or institution of self-government established or constituted by or under the Indian Constitution. Thus, the Supreme Court of India is an institution created by the constitution and is therefore a public authority within the meaning of Section 2(h) of the RTI Act. The commission further observed that the CJI is also designated as a "competent authority" under Section 2(e) of the RTI Act, and Section 28 of the act empowers competent authorities defined in Section 2(e), which inter alia,include the CJI to frame rules to perform provisions of the RTI Act.

The commission held that this rule-making power has been explicitly conferred for the purpose of performing the provisions of the RTI Act. In another judgment, Justice S. Ravindra Bhatt favoured evolving some uniform standards and modalities for declaration of assets by judges. After this judgment, the judges of the Supreme Court and some high courts {Delhi, Kerala, Punjab, Haryana, and Maharashtra) passed resolutions that they would publicly declare their assets and place the information in the public domain. Proactive disclosure is the hallmark of this act, and, if complied with, it will improve record management of public authorities as well as facilitate a people friendly politico-administrative regime.

The RTI Act of 2005 stipulated two important means to achieve the objectives enshrined in its preamble—adjudication in case of inappropriate response from public authorities to a request for information and/or denial of information and effective implementation of Section 4,the latter envisaging effective record management, including digitization and availability in electronic form, proactive disclosure of all information except those prohibited by exemption provisions of the act, and effective dissemination of information for the benefit of citizens. However, the CIC has observed, in the course of hearing various appeals/complaints, that although the RTI Act had been in place for some time now one of the key elements of the law (Section 4 of the RTI Act) was not being implemented in letter and spirit. Although there are ministries/departments and public authorities, which are relatively more transparent and open than others, most of them do not confirm to the matrix of disclosure set out in Section 4(1) (b) of the act as well as practices relating to record management and dissemination of information held by and/or under their control.

The full bench of the commission, vide its Order No. CIC/AT/D/10/000111 dated November 15, 2010, under Section 19(8) (a) of the RTI Act, has directed all public authorities to fulfill their obligations stipulated in Section 4 of the act as per the timeline laid down for each activity. The commission further directed that:

- The information in compliance with Section 4 shall be uploaded by every public authority on the portal setup for the purpose by the CIC.
- Every public authority shall designate one of their senior officers as "transparency officer" (with necessary supporting personnel as required). The transparency officers shall:
  - oversee implementation of provisions of Section 4 and apprise the higher echelons of the management about the progress.
  - act as an interface with the CIC regarding progress of the above.
  - help promote congenial conditions for positive and timely response to RTI requests by CPIOs, deemed CPIOs.
  - act as a contact point for the public in all RTI -related matters.

- The status of submission of the annual reports by ministries/departments/ public authorities, as mandated under Section 25(2) of the RTI Act, is also discouraging. There has been an increasing trend in the number of public authorities not submitting the reports from 2006-11. It is worth mentioning that during 2010-11, 67.5%, submitted their returns. In 2009-10, approximately 77% of public authorities had submitted their reports, whereas approximately 86% of the public authorities submitted their reports during 2008-09 (CIC Annual Report 2010-11). The failure on the part of public authorities to submit annual reports amounts to violation of their statutory responsibility in assisting the CIC in preparation of its annual report.

This is indicative of the fact that the public authorities have so far not been able to make any systemic arrangements in regard to timely submission of annual reports to the commission. The ministries/departments/public authorities have to introspect and create a system so that the response rate reaches 100% every year without any intervention of the central commission.

From successive annual reports of CICs, the following conclusions can be drawn:

- In 2009-10, the commission imposed penalties on various PIOs and deemed PIOs amounting to Rs. 26.80 lakhs u/s 20(1) of the RTI Act of 2005. The respondents filed writ petitions before the High Court of Delhi in five cases, where penalty amounts of Rs.17,500; Rs. 50,000; Rs. 22,500 and Rs. 25,000 had been imposed. The High Court of Delhi stayed the penalty orders of the commission in three cases with respective penalty amounts of Rs. 50,000, Rs. 22,500, and Rs. 25,000; reduced the amount from Rs. 17,500 to Rs. 5,000 in one case; and set aside the order regarding the penalty amount of Rs. 25,000 in another case. Consequently, the penalty amount imposed by the commission during the reporting year 2009-10 is effectively Rs. 2,642,500. The commission has received a compliance report, by way of recovery, in respect to the remaining cases for an amount of Rs. 1,771,725 (CIC Annual REPORT 2009-10).

17.5 RTI: Some Observations

The foundations of our democracy cannot be laid on a deficit of trust. Therefore, the politico-administrative regime in India must encourage itself in building this trust to do our democracy proud. It is indeed heartening to note that the RTI has now become a precursor to other model legislation such as the Delhi Act of 2011 (Right of Citizen to Time Bound Delivery of Services) or the Lokpal Act.

Information flow is an important tool that offers verified data so as to protect individual, community and national interests. All human rights issues require complete transparency. That is why the framers of the RTI law were insistent that there be a "human rights and corruption", override to the blanket exemptions being granted from the provisions of the act to intelligence and security agencies.

There are many prerequisites for the effective functioning of a democracy. Education and an economic leveling of the population are essential. Both being absent, coupled with an administrative system seeped in the age-old culture of secrecy, the RTI is one of the most important tools of citizens to secure entitlements, safeguard constitutional rights, and make a much needed dent in the administrative culture of secrecy. "Knowledge" was the key to the power of bureaucrats so far. It is now the turn of citizens armed with the RTI to use that power. The revamping of our administrative system in this direction would require multipronged measures, which would inter alia include the following:

- The government and the commissions must ensure effective implementation of provisions of Section 4 regarding record management practices and suo moto proactive disclosures to ensure that citizens are not required to file requests for basic and routine information.
- Citizen's charters with firm timelines for efficient delivery of goods and services and mechanism for grievance redressal and routinization of processes.
- All public-private partnership projects should be brought under the ambit of the RTI Act at the signing stage itself by incorporating disclosure norms and scope.
- The political leadership, media, NGOs, and civil society organizations must work together using the RTI Act to raise vital governance issues and carry them to their logical conclusion.
- Evolving a comprehensive training policy with a view to developing the required mindsets among public functionaries in the context of "open government".
- Institution of an effective system of reward for competent service rendered by public functionaries with regard to the dissemination of information and also punishment for those who would be found withholding information in an arbitrary manner.
- Finally, implementation of the RTI would require an efficient information management system with the help of sophisticated information technology.

Information management is a multifaceted process involving the collection, processing, storage, transmission, and use of information. For a developing country such as India, the cost constraints would be much greater because the government will have to bear additional expenses to provide such information to all sections of its population. Knowledge of government schemes, policies, and programmes, especially highlighting the benefits for target groups, needs to be given free of cost to all. The role of the act itself and intermediaries such as NGOs and civil society groups will be crucial in ushering in a new era of open, transparent, and accountable governance.

This is an absolute imperative for all countries, and even more so for a country such as India, which has the unique distinction of having been the world's largest functional democracy for more than seven decades. It is because of the success of our vibrant democracy (albeit with aberrations) that many civil society organizations have been playing a catalytic role in various fields of public life. The more these organizations come forward to enlighten and mobilize the people at the grassroots level, the more would be the realization of the immense potential of the RTI. The RTI is a demand for a share of the power to govern and to question the institutions of governance and an effort to put the brakes on the arbitrary exercise of state power. It is a tool of empowerment for an average citizen and can be catalytic in bringing about change in the culture of governance.

The CIC has come with a landmark resolution to combat unending assaults on RTI activists. According to the resolution, if the commission receives a complaint regarding an assault on or murder of an information seeker, it will examine pending RTI applications of the victim and order the departments to publish the requested information suo motu on their web sites. If the information is made public on the Web every time an activist is attacked, it will defeat the very purpose of attacking an activist. RTI activists have welcomed the CIC move to address the need to take responsibility for the lives of information seekers and protect them from assaults. This resolution is a serious move to protect the rights of whistle-blowers.

Some of the Second Administrative Reforms Commission recommendations related to effective implementation of RTI in its first report, Right to Information-Master Key to Good Governance, are the following:

- The Official Secrets Act of 1923 should be repealed and substituted by a chapter in the National Security Act containing provisions relating to official secrets.
- Ministers on assumption of office should be given an oath of transparency along with the oath of office.

In a long interview given to the author, Shailesh Gandhi, one of the Central Information commissioners, listed three major threats to the RTI in India:

- The government's efforts at diluting the act by increasing the number of "exemptions" and making the legally binding decisions "recommended" instead of mandatory (as they exist now).
- The successful efforts of many public authorities to stall penalties imposed against them by getting "stay" orders from courts. The courts today have insulated themselves from any public scrutiny, and their disregard for the RTI Act and their non-transparent functioning is a great challenge to the RTI.
- Justice delayed can be justice denied. Information commissions have to be much more efficient and effective than the courts. Only approximately 5% of RTI applications come in appeal to the CIC; therefore, it should have the capacity for quick disposal of these cases. (The total cases disposed by the CIC as of October 2011 were 76,366; the total pending cases were 19,000).

The RTI heralds a new age in state-citizen relations in India. It is perhaps the first right that empowers an ordinary citizen to question and seek information from the State bureaucracy that exercises huge discretionary power over their lives. Earlier, the citizen was largely helpless against the administrative state, which was consistently being shielded by the Official Secrets Act or by the cloak of ministerial responsibility. Now, even the poorest citizen of the Indian state has been publicly empowered by the right to hold the State accountable for its acts of omission, incompetence, abuse, or delay in official work. The act would have lacked teeth without the penalty provisions that have given it the due seriousness it deserves.

RTI is truly a game changer. It has democratized information to the citizen's advantage. The citizen is central to the Act. Other countries offer freedom of information while our legislation recognizes it as a right. The exercise of RTI is the simplest form of participatory governance. The Act has changed the power equation of the Indian citizen with the government. It has given the ordinary Indian a tool to exercise his sovereignty —to ask questions and demand answers. The RTI application has forced Panchayats, States and the Centre to disclose information, and has initiated an era of citizen-driven transparency and accountability.

From the beginning, the RTI campaign has strongly advocated that all institutions that use public money and affect public interest must be brought under the ambit of the Act. This includes NGOs, political parties, the media, trade unions, cooperative societies, religious institutions, and many others. Transparency and accountability would be incomplete without ensuring that the private sector is subject to RTI in so far as it affects public interest.

It has brought the energies of public-spirited Indians to the domain of democratic governance. It has helped reduce corruption and arbitrary use of power. Contrary to the allegation that it has resulted in policy paralysis, RTI has and will eventually ensure accountability and efficiency so that bureaucrats and policymakers do their jobs they are paid to do with integrity, effectiveness and efficiency.

17.6 Right to Public Services Acts

Efficient and timely delivery of public services constitutes the heart of good governance. Our experience has shown that an enabling environment created by an effective and competent politico-administrative regime is a pre-requisite for attaining an optimum level of public service delivery. Several instruments of governance, including citizens' statutory entitlements, empowering user groups and transforming accountability of services through effective penalties have been identified as crucial for service delivery reforms. A number of Indian states have enacted legislation to guarantee well-timed delivery of public services as a matter of citizen rights. These laws also contain penalty provisions for public servants who fail to deliver the notified services within the particular time frame.

Right to Public Services Enactments in India comprise statutory laws that guarantee time-bound delivery of various public services rendered by the Government to citizens besides providing mechanisms for punishing errant civil servants who default in providing the services stipulated under the statute. Right to Service legislation is meant to reduce corruption among government officials by increasing transparency and public accountability. Madhya Pradesh became the first state in India to enact the Right to Service Act on 18 August 2010 and several other states like Bihar, Delhi, Punjab, Rajasthan, Himachal Pradesh, Kerala, Uttarakhand, Haryana, Uttar Pradesh, and Jharkhand have introduced similar legislation for guaranteeing the right to service to the citizen.

The common framework of the legislations in various states includes, granting of "right to public services", which are to be provided to the public by the designated official within the stipulated time frame. The public services, which are to be granted as a right under the legislations, are generally notified separately through Gazette notification. Some of the common public services which are to be provided within the fixed time frame as a right under the Acts, include caste, birth, marriage and domicile certificates, electric connections, voter's card, ration cards, copies of land records, etc.

In case of failure to provide the service by the designated officer within the given time or rejected to provide the service, the aggrieved person can approach the First Appellate Authority. The First Appellate Authority, after making a hearing, can accept or reject the appeal by making a written order stating the reasons for the order and intimate the same to the applicant, and can order the public servant to provide the service to the applicant.

An appeal can be made from the order of the First Appellate Authority to the Second Appellate Authority, who can either accept or reject the application, by making a written order stating the reasons for the order and intimate the same to the applicant, and can order the public servant to provide the service to the applicant or can impose penalty on the designated officer for deficiency of service without any reasonable cause, which can range from Rs. 500 to Rs. 10000 or may recommend disciplinary proceedings. The applicant may be compensated out of the penalty imposed on the officer. The appellate authorities have been granted certain powers of a Civil Court while trying a suit under Code of Civil Procedure, like production of documents and issuance of summons to the Designated officers and appellants.

17.7 Institutional Structure

Recently, many Indian states have enacted their respective Public Service Guarantee Acts, as a key administrative reform initiative. These Public Service Guarantee Acts build on the idea of the Citizen Charters which define the quality of public services, these Acts take it a step further by making a citizens' right to public service within the stipulated time legally binding, failing which the concerned officials can be penalized.

Few states such as Madhya Pradesh, Delhi, and Bihar have formulated legal enactments to devise mechanisms for strict implementation of the Act, while other states like Haryana have issued administrative orders for bringing together basic public services under a common e-governance portfolio. Although the legislative framework for these Acts has been established, the objectives of the Act can be achieved only by improving the actual delivery of services. This depends on several factors, foremost among which is the need to strengthen the capacities of service providers by creating adequate and efficient supporting infrastructure along with an attitudinal change.

In every state there are a certain number of services notified under the Act, ranging from 17 in Uttar Pradesh to 265 in Karnataka. These services are being provided from a single window through a Network of Public Service Centres (Jan Suvidha Kendras), which offer citizens the facility to track applications online. There is a two-tier appeal system in all states. The Missions are under one nodal department of the government, e.g. Department of General Administration/ Revenue/Information Technology Administrative Reforms, etc. In some states Right to Service Commissions for the monitoring of this Act have been also established, e.g. Rajasthan and Punjab.

The major services included in most states under these Acts comprise certified copies of many documents like record of land rights, mutation, water supply/ gas/sewerage sanctions, birth/marriage, death certificates, tax clearance/permits/ registrations, driving license, passport, caste, income, handicapped certificates, etc. Punjab is the first state which has brought more than 20 police services under the purview of the Act.

Furthermore, for strengthening the practice of public service guarantee laws across the country there is a need to create informed citizen opinion about the rights of citizens under the Acts. Such awareness will make the Act binding on the service-providers warning them against taking a laid-back attitude towards service-provision. Also, the use of ICT-based tools for tracking and monitoring service delivery can bring about accountability and efficiency which will make it easier to deliver services on time as well as help in quick identification of faulty individuals/departments. Information regarding type of services notified, appellate authorities and penalty provisions are not always clearly displayed/ published in these service centres by the service providers. Due to shortage of staff and poor quality of computers service delivery suffers. Instances of delay and backlog in the clearing of services have happened in all states. Officials often do not adhere to the time limit in the delivery of services. Lastly the slow process of penalizing errant officials does act as a stumbling block in almost all states. Penalty cases are reported pending with appellate authorities who are also slow to act. Despite delays, people usually do not file complaints.

While action on the above problems will certainly smoothen the implementation of the Right to Public Service, it must be emphasized that the legislation is a relatively new one and bottlenecks will continue for a while. Nevertheless, the Acts represent a dedicated effort on the part of State Governments to facilitate accountable, efficient and citizen-centric governance. Its effective implementation now depends upon citizen awareness and assertions as well.

17.8 Unique Features of the Acts

- Centralized monitoring has helped to keep a check on cutting-edge administration.
- Disposal rates have reached an overwhelming 90% in all states.
- Expenditure amount includes only the service specific prescribed service charges, if applicable. This has won public confidence and public participation in governance process.
- There is 100% accountability of every dealing government official under the Acts.
- There is reduction of grievance/petitions by 50% in almost all of these states.
- Data is generated online. This data can really add value to policy makers to plan and act from a citizen-centric perspective.
- Multiple access points like call centre, mobile interface; e-mail access provide easy and responsive public grievance redressal mechanisms.
- Revenue generation has gone up because every application seeking service is accounted for in the system, thus wastage of public money can be avoided.

- With timely delivery of services the image of the government as service provider can hugely improve.

Advantages

De-mystifying Government: The impression of government being a complex and complicated monolith is sought to be replaced by an image of government as a transparent, predictable and efficient service provider. A paradigm shift in citizen- government interaction should follow. The shift is towards citizen-centric governance.

The citizen-interface points: Regular government offices or Special Citizen Service Centres become better equipped from both infrastructure and staffing point of view to give full support to the citizens seeking services. Citizen Help Desks as well as online information allows citizens to obtain the services they desire in single or at the most two visits.

Online as well as Mobile Governance/Call Centre based acceptance of applications from the citizens: In due course, this facility is aimed at extending to the delivery of all services. The information on each step of processing of a given application by a citizen will be made available online as well as through a call centre and SMS. The application forms for all services will be standardized and converted into Online e-Forms. These application forms will be in a universal and common format, and, therefore, the citizen will find them user-friendly and easy to use/fill.

Business Process Reengineering: It is well understood that timely service delivery is critically dependent on modifying/replacing outdated procedures of service processing and delivery. Business Process Reengineering helps to rationalize decision making so that not only the citizen gets timely delivery of services but at the same time the burden of work of government officials is also considerably reduced.

Broadbasing Information Technology: IT will continue to form the backbone to serve citizens better. The Acts aim to achieve inter-operability and cross-communication of multiple databases of government and private systems to use the information therein to deliver services accurately and promptly to user groups.

Integrating Services: These Acts aim at leveraging existing databases of government departments to harness information therein, accurately, quickly / over-the-counter and deliver public services. For example, in case of an applicant seeking repeat service that his family members have already availed, then the service's system will be able to correlate with the existing requests and facilitate quick/over-the-counter decisions. Specified and notified time-bound service delivery through a single-window system is the most important goal of these Acts.

Capital Building: The government servants will be provided full support to discharge their duties by providing actionable information in due time as well as by other support such as emails, login accounts, etc. The Acts should be followed by regular and continuous training programmes for all stakeholders. Training and information workshops are required for both public officials as well as user groups.

Key to Good Governance: Broadly, the citizens' interface with the government (or its agencies) are for the following:

1. Public Services: These are the services to be provided to the citizens pursuant to Acts, Rules, Government Orders, Schemes, Circulars, etc.
2. Public Grievances: These broadly arise in relation to interaction of the citizens with the government or its agencies but do not constitute public services by themselves. For example, allegation of lack of cordial behaviour against a public servant by a citizen will fall in this category (though the dividing line between the public services and grievances is a thin one)
3. Information seeking requests: This is generally covered by Right to Information Act, 2005 & rules there under;
4. Any correspondence from citizens due to or in connection with the affairs of the government: The aim is to become a single point solution to facilitate handling all these interactions, keep a track of the same on the lines of notified services.

Secretariat under the ambit: It is expected that the number of government departments and services under the ambit of Acts will expand continuously and rapidly. These changes will usher in transparent, people-oriented, predictable administration and governance.

Citizens participation enables citizens' feedback and voice in public service delivery.

17.9 Challenges for Sustainability

Framing of an Act does not automatically assure satisfactory implementation. The single portal enabling online monitoring and automated checks and balances can be affected only with a personalized follow-up at the highest level of Chief Secretary and the Chief Minister. The administrative heads have to physically supervise the implementation on a day-to-day basis. Allocating more resources for overcoming shortage of staff and equipment will be necessary to improve the e-readiness of departments and their capacity to handle the workload.

No system can be made sustainable by outside forces alone. The internal motivation of the employees to improve their brand image in the eyes of the public have to be continuously reinforced through training, workshop, seminars, etc., involving both officials, citizens and the media. If an employee chooses to bypass an application (not issue a GSC) —it is only through attitudinal training that this mentality can change, which may take some time. There is still widespread ignorance of these Acts among the public and inadequate computerization of records in most government departments besides the old inertia to act or deliver services on time.

The external motivation for performance-based incentives has been introduced through annual 'Sarvottam Seva' cash awards for Group A, B, C and D employees. Officials who have not defaulted during their service will be recognized for their meritorious work through an appreciation letter to be entered in the Annual Confidential Report.

The Act is only a means to improve the administrative processes for the satisfaction of the citizens. Work studies pertaining to officials' capacity v/s the workload forms a critical input for ensuring good administration. The stipulated time limits have to be certainly reviewed and business processes simplified so that the services are given within an optimum time and the public official capacities are also optimally utilized.

17.10 A Review

There are 20 Indian states that have enacted such legislation, so far (June 2014) and an overarching Central Act is also on the anvil. Today the legislative framework for rights of citizens to receive time-bound services is well-established, but it will be premature to draw any inferences about its effective implementation. Wherever positive results are seen, they are more about sustained efforts, gradual progress and perfect coordination between all levels of the implementation hierarchy.

While it is too early to assess how effectively the Acts are delivering results, some commonalities are clearly visible even now. As a general rule, legislation alone is rarely effective in achieving the desired results. In the present context, time-bound services to citizens will not get delivered only by legislating penalties for delays. While the provision for penalty will make some employees work harder, actual delivery on time will happen when laws are accompanied by complementary governance reforms that build systems capability for timely delivery. The interventions required are simplification and standardization of delivery processes, application of e-governance solutions, adequate and efficient support infrastructure, training and attitudinal change among implementing employees.

17.11 Towards E-Governance

The use of information and communication technologies to improve public service delivery has been widely acknowledged in policy practice in both the Indian states and the Centre since the 1990s. The Central Government's National e-Governance Plan (NeGP), spelled out in 2006, sets out a comprehensive agenda for developing e-governance services, networking infrastructure, state data centres, and village-level centres for delivering core services to citizens (Government of India 2006). This programme is an extension of earlier efforts by a number of states to offer computerized services in ration cards, income certificates, licenses, land records, and income tax payments. From e-Seva in Andhra Pradesh, Nemmadi in Karnataka, and Friends in Kerala to e-Mitra in Rajasthan, Civic Centres in Gujarat, and Sugam in Himachal Pradesh, State Governments have been pioneers in introducing e-governance projects in public service delivery.

Over the last few years, the Indian Government has taken several initiatives to improve the delivery of public services to the citizens through computerized services. It has introduced policies around development and deployment of Information and Communication Technology (ICT) to improve the coverage and timeliness of government services. For this, significant investments have been made varying from computerization of government departments, to creating effective service delivery mechanisms for various citizen-centric services.

17.12 National e-Governance Plan

The National e-Governance Plan (NeGP) has been formulated by the Department of

Electronics and Information Technology (DeitY) and the Department of Administrative Reforms and Public Grievances (DARPG). The NeGP was approved by the Government of India in May 2006 to make all government services accessible to citizens through service delivery outlets. It makes most services available online, ensuring that citizens have speedyaccess to these thereby improving the quality of governance.

NeGP comprises 31 mission mode projects (MMPs), which are further classified as State, Central or Integrated projects. Each State Government can also define five MMPs specific to its individual needs. MMPs have clearly defined scope and objectives, measurable outcomes, service-levels, well-defined milestones and timelines for implementation. MMPs are owned and managed by different Ministries which are entirely responsible for all decisions related to their areas. However, overarching decisions that impact NeGP are taken in consultation with DeitY. The 31 MMPs include: Central MMPs: Banking, Central Excise and Customs, Income Tax, Insurance, MCA21 National Citizen Database, Passport, Immigration Visa and Foreigners Registration and Tracking, Pensions, e-Office

State MMPs: Agriculture, Commercial Taxes, e-District, Employment Exchange, Land Records, Municipalities, Gram Panchayats, Police, Road Transport, Treasuries, Health, Education and Public Distribution System.

Integrated MMPs: Common Service Centres, e-Biz, e-Courts, e-Procurement, EDI for e-Trade, National e-Governance Service Delivery Gateway, India Portal

Implementation of the NeGP requires provision of hardware and-software, IT infrastructure, process re-engineering and change management. The NeGP is a three- tier structure for providing common support infrastructure.

Tier I - The Common Service Centre (CSC) is the front-end delivery point for a variety of citizen services including application forms, certificates, and utility payments such as electricity, telephone and water bills. The objective of NeGP is to develop a platform that enables the Government and non-governmental organizations to align their goals through IT based services for the benefit of citizens.

Tier II: -This includes common support infrastructure that can allow information to be shared electronically between different agencies of the government and with citizens. State Wide Area Networks (SWAN) form the converged backbone network for data, voice and video throughout a State/UT. The objective of SWAN is to interconnect each State/UT headquarter with District Headquarters, and each District Headquarters with the Block Headquarters. The plan is to create; a secure closed user group (CUG) government network for the purpose of delivering services.

Tier HI: The third important infrastructural element of the NeGP is the State Data Centre (SDC). Under the NeGP, it is proposed to have SDCs to consolidate services, applications and infrastructure to provide efficient electronic service delivery. SDCs provide common IT infrastructure to host State-level e-governance applications and data. SDCs provide rich functionalities such as central repositories, secure data storage, online delivery of services, citizen information/ services portal, State internet portal, disaster recovery, remote management and service integration.

The failures of previous initiatives have played an important role in shaping the e-governance strategy of the country. A programmed approach has now been adopted for the implementation of e-governance projects that has helped in saving costs via sharing of core and support infrastructure.

The NeGP programme management structure comprises:

- Prime Minister's Office: provide leadership and periodically monitor the implementation of NeGP.
- National e-Governance Advisory Group: advise the Government on policy issues and strategic Intervention for introduction, of e-governance.
- Apex Committee: oversee the NeGP programmes by providing policy and strategic directions for implementation.
- Planning Committee and Ministry of Finance: allocate funds for NeGP through Plan and Non-Plan budgetary provisions.
- Line-Ministries/Departments: take the ownership of MMPs and conceptualize.
- State Governments/UT Administration: implement State sector MMPs.
- DeitY/NIC: serve as a secretariat to the Apex Committee and assist in managing the projects either directly or through NIC.

E-governance is promoted through a centralized initiative while allowing decentralized implementation model. The NeGP encourages the adoption of the Public Private Partnership (PPP) model to enlarge the resource pool for implementation and functioning of the plan.

17.13 Digital India

Digital India is an ambitious programme of the Government of India to prepare India for a knowledge based transformation by a synchronized engagement with both Central Government and the State Governments to deliver good governance to citizens.

This programme has been envisaged by the Department of Electronics and Information Technology.. The existing/ ongoing e-Governance initiatives would be revamped to align them with the principles of Digital India. The vision of Digital India is to transform the country into a digitally empowered society and knowledge economy. It would ensure that government services are available to citizens electronically. It would also bring in public accountability through mandated delivery of government services electronically.

The Digital India vision provides the intensified impetus for further momentum and progress for e-Governance and would promote inclusive growth that covers electronic services, products, devices, manufacturing and job opportunities. Digital infrastructure will focus on providing high speed secure Internet. Digital empowerment of citizens will pay emphasis on universal digital literacy and availability of digital resources/services in Indian languages.

Requirements of funds for individual project(s) for Digital India will be worked out by respective nodal ministries/departments. To implement this the government is planning to strengthen National Informatics Center (NIC) by restructuring it to support all central government departments and state governments. Digital India consists of three core components: the development of secure and stable digital infrastructure, delivering government services digitally, and universal digital literacy.

As of 31 December 2018, India had a population of 130 crore people (1.3 billion), 123 crore (1.23 billion) Aadhaar digital biometric identity cards, 121 crore (1.21 billion) mobile phones, 44.6 crore (446 million) smartphones, 56 crore (560 million) internet users up from 481 million people (35% of the country's total population) in December 2017, and 51 per cent growth in e-commerce

17.14 Empowering Citizens Through e-Services

Presently, digital transformation of India is on a growth trajectory aiming towards a trillion dollar digital economy by 2025. Government is taking strategic steps to realize the Trillion Dollar Digital Economy potential.

The coverage of Aadhaar (123 crore), Jan Dhan Yojana (36 crore) and mobile connections (118 crore) have moulded the digital profile of India. Each of the individual components of the JAM Trinity enable citizen centric services collectively as well as in individual capacity. Jan Dhan Yojana has provided financial inclusion to unbanked people and thereby, it has enabled banking, pension (PMSBY and PMJJBY) and insurance (Atal Pension Yojana) services to common citizens. Mobiles have also accelerated the accessibility of government services in rural areas helping tremendously to bridge the digital divide.

Digital delivery of services has been strengthened with the help of 3.47 lakh Common Services Centres (CSCs), spread across 2.3 lakh Gram Panchayats in the country that provides digital access in rural areas at an affordable cost.

Various new citizen centric, transformational digital platforms have been developed, such as Bharat Interface for Money-Unified Payment Interface (BHIM-UPI), Government e-Marketplace (GeM), Goods and Services Tax Network (GSTN), Digital Locker (DigiLocker), Unified Mobile App for New-Age Governance (UMANG), Jeevan Pramaan, e-Hospital, MyGov, e-National Agriculture Market (e-NAM), Study Webs of Active-Learning for Young Aspiring Minds (SWAYAM) and National Scholarship Portal (NSP) etc.

The combination of Jan Dhan bank accounts, mobile phones and digital identity through Aadhaar i.e. JAM trinity is helping the poor to get benefits directly into their bank account. A total of Rs. 7.34 lakh crore have been disbursed through Aadhaar based DBT to beneficiaries of 439 Government schemes which, have led to saving of over Rs. 1.41 lakh crore cumulatively by March 2019, by removing fictitious claimants.

Efforts are being made to uplift the marginalised sections with the support of digital technologies, starting from giving ration at reasonable cost with around 23.19 crore Digitized Ration Cards; giving various pensions to the deserving where in 1.99 crore Digital Life Certificates were processed; disbursing scholarships wherein over 1.4 crore applications received digitally and over 2128 crore disbursed in AY 2018-19; employment to unemployed under MGNREGA Scheme with 13.14 crore job cards and 7.75 crore number of DBT Transactions during 2019-20.

It is estimated that in India only about 10 per cent people are English speaking and it is obvious that a large population will be deprived of benefits of technologies due to language barrier. The internet and digital technologies can only be useful to people once it services citizens in local language. Today India has Indian language content in cyberspace in at least 15 languages and the rest would soon be available on the Internet.

Pradhan Mantri Digital Saksharta Abhiyan has been appreciated as the world's largest Government effort to bridge the digital divide. It aims to make 6 crore rural adults digitally literate – one person in every household, out of which 2.21 crore persons have already been trained. Common Services Centres (CSCs) are internet enabled centres allowing near doorstep access to citizens to social services. These front end services delivery outlets are delivering over 350 digital services. A number of important government welfare services for including PMAY, FSSAI, Soil Health Cards, Swachh Bharat Abhiyan, Pradhan Mantri Fassal Bima Yojana, etc have been added on Digital Seva Portal.

As per the data from Electronic Transaction Aggregation and Analysis Layer (eTAAL), the portfolio of electronic services has grown to 3,702 and an average number of electronic transactions on a daily basis (till April 2019) is around 9.5 crore, which can be attributed to both i.e., growing number of transactions as well as increase in consumption of e-Services. This also signifies that the benefits of Digital India have percolated down to a large section of the society

17.15 Some Observations

Technological changes have certainly improved the living status of Indians. The technological advancement is, however, a little slow in the area of computer-aided public delivery of services. It is because of two basic difficulties of this sector, first, is the ready availability of personal computers which is still a costly affair for an average-income earning Indian and the second is ignorance and lack of information of available computer-aided facilities and their huge benefits over the conventional system.

Governments today are taking initiatives to provide basic amenities and facilities electronically. In this way, they want to reach closer to every citizen, provide easy access to government programmes and make it easy for citizens to pay their taxes and bills for services used or accessed. In e-governance, various facilities and functions of government are available to the public through web portals with the help of Internet. Hence, a citizen can access the services with the use of computer and Internet and is saved from the long wait in tedious queues. In the sense of customer-to-customer (C2C) electronic business module, e-governance is Government to resident (G2R) module, electronically connecting administrators with the remotest citizen for welfare of the society and "ease in use" purposes.

In a country like India where Internet penetration and usage are low, and there are a huge number of people who do not have any access to computers, e-services can expand only at the initiative of the government. The government has to reach each beneficiary even if the beneficiary himself finds it difficult to reach for and demand the service. It is only this approach that can ensure that the services are affordable, easily accessible and brought within citizen reach. E-government presents a win-win proposition to all stake holders — the private sector gets new customers and markets, government presents SMART (Simple, Moral, Accountable, Responsive and Transparent) administration to the citizens, and the citizens finally get access to timely and efficient public services with greater transparency and less corruption. India can be a leader among developing countries in e-governance for several reasons: (a) its well-developed IT industry and the Union Government's commitment to make India an IT superpower (b) a cyber legislation in place and (c) a growing telecom and networking infrastructure. Almost 20 states of India now have Public Service Guarantee Acts covering the timely delivery of specified services where citizens interact online at public kiosks where applications are processed e-government applications have been used in India for e-procurement, tax collection, processing licence applications sharing budget/expenditure information, and sharing information across departments. Now, with automation of the processes, there are fewer opportunities for officials to obstruct or delay the process, and speed money to hasten the manual process need not be paid, thereby lowering levels of corruption.

Making e-governance widespread entails bridging the digital divide, enabling access to the Internet in rural areas and setting up information kiosks. A major task is to build institutional capacity for governance reform.

17.16 Role of Non-Governmental Agencies

India has possibly the largest number of active non-government, non-profit organizations in the world. There has been a sharp increase in the number of new NGOs in the past decade in India. *A recent study commissioned by the government showed that there were about 3.3 million NGOs in India (highest in the world)* by the end of 2009, i.e. one NGO for less than an average of 400 Indians. This is because the study, took into consideration only those entities which were registered under the Societies Registration Act, 1860, or the Mumbai Public Trust Act and its variants in other states.

Similarly, in case of finance the government has been the biggest donor, i.e. Rs 18,000 crore was set aside for the social sector in the XI Plan followed by foreign contributors. Individual donors are emerging as the biggest and most important source of funds for the working of NGOs.

It can be noted that a great majority of the NGOs are small and about three- fourths of all NGOs are run entirely by volunteers. About 13% of the NGOs have between 2 to 5 employees; about 5% have between 6 to 10 employees and only about 8.5% NGOs employ more than 10 people (survey conducted by society for Participatory Research in Asia [PRIA]), 73.4% of NGOs have one or no paid staff, although across the country, more than 19 million persons work as volunteers or paid staff in NGOs. More often NGOs are registered as trusts, societies, or as private limited non-profit companies, under Section-25 of Indian Companies Act, 1956. They also enjoy income tax exemption. Foreign contributions to non-profits are governed by Foreign Contribution Regulation Act (FCRA, 1976). There are organizations in India working in the areas of environment, health care, anti-corruption, eradication of child labour, education, protection of human rights of women and children, consumer protection, etc., which have been given an NGO status.

M Venkatarangaiya Foundation formed in 1991 and now functioning in several states like Maharashtra, Madhya Pradesh and Bihar is known for having ceaselessly worked for eradicating child labour from India. The major NGOs involved in environment education and protection include Centre for Science and Environment (CSE), Gandhi Peace Foundation, Bombay Natural History Society, Assam Science Society, etc. It is worth mentioning here that a major effort, no doubt, of the NGO sector in influencing environmental policy in the country has been that of the Narmada Bachao Andolan. The founder of the Bachpan Bachao Andolan has been honoured recently with the Nobel peace prize.

India Against Corruption and Awaaz are very active organizations fighting against corruption in India. A Chennai-based anti-corruption NGO called Fifth Pillar India is yet another organization that introduced a zero rupee note to provide anti-corruption message to Indians. Centre for Social Research has been active in women empowerment issues in India since 1983. Similarly, in order to protect the consumer rights and interests, there are NGOs like Consumer Education and Research Centre. This organization primarily deals with various projects through media, consumer research and monitoring.

In short, NGOs exist in the area of environment, health, education, peace, human rights, consumer rights, women's rights and in every field of social change. Since 1980, many NGO groups across the country have adopted an alternative 'social action' approach by politicizing the issues of poverty, directly challenging many of the social programmes established by the government and thereby fighting against them. The NGO sector has always been in the forefront in providing recovery, relief and rehabilitation after natural calamities and disasters such as floods, droughts, earthquakes and epidemics. In this respect the government also recognizes their significant role.

17.17 Advisory Role to the Government

There are some voluntary organizations that play an active role as advocacy groups. They conduct research on key issues affecting the country and engage with government on policy dialogue. They also conduct regular reviews on the efficacy of developmental projects carried out by the state and national governments. These reviews help in mid-course correction and redefine the targets of such projects. The voluntary organizations have benefit of their outreach on the one hand and also availability of technical expertise on the other. The review of the 11th plan was conducted by a consortium of voluntary organizations after a series of consultations at the state and thematic levels. Even the government considers their role as an important input in policy formation. Since the last two years selected voluntary organizations are also invited by the Finance Ministry for Pre-budget annual consultations. Many consultative committees are formed by various ministries to seek structured input from the voluntary sector. For example, the Centre for Budget and Governance Accountability publishes a journal called Budget Track which acts like a general awareness document on public expenditure and budgetary issues meant to sensitize the average citizen.

The voluntary sector is also engaged in providing critical inputs to the policy makers within the government in other ways. They regularly bring out status reports on climate change, agriculture, industry, fiscal reforms, etc., and submit to the government. They also provide inputs to the members of parliament and state legislatures. These organizations also run advocacy campaigns through the media and popular publications to generate awareness and public support.

17.18 National Policy on the Voluntary Sector

The relationship between the government and the voluntary sector has always been problematic. Sometimes the voluntary sector plays the role of an extended arm of the government by delivering services and projects and also produces a critique of the same. Within the complex realities of the relationship between the government and the voluntary sector, the National Policy on the Voluntary Sector came like a ray of hope. The policy saw the light of the day in 2007 due to the tremendous efforts and the leadership of the Planning Commission. This policy visualized a long-term, sustainable and institutionalized collaboration between the government and the voluntary sector. A need to develop a national policy, which not only defines the relationship between the government and the voluntary sector but also explores the ways to strengthen the sector, have now emerged. Various strategies like capacity building, streamlining the procedures and guidelines, creating synergy between efforts of the government and the voluntary sector have all been outlined. Although, the origin of these efforts could be traced back as far as 1988, the first concrete step was taken by the Planning Commission in March 1994, when a national convention was organized. In these two days of deliberations, the Planning Commission adopted an 'Action Plan' to bring about a collaborative relationship between the Voluntary sector and the Government. It should be noted that while formulating the Tenth Five Year Plan, the Planning Commission had set up a Steering Committee for the active involvement of voluntary organizations in the national development process. On May 17,2007, the "National Policy" was approved by the Government of India.

The announcement of a national policy was whole-heartedly welcomed by the sector as it reflected the seriousness of the government to encourage, enable, and empower an independent, creative and effective voluntary sector as its partner. Broadly speaking, the policy sets out four specific objectives:

- To create an enabling environment for Voluntary Organizations (VOs) that stimulates their enterprise and effectiveness, and safeguards their autonomy.
- To enable VOs to legitimately mobilize necessary financial resources from India and abroad.
- To identify operating systems by which the Government may work together with VOs, on the basis of the principles of mutual trust and respect, and with the shared responsibility.
- To encourage VOs to adopt transparent and accountable systems of governance and management.

The policy aims at improving the engagement between the government and the voluntary sector. The policy outlines instruments of partnership. They are: formal consultation, strategic collaboration, project funding and establishment of joint consultative groups with representatives from NGO's and the government. These could be permanent mechanisms of working together. Although, there has been no systematic analysis of the achievements or failures of the policy but the reviews so far point to many problematic issues. Some of the areas are listed below:

Enabling Environment

The National Policy promised government's efforts towards creating an enabling environment for voluntary organizations by simplifying rules, regulations, capacity building and facilitating funding environment. However, in the meantime a more stringent Foreign Contribution (Regulation) Act, 2010, was enacted, which not only requires re-registration after every five years but also relieves government from accountability towards VOs. On the one hand, the provision of deemed approval is being taken back while on the other hand there is no answerability by the Ministry in case of a delay or arbitrary rejection. Presently, the VOs are not supposed to mobilize people for their democratic rights unless approved by the ministry. Similarly, the proposed Direct Taxes Code intends to tax VOs. The provision of saving has been taken away along with the facility to account on accrual basis. However the definition of "charitable activities" remains confused as it was earlier. The VISA regime for VOs has also been tightened. Hence, inviting external experts and organizing international workshops requires clearance from three Ministries: Home, External Affairs, and the Nodal Ministry. Lastly, the environment for fund generation within India has become more difficult. The VOs have to compete along with the various consultancy firms to partner with the government on various development schemes.

17.19 Role of the Voluntary sector – A Review

The rise of NGOs is an important development since the 1980s. This period also coincides with the demise of the conventional planning era and the rise of a neo- liberal political economy. In what is often characterized as a move from inefficient states to efficient markets, NGOs hold a distinctive mediating position. Given the profound implications of the NGO involvement in development, there is a great need to critically examine the changing relations among NGOs, state agencies, multilateral and bilateral funding institutions and other social groups. This situation has a great bearing on the way in which we conceive the process of social change and the roles of different social actors within it.

The growing prominence of NGOs in the field of development is strongly related to the declining legitimacy of the state. Increasingly, the state is looked upon with suspicion, if not contempt. Least governance is seen as a sign of good governance. Post-development a list ideologies of neo-liberalism choose to espouse the virtues of market enterprise. 'Good governance' is believed now to consist of two functions: facilitating the free play of market forces and enabling decentralized institutions of 'participatory management' to function. Participatory management is the new mantra for the provision of services through local municipalities and Panchayats, as well as in the sphere of natural-resource management. State structures are criticized as being rigidly bureaucratic and corrupt, and, thus, unsuited for performing either welfare or resource-management functions; whereas, NGOs are seen as 'civil society' actors that are more responsive and committed to bringing about social change. The state is seen as consisting of entrenched interests and styles of functioning that make it unwilling and unable to work with people, a role that NGOs are supposed to be good at. Thus, NGOs have emerged to perform a bridging function, taking on functions that the state is unsuited for, and are performing them with lower overheads, greater efficiency and motivation. Increasingly, it is not only funding institutions but the state itself that accepts the presence of NGOs and, in fact, expects them to take over certain tasks. This new set of institutional linkages between the state agencies and NGOs, between state and 'civil society', needs to be explored and researched.

Whereas many NGOs espouse democratic decentralization, the working of their own organizations is often idiosyncratic, with authority being vested in unaccountable charismatic figures. Structures for the redressal of employee grievances, mandatory in most formal organizations, are often absent in NGOs where personalized management practices tend to prevail over more impersonal rule-based procedures. This contradiction has been the source of conflict in many cases, where workers were forced to leave the organization at the behest of the founders. Whereas state structures are at least formally rule-governed, the same is not true of NGOs where the spirit of voluntarism is sometimes used to obscure exploitation and manipulation.

Besides, NGOs often indulge in double standards. When criticizing state structures, they plead for 'openness, transparency and democratic participation'. However, many of them do not seem to observe these norms in their own functioning. Crucial decisions are often taken at the top by the senior leaders without any scope for ordinary workers to participate in decision-making deliberations.

By and large, NGOs that receive external funds are expected to fulfil physical and financial targets, show tangible results (how much money spent, how many trees planted, how many people trained, etc.), but without regard to the quality of the output. Often, the expected output is hard to measure since it is difficult to come up with quantifiable indicators of measurement. The pressing need to meet physical targets (the requirement of bureaucratic accounting practices often forces NGOs to take shortcuts) often results in the more gradual and open-ended process of empowerment being compromised.

While NGOs are often critical of politicians and bureaucracy for misusingand misappropriating public money earmarked for development, the NGO record is not so exemplary. Recently it was reported that many NGOs have not submitted utilization certificates amounting to several crores of rupees. They have been warned that no further grants will be released till they submit utilization certificates for money spent by fund or grant giving organizations, national or international.

When the late Prime Minister Rajiv Gandhi revealed that less than 15% of the total money spent by the government on development programmes reached the targeted beneficiaries, there was a wave of shock and surprise. According to some calculations, this proportion may be 20% in the case of NGOs, which also spend substantial amounts on their own salaries and infrastructure. The difference in terms of benefits to the poor may not be so great at all.

It can be concluded that India has now a vibrant and fast growing NGO sector. They perform a lot of functions in areas including environment, health care, anti- corruption, eradication of child labour, education, protection of human rights of women and children, consumer protection, disaster management and many more. A healthy linkage of government and NGOs is the requirement of the times. It is also of paramount importance that the NGO sector in India, considering its growing social reach should now be subjected to social audit and scrutiny as much as governmental organizations.

Conclusion

In the 21st century, the position of citizens from being mere recipients of public goods and services has now shifted to their being prime movers in the affairs of governance. It is a change from the local beneficiary status to active 'participant status'. In a democracy, the main purpose of public administration is to serve the needs of the people. An accountable, accessible, transparent, participative and responsive administration is urgently required to address the problems of the people. Citizens' grievances against the administration are on an increase and at the same time concerted efforts are being made by the Indian Government to reduce the growing discontent amongst the citizens by providing various channels for the redress of their grievances. The Right to Information, the Citizens' Charter, Public Service Guarantee acts and E-Governance have emerged as more effective and accessible tools to redress citizens' grievances.

Suggested Readings

Awasthi, Ramesh, "*Rural Development through people's Mobilisation: A Case Study of Ralegaon Siddhi,*" *in, Social Change through Voluntary Action*, edited by M.L. Dantwala, Harsh Sethi and Pravin Visaria. New Delhi, Sage, 1998, pp. 69-74.

Bagga, R.K., K. Keniston and R.R. Mathur, *The State, IT and Development*, New Delhi, Sage, 2005.

Basu, Rumki, "*Freedom of Information in India*", *in Public Administration in South Asia*, Meghna Sabharwal, Evan M. Berman (ed.), Taylor and Francis Group, 2013.

Baviskar, B.S. and W. Attwood, *Finding the Middle Path: The Political Economy of Co-operation in Rural India*, Boulder and London, Westview Press, 1995.

Bhatnagar, S., *E-Government: From Vision to Implementation*, Delhi, Sage, 2004.

Centre for Good Governance, A Manual for Public Authorities, Information Officers and Appellate Authorities, Hyderabad, 2006.

----- The RTI Act: *A Guide for Civil Society Organizations*, Hyderabad, 2006.

------ *Information Commission: Roles & Responsibilities*, Hyderabad, 2006.

------ *A Citizen's Guide on Right to Information Act*, Hyderabad, 2008.

Citizen Centric Administration. The Heart of Governance, 12th Report SARC, Government of India, New Delhi, 2009.

Dantwala, M.L., Harsh Sethi and Pravin Visaria (eds.), *Social Change through Voluntary Action*, New Delhi: Sage Publications, 1998.

Dhanagare, D.N. *"Action Groups and Social Transformation in India,"* Lokayan Bulletin, 6 no. 5(1988): pp. 37-59.

Dudeja, V.D., *Information Technology and Practical Management*, New Delhi, Commonwealth Publishers, 2004.

Ghuman, B.S., Ranjeet Singh and Mohammad Sohail, *"Right to Public Service Act: A Tool of Good Governance in India" in Democracy and good governance: Reinventing the Public Service Delivery System in India*, edited by Rumki Basu, Badrul Alam and Furqan Ahmad, Bloomsbury, New Delhi, 2015.

Gupta, P, and R.K. Bagga, *Compendium of e-Governance in India*, Hyderabad, Orient Blackswan, 2008.

Jeffery, Roger and Nandini Sundar (eds.), *A New Moral Economy for India's Forests? Discourses of Community and Participation*, New Delhi, Sage Publications, 1999.

Kedia Sapna *Implementing the Right to Public Service Act,* One World Foundation India 2011.

Kothari, Smitu, *"Social Movements and Redefinition of Democracy," India Briefing*, edited by R. Oldenberg, Boulder, Westview Press, 1993, pp. 131-62.

Mathew, George, *"Decentralised Institutions: Governmental and Voluntary Sector" Economic and Political Weekly*, 34 no. 9(1999): pp. 529-34.

Naib, S., *The Right to Information Act 2005: A Hand Book*, New Delhi, Oxford University Press, 2011.

Prabhu, C.S.R., *E-Governance: Concepts and Case Studies,* Delhi, Prentice Hall of India, 2006.

Raj, B., *E-Governance Techniques: India and Global Experiences,* New Delhi, New Century Publications, 2008.

Rajneesh Shalini Sakala, *"Guarantee of Services to citizens. Management in government/* April June 2013, pp. 41-62.

Ramulu, C.H. Bala and A.V. Reddy, *"State NGO's and Development Experiences in India— Need for a stronger relationship,"* IJPA, LX no. 2 (April-June 2014).

Roy, A., D. Nikhil and S. Pande, *The Right to Information Act 2005: A Social Development Perspective Social Development Report 2008.* New Delhi, Council for Social Development, 2008.

Second Administrative Reforms Commission, First Report, Right to Information: Master Key to Good Governance, New Delhi, Government of India, 2006.

Srivastava, S. and R. Tandon, *"How large is India's non-profit sector?"* EPW, XL no.19 (2005), pp. 1948-52.

Tandon R., *Voluntary action, civil society and the state*, New Delhi, Mosaic Books, 2002

Yojana, *Special issue on Citizen Centric e-Services*, July 2019

ooo

Chapter Eighteen

New Regulatory Agencies

Introduction

Some mechanisms of regulatory exercise were put in place in the Indian Constitution itself and in the laws of the land. The examples are the Election Commission of India under Article 324 of the Constitution for legislative elections at union and state levels and the presidential and vice-presidential elections; Union and State Public Service Commissions for civil service recruitments under Articles 323 to 315; the Comptroller and Auditor General of India for audit of accounts of both orders of governments under Articles 148 to 151; and the Reserve Bank of India (RBI) under RBI Act, 1934, with subsequent amendments.

The Second Administrative Reforms Commission (ARC-II) Report gives a list of only major professional self-regulating authorities operating in India each formed under respective Acts of Parliament (year of enactment within brackets): (a) Bar Council of India (1961), (b) Medical Council of India (1956) presently being reformed as Medical Commission of India, (c) Institute of Chartered Accountants of India (1949), (d) Institute of Cost and Works Accountants of India (1959), (e) Institute of Company Secretaries of India (1980) and (f) Council of Architecture (1972) (Government of India, 2008b, p. 113).

In 1991, there came the paradigm shift in the economic policy regime towards neoliberalism (predicated on bureaucratic deregulation, privatization and business liberalism – nationally and globally) under the P.V. Narasimha Rao Congress government. The effects of these economic reforms are evident in areas such as industrial licensing, financial sector reforms in banking, stock market, telecommunication, electricity, companies affairs, security and exchange, insurance, coal, petroleum, etc. In all these sectors, new regulatory agencies have come under parliamentary statutes with varying degrees of autonomy. Various sectors of national economy, which were earlier managed under direct ministerial and bureaucratic control have now been placed under IRAs, reporting to the Parliament annually. Among the new financial regulatory bodies in India, besides the RBI whose origins go back to British India, there are Securities and Exchange Board of India (SEBI), Pension Fund Regulatory and Development Authority (PFRDA), Forward Markets Commission (FMC), Insurance Regulatory and Development Authority (IRDA), Foreign Investment Promotion Board (FIPB), Financial Stability and Development Council (FSDC), Project Exports Promotion Council of India, Foreign Direct Investment Promotion Board (FDIPB), etc. In various sectors of the national economy such regulatory authorities include Central Electricity Regulatory Commission (CERC), Telecom Regulatory Authority of India (TRAI), etc.

18.1 Some Regulatory Agencies

Telecom Regulatory Authority of India (TRAI)

The Department of Telecom (DoT) in its erstwhile combined policy-maker-operator-licensor role had created the (previous) independent TRAI in March 1997, which was later terminated in late 1999 and reconstituted in 2000.

The TRAI Amendment Ordinance 2000 reconstituted the body into two—the regulator TRAI, and a dispute redressal and adjudicatory body, the Telecom Dispute Settlement and Appellate Tribunal (TDSAT). The Amendment separated the functions of the new TRAI into three operationally distinct areas: (1) a set of recommendatory roles, (2) a set of binding roles, and (3) tariff setting functions.

The achievements of the Indian telecom industry are considered a landmark in the reform process. Since liberalization, India has seen growth in the cellular network reach and tariffs fell across the board. The impact of successful regulation is quite obvious in this sector. The regulatory role encompassed tariff determination for landline telephones, Internet, Internet telephony, cellular phones, cable and broadband connections and interconnections for domestic and international services. In addition the agency had to trigger competition by awarding different services to private and public players. The decision-making process of TRAI has been questioned many times accusing the body of trying to protect the interests of public operators.

However, the power to issue licenses remained with the government. Since the inception of TRAI, its independence has often been challenged. In the case of TRAI political barriers to such independence are quite evident from a study of the sector's regulatory history, as relations between the government and the TRAI have been problematic at all times. TRAI is accountable to the parliament, and regulated companies and consumer groups have appealed against its decisions in the tribunal for telecommunications; many suits have gone to High Courts and the Supreme Court.

An important dimension of independence relates to financing of the regulatory body. As mentioned, if there is no assured and independent funding for the regulator, its decisions may be constrained due to its dependence on the government, thus introducing scope for abuse and manipulation. TRAI has been weak on this front too as it has had to depend on the line ministry for funding.

A regulator also needs to be transparent and accountable to consumers. The prime purpose of a regulator is to defend and promote consumer choice, welfare and quality of service. TRAI has made efforts to solicit consumer participation by regularly consulting consumer groups. But consumer participation is lacking as mostly service providers attend these meetings and very few consumer groups participate actively. TRAI is not authorized to impose penalties and therefore its directives are often not followed by operators.

However, despite these inadequacies, TRAI has been successful in widening access quality of service and reducing price by introducing competition in the market. TRAI has set the standards of following a systematic procedure of decision-making with detailed consultations on tariff philosophies, a series of public consultations and hearings and, finally, reasoned and documented interventions.

The experience of TRAI bolsters the need for a clear division of jurisdiction between the regulator and the government by reducing the dependence of the former on the latter in a very substantive sense.

18.2 Electricity Regulatory Commissions (ERCs)

There are State Electricity Regulatory Commissions (SERCs) besides the Central ERC. The central commission regulates bulk electricity tariffs up to the boundaries of states and interstate transmission tariffs. The CERC also has powers to license private investment in transmission, with the consent of Power Grid Corporation of India Ltd (PGCIL), which is a state monopoly. Tariffs for generation, transmission, distribution within a state, as well as purchase and supply, are regulated by the state bodies. It is also a mandate for CERC to develop a competitive market for bulk electricity. However, electricity regulation in India has had its share of problems. Public ownership of electricity (with embedded distributive politics) has created a political legacy that is likely to delay effective and efficient regulatory regimes in India. The farmers and household consumers are an important subsidized political constituency at the state level and electricity is a state subject. Besides, a regulator needs independence from the government to discharge its functions with neutrality. The role of the government (Central as well as State) is to issue appropriate policy guidelines in consultation with the respective regulator but sometimes there are overlaps in their respective jurisdictions. For example, ERCs are empowered to fix tariffs for user groups but the Central Government has not allowed them to determine tariff at their discretion. The Act allows the State Governments to provide subsidy to deserving consumers but the respective governments have to pay the subsidy amount in advance to the utility. In practice, the governments provide subsidy but do not make equivalent payment to the utility which adversely affects its financial status and quality of service.

Dependence on uncertain budgetary allocations also reduces the independence of regulatory bodies. In India, ERCs, with few exceptions, depend upon state exchequers although the Electricity Act 2003 empowers them to generate revenue through license fees, etc. The lack of financial independence also leads to problems relating to quality and capacity of personnel. The ceiling on salaries imposed by governments prevent the ERCs from appointing high-caliber professionals. At the same time, financial constraints prevent them from conducting adequate skill building training for their personnel.

Policy mandates require regulatory bodies to adopt transparent and participatory decision-making processes. The ERCs provide a forum for citizen participation in the decision-making process but due to lack of awareness and inadequate capacity of consumers, public participation has been weak. This should not happen since every citizen is an electricity consumer.

However, on the positive side, ERCs have been successful in ensuring fast redressal and this in turn has led to an improvement in service standards. To sum up, political issues have played a very important role in the regulation of this sector; by and large, political interests have been able to regulate the regulators. In recent years ERCs have been able to augment transparency and accountability to some extent besides performing their major regulatory functions —licensing, setting tariffs, ensuring maintenance of service standards and promoting competition in the sector.

18.3 Securities and Exchange Board of India (SEBI)

Regulation is important in securities markets as the absence of conditions of perfect condition and information asymmetry among participants do not allow a level playing field for either domestic or foreign investors tapping the Indian financial market. A Presidential Ordinance promulgated on 31 January 1992 accorded the SEBI a statutory status as an autonomous body to govern all the stock exchanges and a large part of securities' transactions.

The SEBI Board comprises a chairman, two members from the ministries of the GOI dealing with finance and law, one from the Reserve Bank of India, and two other members, appointed by the GOI, who are professionals and have experience or special knowledge relating to securities markets. The GOI has the right to terminate the services of the chairman or any member of the board. The decisions of the board are by majority vote, with the chairman having a tie-breaking second vote.

The Board is bound by the directions given by the Central Government on questions of policy, and the board is also obliged to submit a report to the Central Government every year, giving account of its policies, and programmes. Although the board's decision can be appealed to the courts, given the delays of the judicial system, the de facto appellate body is the Ministry of Finance.

Section 11 of the SEBI Act provides that '...it shall be the duty of the Board to protect the interest of investors in securities and to promote the development of and to regulate the securities market by such measures, as it thinks fit'. It empowers the board to regulate the business in stock exchanges, to register and regulate the working of stockbrokers, share transfer agents, bankers, trustees of trust deeds, registrars to an issue, merchant bankers, underwriters, portfolio managers, investment advisors, and such other intermediaries who may be associated with the securities market. It also registers and regulates the working of collective investment schemes including mutual funds, prohibits fraudulent and unfair trade practices and insider trading, regulates takeovers, conducts enquiries and audits of the stock exchanges, etc. An efficient and transparent securities market is impossible without the confidence instilled by a regulatory process that can swiftly detect irregularities and mete out deterrent punishment in a relatively short time.

The technology used in India's capital markets today is one of the best in the world. The establishment over time of the National Stock Exchange (NSE), the National Securities Clearing Corporation of India (NSCCL), the National Securities Depository Ltd (NSDL), the Central Securities Depository Ltd (CSDL), Stock Holding Corporation of India Ltd (SHCIL), etc., has put in place high-quality institutions. Although the credit for these institutions must mainly be given to market intermediaries, SEBI played a part in progressively instituting market best-practices in trading, delivery, and settlement. The development of the NSE as a competitor to the Bombay Stock Exchange, Mumbai, aided SEBI immensely in these objectives. Trading in financial derivatives has started well, the spot market has moved into rolling settlement, yielding important gains in market integrity. Various risk containment measures have also been put in place. The Indian securities market has on several counts shown development in the number of stock exchanges, market capitalization, trading volumes, institutional investors and turnover on stock exchanges. Yet areas of malpractice remain, like vanishing companies, price manipulation and insider trading.

SEBI's primary concern has, rightly, been the equity markets as this is the operational ambit of a large section of capital-market intermediaries. Electronic screen-based trading, dematerialization of securities and rolling settlements have made the equities' markets more safe and transparent and reduced the amount of speculative trading and price rigging.

SEBI has also progressively increased the pressure of various market intermediaries to disclose information. It has to be noted that proprietary information in the intensely competitive segments of capital markets aids innovation and confers an advantage on efficient players. Balancing disclosure of information with ensuring proprietary ownership of information then becomes the basic challenge of securities regulation. On the whole, market perception is that the availability of the currently disclosed information needs to be disseminated more widely amongst investors.

Despite the institution of best practices, SEBI is widely perceived to be a relatively ineffective and toothless regulator. The nature of securities transactions makes credible deterrence a key weapon against fraud. The number and magnitude of the SEBI's fines, as well as its active coordination with the US Department of Justice, is a pointer to the need for such punitive action even in a mature and (more) transparent market. The Harshad Mehta security scandal in India in 1991-92 was an example. Its effect is still being felt with retail investors not having regained their confidence in the securities, markets despite the strengthening of the regulator, SEBI, in the intervening period and the framework of preventive measures and information disclosure requirements now in place. More such fraudulent schemes have emerged since, and have attracted harsh deterrent penalties from SEBI, e.g. Market regulator SEBI in July 2014 barred Gammon India Chairman from the market on charges of insider trading. SEBI alleged that the Chairman sold his holdings in Gammon Infra based on 'unpublished price sensitive information' and barred him from the market till further orders. It's one of the rare cases where the Chairman of a company has come under the scanner for insider trading. (Times of India, 20th July 2014).

In an attempt to meet the long-term financing needs of the infrastructure sector, SEBI has issued guidelines that would pave the way for launching infrastructure investment trusts in India. These trusts will invest public money only into completed and revenue generating infrastructure assets and under-construction projects. The units issued by these trusts, just like mutual funds, will also be compulsorily listed on the bourses thus providing liquidity to investors.

Beginning with the 2002 amendments SEBI has been given sufficient powers of search and seizure of premises, debarring market defaulters of SEBI rules. SEBI has intervened in cases of price rigging, creation of false market, insider trading, takeover of companies without compliance to regulations, price maintenance and market manipulation and irregularities in public issues. Prosecutions in such cases have gone up substantially in recent years with the increased powers of SEBI. However, out of all appeals that are made, in 50% cases the decision is not in SEBI's favour. As it stands now securities laws seems to be quite pervasive, the problem lies in enforcing compliance.

18.4 Competition Commission of India (CCI)

Sustenance of the growth momentum in India, however, calls for more investment and innovation, prompted by dynamic and consumer-friendly markets. Keeping these objectives in mind, the Competition Act 2002 was enacted paving the way for the establishment of the Competition Commission of India (CCI), the institutional framework to support healthy and fair competition in markets. This Act moved away from the earlier emphasis of Monopolies and Restrictive Trade Practices (MRTP) on curbing monopolies to a more directed approach towards promoting competition and thereby increasing efficiency, innovation and competitiveness. Primarily and essentially the Competition Act aims to: eliminate practices having adverse effect on competition; promote and sustain competition, protect interests of consumers and to ensure freedom of trade in markets in the country. The Competition Commission of India was set up on October 14, 2003.

Key provisions of the Competition Act, 2002, are contained in Section 3 to 6. Section 3 and 4 of the Act relating to the anti-competitive agreements and abuse of dominant positions respectively came into force from May 2009. Section 5 and 6 of the Act provide that any person or enterprise that proposes to enter into merger, acquisition or amalgamation which are above a threshold limit in terms of turnover or assets prescribed in the Act and as enhanced are mandatorily required to give notice to the Commission for the assessment of their anti-competitive effect. The Commission may approve these combinations with or without modifications or disapprove in case it is established that such combinations will have appreciable adverse effect on competition.

The CCI has received 382 matters (till July 2014) alleging violations of Section 3 and 4 of the Act relating to anti-competitive agreements and abuse of dominance in diverse sectors such as insurance, travel, transport, cement, automobile manufacture, real estate, pharmaceuticals, financial sector, public procurement and entertainment. It passed final orders in about 285 cases which are around 75% of the cases received. Penalties have been imposed where warranted. The CCI has suggested changes in policies where, after inquiry, it has been found that competition could be enhanced if certain government policies are modified. With regard to Merger and Acquisition cases, since the notification of Section 5 and 6 in June 2011, the Commission has received 130 cases out of which 127 have been disposed of well within the prescribed time line.

Section 49 (3) of the Act lays responsibility on the Commission to take suitable measures for the promotion of competition advocacy, creating awareness and imparting training about competition issues. In pursuance of these objectives, the Commission has organized various workshops, seminars, conferences, interactive meetings with various stakeholders viz., students, industry associations, public sector enterprises, consumer organizations, professional institutes, etc.

Competition is an essential ingredient of a liberalized economy. It is a powerful instrument to help in achieving the macroeconomic policy goals of the country. Increased competition can improve country's economic performance, open business opportunities to its citizens and reduce the cost of goods and services throughout the economy. To make its objective clear, the Commission has adopted vision and mission statements that are read as:

Vision Statement

"To promote and sustain an enabling competition culture through engagement and enforcement that would inspire businesses to be fair, competitive and innovative; enhance consumer welfare and support economic growth."

Mission Statement

"Competition Commission of India aims to establish a robust competitive environment through:

- pro-active engagement with all stakeholders, including consumers, industry, government and international jurisdictions;
- being a knowledge intensive organization with high competence levels;
- professionalism, transparency, resolve and wisdom in enforcement."

The Competition Act, 2002, as amended in 2007, provides for setting up of the CCI, comprising a Chairperson and minimum of two and maximum of six members. In addition, it also provides for establishment of the Competition Appellate Tribunal comprising a Chairperson and two members to hear and dispose of appeals against the orders of the Commission and also to adjudicate on the claims of compensation that may arise from the findings of that Commission. The Competition Appellate Tribunal (COMPAT) was set in May 2009.

The COMPAT is vested with powers to hear and dispose of appeals filed against any direction issued or decision made or order passed by the Competition Commission of India; to adjudicate on claims for compensation that may arise from the findings of the CCI or the orders of the Appellate Tribunal in an appeal against any findings of the Commission and pass orders for the recovery of compensation under the Act.

After the dissolution of the erstwhile MRTP Commission, the government vested the COMPAT with powers to hear and dispose of pending cases, being dealt with by the then MRTP Commission. About 1825 pending cases were transferred to this Tribunal, out of which it has disposed of 1650 cases till the end of June 2013.

Since the establishment of this Tribunal, it has received 218 appeals against the decisions of CCI. Out of these, 106 appeals have been disposed of and remaining 112 are under adjudication.

18.5 The Insurance Regulatory and Development Authority (IRDA)

Constituted under the provisions of the Insurance Regulatory and Development Authority (IRDA) Act, 1999, IRDA of India is also a regulatory authority mandated to bring order and growth in the insurance sector. Its mission, thus, stressed virtues of integrity, growth, viability, fairness and professionalism. Insurance regulation is relatively a new phenomenon in India: considering that pace of change through regulatory reform is definitely quite impressive. Insurance companies need the ability to say liquid, face competition and survive market turbulence. Considering these, regulatory impact on the insurance sector in India during the past two decades has been credible. Regulation has also brought players of worth into the market.

- Core Principles for Service Delivery: IRDA of India has done well to keep close to the 28 Core Principles of Service Delivery, set internationally by the International Association of Insurance Supervisors-a credible standard-setting organisation of 190 jurisdictions in 140 countries. Most enduring has been its success in ensuring disclosures of financial performance, risk exposures, accounting policy and policyholders' rights.
- Assets and Solvency Margins: Insurance contracts, particularly in the life arena, are long-term contracts. They require rigorous asset liability management to see that the delicate balance between risks and returns is not disturbed. In the year 2000, IRDA of India issued Assets, Liabilities and Solvency Margin Regulations and improved it in 2016 to adopt tougher standards of solvency margins for covering insurance market risks of adequate time span.
- Regulation of Insurance Brokers: Insurance regulators evolve regulations on insurance brokers and keep an eye on their conduct. IRDA of India now has, since 2017, fairly elaborate regulations on insurance brokers covering registration, certification, capital, deposit and net worth requirements remuneration and reward system, accounting norms and penalty framework for non-compliance or non-performance. It has been an aspect of norms-setting based on experiential evidence.
- Outsourcing Arrangements: IRDA of India has streamlined outsourcing activities by Indian insures by issuing new regulations in 2017. The guiding approach of the regulations is two-tier: (a) efficacy in oversight and (b) due diligence. Stipulated core functions are not be outsourced, frameworks of risks have to be provided, outsourcing arrangements have to be binding contracts of rights and liabilities and due care has to be taken to monitor and evaluate outcomes. These regulations aim at improving governance and protecting policyholders' interests.

18.6 Regulatory Reform

Despite significant differences across countries most regulatory reforms, especially in the developing countries, encompass an introduction of competition in a semi-liberalized market, redefinition of universal service obligations and privatization of state-owned enterprises. These substantial structural changes also led to significant conceptual, legal and institutional changes in the countries concerned. Not only the regulatory process but also competition law and policy have been among those challenges.

In the past, most developing countries were characterized by significant government intervention in their economies marked by dominance of large state-owned enterprises. Economic liberalization process started in several of these countries from the 1990s and governments adopted policies of deregulation, privatization and liberalization.

Despite these developments, for a variety of reasons competitive markets did not yield positive results initially and governments intervened to correct market failures. There emerged a new form of regulatory governance characterized by the setting up of specialized agencies, seeking to ensure competitive outcomes by making decisions in a transparent and participatory manner, keeping in mind the vital interests of the stake holders/consumers.

Regulators apart from the Government, generally fall into two categories — sector regulators and competition authorities, set up to enforce national competition laws. Competition authorities have a regulatory mandate over competition issues that cover all sectors of the economy. The two sets of regulators share a common goal of protecting economic welfare, consumer interest and enhancing stake holder participation.

Despite common objectives, sector regulators and competition authorities generally have different legislative mandates and their perspective regarding introducing competition in the market may be different. Competition laws seek to protect the process of competition, with a view to maximizing productive and allocative efficiencies. Competition rules tell the agents in the market what they should not do, while sector regulation does the reverse and tells market agents what to do.

Sometimes there is an absence of clearly defined jurisdiction in regulatory matters, leaving a lot of subjectivity as to which of the two authorities can be more effective in handling specific cases. There is, therefore, a need for defining boundaries between mandates as well as understanding respective competencies so that both do the job they are best suited for in the public interest.

India started developing regulatory institutions with the introduction of reforms in 1991. But the regulatory environment which has developed over a period of time does not seem homogeneous across sectors. There are three sets of justifications for regulatory interventions—prevention of market failures, restriction or removal of anti-competitive practices, and promotion of public (consumer) interest.

Post-Independence, India experimented with a mixed economy model with the state retaining control over the commanding heights of the economy, heavy industries and public utilities. While private sector was allowed a narrow niche, the government tried to control it through a network of controls such as licensing and quotas in regard to intermediate goods imports and outputs. The government was not only a producer and regulator of strategic and important goods and services, but also exerted direct control over the domestic output, and the private sector through the pricing mechanism. Given that electoral pressures exerted by various interest groups did affect regulatory actions by the government, such regulation can hardly be labeled as 'independent'.

After 1990, the Indian economy embarked on a process of domestic reform which involved the following elements — delicensing of industries and abolition of output quotas or bounds on outputs of firms, permission for private entry into sectors which were hitherto the monopoly of the government, and liberalization of quotas and tariffs on capital goods' imports. From 1991 onwards, liberalization of the external sector meant that tariff reductions were extended to almost the entire spectrum of merchandise trade and conditions for foreign investment were simplified and liberalized.

The process of domestic reform and external liberalization is a continuing agenda of public policy. However, government monopolies have become extinct and public-private partnerships are on the rise. Besides the private sector co-exists with government firms in many sectors which were previously government monopolies (e.g. electricity and telecommunications). The consensus among decision makers has been that independent regulation is required in such sectors to guarantee a level playing field. As a result, independent regulators have been constituted in various sectors, starting with electricity and telecommunications, and the number is on the rise. The regulatory climate in India is still in transition.

Regulation in India can be placed under three broad heads: economic regulation, regulation in the public interest and environmental regulation.

Economic Regulation

Economic regulation prevents or handles market failure. This is accomplished by rules that proscribe and penalize market distorting behaviour. Examples in the Indian context include The Foreign Trade (Development and Regulation) Act, 1992, for facilitating imports into and augmenting exports from India; and the Electricity Act of 2003, which allows state regulators to fix tariffs for power consumption, thus preventing suppliers from taking advantage of natural monopolies.

Regulation in the Public Interest

This is required where industries fail to meet a standard or uphold something of grave public interest. A classic case is of health and safety, where firms can fall short in protecting employees or the general public from physical damage. Although market competition can make firms more willing to address such issues, the standards adopted may be inadequate or not uniform across the industry. In India, there is very little evidence to suggest that competition in its existing form has had a positive impact on quality.

The Bureau of Indian Standards (BIS) created by the Bureau of Indian Standards Act, 1986 has been setting quality and safety standards for various products, some of which are mandatory. The existence of an authority like BIS helps in laying down rules, especially in a situation of low consumer awareness about quality. A large number of laws and rules to enforce standards are in force but the desired extent of enforcement has not really happened.

Environmental Regulation

In India, environment protection has been given constitutional status. The Directive Principles of State Policy state that protecting and improving the environment is the duty of the state as well as citizens of the country. The GOI has enacted various laws to protect the environment through the Environment (Protection) Act, 1986, as the umbrella legislation. These set standards for emissions and discharge; regulation of the location of industries; management of hazardous waste; and protection of public health and welfare.

Under the EPA, statutory clearances relating to pollution control and the environment are necessary for setting up units in 31 categories of industries. This list includes petrochemical complexes, petroleum refineries, thermal power plants, cement, fertilizers, bulk drugs, dyes, papers, etc.

Ministry of Environment and Forests is the key agency for environmental legislation. However, several states have also enacted their own legislation besides the major ones enacted by the Central Ministry. The State Pollution Control Board (SPCB) established in each state, is responsible for implementing these legislations as well as issuing rules and regulations prescribing the standards for a clean environment. The activities of SPCBs are coordinated by the Central Pollution Control Board (CPCB).

Environmental issues around any industrial project are highly sensitive and quite often lead to civil society activism. Therefore, this aspect requires careful handling both by the Central and State Governments. Due to corruption, administrative delays, popular protests, etc., such clearances are often difficult to acquire. There is need for an independent regulator in this sector.

18.7 Sector Regulation in India: Trends

Sector regulators are important as individual sectors have their own characteristics which, in turn, determine the nature of regulation. These provide orderly procedures, and protect consumers and investors from market failures and anti-competitive actions in a particular sector.

Government efforts have been consistent in promoting competition in the market place. In some areas such as telecom, civil aviation, insurance, railway container traffic, gas distribution, etc., government monopolies have been curbed by allowing the private sector to enter. However, if one examines each sector in detail we find that principles of competitive neutrality (providing a level playing field) have often been compromised or overlooked.

Regulatory trends can be better evaluated by examining performance indicators in business regulation and regulation of key infrastructure sectors. Each sector might have its exclusive regulatory law and policy which is shaped by the ground realities in that sector. Thus, the telecom regulator might advocate for the lowering of entry barriers (for example, multiple and cheaper licenses) to promote competition; however, the water sector might be regulated in a manner aimed to maintain the natural monopoly of the state. While policies/regulations relating to market reforms which apply to the economy as a whole are important, so are sector specific ones. Sector regulation can take account of specific technical nuances that characterize a sector and modify the behaviour of actual and potential participants.

Status of Sector Specific Regulations

S. no.	Sector	Status of regulation
1.	Power	Electricity Regulatory Commissions (ERC's) have a presence in almost all States and at the Centre.
2.	Energy	Absence of any regulator.
3.	Oil & Gas	The Petroleum Natural Gas Regulatory Board (PNGRB) regulates refining, processing, storage, transportation, distribution and marketing of petroleum products.

4.	Coal	The government owns the coal companies, and is the only regulator.
5,	Telecom	Telecom Regulatory Authority of India (TRAI) facilitates competition through regulation and introducing pro- consumer elements relating to quality and access.
6.	Ports	Tariff authority for Major Ports (TAMP), has limited authority in determining tariffs. There are no performance standards, or consumer protection or competition.
7.	Airports	The Airport Authority of India (AAI) is an operator and regulator of airports; and the Director General of Civil Aviation (DGCA) along with the Bureau of Civil Aviation Security is responsible for safety and technical aspects.
8.	Roads	The National Highways Authority of India (NHAI) acts as a regulator.
9.	Railways	The government-owned Indian Railways is both operator and regulator
10.	Water supply and sanitation	Central Ground Water Authority is the only authority to control ground water, pollution and protect the environment.
11.	Social sector	Higher education is regulated by the autonomous bodies like UGC, AICTE and self-regulatory bodies. Independent Regulatory Authority for Higher Education (IRAHE) is under consideration.

Note: Based on Eleventh Five Year Plan (2007-12), Volume I, Inclusive Growth, Planning Commission, Government of India.

After 1991, the government made a paradigm shift in its policies and governance structure in some key infrastructure sectors. Specialized regulatory agencies were established in the telecom, electricity and oil & gas sectors. However, outcomes so far have been mixed and in many cases have fallen short of expectations, one important reason being the lack of actual independence of regulators despite legislative provisions.

Independence of regulators is important in almost all these sectors as the government holds a major share in operations leading to the problem of competitive neutrality. Independence and accountability are required for good regulatory governance. Independence ensures that interests of various stakeholders are accorded due importance in formulating and implementing regulation to prevent regulatory capture by vested interests. Accountability ensures that regulation is based on careful weighing of pros and cons; arbitrary decisions are not taken as consumers have access to facilities for redressal and appellate authorities and courts for remedial action against incorrect regulatory decisions. One basic form of accountability is transparency in the regulatory decision-making process which, to a certain extent, can be achieved through public participation in decision-making processes.

Sector Regulators

Independent sector regulation is a relatively new development in India. After economic reforms, sector regulatory authorities have been set up in various sectors to produce competitive outcomes, i.e. foster greater efficiency in resource allocation and consumer welfare through promotion of competition.

India has regulators for telecom, power, ports and petroleum with a variety of powers to implement their brief which differ widely across sectors. Some regulators, such as TRAI, have been specifically mandated to regulate the entire sector as a whole and even recommend the timing of entry of players, licensing conditions, spectrum management, etc. Similarly, the Central/State electricity regulatory commissions issue licenses which enable entities to transmit, distribute or trade in electricity and enjoy other powers such as rule making, enforcement, imposition of penalties, etc. However, while one of the important functions of the telecom regulator is to promote competition, this is not a function specifically assigned to the electricity regulator.

Others such as Tariff Authority for Major Ports (TAMP) have powers that are more limited than both the electricity and telecom regulator as these only have the mandate to fix tariffs.

Differences abound across regulators. While both telecom and power have appellate authorities where appeals against the regulator's decision can be made, most other sectors have a specialized form of appeal. Further, the tenure of regulators vary between 3 to 5 years across sectors and even the selection process is not uniform across sectors.

Thus, the existing regulatory framework in India is uneven across different sectors of the economy. This diversity can be explained by the fact that institutional arrangement regarding regulatory design and the powers given to a regulatory authority both require political decisions. However, the efficacy of regulation in every sector depends on the extent of independence, accountability and transparency in procedures and processes.

Regulatory efficacy demands functional independence which calls for the regulator maintaining true neutrality and distance from user groups and the government. One aspect of such autonomy is the ability of the regulator to access funds from sources other than, the line ministry. Independence also requires fulfillment of other prerequisites—regulators once appointed should have fixed tenure and immunity from removal except in the case of gross incompetence or financial impropriety.

Again on the lines of what has been mentioned above, there is no uniformity in the independence and funding of different regulators. While the Finance Ministry has been proactive in providing secure funding and resultant independence to the regulators reporting to it, this principle has been largely ignored by many other ministries. If this principle is indeed followed by other ministries, there would be improvements in regulatory effectiveness, efficiency, transparency and accountability.

Independence should go hand in hand with accountability. Along with independence, all regulators need to be accountable. Accountability is of two types: political and legal. Political accountability involves reporting to the line ministry/ legislature which may have a special committee to scrutinize and debate its contents. Legal accountability enables those aggrieved by a regulatory decision to issue a formal complaint or appeal.

In general, regulatory bodies in India are required to submit their annual reports and/ or audited accounts to the legislature. However, in most such cases, regulatory bodies are made accountable to the legislature through the line ministry. Legislative oversight over the regulator's performance does not seem to be effective as annual reports submitted by regulators are hardly discussed with any seriousness in Parliament.

As mentioned earlier, legal accountability allows review of a regulator's specific decisions. It is important to ensure that the review process does not create a second layer of regulation, as experienced in the telecom sector. In the telecom sector the powers of the appellate tribunal, Telecom Disputes Settlement and Appellate Tribunal (TDSAT), is quite wide. The TDSAT and not the TRAI has been empowered to settle disputes. This division of labour has adversely affected the performance of the telecom regulator as any issue can be presented as a 'dispute'. Nevertheless, there are some benefits--judicial review is considered important in guarding against decisions by a regulatory agency which fall outside its statutory mandate or fail to follow established administrative procedures'. TDSAT has taken decisions in certain cases where TRAI has seemingly not followed due process.

Appellate powers are also not uniform across sectors. Unlike TDSAT, the Securities Appellate Tribunal (SAT) can only entertain appeals against the decisions of the capital market regulator, SEBI.

The regulatory process must incorporate some crucial steps to ensure transparency. For example, stakeholders must be made aware of the regulatory process and should be given opportunities to present their views freely. In certain cases, regulatory legislation in India has made provisions to guarantee a transparent regulatory process. For example, in the electricity and telecom sectors, it has been mandated that regulators should ensure transparency while exercising their powers and discharging functions. TAMP has attempted to introduce transparency through guidelines. No provision in regard to transparency exists in the Competition Act, but a provision does exist in the general governance principles expounded by the government. Furthermore, the Right to Information (RTI) Act empowers citizens to seek information on any matter from any government department or undertaking.

18.8 The Government and the Regulators

The role of the regulator is to achieve mandated policy objectives and maintain competitive conditions in the market by ensuring a level playing field. On the other hand, the role of the government is to spell out long-term objectives and developmental vision.

However, while in theory the government and regulators have distinctly different roles, in reality the regulator and policy makers also share common responsibilities ensuring orderly and sustained growth of the sector, attracting private investment, enhancing consumer protection and so on.

Given that regulatory bodies are often created to achieve predetermined policy objectives, proper interaction between them becomes very important. At the same time, it is equally important to ensure that the regulator's domain is not encroached upon by the government in the name of achieving policy objectives. This calls for creating a clear distinction between policy and regulation, which is yet to be followed in India.

In India, regulatory reforms, which have accompanied economic reforms, have been marked by lack of consumer awareness and participation. Consumers, being largely unorganized, have been often bypassed by the reform process (except in a few cases where consumer concerns have been highlighted by the media) which has been influenced more by a strong business sentiment rather than consumer sentiments.

In India, a few sector regulators such as Central Electricity Regulatory Commission (CERC) and TRAI have created participatory mechanisms by constituting Advisory Committees with representation from consumers and other stakeholders. The telecom sector has a Common Charter of Telecom Services, which requires service providers to promote consumer participation in the process. In electricity, even state level regulators have some consumer representation in certain cases.

To strengthen the forces of competition in the market, both competition law and policy (to be forced by the Competition Commission of India) and market regulatory laws (to be enforced by the regulators) are required. These complement each other. The difference between the two forms of intervention in the market process should, however, be marked. A regulator tells the firms what these have to do. A regulator examines issues of technology, cost and process in the industry regulated by it. The Competition Authority, on the contrary, tells the firms what they should not do, i.e. price fixing, predatory pricing, creating cartels, discriminatory treatment, etc. The role of the Competition Authority is that of an adjudicator that acts against anticompetitive practices.

Further, a sector regulator has a narrow focus, whereas the competition authority has an economy wide mandate. The differences in domain also result in differences in views and create tensions between the competition authority and the sector regulator.

In India, there is very little evidence to suggest that regulation has had a positive impact on quality. In certain cases, there is free competition without adequate consumer information and awareness about quality. This leads to price competition being associated with scarce attention paid by firms to quality—a state of affairs which is far from ideal despite the presence of competition. The regulatory authorities laying down standards (safety, performance, etc.) do not have the teeth to implement the standards and penalize the providers/sellers for non-compliance. Without penalties, service providers are unlikely to have an incentive to invest in resources for improving the Quality of Service (QoS). A related problem with standards is the low level of consumer awareness on issues such as safety, which means there is not enough demand pull to make industry interested in implementing safety standards.

In sectors such as telecom and electricity, there is a visible regulatory initiative to improve quality but without adequate legislative backing. TRAI is to be commended for drawing attention to QoS and establishing standards. TRAI provides guidelines for service providers and publishes periodical survey reports assessing quality of service and customer satisfaction.

Redressal of Grievances

A redressal mechanism is an essential component of the competition legislation of any country. In India, too, the MRTPA (Monopolies and Restrictive Trade Practices Act) has inbuilt grievance redressal provisions. However, over the years, because of factors like inadequate budgetary allocation and lack of autonomy the MRTPC (the predecessor of

Competition Commission of India governed by MRTPA) has not been very effective in providing redress and consequently pending cases have kept piling up.

The CCI is expected to serve consumers better in terms of redress. Among other things, the Competition Act allows individual consumers or their associations to present their grievances for redress before the CCI. However, cost considerations and other factors may deter individual consumers or local consumer groups from approaching the CCI. The need for regional benches of the Commission is again felt in this context.

Other than competition law, Consumer Protection Act of 1986 (COPRA) provides a three-tier, simple, quasi-judicial machinery —at the national, state and district levels—for the purpose of redress. While COPRA is a comprehensive piece of legislation its enforcement is plagued by inordinate delays in the delivery of justice, implementation of orders, etc.

In addition to the above, some sector regulators such as telecom, electricity and insurance also have redressal mechanisms: generic complaint redress by TRAI, telephone adalats (courts), grievance redress mechanisms of state electricity commissions, the consumer grievance redress cell of the Insurance Regulatory Development Authority (IRDA), insurance ombudsman, banking ombudsman, etc.

18.9 Future Trajectory

The Government realizes that the sectoral approach to independent regulation in India has been associated with the evolution of an uneven regulatory environment. There are no regulators in some sectors, partial regulators in others and relatively comprehensive regulators in yet others.

The government is also planning to reform the institutional framework of regulatory commissions, their role, functions and relationship with the executive and legislature, their interface with markets and the public, and processes and methods of regulation including rule making and dispute resolution as follows:

- Empowering all regulators to make and enforce regulations; issue licenses and impose punitive measures, including suspension or cancellation of licenses; and setting performance standards and determine tariffs.
- Ensuring independence of regulatory bodies: the government is planning to make the selection process transparent and shorn of interference. To ensure this, the chairpersons and members of regulatory bodies may be appointed by the President of India on the recommendation of the Prime Minster. The Prime Minster can choose these names from a panel of two or three names empanelled by a committee comprising the Chairperson of the Union Public Service Commission (UPSC), Cabinet Secretary and Chairperson of the respective regulatory body. Similar arrangements are planned at the state level. The removal has to be approved by an enquiry conducted by a sitting judge of the Supreme Court or the High Court and approval by the President of India or the government as the case may be.
- Introducing multi-sector regulators. The government is contemplating the establishment of multi-sector regulators for (i) communications; (ii) transport;

and (iii) electricity, fuels and gas (iv) energy. This would eliminate proliferation of regulatory commissions, help build capacity and expertise, promote consistency of approach and save on costs. At the state level, a single regulatory commission for all infrastructure sectors may be more productive and cost-effective. States should be encouraged to consider this approach and the scope of their existing electricity regulators could be extended to other sectors.

Independent regulatory agencies have now established themselves as useful administrative entities of governance in India. Their number has increased, particularly since the 1991 economic policy paradigm shift, and there has been an intense institutional learning all along. Not all agencies have regulated equally well-we have the example of electricity regulation on one hand and food safety regulation on the other. Even in the electricity sector, regulatory impact improved gradually. Much depended on the will of the holders of the executive power in Departments to loosen their profiteering grips in favour of public interest: scrutiny of amendments to the principal acts of regulation eloquently reveals the intent. From a knowledge management point of view, things improved only to the extent to which agencies exposed themselves to the global professional standards of norms-setting in regulation and adopted them situationally. As administrative entities, independent regulatory agencies have to prove their 'independence' at every determining point: they have a duty to make stakeholders realise that they have a perfect understanding of facts and that they are really beyond the power of capture.

The quest in the regulatory governance in India today is on fine-tuning the balance between autonomy and control. The problem, also is in adequately regulating sectors such as social care and livelihood security. A policy design is needed in which the government and its independent regulatory agencies have mutually reinforcing roles. Regulation is not only about vibrant competitive markets for production; it is equally an instrument of justice for the consumers of different purchasing power in society.

Conclusion

Regulatory agencies in India were necessitated by the New Economic policies in India after 1991. At the level of the Central Government, the initiatives are quite satisfactory but State Governments have been quite lethargic in the creation of new regulatory agencies.

Many sectors remain unexplored from a regulatory point of view. Sectors which deserve attention are the social (health and education) environment and retail sectors. Both play a significant role in the Indian economy from the point of view of human development and employment generation respectively.

Another issue that needs to be given importance is stimulation of competition in natural monopolies through public-private partnerships (PPPs). This is particularly relevant in the case of sectors such as railways and other infrastructure areas. More than 20 years of independent regulation in India have been characterized by the government's inability to create or follow a clear or consistent approach. Quite often there is no clarity about the objectives that the government wishes to follow in any sector. At times, the regulatory mandate falls short of what is required for achieving the stated policy objectives. A multi-stakeholder approach is often absent in most of the sectors and given opaque regulatory mandates as well as limited regulatory capacity, this evolving form of governance has failed to develop 'teeth' or evolve a cogent and coherent approach that can be truly 'independent' in its functioning.

Suggested Readings

Bhattacharya, Aditya, and Oindrila De, "*Cartels and the Competition Commission*," EPW, XCVII no. 35 (2012).

Bhattacharya, Saugata, and Urijit R. Patel, *New Regulatory Institutions in India: White Knights or Trojan horses? in Public Institutions in India: Performance & Design*, eds. Devesh Kapur and Pratap Bhanu Mehta, New Delhi, OUP, 2005, pp. 406-56.

Bose, Suchismita, *"Securities Market Regulations: Census from US and Indian experience,"* Money and Financel CRA Bulletin, Jan-June, 2005.

Dokeniya, Anupama, *Reforming the State: Telecom Liberalization in India*, Telecommunications Policy 23, pp. 105-128, 1999.

Dubash, Navroz K., "*Independent Regulatory Agencies: A Theoretical Review with Reference to Electricity and Water in India*," EPW, XLII no. 40 (0ct. 4., 2008).

Indian Journal of Public Administration Special Issue : "Independent Regulatory Authorities in India: A Comparative Perspective" vol. 64, Issue 3, September 2018

Mukherji, Rahul *"Managing Competition: Politics and the Building of Independent Regulatory Institutions,"* India Review,. 3 no. 4 (2004): pp. 278-305.

Sinha, Nikhil, *The Political Economy of India's Telecommunication Reforms, Telecommunications Policy* 20, pp. 23-38, 1996.

OOO

Chapter Nineteen

Administrative Reforms

Introduction

Reforming the administrative system in India to increase the effectiveness of policy making and execution is an ongoing and deliberate exercise. External developments such as advancements in technology and globalization are exogenous pressures on the public administration to meet the increasing expectations of the public for effective service delivery, transparency and accountability.

The purpose of reform is to revisit the structure and functions of the bureaucracy to make it a dynamic and efficient mechanism of service delivery built on values of integrity and effectiveness. Reforms are expected to raise the quality of service delivery and enhance the performance capacity of the administrative system to deliver these services.

Administrative reforms involve rationalization of government structures and functions to make them more efficient and competent. Governance reforms focus on the improvement of the legal and policy frameworks that facilitate effective decision making and create citizen participatory mechanisms. Civil service reforms are aimed at making effective policy decisions within public agencies and strengthening administrative capacity to perform core governmental functions.

Successive Indian governments have undertaken several civil service reforms aimed to improve its functioning and the delivery of public services. These reforms have focused on a variety of topics that range from structure, recruitment, capacity building, introduction of smart and open governance that embrace technology, or develop public-private partnerships to improve service delivery.

19.1 Reforms in the Post-Liberalization Era: The Precursors

Since the adoption of the new economic policy in the early 1990s in India, there have been attempts at dismantling the centrally directed framework of planned development. This was also when the international donor agencies exercised considerable influence on the domestic economy by attaching conditional ties while giving aid. These conditional ties were, at the outset, mere prescriptions for good governance but later became modalities for reform in the overall framework of governance itself. Reforms in administration in India in the 1990s have been basically driven by the measures of economic liberalization.

The Indian response to liberalization came in the form of post-1991 structural Adjustment Policies which suggested several steps to free the Indian economy from unnecessary bureaucratic controls though from within the overall control of the state.

Four specific steps were taken. First, the government decided to abolish 'industrial licensing policy', except for a short list of industries related to security and strategic concerns, social concerns, hazardous chemicals, and overriding environmental considerations. Second, the government also endorsed direct foreign investment up to 51% foreign equity in some high priority industries. To avoid bottlenecks, an amendment to the 1973 Foreign Exchange Regulation Act was suggested, Third, it was also decided to withdraw protection of the 'sick' public sector units and there would be 'a greater thrust on performance improvement' to ensure accountability of those involved in these state-sponsored enterprises. Finally, the 1991 policy sought to remove 'the threshold limits of assets' in respect of those companies functioning under the Monopolies and Restrictive Trade Practices Act (MRTP)'. By seeking to amend this act, the 1991 policy suggested elimination of the requirement of prior approval of the union government for establishment of new enterprises, expansion of enterprises, merger, amalgamation and takeover, and appointments of directors under certain circumstances. Quite clearly, the focus of the policy was on increasing privatization, de-licensing, and decentralization.

The role of the command and control structure of the government received a new meaning in the regime of economic reforms. Major initiatives towards restructuring of public sector enterprises (PSEs) were started, in view of their low productivity, over staffing, lack of technological upgradation, and low rate of return. In order to raise resources and ensure wider public participation in PSEs, it was decided to offer its shareholding stake to mutual funds, financial institutions, general public and workers. Similarly, in order to revive and rehabilitate chronically sick PSEs, it was decided to refer them to the Board for Industrial and Financial Reconstruction (BIFR). The policy also provided for greater managerial autonomy to the Board of PSEs. In order to promote the role of the private players, the National Mineral Policy (1993) de-reserved thirteen minerals for exploitation by the private sector, while the National Telecom Policy, 1994, allowed private participation in basic telecom services. The Air Corporation Act, 1994, enabled private air taxi companies to operate on regular domestic routes. The National Highways Act was amended to enable levy of toll on users of national highways (GOI 1997). The new economic policy of 1991, thus, envisaged a roll-back of the state and placed a greater reliance on the market for national development.

In the post-1990s, there were sporadic attempts at disinvestment in public sector enterprises, but these got embroiled in controversies, culminating finally in the setting up of the Disinvestment Commission in 1996. The Fifth Central Pay Commission (CPC) Report (1994) stated that it is increasingly felt that in capital intensive infrastructural sectors like energy, telecommunications, roads, ports, and others, the shortfalls in investment are so large that a massive infusion of private investment would be required. Many states initiated special measures to attract FDI for greater industrialization in their region. Several states introduced single-window systems for faster processing of applications for setting up industrial enterprises and liberal incentives were offered to industrialists for setting up industries in backward areas. The impact of these reforms may be gauged from the fact that total foreign investment in India grew from a minuscule US$132 million in 1991-92 to US$5.3 billion in 1995-96. As a part of economic reforms, creation of statutory independent regulatory mechanisms also gained wider support.

For the telecom sector in 2000, the government reconstituted the erstwhile regulatory body in two, namely, the Telecom Regulatory Authority of India as a regulator and the Telecom Dispute Settlement and Appellate Tribunal for settling disputes.

Another significant development in the post-1990s was the decentralization and empowerment of localities for grass roots governance. The 73rd and 74th Constitutional Amendments signaled momentous changes in terms of grass roots people's empowerment by providing for (a) regular elections, (b) minimal suppression of Panchayati Raj bodies through an administrative fiat, (c) regular finances through statutory distribution by finance commissions and (d) reservation of seats for the weaker sections of society including women. Given the clear legal sanction for decentralization, there is no doubt that decentralization through Panchayats could bring about an enormous change in the way our democracy functions.

In the 1996 conference of chief secretaries, the focus was on having an accountable, open, and citizen-friendly government. It recognized that the public image of the bureaucracy was one of inaccessibility, indifference, procedure orientation, poor quality and sluggishness, corruption, and non-accountability which needed to change in the post-liberalized era.

The conference initiated a national debate on effective and responsive administration which culminated in an Action Plan discussed and adopted in the conference of chief ministers on 24 May 1997. The Action Plan had three components:

- Accountable and citizen-friendly government.
- Transparency and right to information.
- Improving the performance and integrity of the public services.

In order to have an accountable and citizen-friendly government, the Action Plan specified that all the Central and State Governments would formulate a Citizen's Charter for departments and facilitate at various levels effective mechanisms for redressal of public grievances from the secretariat downwards to the village. The Action Plan also recognized the need for greater decentralization and devolution of administrative powers at all levels. It emphasized people's participation in consonance with the spirit of the 73rd and 74th Amendments of the Constitution, involvement of the people and voluntary agencies in the delivery of services and devolution of administrative powers. The conference recognized that secrecy and lack of openness in transactions was largely responsible for corruption in official dealings. Thus, steps needed to be taken to ensure easy access of the people to all information relating to government activities and decisions. In this regard, the government would take immediate necessary steps for examining the report of the working group on Right to Information and for introducing a legislation in the parliament for the freedom of information. The Action Plan also aimed at imposing the performance and integrity of the civil services. It was agreed that elimination of corruption in public services would require prevention, surveillance, and deterrent prosecution. For this, investigation agencies and vigilance machinery would be strengthened. It was agreed that institutional arrangements should be evolved for enabling objective and transparent decisions as postings, promotions, and transfers of officials, particularly those working in key areas to ensure stability of tenure and depoliticized postings at all levels to sustain the morale of the civil services.

True to the spirit, expressed in the 1996 Chief Secretaries conference, the Fifth CPC recommended (a) downsizing the government through the corporatization of activities, which involves 'malfunctioning of goods or the provision of commercial services' (b) transparency, openness, and economy in government operation through the 'privatization of activities where government does not need to play a direct role' and also 'contracting out services which can be conveniently outsourced to the private sector' (GOI 1997); and (c) the contractual appointment in selected areas of operations 'for the purpose of maintaining a certain flexibility in staffing both the lateral entry of experts, moderating the numbers deployed depending on the exigencies of work and ensuring availability of competent and committed personnel for certain sensitive/specialized jobs'. (GOI 1997)

The Central Government has been advised to go for a 30% reduction in the strength of the civil services, as the Pay Commission felt that it would be unwise to let the government sector continue as 'an island of inefficiency' and 'inertia. The normal procedure of voluntary retirement after completing 20 years would be continued. Alongside this, the commission recommended a special scheme of voluntary retirement in the departments where surplus manpower was identified. In such cases, there would be a provision for the selective retirement of persons, the initiative always resting with the government for a golden handshake. The Pay Commission also stated that the role of the government will be more in evolving the policy of governance and less in the actual governance itself. Most government departments will have to function as facilitators rather than inhibitors of growth. New regulators will have to be evolved and enforced so as to provide a level playing field as between the public and private sector enterprises, as also between domestic and foreign companies. The administered price mechanisms will have to be replaced by mechanisms based on market-determined prices. (GOI 1997)

The other significant recommendations of the commission concerns 'openness' in administration. Defending the repeal of 'the Official Secrets Act of the old colonial days', the commission insisted on openness which 'means giving everyone the right to access to information about the various decisions taken by the Government and [knowing] the reasoning behind them' (GOI 1997). As an integral part of civil service reform, the commission insisted on the formation of efficient grievance redressal machinery that has to be effective, speedy, objective, readily accessible, and easy to operate' (GOI 1997). Drawing upon the examples of Canada, UK, and Malaysia where effective grievance redressal cells have been functioning efficiently, the idea of a Citizens Charter defining the rights of the customers of government schemes and services was mooted by the commission. The recognition and the procedures suggested in this connection are of crucial importance from the point of debureaucratizing government and making it citizen-friendly. The issues, raised by the Pay Commission figured prominently in the 1997 Conference of Chief Ministers where an action plan was adopted to (a) make the administration accountable and citizen-friendly, (b) ensure transparency and right to information, and (c) adopt measures to cleanse and motivate the civil services.

The Sixth CPC, not only had to evolve a proper pay package for the government employees but also to make recommendations rationalizing the governmental structure with a view to improving the delivery mechanisms for providing better services to the common man. The main recommendations of the commission which have a bearing on good governance are as follows:

- Diminishing layers: The commission has recommended reducing the layers within the government structure so that decision-making and delivery is expedited. From thirty-five standard pay scales, the grades have been reduced to twenty, spread across four distinct running pay bands, one apex scale and another grade for the post of Cabinet Secretary and equivalent.
- Restoring motivation in public services: Government employees have to be motivated to take pride in public services. Thus, the commission has recommended various measures for job enhancement and job enrichment. The functions presently being discharged by assistants and private secretaries will now be carried out by executive assistants. Upgradation of all posts in Group D in the government to Group C, along with their retraining and multitasking will provide enlargement and enrichment of functions and responsibilities to a large section of government employees.
- Delegation with accountability: Restoring delegation with accountability at each level in the decision-making process is one of the main thrust areas proposed by the commission. Upgradation of the critical cutting-edge jobs like teachers, staff nurses, constables, and so on, has been recommended. Strengthening the decentralized levels with parity between fielder offices and the secretariat has also been recommended as the motivation and performance of the field and programme officers is critical to improve service delivery for the common man.
- Ensuring the best possible talent; The commission has recommended the lateral entry at higher levels in the government to ensure availability of the best possible talent from within and outside government with performance contracts. It suggests a shift from career-based to post-based selection in the higher echelons of government in order to get the best domain-based expertise. A higher start and better incentives have been recommended at the initial entry level so as to attract a younger talented profile. No increase in retirement age is recommended as an active younger employee profile is best suited for the tasks ahead. Additionally, it argues for a market-driven compensation package for posts requiring special expertise and professional skills.
- Performance-related incentive scheme (PRIS): The introduction of a PRIS is designed to reward performance, innovation, creativity, and responsive delegated administration of stakeholder interface for inclusive outcomes and service delivery. This will be a budget neutral tool for results-based management with performance targets, standards, indicators and greater accountability.

The Sixth CPC mission is a landmark in the evolution of India's civil services. This is not only a pay commission in the usual sense of the term but it has also sought to reform the structure of the bureaucracy in the light of emerging global trends. By suggesting significant changes in personnel administration the commission translated into reality the drive towards debureaucratization.

Information technology (IT) has emerged as a major instrument for ushering in administrative reforms. A major initiative taken by the government for ushering in e-governance on a national scale, called the National e-Governance Plan (NeGP) was approved on 16 May 2006. The NEGP consists of 27 Mission Mode Projects (MMPs) encompassing central MMPs, 11 state MMPs, and 7 integrated MMPs that span multiple backend ministries/ departments. It is being implemented at the central, state, and local government levels. The Indian Portal project is an MMP under the NeGP which aims at providing a single-window access to the information and services of the Indian government at all levels from Central Government to State Governments to district administration and Panchayats for the citizens, business, and overseas Indians. An assessment report released in November 2008 of the three state-level e-government projects—vehicle registration, property registration, and land records (data selected from twelve states across India) —has the following key findings: (GOI 2008)

- The number of trips to government offices has reduced from 8 trips to 1-2 trips.
- Waiting time at the offices has reduced in the range 20-40%;
- There has been direct cost saving to citizens in the range of C 50-100.
- In land records projects, there has been a significant improvement in the perception of citizens. (Singh 2009)

The e-governance initiatives introduced by various government agencies include the setting up of single-window system in government offices, public grievance redressal systems, creation of online reservation in domestic rail and air travel, and so on. This has benefited the general public by improving the quality in delivery of services of these agencies. A few states like Andhra Pradesh and Maharashtra have taken the lead in making e-governance an integral part of the efforts at good governance. In a country like India, if access to IT was not restricted because of poor infrastructure, high costs, and lack of opportunity, the benefits in terms of service delivery would be phenomenal.

19.2 Rationalization and Reorganization

It has been felt that some of the functions handled by the Central Government should be transferred to the State Government and similarly few of the functions of the State Government should be delegated to the local authorities. The Fifth CPC had observed that few functions of the Government such as direct participation in manufacturing, mining and economic services should be divested to PSEs. In order to achieve this, few Ministries/ Departments have been abolished or amalgamated with other Ministries/Departments. Continuous efforts are being made to abolish departments and agencies to evolve compact governance structures. Apart from reduction in the quantum of work due to rationalization of functions, the Government has been implementing steps to improve efficiency and reduce the number of employees through structural changes and the use of technology.

Several Ministries/Departments have set-up separate and autonomous agencies for specific thrust areas. A popular approach at the State level has been to decentralize departmental responsibility and entrust the execution of schemes to arms-length agencies such as corporations and autonomous boards.

For rationalizing and reorganizing Ministries/Departments, the Second ARC has made several recommendations to the Government. They have made recommendations on recasting of Allocation of Business Rules to make them more focused on the goals and outcomes of each Ministry and Departments and to bring uniformity in the roles and responsibilities of various Ministries/ Departments.

The Ministry of Railways is an excellent example of a government body that has separated policy and execution. The Railways has granted autonomy to zonal and divisional managers in areas such as finance and personnel. In 1974, the Indian Railways established Rail India Technical and Economic Services (RITES) Ltd., to provide consultancy services in rail transport management to operators in India. Over time, RITES has evolved into a multi-disciplinary consultancy engaged in planning and consulting for other infrastructure services including airports, ports, highways and also urban planning.

19.3 Performance Monitoring of Ministries and Departments

The performance management function of the Government is carried out by the Performance Management Division within the Cabinet Secretariat. The Performance Management Division is headed by a Secretary to the GOI. This Division is responsible for designing the performance management system in the Government.

In September 2009, the Government supported by the Performance Management Division, introduced the Performance Monitoring and Evaluation System (PMES) to measure the performance of Government Departments in a fair and comprehensive manner. The performance of a Department is evaluated by measuring the performance of all schemes and projects implemented by the department in terms of financials, quantitative/qualitative impact and static and dynamic efficiency. The PMES provides a unified and single view of departmental performance. By focusing on areas that are within the control of a Department, PMES also ensures fairness and high levels of motivation.

Result Framework Document (RFD) introduces explicit prioritization with the help of weights attached to various objectives and performance criteria. Instead of a single point target, RFDs introduce a concept of scale. Most departments face multiple principals (GAG, CVC, Parliament, Courts, etc.,) who have multiple (and often conflicting) goals. This leads to fuzziness regarding expectations. RFDs reduce this fuzziness and provide clear goals to public managers. This leads to improvement in management of Departments.

At the beginning of each financial year, each Department prepares a Results Framework Document (RFD) consisting of the priorities set out by the Minister concerned, agenda as spelt out by the Government from time to time. The Minister incharge decides the priorities among the departmental objectives.

The RFD addresses three basic questions; (a) department's main objectives for the year (b) actions proposed to achieve these objectives (c) the degree of progress made in implementing these objectives, i.e. what are the relevant success indicators and their targets.

RFDs are discussed and finalized by the Ministers/Departments after thorough discussion with the Ad hoc Task Force (ATF) consisting of retired civil servants, domain experts, and leading management experts. This process helps the Ministries/ Departments in arriving at realistic performance targets. The RFDs so reviewed are approved by the High Power Committee (HPC) on Government performance headed by the Cabinet Secretary.

At the end of the year, all ministries/departments are required to review and prepare a report listing their respective achievements against the agreed targets in the prescribed format. This report is expected to be finalized by 31st May each year.

From the year 2011-12 onwards, as many as 72 ministries/ departments have finalized Results-Framework Documents. Thus, effectively 80 ministries/departments and 800 Responsibility Centres stand covered under the RFD system. By May 1st, 2012, states like Maharashtra, Punjab, Kerala, Himachal Pradesh, Karnataka, Assam, Haryana, Chhattisgarh, Tripura, Rajasthan, Andhra Pradesh, J & K, Mizoram have already adopted RFD policy and are at various stages of implementation.

In order to build capacity on performance management in Government, as many as 30 workshops have been conducted across the country in collaboration with IIM Ahmedabad and Lal Bahadur Shastri National Academy at Mussoorie. Some administrative bodies are Department of Administrative Reforms and Public Grievances, National Informatics Centre (NIC), and various State Governments.

PMD has, in collaboration with NIC, developed a powerful software to automate monitoring and evaluation of performance based on RFDs. This software is called RFMS (Results-Framework Management System).

19.4 Social Audits

The term social audit can be defined as the process of improving efficiency and effectiveness of governance through the participation of concerned people. Social audit is a process for enforcing accountability and transparency in the development initiatives of local agencies by providing the details on usage of resources, both financial and non-financial, through a public platform. The social audit process provides an opportunity for people to participate in the process of analyzing the status of public sector programmes. The advantages of conducting social audits are:

- Community participation in local planning.
- Increases accountability and transparency.
- Improves local decision-making process.

While conducting social audit, factors such as the need of people, government understanding of the need and the actual work done are important parameters that are considered. The social audit process also helps in strengthening democracy in governance and improves grievance redressal mechanisms.

According to the Constitution (73rd Amendment) Act, 1992, the Gram Sabhas are empowered to conduct social audits along with other functions. The Gram Sabhas have been entrusted with the responsibilities of reviewing, planning and executing village development plans in the presence of people. The Gram Sabhas have to monitor the execution of work within the Gram Panchayat. Gram Sabhas are expected to conduct regular social audits of all the projects and schemes taken up by the Gram Panchayats.

However, the scope of social audit is restricted and localized covering only select aspects out of a wide range of audit perspectives in terms of financial compliance and performance. The monitoring through social audit is informal and unprocessed. Citizens can also call for a social audit of any public process where the government audit has been unsatisfactory. These audits should be used as a supplemental audit process along with government audit to improve accountability.

The MNREGA conceptualized on September 7, 2005, aims at enhancing the livelihood of people in rural areas by guaranteeing hundred days of wage-employment in a financial year to a rural household whose adult members volunteer to do unskilled manual work. The employment is generated in several areas such as flood control and protection, water conservation and harvesting, rural connectivity, land development, irrigation facility and renovation of traditional water bodies.

The social audit tool has enabled the rural communities to monitor and analyze the quality, of MNREGA as well as mobilize awareness and enforcement of their rights. All the states have been directed to form an independent social audit committee to facilitate the process of social audit.

The social audit process includes public vigilance and verification through social audit forums such as public hearings, where information is read out publicly. People are given an opportunity to question officials, seek and obtain information, verify financial expenditure and critically evaluate the quality of work as well as the functioning of the programme staff. One of the best examples of the social audit tool being used ably and efficiently is in the state of Andhra Pradesh. The social audit work initially started in the districts of Nalgonda, Medak, Mehbubnagar and Ananthapur, was subsequently spread to all 22 districts. By 2010, it was found that out of Rs. 2866.48 crore expenditure audited, an amount of Rs. 29.40 crore was misappropriated, which is around 1.03% of deviation (DARPG - GOI - 2012).

19.5 Other Initiatives: Civil Services Day

From the year 2006, GOI has started celebrating 21st of April every year as 'Civil Service Day' as an occasion for the civil servants to rededicate themselves to the cause of citizens and renew their commitment to public service and excellence in work. The first such function was held in Vigyan Bhawan on 21.04.2006. On the occasion, civil servants are awarded by the PM for their excellent work done in the field of public administration. On 21st April the first Home Minister of the country Shri Vallabhbhai Patel addressed the first batch of

Indian Administrative Services officers and so it has been chosen as the date for celebrating the Civil Services Day.The GOI has instituted Prime Minister's Awards for excellence in 'Public Administration' to acknowledge, recognize and reward the extraordinary and innovative work done by officers of the Central and State Governments. The Scheme rewards the outstanding and exemplary performance of civil servants. Discharge of routine duties and responsibilities and/or implementation of programmes/projects in the normal course are not considered as qualifications for the Award. Initiatives and projects whose qualitative and quantitative outcomes/results are of a very high order, and benefit a large number of citizens/stakeholders could be considered. All serving officers of the Central and the State Governments, either individually or as a team or as organizations, are eligible for the Awards. A maximum of 15 Awards are given under individual, team and organization categories.

19.6 State of the Governance Report (SOGR)

The GOI has initiated a study for measuring governance at State level to provide a tool which could be issued by State Governments to identify areas which need improvement. It was the expectation that assessing the state of governance for identifying parameters would help the policymakers and development practitioners to understand implications of certain decisions.

Keeping these objectives in mind, the department initiated this project to develop a framework and an appropriate methodology for assessing the 'state of governance' in a State with a focus on the poor. The project recognizes the basic linkages between quality of governance, service delivery and poverty reduction.

The state of government report methodology was finalized after extensive consultations with a broad spectrum of people. The draft methodology was presented to a wide range of audience at a national level workshop on March 27, 2009, where representatives from academia, civil society, research bodies, senior officers from Central Line Ministries, State Government representatives (where the pilot was undertaken), Planning Commission and multilateral agencies were invited.

19.7 Study on Social Accountability Mechanisms

A study was initiated by the central government entitled "Social Accountability Mechanisms" which would explore ways and means of enhancing the ability of citizens (especially the poor and marginalized) to engage with public servants and politicians in a more informed, direct and constructive manner so that the services under the National Programmes were effectively delivered. The National Institute of Administrative Research (NIAR), a unit of Lal Bahadur Shastri National Academy of Administration (LBSNAA), Mussoorie, was entrusted with the assignment for developing necessary generic tools/ framework relating to social accountability which could also be adopted in various social sector schemes/programmes of the GOI.

Social accountability is an approach towards building accountability that relies on civic engagement, i.e. in which its ordinary citizens and or civil society organizations who participate directly or indirectly are entitled to exact accountability. Social accountability initiatives derive from the core goals of promoting poverty reduction and effective and sustainable development. The three main arguments underlying the importance of social accountability are: (i) governance; (ii) increased development effectiveness; and (iii) empowerment. Social accountability mechanisms refer to a broad range of actions (beyond voting) that citizens, communities and civil society organizations can use to hold government officials accountable. These include citizen participation in public policy making, participatory budgeting, public expenditure tracking, citizen monitoring of public service delivery, advocacy campaigns, etc.

19.8 Second ARC Reports

The Second Administrative Reforms Commission (ARC) was constituted on 31.08.2005, as a Commission of Inquiry, under the Chairmanship of Shri Veerappa Moily for preparing a detailed blueprint for revamping the public administrative system. The Commission was requested to suggest measures to achieve a proactive, responsive, accountable, sustainable and efficient administration for the country at all levels of the Government. It has presented the following 15 Reports to the Government for consideration:

1. Right to Information: Master Key to Good Governance (9.6.2006)
2. Unlocking human capital: Entitlements and Governance - a Case Study (31.7.2006)
3. Crisis Management: From Despair to Hope (31.10.2006)
4. Ethics in Governance (12.2.2007)
5. Public Order : Justice for each ... Peace for all (26.6.2007)
6. Local Governance (27.11.2007)
7. Capacity Building for Conflict Resolution—Friction to Fusion (17.3.2008)
8. Combating Terrorism (17.9.2008)
9. Social Capital-A Shared Destiny (8.10.2008)
10. Refurbishing of Personnel Administration—Scaling New Heights (27.11.2008)
11. Promoting e-Governance-The Smart Way Forward (20.01.2009)
12. Citizen Centric Administration—The Heart of Governance (30.3.2009)
13. Organisational structure of GOI (19.5.2009)
14. Strengthening Financial Management System (26.2.2009)
15. State and District Administration (29.5.2005)

The Government constituted a Group of Ministers (GoM) on 30th March 2007 to consider the recommendations of the Second ARC and to review the pace of implementation of the recommendations as well as to provide guidance to the concerned Ministries/Departments in implementing the decisions. It has since been reconstituted under the Chairmanship of Union Finance Minister on 21.08.2009. The Core Group on Administrative Reforms (CGAR) under the Chairmanship of Cabinet Secretary has finished examination of all the 15 reports.

This GoM has so far considered 15 reports. Their decisions on these reports are at various stages of implementation.

Conclusion

The Indian bureaucracy at the Central and State levels form the basic framework of administration in India. It is entrusted with formulating and implementing policies, maintaining law and order and delivering public services. The Civil Service in India, (consisting of All India Services, Central Civil Services and the State Civil Services) constitutes the backbone of the public governance system in the country. The civil service has played a vital role in the task of nation building, while adhering to the basic tenets laid down in the Constitution. In India's post-globalized era, competition in service delivery and changed mindsets of Indian citizens have been the biggest catalysts of administrative reform in the post-1991 era.

Efficient and Open governance is the key to strengthening peoples' participation in a democracy. Access to information can empower the citizens to demand and receive information regarding any executive action. This fosters a culture of accountability and transparency as government records become open to public scrutiny. Transparency in government organizations makes them function objectively, thereby leading to efficient and effective governance.

In line with this, the GOI enacted the Right to Information Act in 2005 to empower citizens and promote transparency. This watershed legislation has become one of the hallmarks of an attempt to good governance in India.

India has undergone a transformation in terms of growth, urbanization, technological change and increased citizen awareness. There is an increasing need to build a dynamic civil service adept at adjusting to change and this can be done by bringing in a process of personnel management reforms. The key to good governance will be to instill this as part of administrative culture and encourage civil servants to be more trained in citizen-centric administration. Government monopolies are gone and the administrator of today has to adjust to competition from the private and voluntary sector for service delivery. The citizen is now a consumer in the market who expects much better quality and standards of service.

We have now moved from the era of government to governance. Most of the government structures are based on the Weberian model of division of work—a well- defined hierarchy, adherence to rules and, by and large adoption of an impersonal work ethics. To foster quick decision-making, there is a need on the part of the Central Government to delegate some of the tasks to State Governments, who in turn need to delegate and involve local administrative bodies. This is the way a three-tier public governance system should work. State Governments should also encourage local bodies to outsource specific functions to public or private agencies, as may be appropriate, through enabling guidelines. The Central and the State Governments can also consider partnering with Non-Governmental Organizations (NGOs) to ensure that the programmes and policies are implemented at the grass-root level and the desired benefits are available to all targeted group of citizens.

Public-Private Partnerships (PPPs) refer to joint ventures in developmental areas between the Central and/or the State Governments and the private sector that is coordinated through power sharing and joint decision-making mechanisms. This model may work in case of projects that are constrained by lack of public financial resources and low level of skills and capacity. Private agencies can help overcome these challenges by partial funding and expediting the delivery of public services. They can bring in specialized expertise (project and change management) and facilitate faster development of technologies. PPPs facilitate pooling of human and financial resources, professionalism, and participation of civil society in governance.

Embracing technology should be the key priority for the civil servants. In a bid to streamline operations and increase efficiency, the Central Government has embarked upon a massive e-governance programme, as part of which a number of systems are being automated and data is being digitized. To ensure that the e-governance programme achieves its objectives, it is important to educate civil servants themselves in the use of technology. The Central and the State Governments are taking many steps in this direction and implementing training schemes that make civil servants aware of the use of technology. However, this has to be a concerted effort and will be effective only if the civil servants across all levels undergo training and imbibe the use of technology in their day-to-day operations.

Various attempts have been made over the years to reform administration. We have experimented with performance budgeting, zero-based budgeting, the desk officer system, lateral entry of distinguished persons from outside at high levels in governance, different kinds of performance appraisal systems, new training methods, merging and de-merging departments, moving forward briskly on introduction of digital governance and introducing a quality control system called Sevottam. The experiment with "results framework documents" a few years ago was an attempt to create system reform by laying down objectives, assigning weights, developing a scoring system and enabling each entity in the governance system to assess its own performance. Therefore a variety of changes have been tried.

In December 2018, the NITI Aayog released Agenda 2022 with a foreword by Prime Minister Narendra Modi. Currently only 4,000 IAS officers administer populations the size of countries. This is done despite a shortage of nearly 1,500 IAS officers. If Agenda 2022 is to become a reality, state-level capacity needs to be fortified. Both at the Centre and more so in the states, there should be sizeable induction of professionals but only by following rigorous and transparent processes for selection.

We have a new government and fresh opportunities. We have many things to do in administration: linking inputs to outputs, evolving strong monitoring systems, building a system of incentives and penalties, integrating career progression at higher levels with performance over the years, digitising service delivery, reorienting our financial systems and so on. Instead of adhocism through commissions, committees and reports, we need to mainstream the process of administrative reform through political support and execution at the highest level.

Today's fast-changing India warrants the availability of well-rounded professionals, people who not only have the knowledge, but who are also adept at understanding the dynamics of the 21st century. *India is now the fastest growing economy in the world with the largest pool of scientific manpower and the largest electorate of young voters*. We need the best-trained personnel to man one of the largest public administrative systems in the world such as ours. An active synergy between politicians, civil servants, domain experts and proactive citizens can make this happen—to reach standards of excellence in public service delivery.

Suggested Readings

Action Plan for Effective and Responsive Administration, Statement Adopted at the Conference of Chief Ministers, New Delhi, 1997a

Administrative Reforms Commissions Reports, New Delhi, Ministry of Home Affairs, 1966- 70.

Appleby, Paul H., *Public Administration in India: Report of a Survey*, Cabinet Secretariat, GOI, 1953.

Chakravarty, Bidyut and Mohit Bhattachavya (eds.), *Administrative Change and Innovation: A Reader*, New Delhi, OUP, 2005.

Medury, Uma, *Public Administration in the Globalization Era: The New Public Management Perspective*, New Delhi, Orient Black Swan, 2010.

Public service in India: A country profile, DARPG, GOI, 2012.

Report of the Fifth Central Pay Commission, Vol. L Ministry of Finance, GOI, 1997b.

Report of the National Police Commission, New Delhi, GOI, 1981.

Second ARC, Reports, GOI

Singh, Sujata, *Reforms in Governance: Six Decades of Administrative Reforms*, New Delhi, Indian Institute of Public Administration, 2009.

The Report of the Fifth Pay Commission, Vol. 1, New Delhi, GOI Press, 1997c.

OOO

Epilogue: Where do we go from here?

Introduction

Democracy in India

In pre-independence India, the demand for democratization was not an essential part of the anti-imperialist struggle for national independence. As the nationalist struggle gained momentum it widened its social base as larger and larger sections of people were brought within its fold. Thus it seemed inevitable that Independent India should have a democratic set-up. There was complete unanimity among the constitution- makers about the choice of democracy as a system of governance for Independent India Democracy seemed a visible symbol of our newlywon independence being actualized through self-rule. It took us more than sixty years to institutionalize the political foundations (rule of law, multi-party system, free and fair elections, vibrant press and dynamic judiciary) of this democracy, though it was given to us at one stroke by our constitution. Institutionalizing the formal features of a democracy isn't easy in an unequal, class-divided, developing society with low levels of human development. Now in the second decade of the 21st century we do believe that we have gone beyond the formal system of democratic governance. The increasing role of NGOs, women's groups, human rights and grassroots movements questioning the existing paradigms of development, the increasing importance of public litigation cases, etc., are an evidence of the growing influence of civil society in the public policy process in India.

In the political discourses on Indian democracy in the 20th century, India had been increasingly described as a 'lame duck' democracy or an 'ungovernable' one. These debates have arisen not only because of the persistence of insurgency in the North-East, and Kashmir but also due to the existence of the ever-present threat of the failure of the Central parliamentary government. The persistence of a hung parliament in several recent elections had led to the formation of coalition governments at the Centre and the States since 1989. This led to non-Congress opposition (national and regional) parties tasting power for the first time —working out a consensus agenda of government and learning to respect the limits and possibilities of public position and power. This effort to arrive at a national consensus on major issues facing the nation was a healthy by-product of the coalition era (1989-2014) in national politics.

The literature on the issue of ungovernability of India started with Morris-Jones (The Government and Politics of India, 1989) and continued with Atul Kohli (Democracy and Discontent, 1991). It is a fear of system failure based on the general rise in lawlessness, increasing use of violence, breakdown of law and order, criminalization of politics and a rising trend towards de-institutionalization and scant respect for the rule of law by the politicians. India's problems of governance are a part of the process of institutionalization itself, it must be admitted that our democracy is more vibrant today than it ever was before —with an alert press, a sensitive judiciary, grassroots NGOs and increasing number of citizen groups building up a strong culture of dissent within an essentially feudal hierarchical society. India has sustained her democracy in extreme paradoxical and vulnerable conditions (social cleavages, weak fledgling institutions) and therein lies her strength for the future.

Lloyd and Susanne Rudolph see the state in India (In Pursuit of Lakshmi, 1987) as a polymorphous creature of manifold forms and orientation. It is a liberal state, a capitalist state, and also a socialist state, depending on whose pressure it yields from time to time. The point is, one must finally argue that there is a certain amount of autonomy that the Indian state does exercise, despite the multiple (class caste/region) pressures under which it is constantly subject to. This autonomy is the autonomy granted to it by the democratic political process where the public policy agenda will ultimately be geared to the greatest good of the greatest number (euphemistically called the 'public interest'), however, that may be interpreted at a particular point of time by the state.

The contemporary state versus civil society discourse had found a vocal exponent in the writings of Rajni Kothari (State Against Democracy, 1988). He argued that many recent developments have gradually belied the hope that parties and governing institutions will serve the interest of civil society. The state has become both too omnipotent and too repressive of the social order and it has thus ceased to be representative besides lacking the 'capacity' to fulfill public needs and aspirations. All this and more have led to major social segments evolving their own politics — as evidenced by the development of political activity and grassroots movements focusing on the specific demands of women, Dalits, tribals, Muslims and OBCs, the Naxalite movement, militant struggles for regional autonomy, and ecological movements. In such a scenario there is a need to refocus on ways to reconnect the state and the citizen by reinventing democratic capacity to serve citizen needs. In fact, compulsions of electoral politics should force political parties to broaden their appeal rather than base themselves on constricting religious, regional, caste or ideological grounds. In a pluralist and diverse society like India, especially in a democratic context, the basis of one kind of politics (e.g. communal) gets modified or controlled by other strong contenders (e.g. regional/class/caste-based) or issues. No community, caste/class is a monolith in India, besides having regional variations. In a pluralist society like India sharing of power is the only way to sustain our democracy.

Within a democratic polity, power may be unequally distributed. Who gets what, when and how will greatly depend on the distribution of the sources of power in society, namely, wealth, social status, legality, population, control over employment, technology and media. In the context of India, the rich landed gentry, affluent middle and small farmers, the industrialist, the work force in the organized sectors (through their trade unions) have successfully managed to bargain for and influence political decisions in their favour. A large part of the rural and urban workforce in the unorganized sector is left out of the process of democratic bargaining. There is practically no regularity of employment or any social security cover guaranteed to them by their employers. It is these groups that have to be given a stake in our democracy.

The need for Indian democracy to continually justify itself in economic terms is unfortunate but that is inevitable in the context of a developing country. Political democracy does not exist in a vacuum. It has certain parameters like liberty and equality. Even with guaranteed civil and political rights, economic failures can jeopardize democracy. Since the liberalization of our economy began in the 1990s a lurking suspicion remained that the state was attempting to abdicate its responsibilities, especially in the developmental sectors. A regulatory state in the context of a country like India would only show a bias in favour of the existing beneficiaries of development if it tried to roll back suddenly. Widening of the social base of development, to include more and more beneficiaries within its fold, is a continuing need of the democratic Indian state. If there have been reasons for despair, there are ample reasons for hope in the Indian democratic developmental experience as well. Let us not expect growth miracles alone from the Indian state for that is not enough. What we need are committed public policy implementers with a 'human development' vision, and feasible policies to implement that vision with honesty and integrity. That is the least the citizens of the largest democracy in the world have a right to expect and deserve.

The India Story: Gains and Asymmetries

At the second decade of the 21st century, let us look at the India story a little more closely. In the last two decades, since 1991, the country has seen some strong macro- economic gains and the role of the Indian state today cannot be said to match any stereotypical image of a minimalist state. The Indian regulatory state (post-1991) has initiated many administrative and Rights-based initiatives, which have made a definite impact on public governance. Decentralization has taken on new meanings after the 73rd and 74th constitutional amendments and the concept of a Rights-based approach to development has acted as a linking pin catalyzing the post-globalized public discourses on democracy, development and good governance. Many issues have been raised: growth vs. equity, the role of the state in the social sector, the model of development we choose to espouse in a society which has transited from a 3% rate of growth to a robust and sustainable 8 to 9%, welfare in a globalizing economy or a bottom line agenda of good governance, etc. These are crucial issues on which a societal consensus needs to emerge in the 21st century. From 2005 onwards, largely powered by the services sector the economy has been growing at a rate of 8 to 9% per annum and is the fastest growing economy in the world. Yet this growth is not without its asymmetries. An agricultural sector growth at only 3%, a near stagnant industrial sector, environmental degradation, regional inequalities and inadequate investments in the social sector are the worrying aspects of this era. If poverty is to be measured by relative deprivation in basic public goods then more than 70% of India is still deprived. Ninety per cent of India's workforce is in the unorganized sector with minimal social security. It is in this context that the record of the Indian state in providing social goods to the citizens comes up for serious debate in the public domain.

New Rights Discourse

One of the paradoxes of the Indian globalized era is the fact that it is during this era that the state has enacted several important laws that make work, education, information and food a right. The state has also taken major initiatives in the public health sector like the National

Rural Health Mission. State spending in the social sector has significantly risen and social security schemes for the unorganized sector have also been flagged off by the Centre and the States. Many of the leading campaigns for New Rights or for the upgradation of the provisions in the Directive Principles of state policy have come from civil society initiatives or judicial activism. All campaigns draw upon the language of rights. The Supreme Court in different judgements have expanded the ambit of certain rights, e,g. the right to life has now come to mean the right to food, livelihood, health, clean environment, education and information as well. In the post-globalized era, India has not followed the classical model of globalization—that of retreat of the state from the social sectors. Electoral pressures, grassroots demands and the need of the state to garner legitimacy have ensured that the state continues to provide a minimum package of social goods to its citizens.

The command and control economy of the pre-1991 era in India with largely affirmative action ensured the growth of a 400 million strong middle class when the post-globalized state took over. The middle class acts as the greatest bulwark of a healthy democracy and have been the greatest beneficiaries of the pre-1991 planning era. Development in today's age includes both economic growth and human development. Globally we are the fastest growing economy yet our ranking in human development is 130 out of 189 nations according to UNDP Human Development Report 2018. This is an obvious mismatch. Both economic growth and human development are investment reliant. If in an age of globalization, the private sector funds the first, then state funds compulsorily need to go to the second.

It is the experience of developed countries today that higher growth (we have averaged above 7% growth rate in the last decade) is an essential pre-condition to better equity. Our high savings rate (32% of G.D.P.) and investment rate (30% of G.D.P.) with a predominantly internally financed economy can be rated as substantive achievements. Only China and South Korea among the larger economies have a better record in these two aspects. However, India is characterized by economic under-achievement and a 'soft state' status. The test of a successful democracy has always been absorption of as many demands as possible within the body politic.

With an 8-10% growth rate, for the first time in India's political history equalizing citizen rights has become a realistic target for Indian public policy makers. The entire development discourse in India should now be centred on developing feasible public policy options in terms of giving hitherto excluded groups economic entitlements like work, food, education, health care and housing. Higher growth is an essential precondition to better equity but its attendant inequalities need consensual equalizing public policy interventions in every democracy

Democracy eventually gives everyone a promise and a hope to be included in citizen entitlements. Part IV of the Indian constitution constitutes the core of the promise of socio-economic justice to be progressively realized through enhanced state capacity. The day of deliverance has finally arrived when public power can match promised public outcomes.

Good Governance in India: Post-1991 Efforts

The good governance debate in the context of globalization and liberalization is ongoing in developing countries since the 1990s. The Second Administrative Reforms Commission (SARC) has produced 15 Reports and action has been taken on many of them, unlike half-hearted efforts at administrative reform in the earlier decades. Looking at the Indian scenario, a classification of reforms undertaken by the government of India since the 1990s can be listed as follows:

1. Reforms that pertain to the legal basis of government action: The Jain Commission which reviewed administrative laws sought repeal of over 300 central laws. The constitutional amendments impart stability to the rural and urban local self-governing institutions and legislation for an effective set of vigilance bodies also belong to this category.
2. Comprehensive or specific reforms of administrative structure, size and design: The application of Total Quality Management (TQM) concepts would clearly be within this reform category. Procedural reforms in financial decentralization and delegation meant to speed up internal or inter-departmental operations are also in the anvil. E-governance projects in several states, introduction of Results Framework Documents in Ministries are all efforts in this category.
3. Reforms for more active partnerships between the government, private/voluntary sectors and citizens: These include the all-important interface with citizens (Right to Information, Citizen's Charters and Public Service Guarantee Acts etc), local self-governance institutions (the municipalities and panchayats), NGOs, registered associations (for instance of residents of urban localities, or societies), elected and other public representatives. The social audit component of MNREGA is another pioneering conception.

Initiatives by State Governments

Starting with Madhya Pradesh in 2010, another 20 State Governments (SGs) have so far enacted the Right-to-Public Services Guarantee Acts albeit under different names, with five declared intents: (a) assurance of the service, (b) service within a stipulated time frame, (c) holding designated officers accountable, (d) a system of grievance redressal by two stage appeal, and (e) a system of penalty and fine for delay/ denial in service. Some of these SGs are of Rajasthan, Delhi, Jammu and Kashmir (J&K), Bihar, Punjab, Uttar Pradesh, Himachal Pradesh, Uttarakhand, Karnataka, Jharkhand and Haryana. The model for all these Acts has common characteristics. The departments are free to declare a few or all of their services to come under its purview. A department that wishes to declare that a service would come under the legislation must designate a responsible officer to provide the service, a first appeal officer and a second appeal officer for each declared service, determine the fine or penalty for failure to provide acknowledgement, delay in service or its denial. The citizen is required to submit applications with supporting documents and mandatorily get an acknowledgement.

Since the services that come under this Act are dependent on departmental willingness, their number varies from as low as 17 in Uttar Pradesh to 265 in Karnataka. The service may include documents (certificates, licenses, permits), cash (pension, stipends) and kind (electricity/water connections). The nature of these services can be classified as regulatory (trade, licence), administrative (birth, caste certificate), basic (water, electricity), and welfare (pension, stipend) services.

What is more striking about these Acts is that they are all initiated by State Governments. This is in stark contrast to the plethora of rights-based legislations in the last decade or more, which came primarily out of a large number of civil society organizations' advocacy efforts with the union government and parliament. Right to Information (RTI) Act 2005, Forest Rights Act (FRA) 2006, Mahatma Gandhi National Rural Employment Guarantee Act (MGNREGA) 2005, Child Labour (Abolition and Rehabilitation) Act 2006, Right to Education (RTE) Act 2009 and the Food Security Act 2013 can be classified as central legislations pushed for by civil society for enabling and empowering particular groups of citizens. All of these rights-based legislations were enacted as Central Acts with a clear mandate for the states to implement by framing appropriate rules.

The experience of actual implementation of these rights-based legislations tells us a different story. While these legislations have certainly raised public expectations, they have not translated into any internal movement for reform within the structures of governance. Neither have they improved the internal efficiency, accountability or transparency of the system nor have they improved the downward accountability of the departments/ authorities towards their constituencies. Except perhaps, the RTI, other such Central legislations have not made administration ordinarily accountable.

Therefore, it is encouraging to note the enthusiasm of the State Governments in pushing for the Service Guarantee Acts since 2010. This is manifested in the fact that all these State Governments are taking proactive steps to digitize parts or the whole of the service delivery system connected with these services, with clear internal control and built in transparency in the procedures of implementation. One good example is Bihar, where the designated monitor can track each application by name on the computer screen. Other software versions being piloted elsewhere even have the provision for the citizen to track his/her own application as it goes through the various stages of processing. The initial results are encouraging and Bihar has already received 99 lakh applications for various services, of which almost all have been attended to. The average rate of disposal seems to be 98%, an appreciable achievement indeed. Similarly, Madhya Pradesh has received more than 1 crore requests and has attended to them all.

Cost of Governance in India Today

We have one of the largest government sectors in the world today. The cost of governance of India by the roughly 800 politicians at the Centre, the 6000 in the 29 states and approx. 2.15 crore employees of the Central and State Governments cost the country about 1800 crore a day. This study excludes the 3 million representatives of the people at the Panchayat level. About 1.87% of Indians govern 1000 million people. This comes to about US $ 138 billion or nearly 30% of India's GDP.

The Public Affairs Centre, Bangalore surveyed 37,000 households in 24 states of India to focus on the Five Basic Services in which the government of India has invested thousands of crores including drinking water, health and sanitation, education and child care, the public distribution system and road transport. Their findings regarding government run delivery systems are listed below:

- Only 13% of the users are satisfied with the public health system.
- Less than 10% are content with the public distribution system.
- Barely 16% are satisfied with teachers in government schools.
- Just 5% are satisfied with public sanitation in public places.
- Only a fifth are satisfied with the public transport system. [Samuel Paul (et al) Who benefits from India's Public Services (2006)]

What should the Government Do?

The policy makers must realize that poverty eradication is not only a development goal but also a major human rights challenge of the 21st century. A minimum standard of decent living, adequate nutrition, healthcare, education, and employment are not just Development Goals they are also Human Rights. One-third of India's population lives below the poverty line and constitute one-third of the world's extreme poor, one-third is illiterate, nine out of ten households don't have access to toilets, one out of six villages is yet to get electricity and two out of five do not get drinking water. It also had the highest number of infant deaths in the world in 2012. Poverty reduction was sluggish, coming down from 49.4% in 1994 to 42% in 2005, 32.7% in 2010 to 20% in 2019. Almost 60% of people who defecate in the open reside in India which also accounts for 17% of global maternal deaths. In fact the sustainable development Goals cannot be met globally if they are not reached in India.

Citizen rights have to be defined and compared in terms of both entitlements and deprivation on a pan Indian scale, e.g. inter-state comparisons in growth and human development indicators would initiate meaningful debate on the wide range of variations in terms of policy successes and failures within India itself. For instance, a citizen of Bihar may get quite a different package of entitlements and access in terms of basic public goods and services than probably a resident of Kerala (an Indian state whose human development indicators are very high even by global standards).

These are the Core areas where the government has to be proactive. The success of any developmental philosophy in Indian democracy needs to be judged only by one touchstone —Public Interest as defined at the grass roots in terms of public goods and utilities provided to the people.

If we want a new public governance system these new questions have to be dissected in practice. They are:

- How do we manage policy execution in a manner that the declared public policy be carried out in practice? (the policy implementation question)
- How do we ensure organizational and individual service performance and standards? (the audit and targets question)

- How do we hold public managers accountable? (the scrutiny question)
- How do we incentivize staff for optimal productivity in public agencies? (the rewards question)
- How do we ensure long run organizational sustainability? (the change and innovation question)

Understanding Basic State Capacity:

It has been increasingly felt that we need to focus on how governance works and the need to reinvent public service delivery systems in India. Political Science has focused largely on democratic institutions in recent years but far less on *the understanding of basic state capacity, the absence of which often undermines democracy*. Do democratic governance systems comparatively work better to ensure improved public delivery systems in the long run? Do public powers in democracies necessarily match human welfare and better public outcomes? These are serious questions that ought to be debated in the public domain. Democracy and good governance are separate and distinct phenomena, but worldwide empirical evidence has proved that regimes reflecting both dimensions are necessary to achieve many aspects of human security.

India's performance with respect to the Millennium Development Goals (MDGs) — eradicating extreme poverty and hunger, achieving universal primary education, promoting gender equality and empowering women, reducing child mortality, improving maternal health, combating HIV/AIDS, malaria and other diseases, ensuring, environmental sustainability and developing a global partnership for development —which were to be reached by 2015 has been quite dismal.

The poor (calculated to be one-third of our population) suffer from chronic hunger and malnutrition despite India being a food surplus state. The Food Security Act passed in 2013 promises subsidized food to 67% of the population. If implemented properly it can and should eradicate extreme forms of hunger and malnutrition. India must meet the globally accepted norm of government spending (atleast 6% of GDP) on education rather than the roughly 4% that they now spend. This is essential if the school dropout rate of about 50% by Class X is to be brought down and the gross enrolment ratio in higher education is raised beyond the current 16-17%.

About 50% of India's 1.3 billion population is less than 25 years old. One crore jobs per year are needed to provide employment to our youth for the next 10 years. The government will need to ensure that the employment expectation of its youth are met by educating and giving them skill sets for the job market—a need that cannot be fulfilled via government sector employment or government funded schemes alone. The participation of the private sector is critical for job creation. Micro, small and medium enterprises currently generate the largest employment (nearly 6 crore) after agriculture. The government needs to promote these industries in a big way in order to generate employment. With just 2% of the youth having technical education, the skills gap is becoming a gigantic problem. Vocational technical curricula need to be upgraded and dynamically linked to labour market demands.

India's public health spending barely accounts for 1% of GDP, among the lowest in the world. India's IMR is 42 deaths per 1000 live births and MMR is 179 deaths per 100000 live births, worse than Nepal or Bangladesh. More than 72% of the money people spend on healthcare is on buying medicines.

Indian women's work participation rate is one of the lowest in the world —a mere 20% of the 15+ female population, and unemployment among women graduates is the highest in India, i.e. about 60%.Government needs to legislate and implement equal pay for equal work besides 33% reservation for women in Central and State legislatures.

Development in today's age includes both economic growth and human development. Globally we are the fastest growing economy yet our ranking in human development is 130 out of 189 nations. It is the experience of developed countries today that higher growth is an essential pre-condition to better equity. With high growth rates in the last decade, for the first time in India's political history public power can match public outcomes in human development.

Two eminent economists have recently approached the problem of India's continuing struggle with growth from different angles. Jagdish Bhagwati and Arvind Panagariya in their book Why Growth Matters (2013) argue that reforms driven economic growth in India has reduced poverty, and it can provide a data rich economic story from which we might address the central moral challenge facing the world: which strategy will lift the greatest number of people from extreme poverty? The authors assert that the experience of China, India and East Asia, demonstrate how growth is stimulated and sustained within the policy framework that exploits the opportunities provided by integration into the world economy and also relies on a sophisticated use of market incentives in guiding production and investment. When China reduced people in poverty by 220 million between 1978 and 2004, it was hailed as the greatest poverty reduction in history. India has just reduced its number of poor from 407 million to 269 million, a fall of 138 million in seven years between 2004-05 and 2011-12. This is faster than China's poverty reduction rate at a comparable stage of development. This is no small achievement for a democracy, therefore Bhagwati and Panagariya two famous Indian economists are optimistic about India's slower but surer growth prospects.

Amartya Sen and Jean Dreze, however, in their latest book An Uncertain Glory; India and its Contradictions 2013) lament the underachievement in health and education revealed by India's social indicators in spite of years of rapid economic growth. They argue that growth has not altered the reality of entrenched inequality in the Indian social system. The elite, defined by caste, class, privilege and gender, stay unaffected by the plight of other classes and are indifferent towards working on an improvement on that front.

They argue that only a market-oriented state can ensure an inclusive democracy by adopting a rights-based approach to development where the state reaches out directly to its citizens by guaranteeing a minimum basket of public goods to all. This is a view seconded by Sunil Khilnani (Times of India, January 14, 2012) as well. For all the real and impressive strength of India's private initiatives since 1991 in augmenting India's growth, given the scale at which India's problems have to be tackled, and that solutions must deliver a certain uniformity or universalism of outcome, private action can't be a substitute for government action. Khilnani gives an example to prove his point. Given the scale, and the need to be able to ensure universal standard (so that someone educated in Assam is employable in Kerala) it is the state system that is most likely to be able to deliver this. The need of the hour in India is to rediscover the necessity of the state, renegotiating the compact, between the state, markets and society. India is the world's largest democracy, we need to make it the deepest one.

The available evidence indicates that India has only 1.6 government personnel for every 100 residents (including the personnel in the union state and local governments besides Public Sector Undertakings) as compared to much higher figures of 3.3 in South Africa, 3.9 in Mexico, 5.9 in Brazil, 7.2 in Germany, 10.1 in the UK, and 10.6 government personnel for every 100 residents in Canada (data from Centre for Budget and governance Accountability Reports 2014).

Understanding the Indian Model of Governance

The greatest tragedy of India has been that despite huge resources and potential strengths, she seems to have been delegated to be a superpower-in-waiting status globally. The quality of governance offered by our democracy is still mediocre and 'soft'. Democracy has succeeded despite low-income economy, widespread poverty, illiteracy, and ethnic diversity. Indian democracy has protected its elite without fully excluding the weaker groups (Atul Kohli, Poverty and Plenty in the New India: Politics, Economics and Inequality, 2012). Judged by developing country standards India's greatest asset has been that she has been ruled by civilian elected governments throughout its post-independent history with a competent civil service which unfortunately has not worked to its true potential. The Indian civil service has always underperformed and has never been answerable to the public directly. Unlocking India's potential and taking her rightful position in the committee of nations will require, above all, *a strong visionary political leadership, and a world class public administration to manage a country of such continental proportions as India*. Public systems are managed by politico-administrative regimes and every developed state today rests on the strong and able shoulders of good and efficient governance systems which deliver public goods and services efficiently to the people. India will face huge challenges and some of them are discussed below.

- If India does not respond adequately to climate change, clean up its soil, water and rivers, revive its forests, millions of its citizens will be at risk. India like all other developing countries is still groping for an ideal environment development trade off.
- Human development is the second challenge that our regime will have to take care of. India is a fast-growing economy in the world with a human development ranking which is poorer than some of her South Asian neighbours and even of sub-Saharan Africa.
- The third vital challenge is infrastructure which is woefully inadequate for a country like India. Our public transport, sewage management, energy and communication systems are sub-standard, erratic and poor as compared to other developing countries.
- Our "Soft" state status is our biggest liability. India has one of the largest administrative systems with one of the poorest public service delivery systems in the

world. Their salaries (public servants) constitute 30% of our GDP. The fault lies not in the democratic system which is often perceived to be corrupt, inefficient and slow moving, but in the translation of electoral promises into effective delivery systems for citizens. There is a need to rebuild a relationship of faith and trust between the state and the citizen in Indian democracy. Given our practice of democracy in the last sixty years, this can best be realized through institutionalized statutory citizen entitlements enabling the demand for reasoned answers from the bureaucracy.

In federal systems, good governance is a partnership between the Centre and the States acting individually or sometimes in unison to ensure citizen entitlements. After 1991, the contribution of states to good governance initiatives has become significant and noticeable. Today we talk of the Gujarat and the Bihar models of governance in terms of their contribution to infrastructural development and provision of delivery systems to the people. Madhya Pradesh and Chhattisgarh have made significant innovations in decentralization, education and health delivery, Maharashtra in employment guarantees, Kerala in land reforms, education, public health and community development, Tamil Nadu in the health sector, Mizoram and Himachal Pradesh in the communication and education sectors. The Right to Information movement and many other reform movements were pioneered by the state of Rajasthan.

Individual civil servants have done their bit too. Since 2006, when the Prime Minister's Excellence in civil service awards were introduced, efforts made by individual or group of civil servants to change administrative processes, or delivery systems in order to benefit the citizens have come to the forefront. Such best practices remain an inspiration for others to follow and need to be documented.

Within the international community, democracy and good governance are widely advocated as intrinsically desirable and important public goals. The challenge for democracies is therefore not simply to strengthen downward electoral accountability so that vote-seeking politicians have an incentive to pay attention to citizen needs. It is equally important to endow the public governance systems with the capacity, technical skills and resources so that elected leaders can deliver things that most citizens want: food and nutrition, education, basic health care and sustainable livelihoods. With the growth rates we have today, public power and resources can match effective and efficient public service delivery systems and citizen entitlements. Therefore it is an imperative to look at the good governance practices initiated by the Centre or the States in different sectors —infrastructure, education, health, urban civic services, etc., with visible or measureable impacts on the lives of citizens.

It is no exaggeration to say that the challenges facing the Indian administrative system are as unique and unparalleled in scale and diversity as the Indian developmental experience and therefore there is no shame in advertising and owning up to one's achievements and failures so far. Nothing in this record goes to make the future trajectory look wholly pessimistic or wholly optimistic. The attitude should be one of cautious optimism that we should be able to overcome all that has held us back so far. We never pushed ourselves to the limit and therefore remained underachievers so far.

There has been more continuity, than change in the pattern and functioning modes of Indian administration. More paradigmatic and transformational shifts are the need of the hour in the 21st century, if we are to give the citizens of the largest democracy the quality of public service they deserve.

Public administration in India, if conceptualized in Weberian terms, with its rigid, rule-bound and hierarchic characteristics, will be an inadequate tool of analysis to understand the complexities of the Indian model of governance as it exists today. The Indian model was structured on the Weberian mode long back by the British, but even during the 1950-90 era, the structure was considered inappropriate for administering development which required more dynamism and flexibility. Today the typical Weberian model is still inadequate to meaningfully represent "governance": besides the government is only one of many actors in the complex web of service providers in India today. The new governance style is obsessed only with "implementation strategies" in which bureaucracy plays a supportive role to market and civil society. Adherence to rules and to procedure has a bureaucratic connotation and what is important is to get the job done. The result is that there is a growing tension between a bureaucracy whose bedrock is neutrality and pursuit of public interest and a new governance style that sees bureaucracy as a backbone of support for neo-liberal policies and promotion of private interest. It would also be very problematic if bureaucrats seem to be measured on their ability to facilitate private business and the functioning of the market. The quest for a New Public Service based on new citizen-centric parameters of governance is just unfolding and how Indian public administration responds to these new directions needs to be carefully watched, researched and analyzed in future.

India positives

India and China are often compared, regarding their respective governance outcomes. China was poorer than India until the 1980s. Today it's seven times richer. It was more polluted than India just five years ago, today it's less polluted.

But there are signs that the pace of change is improving in India too. Official estimates of access to basic sanitation (toilets) went up from 39% in 2014 to 99% of the population in December 2018. Highway construction doubled between 2014-15 (4,400 kilometers) and 2018-19 (10,800 kilometers) and Indians are consuming more data per day than any other country – including China.

When extreme poverty (people living on $1.9, or less, a day) reaches negligible numbers, there will still be masses living in deprivation – deprived of good education, healthcare, a house, insurance. But that shouldn't stop us from celebrating the fact that our decades of fighting against extreme poverty and illiteracy may soon end, as will the struggle to access basic amenities like electricity, roads, internet and toilet by the masses in India.

Given its population, India is crucial to achieving the massive improvements needed to meet UN's Sustainable Development Goals. Open defecation is one area where the country has made strides with the Swachh Bharat programme when between 2000 and 2017, India reduced open defecation by half, the private sector wasn't allowed in telecom until 1991, and then only for value-added services like mobile calling and paging. In 1994, private companies were allowed to invest in telecom, starting a revolution that has made India the world's second-biggest wireless market after China. Where only 1 in 10,000 Indians had a mobile phone in 1995, now 8,900 of every 10,000 have them.

From Low- Capacity to High- Capacity State

Contrary to popular belief, the Indian state is one of the smallest among major nations on a per capita basis. While India's population increased from 846 million to 1.2 billion between 1991 and 2011, total public sector employment actually decreased from 19.1 to 17.9 million. Over this period, the absolute size of the elite Indian Administrative Service (IAS) dropped by 10 per cent; by 2010, the total strength of the IAS and the Indian Police Service (IPS) was less than 11,000, while the vacancy rate stood at 28 per cent. In foreign affairs, the strength of the Indian diplomatic corps is less than that of Sweden's. India's judicial system presently has a backlog of more than 3 crore cases. Compounding the fact that India has one of the lowest per capita police rates among major countries (1.3 constables lowest per 1,000 citizens), official estimates of police vacancies stand around 23 per cent (0.5 million of 2.2 million posts vacant)

This 'state capacity' – the ability of the state to effectively design and implement public policies-varies greatly across India. The Indian state is not failing but is seen to be only too often 'flailing' (Pritchett 2009). It can successfully manage highly complex tasks, but fails in executing relatively simple ones. On the one hand, India can organize elections for 850 million eligible voters, conduct a census for 1.3 billion people, and run a highly effective midday meal programme, the largest in the world for that age group of children. Yet, on the other hand, its record in providing basic public services, from health to education and water to sanitation, ranges from modest to dismal.

Undoubtedly, the expansion of India's private sector and vibrant civil society will substitute for some of the short-comings of the public sector in the foreseeable future. *Nevertheless, there is a wide range of core functions, from regulation to security, from social inclusion to public goods provision, where the state is – and will be – indispensable.* This is particularly true for India's vulnerable population-such as its 300-million-odd poor or members of marginalized minority groups-who rely on public assistance to meet their most basic needs. These vulnerable populations, unlike India's middle and upper classes, do not have a viable 'exit' option from the public sector and its myriad deficiencies. (Kapur etal 2017)

In Public Administration the Indian state was often institutionalized in terms of officials be held accountable to and by their superiors, not by either the public or by independently defined standards of performance. One of the landmark shifts in public discourse has been the demand to institute more accountability downward. This is the idea that state officials should satisfy some independent standards of what they do for citizens, rather than simply for their superiors. Institutions are struggling to initiate new practices of performance evaluation that are more citizen-focused in India today.

Conclusion

"After attaining Swaraj (self-rule) we need to have Suraj (good governance)" — Mahatma Gandhi.

It has been more than 70 years of our democratic Republic therefore we should not still call ourselves a nation in "transition". The first fifty years witnessed democratic movements for the representation of people's diversities in our parliament, the government, and all major decision making bodies. That battle is not yet over but we have now moved beyond procedural democracy towards implementing a more substantivist notion of democracy. We have now moved beyond the context of representativeness to looking at the core of citizen entitlements, i.e. how can a citizen be truly empowered in a democracy. Unequal citizen access to basic public goods and services is a bane of our democracy. It is now well understood that building state capacity to deliver citizen needs and aspirations is the primary task of good governance in any democratic state. Democracy means different things to different people —to many it means the capacity to vote and be voted to public office and also the power to change governments.lt also means civil and political rights for the people. However, in India thanks to our practice of democracy for six decades, we are now rightly asking for more rights and increased state capacity to implement those rights. The fact that good governance is a pre-requisite for a good substantivist democracy is completely acknowledged in democratic theory and practice.

Today, many civil society activists have given a rousing call to wage a second "freedom struggle" against corruption, poverty, disease and deprivation "Good Governance" has almost become a buzzword the world over, in both developed and developing countries. Some elements of good governance are universally recognized, some others have found acceptance only in certain countries. Those in the first category, which have been accepted universally, include public accountability and transparency in administration, rule of law, participative governance, predictability in decision making, citizen-centric administration and respect for human rights.

The Second Administrative Reforms Commission (SARC) summarized the core principles of Good Governance thus:

- Rule of law which requires that laws and their implementation be transparent, predictable, equitable and credible.
- Accountability at each level of administration
- Minimization of unfettered discretion
- Putting the citizen first
- Government to be built on a strong ethical foundation
- Principle of subsidiarity, which implies both devolution and delegation of authority.

The ability of the state to provide the institutions that support growth and human development is often referred to as 'good governance'. Whichever way one looks at it India is still far from being a recipient of the products of good governance. Therefore it is heartening to note that for the first time in India's electoral history at the Centre, 'good governance' figured prominently in the 16th and 17th National Elections. Even in the recent past, several State Governments (Andhra Pradesh, Chhatisgarh, Delhi, Odisha, Madhya Pradesh and Sikkim) have come back to power on their records of good governance.

Though the term 'good governance' does not appear in the Indian Constitution, the fundamental rights (Part III) and directive principles (Part IV) of state policy taken together encompass all the characteristics of good governance. It is often said that China is troubled with a democratic deficit while India struggles with a governance deficit! To assume that globalization in India will imply contracting the role of the bureaucracy is mere wishful thinking. In fact, an emphasis on increased public expenditures on social sectors such as food, security, education, health care and rural development will mean a substantial expansion of the bureaucracy. Even the New Rights regime that has been ushered in, will require the administration of these Rights into citizen entitlements. Therefore the sphere of the bureaucracy cannot really be curtailed in the years to come. It remains a pivotal institution in the implementation of public policies. It has not yet adjusted to the new paradigm of governance and continues to reform very slowly. This is one of the foremost challenges of good governance in India today.

Administrative reforms have been a permanent item on the agenda of governance. According to one estimate over 600 committees and commissions have gone into the question of administrative reforms in the states and at the centre since Independence. The last one in this chain is the Second ARC which submitted its 15 volume report to the Centre. However, one can look at this issue of reform with a little more optimism now. *The single most important catalyst of administrative reform in this country has been the liberalization of the economy, unbundling of government monopolies and the opening up of the public sector to competition in the market.* Competition truly triggered off change in the way government worked! Many of the Second ARC report suggestions have been officially accepted by the government.

The new rights given to the people, e-governance, computerization of government records, Citizen Charters, Public Service Guarantee Acts and increasing judicial activism will change the face of the government in the years to come. It is also important to note that the states have an important role to play in ushering in administrative reform since all development schemes and programmes are implemented by them. It is heartening to see that states today are vying with each other in projecting their rates of growth, bringing out Human Development Reports and publicizing their initiatives on good governance. Towards this end it is imperative that an index of good governance be compiled which will enable interstate comparisons on the performance of different states. Recent elections to state legislatures and the Lok Sabha have shown that good governance can also become good politics. The comparable index can include the rate of growth of state domestic product, rate of reduction in poverty, implementation of important social sector schemes, IMR and MMR rates, school dropout rates, custodial death, communal violence, human rights violations and extent of openness of governmental decision making (Madhav Godbole, Good Governance Never on India's Radar, 2014)

Recognition of this Governance Index (for interstate comparison) should act as a precursor to 'good governance' being recognized as a fundamental right of every Indian in the world's largest democracy.

It is important for us to know and believe that in our journey towards greatness as a nation, democracy has been our greatest asset and despite huge domestic problems our commitment to democracy remained strong. The strength of democracy lies in understanding the huge potential and opportunities offered to solve the problems that so many Indians continue to face. Poverty, relative inequality, lack of social opportunities for the marginalized, all of these can be addressed by vigorous planning and initiation of implementable policies through good governance practices in the Centre and the States of India.

Index

D

E

F

Q

R

S

T

U

V

W